ASPEN PUBLISHERS

Rigos Bar Review Series™

Multistate Bar Exam (MBE) Review

Volume 2: Evidence, Constitutional Law, and Criminal Law and Procedure
(Course 5333)

Wolters Kluwer
Law & Business

AUSTIN   BOSTON   CHICAGO   NEW YORK   THE NETHERLANDS

James J. Rigos
230 Skinner Building
1326 Fifth Avenue
Seattle, WA 98101
Telephone: (206) 624-0716
Fax: (206) 624-0731
rigos@rigos.net

To contact Aspen Publishers' Customer Care, e-mail customer.care@
aspenpublishers.com, call 1-800-234-1660, fax 1-800-901-9075,
or mail correspondence to:

Aspen Publishers
Attn: Order Department
PO Box 990
Frederick, MD 21705

Printed in the United States of America.

1 2 3 4 5 6 7 8 9 0

ISBN 978-0-7355-7334-5

This book is intended as a general review of a legal subject. It is not intended as
a source for advice for the solution of legal matters or problems. For advice on
legal matters, the reader should consult an attorney.

Magic Memory Outlines® is a registered trademark owned by Rigos Professional
Education Programs, Ltd.

About Wolters Kluwer Law & Business

Wolters Kluwer Law & Business is a leading provider of research information and workflow solutions in key specialty areas. The strengths of the individual brands of Aspen Publishers, CCH, Kluwer Law International and Loislaw are aligned within Wolters Kluwer Law & Business to provide comprehensive, in-depth solutions and expert-authored content for the legal, professional and education markets.

CCH was founded in 1913 and has served more than four generations of business professionals and their clients. The CCH products in the Wolters Kluwer Law & Business group are highly regarded electronic and print resources for legal, securities, antitrust and trade regulation, government contracting, banking, pension, payroll, employment and labor, and healthcare reimbursement and compliance professionals.

Aspen Publishers is a leading information provider for attorneys, business professionals and law students. Written by preeminent authorities, Aspen products offer analytical and practical information in a range of specialty practice areas from securities law and intellectual property to mergers and acquisitions and pension/benefits. Aspen's trusted legal education resources provide professors and students with high-quality, up-to-date and effective resources for successful instruction and study in all areas of the law.

Kluwer Law International supplies the global business community with comprehensive English-language international legal information. Legal practitioners, corporate counsel and business executives around the world rely on the Kluwer Law International journals, loose-leafs, books and electronic products for authoritative information in many areas of international legal practice.

Loislaw is a premier provider of digitized legal content to small law firm practitioners of various specializations. Loislaw provides attorneys with the ability to quickly and efficiently find the necessary legal information they need, when and where they need it, by facilitating access to primary law as well as state-specific law, records, forms and treatises.

Wolters Kluwer Law & Business, a unit of Wolters Kluwer, is headquartered in New York and Riverwoods, Illinois. Wolters Kluwer is a leading multinational publisher and information services company.

Editorial Direction

James J. Rigos is an Attorney-CPA, a graduate of Boston University Law School, and Editor-in-Chief of the creating team of this Bar Review Series, owner of Rigos Professional Education Programs, Ltd., and an author for Aspen Publishers. He has written and lectured for professional associations and for Bar- and CPA-exam review programs for over a quarter of a century. For many years he has served as a national Director of the American Association of Attorney-CPAs. He has also created a series of CLE and CPE courses focusing on professional ethics.

Acknowledgments

This work product was substantially enriched because of the robust encouragement and editorial involvement of many thoughtful individuals. Aaron Rocke, Sidney Tribe, Tracy Duany, Jason Stonefeld, Tom Smith, Bryan Brown, Kevin Stemp, Gina Lowe, Matt Conrad, Joanna Roth, Steve Johnson, and Carolyn Plant made significant drafting contributions. Law School Professors Janet Ainsworth, Jim Bond, Mark Chinen, David DeWolf, Sam Donaldson, Christian Halliburton, Gregory Hicks, and Karl Tegland made important suggestions on substantive improvements and reviewed the Rigos Bar Review Series textbooks. A special thanks to our past students for their many suggestions of substantive improvement and creative new learning aids. All their recommendations and successes are a part of every page of this Rigos Bar Review Series. The direction and guidance of Steve Errick's team (especially Melody Davies, Carol McGeehan, and Barbara Lasoff) from Aspen Publishers made this all possible.

RIGOS BAR REVIEW SERIES

MULTISTATE BAR EXAM REVIEW (MBE)

Table of Contents

This Rigos Bar Review Series Multistate Bar Exam (MBE) Volume 2 of the two-part series contains the following subjects and contents:

Rigos Bar Review Series Multistate Bar Exam (MBE) Volume 1 of the two part series contains the following subjects:

RIGOS BAR REVIEW SERIES
Other Products in the Series

MULTISTATE ESSAY EXAM (MEE) REVIEW

- Succinct explanations of the most frequently-tested legal principles **provide you only the information needed to answer MEE essays**.
- **Strategies for issue-spotting and techniques for analysis** help build your confidence as you go.
- **Identifies "tips" and "traps" often encountered on the MEE**, to help you avoid common mistakes and pitfalls.
- Introductory chapter on exam strategies **tells you exactly what to expect at the exam**, advises you how to prepare, and takes the mystery out of the MEE.
- Acronyms assist you in memorizing legal elements and perfecting your approach to the essays.
- All topics are presented in an **easy-to-read, outline format**.

MULTISTATE PERFORMANCE TEST (MPT) REVIEW

- Provides **detailed instructions on the best approach to use in answering** the types of MPT questions on the exam.
- Organized so there is **an entire chapter devoted to each popular MPT-format question**.
- Includes a flowchart illustrating the frequency of MPT tasks that show up on the exam.
- Identification of common pitfalls and traps **helps familiarize you with the typical distracters used by the examiners**.
- **Seven simulated exam questions, categorized by topic with full sample answers** provided help you gauge your progress and reinforce MPT practice.
- Explanations are compact, yet **comprehensive enough to give you confidence that you have learned all the important information you need** to pass the exam.

MULTISTATE PROFESSIONAL RESPONSIBILITY EXAM (MPRE) REVIEW

- Topics are presented in an **easy-to-read outline format, allowing you to find quickly what you need** and providing a more focused approach to studying.
- Content is extensive, yet not overwhelming, and **supplies you with only the information you need to know to pass the MPRE**.
- Focuses on the finer distinctions of the rules in order to **help you eliminate possible wrong answers on the exam**.
- **Hundreds of sample questions**, organized by subject, offer extensive MPRE practice, as well as full answer rationales.
- **A mock 2-hour/60 question practice exam helps you simulate a real MPRE test-taking experience**.
- Acronyms provide a **framework for memorization of issues and rules**.

Ask your bookstore about **Rigos Bar Review Series** products from Aspen Publishers or visit us online at *http://lawschool.aspenpublishers.com*.

Multistate Bar Exam (MBE) Review

Review

Volume 2: Evidence, Constitutional Law, and Criminal Law and Procedure
(Course 5333)

RIGOS BAR REVIEW SERIES

MULTISTATE BAR EXAM REVIEW (MBE)

PREFACE

Table of Contents

RIGOS BAR REVIEW SERIES

MULTISTATE BAR EXAM REVIEW (MBE)

PREFACE

I.   INTRODUCTION

Welcome. This introduction is an overview of the Rigos Bar Review Series Multistate Bar Exam (MBE) Review. It describes the MBE process including how the exam questions are created and graded. The question characteristics and related suggested approach tips are covered. Also detailed is our recommended organized preparation program you should follow to ensure that you score high on the MBE at the first sitting. The information in this preface is important. It should be thoroughly studied and understood before you start your Rigos Bar Review Series MBE review program. Refer back frequently.

Candidates in jurisdictions that administer the Multistate Essay Exam should use the *Rigos Multistate Essay Exam Review — MEE* in conjunction with this MBE program. Our MEE course contains practice essay questions to supplement the text contained in this program.

A. <u>Successful Rigos Candidates' Comments</u>

"I chose the Rigos Bar Review program because it seemed to offer a focused approach to passing the bar, and I am happy to say that it provided just that. The materials and the practice questions taught me what I needed to know and how to use what I had learned. There were no surprises on the exam. I was able to answer the questions quickly and confidently." – G. Pisarski, Esq.

"I felt that the course content and structure were superb, and that the concise nature of the materials kept me focused on what was important for the exam, rather than sending me on some theoretical wild goose chase through lengthy legal quagmires." – R. Hulshoff, Esq.

"While the outlines are brief, they are nothing less than outstanding in their coverage. The Magic Memory Outlines® *are so good that my friends who had enrolled in other review courses used them to distill the information down to a manageable size."* – J. Berryman, Esq.

"The amount of material was manageable. Where the other courses' outlines seemed overwhelming, the Rigos Bar Review presented an amount of information for each subject that could be approached and conquered in a short period of time. The acronyms were a life-saver for approaching the commercial code and contract subjects. They provided a framework for dealing with the issues and rules. The information on grading gave me a realistic expectation of the exam. Your course made the whole process seem much less intimidating." – R. Church, Esq.

"The Magic Memory Outlines® *were very helpful. I recommended the Rigos Bar Review to the other firm associates even before I found out I had passed the bar.   The combination of superior passing rate and panic free study materials makes this the clear choice in review courses. I would highly recommend the Rigos Bar Review Series to every law student preparing for the bar."* – N. Montstream, Esq.

"Concise material that doesn't create information overload. The material is organized in a fashion that is focused, sensible, and understandable. It focuses on the fine line distinctions which are so frequently tested on the MBE" – G. Cook, Esq.

"The Rigos Bar Review seamless process was incredibly effective and I went into the bar exam confident that I would pass." – J. Piza, Esq.

B. Focused, Positive Mental Attitude

What the mind can conceive, dedicated hard work can achieve. You must believe you can and will pass the bar exam and become a successful attorney at law.

1. Join the Winning Team: The Rigos professional review courses have over 100,000 professional alumni who have used our structured programs to pass their professional entrance exams. Therefore, your objective of passing the MBE at the first sitting is very attainable.

2. Success-Focused Program: Exam confidence is the result of a well-organized and well-executed preparation program. Students following the complete Rigos Bar Review Series seamless program are geared for exam success.

C. MBE Exam in General

The MBE is a testing product of the National Conference of Bar Examiners (NCBE). The MBE takes one full day of testing and is scheduled for the last Wednesday in February and July. It is required in all but a handful of states. Over 60,000 students a year sit for the MBE. The student must complete two sets of 100 multiple-choice questions in morning and afternoon sessions of three hours each. Both the actual MBE test booklets and this Rigos Bar Review Series text are printed in 12-point type.

II. QUESTION DETAILS

The MBE has 200 four-stemmed multiple-choice questions, 100 in each morning and afternoon set. The subjects of Contracts and Torts have 34 questions each. The other four subjects (Criminal Law and Procedure, Constitutional Law, Evidence, and Property) have 33 questions each. The exam tests the six subjects in random order.

A. Question Source

1. Organization: The NCBE has six MBE Drafting Committees monitoring the six MBE subjects tested. There are five people per committee with broad representation from law school professors, professional bar examiners, and practicing attorneys.

2. New Questions: The NCBE creates new questions on an ongoing basis to refresh the test bank of potential questions and promote breadth of topic coverage. Law school professors and practitioners are a fertile source for new questions. Proposed new questions are subject to multiple reviews by Committee members to ensure they are well drafted, accurate, unambiguous, and fairly test the subjects.

3. Broad Input: Each participating state bar association may submit comments to the Committee prior to acceptance of a new question. A thorough review of all questions is made prior to printing each final published exam.

B. Grading System

1. Scoring: Every right answer you choose is worth one point regardless of the question's degree of difficulty. There is no penalty for wrong choices. The average raw score is about 125 to 130 out of 200.

a. Scaled for Difficulty: The final number of right answers reported for a particular exam depends upon that exam's overall difficulty. The NCBE has a scaled ("equating" is their descriptive term) difficulty system, so the final score awarded to students is comparable from exam to exam. The additional scaling points typically run between 10 and 20 points. Thus, the final equated score averages around 135 to 140.

b. Ensure Consistency: The examiners' analysis of answers and the scaling system is intended to correct the effect of any bad questions on a particular exam. This ensures grading consistency and comparisons from exam to exam.

2. State Passing Rate: Each jurisdiction decides how to combine the MBE scaled score with their own state specific testing. Nationally, about 60% of the students receive a "passing" scaled score, although this percentage varies from state to state (for a breakdown go to http://www.ncbex.org/uploads/user_docrepos/BEMaystatsweb_01.pdf). In states that permit students from non-ABA-approved law schools to sit, the pass rate may be significantly lower.

a. State Rules Vary: Most states combine the MBE and essay scores using various formulas and weights. Some allow a waiver on the essays if you achieve a certain MBE score. A few accept MBE scores from other jurisdictions.

b. Particular State: For details of the passing statistics and particular grading method used in your jurisdiction, you should check with your individual state bar association. Go to www.abanet.org/barserv/stlobar.html for an online listing of state-by-state bar exam information.

C. Question Approach

1. Focus: The fundamental legal principles of the American Law Institute's (ALI) Restatements of Law are the testing focus. Statutes and local or minority case law positions are not usually tested. The MBE questions concentrate on analysis and the detailed black letter law rules, not the usual broad concepts found in law school or bar exam essay questions.

2. Call of the Question: The facts of a question provide the foundation to test the applicable legal rule.

a. Facts Lead to Requirements: The facts are presented in either single or multiple paragraph format. Over the past few years the fact patterns have become longer, creating more time pressure. The facts lead to a requirement sentence containing a "call of the question." The correct answer is the one alternative which is the most directly responsive to the call of the question.

b. Requirement Position: The student is usually required to take either the position of a judge (decide the likely outcome) or an advocate (best or worst argument). A few questions call for the candidate to choose the most effective structuring of a transaction or legal problem. You may also be asked to give a client an opinion on the best course of action. The reasoning is more important than the likely outcome.

3. **Candidate Approach:** About one-third of the exam questions are quite difficult.

   a. **Systematic Approach:** A systematic approach to correct answer selection helps. An enlightened guessing system is also useful (see detailed suggestions below). Detailed analysis of all four alternatives is necessary; instinctive answers are often wrong because fine-line distinctions are everywhere on the MBE.

   b. **Tricks Abound:** There is usually some merit in each of the four alternatives, but some small factual difference or nuance of the determinative legal rule makes one alternative a more compelling answer. The examiners work hard to make the red herrings and distracters seem quite attractive.

D. Subjects Tested

There are six substantive subjects tested on the MBE. The NCBE does issue content specification outlines with rough percentage distributions. We have summarized the topic coverage as follows:

1. **Contracts and UCC Article 2:** Expect over two-thirds of the testing to be under the common law "SIR" topics (services, intangibles, and real estate). The questions will also cover various provisions of UCC Article 2 sale of goods, especially where there is a different or expanded treatment under the UCC as compared to the common law. The majority of the testing focus is on the formation elements (especially offer and acceptance issues, defects in meeting of the minds, and statute of frauds compliance), performance (especially reasons for non-performance), and remedies. Many MBE authorities believe that the contract questions test both deeper and broader that the other five subjects.

2. **Torts:** Expect up to half of the questions in this common law topic to cover various aspects of negligence in some detail. Up to one-quarter of the questions may be on claims asserted under strict liability and product liability theories. The remaining questions are spread over the other tort topics fairly evenly. The emphasis is on the elements of the tort action that P must prove to make a prima facie case and the various defenses that may be asserted by D.

3. **Property and Future Interests:** These are common law topics. Future interests are about one-quarter of the subject testing and may involve quite difficult questions. Acquisition of property by deed or adverse possession is heavily tested. Easements, conveyances and recording are also frequent topics. Restrictive covenants have reasonable coverage and landlord-tenant issues receive some attention. Testamentary devises and rights in personal property are lightly tested.

4. **Evidence:** Almost all the testing in this subject is from the Federal Rules of Evidence (FRE). The usual call of the question is to analyze the reasons why a particular item of evidence is admissible or inadmissible under the facts presented in the question. Admissibility of evidence and hearsay evidence constitute two-thirds of the testing. The focus is most frequently on the particular rules that exclude or limit admissibility.

5. **Constitutional Law:** The emphasis is on the US Federal Constitution's effect on the actions and powers of the three branches of federal government: the Executive, Legislative, and Judicial. In addition, the constitutional limits establishing what a state may or must do in

enforcing their laws is tested. Approximately half the questions test individual rights with the candidate usually required to determine whether a statute is valid or invalid.

6. Criminal Law and Procedure: The testing concentrates on the basic common law criminal rules, although some questions focus on the modern majority rules of statutory modifications. Criminal procedure questions emphasize US constitutional limitations on the states' ability to introduce evidence to convict a criminal defendant. The emphasis is on the controlling standards and appropriate procedural requirements the states must meet in the prosecution process.

III. MBE QUESTION CHARACTERISTICS

A. Comments and Pitfalls

The following question approach tips are extremely important. Tests show that avoiding the MBE question pitfalls may add up to 10% more right choices on uncertain questions. The exam tests not only your knowledge of the black letter law but also your MBE question analytical skills, which can only be developed through practice.

1. Format: All the MBE questions are multiple-choice with four alternatives. All levels of difficulty are represented and there is no pattern to the sequence.

2. Preferred Answer Objective: Look for the best alternative. Often one pair of answers concludes that A will prevail while the other concludes that B will prevail. The rationale supporting the conclusion thus becomes the determining factor.

a. Objective: This may mean the most nearly correct or conversely, the least incorrect answer. There is often some truth in each alternative; the best alternative must be the most completely correct and it must relate to the facts. Look for the fact(s) in the question that make one alternative more compelling than the others. Appreciate the difference between the command adverbs "may" and "shall"/"must."

b. Problems: Typically, two of the four alternatives are the same or very close in outcome, and both may sound accurate. An alternative may reach the right conclusion for the wrong reason or for a reason less compelling than another alternative's rationale. Watch out also for incomplete definitions of the determinative rules of law, particularly legal rules that have more than one requirement, but only one requirement is stated in the question.

3. Negatives: A few questions have negatives in the facts, the call, or the alternatives. This means that the correct choice is the worst, least helpful, least likely, or most false alternative. The candidate must reason very carefully through the alternatives and reverse the normal frame of reference. The "true-false" approach discussed in item 4 below is often quite helpful in dealing with negatives. If looking for the negative, the false or incorrect alternative is the best choice.

4. Try a True-False Approach: For some questions it may help to use a true-false analysis for each of the four alternatives. This is where you evaluate each answer option by asking the question, "Is this statement true or false?" The true-false approach is especially useful for questions having a negative call. Ideally you will end up with a 3-1 split; the odd one out is usually the right answer.

5. Absolutes: Be on the alert for sweeping exclusionary words such as "all," "always," "none," "never," "under no circumstances," or "solely." An alternative containing such words is so broad that it is unlikely to be correct. Ask yourself "is there any exception?" The more narrowly stated, inclusive alternative, is usually preferable to an "open door" option.

6. Nonsense Theory: Occasionally the MBE will include answer options containing a nonsense principle, concept, or theory such as "res gestae" or "doctrine of changed circumstances." A good rule of thumb is that such an alternative is wrong unless you have seen the theory in the Rigos Bar Review Series texts.

7. Be Selective: More facts or law may be given in the question than is necessary.

a. Distracters: Red herrings are often present in the facts. The examiners are very clever in creating attractive factual distracters. They are designed to support logic that leads to one of the wrong alternatives.

b. Detail May Be Coding: Also look for seemingly meaningless detail because such a reference may provide a necessary fact required for the application of a controlling legal rule. An example is a transaction between a wholesaler and a retailer; they are both considered "merchants" and this is necessary to the applicability of some UCC provisions. If dates or dollar amounts are given, they are usually necessary for the correct conclusion.

8. Analyze Modifiers in the Alternatives: Many answer alternatives begin with the conclusion (e.g., "P will prevail," "P will not prevail," or "D's defense will be effective"). This is then followed by a conditional or limiting modifying word ("because," "since," "if," "only if," or "unless") and a statement of a supporting legal reasoning or rationale. Picture the below three element skeleton.

Conclusion | **Conditional or Limiting Modifier** | **Supporting Reasoning or Rationale**

a. "Because," "Since," or "As": These conditional requirement modifiers indicate the following rationale is usually the reasoning necessary to satisfy the legal conclusion.

(1) Example: "Alice prevails because she validly accepted thus creating a contract that is binding on the offeror." "Alice prevails" is the conclusion, "because" is the conditional modifier, and "she validly . . . offeror" is the legal rationale.

(2) Reasoning Requirements: The reasoning must be consistent with the facts given in the question. The reasoning must also resolve the central legal issue in the question.

b. "If" and "Only If": This limiting modifier indicates the following rationale need only be possible under the facts; it is not required to be totally consistent, as in "because" or "since" questions.

(1) Example: "Baker prevails if (or "only if") she reasonably relied." "Baker prevails" is the conclusion, "if (or only if)" is the conditional modifier, and "she reasonably relied" is the legal rationale.

(2) Reasoning Requirement: The "if" modifier can – and usually does – go beyond the given question facts to create a more compelling factual argument to support the legal conclusion. "Only if" is similar except it creates an exclusive condition that must be satisfied. An "if" or "only if" modifier also requires you to reason through the other three alternatives to be sure there is not a better "if" or "only if" argument.

c. "Unless": This conditional modifier usually has a rationale following that addresses more of the required legal reasoning than the other modifiers.

(1) Example: "Carol prevails unless she had actual, constructive, or inquiry notice of the encumbrance." "Carol prevails" is the conclusion, "unless" is the conditional modifier, and "she had actual, constructive, or inquiry notice of the encumbrance" is the legal rationale.

(2) Reasoning Requirement: This "unless" reasoning must be necessary for the application of the controlling principles of law. If there is any other reason or way that the result can occur, an "unless" alternative is incorrect. Again, you should reason through all the other alternatives to be sure there is not a better argument.

9. Remember our Default Rules: Some topics in some MBE subjects are very challenging. Examples are future interests in property and some UCC topics like remedies in sales contracts. The time necessary to analyze and answer these questions may not be efficient and often there remains a high degree of uncertainty even after the effort. By eliminating wrong answers you can usually reduce the choice to two alternatives and use the following default rules. They provide a logical basis for an educated guess.

a. Longest Alternative: Everything else being equal, the longer alternative is slightly more likely to be the correct answer than a shorter alternative. A correct answer must usually contain all the required information and reasoning of the governing black letter law necessary for the best choice. A fragmented alternative is less attractive. This concept favors the more detailed alternative; this is usually the one with the most technical words and specific terminology.

b. Precision: Everything else being equal, the more precise the alternative the better. Vagueness is never encouraged in the law. The three incorrect alternatives in such a question will contain distracters to create confusion.

c. Easier to Prove: An answer choice that the facts suggest is easier to prove is preferred to one that has more complicated legal requirements.

d. Opposite Answer: If only two of the four alternatives are opposite (e.g., P wins because … as contrasted to … P loses because …), one of the two opposites is likely to be the best answer to the question. This technique may also be applied if a similar rationale supports opposite answer outcomes (e.g., P wins because … as contrasted to … D wins because …).

e. Another Legal Subject: An alternative that includes another legal subject is usually wrong. Only infrequently do questions crossover between subjects and almost never is the alternative that refers to the other subject the correct answer.

f. Eliminating Wrong Answers: It may be helpful to understand that there are three common reasons that an MBE answer choice is wrong:

(1) Legal Rule Misstatement: The statement of the rule may be wrong or, more frequently on the MBE, is an incomplete statement of the legal principle.

(2) Factual Misstatement: The facts required to support the alternative may not be stated in the question fact pattern at all. The alternative's facts may also go clearly and impermissibly beyond what is given in the question. In a few instances, the facts of the alternative directly contradict the facts in the question. Read the question carefully.

(3) Legal or Factual Irrelevancy: The law or facts in the answer may be accurate as stated but do not focus on the central determinant concern of the question. Again, the central determinant concern usually involves an element of law that P must prove to establish a prima facie case thus avoiding a summary judgment of dismissal or directed verdict.

B. Approach to MBE Questions

Parts of this section refers to practicing exam-type questions on paper. If you want to use the CD-ROM feature, make sure you also review the instructions in Section V infra.

1. Stay Within Time Allocation:

a. Pace Yourself: Carefully manage your time as you proceed through the questions. The trend is towards longer fact patterns but you should answer every question. There are 100 question in each of the two 180-minute (3 hour) sessions. This is an average of 1.8 minutes per question. You need to work up to this pace.

b. Time Management: Start working questions with a 3 minute maximum (or 10 in 30 minutes). One third of the way through your study period drop to 150 seconds each, the next third to 120 seconds each, the final third to 108 seconds each.

c. Procedure: It is important to work as quickly as possible without sacrificing thoroughness and accuracy. Read intensely and analyze the fact pattern carefully because you only have time to read it once. If a particular question is giving you difficulty, either skip it or make your best educated guess and mark it in the margin.

2. Series Questions: Many of the MBE questions include a common fact pattern followed by a series of 2 to 4 related questions. On a time-per-question basis, analyzing the facts in these questions is usually more efficient than single questions. Still, if you find them too taxing, perhaps skip the series question for subjects in which you feel weak the first time through. If you do skip some of the series questions, make sure you also skip blackening those bubbles on the MBE answer sheet.

3. Analyze Facts and Law: You need to analyze both the facts and the law. Try to understand the precise facts of the question separately from the four alternative choices presented below. The facts in the question are always developed chronologically. As you read the facts, circle all the people's names in the question book; every new person adds another potential legal relationship and set of claims. Analyze the facts carefully; selecting a wrong answer usually occurs because the candidate failed to appreciate the consequence of a significant fact. For some of the most complicated questions it may be helpful to quickly create a chronological skeleton diagram of the events.

4. Go Through Questions Twice: Initially, go through all the questions in order. Time is so precious it is usually a mistake to not do every question in order the first time through. Still, some candidates use a two-step approach.

a. First Time Through: The first time through, every question should be put into one of three categories. You can do this with notes to yourself in the margins, on a separate sheet of paper, or in your head.

(1) Sure of Subject: If you are reasonably competent in the subject, answer all the subject's questions and move on. This applies even if you are not sure of the exact details of the issue being tested. Circle your alternative choice – A, B, C, or D – on the question sheets.

(2) No Clue? Skip It: If you have great difficulty with a question's subject or if the particular question would take too long, skip it. Do not get frustrated by the skipped questions or spend more than 10 seconds before deciding to skip.

(3) Unsure? Take Your Best Shot: If you have some idea, but are unsure which alternative is the best answer, make your best educated guess. After you eliminate the wrong alternatives, you will usually be down to two choices. If you have spent more than 20 seconds on the question you must commit, there is just not enough time to waste on second-guessing. Answer the question and mark the margin, come back later and check the answer.

b. Second Time Through: After you have gone through all 100 questions once, look at the time left and count the skipped questions. Calculate the time per question you have left. Keep on your new time schedule. You must answer every question.

(1) Do Skipped Questions First: The second time through, work the skipped questions first. Do not exceed the average remaining time. Do not get hung up; some of the series questions intentionally have very long and complicated fact patterns. If still unsure after a reasonable intellectual effort, use the default rules discussed above.

(2) Review Marked Questions Last: After the skipped questions are completed, turn to questions you marked in the question book to determine if you see anything new. The questions you have worked may have jogged your memory. If the uncertainty is still present, go with your first judgment; it is probably your best shot at the correct answer.

5. Answer Sheets are Critical: Attention to detail here is critical. A mistake in marking the right number on the official bubble answer sheet can be fatal. Always circle your answer choice on the examination book just before you mark the answer sheet so you have a cross-check. Every 20 questions (36 minutes on average) you should consciously cross-check the numbering on both documents to be sure you did not make a transposition error. This is especially necessary if you have skipped answering some of the questions the first time.

IV. RECOMMENDED MBE PREPARATION PROGRAM

A. Substantial Effort Necessary

A large time commitment is necessary to achieve MBE success. The details of the rules tested take time to absorb and synthesize into your own Magic Memory Outlines®. This knowledge must then be directed towards the MBE multiple-choice method of testing.

1. Disassemble Book: Carefully take the book apart at the perforated line a few pages at a time and place everything in a three-ring binder. This will allow you to study more efficiently by spreading out the various parts of your book for easy reference.

2. You Must Work Questions: Familiarization with the examiner's fine-line distinctions and various tricks is best mastered by working hundreds of MBE-patterned questions. This Rigos Bar Review Series text contains a compendium of over 1,700 questions of varying degrees of easy, average, and hard difficulty. Overall our questions are more complex and contain more tricks than the MBE so that you may find the actual exam questions seem somewhat superficial. The focus is on the most frequently asked topics on the MBE.

3. Time Commitment: The total necessary preparation time depends upon how long ago you studied the subjects in law school and how efficient you are in the MBE learning process.

a. Time Variables: Our successful students report an average of 20 to 40 hours per chapter or about 200 hours average in total. Some get by with less time, but for others it takes a greater effort.

b. Do It Right: It is a mistake to underestimate the necessary effort required to pass the MBE. This is a very competitive exercise and you never know when you cross the passing line. The prudent approach is to aim for a healthy margin of safety.

4. Schedule and Calendars: A well-organized effort is necessary. Use our weekly calendars to schedule out all the necessary time. Work backward from the MBE exam date.

5. Three-Hour Time Blocks: Get used to studying in three-hour solid blocks of time without a break. You may have to work up to this. On the final page of this Preface, you will find an overall seven-week planning sheet and a week-by-week calendar.

B. Six Element Success Program

The Rigos Bar Review Series MBE Review is most effective when used in a structured learning environment. A multi-step approach works best because the student is exposed to the substantive law and question nuances from many different viewpoints. The result is a complete preparation program and a seamless process that leaves nothing to chance. The total integrated preparation effort is more effective than the sum of the individual parts.

1. Preview Text Chapter-by-Chapter: Start by reading all the pages of this text in one sitting to acquaint yourself with the MBE subjects upon which the exam questions are based. Then go through every chapter individually in much detail. Be sure to allocate sufficient time for the important four learning steps described below. Your Rigos Review covers only what is tested on the MBE, not the broader coverage found in some law school courses or other bar review courses.

2. Detailed Study of Chapter: Study each chapter's text slowly and carefully. You must know the black letter law thoroughly. Pay particular attention to the MBE Tips that point out areas of testing concentration or technique suggestions. Highlighted in the text and tips are important facts or legal rules upon which the fine-line distinction answers frequently turn.

3. Preparing Your Own Magic Memory Outline®: This is essential to success.

    a. Summarize Your Knowledge: You need to prepare a summary of every chapter in your own words. This is best accomplished using the Magic Memory Outlines® that are printed both in the book and on the CD-ROM software templates. The words in the Outline correspond to the bold headings in the text.

    b. Capture the Essence: Your job is to summarize the text by capturing the essence of the rule and entering your summarized wording into your own outlines. Aim for concise yet comprehensive statements of the rule. Focus on the required technical elements of the legal principles. Integrate any helpful "learning question" information into your outline.

    c. Memorize Your Outlines: After you have completed your own Magic Memory Outline® for the whole chapter, read it over carefully once or twice. You need to commit your Magic Memory Outline® to rote memory. Every week between your Outlines preparations and the actual MBE exam read over your Magic Memory Outlines® at least once.

4. Work Chapter's Questions:

    a. Work Questions: Next, work the practice questions at the end of the chapter. These questions are not necessarily in the same order as the topics in the chapter, but the Chapter's Question Maps will serve as a cross-reference. The questions preceded by a bold F at the right refer to final exam questions. A few questions contain alternatives from rules in subsequent chapters. Lay the question sheets alongside the answer sheets to save having to flip back and forth. It is usually worthwhile to review the answer rationales since they reinforce the relevant fine-line distinctions tested within that rule of law.

    b. CD-ROM Option: The same book questions are also on the CD-ROM so you can also use the software to work the questions in order. On the CD-ROM Question Map software, a question pertaining to that topic will pop up if you click on the question.

    c. Do a Few At a Time: Work the chapter questions in small bites. Make sure you stop after a few questions to check the answer rationales while the facts are still fresh in your active memory. Some students refer to the answer rationales after every question.

    d. Learn From Mistakes: The objective is to learn from your mistakes by reviewing the answer rationales while you still remember the details of the question. It is good to miss a few; they will help you become familiar with the MBE nuances, tricks and fine-line distinctions. Put a red star alongside (or if you're working on the CD-ROM, note on a sheet of paper) every question you missed. Missed questions should be worked again just prior to taking the actual MBE.

5. Take the Practice Exam: Volume 2 contains a simulated MBE exam. There are 200 questions in random order broken down into two groups of 100 each. While many of the questions in the text are intentionally easier or more difficult, the Final Exam has approximately the same overall difficulty as the actual MBE.

       a. Solid Block of Time: It is best to create actual exam conditions. Time yourself and work as quickly as you can without sacrificing accuracy.

       b. Answer Corrections: The answers do not follow the individual questions. Correct all your answers after you complete the full exam.

       (1) Learn From Your Mistakes: When you refer to the answer rationales, be sure to understand why you picked the wrong choice. The fine-line distinctions are critical. Again, it is usually worthwhile to review the answer rationales to all of the four alternatives because they reinforce the details of the relevant issue. More than one answer rationale may be identical if the alternatives are incorrect for the same reason.

       (2) Mark Mistakes: Again, put a red star in the margin alongside every question you missed and work them again the day right before sitting for the actual MBE. If you are using the software, make note of the questions you missed on a sheet of paper.

       6. Update and Memorize Magic Memory Outlines®: As you work the end of the chapter and the practice exam questions, you may want to supplement and update your Magic Memory Outlines®. Key determinative facts have a tendency to repeat themselves on the MBE even though the scene of the questions may be superficially different. Your self-prepared Magic Memory Outlines® should be committed to memory by reading them over many times.

C. Other Study Tips

       1. Keep Working Questions: You should continue to work practice MBE questions by mixing topics from different chapters. Make your own exams with the Rigos Bar Review Series CD-ROM software. You may work 5, 10, 20, or 100 random questions at a time. When you have a few spare minutes try working a number of short exams. Review every learning, chapter, and practice exam question you missed in your preparation process shortly before sitting for the actual exam (these questions should have a red star alongside them). Learn from your mistakes.

       2. Study Time Blocks: Concentration during your study time is critical. We recommend you build your studying block time to a full three hours. This will not be easy at first but the Rigos Bar Review Series CD-ROM "make your own exam" software will help. This will build up your stamina and concentration intensity so that you don't have to take breaks during the actual exam.

D. Additional Rigos Tools and Assistance

    If you are also using our MEE volume, we have an additional service that overlaps with this MBE text coverage. This three-pronged assistance program is available for an additional charge. Go to www.rigos.net for registration.

       1. Help Desk: If you have substantive legal questions about the text and/or practice questions, send them to our experts at rigoshelpdesk@gmail.com. Please put the subject of your questions in the email subject line, such as "Contract question." You can ask more than one question in an email, but please keep the questions to one subject, such as contracts. So one email with two contract questions would be fine.

2. Subitting Essays for Grading: You should email your essay answer as an email attachment to rigosgrading@gmail.com. Please send only one essay per email, as each question is being graded by a different grader. Do not send anything but essays to this email address. The graders are all former Rigos students who know the substance of our texts, details of our "seamless process," and the Bar exam grading system very well. Put the essay name in the email subject line so the correct grader will pick up your essay. Please identify your essays with your last name. An example is a student named John Smith and the essay named Able v. Baker would be labeled Smith-Able and Baker.doc.

3. Mentoring: After we grade five essays, a former successful Rigos student will contact you to discuss your progress. While the grader will focus on your presentation style and legal content, feel free to ask questions about other concerns of your Bar exam preparation.

V. HOW TO USE THE RIGOS BAR REVIEW SERIES CD-ROM SOFTWARE

There are many ways to work the questions contained on this software. You can mix and match the techniques below. With 1700 questions, you won't soon run out of new challenges.

A. Straight Through

You can also work practice questions from one subject at a time in order.

1. How It Works: The questions will appear one at a time beginning with Learning Question Number 1 for that chapter. You can work questions in order, just as you would in the text, until you want to stop. They are designed to reinforce the textual study.

2. How to Use It: Go to the main page and click the chapter you want to work (for example, Chapter 1, Contracts). The questions will appear in the same order as in the text, and you can work them from beginning to end. If you are reading the text material you can use this software feature to work through the Learning Questions in order. Read the fact pattern and call of the question thoroughly, and then click on your selection, "A," "B," "C," or "D." When you make your answer selection, a window will open and indicate whether your choice was correct or incorrect and why.

B. Final Exam

1. How It Works: The Final Exam is a mock MBE with the same number of questions, difficulty range, and time constraints as the actual MBE. It is timed at 180 minutes per 100-question set. It is designed to be your final review of what you have learned as well as a practice run for the MBE. It should give you confidence when you go in for the real MBE.

2. How to Use It: When you are ready, go to the main page and click "Chapter 7, Final Exam." The final exam contains 200 questions, 100 for the morning set and 100 for the afternoon. It is timed at 180 minutes for each set. Work the a.m. exam straight through without stopping. Take a one hour break, and then work the p.m. set. Unlike your practice sessions, the correct answers will not be revealed until you have completed the whole exam.

C. Make Your Own Exam

This feature allows you to create organized practice sessions in sets of 5, 10, 20, or a specified number of questions of your own choosing with the click of a mouse.

1. How It Works: The questions appear in random order from all of the six MBE topics. You should review all of the answer rationales to gain a depth of subject understanding. You can use this feature as many times in a row as you wish, and you will constantly get new questions. You should be working many questions without stopping, to build stamina.

2. How to Use It: To use this feature, simply click the "Make Your Own Exam" button on the main page. Choose the number of questions that you want to work: click "5," "10," "20," or type any whole number into the white box and click "X." The questions will come on the screen one at a time. Read the fact pattern and call of the question thoroughly, and then click on your selection, "A," "B," "C," or "D." When you make your answer selection, a window will show whether your choice was correct or incorrect and why. If you find it helpful, you can read all four answer rationales to gain a more thorough understanding of the subject.

VI. EXAM SITE TIPS

A. Be Punctual

1. Consider a Convenient Hotel: If you live far away or have transportation problems, consider booking a hotel room near the exam site. Many authorities advise staying alone so there are no distractions. It is best to walk from your hotel room to the exam site; this avoids all the uncertainties and stress of traffic, bus, train, or subway travel.

2. Arrive Early: Don't be rushed on the morning of the exam. Arrive early on exam day at the exam-site before the scheduled starting time. Avoid hurrying or arriving late because it is disconcerting and may adversely affect your composure. Check in at the registrar's desk. Look over the facilities and restroom locations.

3. Improve Morning Performance: If you are usually a late riser, practice getting up early every morning for a week before the exam. First thing in the morning, do one or two dozen questions from varied subjects to get into the test-taking mental routine as you start the day. Use the "Make Your Own Exam" feature on the Rigos Bar Review Series CD-ROM software.

B. What to Bring With You

1. Admission Card: Candidates should bring to the exam site the written instructions and the admission card provided by the state bar testing authority. Also bring two pieces of backup identification bearing your signature and picture, preferably a driver's license. Take an accurate watch to both morning and afternoon exams.

2. Comfort and Practicality: Dress comfortably in the clothes that make you feel the best. You can bring a cushion to soften the chairs if you like. Some candidates who are easily distracted bring earplugs. If you are going to use earplugs in the actual exam, use them while working questions during the preparation period.

3. Snacks: Food and beverages are not usually allowed in the exam room. Do not consume a large meal or massive liquids just before the exam. Restroom breaks are possible but cost you valuable time and break your concentration. Time is very precious in this exercise. Your studying should have expanded your ability to sit and concentrate for three-hour blocks. Go for foods that provide energy and are easy to digest (raisins, peanuts, apples, oranges, bananas, energy bars), but that do not give you a letdown or make you feel tired.

C. Focus Only On the MBE

1. Preserve Your Mental Energy: Get a full night's sleep before you take the exam. Fight to keep mentally sharp and intense for the full two three hour sessions. If you find your mental intensity weakening in the last hour, pause, close your eyes and take four deep breaths.

2. Concentrate on the Task: Imagine you and the exam booklet are in a glass box. During the 180 minutes in each MBE session, the only thing that you should think about is making your best effort on this exam. Personal problems should be left outside the exam room. Use the time management techniques you have learned and practiced in the course.

D. Be Confident

1. Relax: Consciously attempt to relax; deep, slow breathing will facilitate this mental state. Don't listen to the pre-exam chatter of the other nervous candidates. You do not want their test anxiety to affect you. It is too late to add anything to your knowledge and this distraction will only confuse and drain you. It is better not to talk to anyone. If the other candidates are bothering you, take a little walk away from them to relax.

2. Confidence and Poise: Get psyched up to make the MBE your finest intellectual effort. Approach the exam with mental confidence and poise. Think of the MBE as a game that you are going to win. Don't get discouraged by early difficult questions. Think of them as opportunities to use your keenly developed MBE analytical skills. Work quickly without sacrificing accuracy. Many of your competitors have not followed a thorough review program and are there "for practice." Rigos Bar Review Series® candidates are there to pass.

3. Contemplate the Moment: Just before the examiner says "Start your exam," contemplate the moment. Close your eyes and picture the bar admission ceremony in which you will be sworn in. For lawyers, this is our professional rite of passage and you will only do it once. Prepare yourself mentally to go for every grading point and make a commitment not to leave either session early. The most important race of your professional life has just begun.

E. Go the Distance

Fight to the end of both exam sessions. Don't leave any questions unanswered. The difference between a passing and failing score can get down to one or two extra correct questions. Only the inexperienced or the foolish leave any exam session early.

VII. CONCLUSION

This MBE exam is very passable. The Rigos Bar Review Series seamless preparation program works well for those candidates willing to work well at it. There is simply no short cut to planning and following a thorough complete preparation program. Plan to spend the necessary time and distribute all six subjects over at least seven (7) weeks until the exam using the planning calendars on the next page. This allows you to break the effort down into manageable modules. Leave time at the end for the practice exam and a final review of your Magic Memory Outlines®. Plan your success program and stay on schedule week-by-week.

After you get your results, please complete and fax or mail in the student evaluation at the end of this book. It will help us to improve our course for other students, and we may publish your ideas and thoughts. Good luck on the MBE and in your legal career.

James J. Rigos
Editor-in-Chief
Seattle, Washington

MULTISTATE BAR EXAM REVIEW (MBE)

OVERALL SEVEN-WEEK PREPARATION PLANNING CALENDAR

For _____, candidate

Date: _____

7 Weeks Prior. Use Weekly Planning Sheet to accomplish steps 1 through 4 of the Six Element Success Program for Chapter 1 Contracts.

Date: _____

6 Weeks Prior. Use Weekly Planning Sheet to accomplish steps 1 through 4 of the Six Element Success Program for Chapter 2 Torts.

Date: _____

5 Weeks Prior. Use Weekly Planning Sheet to accomplish steps 1 through 4 of the Six Element Success Program Chapter 3 Property and Future Interests.

Date: _____

4 Weeks Prior. Use Weekly Planning Sheet to accomplish steps 1 through 4 of the Six Element Success Program for Chapter 4 Evidence.

Date: _____

3 Weeks Prior. Use Weekly Planning Sheet to accomplish steps 1 through 4 of the Six Element Success Program for Chapter 5 Constitutional Law.

Date: _____

2 Weeks Prior. Use Weekly Planning Sheet to accomplish steps 1 through 4 of the Six Element Success Program for Chapter 6 Criminal Law and Procedure.

Date: _____

1 Week Prior. Use Weekly Planning Sheet to review all topics, memorize Magic Memory Outlines®, use the "Make Your Own Exam" software feature, and work the Rigos Bar Review Series® practice exam. Go over every question you missed during this review.

Exam Week: Monday, _____. Review all missed questions and solutions.

Tuesday, _____. Read over Magic Memory Outlines®.

Wednesday, _____, 20____. Sit for and pass the MBE.

RIGOS BAR REVIEW SERIES

MULTISTATE BAR EXAM REVIEW (MBE)

WEEKLY PLANNING SHEET

WEEK: From Monday _____ **to Sunday** _____.

THE MBE IS _____ **WEEKS AWAY**

WEEKLY OBJECTIVES:

Subject	Topic Studied	Prepare MMO	Do Learning Questions	Do Chapter Questions

Time	Monday	Tuesday	Wednesday	Thursday	Friday	Saturday	Sunday
6-7:00am							
7-8:00							
8-9:00							
9-10:00							
10-11:00							
11-12:00							
12-1:00pm							
1-2:00							
2-3:00							
3-4:00							
4-5:00							
5-6:00							
6-7:00							
7-8:00							
8-9:00							

CHAPTER 4

EVIDENCE

RIGOS BAR REVIEW SERIES

MULTISTATE BAR EXAM REVIEW (MBE)

CHAPTER 4

EVIDENCE

Table of Contents

CHAPTER 4

EVIDENCE

I. INTRODUCTION

A. Preliminary Matters

1. MBE Evidence Focus: The MBE consists of 33 evidence questions as part of the 200 question multiple-choice format. Up to half of the questions test the two main topics of the hearsay rule (and exceptions) and relevance (and the reasons for excluding relevant evidence). The remainder of the questions are evenly spread over this chapter's contents. Study them closely and follow the steps to success!

2. Workbook Format: This Rigos Bar Review Series chapter on Evidence has three parts: (1) the Magic Memory Outline®, (2) Substantive Outline, and (3) practice questions at the end of the chapter. Within the Substantive Outline, you will find references to Rigos Learning Questions (1-71) at the end of the chapter that pertain to each of the topics you are studying. When prompted in the text, go and work the referenced Learning Questions. This will reinforce your learning and build your confidence!

3. Learning Questions: When answering the Learning Questions, the analysis is more important for your learning of the concepts than arriving at a correct answer. Analyze not only why a certain answer is correct, but also why the other answers are incorrect or less correct than the preferred answer. You will then arrive at an optimum result.

4. Practice Questions and Sample Exam: Once you have completed the entire chapter on Evidence, answer the remaining practice questions to assess your strengths and weaknesses. At the end of the workbook and on the CD-ROM, you will find a 200 question sample exam with 33 more evidence questions interspersed throughout.

5. MBE Tips: You will find "MBE Tips" throughout this chapter. These tips succinctly state important points and exam tips. Watch them to learn about common MBE tester tricks and complex areas that are frequently tested.

6. Federal Rules of Evidence: The MBE tests the Federal Rules of Evidence (FRE) exclusively – not the common law. An extremely fertile area for testing is where there is a different treatment between the FRE and common law. Know these rules particularly well and look for questions to come up on the MBE that attempt to "trick" you by leading you toward the common law rule.

B. Answer Strategies

The thrust of all the questions is the basis on which a person's testimony or an item of evidence will be determined to be admissible or inadmissible. Keep the suggestions below in mind while answering the questions.

1. Admissibility for Other Purposes:

a. Objective: Determine just what the proponent of the evidence is trying to accomplish. It may seem the proponent is trying to introduce character evidence when in actuality the evidence is offered to impeach a witness. Do not be fooled into believing that because an item of evidence is inadmissible for one purpose that it is inadmissible for any other purpose simply because the jury may make an improper inference.

b. Example: Evidence of an accused's prior conviction for perjury may be admitted at a present perjury trial to impeach him if he takes the stand as a witness. This evidence may have been limited in the case-in-chief under the "evidence of other crimes or acts" rule, FRE 404(b). However, even though the evidence may also tend to show action in conformity with those past acts, this does not prohibit its admission during impeachment.

2. Process of Elimination: Many times, the correct answer may be arrived at by eliminating two or three of the answers. Try a true-false approach for every alternative. Often, one or two of the answers will not even be applicable to the facts.

3. Nonsensical Answers: If an answer states a doctrine you do not recognize, chances are it is not correct. After studying the following Rigos Bar Review Series text, you will feel confident in recognizing all the important rules that the MBE tests.

4. Old Common Law Rules: An answer may seem correct under the Common Law Rules of Evidence. The MBE tests only the Federal Rules of Evidence (FRE). Although the MBE does not specifically test on differences between the two, mastery of the Federal Rules is imperative to prevent being deceived by a Common Law answer.

5. Overruled or Sustained: When you see this as an option, remember that overruled means the objection fails and the evidence is admitted. If sustained, the objection is successful and the evidence is excluded.

C. Common Answers

The following answers are offered with some regularity. Some are deceptive, but others require closer scrutiny as they are possibly correct.

1. Inadmissible Because of Witness Incompetency: This answer is very often incorrect because the threshold of competency is very low.

2. Inadmissible because of "X": Many times, one will wish to find the evidence admissible at any cost. Rephrase this answer to yourself as "Inadmissible under any of the other three answers."

3. Inadmissible Because Prejudice Outweighs Probative Value: Be sure that the prejudice *substantially* outweighs the probative value. Generally, only the evidence that would cause the jury to decide on emotion rather than on the facts will approach this threshold.

> **MBE Tip:** A common error is to assess very damaging evidence as "unduly prejudicial." Remember that all evidence is prejudicial to some extent; that is why attorneys try to get it in at trial. Only if the evidence is unhelpful to the case and is introduced primarily to make the jury like or dislike the defendant will it be inadmissible.

4. Inadmissible Because Declarant is Available to Testify: This only applies to the hearsay exceptions in Rule 804.

5. Best Evidence Rule: This is a popular distracter. The best evidence rule applies only to proving the contents of writings. It does not, as many seem to infer from the name of the rule, operate to exclude inconclusive or "weak" evidence.

II. GENERAL PROVISIONS UNDER THE FRE

A. Sources and Applicability of Law

1. Federal Rules Orientation: The MBE questions are based on the Federal Rules of Evidence (FRE).

2. Application – FRE 1101: The Federal Rules of Evidence apply to all Federal Courts, except in the following situations listed in Rule 1101(d) & (e) where the rules do not apply:

a. Questions of Fact: Preliminary questions of fact are to be determined by the Court under FRE 104.

b. Grand Jury Proceedings: The FREs do not apply to Grand Jury Proceedings.

c. Miscellaneous Proceedings: FREs do not apply to extradition, sentencing, issuing warrants, and criminal summonses.

3. Preliminary Determinations – FRE 104: The rules do not apply to preliminary determinations necessary to decide the admissibility of evidence except the rules concerning privileges. For example, the qualifications of an expert witness can be established by evidence that would otherwise be inadmissible (e.g., hearsay).

B. Court Discretion

There are few absolutes in evidence. Nearly all of the rules give the court discretion to do what seems fair on the facts and circumstances presented in the particular case. Always keep your mind flexible and imagine what a court would do to avoid a manifest injustice if the facts seem extreme. Rule 102 states: "These rules shall be construed to secure fairness in administration, elimination of unjustifiable expense and delay, and promotion of growth and development of the law of evidence to the end that the truth may be ascertained and proceeding justly determined."

MBE Tip: During the exam, always remember that the rules of evidence reflect a common sense rationale in the interest of fairness. Thus, if you spot an issue but forget the particular details of the rule, employ a common sense approach to the issue that would promote fairness in the pursuit of the truth.

C. Judicial Notice – FRE 201

1. Basic Rule: In a civil case, judicial notice conclusively establishes a fact. In a criminal case, the prosecution's burden of production on that issue is satisfied. A court may take judicial notice of a fact not subject to reasonable dispute. This will arise in one of two circumstances:

a. Generally Known: If the fact is known by the public at large and not reasonably disputable, it is subject to judicial notice. "The sun sets in the west" is an example of this kind of fact.

b. Capable of Accurate and Ready Determination: If consultation of "sources whose accuracy cannot be reasonably questioned" (like a dictionary or a calendar) will reveal the fact, it is appropriately subject to judicial notice.

2. Examples: Examples would be that Los Angeles is in California, or that July 17, 2000 was a Monday. Taking notice of lesser known facts may be error. For example, it would be error to take judicial notice of the fact that headrests in automobiles are standard safety equipment; evidence of this fact would be necessary. While most people know that headrests come standard in modern automobile, the fact that they are *safety* equipment (as opposed to comfort or some other use) is lesser known.

3. Discretionary Notice: The court has discretion to take judicial notice of certain kinds of facts. The court may take such notice *sua sponte* or upon the request of one of the parties. The kinds of facts subject to discretionary notice are:

a. Laws of Foreign Countries;

b. Regulations of Private Agencies;

c. Municipal Ordinances; and

d. Matters of Local Geography.

4. Mandatory Notice: If a party so requests, a court must take judicial notice of the following kinds of facts:

a. Federal and State Law; and

b. Indisputable Facts and Scientific Propositions.

5. Any Time: Judicial notice may be requested and/or taken at any time during the proceeding. Parties have the right to be heard regarding the propriety of taking judicial notice.

> **MBE Tip:** Any time a court accepts a fact without testimony, look for an answer discussing judicial notice.

D. Evidentiary Rulings – FRE 103

Although rulings on evidence are final at the trial level, erroneous rulings (either to admit or to exclude) can be the basis for an appeal. However, a substantial right of a party must be affected for appeal to be available. A timely and specific objection or offer of proof, is required to preserve the issue for post-trial motions and appeal. The court is under no obligation to enforce the rules of evidence on its own initiative.

1. Objection: If the ruling is to admit evidence, counsel must make a timely and specific objection in order to have evidence excluded. The objection must be made before the evidence is admitted, or as soon thereafter as possible by a motion to strike.

2. Specific Grounds: The grounds for the objection must be specified. There are two exceptions.

a. Obvious: If the grounds for the objection are obvious from the context, a general objection will suffice. For example, if a witness is recounting a telephone conversation and counsel has already stated "Objection, hearsay" nine times in a row, and the tenth time counsel says simply, "Again, objection," this will likely suffice.

b. Plain Error: If the admission or exclusion of the evidence in question constitutes "plain error," it may constitute denial of a fair trial, and thus grounds for appeal, even in the absence of an objection.

3. Offer of Proof: If the ruling is to exclude evidence, counsel must make the substance of the evidence known to the court. The only exception is if the substance of the evidence is apparent from the context of the questions asked.

E. Preliminary Questions and Conditional Relevance – FRE 104

In determining preliminary facts such as the qualifications of a witness, the existence of a privilege, or the admissibility of evidence, the Court need not be bound by the rules of evidence except the rules concerning privilege.

1. Burden of Proof: In establishing preliminary facts, the burden of proof is on the party seeking to establish the facts (the proponent). The proponent must establish the preliminary facts by a preponderance of evidence.

2. Ruling Not Conclusive: Although the court may rule that preliminary facts are admissible, it is still up to the jury to determine the weight and credibility of those facts.

3. Conditional Relevance: When the relevancy of evidence is dependant upon a condition precedent, the Court will admit the evidence subject to fulfillment of the condition.

4. No Fifth Amendment Waiver: A criminal defendant does not waive his Fifth Amendment privilege against self-incrimination by testifying on a preliminary matter.

5. Privileges Apply: Although the evidentiary standards are relaxed at this preliminary stage (for example, hearsay may be used) the rules regarding privilege still apply.

F. Limited Admissibility – FRE 105

1. Permissible Purpose: Under Rule 105, evidence may be inadmissible for one purpose but admissible for another. For example, a prior conviction may be barred by Rule 404(b) to prove the D is a criminal type, but admissible under Rule 609 to impeach the D if he or she testifies as a witness. In this situation, the court gives a limiting instruction, cautioning the jury to consider the evidence only for the permissible purpose.

2. Analysis: Any question regarding admissibility will involve more than one analysis. For example, an out of court statement must be analyzed on relevancy and hearsay. Character evidence, if admissible, may also be subject to an FRE 403 prejudice analysis. In short, keep your mind open. Often, there are several valid objections to the admissibility of evidence.

G. Remainder of Related Writings or Recorded Statements – FRE 106

This rule is also called the rule of "completeness." If one party introduces part of a recorded statement or a document, that party has waived the right to object to another part of that same statement or document.

> **MBE Tip:** On the MBE, the admissibility of evidence may turn on the purpose for which it is being offered. Be sure you understand the purpose before answering the question.

H. Presumptions and Burden of Proof – FRE 301

1. Burden of Production: If P has the original burden of production on issue X, P must produce evidence that X exists. If P does not satisfy this burden, the court will decide the issue as a matter of law and will not permit the jury to consider it.

2. Burden of Persuasion: If P has the burden of persuasion on an issue, that means if the jury is not convinced to the level of the required standard of proof, P loses on that issue.

a. Standard of Proof: For criminal cases, the standard is always "beyond a reasonable doubt." For most civil cases, the standard is a "preponderance of the evidence." For civil cases involving fraud, disbarment, and the validity of a deed or will, the standard is "clear and convincing evidence."

b. Example: On a claim of negligence, P will always have the burden of persuasion to prove all required elements. D will then have the burden of persuasion on any affirmative defenses.

3. Effect of Presumptions: In a civil case, a presumption satisfies one party's burden of production and "shifts" the burden of production to the other party. However, presumptions under the law do not shift the burden of persuasion; the burden of persuasion always remains with the original party.

> **STOP!** Go to page 91 and work Learning Questions 1 to 6.

I. Federal Law in Civil Actions and Proceedings – FRE 302

In civil cases, the effect of a presumption regarding a claim or defense raised pursuant to that state law is governed in accordance with the laws of that state.

III. RELEVANCE

A. Definition of "Relevant Evidence" – FRE 401 & 402

"Relevant Evidence" is that which (1) has probative value and (2) is material to the case. Although the evidence must be reliable, it does not have to be conclusive to be admissible.

1. Probative Value: The rule requires only "some tendency" to make the existence of any fact more or less probable. Do not confuse this requirement with sufficiency. The evidence offered need not be enough by itself to sustain a verdict, so long as it is relevant. Circumstantial evidence is acceptable.

2. Materiality: The evidence must bear on a fact in issue: look for a link between the evidence offered and the applicable substantive law (i.e., elements of a tort, defense, or crime).

3. Both Elements: Evidence must meet both elements to be relevant. However, relevant evidence is not automatically admissible. Relevant evidence is still subject to Constitutional requirements, Federal statute, or other Federal Rules of Evidence. Evidence that is not relevant is not admissible.

B. Examples

1. Undisputed Evidence: Evidence that is not in dispute may be probative, but not necessarily material because it is already established. Therefore, it is irrelevant.

2. Rebuttal: Evidence that is irrelevant during the P's case in chief may become relevant during D's case in chief. For example, evidence rebutting an affirmative defense.

3. Conduct Suggesting Guilt: Evidence of such behavior is nearly always relevant and admissible. Examples are fleeing from scene of crime, hiding from police, changing appearance, using an alias, or refusing to take a breath test in a DUI case.

4. Inadmissible Relevant Evidence:

a. Similar Accidents or Injuries: These are inadmissible to show negligence in the present case, but may be admissible on a narrower issue or for a limited purpose (i.e., to show notice or knowledge of a dangerous condition), accompanied by a limiting instruction. For example, in a products liability case, reports to the manufacturer about similar injuries are admissible to show the manufacturer was aware of the danger.

b. Similar Contracts: These are inadmissible to show terms of the contract in question, but may come in for the limited purpose of showing definitions, industry or trade usages, past course of dealings, etc.

5. Violation of Law or Industry Standard: In a civil case, D's violation of an applicable statute or administrative regulation may be admissible to demonstrate negligence or unsafe product. D's violation of an industry standard or similar standard not having the force of law may likewise be admissible. The principal requirement is relevance. The proponent of the evidence must demonstrate that:

a. Applies: The law or standard applies to D's conduct and to the situation presented, and

b. Probative and Material: Its violation is both probative and material on the issue of negligence or unsafe product. The question of whether the violation constitutes negligence per se is governed by tort law, not evidence law.

6. D's Financial Condition: In a criminal case in which D is charged with theft or a similar crime, D's poverty, alone, is inadmissible to show a motive for the crime. However, it becomes admissible when coupled with additional evidence, such as a sudden improvement in D's financial condition after the alleged crime.

7. Demonstrative Evidence: Photos, video, diagrams, etc., are generally favored by the court, as long as it is a reasonable representation of the facts depicted.

MBE Tip: Keep clear the difference between demonstrative and admissible evidence. While demonstrative evidence may be used, it cannot be taken back to the jury room during deliberations unless it is properly admitted.

---

a. Admissibility: The test is whether the demonstrative evidence is a "reasonable representation" of the facts depicted. Usually this is satisfied by testimony from an "authenticating witness," who says the photo, the model, or the like, is an accurate depiction. However, if the demonstrative evidence is for illustrative purposes only, the evidence is not admitted as an exhibit and is only viewed by the jury during the proceedings.

b. Photos: Photos must be recent and clear enough to be relevant.

c. Models: A model must be accurate enough to be useful to the jury.

8. "Real" Evidence: Something that actually played a part in the case requires a showing of the chain of custody (where item has been, who has handled it) to rule out tampering. This is especially important for fungible substances.

9. Witness Bias: Nearly always relevant to their testimony credibility.

C. Balancing Against Prejudice – FRE 403

Relevant evidence may be excluded if its probative value is substantially outweighed by any of these four factors:

1. Danger of Unfair Prejudice: Some prejudice is allowable; only "unfair" prejudice is excluded. Unfairly prejudicial evidence may inflame the jury into making a decision on the basis of emotion rather than fact.

a. "Too Good" Not Enough: Evidence that is simply "too good" or "too powerful" cannot be excluded on that basis alone. All evidence is "prejudicial" to a party.

b. Examples: Possibly unfairly prejudicial evidence would include gruesome autopsy photographs and evidence. One example is the trial of the D.C. snipers, when the court had to decide whether to admit the testimony of grief-stricken relatives of people who were allegedly killed by the defendant in the same "spree," but whose deaths were not the subject of the prosecution before the court.

2. Marginally Relevant: When the mere fact of a prior conviction is an element of the crime presently charged (e.g., the crime of owning a firearm with a prior felony conviction), the prosecution may be required to accept D's offer to stipulate to the prior conviction, thus keeping the nature of the prior conviction from the jury. The reason for this is that the nature of the prior crime is marginally relevant yet could be highly prejudicial.

3. Confusion: The evidence should not create confusion of the issues or mislead the jury. This does not mean that confusing evidence is by definition irrelevant. Rather, irrelevant evidence is confusing because the jury does not know what purpose it serves.

4. Considerations of Undue Delay: The evidence cannot create a waste of time, or needless presentation of cumulative evidence. "Asked and answered" is the usual objection. The rule could also be used, for example, to exclude a photograph that is too fuzzy to be helpful. There are no hard and fast rules; the trial court has discretion.

> **MBE Tip:** Rule 403 does not authorize a judge to exclude evidence on the grounds that it lacks credibility. Credibility is for the jury alone to decide, after hearing all the evidence.

> **STOP!**   Go to page 92 and work Learning Questions 7 to 11.

IV. CHARACTER EVIDENCE – FRE 404 & 405

A. Character Evidence Generally – FRE 404(a)

Evidence of a person's character is evidence of a person's natural tendencies or evidence showing what kind of person he or she is. Examples would be honesty, peacefulness, sobriety, etc. By definition, this evidence is partly judgmental and is generally not admissible for the purpose of proving action in conformity with that character on a particular occasion. There are different exceptions for civil and criminal cases:

> **MBE Tip:** The issue of introduction of character evidence is very complex and commonly tested on the MBE. Pay attention to the type of case (civil or criminal), the person against whom the evidence is offered (plaintiff/victim/defendant/witness), and the purpose of the evidence.

1. **Civil Proceeding:**

    a. Character At Issue: If character is actually at issue, character evidence is admissible (i.e., truth of a libel/slander accusation, employing a person of questionable character, parental fitness in a custody dispute); these cases are very rare.

    b. Character Not At Issue: Where character is not at issue (the more typical civil case), character evidence is not admissible to prove negligence or other liability. Character evidence may only be admissible for impeachment under FRE 608 (see below).

2. **Criminal Proceeding:** Evidence of a character or trait thereof is not admissible to prove action in conformity therewith, except:

    a. Character of Accused – FRE 404(a)(1):

        (1) Offered by Accused: A criminal D is entitled to introduce pertinent evidence of good character relevant to the crime with which he is charged. The character evidence must be relevant to the crime charged.

        (2) Offered by Prosecution: The prosecution may introduce character evidence under two circumstances:

            (a) Rebuttal: To rebut the accused's character evidence when the D "opens the door," or

            (b) Victim: If the accused offers a victim's character trait under 404(a)(2), the prosecution may introduce the same character trait of the accused.

    b. Character of Victim – FRE 404(a)(2): A pertinent trait of the victim's character may be offered:

        (1) Accused in Criminal Proceeding: By the accused. This is limited to circumstances where the victim's character is pertinent, which is rare. If evidence of the victim's character is allowed, the prosecution may offer victim character evidence in rebuttal.

        (2) Victim's Peacefulness in Homicide Where Self-Defense is Raised: By the state. In the case of homicide, the prosecutor may introduce evidence of the peacefulness of the victim to rebut a D's claim of self-defense.

        (3) Sexual Assault: Rarely. For the rule on evidence of the alleged victim's character in cases of sexual assault, see FRE 412 below.

    c. Character of Witness – FRE 404(a)(3): See Rules 607, 608 and 609 for evidence regarding the character of a witness.

B. Other Crimes, Wrongs, or Acts – FRE 404(b)

This rule applies to both civil and criminal cases. It essentially prohibits the use of evidence of past misdeeds in an attempt to prove that the party committed the current misdeed. However, as always, the rule has exceptions.

1. Inadmissible as to Character or General Propensities: A person's prior misconduct is not admissible to show that the person is a certain "type" or has a certain trait that makes it more likely that the person committed the crime charged or was negligent. The law shuns the notion that "once a criminal, always a criminal" or "once negligent, always negligent." In other words, a person's prior misconduct is inadmissible to demonstrate the person's general propensities. For exception in cases of sexual assault, see Rule 413 *et seq*.

2. Admissible for Other Purposes: Character evidence may be admissible for other purposes, so long as the prosecution gives reasonable notice of its intent to do so. The Rule lists some non-exclusive other purposes such as modus operandi, opportunity, intent, preparation, plan, knowledge, identity, absence of mistake or accident. Examples include:

a. Rebutting Claim of Accident: David is accused of assaulting Pamela, but claims it was an accident. Pamela's evidence that David assaulted Victoria last week is inadmissible to show David as violent, but may come in to rebut the "accident" defense.

b. Common Scheme or Plan: D is arrested after a crime spree, but charged with only one of the crimes. The other crimes are inadmissible to show D is a criminal, but may be allowed to show that this crime was part of a larger criminal scheme (D's "modus operandi").

c. Identity: Daniel is charged with theft in Seattle on May 15, but claims he was in New Orleans on that day. Evidence that Daniel assaulted Peggy in Seattle on May 15 cannot come in to show D is a criminal type, but it can come in to show that he was present to commit the theft.

MBE Tip: The key to admissibility of character evidence is to be able to articulate how in some way that the evidence is relevant *other than* to demonstrate a person's action in conformity with the character trait.

C. FRE 404 Character Evidence Chart

Type of Case	Type of Character Evidence	Party Offering	Purpose of Introduction of Evidence	Admissible?
Civil	General	Either	Prove conformity therewith	NO
Civil	General	Either	Character is at issue	YES
Civil	General	Either	Impeach witness	YES
Civil	Other Crimes, Wrongs, or Acts	Either	Prove conformity therewith	NO
Civil	Other Crimes, Wrongs, or Acts	Either	Proof of motive, opportunity, intent, preparation, plan, knowledge, identity, absence of mistake	YES

Type of Case	Type of Character Evidence	Party Offering	Purpose of Introduction of Evidence	Admissible?
Criminal	General	P	Prove conformity therewith	NO
Criminal	General	D	Prove innocence; impeach witness; challenge witness' character	YES
Criminal	General	P	Rebut; impeach witness (if D "opens the door")	YES
Criminal	Other Crimes, Wrongs, or Acts	P	Conformity therewith	NO
Criminal	Other Crimes, Wrongs, or Acts	P	Proof of motive, opportunity, intent, preparation, plan, knowledge, identity, absence of mistake	YES
Criminal	Other Crimes, Wrongs, or Acts	D	Prove innocence; impeach witness; challenge witness' character	YES

Type of Case	Type of Character Evidence	Party Offering	Purpose of Introduction of Evidence	Admissible?
Criminal – Rape	General	P/D	Character of Victim	NO
Criminal – Rape	Other Crimes, Wrongs, or Acts	P/D	Character of Victim	NO
Criminal – Rape	Other Crimes, Wrongs, or Acts	P/D	Prove D was not source of semen; prove consent via past sexual acts	YES

MBE Tip: Remember that all evidence is still subject to a balancing test for prejudicial harm under Rule 403. Keep this in mind in any Rule 404(b) analysis on the exam.

D. Methods of Proving Character – FRE 405

If it is admissible for one of the purposes under 404(b), character evidence may be introduced in one of two ways, depending on whether the character trait in question is essential to the charge, claim, defense, or proof:

1. Reputation or Opinion: If the character trait is not essential, then evidence of the trait may be introduced by reputation or opinion.

a. Reputation: Reputation evidence must relate to a party's reputation in a neutral and generalized community, such as the party's neighbors or co-workers. A party's reputation in a smaller or non-neutral community (e.g., among law enforcement officers or within the party's family) will usually be inadmissible.

b. Opinion: Opinion evidence is the testimony of one person as to his or her own generalized opinion regarding the D's character. Examples of specific instances of conduct leading to a reputation/opinion may be inquired upon on cross examination if the other party "opens the door," but may not be introduced on direct (but see below).

2. Specific Conduct: Evidence of specific instances of conduct may be admitted if the character trait is an essential element of a charge, claim, defense, or proof.

MBE Tip: FRE 404 and 405 must be read together to make sense. 404 describes those circumstances in which evidence of a character trait is admissible. If the evidence passes the 404 test, then proceed to a 405 analysis to determine which kind of evidence is permissible. The answer will depend on whether the character trait at issue is an essential element of the charge or claim.

E. Victim's Sexual History – FRE 412

1. General Rule of Inadmissibility: In any civil or criminal proceeding, a victim's past sexual behavior is generally not admissible.

MBE Tip: For the purposes of the MBE, it is unlikely that the testers would write a question where the correct response is the admission of a victim's past sexual behavior. If in doubt, choose the response that excludes the evidence under FRE 412.

---

2. Exception: Instances of admissible sexual behavior are

a. Criminal Proceedings:

(1) Proof of Physical Evidence: Evidence of a victim's specific sexual acts with others offered to prove that the accused was not the source of the semen or other physical evidence;

(2) Proof of Consent: Evidence of past sexual behavior between the victim and accused to prove consent;

(3) **Protection of Constitutional Rights:** Other evidence offered in a criminal case, the exclusion of which would violate the constitutional rights of the accused.

  b. **Civil Proceedings:**

   (1) **Otherwise Admissible:** Evidence of a victim's sexual behavior if otherwise admissible by these rules and probative value outweighs prejudicial value,

   (2) **Reputation at Issue:** Evidence of a victim's reputation if the victim places the reputation in controversy.

F. Evidence of Similar Crimes in Sexual Assault and Child Molestation Cases – FRE 413

  This rule is an exception to the Rule 404(b) prohibition on propensity evidence. In both civil and criminal proceedings involving sexual assault or child molestation, evidence of past sexual assault or child molestation is admissible for "its bearing on any matter to which it is relevant."

STOP! Go to page 92 and work Learning Questions 12 to 19.

V. HABIT AND ROUTINE PRACTICE – FRE 406

A. Establishing Habit or Routine Practice

  1. Conformity: Evidence of a person's habit or of the routine practice of an organization to show conformity therewith is generally admissible, whether corroborated or not and regardless of the presence of eyewitnesses.

  2. Habit: "Habit," however, is narrowly defined. It means automatic behavior without premeditation. Examples include always turning right coming out of the driveway or always blowing a whistle at a railroad crossing.

  3. Routine Practices: Routine practices of an organization are admissible to show conformity therewith on the occasion in question (i.e., mailroom procedures or a standard chain of review of common forms).

  4. Method of Proof: Evidence of habit may be introduced either by general opinion testimony or by specific instances of conduct. If specific instances are offered, they must be sufficient in number to constitute a finding that the behavior is a habit or routine practice.

MBE Tip: A habit is a semi-automatic response. The test is whether you would have acted the same way if the stimulus were removed; if you would have had to think about it (the act), then it is not a habit. If the response is characterized in the MBE fact pattern as "often," "frequently," or "sometimes" occurring, the odds are that the behavior will fall short of the definition of a "habit" according to the rule. If the response is characterized as "always" or "regularly" occurring, then it is probably a habit.

B. Habit Distinguished from Character

Habit is distinguishable from character. Character is a general pattern of behavior or a personality trait; habit when a party always performs a specific act or set of acts when a particular set of circumstances occurs.

VI. SUBSEQUENT REMEDIAL MEASURES – FRE 407

A. Generally Inadmissible

The law encourages parties to take remedial or corrective measures after an accident. When such measures are taken, evidence of subsequent measures is not admissible to prove culpable conduct in connection with the event in question. This arises in product liability cases if a product was redesigned after an injury even if it would prove feasibility of design.

B. Examples of Inadmissible Remedial Measures

Examples are warning signs, systemic improvements, safety measures, retraining, redesign of a product, etc. Although some states admit evidence of subsequent changes in design to prove prior defects, the Federal Rules do not allow this.

C. Exception

Evidence of subsequent remedial measures may be offered for more narrowly defined purposes such as (1) proving ownership or control, (2) proving feasibility of precautionary measures if the potential success of such measures is in controversy (distinguished from feasibility of alternate design), or (3) impeachment. For these purposes, an exception is made and the evidence is admissible.

MBE Tip: Questions that demonstrate the above exception are common. For example, look for cases where P seeks to admit a subsequent remedial measure to establish D's ownership or control of the property involved with a negligence action. The remedial measure is admissible for this purpose.

VII. OFFERS OF COMPROMISE – FRE 408, 410

Settlement negotiations in both the civil and criminal contexts are usually inadmissible. The law intends to encourage settlements.

A. Civil Proceeding – FRE 408

1. Generally Inadmissible: An offer of compromise in a pending civil claim is not admissible to prove validity of the claim.

MBE Tip: The rationale for this rule is to remove what would otherwise be a disincentive toward settlement negotiations. Therefore, the statement does not have to be particularly damaging or compromising to be excluded.

---

2. Exception: An exception is made to allow evidence of a settlement to show bias or prejudice of a witness, or to rebut an accusation of undue delay. However, such may still be excluded under Rule 403.

3. "No Severance" Rule: A party may not circumvent the rule against introducing offers of compromise by severing statements of culpability from the actual offer of settlement.

      a. Example: For example, just following a collision, the D approaches the P and says, "I'm so sorry, it's all my fault. Please let me pay for the damages." The P cannot introduce the first sentence by omitting the second – both are considered statements made as an offer of compromise and are excluded.

      b. Exception: When the offer is specifically an offer to pay medical expenses, statements may be severed (see Rule 409).

B. Criminal Proceeding – FRE 410

      1. Generally Inadmissible: In both civil and criminal cases, the fact that a party entered into discussions regarding the entering or withdrawal of a settlement or plea is inadmissible. Statements made to the prosecutor during plea discussions are likewise inadmissible. But admissions made during police questioning are admissible. In borderline cases, the test is to ask: (1) did D subjectively believe he/she was engaged in plea negotiations, and (2) if so, was the belief reasonable from an objective point of view, based on the circumstances?

      2. Exception: Such pleas, offers, or statements are admissible in a criminal proceeding for perjury or false statement if the statement was made by the D under oath and in the presence of counsel. Also, another contemporaneous statement already admitted may in fairness allow for admission of the first statement.

VIII. PAYMENT OF MEDICAL EXPENSES – FRE 409

      A gratuitous offer to pay someone's medical expenses is admissible. However, if it is made as a settlement offer, it is inadmissible. This is a narrower exclusion than in rules 408 and 410. Statements regarding offers to pay medical expenses as settlement are not subject to the "no severance" principle under FRE 408. This means that statements of culpability made in connection with an offer to pay medical expenses may be introduced, as long as the offer itself is omitted.

> **MBE Tip:** The difference between a settlement offer and an offer of payment of medical expenses is the intent of the offeror. If the offer is made gratuitously, it is an offer to pay medical expenses and other related statements will be admissible. If the offer is made with the expectation of a release of liability, it is a settlement offer and other related statements are inadmissible.

IX. LIABILITY INSURANCE – FRE 411

A. Generally Inadmissible

      Evidence that a person was or was not insured against liability is not admissible to prove liability for negligence.

B. Exception

When offered for another purpose, such as proof of agency, ownership, control, bias or prejudice of a witness, such evidence may come in. The exceptions are narrowly construed and must still pass the Rule 403 prejudice barrier.

STOP!	Go to page 94 and work Learning Questions 20 to 24.

X. PRIVILEGES

Privileges are exclusionary rules designed to serve the higher purpose of fostering certain important relationships where confidentiality and client disclosure to a professional are essential. Privileges apply to all stages of legal proceedings, including discovery.

MBE Tip: The source of privileges in Federal Courts is the common law, rather than statute or formal rule of evidence as in many state courts. The FRE does not contain specific rules on privilege. This area is not heavily tested on the MBE, but you may encounter one or two questions on privilege.

A. General Approach to Privileges

1. Legitimate Relationship Required: There must be a professional relationship or legitimate marriage in fact.

2. Confidentiality Intended: Any protected communication offered within the privileged relationship must have been made confidentially. A third party cannot have been present to overhear the protected communication unless the third party's presence was necessary to promote the relationship (e.g., nurse, legal secretary, guardian).

3. "Holder" May Choose to Assert or Waive Privilege: Each privilege belongs to a "holder" who is then entitled to assert or waive the privilege.

a. Assertion: The "holder" is usually the non-professional in the relationship (i.e., patient, client, etc.). The professional may also assert the privilege on behalf of the holder (i.e., attorney may assert privilege concerning confidential communications with one of his clients), but cannot waive the privilege on behalf of the holder.

b. Waiver: Waiver is often an affirmative act (disclosing privileged information to a third party, or filing suit against the hearer of the communication). Waiver can also follow an act of omission (failing to assert privilege while under oath). Waiver, once employed, may not be retracted. The rule is once privilege is waived, it is forever waived.

4. More Than Just Verbal Communications: Much like the rules about freedom of expression, privilege rules have been expanded to include not just written and spoken verbal conveyances, but also assertive conduct (like a "thumbs-up" gesture or nodding head).

B. Attorney-Client Privilege

The client is the holder of this privilege and can assert this privilege to prevent his or her own testimony or to prevent the testimony of the attorney. An attorney can assert this privilege only on behalf of his or her client.

1. Necessary Element – Relationship Must Exist: The privilege does not arise until an attorney-client relationship exists. In general, the test is whether the communications were made when the client believed he or she was consulting a lawyer and manifested an intention to seek professional legal advice.

2. Necessary Element – Confidentiality Expectation: The privilege applies only to communications intended as confidential. The presence of third persons may destroy the privilege. Examples are conversation made in a public place like an elevator, a courthouse hallway or in the presence of an unprivileged third party.

3. Exceptions:

    a. Crime or Fraud: If the communication was made in furtherance of a future crime or fraud, then communication is not protected.

    b. Attorney-Client Dispute: The privilege disappears if the communication is relevant to an attorney/client dispute such as a lawsuit for malpractice or fees.

    c. Attesting Witness: If the communication concerns an attested document to which the lawyer was an attesting witness, an exception applies. For example, if a client tells the lawyer that he believes the opposing party lied, and that statement is then made part of the lawyer's sworn affidavit, communications relevant to that statement in that affidavit are not privileged.

    d. Joint Clients: If former joint clients are currently in their own dispute, communications to the lawyer relevant to a matter of common interest, made during the time when joint representation was still in effect, are not privileged.

MBE Tip: Watch out for the presence of a third person to the communication. If the presence is necessary for the communication to occur, privilege is not destroyed. For example, a nurse who keeps the client awake or an interpreter who facilitates communication will not destroy a privilege.

C. Marital Communication Privilege and Spousal Incompetency

There are two types of spousal privileges to be distinguished: (1) privilege for confidential communications made during marriage and (2) spousal incompetency. Each operates independently of the other.

1. Rule One: Traditional Privilege for Confidential Communications: This is available in civil and criminal cases. This privilege protects the (confidential) communication made or exchanged between spouses during the marriage – even if the spouses are later divorced. The holder is the non-testifying spouse; thus one spouse can prevent the testimony of the other.

2. Exceptions: The Communication Privilege is not applicable to the following four situations:

    a. Lawsuit: In a lawsuit between the spouses;

b. Competency: In a competency proceeding against one of the spouses by the other spouse or by a third party;

c. Prosecution of Crime Against the Other Spouse: When one spouse being prosecuted for a crime against the other; or

d. Planning Crime or Fraud: The communication was made to aid the planning or commission of a crime or fraud.

> **MBE Tip:** Marital Communication Privilege applies to statements only. Marital Communication Privilege would not prevent a spouse from testifying as to the other spouse's actions. However, see Spousal Incompetence below.

3. Rule Two: Spousal Incompetence: This is an incompetency of a witness issue, not a true privilege. Nonetheless it is sometimes called marital testimonial "privilege." It is distinguishable from the "marital communication privilege." The principle of spousal incompetence prevents a spouse from being compelled to testify against the other while married; it expires upon divorce.

> **MBE Tip:** Marital Privilege and Spousal Incompetency may overlap, such as when the spouses are still married and the testimony sought is regarding a confidential marital communication. In such cases, either rule may be applied.

TIME OF COMMUNICATION	SPOUSAL INCAPACITY "PRIVILEGE" (WITNESS INCOMPETENCY) Available?	MARITAL COMMUNICATION PRIVILEGE Available?
Before Marriage	Yes, spouse is incompetent to testify as to all communications before or during marriage	No, confidential communications prior to marriage are not protected
During Marriage	Yes	Yes
After Marriage	No, spouse may now testify as to any communications made at any time (except those that were confidential during marriage)	Yes, but only as to confidential communications that occurred during the marriage

D. Physician-Patient Privilege

A patient may assert a privilege regarding communication with his or her physician for the purposes of treatment. The physician may assert the privilege on behalf of the patient, but may not waive the privilege on behalf of patient. Note that this privilege does not apply to personal injury suits brought by the patient, nor to malpractice actions that the patient brings against the physician.

> **STOP!** Go to page 94 and work Learning Questions 25 to 29.

XI. WITNESS COMPETENCY

A. General Rule of Competency – FRE 601

Every person is competent to be a witness except as provided by statute or by court rule. The state law of witness competency governs in a claim brought in that state court.

B. Disqualifications of a Witness

1. **Untruthfulness:** Witness has a lack of appreciation of truthful testimony.

2. **Lack of Observation:** Witness lacks observation/perception. See Rule 602.

3. **Lack of Memory:** Witness lacks recollection of the events in question. See Rule 612.

4. **Uncommunicative:** Witness lacks ability to communicate.

MBE Tip: Do not assume that someone falling within a particular class (e.g., insane, infant) automatically meets the above criteria. Membership in a class does not *per se* prove any of the above disqualifying criteria.

C. Personal Knowledge – FRE 602

A lay witness must testify on the basis of personal knowledge. For example, if the witness did not see the stoplight, she cannot testify as to what color it was.

1. **Own Testimony:** Evidence of personal knowledge may consist of the witness's own testimony such as "I saw the light and it was green." However, simply stating "The light was green," requires the foundation that the witness saw the light.

2. **Equivocating Witness:** This rule does not prevent a witness from qualifying her knowledge with words like "I think," "As I recall," or "Probably . . .," etc. Equivocation goes to the weight, not admissibility of testimony. Weight is for the jury to consider.

MBE Tip: This rule seldom results in the exclusion of testimony. Objections are often mistakenly made regarding weight, not admissibility.

D. Judge as a Witness – FRE 605

The judge presiding at the trial may not testify in that trial as a witness.

E. Juror as Witness – FRE 606

A member of the jury may not testify as a witness before that jury in the trial of the case in which the juror is sitting.

XII. WITNESS CREDIBILITY/IMPEACHMENT

A. Generally – FRE 607

1. Impeachment Defined: Impeachment is the practice of introducing evidence not on the merits of the case itself, but to cast doubt upon the credibility of a witness. The credibility of a witness may be attacked by any party, including the party calling the witness. Impeachment evidence is usually offered to demonstrate the following:

a. Bias: Witness bias, either actual (witness states a bias in favor of a particular outcome) or implied (witness has a personal relationship with a party or attorney) is strong grounds for impeachment.

b. Mental or Sensory Perception Problems: If an impairment would interfere with the witness' proper recitation of an event, this may be grounds for impeachment. For example, bad eyesight or hearing, or a poor memory.

c. Contradiction of a Witness' Testimony: Usually a direct contradiction is grounds for impeachment. Merely a different recollection about an unimportant detail will not suffice.

d. Character or Prior Conduct of a Witness: In some circumstances, the character or prior conduct of a witness is admissible to impeach if it is relevant. See FRE 608.

e. Prior Convictions of Witness: Criminal convictions for crimes involving untruthfulness.

f. Inconsistent Statements of a Witness: Prior statements made to police or in preliminary proceedings can be used to impeach.

2. Contradiction with Extrinsic Collateral Evidence Prohibited (Collateral Facts Rule): When not otherwise prohibited, extrinsic evidence used to impeach a witness by contradiction must be relevant to a substantive issue in the case.

a. Example: For example, Witness 1 states "I saw D run the red light, I was wearing a blue jacket at the time." Witness 2 could testify "D did not run the red light," because it directly contradicts a substantive factual issue stated by Witness 1. Witness 2 cannot state, "Witness 1 was wearing a red jacket at the time, not blue." Though this casts doubt upon Witness 1's memory by contradicting his statement, this contradictory evidence is not material to the issues at trial and its only purpose is to cast doubt upon Witness 1's memory. The color of Witness 1's jacket is collateral to the issues at trial.

b. Exception: If there were a videotape of the collision, and the tape showed Witness 1 wearing a red jacket, the tape would not be collateral because it is relevant to a substantive issue. Witness 1 can be cross-examined on the color of the jacket because such questioning is not extrinsic evidence.

MBE Tip: The credibility for recollection of a witness may not be attacked with introduction of extrinsic evidence if the facts in the evidence has no other purpose than to cast doubt on the credibility of the testimony. This is known is the "Collateral Facts Rule."

---

3. Use of Impeachment Evidence as Substantive Evidence: Evidence that impeaches a witness may be used as substantive evidence as well, so long as the evidence is not excluded under any other rule such as hearsay.

    a. Admission With Limiting Instruction: If the impeachment evidence is not admissible substantively, then the Court gives a limiting instruction to the jury that the evidence may be considered only for impeachment purposes.

    b. Example: Extrinsic evidence of a prior inconsistent statement by a witness (not a party) would be admissible as impeachment evidence under FRE 613. This evidence may be inadmissible as substantive evidence under hearsay rules.

> **MBE Tip:** Once an accused testifies, under FRE 404(a)(3), he or she becomes a witness subject to impeachment rules 607, 608, & 609, which includes impeachment by prior conviction.

B. Character or Conduct of the Witness – FRE 608

1. Opinion or Reputation Evidence of Witness's Character – FRE 608(a): The credibility of a witness may be attacked or supported by evidence in the form of opinion or reputation only for truthfulness or untruthfulness.

    a. Reputation in Neutral Community: Reputation evidence must relate to the witness's reputation in a neutral and generalized community, such as the witness's neighbors or co-workers. A witness's reputation in a smaller or non-neutral community (e.g., a witness's reputation among local law enforcement officers) is inadmissible.

    b. Truthfulness: Evidence of the witness's truthful character may be introduced only in rebuttal to evidence of untruthfulness.

2. Specific Instances of Conduct – FRE 608(b): Specific instances of conduct, *other than conviction of a crime*, which concerns a witness's character for truthfulness or untruthfulness may be introduced only by cross-examination of a witness. They may not be proven by extrinsic evidence.

    a. Witness' Own Acts: A witness may be asked about his or her own prior acts that reflect for truthfulness or untruthfulness only upon cross-examination.

    b. Other Witness' Acts: If witness 2 testifies to the character of witness 1, witness 2 may testify about witness 1's prior acts only upon cross-examination.

C. Impeachment by Evidence of Conviction of Witness – FRE 609

> **MBE Tip:** Rules 608 & 609 allow for the introduction of character evidence of an accused if he testifies as a witness. For example, if a criminal D on trial for perjury takes the stand, his prior perjury conviction may be introduced for the purpose of attacking his credibility at the same time collaterally implying that the D has a propensity for perjury.

1. General Rule: For the purpose of attacking the credibility of a witness, evidence of the following types of crimes may be admitted:

a. Felonies: For any witness *other than the accused,* all crimes punishable by death or more than one year in prison (typically felonies) are admissible. When the witness is the accused, a prior felony may be admitted if the court determines that the probative value outweighs the prejudical effect.

b. Dishonesty: All crimes involving dishonesty (fraud, theft, etc.) or false statement, regardless of length of punishment are admissible.

c. Other Crimes: Crimes not falling into the above two categories are not admissible to attack the credibility of the witness under this rule. Typically, misdemeanors will not be admissible.

2. **Time Limit – 10 Years:**

a. Rule: Conviction of a felony or a crime involving dishonesty is not admissible if the conviction (or release from prison) was more than ten years ago.

b. Exception: However, if the court determines that the probative value of the conviction supported by specific facts and circumstances substantially outweighs its prejudicial effects, the court may admit evidence of a conviction that sits outside the ten year limit. This is allowed in the interests of justice, so long as the offering party gives advanced, written notice of such intent.

3. **Effect of Pardon, Annulment, or Certificate of Rehabilitation:** Evidence of a conviction is not admissible under this rule if the conviction was the subject of a pardon, annulment, or equivalent procedure where one of the following applies:

a. No Subsequent Felony: The person had not been convicted of any subsequent felony, or

b. Innocent of Charge: The pardon, etc., was based on a finding of innocence.

4. **Juvenile Adjudications:** Evidence of juvenile adjudications is generally not admissible under this rule. However, evidence of a juvenile adjudication may be used to impeach an adult witness who is not a D.

MBE Tip: The restrictions on impeachment evidence in Rules 608 & 609 do not apply to evidence showing bias. Bias may always be shown by prior acts that might otherwise be inadmissible character evidence. Example: Witness's membership in the same violent gang as the D may be admitted to show bias in favor of the D.

D. Religious Beliefs – FRE 610

Religious beliefs are not admissible for the purpose of attacking or bolstering witness credibility. However, religious beliefs may be admissible for another purpose such as bias.

E. Prior Witness Statements – FRE 613

1. **Inconsistent:** A prior witness statement that is inconsistent with or casts doubt upon her present trial testimony may be admitted into evidence.

2. Example: Witness A states that D ran a red light. That testimony is material to P's case. If witness B heard A previously state that the light was green, B may testify to such. However, witness A must be given an opportunity to explain the statement and opposing counsel must have an opportunity to interrogate the witness about the statement. This provision does not apply to an admission by party opponent under Rule 801(d)(2).

3. Purpose of Evidence: A statement offered only for impeachment is not subject to the hearsay rule. This is because the statement is not offered to prove the truth of the matter asserted, rather the fact that the statement was made.

4. Collateral Facts Rule Applies: As explained above, if a prior inconsistent statement is revealed with extrinsic evidence (FRE 613(b)), that evidence must be relevant to a substantive issue at trial.

MBE Tip: Extrinsic evidence may be used to introduce a witness's prior inconsistent statement. Don't confuse the prior statement with specific instances of <u>conduct</u> that *may not* be introduced with extrinsic evidence. Compare FRE 608(b) and FRE 613(b). Prior witness statements are still subject to the prohibition on impeachment evidence of collateral matters.

STOP!   Go to page 95 and work Learning Questions 30 to 38.

XIII. WITNESS PRESENTATION AND INTERROGATION

A. Mode and Order of Interrogation and Presentation – FRE 611

1. Scope of Cross-Examination: Cross-examination is limited to the subject matter of the direct examination and matters affecting the credibility of the witness.

2. Leading Questions: Leading questions are permitted on cross-examination. Leading questions should not be used on direct examination except as necessary to develop the witness's testimony.

3. Exception: When a party calls a hostile witness, an adverse party, or a witness identified with an adverse party, leading questions may be used on direct examination. The assumption is that an adverse witness will not want to be "led" so leading questions are harmless.

B. Writing Used to Refresh Memory – FRE 612

Rule 612 is "out of place" in the outline of rules because it does not relate to impeachment. Instead, it relates to helping a friendly witness recall factual details. If a witness is forgetful, a writing or anything else (i.e., song, scent, photograph) may be used to help refresh the witness's memory.

1. Oral Testimony: The witness must testify orally after having his memory refreshed. He/she may not read from the document used to refresh, but must testify from memory.

2. Need Not Be Admitted: Note that the writing or other item need not be introduced as evidence.

3. Opposing Counsel May Request Admittance: Opposing counsel has the right to inspect anything used to refresh the witness's memory and may introduce it into evidence if it meets other requirements of admissibility.

4. Privileges Are Waived: If the material was previously protected from disclosure by a privilege, counsel using the material to refresh the witness's memory is deemed to waive the protection.

> **MBE Tip:** If the writing itself is introduced as evidence, it must meet the other requirements of admissibility such as authenticity and hearsay.

C. Calling and Interrogation of Witness by Court – FRE 614

The Court may call or interrogate any witness. Objections may be made. The Court must refrain from demonstrating or suggesting any bias or partiality to any witness or argument.

D. Exclusion of Witness – FRE 615

At the request of a party, the Court may exclude a witness from the proceeding, so that they cannot hear the testimony of other witnesses.

XIV. OPINION AND EXPERT TESTIMONY

A. Opinion Testimony by Lay Witnesses – FRE 701

Opinion testimony by a lay witness is not automatically excluded by the FREs. (It is automatically excluded under the common law rules of evidence). Therefore, it is the judge's discretion whether to admit opinion testimony, so long as any opinion testimony meets the following criteria:

1. Rationally Based on the Witness' Perception: This witness focus is consistent with the Rule 602 requirement of personal knowledge for any witness testimony.

2. Helpful to a Clear Understanding of the Testimony or Determination of a Fact in Issue:

a. Factual Testimony: Lay opinions may be stated to help determine a fact in issue. For example, a witness would be allowed to draw a conclusion that a certain liquid was gasoline. This reflects most people's familiarity with gasoline although the witness could be wrong. The alternative would be limiting testimony to only the witness's observation that the liquid was amber in color, gave off strong fumes, and ignited when a match was set to it.

b. Helpful to Jury: Since the jury may not otherwise reach the conclusion that a liquid described in technical terms was gasoline, the witness's conclusion is helpful. Of course, opposing counsel would be allowed to cross-examine the witness on the witness's experience with gasoline that could cast doubt on the witness's testimony.

3. Not Based on Knowledge Within Scope of FRE 702: A lay witness may not give an opinion based on scientific, technical, or other specialized knowledge governed by FRE 702. If the witness can qualify as an expert, then an opinion may be given under FRE 702.

4. Examples:

a. Opinion: "Jim was happy." "My house is worth $200,000.00." "This is Sandra's handwriting."

b. Perception: "Jim was smiling." "Houses just like mine sell for $200,000.00." "This handwriting has these distinct characteristics, which I have also seen in Sandra's handwriting."

c. Observation: The above opinions are based on firsthand observation, which is still a strict requirement of admissibility. Therefore, counsel will need to lay the foundation of firsthand knowledge before eliciting the opinion from the witness.

> **MBE Tip:** Because the allowance of lay opinion is within the court's discretion, it is unlikely that a correct answer on the exam will be exclusion of the testimony because it is an opinion. Because Rule 701 favors inclusion to help the jury, look for other reasons to exclude such as lack of personal knowledge (see Rule 602).

B. Testimony by Experts – FRE 702

If scientific, technical, or other specialized knowledge will assist the trier of fact to understand the evidence or to determine a fact in issue, an expert witness may testify in the form of an opinion.

1. Requirements: The following requirements must be met to the judge's satisfaction:

a. Reasonable Basis: The testimony is based upon sufficient facts or data.

b. Reliable Principles: The testimony is the product of reliable principles and methods.

c. Application: The witness has applied the principles and methods reliably to the facts of the case.

2. Qualification of Experts: The witness must be qualified by knowledge, skill, experience, training, or education.

> **MBE Tip:** Note that formal education is not required; for example, a lifelong hobby can qualify a witness as an expert in that hobby. If qualification as an expert is raised on the MBE, don't discount informal experience.

3. Helpfulness: The opinion must be helpful to the trier of fact. This means the subject matter must be beyond the common understanding and normal knowledge of lay jurors. Expert opinion is not admissible if the jury does not need help understanding a matter of common experience such as intoxication or identifying gasoline.

4. Reliable Methods: There are three conditions to fulfill for an expert's methods to be deemed "reliable":

a. Reliable Principles and Techniques: A condition to admissibility of an expert's opinion is that the testimony must be based on reliable principles and methods.

b. Sufficient: Furthermore, the facts or data upon which the opinion is based must be sufficient to support the opinion.

c. Reliably Applied: Finally, the principles and methods must be reliably applied to the facts.

5. Example: The witness is an astrologer who will testify that it was physically impossible for D to have committed the crime because Aries was ascending that day precluding D's ability to get out of bed. Believe it or not, the judge has discretion to admit this testimony if astrology could be proved a reliable principle or method because acceptance of the principles in the scientific community is only a factor for the judge's consideration.

6. Some State Rules Differ: Many states follow the strict exclusion rule that the scientific basis of expert testimony *must* be accepted in that scientific community.

C. Basis for Expert Opinion – FRE 703

Expert opinion must be based on more than mere conjecture or speculation; there must be some reasonable basis for an opinion.

1. Facts Known to Expert: The facts or data in the particular case upon which an expert bases an opinion or inference may be those perceived by or made known to the expert at or before the hearing. This includes hypothetical facts upon which the expert is asked to offer an opinion or conclusion.

2. Need Not Be Admissible Facts: The facts or data need not be admissible into evidence (may be hearsay) if they are of a type reasonably relied upon by experts in the particular field in forming opinions or inferences upon the subject. As a practical result, assuming the expert's reliance is reasonable, counsel cannot object that the expert is basing an opinion on "facts not in evidence."

3. Proponent May Not Disclose Inadmissible Facts: If the opinion is based on inadmissible facts, those facts may not be disclosed by the proponent to the jury. There is no prohibition on opposing counsel conducting a cross-examination of the witness on the inadmissible facts.

MBE Tip: Occasionally courts have excluded expert opinion because it was based upon nothing but assumptions and speculation. More often, however, such objections go to the weight of the facts upon which the expert is relying, not admissibility. The court has discretion to make this determination.

D. Opinion on the Ultimate Issue of Fact – FRE 704

1. Not Objectionable: Testimony by either experts or lay witnesses in the form of an opinion or an inference that would be otherwise admissible is not objectionable simply because it embraces an ultimate issue to be decided by the trier of fact. Examples: "D was driving too fast for the conditions;" "D was intoxicated;" "The substance found in D's car was cocaine."

2. Legal Conclusion Prohibited: The witness cannot, however, give an opinion on the ultimate legal conclusion to be made by the trier of fact. The test for determining admissibility is usually whether the words chosen are ordinarily understood by the jury as lay persons or are legal terms of art with meanings of which the jury might be unaware.

3. Example of Legal Conclusion: "D is guilty as charged;" "D had no reason to defend himself;" "D was not negligent." A witness can say there was a "murder;" or say that the guardrail was "inherently dangerous." However, a witness cannot say "D committed second degree assault."

E. Disclosure of Facts or Data Underlying Expert Opinion – FRE 705

1. Foundation Unnecessary: The expert may testify in terms of opinion or inference and thus give reasons without prior disclosure of the underlying facts or data, unless the judge requires disclosure. There is no need to "lay a foundation" by bringing out the basis first. However, the expert may be required to disclose the underlying facts or data on cross-examination.

2. Hearsay: There is a question as to whether or not the expert may deliberately disclose the basis or underlying data if that information would otherwise be inadmissible as hearsay. The answer is that the expert may reveal the basis, but the court will give a limiting instruction, directing the jury not to consider it as substantive evidence. The court has discretion to exclude such evidence altogether under Rule 403's balancing test.

> **STOP!**   Go to page 96 and work Learning Questions 39 to 46.

XV. HEARSAY

> **MBE Tip:** The hearsay rule and the numerous exceptions are the most frequently tested evidence topics on the MBE.

A. Rule of Exclusion – FRE 802

Hearsay is excluded from evidence unless specifically excepted by rule. Note that a piece of evidence must first meet the definition of hearsay to be excluded under this rule. However, even if the statement does not meet the definition, or is excepted from hearsay, the statement may still be subject to other rules of exclusion (relevance, character, prejudicial).

B. Definitions – FRE 801

1. Hearsay: Hearsay is a statement, made by the declarant outside of the particular proceeding, and the statement is offered to prove the truth of matter asserted in the statement. A statement must meet this definition to be excluded as hearsay.

> **MBE Tip:** Remember, a statement that does not fit the definition of hearsay is *non*-hearsay, while a statement that fits the definition is hearsay, but may be subject to an exception. This is an important distinction, since the MBE may test knowledge of non-hearsay as well as the exceptions.

a. Statement: A "statement" is (1) an oral or written assertion or (2) nonverbal conduct intended as an assertion of fact.

b. **Declarant:** A "declarant" is the person who makes the statement in question.

c. **Truth of the Matter Asserted:** Logically, to be excluded under Rule 802, a statement must meet the definition of hearsay. A statement offered for a purpose other than to prove the truth of the matter asserted is not hearsay. If the jury's belief in the truth of the statement is necessary to the proponent's case, then the statement is hearsay.

d. **Examples of Non-Hearsay:** The following are typical examples of statements not offered to prove the truth of the matter asserted therein:

(1) Statements of Independent Legal Effect: These statements have legal effect regardless of the truth or falsity of the statement. "I give you my WorldCom stock" conveys an interest by the mere utterance; whether the statement is true or not.

(2) Statements Offered to Prove the Statement Was Said: Typically, this is to prove notice or duress.

(a) Example: "These floorboards are loose," can demonstrate notice to an owner in a premises liability case when knowledge of condition is an element; "Sign this contract or I'll break your knees," can show duress; "Professor Smith is a communist," can establish defamation.

(b) Statement Sufficient: The truth of the statement need not be believed to support a party's case, rather just the fact it was said. Note that the jury may infer the truth, but that is not the purpose for which the statement is offered.

(3) Statements Offered to Show Declarant's Perception: When the mental perception of a person based upon a statement is relevant to the case, then the truth or falsity of a statement is not at issue.

(a) Example: To assert a claim of self-defense D could testify, "Bob told me Victim wanted to kill me." This establishes the D's fear of imminent harm. Whether or not it is true that Victim did want to kill D does not matter; only the fact D heard the statement. Also, the declarant's description of an item or event may be offered not to prove that the perception was accurate, but rather to prove that the declarant perceived the item or event.

(b) Example: Declarant's statement "Old Main at the University of Arizona is painted white on the inside," may be offered to support a contention that declarant has been inside of Old Main. This does not support a contention that the walls are indeed white.

e. **Conduct as an Assertion:** The statement must also be intended by the declarant to be an assertion.

(1) Inference: A verbal or written statement is usually intended as an assertion. However, certain types of conduct may lead a witness to infer a fact. Only if the conduct was intended to assert a fact, will the conduct be hearsay.

(2) Example: If one asks the declarant "Is it raining outside?" and in response, the declarant holds up a wet umbrella, the declarant was asserting that it is indeed raining outside. However, if the declarant merely shakes the water off the umbrella when entering a building, the shaking is not an assertion that it is raining though one may infer such.

> **MBE Tip:** Be careful when assessing conduct as an assertion. It will almost always be in response to a request for information. If the fact pattern describes the conduct as an unsolicited assertion, it is probably not assertive conduct.

f. **Silence as an Assertion:** See adoptive admission in 2(b)(2) below. Obviously, an adoptive admission is also an assertion.

2. Statements That Are Non-Hearsay Despite Meeting Definition – FRE 801(d): A statement may meet the above definition, but still be "non-hearsay" by rule if it meets the criteria of either **a** or **b** below:

a. **Prior Statement by Witness – FRE 801(d)(1):** The declarant testifies at the trial or hearing and is subject to cross-examination concerning the statement, and the statement is:

(1) Inconsistent: Prior testimony is inconsistent with the declarant's current testimony, and was given under oath at a prior proceeding subject to the penalty of perjury; or

(2) Consistent: Prior testimony is consistent with the declarant's testimony *and* is offered to rebut an express or implied charge of recent fabrication or improper influence or motive; or

(3) Identification: An identification of a person made after perceiving the person (i.e., identification in a lineup or shortly after a crime) is not hearsay.

> **MBE Tip:** A statement is non-hearsay under 801(d)(1) *only* when the declarant is also a witness.

b. **Admission by Party-Opponent – FRE 801(d)(2):** The statement is offered against a **party** and is:

(1) Own Statement: That party's own statement, or assertive conduct, in either an individual or a representative capacity.

(2) Adoptive Admission: A statement that the party has adopted as his own or has manifested a belief in its truth (known as an "adoptive admission"). An adoptive admission must meet all of the below three criteria to be admissible:

> **MBE Tip:** The admissions exception is very broad and opens the door to virtually anything the opposing party has said or written. It does not have to be a statement "against interest." Typical examples are letters or diaries written by the opposing party, opposing party's deposition, or answers to interrogatories.

(a) Heard: The party heard and understood the statement,

(b) Not Denied: The statement was false and of such a nature that a reasonable person would deny it, and

(c) No Response: The party was able to respond to the statement, but did not.

(3) Authorized: A statement by a person authorized by the party to make a statement concerning the subject; or

(4) Agent: A statement by the party's agent or employee when the agent or employee:

(a) Scope of Agency: Acts within the scope of the agency or employment, and

(b) During Agency: Made during such agency or employment (Under the Federal Rules, the agent or employee need not have authority to make the admission).

(5) Co-Conspirator: A statement by a co-conspirator of a party during the course and in furtherance of the conspiracy. (Evidence other than the statement must first establish the conspiracy.)

STOP! Go to page 97 and work Learning Questions 47 to 51.

C. Hearsay Exceptions; Availability of Declarant Immaterial – FRE 803

> **MBE Tip:** These exceptions are heavily tested on the MBE. It is vital to remember that the hearsay exceptions under Rule 803 apply *regardless* of whether the declarant is present.

Admissible hearsay must meet a specific exception. The following statements are exceptions to the exclusion by the hearsay rule, and apply in all cases, civil and criminal, whether the declarant is available to testify or not. The presence or absence of the declarant makes no difference.

1. Present Sense Impression – FRE 803(1): A statement describing or explaining an event or condition made while the declarant was perceiving the event or condition, or immediately thereafter. An example is a statement about a phone call, immediately after hanging up: "That was Herman on the phone, and he told me he was coming over here to discuss the contract."

> **MBE Tip:** The key to the present sense impression exception is that the perception and statement are contemporaneous with the event. The passage of time eliminates this exception. Distinguish from a situation where the declarant described the event some time after its occurrence.

2. Excited Utterance – FRE 803(2): A statement relating to (but not necessarily describing) a startling event or condition made while the declarant was under the stress of excitement caused by the event or condition. The event causing the emotional excitation need not have occurred immediately prior to the utterance. Examples are a 911 call for help; a hysterical statement describing a horrific automobile accident; a victim's sobbing declaration.

3. Then-Existing Mental, Emotional, or Physical Condition – FRE 803(3): A statement of the declarant's then-existing state of mind, emotion, sensation, or physical condition.

a. Includes: This includes intent, plan, motive, design, mental feeling, pain and bodily health as currently being experienced by the declarant. Watch for phrases like "I do," "I intend," "I will," "I am," as they all indicate a then-existing state of mind or intention.

b. Excludes: However, statements regarding a declarant's state of mind or beliefs are not admissible to prove causation. Thus, "I believe my current leg pain was caused by yesterday's car collision," is inadmissible as part of the statement relates to a past event. A statement describing a *past* mental, emotional, or physical condition is not admissible unless the statement relates to declarant's will.

4. Statements Made for Medical Treatment – FRE 803(4):

a. Relevant to Treatment: This is a statement made to a clinician to help the clinician treat or diagnose the declarant's illness or injury, even if the clinician is retained only for expert testimony. However, the facts in the statement must be relevant to the treatment.

b. Fault Excluded: Statements attributing fault are technically excluded. "I was beaten" would be admissible as the cause of injury will assist the clinician in her treatment or diagnosis. "I was beaten *by my husband*," is not because who caused the injury does not assist the clinician in her diagnosis or treatment. However, many courts will admit these statements on the theory that they are necessary to prevent future injury to the patient (i.e. potentially recurrent spousal or child abuse).

5. Recorded Recollection – FRE 803(5): When a knowledgeable witness has insufficient recollection to testify fully and accurately about a matter, and an accurate or factually correct record concerning the matter is shown to have been made or adopted by the witness when the matter was fresh in the witness's memory, the record may be read into evidence. It may not itself be received as an exhibit unless offered by an adverse party.

a. Examples: Some examples of recorded recollections are police reports, court reporter's notes, journalist's notes, entries in business records (note that some of these may also be records of regularly conducted activity).

b. Foundation – PIFA: To lay a proper foundation, the following must be shown. Failure to meet any of these four "PIFA" elements will render the recollection inadmissible.

(1) Pertinent: The record pertains to a matter about which the witness once had personal knowledge;

(2) Insufficient Present Recollection: The witness now has insufficient recollection to testify *fully and accurately* (thus partial recollection or insufficient recollection of details would not negate this element);

(3) Fresh When Adopted: The record was made or adopted (witness agreed to accuracy at the time of preparation) by the witness when the matter was fresh in the witness's memory; and

(4) Accurate: The record reflects the witness's prior knowledge accurately.

> **MBE Tip:** Do not confuse this with a Rule 612 writing used to refresh memory, the contents of which are not offered into evidence. Also, this type of evidence is still subject to "Best Evidence" requirements under Rule 1002.

6. Records of Regularly Conducted Activity (Business Records Exception) – FRE 803(6): Records kept in the ordinary course of business are admissible. The rationale is that the business has a strong incentive to keep accurate records for the purposes of taxation, accounting, etc. To qualify as a business record, the document must meet the following requirements through the testimony or certification of a witness with knowledge that:

a. Regularly Conducted: The record is of a regularly conducted activity.

b. Near in Time: The record was created in the regular course of business near in time to the activity, condition, or event.

c. Personal Knowledge: The record is based on personal knowledge of someone in the business who made the recording.

d. Regular Practice: The recording was a regular practice of the business.

e. Reliable: The record is reliable for truthfulness (no motive to fabricate) – records prepared in anticipation of litigation fail this element.

> **MBE Tip:** Watch for hearsay within hearsay. If a business record is based on a statement obtained by a declarant not in the business, then it will not be admissible unless the statement qualifies under another hearsay exception.

7. Learned Treatises – FRE 803(18): A learned treatise or periodical may be used to supplement the testimony of an expert on direct examination.

a. Foundation: As a matter of foundation, counsel must establish that the expert relied upon the publication and that it is authoritative. The expert may only read relevant portions to the jury. The publication itself is not admitted as an exhibit.

b. Cross-Examination: A learned treatise or periodical may also be used on cross-examination of an expert for purposes of impeachment. On cross-examination, counsel must establish that the publication is authoritative, but not that the expert actually relied upon it. The contents of the treatise may be substantive as well as impeachment evidence.

> **STOP!** Go to page 98 and work Learning Questions 52 to 55.

D. Other Hearsay Exceptions; Availability of Declarant Immaterial

> **MBE Tip:** The following exceptions are not heavily tested on the MBE, but are presented here for completeness of study.

1. Absence of Entry in Records – FRE 803(7): Lack of a record of an activity that would otherwise be recorded and admissible as a Record of Regularly Conducted Activity is admissible to show lack of an occurrence.

2. Public Records – FRE 803(8):

a. Rule: Copies of all records and documents on record or on file in the offices of the various departments of the United States and of any State or Territory within the United States, when duly certified (under seal where appropriate) by custodial officers of such documents, shall be admitted into evidence. The record must be government generated and simply state facts.

> **MBE Tip:** A record that expresses an opinion or discretionary finding (such as an administrative determination) do not fall within this exception. Note that these records are also self-authenticating under FRE 902.

b. Examples: Driving records, official weather reports, official records of births and deaths, or a sheriff's written proof of service (often called a "return of service").

3. Records of Vital Statistics – FRE 803(9): Records or data compilations, in any form, of births, fetal deaths, deaths, or marriages are admissible, if the report was made to a public office pursuant to requirements of law.

4. Absence of Entry in Records of Vital Statistics – FRE 803(10): The absence of such a record where one should or is alleged to exist may also be introduced and is not hearsay. For example, if a D claims to be 28 years old and there is no entry of her birth record 28 years prior, that absence of record may be introduced.

5. Records of Religious Organizations – FRE 803(11): Births, Deaths, Marriages, Genealogy, or other personal or family history contained in regularly-kept record.

6. Marriage, Baptismal, and Similar Certificates – FRE 803(12): Statements of fact contained within the certificate that the maker performed the marriage.

7. Family Records – FRE 803(13): Statements of fact concerning family history contained in family bibles, genealogies, charts, engravings, or inscriptions.

8. Records of Documents Affecting an Interest in Property – FRE 803(14): Deeds recorded in a public office and a statute authorizing same.

9. Statements in Documents Affecting an Interest in Property – FRE 803(15): A statement within a document purporting to establish or affect an interest in property if the statement is relevant to the purpose of the document.

10. Statements in Ancient Documents – FRE 803(16): Statements in a document in existence 20 years or more whose authenticity is established are admissible. See Rule 901 for authenticity requirements. Examples are old newspapers, reference books, deeds.

11. Market Reports, Commercial Publications – FRE 803(17): Market quotations, tabulations, lists, directories, or other published compilation generally used and relied upon by the public or person in a particular occupation are admissible.

12. Reputation Concerning Personal or Family History – FRE 803(19): Reputation among family members concerning a person's birth, adoption, marriage, divorce, death, ancestry, or other personal or family history.

13. Reputation Concerning Boundaries or General History – FRE 803(20): Reputation in a community, arising prior to the controversy, as to boundaries of or customs affecting lands in the community, or general history of significance to the relevant community.

14. Reputation as to Character – FRE 803(21): Reputation of a person's character among associates or in the community.

15. Judgment of Previous Conviction – FRE 803(22): A final judgment after trial or guilty plea (but not nolo contendere) adjudging guilt of a crime punishable by death or imprisonment of more than one year are admissible, but only to prove a fact essential to the judgment. Excluded when the government offers judgments of one other than the accused in a criminal prosecution for purposes other than impeachment.

16. Judgment as to Personal, Family, or General History, or Boundaries – FRE 803(23): Judgments as proof of matters of personal, family, or general history, or boundaries, essential to the judgment, if the same would be provable by evidence of reputation.

> **MBE Tip:** The list of 803 exceptions is long and daunting. Use common sense to evaluate whether an 803 exception applies: if it is the kind of information generally relied upon in society.

E. Hearsay Exceptions; Declarant Unavailable – FRE 804

Unlike Rule 803 exceptions, the following exceptions require that the declarant be unavailable.

1. Definition of Unavailability: "Unavailability as a witness" includes situations in which:

a. Privilege: The declarant is exempted from testifying on the ground of privilege; or

b. Refusal to Testify: The declarant refuses to testify concerning the subject matter of the declarant's statement despite a court order to do so; or

c. Lack of Memory: The declarant testifies to a lack of memory of the subject matter of the declarant's statement; or

d. Death or Infirmity: The declarant is unable to be present or to testify at the hearing because of death or then-existing physical or mental illness or infirmity; or

e. Absence: The declarant is absent from the hearing and the proponent has been unable to procure the declarant's attendance by process or other reasonable means. Or, in the case of a statement under 804(b)(2–4) below if the proponent has been unable to procure the declarant's attendance *or testimony*.

f. Wrongdoing by Proponent: A declarant does not meet the definition of unavailable if the exemption, refusal, claim of lack of memory, inability, or absence is due to the procurement or wrongdoing of the proponent of a statement for the purpose of preventing the witness from attending or testifying. Examples are counsel flew the declarant to another country or counseled declarant not to talk.

2. Hearsay Exceptions – FRE 804(b): The following are *not* excluded by the hearsay rule if the declarant is unavailable as a witness:

a. Former Testimony – FRE 804(b)(1): Testimony given by a witness at a prior hearing or deposition, if the party against whom the testimony is now offered had an opportunity or motive to develop the testimony by direct, cross or redirect examination. For example, W testifies in D's criminal trial. A mistrial is declared, but before the second trial, W dies. W's testimony from the first trial is admissible under this exception.

> **MBE Tip:** Do not confuse the Rule 804(b)(1) Former Testimony exception with a Rule 801(d)(1) Prior Statement by Witness. Prior Statement by Witness refers to situations where the witness *is* available, but there is a potential inconsistency.

b. Statement Under Belief of Impending Death – FRE 804(b)(2): A statement made by a declarant (1) while believing that his or her death was imminent, and (2) concerning the cause or circumstances of the imminent death. This rule applies in all civil cases, but only in criminal prosecutions for homicide of the declarant. The declarant need not be dead, but only unavailable.

> **MBE Tip:** It is imperative that in an exam question the declarant express a belief in imminent death, though the declarant need not die. Conversely, the fact that the declarant did die does not establish a belief in imminent death.

c. Statement Against Interest – FRE 804(b)(3): A statement that is so far contrary to the declarant's pecuniary or proprietary interest, subjecting the declarant to criminal or civil liability, or rendering invalid a claim by the declarant against another; such that a reasonable person in the declarant's position would not have made the statement unless the declarant believed it to be true.

(1) Not Merely Embarrassing: This exception does not include statements that simply expose the declarant to ridicule or disgrace. Personal knowledge by the declarant is required.

(2) Criminal Case: An exception is in a criminal case, a statement tending to expose the declarant to criminal liability and exculpating the accused is not admissible unless corroborating circumstances clearly indicate the trustworthiness of the statement.

> **MBE Tip:** Do not confuse a statement against interest with an admission *by party opponent*. A party opponent is by definition available, so Rule 804 exclusions do not apply. Conversely, in order to be excepted under Rule 804 the declarant cannot be a party; the declarant *must* be unavailable. Also, a Rule 801 admission may be self-serving, a statement against the interest cannot.

d. Statement of Personal or Family History – FRE 804(b)(4): This is either:

(1) Own Statements: A statement concerning the declarant's own birth, adoption, marriage, divorce legitimacy, relationship by blood, adoption, ancestry, or other fact of family history *even despite the declarant's lack of personal knowledge,* or

(2) Other Statements: A statement concerning the birth, adoption, marriage, divorce legitimacy, relationship by blood, adoption, ancestry, or death also, of another person, if the declarant was related to the other by blood, adoption, or marriage or was so intimately associated with the other's family as to be likely to have accurate information concerning the matter declared.

e. Forfeiture by Wrongdoing – FRE 804(b)(6): A statement may be offered against a party who has attempted to and did procure the unavailability of the declarant as a witness.

> **MBE Tip:** Frequently on the MBE, the previous declarant of the statement identifying the criminal D is dead. This by itself does not meet any of the FRE 804 exceptions and thus such evidence is to be properly excluded, unless it is former sworn testimony.

F. Hearsay Within Hearsay – FRE 805

Hearsay included within hearsay is not excluded under the hearsay rule if each part of the combined statements conforms with an exception to the hearsay rule provided in these rules. For example, at trial a police accident report is offered. The accident report can get in under the Business Records exception or the Public Record exception. The statements of the witnesses documented on the accident report may get in under Admission by a Party, Statement Against Interest, Present Sense Impression, or Excited Utterance.

> **MBE Tip:** Think of "levels" or "layers" of hearsay. For each layer, does the statement meet the definition of hearsay? If so, does a separate exception apply? If any layer of hearsay does not meet an established hearsay exception, then the statement is inadmissible.

G. Credibility of Declarant – FRE 806

1. Impeachment: When hearsay, or a statement defined under Rule 801(d)(2)(C-E), is admitted pursuant to a hearsay exception, the out-of-court declarant may be impeached just as if he were present and testifying as a witness. The opportunity for the declarant to deny or explain is not required.

2. Cross-Examination: A party against whom a hearsay statement was admitted may call the declarant as a witness and interrogate him or her as if on cross-examination.

H. Residual Exception – FRE 807

Hearsay not excepted from exclusion under Rules 803 & 804 may still be admitted if the following three criteria are met:

1. Material Fact: The statement is evidence of a material fact,

2. Probative: The statement is more probative on the point for which it is offered than any other evidence, which the proponent can procure through reasonable efforts, and

3. Interest of Justice: The general purposes of these rules and the interests of justice will best be served by admission of the statement into evidence.

Thus, impeachment hearsay would not be excepted under this rule. Also, the hearsay must be the most probative of any other evidence.

> **STOP!** Go to page 99 and work Learning Questions 56 to 60.

XVI. DOCUMENT AUTHENTICATION AND IDENTIFICATION

Documentary evidence cannot stand on its own. It must be proved to be what the proponent claims it to be. The document can be self-authenticating or authenticated by other means.

A. Authentication and Identification Required – FRE 901

The requirement of authentication or identification, as a condition precedent to admissibility, is satisfied by evidence sufficient to support a finding that the matter in question is what its proponent claims. In practice, the requirement is easily satisfied in most cases. This rule pertains mainly to documents and other tangible evidence such as photographs, and the identification of voices.

B. Acceptable Methods – FRE 901(b)

The following is a list of acceptable methods of authentication and identification.

1. Testimony of Witness With Knowledge: This is testimony by one who would have reason to know that a matter is what it is claimed to be. The maker of, or a witness to, the creation of the document may testify to authenticity.

a. Special Knowledge: The authenticating witness has knowledge that facts in the writing were known only to herself and the writer. For example, A told the witness, "I wrote to Madame Versant that I was admitting liability due to my bad horoscope." The witness could relate this special knowledge to establish that the memo was written by A.

b. Maker's Admission: The maker may testify that she did indeed make the writing.

c. Witness to the Creation: A witness can testify that she saw the writer create the writing.

d. Out-of-Court Admission: An out-of-court statement regarding the authenticity of the document is subject to hearsay rules.

e. Expert Opinion on Handwriting: An expert can compare the signature on a document with an authentic signature.

2. Photograph or Drawing: Testimony by a witness who saw the scene in question and testifies the photograph or drawing is a fair and accurate representation. If the witness took the picture, then she is a witness with knowledge.

3. Non-Expert Opinion on Handwriting: Non-expert opinion as to the genuineness of handwriting is based upon familiarity acquired prior to litigation. Examples include a sister testifying as to her sibling's writing in a journal, correspondence, or on a deed.

4. Distinctive Characteristics: Appearance, contents, substance, internal patterns, or other distinctive characteristics, taken in conjunction with circumstances. For example, the authenticity of page 3 of a five page letter is in dispute. Assuming the other pages are authentic, if page 3 "fits" within the letter, it will be authentic.

MBE Tip: The bar frequently tests the admissibility requirements of authentication. An expert is not usually required; only someone with personal familiarity.

---

5. Voice Identification: Identification of a voice, whether heard firsthand or through mechanical or electronic transmission or recording, by opinion based upon hearing the voice at any time under circumstances connecting it with the alleged speaker. Of course, the witness must have prior knowledge of the maker's voice.

6. Telephone Conversations: Telephone conversations, by evidence that a call was made to the number assigned at the time by the telephone company to a particular person or business, if

a. Identification: In the case of a person, circumstances, including self-identification, show the person answering to be the one called, or

b. Reasonable Content: In the case of a business, the call was made to a place of business and the conversation related to business reasonably transacted over the telephone.

c. Return Call: If caller calls Bob at his place of business, leaves a message, and someone returns the call identifying himself as Bob returning the prior call, the voice of Bob is authenticated.

7. Ancient Documents or Data Compilation: Evidence that a document or data compilation, in any form:

a. Not Suspicious: Is in such condition as to create no suspicion concerning its authenticity;

b. Likely Place: Is in a place where it, if authentic, would likely be found, and;

c. 20 Years Old: Has been in existence 20 years or more at the time it is offered.

C. Self-Authentication – FRE 902

Due to the typical accuracy of the following documents, additional evidence of authenticity is not required as a condition to admissibility:

MBE Tip: Self-authentication only refers to official documents. If self-authentication is an option on the MBE, be wary unless it is an official publication or is under some kind of seal or oath.

---

1. Domestic Public Documents Under Seal: Public documents bearing a proper seal and attesting or executing signature.

2. Domestic Public Documents Not Under Seal: Authenticity of non-sealed public documents are established if 1) the signing officer had no seal to use when the document was signed, and 2) a current public officer who works for the same public entity certifies under seal that the signature is genuine.

3. Foreign Public Documents: A foreign public document is authenticated by the fact it is signed by a public official authorized to do so under the laws of a foreign country, and has a final certification by a U.S. Consular agent.

4. Certified Copies of Public Records: Copy of an official record certified by the custodian as authentic.

5. Official Publications: Books, pamphlets, or other publications purporting to be issued by public authority.

6. Newspapers and Periodicals: Newspapers, magazines, and other periodicals.

7. Trade Inscriptions: Signs, tags or labels affixed in the course of business and indicating ownership, control, or origin.

8. Acknowledged Documents: Documents accompanied by a certificate of acknowledgement by a notary public.

9. Commercial Paper and Related Documents: Commercial paper, signatures thereon, and documents relating thereto.

10. Act of Congress: Any signature, document, or other matter declared by Act of Congress to be authentic.

11. Certified Domestic Record of Regularly Conducted Activity: A record accompanied by a declaration of its custodian or other qualified person certifying that the record was kept properly. The proponent must then give notice to adverse parties and make the declaration available for inspection. For a record to be kept "properly" means that:

a. **Near in Time:** The record as made at or near in time to the occurrence by or through information transmitted by a person with knowledge,

b. **Regular Course:** The record was kept in the course of regularly conducted activity, and

c. **Regularly Conducted Activity:** The record was made as part of a regularly conducted activity, as opposed to a unique record made in response to an extraordinary event.

12. Certified Foreign Record of Regularly Conducted Activity: This falls under the same requirements as 11 above, but is applicable in civil cases only. Also, the declaration must be made under the penalty of the laws of perjury of the country of origin.

XVII. BEST EVIDENCE RULE

The best evidence rule simply states that to prove the contents of a writing, the writing must be produced. The best evidence rule applies only when attempting to prove the actual content of a writing, recording, or photograph. It does not apply when attempting to prove underlying or related events. For example, a business keeps written records of certain transactions. If the business wishes to use the records themselves as evidence, it must comply with the best evidence rule. But if employees wish to give oral testimony about the underlying transactions from memory, they are free to do so without satisfying the best evidence rule.

A. Definitions – FRE 1001

1. Writings and Recordings: "Writings" and "recordings" consist of letters, words, sounds, numbers, or their equivalent, set down by handwriting, typewriting, printing, photostatting, photographing, magnetic impulse, mechanical or electronic recording, or other form of data compilation.

2. Photographs: "Photographs" include still photographs, x-ray films, video tapes, and motion pictures.

3. Originals: An "original" of a writing or recording is the writing or recording itself or any counterpart intending to have the same effect by a person executing or issuing it. An "original" of a photograph includes the negative or any print from the negative. If data is in a computer, any printout or other readable output shown to reflect the data accurately is an "original."

4. Duplicate: A "duplicate" is a counterpart produced (1) by the same impression as the original, (2) from the same matrix, (3) by means of photography, including enlargements and miniatures, (4) by mechanical or electronic recording, (5) by chemical reproduction, or (6) by other equivalent techniques which accurately reproduce the original.

B. Requirement of Original – FRE 1002

To prove the content of a writing, recording, or photograph, the original is required, except where the FREs or law provide otherwise. FRE 1003 below is the biggest exception.

> **MBE Tip:** An answer on the MBE purporting to exclude the evidence as failing the best evidence rule is a common trap. The best evidence rule applies only when the material terms of a writing are being proved or the witness is testifying relying on the writing. If the witness is testifying to a collateral matter, the best evidence rule does not apply.

C. **Admissibility of Duplicates – FRE 1003**

A duplicate is admissible to the same extent as an original unless (1) a genuine question is raised as to the authenticity of the original or (2) in the circumstances it would be unfair to admit the duplicate in lieu of the original.

> **MBE Tip:** Look for a credible allegation that the duplicate has been tampered with. In this instance the original document is required.

D. **Other Evidence of Contents – FRE 1004**

To prove the content of a writing, recording, or photograph, the original (or a duplicate) is required, unless:

1. Original Lost or Destroyed: All originals are lost or have been destroyed, unless the proponent lost or destroyed them in bad faith; or

2. Original Not Obtainable: No original can be obtained by any available judicial process or procedure; or

3. Original in Possession of Opponent: At a time when an original was under the control of the party against whom offered, that party was put on notice, by the pleadings or otherwise, that the contents would be a subject of proof at the hearing, and that party does not produce the original at the hearing; or

4. Collateral Matters: The writing, recording, or photograph is not closely related to a controlling issue. The terms in question must be material.

E. **Public Records – FRE 1005**

Contents of official records may be authenticated in accordance with Rule 902 or by testimony of a witness who has compared it to the original. If a copy cannot be obtained with reasonable diligence, other evidence of the contents may be given.

F. **Summaries – FRE 1006**

Where the contents of voluminous writings, recordings, or photographs cannot conveniently be examined in court, they may be presented in the form of a chart or summary. The originals, or duplicates shall be made available for examination or copying, or both, by other parties at a reasonable time and place unless the court orders that they be produced in court.

G. Admission – FRE 1007

Authenticity may be proved by testimony, deposition, or written admission by a party against whom the document is offered without accounting for the non-production of the original.

H. Function of Court and Jury – FRE 1008

When admissibility is conditioned on another fact, the fulfillment of that fact is to be determined by the Court under Rule 104. An issue as to the existence of the writing, the originality of the writing, and/or whether other evidence correctly reflects the contents is for the trier of fact.

> **STOP!** Go to page 100 and work Learning Questions 61 to 71.

XVIII. FINAL CHAPTER REVIEW INSTRUCTIONS

1. Completing the Chapter: Now that you have completed your study of the chapter's substantive text and the related Learning Questions, you need to button up this chapter. This includes your preparing your Magic Memory Outlines® and working all of the subject's practice questions.

2. Preparing Your Own Magic Memory Outline®: This is essential to your MBE success. We recommend that you use our software template in this process. Do not underestimate the learning and memory effectiveness derived from condensing the text chapter into your succinct summaries using your own words. This exercise is covered in much more detail in the preface and on the CD-ROM.

    a. Summarize Knowledge: You need to prepare a summary of the chapter in your own words. This is best accomplished using the Rigos Bar Review Series Magic Memory Outlines® software. The words in the outline correspond to the bold headings in the text.

    b. Capture the Essence: Your job is to summarize the substance of the text by capturing the essence of the rule and entering your summarized wording into your own outlines. Go to the text coverage and craft your own tight, concise, but yet comprehensive statements of the law. Take pride in your skills as an author; this is the best outline you have ever created.

    c. Focus: Focus your attention and wording on the required technical elements necessary to prove the relevant legal principles and fine-line distinctions. Integrate any helpful "learning question" information into your outline.

3. Memorize Outline: After you have completed your own Magic Memory Outline® for the whole chapter, read it over carefully once or twice. They are the best book ever written. Refer back to your Outlines frequently.

4. Work Old Questions: The next step is to work all the final questions of each chapter. These vary in degree of difficulty, but the ones towards the end tend to concentrate on fact patterns and issues at the most difficult testing level. Consider using the Question Map on the CD-ROM. Click on the questions under the subject and topic you have just studied. This allows you to cross relate the subjects and related MBE testing.

a. Question Details: Again, it is usually worthwhile to review the explanatory answer rationales as they reinforce the relevant principles of law. If you are still unsure of the controlling rule, refer back to the related portion of the text. This will help you to appreciate the fine-line distinctions on which the MBE questions turn.

b. Do a Few Questions At a Time: Work the final chapter questions in sequence. Make sure you stop after no more than a few to check the answer rationales. Do this frequently so that the facts of the individual question are still in active memory.

c. Work Them All: We have tried to pick questions with an average or higher probability of reappearing on the MBE. You should at least read all the questions and ponder their answers. Every question and answer has some marginal learning and/or reinforcement value. On the MBE you will recognize many of the actual MBE questions as very similar to the ones in your Rigos Bar Review Series review books.

d. Learn From Mistakes: The objective is to learn from your mistakes by reviewing the explanatory rationales while you still remember the factual and legal details of the question. It is good to miss a few; they will help you become familiar with the MBE fine-line distinctions. The examiners' use of distracters, tricks, and red herrings is repetitive.

e. Flag Errors: Put a red star in the margin of the book along side every question you missed. Missed questions should be worked again the day right before the MBE. Do not make the same mistakes on the exam.

f. Essays: Candidates in jurisdictions that administer the Multistate Essay Exam should refer to the *Rigos Bar Review Series Multistate Essay Exam Review — MEE* for practice essay questions.

5. Practice Exam: After you complete the last chapter, you should take the 200 item practice exam. There is detailed information covering this simulated MBE test in both the preface and at the beginning of the exam in Volume 2. This is important because you need to build your concentrated attention time span. You also need to get intellectually used to jumping between unrelated topics and subjects.

6. Make Your Own Exam: The Rigos Bar Review Series software allows you to pick 5, 10, 20 or 100 questions at random from all six MBE subjects. This is an important feature because you must become comfortable with switching intellectual gears between different subjects. If you are not an early riser and/or get going slowly when you get up, try working 10 or 20 questions using the "Make Your Own Exam" software the first thing every morning.

7. Update Your Magic Memory Outline®: The fine-line distinctions in the question and answer rationales will improve your understanding of how the MBE tests the law. Consider updating your Magic Memory Outline® while the question testing environment is still fresh in your mind.

8. Next Chapter: It is now time to go to the beginning of the next subject. Begin by previewing the chapter. Scan the typical coverage.

Magic Memory Outlines®

XVI. DOCUMENT AUTHENTICATION AND IDENTIFICATION

RIGOS BAR REVIEW SERIES

MULTISTATE BAR EXAM REVIEW (MBE)

CHAPTER 4

EVIDENCE

Question Distribution Map

> Numbers immediately following the topic are the chapter question numbers. The **boldface** numbers preceded by "F" are the final exam question numbers. For example, for the topic "H. Presumptions and Burden of Proof – FRE 301" below, questions 5, 6, and 214 are in the chapter questions on pages 4-91, 4-91, and 4-127, respectively; questions **F40**, **F55**, and **F144** are in the final exam on pages 7-459, 7-463, and 7-484, respectively.

XV. HEARSAY

XVII. BEST EVIDENCE RULE

MEE Candidates: If your jurisdiction administers the Multistate Essay Exam in addition to the MBE, please refer to the *Rigos Bar Review Series Multistate Essay Exam Review — MEE* for practice essay questions and sample answers covering evidence.

Evidence
Learning Questions

Assume all jurisdictions use the Federal Rules of Evidence.

1. In a civil case, when the Court takes judicial notice of a fact, that fact is
   (A) Conclusively established.
   (B) Still must be proved with other evidence.
   (C) The moving party's burden of production is satisfied.
   (D) The other party may rebut with other evidence.

2. In a criminal case, when the Court takes judicial notice of a fact
   (A) That fact is conclusively established.
   (B) That fact must still be proved with other evidence.
   (C) The prosecution's burden of production is satisfied.
   (D) A text or other reference source must be consulted.

3. For which of the following facts, would it be error to take judicial notice in a civil case?
   (A) The fact that the sky is blue.
   (B) The fact that New York City is in New York State.
   (C) The fact that the Columbia River empties into the Pacific Ocean.
   (D) The fact that air bags are standard safety equipment on automobiles.

4. D is on trial for embezzlement. During the prosecution's case in chief, evidence of D's prior conviction for embezzlement is offered into evidence. The Court sustains the objection, ruling that prior convictions may not be admitted to demonstrate that D is a criminal type. During D's case in chief, D testifies that he is honest and would never do such a thing. In rebuttal, the prosecution again offers the evidence of conviction to impeach D's testimony. What must happen for the evidence to be admitted?
   (A) The Court must tell the jury that they may consider the evidence only to determine the D's credibility.
   (B) The Court must tell the jury that they may consider the evidence not only as impeachment evidence, but also for its substantive value.
   (C) The Court must tell the jury that evidence of a prior conviction is determinative of a witness's credibility.
   (D) The Court must not comment on the evidence in any way.

Questions 5 and 6 share common facts.

5. Suppose that in Anystate, U.S.A., it is negligence per se to allow your dog to run loose. D's dog, while running loose, bites P. P sues and during his case in chief, produces evidence that D's dog was running loose at the time he was bitten. This evidence has what effect?
   (A) The D's negligence is presumed.
   (B) The D's negligence is presumed until he offers evidence in rebuttal.
   (C) The jury may consider whether the dog running loose and biting P was negligent.
   (D) P has not proved anything.

6. D from above is charged with criminal negligence based on the same facts. What effect does the prosecution's introduction of

the fact that D's dog was running loose at the time of the bite have?

    (A) The D's negligence is presumed.

    (B) The D's negligence is presumed until he offers evidence in rebuttal.

    (C) The jury may consider whether the dog running loose and biting P was negligent.

    (D) The prosecution has not proved anything.

Questions 7 and 8 share common facts.

7.   P is suing D for negligence (failure to exercise due care) resulting from a rear-end automobile collision. Which of the following facts is relevant to P's case?

    (A) The fact D was not carrying a license to drive.

    (B) The fact D was driving too fast for the weather conditions.

    (C) The fact that the license plate on D's car was expired.

    (D) The fact that D was driving a Gremlin.

8.   Same facts as above, except P is able to establish D's negligence on summary judgment. P then moves to admit evidence of items A & B from above at trial. Which is correct?

    (A) Irrelevant, not probative of negligence.

    (B) Irrelevant, not material to establish P's case at trial.

    (C) Relevant, material to establishing P's negligence.

    (D) Relevant, probative of P's negligence.

9.   D is on trial for embezzlement. The prosecution wishes to introduce evidence that D makes $15,000.00 per year and has a net worth of $5.00 to establish a motive for the embezzlement. What else, if anything, must the prosecution offer to establish the relevance of this evidence?

    (A) None, poverty alone is sufficiently relevant to show motive for embezzlement.

    (B) The fact that after the money disappeared, D bought a very expensive sports car.

    (C) The fact that D is a compulsive gambler.

    (D) The fact that D inherited 2 million dollars.

10. Doctor Witness testifies on behalf of P in P's suit for personal injuries. Which of the following questions will be permitted on cross-examination?

    (A) "Isn't it true that the only way your bill will be paid is if P recovers?"

    (B) "Isn't it true that you were once cited for sleeping in a park?"

    (C) "Isn't it true that your wife is a communist?"

    (D) "Isn't it true that your Doctoral Degree is in Post-Modern Feminist Thought?"

11. P is suing D for breach of contract. P needs to prove that D failed to personally deliver 20 widgets at 2:00 p.m. on Friday as required by the contract. D denies he failed to do this claiming he delivered the widgets at the specified time. Which item of evidence will not be admitted?

    (A) The fact that D was seen at Safeco Field at 2:00 p.m. on Friday.

    (B) Testimony by a witness who states "D told me he failed to deliver the widgets as required by the contract."

    (C) Testimony by a witness who states "D told me that he couldn't perform on the contract because he wanted to attend a pro-Taliban rally in downtown Seattle at 2:00 p.m. on Friday where he had been invited to speak against the U.S. and in favor of Osama bin Laden."

    (D) The fact that D was at a bar drinking beer at 2:00 p.m. on Friday.

12. D is on trial for murder. Prosecutor (P) offers evidence of D's prior conviction of murder. Which of the following must occur first to admit this evidence?

(A) Expert testimony establishing that once a person has murdered, they are more likely to commit a subsequent murder.

(B) Testimony that D has always been a peaceful person who would never harm a fly.

(C) Testimony that the victim was a peaceful person.

(D) None – the evidence comes in on its own.

13. D is on trial for a robbery that occurred in Los Angeles on January 1. P offers evidence that D was charged with assault in an unrelated incident on the same day in Los Angeles. Which of the following is a condition precedent to the admission of the assault evidence?

(A) The assault victim was first aggressor.

(B) The robbery involved an assault as well.

(C) The robbery victim was first aggressor.

(D) D claims that he was in Las Vegas on January 1.

14. Heather is a radical leftist who is charged with giving the middle finger to a police officer. The Prosecution offers Heather's previous five convictions for giving the finger to police officers. Which of the following is a condition precedent to admission of the previous convictions?

(A) Heather claims she was giving the finger to a rich capitalist who was walking behind the police officer.

(B) Heather must testify.

(C) Testimony that Heather has a reputation for such things.

(D) There is no condition precedent, the evidence comes in on its own.

15. In a divorce proceeding, the Court orders a parental fitness hearing. The wife offers evidence that the husband is a violent drunk. Characterize this evidence.

(A) Inadmissible character evidence.

(B) Inadmissible to prove that the husband will be a drunk in the future.

(C) Admissible because character is at issue.

(D) Admissible provided the evidence is offered for a purpose other than to prove action in conformity therewith.

16. Professor McGaff sues Garrett for defamation when Garrett stated "Professor McGaff is a communist, a liar, and stupid." Which of the following is not admissible?

(A) Professor's membership card in the Communist Party.

(B) Professor's five previous perjury convictions.

(C) Professor's law school transcript.

(D) Professor's previous Driving While Intoxicated conviction.

17. D is charged with a daring nighttime burglary of the Crown Jewels from the Tower of London (ignore jurisdictional issues). The burglar left a single red rose as a calling card in the empty jewel case. The prosecution offers the testimony of five burglary victims, for which D was convicted, who testify that a single red rose was left at the scene of each of the burglaries. For which purpose may this evidence be admitted?

(A) To show that D is the likely crown jewel burglar.

(B) To show that D is the criminal type.

(C) To rebut D's denial that he is not the criminal type.

(D) To bolster the credibility of the five witnesses.

18. D is on trial for perjury. D claims to be an honest person while on the stand. Which of the following is not a permissible method of proving character?

(A) On direct examination: "In my opinion, D is a dishonest person."

(B) On direct examination: "In the general community, D has a reputation as a dishonest person."

(C) On direct examination: "On January 1, I heard D lie to his wife."

(D) On cross-examination: "My poor opinion of D as a liar is due to my witnessing him lie to his family numerous times."

19. D is on trial for molesting Child V. Which of the following may be admitted into evidence?
- (A) D's previous conviction of molesting children.
- (B) D's previous conviction for perjury.
- (C) D's previous conviction for assault.
- (D) D's previous conviction for burglary.

20. Which of the following qualifies as routine practice, as opposed to a habit?
- (A) A train engineer who has blown the train whistle at every crossing for the past 20 years.
- (B) Washing one's hands before every meal one's entire life.
- (C) A factory that fills out an incident report every time a worker is injured.
- (D) A factory worker who runs a machine, resetting the safety lever 30 times per day.

21. In regards to evidence of a subsequent remedial measure, which of the following is not correct?
- (A) Admissible to prove negligence.
- (B) Admissible to prove notice.
- (C) Admissible to prove feasibility of safety measures.
- (D) Admissible to prove ownership or control.

22. In which situation will the statement by D, "I am so sorry that I was negligent and you were hurt as a result" be admissible?
- (A) If the statement was made right after D offered to settle P's claims.
- (B) If the statement was made during a meeting with the prosecutor regarding a plea agreement for criminal negligence.
- (C) If the statement was made right after D offered to pay P's medical expenses.
- (D) If the statement was made in a settlement letter sent to P in which

the D discusses P's medical expenses.

23. With respect to evidence that the D did or did not possess liability insurance, which of the following is not correct?
- (A) Admissible to prove ownership or control over an automobile.
- (B) Admissible to prove the existence of an agency relationship.
- (C) Admissible to prove witness bias.
- (D) Admissible to prove negligence.

24. P is suing D for injuries sustained when D slipped on an icy sidewalk allegedly owned by D. D denies owning the portion of the sidewalk upon which P slipped. Which of the following is not admissible?
- (A) The fact that D subsequently contracted with Bob to keep the sidewalk clear of ice.
- (B) The fact that D sent a letter to P offering to pay P a large amount of money because as D stated in the letter "I may be subject to liability."
- (C) The fact that D added a "slip and fall" endorsement to his premises liability insurance policy.
- (D) The fact that upon offering to pay P's medical bills, D admitted to owning the sidewalk.

25. In which of the following situations does a privileged communication exist?
- (A) Doctor Bob asks Lawyer a legal question at a cocktail party.
- (B) A married couple loudly arguing in public.
- (C) Larry consults with his Lawyer in a private office in order to plan an insurance fraud scheme.
- (D) A husband tells his wife "I think I was negligent today."

26. In which of the following situations could a spouse be compelled to testify regarding a communication between the two?

(A) A communication made before marriage between a couple now divorced.

(B) A communication made between a currently married couple during their marriage.

(C) A communication made between a currently married couple before their marriage.

(D) A communication made during marriage between a couple now divorced.

27. In which situation will the client be able to invoke attorney-client privilege?

(A) When the client refuses to pay the attorney's fees.

(B) When the client consults with the attorney as to the best way to get away with fraud.

(C) When the client asks the attorney to represent him in defending against a charge of fraud.

(D) When the client discusses a legal matter in the presence of a "man on the street."

28. In which of the following situations is marital privilege present?

(A) In a divorce proceeding.

(B) In a mental competency proceeding.

(C) In the planning or commission of a crime.

(D) In a lawsuit by a third party against one of the spouses.

29. In which situation will one spouse be competent to testify against the other?

(A) Husband is accused of assaulting his wife.

(B) Husband is accused of planning a crime.

(C) Husband is subject to a mental competency proceeding.

(D) Husband is accused of assaulting his next door neighbor.

30. In which of the following situations will a witness be competent to testify?

(A) The witness refuses to take the oath.

(B) The witness is newly deaf and just had her larynx removed and has not yet learned sign language.

(C) The witness has been stricken with amnesia.

(D) The witness is insane.

31. Which of the following witness statements is not admissible in and of itself?

(A) "The light was green."

(B) "I was watching the light at the time of the collision and it was green."

(C) "If I remember correctly, I saw that the light was green."

(D) "I'm not exactly sure, but I'm fairly certain that when I saw the light it was green."

32. P is suing D for damages resulting from D's throwing a brick through the P's window. D states that it was not him who threw the brick. Witness testifies "I saw D throw the brick and he was drinking a Daff Beer at the time." Which of the following evidence is inadmissible as impeachment evidence?

(A) A videotape showing someone other than D throwing a brick through the window drinking Daff Beer.

(B) Testimony of D stating that he could not have been drinking Daff Beer because he is allergic to alcohol.

(C) Testimony of D that he did not throw the brick through the window, rather it was his twin brother E.

(D) The fact Witness is a convicted perjurer.

33. D is accused of car theft. D calls Homer to testify that at the time of the theft, Homer and D were together at a pool hall. What question may be asked on cross-examination?

(A) "Isn't it true that D was once arrested for shoplifting a pen?"

(B) "Isn't it true that D has a reputation for theft?"

(C) "Isn't it true that D threatened you to testify in his favor?"

(D) "Isn't it true that at the time of the crime, you were not playing pool, but air hockey?"

34. W1 testifies on behalf of P. P would like to ask W2 about W1's good reputation for truthfulness. What if anything must happen before W2 can testify about that?

(A) The accused must put his character in issue.

(B) The credibility of W1 must be attacked.

(C) Nothing, a witness can be impeached by any party including the party calling the witness.

(D) Nothing, specific instances of conduct cannot be proved with extrinsic evidence.

35. P calls Witness to testify on his behalf. Witness testifies very favorably for P. D knows about an incident where Witness lied to his landlord about his ability to pay rent. How can D get this into evidence?

(A) Call the landlord to testify about the incident.

(B) Introduce Witness's bank statement that shows Witness had enough money to pay the rent.

(C) Question Witness about the incident on cross-examination.

(D) He can't. P must first bolster the credibility of Witness before D can attack it.

36. D is on trial for assault. D takes the stand in his own defense and denies being the assailant. If the prosecutor wishes to attack D's credibility, which of the following is permissible?

(A) Introduce D's five year-old conviction for embezzlement.

(B) Introduce D's attempted murder conviction for which he has been out of prison for one year.

(C) Introduce D's 7-year-old juvenile conviction for perjury.

(D) Call a witness who will testify that D kicked her dog on one occasion.

37. In which situation will a witness's religious beliefs be admissible?

(A) To show that the witness is less likely to lie.

(B) To show that the witness takes the oath seriously.

(C) To show that the witness is more likely to lie.

(D) If religious belief is an essential element of a claim or defense.

38. Witness testifies on P's behalf. Witness states "I saw D's car run the red light." D knows that Witness stated to a police officer that the light was green when D entered the intersection. Which of the following is not a permissible way to impeach the witness?

(A) Question Witness about the statement on cross-examination.

(B) Call the police officer to testify as to what Witness told him.

(C) Call another witness who will state that Witness told him "I did not see the color of the light."

(D) Call another witness who will state that Witness also said that the incident happened on a Tuesday when it actually happened on a Wednesday.

39. On direct examination Witness is questioned as an expert by P regarding her knowledge of accounting professional standards. On cross-examination, D asks Witness "Isn't it true that an attorney must also adhere to professional standards?" Upon objection what result?

(A) Sustained, outside the scope of direct.

(B) Sustained, leading question.

(C) Overruled, within the scope of direct.

(D) Overruled, leading questions allowed to develop witness's testimony.

40. Witness is being questioned by P. P asks, "Please describe in detail the events of last Tuesday." Witness answers, "I don't recall in detail those events, but I took down some notes that I have with me. I'll

look at them to help me remember." What must happen in order for the witness to use the notes?

(A) The notes must be offered and admitted into evidence.

(B) Opposing counsel must be allowed to inspect the notes.

(C) The notes must be read into the record, but the notes themselves not admitted into evidence.

(D) Nothing-The witness may use the notes.

41. Which of the following is not permissible lay witness opinion testimony?

(A) "D was obviously intoxicated when I saw him."

(B) "The substance upon which I saw P slip looked like grease."

(C) "I saw the D and he was upset."

(D) "The roof on my house was not designed or built to industry standards."

42. Which of the following opinions is admissible?

(A) "The D is guilty."

(B) "The P's injuries were proximately caused by the automobile collision."

(C) "The D was negligent."

(D) "I examined the D, and in my opinion, he is not mentally capable to have the mens rea for the crime."

43. Which of the following will not qualify a witness as an expert?

(A) In an admiralty case, the witness spent 20 years as master of a commercial vessel and will testify as to standards of care in commanding a vessel at sea.

(B) In a case for negligent design, the witness holds a Master's Degree in Engineering and will testify as to the proper design required.

(C) In a case of legal malpractice, the witness is a law professor who has studied the legal subject area and will testify as to the proper application of the law.

(D) In a medical malpractice case, the witness is a truck driver who has had an injury similar to the one claimed by P and will testify as to the causation of such an injury.

44. Upon which of the following facts may an expert opine?

(A) Those facts personally perceived by the expert witness.

(B) Those facts made known to the expert witness.

(C) Both A & B.

(D) Neither A nor B.

45. The facts upon which an expert bases her opinion must be

(A) Known to or perceived by the expert.

(B) Accepted within the scientific community.

(C) Admissible in and of themselves (may not rely on hearsay for example).

(D) Of a type reasonably relied upon by experts in the field.

46. If an expert gives an opinion based on certain facts, those facts must be testified to by the expert

(A) Prior to giving the opinion.

(B) If elicited upon cross-examination.

(C) During the expert's qualification hearing.

(D) Only if the expert is court appointed.

47. Which of the following statements is made to prove the truth of the matter asserted therein?

(A) In a defamation case: "P has a sexually transmitted disease."

(B) In a murder prosecution: "Sally said she saw D kill victim."

(C) In a premises liability case: "Mr. Shopkeeper, did you know there is ice on the sidewalk in front of your store?"

(D) In a prosecution for kidnapping: "Victim told me that the inside of D's apartment was painted with pink and green stripes."

48. Which of the following is non-assertive conduct as to whether it is/was raining outside?

- **(A)** Bob's secretary sees Bob glance out a window on his way out of the office, turn around, and take an umbrella off the coat rack.
- **(B)** Upon Bob's return, the Secretary asks, "Is it raining outside?" Bob takes off one of his shoes and pours water out of it onto her desk.
- **(C)** Upon Bob's return, the Secretary says, "It's raining." Bob looks at her and furiously shakes out his umbrella.
- **(D)** Upon Bob's return, the Secretary asks, "Is it raining outside?" Bob shakes his head.

49. Determine which of the following out-of-court statements by a witness is hearsay.

- **(A)** A statement given to an insurance adjuster inconsistent with the witness's current trial testimony.
- **(B)** A statement made at a previous trial inconsistent with the witness's current trial testimony.
- **(C)** A statement made at a deposition inconsistent with the witness's current trial testimony.
- **(D)** A statement made to a police officer identifying D as the perpetrator of a robbery.

50. D CEO and his corporation are being sued for an intentional tort. Determine which of the following out-of-court statements offered against the D is hearsay?

- **(A)** D's wife said, "Of course my husband's company is liable."
- **(B)** D states to an investigating officer, "I did it on purpose."
- **(C)** D states to a friend, "I don't remember what happened."
- **(D)** D Corporation's Public Relations Spokesperson states, "The President of Mega Co. has asked me to say we are very sorry that our toxic chemicals spilled into the public aquifer."

51. Which of the following is an adoptive admission?

- **(A)** In the presence of a witness, P accuses D of negligent driving. D says nothing.
- **(B)** Same as A, except D is deaf.
- **(C)** Same as A above except after hearing the accusation, faints from his injuries.
- **(D)** Same as A above except D responds, "You are a filthy liar."

52. Which of the following statements will most likely not be admitted into evidence?

- **(A)** Declarant is standing on a street corner with her friend witness. Declarant then says, "Hey, that car [driven by D] just ran a red light."
- **(B)** Declarant is crossing the street when her ex-husband clips her sending her onto the ground. She shouts, "John, you jerk! Watch where in the hell you are going!"
- **(C)** Declarant returns home from work. Her husband asks how her day went. "Well, this morning on my way in to work, I saw [D] run a red light, and strike [P]."
- **(D)** Declarant returns home from work and tells her husband, "I got fired today. I'm so upset. It's discrimination."

53. In order to admit a recorded recollection as an exception to hearsay, which of the following are not required?

- **(A)** The witness once had personal knowledge of the events or facts recorded.
- **(B)** The witness has a total but inaccurate recollection of the events.
- **(C)** The events or facts were fresh in the witness's knowledge when recorded.
- **(D)** The record is an accurate reflection of the witness's knowledge at the time of the recording.

54. P is an employee in the factory owned by D Corp. P is injured. P's supervisor immediately calls the risk management department who tells him, "Have all the witnesses make a written statement as per our established procedure. We want to be prepared for any potential lawsuit by the government." Would the statements qualify as Records of a Regularly Conducted Activity?

(A) Yes, because D Corp. took the statements pursuant to established procedure near in time to the incident.

(B) Yes, because the statements were made by persons with personal knowledge of the incident.

(C) No, because the statements were made in anticipation of litigation.

(D) No, because taking witness statements was not a regular practice of D Corp.

55. P Patient is suing D Doctor for medical malpractice. P alleges that D used an improper surgical technique when removing P's appendix. P calls Expert Witness who on direct examination states "According to the book 'Appendectomy Illustrated' upon which I relied in forming my opinion and which is authoritative within the surgical community, an appendix should be removed using a number four scalpel." On-cross examination, D's attorney would like to bring to the jury's attention a passage in "Appendectomy Illustrated" that states that a number five scalpel is also acceptable. What is the permissible way to get that passage to the jury?

(A) Offer the relevant passage into evidence.

(B) Have the expert read the relevant passage into the record.

(C) Admit the entire treatise into evidence with a limiting instruction that the evidence therein is for impeachment purposes only.

(D) Admit the entire treatise into evidence for impeachment or substantive evidence.

56. In which of the following situations, is the declarant unavailable for the purposes of a hearsay exception?

(A) The declarant is on the witness stand yet refuses to answer questions even though ordered to do so by the Court.

(B) The declarant is on vacation when service of process was attempted for the first time a week prior to trial.

(C) The declarant was murdered by the proponent of the statement.

(D) The declarant has suffered partial amnesia, but can remember most of the subject matter of the statement.

57. Which of the following does not qualify as admissible under a hearsay exception?

(A) "Bob shot me and I'm going to die." Declarant lives.

(B) "Bob shot me, but he missed anything vital, so I think I'll pull through." Declarant then dies.

(C) Declarant testifies in a trial involving two parties. A mistrial is declared. Before the second trial, declarant dies. The proponent offers the transcript of declarant's testimony from the first trial.

(D) Declarant states, "I do not have title to Blackacre even though everyone thinks I do."

58. P's medical records contain the following written statement by P's doctor, "Patient complains of arm pain secondary to motor vehicle accident." P offers the records into evidence. Which of the following hearsay exceptions will get this record into evidence?

(A) Then existing mental, emotional, or physical condition.

(B) Record of a regularly conducted activity, and Statements for purpose of medical diagnosis.

(C) Recorded recollection, and Statements for purpose of medical diagnosis.

(D) Present sense impression, and then existing mental, emotional, or physical condition.

59. In which situation may the declarant be impeached as if he were present and testifying?

(A) The statement is the party's own statement.

(B) A prior statement by a witness regarding identity of a person.

(C) A statement by a co-conspirator.

(D) The statement is the party's adoptive admission.

60. Which of the following is not an element of the residual hearsay exception?

(A) The statement is evidence of a material fact.

(B) The statement is the most probative piece of evidence.

(C) The admission of the evidence will best serve the purposes of the Rules and the interest of justice.

(D) The statement can be corroborated for reliability.

61. What is the burden of proof a proponent must satisfy in order to authenticate the evidence?

(A) Evidence sufficient to support a finding of authenticity.

(B) Evidence, a preponderance of which, supports a finding of authenticity.

(C) Clear and convincing evidence, which supports a finding of authenticity.

(D) Proof beyond a reasonable doubt, which supports a finding of authenticity.

62. Which of the following is not an acceptable method of authenticating a document?

(A) A lay witness compares the signature on the document with an authentic signature.

(B) An expert witness testifies that she created the document.

(C) A witness testifies that she witnessed the creation of the document.

(D) A witness testifies that she heard the D admit to creating the document.

63. Which is a correct statement as to authenticating a photograph?

(A) The photographer must testify as to taking the photograph.

(B) Testimony by a witness who has been at the scene that the photograph is a fair and accurate representation thereof.

(C) The photograph must have distinctive characteristics.

(D) The opposing party must admit that the photograph is authentic.

64. In which situation is a voice over the telephone not authenticated?

(A) X calls Y's place of business and leaves a message for Y. X gets a telephone call five minutes later and the caller states, "Hello, this is Y returning your telephone call."

(B) X receives a telephone call where the caller identifies himself as Y.

(C) X looks up Y's telephone number in the directory, dials the number, and the call is answered by "Hello, Y speaking."

(D) X calls Y's place of business and speaks to a person identifying himself as Y and the two discuss business.

65. Which is not an acceptable way to authenticate a page in a letter?

(A) Have a witness familiar with the maker's handwriting testify that the handwriting belongs to the maker.

(B) Bring to the Court's attention that the page in question states in the margin "Maker's letter page 3 of 5." Authentication of the other pages is already established.

(C) Have the maker's sister testify that the handwriting is the maker's.

(D) The letter is proved to be fifteen years old.

66. Which of the following is most likely to negate authenticity of an "ancient document"?

(A) The document is proved to be 225 years old.

(B) The document was found in the County Recorder's Office where such documents are located.

(C) Neither party disputes authenticity.

(D) The document is printed in Times New Roman font on a sheet of clean white paper. All other documents of the same age are handwritten on yellowing, crumbling paper.

67. Which of the following is not a self-authenticating document?

(A) Market reports or commercial publications.

(B) A certified copy of a deed.

(C) A book published by the Federal Government.

(D) The New York Times.

68. Which of the following is considered "Best Evidence" under the Rules?

(A) Live testimony regarding the contents of a document.

(B) Testimony of a witness with firsthand knowledge instead of hearsay.

(C) An original document in order to prove the contents thereof.

(D) An original document that records a witness's observations of an event.

69. When may evidence other than the document itself be admissible to prove the contents of a document?

(A) The document does not regard an issue central to the case.

(B) The document is in the possession of the opposing party.

(C) The document is located in another state.

(D) Only a duplicate is available.

70. What affect does an opposing party's admission to the contents of a document have?

(A) None, the document must still be produced.

(B) The proponent need not produce the original.

(C) None, provided that the original is not obtainable.

(D) A presumption of the contents of the document arises.

71. In order to admit a summary of voluminous documentation, what must the proponent do?

(A) The underlying documents must be admitted into evidence.

(B) The underlying documents must be produced in court.

(C) The party against whom the summary is offered must not object to the summary.

(D) The underlying documents must be made available to opposing parties.

Evidence
Practice Questions

Questions 72-75 share common facts.

72. Jones is on trial for vandalism in Seattle during the WTO riots. The State introduces a videotape of Jones throwing a garbage can through the window of a coffee shop. In his defense, Jones calls his chapter president of Spoiled Rich College Kids United who testifies that Jones has a reputation for honesty within the college activist community. The prosecution timely objects. What result?

(A) Admissible, relevant to show Jones' character for truth.

(B) Admissible, relevant to dispute the charges.

(C) Not admissible, character evidence cannot be introduced by the accused unless first attacked by the other party.

(D) Not admissible, not a relevant character trait.

73. Jones is also charged with assaulting a police officer. The primary evidence is the testimony of the officer who states that a black clad and masked person with a red "A" on his shirt spit in his face. The prosecution then introduces a certified copy of a State Court judgment finding Jones guilty 14 years ago for spitting in a police officer's face while wearing black clothing with a red "A" and a mask. Upon a timely objection, what result?

(A) Admissible, probative value outweighs prejudicial effect.

(B) Admissible, but not to prove that Jones has a propensity for spitting in police officer faces.

(C) Not admissible, conviction is more than ten years prior.

(D) Not admissible, specific acts cannot be proved with extrinsic evidence.

74. Jones is the victim of a vast right-wing conspiracy. He is now charged with lewd conduct after allegedly "mooning" the WTO delegate from Uruguay. The prosecution wishes to introduce documents charging Jones with "hate speech" after he referred to another delegate in a racially derogative way; but he was not convicted. If Jones timely objects, what result?

(A) Inadmissible, Jones was never convicted.

(B) Inadmissible, prejudice outweighs probative value.

(C) Admissible, probative nature of the evidence outweighs prejudice.

(D) Admissible, shows common scheme or plan.

75. Jones gets a high paying job and buys a yacht. His friend Heather scoffs, "That is an obscene monument to capitalism, and I'd like to use it to run down Bill Gates because I hate him. He has gotten rich off the backs of his employees. He exploited them." Jones hands the keys to Heather and says "Have fun." Heather takes the boat and sees Bill Gates swimming. She runs him down killing him. His estate sues Heather (wrongful death) and Jones (negligent entrustment).

The estate wishes to call Peter who will testify that Jones was aware that Heather had a propensity to run down prominent businessmen using various vehicles. Upon Heather's objection, what ruling?

(A) Not admissible, evidence of Heather's character is not admissible.

(B) Not admissible, specific instances of conduct cannot be introduced by extrinsic evidence.

(C) Admissible, the evidence goes to Jones' knowledge of Heather's dangerous propensities.

(D) Admissible, but cannot be used against Heather, only Jones.

76. Gunther is charged with cruelty to animals. Some of the evidence the prosecution wishes to introduce is testimony to the fact that Lumbo the elephant exhibits fright whenever Gunther approaches, but not when anyone else approaches. If Gunther objects, what result?

(A) Not admissible, the prosecution must produce the best evidence.

(B) Not admissible, prejudice outweighs probative value.

(C) Admissible, evidence of guilt.

(D) Not Admissible, evidence is insufficient to sustain prosecution's burden.

77. Anthony sues Bob for battery. Anthony offers the testimony of Charlie who will state that he saw Bob drinking a beer two hours before the alleged battery. Bob timely objects to the testimony as irrelevant. The judge should rule

(A) For Anthony because it will help establish Bob's intoxication.

(B) For Anthony because intoxication may be a defense to the tort of battery.

(C) For Bob because intoxication is not a defense to an intentional tort.

(D) For Bob because drinking a beer does not help establish any of the elements of battery.

Questions 78-83 share common facts.

78. Dave is on trial for the murder of Erin. The prosecution offers the testimony of Frank who heard Erin accuse Dave of embezzling from their partnership. Dave timely objects to Frank's testimony as irrelevant. The judge should rule

(A) For the prosecution because Erin's accusation may have motivated Dave to murder her.
(B) For the prosecution because Erin's accusation demonstrates that Dave was dishonest.
(C) For Dave because Frank's testimony is insufficient to sustain a guilty verdict.
(D) For Dave because Frank's testimony is circumstantial evidence.

79. Same facts as above, except Frank's testimony is that he saw Dave dispose of bloody clothing after returning home from his work as a butcher. Dave timely objects. What ruling and why?

(A) For the prosecution because disposing of bloody clothes demonstrates that Dave was trying to hide something.
(B) For the prosecution because the testimony is relevant.
(C) For Dave because the testimony is prejudicial.
(D) For Dave because the testimony is irrelevant.

80. Dave takes the stand in his own defense. Which of the following is a proper impeachment question on cross-examination?

(A) "Is it not true that you were convicted of assault and served two years in prison?"
(B) "Is it not true that you are an atheist, thus you have no reason to tell the truth?"
(C) "Is it not true you were reprimanded by your Law School for claiming to be on Law Review when you never actually were?"
(D) "Is it not true you were arrested for perjury?"

81. Dave states on the stand that his law school never reprimanded him. The prosecution offers into evidence a letter from the Dean to Dave reprimanding Dave for going overtime on an exam. If Dave objects, what result?

(A) Sustained, because the letter is extrinsic evidence.
(B) Sustained, because Dave has not had an opportunity to explain or deny the statement in the letter.
(C) Overruled, because the letter is a prior inconsistent statement.
(D) Overruled, because the letter is offered to refresh the witness's memory.

82. Dave calls his best friend Goler to the stand to testify as a character witness. Goler testifies "It has always been my opinion that Dave is honest and peaceful." The prosecution on cross-examination asks "Is it not true that you once sent a letter stating 'Dave is a violent liar.'" What ruling on Dave's timely objection?

(A) Sustained, the statement is extrinsic evidence.
(B) Overruled, prior statement by witness.
(C) Sustained, the letter was not disclosed to Goler before questioning about it.
(D) Overruled, unless the letter is merely used to refresh Goler's memory.

83. Upon further cross-examination, the prosecutor asks "Is it not true that Dave saved your life during the Gulf War?" Dave timely objects, what result?

(A) Sustained, irrelevant to Goler's credibility.
(B) Sustained, prejudicial.
(C) Overruled, shows possible witness bias.
(D) Overruled, shows Goler's propensity for truth.

84. P is suing D for breach of contract. P then telephones D and says "I'll settle for twenty dollars because it is questionable whether the terms of the contract were clear." D rejects the offer. At trial, D tries to testify about P's statement. On P's timely objection, what result?

(A) Not admissible, hearsay.

(B) Not admissible, but only the offer itself, not the fact P admitted the weakness of his case.

(C) Admissible, hearsay, but subject to an exception.

(D) Not admissible, both offer and admission are inadmissible.

85. Delores was furiously chatting on her cell phone when she ran down Penelope. The next day Delores visits Penelope in the hospital and says "I will pay for all your medical expenses; I am very sorry I was negligent." At trial, Penelope wishes to testify about the statement. Upon Delores' objection, what result?

(A) The entire statement is admissible.

(B) Only the offer to pay is admissible.

(C) Only the admission of negligence is admissible.

(D) The entire statement is not admissible.

86. In which of the following situations is the evidence most likely to be admitted?

(A) P's attorney examines her about her relationship with D. Upon cross-examination, D's attorney questions P further about the relationship.

(B) P is suing D for damages arising from negligence. In his answer, D admits to negligence, but denies the damages. P calls Witness to testify as an expert that D's conduct was negligent.

(C) In a murder trial of D, P offers into evidence autopsy photos in order to prove that the victim was killed.

(D) P calls Witness as the tenth witness to testify that D has a reputation for dishonesty.

87. Doris is walking by Henry's store when she trips over a dislodged piece of sidewalk. She sues Henry alleging that he knew or should have known of the dangerous condition. Henry takes the stand and testifies that since he had the sidewalk installed no one has tripped over it. Doris objects to this testimony. What result?

(A) Overruled, relevant to an issue in the case.

(B) Overruled, but subject to a limiting instruction.

(C) Sustained, negative evidence is inadmissible.

(D) Sustained, not relevant to an issue in the case.

88. Dr. Witness testifies as a witness for P on the causation of P's injuries. On cross-examination D's attorney reads from "Astrological causation of injury" a passage that disagrees with the doctor's testimony. The doctor scoffs at the passage and declares that the text is non-authoritative. Upon P's objection what ruling on the admissibility of the passage?

(A) Not admissible, not authenticated.

(B) Not admissible, not determined as authoritative.

(C) Admissible, but only to impeach the doctor's testimony.

(D) Admissible, to impeach and as substantive evidence.

89. Polly is suing Domingo for injuries resulting from an automobile collision. She alleges that he ran a stop sign. Domingo states that there were no stop signs, and as the car on the right he had the right-of-way. The collision happened at night. Polly introduces a photograph taken the next day in daylight. The photograph clearly shows a stop sign on the street upon which Domingo was traveling. Polly testifies that the photo is an accurate depiction of the placement of the stop signs at the time of the collision. Domingo objects, what result?

(A) Sustained, the photo does not depict the intersection at the time of the collision.

(B) Sustained, the photographer must testify to authenticity.

(C) Overruled, the photo is authenticated.

(D) Overruled, photographs do not need authentication.

Questions 90 and 91 share common facts.

90. Captain Ron contracts with Meteorologist Mary to notify him in the event of rapidly dropping barometric pressure, which is a good sign of an approaching storm. Before his last departure, Mary tells Ron that the pressure is holding steady. Twelve hours later a Nor'Easter strikes sinking Ron's ship. Ron sues Mary alleging that she broke her contract to warn of dropping pressure. In her defense, Mary offers into evidence a certified copy of a National Weather Service report for the day the storm struck that recorded the barometric pressure. The pressure never fell. Upon Ron's objection, what result?

(A) Admissible, exclusion based upon Authentication and Hearsay is not applicable.
(B) Not admissible, the report has not been authenticated.
(C) Not admissible, the report is hearsay not subject to an exception.
(D) Admissible, provided the person compiling the data testifies to the authenticity of the report, but not necessarily to the facts therein.

91. Mary calls a famous meteorologist as an expert witness. Mary's attorney's first question to the witness is "What was the barometric pressure on the day of the storm?" Ron objects. What result?

(A) Overruled, experts may testify based on hypothetical information.
(B) Overruled, the witness's fame establishes his expertise.
(C) Sustained, expert witnesses must base their opinions on admissible evidence.
(D) Sustained, foundation for the opinion must first be established.

92. Sally is called as a witness in Paul's suit against Deidre. Sally testifies "I did not see the collision, but based on the fact the Paul was so badly injured, Deidre must have been going at least seventy miles-per hour." Upon Deidre's objection what result?

(A) Excluded, not based on personal knowledge.
(B) Excluded, Sally is not an expert.
(C) Admitted, expert opinion is not required because it does not take specialized knowledge or training to testify as to a car's speed.
(D) Admitted, best evidence available.

93. Bob is prosecuted for possession of marijuana. The only evidence the prosecution has is the testimony of Jones, a long-time pot-head, who states that he and Bob smoked Bob's marijuana on several occasions. Defense objects to Jones' identification of the substance as marijuana. Rule on the admissibility of Jones' testimony regarding the identification of the marijuana.

(A) Not admitted, Jones is too unreliable due to his drug use.
(B) Not admitted, Jones is not trained to recognize marijuana.
(C) Admitted, Jones is an expert.
(D) Admitted, lay opinion.

94. Bob is prosecuted for possession of cocaine. The prosecution's chief witness is a ten-year crime-lab technician who will testify that he tested a sample of a substance taken from Bob by police. The test came up positive as cocaine under a test used by most crime labs across the country. The testimony is

(A) Admissible, expert opinion.
(B) Not admissible, whether or not the substance is cocaine is an issue for the trier of fact.
(C) Not admissible, the opinion is not based on items in evidence.
(D) Not admissible, the expert does not have personal knowledge of the facts.

95. Billy-Joe and Bobbie-Sue are a married couple with nothing better to do. While dining together one night, Billy-Joe confesses "Before we were married, I shot a man while robbing his castle." Billy-Jack, a detective down in Texas, overhears the conversation and arrests Billy-Joe. At Billy-Joe's murder trial, Bobbie-Sue is called by the prosecution and asked about Billy-Joe's statement. Which objection will the judge sustain?

(A) Hearsay.
(B) Marital Communication Privilege.
(C) Specific instances of conduct cannot be proved by extrinsic evidence.
(D) None, the statement is admissible.

96. Jerry goes to an attorney's office where in the presence of attorney and a court reporter, gives a sworn statement confessing to the conspiracy of the murder of JFK and implicating several others in the plot. Jerry meets a mysterious death some days later. JFK's estate sues Jerry's estate for the murder and calls the court reporter to testify to the contents of Jerry's statement. What result?

(A) Admissible, privilege ends on the death of the client.
(B) Admissible, the presence of the court reporter destroyed any privilege.
(C) Not admissible, the privilege is not destroyed.
(D) Not admissible, hearsay.

Questions 97 and 98 share common facts:

Gary is a bartender at the Unicorn Tavern. He is serving Bob and Cheryl when he hears Cheryl say "Bob, if you leave me, I will kill you." Bob then says "Let's talk about this at home." Bob's body is then found at his and Cheryl's house.

97. Cheryl is placed on trial for Bob's murder. Gary is called to the stand to testify to Bob and Cheryl's statements. Which of the statements are admissible?

(A) Bob's statement only because he is not available.
(B) Cheryl's statement only because it is not hearsay.
(C) Both statements are excepted from hearsay.
(D) Neither, both statements are hearsay subject to no exception.

98. The first trial ends in a hung jury. Gary's National Guard unit is activated and he is sent to Kerblekistan during the time of the second trial. The prosecution would like to offer the transcript of Gary's testimony from the first trial. What additional facts are needed to admit the transcript?

(A) The prosecutor contrived Gary's assignment because he is not credible on the stand.
(B) The testimony regards the state of mind of the declarant.
(C) Gary reiterates his testimony to his company chaplain after being wounded on the battlefield.
(D) Gary is beyond service.

99. Richard was inspecting a roof when unbeknownst to him he stepped on a weakened portion of the roof, fell through, and landed ten stories below. A witness who comes to his aid hears Richard state, "The roof was rotted." Witness looks up and clearly sees rotted wood in the spot Richard fell through. Richard dies and his estate brings a wrongful death action against the owner of the building. The owner approaches Witness and says, "I will give you $50,000.00 to testify that the wood was not rotted." If the Witness testifies to the owner's statement, what result?

(A) Admissible, hearsay subject to an exception.
(B) Admissible, not hearsay.
(C) Not admissible, hearsay not subject to an exception.
(D) Not admissible, no indication Richard thought he was dying.

100. Ronald is sued by Betty for the tort of battery. Ronald calls Warren to testify that Ronald has a reputation for peacefulness in the general community. If Betty objects what result?

(A) Admissible, character evidence may be offered by the accused.
(B) Admissible, for other purposes.
(C) Not admissible, character evidence may not be offered to show action in conformity therewith.

(D) Not admissible, Betty must first attack Ronald's character.

101. Percy is involved in an automobile collision that leaves several dead. One of the estates sues the bar at which Percy had been drinking. The estate calls Dave a bar patron who will testify that he saw and heard Doris tell the bartender, "Look at Percy, he's stumbling around drunk and vomiting." Percy objects, what result?

(A) Admissible, hearsay subject to an exception.

(B) Admissible, not hearsay.

(C) Not admissible, Doris is not an expert on intoxication.

(D) Not admissible, hearsay not subject to any exception.

102. Hamlet brings a wrongful death action against his uncle for his father's death. Hamlet wishes to enter into evidence the records of the church showing that his father died on January 2, a day the uncle was present. The uncle testifies that he was in Norway negotiating with Fortinbras on the day of the death. He offers into evidence the guest logbook of Fortinbras' castle filled out by the gate guard showing January 2 as the entry date. What is the admissibility of each of these documentary exhibits?

(A) The church records are not admissible, hearsay.

(B) The logbook is not admissible, hearsay.

(C) Neither are admissible, hearsay.

(D) Both are admissible.

103. Hadley is suing Baxendale for defective design of a driveshaft. His allegation is that the diameter of the shaft when made was too big. Hadley wishes to introduce blueprints showing the specifications of the shaft. The blueprints, unfortunately, are thirty (30) years old. What ruling on the admissibility of the blueprints?

(A) Not admissible, hearsay.

(B) Not admissible, age makes the blueprints unreliable.

(C) Admissible, hearsay but subject to an exception.

(D) Admissible, not hearsay.

104. Stone and Hauser are well known to be enemies. Hauser's wife returns home to find him lying in a pool of his own blood. With his last breath, Hauser says. "That Stone tried to stab me to death. Call 911 and I will live." Hauser's wife, who also hates him, does nothing. He dies. The prosecution calls the wife to testify about Hauser's last words in Stone's murder trial. What is the best objection to this testimony?

(A) Hearsay.

(B) Irrelevant.

(C) Prejudicial.

(D) Dead Man's Statute.

105. Patricia is called to the stand to testify regarding events from ten years ago. Her memory of the detailed events is not clear; however, she did take notes at the time. How can the notes be used?

(A) The witness may not look at the notes.

(B) The witness may look at the notes, so long as they are then entered into evidence as a documentary exhibit.

(C) The witness may look at the notes, so long as the notes are available at the hearing for opposing counsel to examine.

(D) The witness may only read the notes into the record, but then counsel must enter the notes into evidence as a documentary evidence.

106. Hoffman is on trial for assault. The prosecution must establish that the assault occurred in King County, the venue of the trial. The victim testified that the assault occurred in Seattle, Washington. The judge takes judicial notice of the fact that Seattle is located in King County. What effect does judicial notice have?

(A) The prosecution's burden of production is satisfied.

(B) The fact is conclusively established.

(C) The burden of production is shifted to the D.

(D) The fact is conclusively established unless the D objects.

Questions 107 and 108 share common facts:

107. P Percy sues D Anarchist for damage to Percy's store window. Percy calls Uma Undergraduate to testify that Anarchist threw an object through the window. However, once on the stand she states that it was a policeman, not Anarchist, that threw the object. Percy then calls Clancy Cleancut who testifies that Anarchist did indeed throw a brick through the window. What ruling on Clancy's testimony?

(A) Not admissible, because Percy did not disclose Clancy as a witness.

(B) Admissible, because Clancy's testimony is relevant.

(C) Not admissible, because Clancy's testimony contradicts another P witness.

(D) Admissible, because Uma did not testify the way she was supposed to.

108. Anarchist cross-examines Clancy and asks, "Isn't it true that you were wearing a blue coat that day?" Clancy replies, "No, it was red." Anarchist then seeks to introduce videotape showing Clancy next to the smashed window in a blue jacket. How should the judge rule on the admissibility of the tape?

(A) Not admissible, because specific instances of conduct cannot be proved by extrinsic evidence.

(B) Admissible, because it casts doubt on Clancy's recollection.

(C) Not admissible, because the color of Clancy's jacket is collateral to the issues at the trial.

(D) Admissible, because it is impeachment evidence.

Questions 109 and 110 are based on the following:

Able brings an action against Betty for breach of contract for the lease of commercial property to be used by Betty for her retail business. A material term of the contract required Betty to procure liability insurance, which Able alleges she has not done. At trial, Able's attorney seeks to introduce the testimony of Betty's employee Carol who will state "Betty told me she does not have liability insurance on her leased property." Betty objects based on both hearsay and evidence of insurance coverage.

109. How should the judge rule on Betty's timely objection specifically on the evidence of insurance coverage?

(A) For Betty because evidence of insurance coverage, or lack thereof, is not admissible upon the issue of whether she acted negligently or otherwise wrongfully.

(B) For Betty because Carol's testimony is in regards to an out-of-court statement offered for the truth of the matter asserted.

(C) For Able because the testimonial evidence is offered for a purpose other than negligent or wrongful conduct.

(D) For Able because all relevant evidence is admissible.

110. How should the judge rule on Betty's timely objection on hearsay to Carol's testimony?

(A) For Betty because Carol's testimony is in regards to an out-of-court statement offered for the truth of the matter asserted.

(B) For Able because Carol's testimony is being offered against Betty and is Betty's own statement.

(C) For Betty because Carol's testimony is in regards to insurance coverage.

(D) For Able because Carol's testimony is being offered against Betty and is a statement by her agent or servant.

111. Jeff is on trial for the sexual assault of Karen. Karen's assailant wore a Halloween mask during the assault. The prosecution seeks to introduce evidence that Jeff was convicted 12 years ago of sexual assault for which he served one year and a day in prison. During that prior assault he wore a Halloween mask. Jeff timely objects to the evidence of his past conviction. What ruling and why?

(A) For the prosecution because this evidence is admissible for its bearing on any relevant matter.

(B) For the prosecution because this evidence is admissible for a purpose other than proving action in conformity therewith.

(C) For Jeff because this evidence is of a conviction more than ten years ago.

(D) For Jeff because this evidence is of another crime to prove action in conformity therewith.

112. Jeff from above is called to testify on behalf of Larry in Larry's Personal Injury suit. Jeff testifies as to his observations of how Larry's injuries have affected his daily life. On cross-examination, defense counsel asks "Is it true that you were convicted of sexual assault?" Larry's attorney timely objects. What ruling and why?

(A) For D because past sexual assaults are admissible for its bearing on any matter to which it is relevant.

(B) For D because past crimes punishable by death or imprisonment greater than one year are admissible to impeach a witness.

(C) For Larry because Jeff's conviction was not for a crime involving dishonesty and false statement.

(D) For Larry because more than ten years has elapsed since Jeff's release from prison.

113. Sal is on trial for the murder of Tom his business partner. Tom was killed by a single gunshot fired from a rifle of the same caliber as one owned by Sal. In fact, there are millions of rifles that use the same caliber bullet as the one that killed Sal. This is the only evidence that could possibly link Sal to the murder. The prosecution seeks to introduce Sal's rifle into evidence. The rifle is a Remington "Widowmaker" sniper rifle, the same model used by SWAT teams and military Special Operations forces. Sal timely objects. The judge should

(A) Exclude the rifle from evidence because the possible prejudice of the model name "Widowmaker" outweighs the probative value.

(B) Exclude the rifle from evidence because as the only prosecution evidence it is insufficient to sustain a guilty verdict.

(C) Admit the rifle into evidence because it is relevant.

(D) Admit the rifle into evidence, but instruct the jury to not be prejudiced by the name "Widowmaker."

114. Sal from above calls Vernon as a witness to testify that Sal has a high reputation in the community for peacefulness. Sal then wishes to call Wendy who will testify to Vernon's reputation for truthfulness. The prosecution objects to Wendy's testimony. The Judge should

(A) Allow Wendy's testimony as a character witness for another witness.

(B) Allow Wendy's testimony because it supports another witness's credibility.

(C) Bar Wendy's testimony because Sal has opened the door to prosecution attack of his character.

(D) Bar Wendy's testimony because Vernon's character has not been attacked by the prosecution.

115. The prosecutor wishes to introduce evidence that Vernon was sued by his former employer for theft and embezzlement. What is the best way to accomplish this?

(A) Question Vernon about the suit on cross-examination.

(B) Call Vernon's former employer to testify regarding Vernon's thievery.

(C) Offer into evidence a certified copy of the verdict and judgment against Vernon.

(D) Cross-examine Wendy of her knowledge of Vernon's thievery.

116. Tom was killed at 6:30 p.m. on a Saturday night. Sal wishes to offer the testimony of his friend Bruce who will state that he has seen Sal with his "Widowmaker" rifle at the gun club on every Saturday from 5:00 p.m. until 6:00 p.m. for the last ten years. Bruce will then testify that every time Sal finished shooting he always disassembled and cleaned his rifle, which always takes until 7:00 p.m. On the evening in question, Bruce went with Sal to the gun club, but had to leave early for a church function. The prosecutor objects to Bruce's testimony. The Judge should rule to

(A) Exclude the testimony because it is not based on first hand knowledge.

(B) Exclude the testimony because it attempts to use religious beliefs to enhance Bruce's credibility.

(C) Allow the testimony because it is relevant to demonstrate that Sal had probably disassembled his rifle at the time Tom was killed.

(D) Allow the testimony because it may be admissible for another purpose such as intent, plan, preparation, or knowledge.

117. Tom's estate files a wrongful death suit against Sal. The attorneys for each party enter into lengthy and extensive settlement negotiations, but do not conduct any discovery or other pre-trial pleadings. After one year, with settlement negotiations continuing Sal brings a motion to dismiss the suit alleging the estate has taken no action on the suit. The estate's attorney prepares an affidavit detailing the numerous settlement offers given by each party. Sal moves to strike the affidavit. What result?

(A) Strike the affidavit because evidence of settlement offers is not admissible.

(B) Strike the affidavit because an attorney cannot be a necessary witness in a case he is involved in as counsel.

(C) Allow the affidavit because it is not evidence of plea discussions.

(D) Allow the affidavit because it rebuts Sal's contention that the estate has taken no action in the case.

118. Tom did not die until several days after he was shot, though he was never conscious. Tom's wife saw Sal in public and loudly accused him of shooting Tom. Sal replied "I will pay for Tom's medical bills." Tom's estate wishes to offer the testimony of the wife repeating Sal's statement. Which is the best answer to the question of admissibility of the Wife's testimony?

(A) Admissible as an admission by party opponent.

(B) Inadmissible because it regards an offer to compromise.

(C) Inadmissible for the purpose to prove liability for Tom's death.

(D) Inadmissible because the prejudice outweighs the probative value.

119. Tenant falls down stairs lacking a handrail at his apartment building, injuring himself. He sues Landlord, Inc., a large property management company he believes owns the building, alleging that the lack of a handrail is negligence. Landlord, Inc., answers by denying ownership of the building. To rebut this denial, Tenant offers into evidence the testimony of Contractor who will state that he was hired by Landlord, Inc., to install a handrail after the injury. Landlord, Inc., objects. What result?

(A) Admissible to show Landlord, Inc.'s ownership of the apartments.

(B) Admissible because Contractor can authenticate any written work orders.

(C) Inadmissible because actions taken after an injury that could have prevented the injury cannot be used to prove negligence.

(D) Inadmissible because Contractor's testimony is hearsay.

120. Harold married Wanda on January 1, 2000. On December 31, 1999, Harold told Wanda "I murdered Gary." Harold and Wanda are divorced December 31, 2000. Harold's trial for murder begins January 1, 2001. The prosecution calls Wanda as a witness to testify as to Harold's confession to her. What is the best way to exclude Wanda's testimony?

(A) Spousal Incompetancy.

(B) Marital Communication Privilege.

(C) Object based on Hearsay.

(D) Plead guilty to end the trial.

121. Cathy sues Arnold Attorney for legal malpractice resulting from Arnold's failure to file Cathy's personal injury suit within the applicable statute of limitations. Arnold intends to testify on his own behalf. Cathy brings a motion to bar Arnold from discussing the fact that Cathy ordered him not to file the suit. What result?

(A) Arnold's testimony is barred because Cathy has not waived the Attorney-Client privilege.

(B) Arnold's testimony is barred because he is offering an out of court statement for the truth of the matter asserted.

(C) Arnold will be allowed to testify because Cathy cannot assert Attorney-Client privilege because the privilege is inapplicable.

(D) Arnold will be allowed to testify because an inequitable result would otherwise occur.

122. Donald is called as a witness by P to testify regarding a collision he witnessed. Defense counsel objects as to Donald's competency. The judge holds a competency hearing in which Donald confirms that he is under psychiatric care for schizophrenia. The court then hears testimony by Donald's brother who states "In my opinion, and in his reputation in the community, Donald is a liar." What should the judge decide?

(A) Donald is competent to testify notwithstanding his mental illness and reputation as a liar.

(B) Donald is competent to testify because his credibility may be attacked by any party.

(C) Donald is incompetent to testify due to his mental illness.

(D) Donald is incompetent to testify because he is a known liar.

Questions 123 - 129 share common facts:

123. Alan is on trial for armed robbery. Alan calls Bob to testify regarding Alan's reputation for peacefulness and honesty. Upon cross-examination, the prosecution asks "Isn't it true that you and Alan were members of a prison gang that requires absolute loyalty to each other?" Alan objects. How should the judge rule?

(A) Sustain the objection because the prosecutor seeks to establish Alan's propensity to commit crime.

(B) Overrule the objection because it attacks Bob's credibility as a witness.

(C) Sustain the objection because Alan has not placed his character in issue.

(D) Overrule the objection because this is a specific instance of conduct concerning Bob's character for untruthfulness elicited under cross-examination.

124. Same facts as above. Alan calls Charlie who testifies that Bob has a high reputation for truthfulness due to his devout religious beliefs. On cross-examination the prosecutor asks "Isn't it true that Bob has lied to his priest?" Alan objects. How should the judge rule?

(A) Sustain the objection because references to a witness's religion are inadmissible.

(B) Sustain the objection because this statement can only be elicited by cross-examination of Bob.

(C) Overrule the objection because conduct probative of untruthfulness may be inquired into by cross-examination.

(D) Overrule the objection because the prosecutor failed to timely object to Charlie's testimony.

125. Alan takes the stand in his own defense. After his testimony, the prosecution offers into evidence a certified copy of a guilty judgment on the verdict entered against Alan five years ago for "Spitting on a sidewalk," a crime punishable by five years in prison. If Alan objects, which of the following is the best argument in support of exclusion of the evidence?

(A) The judgment is extrinsic evidence of a specific instance of conduct.

(B) The crime does not involve dishonesty or false statement.

(C) The prosecution failed to give the defense adequate notice (pursuant to 404(c)(1)) of its intent to introduce the past crime.

(D) The crime was not punishable by death or imprisonment greater than one year.

126. At Alan's trial, the prosecution calls the store clerk who was robbed. The clerk testifies that the robber wore a Halloween mask of Bill Clinton and said "It depends on what your definition of 'is' is." The prosecutor then offers into evidence Alan's 20 year old conviction for numerous armed robberies during which he wore Halloween masks of various presidents and uttered a famous phrase of each president. Alan objects. The judge should rule as follows:

(A) Overrule the objection because the evidence is offered for a purpose other than to prove action in conformity therewith.

(B) Sustain the objection because it has been more than 10 years since his conviction.

(C) Overrule the objection because the evidence is that of a habit.

(D) Sustain the objection because this evidence may lead the jury to believe that Alan has a propensity to commit robbery.

127. Alan calls David as an alibi witness. David states "I was with Alan at the Spar Tavern shooting pool at the time of the robbery." On cross-examination the prosecutor asks David if he told Mary that he was home alone at the time of the robbery. Alan objects. How should the judge rule?

(A) Sustain the objection because of hearsay.

(B) Overrule the objection because prior inconsistent statements are always admissible.

(C) Sustain the objection because David was not afforded an opportunity to explain or deny the statement.

(D) Overrule the objection because a witness may be examined regarding his or her own prior statement.

128. Same facts as above, except instead of cross-examining David, the prosecutor calls Mary and asks "What did David tell you regarding his whereabouts shortly after the robbery?" Alan objects. How should the judge rule?

(A) Sustain the objection because a specific instance of conduct cannot be introduced with extrinsic evidence.

(B) Overrule the objection because this is a prior inconsistent statement by a witness.

(C) Sustain the objection because David's prior statement was not made under oath.

(D) Overrule the objection because the statement is an admission.

129. The prosecutor asks David, "Do you remember the statement you gave to the Detective who was investigating the robbery?" David says no, but acknowledges giving the statement. After showing the Detective's notes regarding the statement to Alan's attorney, the prosecutor asks David to read the Detective's notes and then asks "What did you tell the detective?" Alan objects. How should the judge rule?

(A) Overrule the objection because the notes are a recorded recollection.

(B) Overrule the objection because the notes are writings used to refresh witness memory.

(C) Sustain the objection because the prosecution has not demonstrated that the notes were made or adopted by David when the matter was fresh in his memory.

(D) Sustain the objection because the prosecution has not demonstrated that the notes accurately reflect David's knowledge correctly.

130. P is suing D for breach of contract. Counsel for defense calls the P as a witness. The first question is "Sir, when did you stop beating your wife?" Counsel for P objects. What is the best objection to make?

(A) Leading.

(B) Prejudicial.

(C) Outside the scope of direct examination.

(D) Defamatory.

131. Witness is called to testify regarding a motor vehicle collision that occurred at a four-way stop intersection. Witness confirms she did not witness the actual collision, but came upon the scene after. She saw two cars with obvious damage, but not touching each other. One of the cars had a smashed front-end with steam escaping from the radiator. The other had a dented door. If asked what she saw, what response is least likely to arouse an objection.

(A) "Two cars that had collided with each other."

(B) "Two cars that had collided, one of which obviously ran the stop sign."

(C) "The car with the front-end damage ran the stop sign."

(D) "The car with the door damage entered the intersection first."

132. Personal Injury P calls his crystal healer Guru to testify regarding his injuries. Guru states "Based on my twenty year practice as a crystal healer in Sedona, Arizona at the prestigious 'Energy Vortex Healing Center,' my examination of P, and statements by Mr. Centauri, a space alien with whom I consulted, it is my opinion on a more probable than not basis that P's unbalanced aura was proximately caused by D." Which of the following is the most likely?

(A) The Judge must exclude the testimony because crystal healing is not recognized by the mainstream scientific community.

(B) The Judge must exclude the testimony because it contains hearsay.

(C) Admit the testimony because Guru is an expert in crystal healing.

(D) Admit the testimony because Guru correctly stated the causal relationship.

Questions 133 and 134 share common facts:

133. Doug sees Paul run a red light. Later, Doug tells Wendy "Paul ran a red light." At Paul's trial, the prosecutor calls Wendy who states "Paul ran the red light." What objection would you make?

(A) Hearsay.

(B) Lack of personal knowledge.

(C) Prejudicial.

(D) Irrelevant.

134. Same as above except Wendy states "Doug told me Paul ran the red light." What objection?

(A) Hearsay.

(B) Lack of personal knowledge.

(C) Prejudicial.

(D) Irrelevant.

135. Albert is being sued for premises liability. A necessary element of liability is that the landowner had notice of the condition. P alleges she slipped on ice in front of Albert's business. Prior to P's slipping, Bob told Albert in the presence of David, "There is ice in front of your business and you are under a legal duty to remove it." David is called to testify what Bob said to Albert. After timely objection, what ruling?

(A) Exclude as hearsay.

(B) Admit because it is not hearsay.

(C) Admit because it is an admission by party opponent.

(D) Admit as a prior statement by witness.

Questions 136 and 137 share common facts:

136. In a capital murder case, possible exculpatory evidence is that it was raining on the day of the murder. Unbelievably, the only person who has knowledge of that fact is Cindy. Cindy will testify that on the day after the murder she asked her now deceased husband if it had rained the previous day. He responded by holding up his $200.00 Italian loafers that were obviously ruined by water. Cindy knows he had worn those shoes outside on the day of the murder. What is the best way to characterize Cindy's testimony?

(A) Not hearsay, admissible.

(B) Hearsay, but admissible.

(C) Hearsay, not admissible.

(D) Not hearsay, inadmissible.

137. Same facts as above, except Cindy will testify that she saw her husband open his umbrella on the way outside on the day of the murder. What is the best way to characterize Cindy's testimony?

(A) Not hearsay, admissible.

(B) Hearsay, but admissible.

(C) Hearsay, not admissible.

(D) Not hearsay, inadmissible.

138. P calls Whitney who testifies that D ran the red light. P then calls Xavier who testifies that Whitney told him the same thing shortly after the incident. Which of the following is correct regarding Xavier's testimony of Whitney's statement?

(A) Admissible because Xavier is subject to cross-examination regarding the statement.

(B) Admissible because Xavier's testimony is one of identification.

(C) Not admissible because the defense has not implied an improper motive upon Whitney.

(D) Not admissible because Xavier's testimony is extrinsic evidence of Whitney's truthfulness.

139. Paul sues Dan for breach of contract for the sale of Paul's property to Dan. Paul testifies that he verbally offered $100 for the property and Dan said "I accept your offer." Dan objects to Paul testifying to Dan's statement. Which ruling is the judge most likely to make?

(A) Admissible, exception to hearsay exclusion.

(B) Admissible, not hearsay.

(C) Not admissible, hearsay not subject to any exception.

(D) Not admissible, subject to exclusion by another rule of evidence.

140. In a contract dispute, Drake asserts an affirmative defense of duress. He takes the stand and testifies "Piper told me 'Agree to my offer or I will kill your cats.'" Piper objects to Drake testifying regarding the statement. What ruling and why?

(A) Not admissible, hearsay.

(B) Not admissible, self-serving.

(C) Admissible, hearsay but excepted as statement against interest.

(D) Admissible, not hearsay.

141. Peter is called to testify in Paul's robbery trial. Peter testifies, "Paul robbed me at gunpoint." Paul then calls David who testifies, "Peter told me 'Oh my God! I was just robbed by Sal.'" How should the judge rule?

(A) Admissible, non-hearsay.

(B) Admissible, hearsay, but subject to an exception.

(C) Not admissible, hearsay not subject to any exception.

(D) Not admissible, extrinsic evidence.

142. Jack and Jill are on trial for murder. The prosecutor calls Bob who testifies, "Jack and I were sitting around drinking beer and he told me 'I killed him myself, but Jill will take the blame.'" What is the best way to characterize Jack's statement to Bob?

(A) Admissible, admission by party opponent.

(B) Admissible, statement against interest.

(C) Admissible, statement by coconspirator.

(D) Not admissible, hearsay not subject to an exception.

Questions 143 - 150 share common facts:

143. Pure-hearted P is suing Mega, Inc., a large, evil corporation accused of polluting the habitat of baby ducks. At issue, is whether Mega, Inc.'s Chief Engineer altered a diversion valve to spew pollution onto the baby ducks. The case is made possible by Whistleblower Wally, the human resources manager who told Sierra Club Sue, "Even though I have nothing to do with the Engineering Department, I know for a fact that this company did alter the valve." Sue now wants to testify as to Wally's statement. What ruling?

(A) Admissible, hearsay, residual exception because stopping a polluter is in the interest of justice.

(B) Admissible, not hearsay, admission by party opponent.

(C) Admissible, hearsay subject to an exception.

(D) Not admissible, hearsay subject to no exception.

144. Same circumstances as above, except Sue wishes to testify that she was speaking with Wally over the phone when he said, "Sue, you won't believe this, but I'm looking out my window watching those goofballs from Engineering alter a diversion valve." What ruling?

(A) Admissible, hearsay, residual exception because stopping a polluter is in the interest of justice.

(B) Admissible, not hearsay, admission by party opponent.

(C) Admissible, hearsay subject to an exception.

(D) Not admissible, hearsay subject to no exception.

145. Same circumstances as above, except that Wally says, "Sue, I am so sad and disillusioned with this company; I am sick to my stomach and am losing sleep over the fact that we altered the diversion valve." What ruling and why?

(A) Admissible, hearsay, residual exception because stopping a polluter is in the interest of justice.

(B) Admissible, not hearsay, admission by party opponent.

(C) Admissible, hearsay subject to an exception.

(D) Not admissible, hearsay subject to no exception.

146. Wally is suing Mega, Inc., for emotional distress. Mega, Inc., has alleged that Wally made up his symptoms well after the spill. Sue will testify that before the spill, but after the alteration of the valve Wally told her "Sue, I am so sad and disillusioned with this company; I am sick to my stomach and am losing sleep." What ruling?

(A) Not admissible, hearsay not subject to any exception.

(B) Admissible, hearsay subject to an exception.

(C) Admissible, not hearsay.

(D) Not admissible, excluded under admission by party opponent exception.

147. Bob is an employee of Mega, Inc., the same evil corporation that polluted baby ducks. Bob sees his physician Dr. Julius Hibbert and tells him "My hair and teeth are falling out, I am suffering from abdominal cramps, and I am convinced it is due to Mega Inc.'s use of Dihydrogen Monoxide to which I have been exposed." Which is the best reason to admit Dr. Hibbert's testimony regarding what Bob told him?

(A) None.
(B) Present sense impression.
(C) Then-existing mental, physical, or emotional condition.
(D) Statements for purposes of medical diagnosis or treatment.

148. Bob calls Wally as a witness to testify regarding an injury that occurred the day after the valve was altered. Wally witnessed the injury, and filled out a company injury report on the spot. In the report he states, "I saw Joe, an independent contractor, get injured. Joe told me that he was in pain." On the stand, Wally admits that he fills out at least three injury reports each day and states that even if he reviewed the report he would not remember the events. You are Bob's Attorney. What should you do?

(A) Have Wally review the report and testify based on his refreshed recollection.
(B) Have Wally read the entire report into evidence.
(C) Have Wally read the report except for Joe's statement to him because it is hearsay.
(D) Offer the report into evidence, but strike Joe's statement because it is hearsay.

149. Joe is suing Mega, Inc. for damages resulting from injuries sustained when the diversion valve failed. Mega, Inc. denies that valve failure caused the injuries. Instead of the facts above, Wally does not personally witness the injury. He is notified that Joe, an independent contractor, has been injured. He interviews Joe three days later and records Joe's statement "I was scalded by gaseous DiHydrogen Monoxide when the diversion valve failed," in an accident report pursuant to company policy. Wally remembers the incident very clearly, as that was the only injury to occur

in the last 10 years. Joe offers the report into evidence. What result?

(A) Not admissible, hearsay not subject to an exception.
(B) Admissible, not hearsay.
(C) Admissible, hearsay but subject to an exception.
(D) Not admissible, hearsay within hearsay each level not subject to an exception.

150. Same facts as above, except no report is created at the time of the injury. After Joe files suit, the V.P. of Legal Affairs directs Wally to investigate and take statements from other witnesses to the injury to help prepare Mega, Inc.'s defense. Several witnesses state "Joe was 100% at fault for his own injury, he failed to relieve the pressure on the valve before opening it," which Wally dutifully records in a report to the V.P. Unfortunately, all of the witnesses meet mysterious and untimely deaths. Counsel for Mega, Inc. offers the report into evidence. What result?

(A) Not admissible, hearsay not subject to any exception.
(B) Admissible, hearsay subject to an exception.
(C) Admissible, not hearsay.
(D) Not admissible, not hearsay, but excluded under another rule of evidence.

151. Sara is suffering from a broken arm sustained in a motor vehicle collision. She brings suit, but needs an expert to testify as to causation. She goes to Dr. Flibble and tells him, "My arm is in tremendous pain, it broke due to striking it on my car door in a motor vehicle collision, when the D ran a stop sign." How much of Sara's statement may Dr. Flibble relate via testimony?

(A) None, Dr. Flibble was retained exclusively for expert testimony, not treatment.
(B) "My arm is in tremendous pain."
(C) "My arm is in tremendous pain, it broke due to striking it on my car door in a motor vehicle collision."
(D) "My arm is in tremendous pain, it broke due to striking it on my car

door in a motor vehicle collision, when the D ran a stop sign."

152. Arnie is on trial for the murder of Bret. The prosecution calls Mr. Tallman who found a dying Bret and heard him exclaim with his last breath, "That jerk Arnie stabbed me, but I think he missed anything vital." What ruling and why?

(A) Not admissible, hearsay not subject to any exception.

(B) Not admissible, not hearsay, but excluded under a different rule of evidence.

(C) Admissible, hearsay, but subject to an exception.

(D) Admissible, not hearsay.

153. Earl's will is offered for probate. Dan contests the will by testifying as to Earl's deathbed statement "I am about to die. I now know that at the time I executed the Will, I was suffering from a delusion." Is Earl's statement admissible and why or why not?

(A) Admissible, statement under belief of impending death.

(B) Admissible, then existing emotional, mental, or physical condition.

(C) Admissible, not hearsay.

(D) Not admissible, not hearsay, but excluded under another rule of evidence.

Questions 154 – 156 are based on the following:

Percy P is suing Donald for the tort of battery. Percy calls Wendy to testify that she saw Donald strike Percy. However, Wendy testifies that it was not Donald who struck Percy.

154. Percy calls Xavier to testify that he saw Donald strike Percy. How should the judge rule on Xavier's testimony?

(A) Admissible because Percy was caught off-guard by Wendy's testimony.

(B) Admissible because Xavier's testimony is relevant to issues at

trial.

(C) Not admissible because one may not impeach their own witness.

(D) Not admissible because it is unfair to Donald.

155. On cross-examination, Donald's attorney asks Xavier if he was wearing eyeglasses at the time of the battery. Xavier replies, "No, I do not need them." Donald then calls Dr. Smith, Xavier's optometrist to testify that Xavier wears reading glasses on occasion. What ruling as to Dr. Smith's testimony and why?

(A) Admissible to impeach Xavier's credibility.

(B) Admissible to impeach Xavier's memory.

(C) Not admissible because a witness's prior acts cannot be proved through extrinsic evidence.

(D) Not admissible because whether or not Xavier wears eye glasses is collateral to the issues at trial.

156. Donald calls Ray to testify regarding Xavier's reputation for truth in the community. Ray admits he has never met Xavier. What ruling as to Ray's testimony?

(A) Not admissible because Ray does not know Xavier.

(B) Not admissible because it is character evidence.

(C) Admissible because it will impeach Xavier's testimony.

(D) Admissible because Ray does not know Xavier and is thus more credible.

Questions 157 and 158 share common facts:

Paul was a passenger in Dan's car when he was injured. Paul sues Dan for negligence. Dan denies any negligence or that Paul was injured.

157. Paul's attorney seeks the introduction of a transcript from Dr. Jones' deposition. In the deposition, Dr. Jones stated that he examined Paul one week after the injury occurred and found a recently incurred broken arm. Dr. Jones dies one week before trial. What ruling on the admissibility of the Doctor's testimony?

(A) Admissible, present physical, mental, or emotional condition.

(B) Admissible, former testimony.

(C) Not admissible, irrelevant.

(D) Not admissible, hearsay not subject to any exception.

158. Dan calls Wanda Witness to testify that Paul said to her "My broken arm was nearly healed from a prior break when Dan's negligence caused it to break again." What ruling on Wanda's testimony?

(A) Admissible as an excited utterance.

(B) Admissible as a statement for the purpose of medical diagnosis.

(C) Admissible as an admission by party-opponent.

(D) Not admissible as hearsay not subject to any exception.

159. P sues D Corporation for injuries. D's attorney requests the risk manager to memorialize the incident in a letter to the attorney. P demands that the letter be produced at trial. What result?

(A) Produce the letter because it is a record of a regularly conducted activity.

(B) Produce the letter because it is not privileged.

(C) Withhold the letter because it is attorney-client communication.

(D) Withhold the letter because it is hearsay not subject to an exception.

160. D Dirk is on trial for armed robbery. At trial, the prosecution offers evidence of Dirk's past armed robberies and his reputation in the community as a thief and robber. What ruling on this evidence?

(A) Admissible to prove that it is more likely than not that Dirk is the robber.

(B) Admissible to impeach the credibility of Dirk's testimony.

(C) Not admissible to prove Dirk committed the robbery in question.

(D) Not admissible because the prosecution failed to provide

reasonable notice of its intention to use the evidence.

161. A blue car skids through an intersection into a red car. The red car's driver does not know which of two people were driving the blue car. Dave and Tom were in the blue car and approach the red car. Dave states in the presence of the red car driver, "Tom, you idiot. Didn't you see that stop sign?" Tom says nothing. The red car driver sues Tom and wishes to testify at trial as to the exchange between Dave and Tom. What ruling and why?

(A) Admissible, statement of a co-conspirator.

(B) Admissible, adoptive admission by party-opponent.

(C) Not admissible, silence is never an adoptive admission.

(D) Not admissible, unless Dave is also a party.

162. James is attacking the validity of his father's will executed ten years ago. James offers a contemporaneous affidavit by the father's doctor opining that the father was mentally incompetent at the time of the execution. What ruling on the admissibility of the affidavit?

(A) Not admissible, dead man's statute.

(B) Not admissible, hearsay without exception.

(C) Admissible, ancient document.

(D) Admissible, statement for the purpose of medical diagnosis.

163. Jane is being sued for breach of contract. The P's evidence consists of a letter purporting to bear Jane's signature. Jane denies the signature is hers. P calls a former co-worker to identify the signature on the letter. The former co-worker states that she is familiar with Jane's signature and the letter does indeed bear Jane's signature. Will the letter be admitted into evidence?

(A) No, the co-worker has not been qualified as an expert witness.

(B) No, unless the co-worker can testify that she saw Jane sign the letter.

(C) Yes, a lay expert may testify regarding a signature with which he or she is familiar.

(D) Yes, the co-worker's familiarity with Jane's signature makes her an expert.

Questions 164 and 165 are based on the following:

Clumsy Clancy slips and falls on some ice on a sidewalk in front of a video store and dry cleaners, which are located side by side. It is unclear which of the two businesses had control over the sidewalk. The elements of premises liability are notice and control over an unsafe condition. Clancy sues both. Both allege contributory negligence as an affirmative defense.

164. The video store offers evidence that to the best of their knowledge no patrons have ever slipped and injured themselves when the sidewalk has been icy. Is this evidence admissible?

(A) Yes, because it is relevant to the Video Store's notice.

(B) Yes, because it is relevant to show that Clancy did not exercise the same care as have other patrons.

(C) No, because it is irrelevant to the Video Store's exercise of due care.

(D) No, because it is prejudicial to Clancy.

165. Clancy wishes to introduce evidence that after his fall the video store received a letter from the landlord acknowledging that the video store shoveled the ice off of the sidewalk as required by the lease. Is this letter admissible?

(A) Yes, because it shows that the video store had knowledge of the unsafe condition.

(B) No, subsequent remedial measures are not admissible.

(C) No, unless Clancy can prove that the ice was more dangerous than a bare sidewalk.

(D) Yes, because it goes to control over the sidewalk.

Questions 166 and 167 are based on the following:

Lynx sues the Golden Eagle after he is hit by a golf ball. Lynx alleges that the Golden Eagle failed to yell "Fore" after swinging at the ball.

166. Lynx testifies that he was wearing a maroon shirt that day. Golden Eagle will call Steve to testify that Lynx's shirt was orange. Steve's testimony is

(A) Admissible, relevant.

(B) Admissible, impeaches Lynx's memory.

(C) Not admissible, irrelevant to Tiger's memory.

(D) Not admissible, extrinsic evidence of a collateral matter.

167. Lynx testifies that he was standing behind a safety net when he was hit. The course pro will testify that after being struck, Lynx stated, "I should have been standing behind the safety net." What ruling on Pro's testimony?

(A) Admissible as a statement against interest.

(B) Admissible as prior inconsistent testimony.

(C) Not admissible as hearsay subject to no exception.

(D) Admissible as admission by party opponent.

Questions 168 – 170 are based on the following:

P sues D Railroad Company for injuries after P drove his car across tracks and was struck by a train. P alleges that the crossing signals were not operating nor did the train blow its warning whistle.

168. Railroad Company calls Witness 1, a passenger in P's car, to testify that "We should not have tried playing chicken with the approaching train." What ruling on the admissibility of this testimony?

(A) Admissible, admission by party opponent.

(B) Admissible, not hearsay.

(C) Not admissible, hearsay with no exception.

(D) Not admissible, lack of personal knowledge.

169. Railroad company calls Witness 2 to corroborate Witness 1's testimony by confirming that right after the collision, Witness 1 told him the same thing. What ruling?

(A) Admissible, admission by party opponent.

(B) Admissible, statement against the interest.

(C) Not admissible, hearsay, no exception.

(D) Not admissible, prejudicial.

170. Witness 2 is called to testify that he was standing with Witness 3 right before the collision when Witness 3 exclaimed, "Oh my! That car is trying to play chicken with the train! They are going to be killed! Oh, the humanity!" Witness 3 died from fright right after. What ruling?

(A) Admissible, dying declaration.

(B) Admissible, present sense impression.

(C) Admissible, declarant unavailable.

(D) Not admissible, hearsay with no exception.

Questions 171 and 172 are based on the following:

Mega Co. and its vendor Vend Co. consult with the senior partner of Dewey, Cheatum, & Howe about a product liability case initiated by P for injuries caused by a Mega Co. product of which a part was made by Vend. Co. Both parties discussed their potential liability. In its answer, Mega. Co. cross-claims against Vend Co.

171. P calls Vend Co. and asks Vend Co. to repeat the statements of Mega Co. in the conference. What ruling on the admissibility of the statements.

(A) Not admissible, privileged conversation.

(B) Admissible, no privilege.

(C) Admissible, admission by party opponent.

(D) Not admissible, hearsay with no exception.

172. Vend Co. calls its employee who was present at the conference to testify as to Mega Co.'s statements. What ruling?

(A) Admissible, relevant to rebut Mega Co.'s cross-claim.

(B) Admissible, no privilege.

(C) Not admissible, hearsay without an exception.

(D) Not admissible, still a privileged conversation.

Questions 173 – 176 are based on the following:

A Seccna 172 (a light single propeller airplane) stalls short of the runway, killing all aboard. After the crash, Seccna begins installing a stall warning indicator on all of its production aircraft. The estate of a passenger sues for defective design in not installing a stall warning indicator. Seccna alleges that it was not feasible to install the indicator in the 172.

173. Is the evidence of the installation admissible?

(A) Yes, relevant to prove feasibility of installing the indicator.

(B) Yes, relevant to prove Seccna's negligence.

(C) No, subsequent remedial measures are not admissible.

(D) No, installation of the warning indicator insufficient to prove that lack of a warning indicator proximately caused the crash.

174. Seccna introduces evidence that the pilot had failed to take his heart medication. The evidence is a statement in the pilot's wife's diary that the pilot refused to take his medication. What ruling on this writing?

(A) Admissible, the wife is unavailable due to marital privilege.

(B) Admissible, best evidence.

(C) Not admissible, hearsay.

(D) Not admissible, best evidence.

175. Same as above, except the wife is called to testify that her husband stopped taking his medication. What result?

- (A) Admissible, subject to an offer of proof on relevance.
- (B) Admissible, provided that the diary is made available to opposing counsel.
- (C) Not admissible, the contents of a writing must be proved with the writing admitted into evidence.
- (D) Not admissible, hearsay.

176. Seccna calls an air traffic controller who was talking to the pilot and will testify that the pilot stated, "I forgot to put fuel in the airplane." Is this statement admissible?

- (A) Yes, admission by party opponent.
- (B) Yes, exculpates Seccna.
- (C) No, hearsay with no exception.
- (D) No, irrelevant to negligence claim.

177. Bubo brings an action to eject some squatters from his home after returning from the Lovely Mountain. The squatters allege an affirmative defense of adverse possession. Central to the case is the date upon which he left for his adventure. Bubo testifies that it was on a Thursday and he remembers the fact because the day before he hosted Elf for tea and wrote on his engagement tablet "Elf Tea Wednesday." Is the testimony regarding the engagement tablet admissible?

- (A) Yes, provided the underlying document is made available to opposing counsel.
- (B) Yes, because the engagement tablet is collateral to the issues at trial.
- (C) No, best evidence: The engagement tablet itself must be offered into evidence.
- (D) No, hearsay not subject to any exception.

178. Witness finds victim lying in a pool of blood. Victim states, "Peter stabbed me. Since I am dying, I must clear my conscience. I shot T.R." Victim survives and is prosecuted for the shooting of T.R. Can witness testify as to Victim's statement?

- (A) No, hearsay.
- (B) Yes, dying declaration.
- (C) Yes, admission by party opponent.
- (D) No, declarant is available.

Questions 179 – 183 share common facts:

179. Polly comes home to find her apartment trashed and graffiti scrawled on the wall. Knowing her ex-boyfriend, Justin, probably did it, she telephones his home. A voice picks up and says, "Hello, Justin speaking." Polly says, "You SOB. How could you trash my apartment like this?" The voice starts laughing and hangs up. If Polly brings suit against Justin, what is the best way to characterize this conversation?

- (A) Hearsay subject to an exception, and authenticated telephone voice.
- (B) Hearsay with no exception, and unauthenticated telephone voice.
- (C) Hearsay subject to an exception, but unauthenticated telephone voice.
- (D) Hearsay with no exception, but authenticated telephone voice.

180. Polly offers a photograph of her apartment to prove the extent of the damages. What else is needed to admit the photograph?

- (A) The testimony of the photographer.
- (B) Testimony that the photograph was taken within a reasonable time of Polly's arrival home.
- (C) Testimony that the photograph accurately depicts the damage to the apartment.
- (D) Testimony that the photograph is actually of her apartment.

181. Polly calls Handyman to testify that he, erroneously thinking Justin still lived in the apartment, let Justin in to Polly's apartment. Polly then offers a copy of a log supposedly filled out by Handyman every time he lets a tenant into an apartment. Justin objects to the log. What result?

- (A) Admitted, the log is an admission that Justin was in the apartment.
- (B) Admitted, hearsay subject to an exception.

(C) Not admitted, hearsay not subject to an exception.

(D) Not admitted, no authentication.

182. Justin has been charged with breaking and entering. Justin calls his employee George to testify that Justin is very religious and is not the type of person who would do such a thing. Is George's testimony admissible?

(A) Yes, this kind of character evidence is admissible.

(B) No, character evidence is not admissible to prove or disprove action in conformity therewith.

(C) No, religious beliefs are not admissible.

(D) Yes, hearsay subject to an exception.

183. On cross-examination, George is asked, "Are you aware that Justin has trashed the apartments of his last three girlfriends?" George answers, "Yes." Upon a timely motion to strike, what ruling?

(A) Admissible to impeach George's testimony.

(B) Admissible as substantive evidence of Justin's propensity to trash apartments of ex-girlfriends.

(C) Not admissible, prior bad acts cannot be proved with extrinsic evidence.

(D) Not admissible, collateral matter.

Questions 184 – 191 share common facts.

184. The police are called to Polly's apartment. They find Justin shot to death and recover Polly's handgun that has been fired. Polly is charged with murder. Her defense is that Justin came to her apartment to kill her and she shot him in self-defense.

Polly calls three of Justin's ex-girlfriends who testify that Justin had a propensity to come to their apartments and assault them and threaten them with death often with a deadly weapon. Is this testimony admissible?

(A) Yes, not hearsay.

(B) No, character evidence of one not accused is not admissible.

(C) No, the victim is not available to rebut the character evidence.

(D) Yes, character evidence of the victim is admissible.

185. The prosecution calls George to testify as to Justin's peaceful nature. Polly objects. What result?

(A) Admissible, provided there is some evidence that Justin was the aggressor.

(B) Admissible, character evidence of the victim offered by the prosecution is admissible.

(C) Not admissible, the victim's character may not be introduced to prove action in conformity therewith.

(D) Not admissible, best evidence requires Justin to testify.

186. The prosecution calls Officer Friendly who will testify that Justin was not dead when he arrived at the apartment and that Justin told him, "Polly shot me and now I'm going to die." What ruling on the admissibility of this statement?

(A) Admissible, dying declaration.

(B) Admissible, declarant unavailable.

(C) Not admissible, irrelevant.

(D) Not admissible, prejudicial.

187. Assume that the Judge excluded the testimony of the three ex-girlfriends. Polly takes the stand and testifies that Justin was the first aggressor. The prosecution now wishes to call George to testify that Justin had a peaceful nature. Is George's testimony now admissible?

(A) Yes, a victim's character is admissible to rebut self-defense.

(B) No, a victim's character is admissible only when the D brings it up first.

(C) Yes, the victim is not the accused.

(D) No, Justin is not a witness, therefore he cannot be impeached.

188. Polly calls Officer Friendly for her case in chief. Polly's attorney asks, "What else did Justin say before he died?" Officer Friendly replies, "Justin said, 'I tried to kill Polly,' right before he told me that Polly shot him." Is Officer Friendly's testimony admissible?

- (A) Yes, dying Declaration.
- (B) Yes, statement against interest.
- (C) No, unless Justin was a party.
- (D) No, hearsay with no exception.

189. Justin's estate sues Polly for wrongful death. The estate calls Officer Friendly who will testify that Polly said, "Oops, I was cleaning my pistol and it went off striking Justin. I sure was negligent." Is this testimony admissible?

- (A) Yes, statement against interest.
- (B) No, hearsay without an exception.
- (C) Yes, admission by party.
- (D) No, opinion on an ultimate issue that must be left for the jury.

190. The estate calls the Personal Representative who will testify that Polly said, "I am so sorry that I was negligent; here's ten dollars to settle your claim against me." Is this statement admissible?

- (A) No, offer of compromise or settlement.
- (B) Yes, the statement embraces issues in addition to an offer of compromise.
- (C) No, embraces an ultimate issue to be decided by the jury.
- (D) Yes, but only the part of the statement admitting negligence.

191. The estate calls Surprise Witness Wendy who will testify that she heard Dana say, "Polly said, 'I confess. I called Justin over telling him I wanted to get back together. Then I shot him. I would have gotten away with it too if it weren't for you meddling kids.'" What result?

- (A) Inadmissible, embraces ultimate issue.
- (B) Inadmissible, hearsay without exception.
- (C) Admissible, admission by party.
- (D) Admissible, statement against interest.

192. Wally Witness saw a complex series of events resulting in an injury. He wrote a detailed account of what he saw. At trial, he testifies to the events he saw. He can't remember one detail, so Wally pulls the writing from his pocket to consult it. What must happen next?

- (A) The writing must be entered into evidence.
- (B) Opposing counsel must be allowed to inspect the writing and to cross-examine Wally about it.
- (C) Wally must read the writing into evidence.
- (D) Wally must state that he regularly records such events.

193. Doctor Doomuch is called as a P's witness in a wrongful doggy death case. The Doctor testifies that he performed a doggy autopsy upon "Muffin," the P's 250 pound Bull Mastiff. The Doctor states that he followed the procedures established by the Board of Certified Doggy Pathologists in performing the autopsy and found a surgical instrument inside Muffin, which the Doctor opines was the cause of death. The instrument has not been entered into evidence. Is the Doctor's testimony admissible?

- (A) No, doggy autopsies are not recognized in the veterinary community.
- (B) No, an expert cannot base testimony on items not in evidence.
- (C) Yes, provided that the instrument is merely admissible, but not necessarily in evidence.
- (D) Yes, an expert may base testimony upon items not in evidence.

194. Bob is on trial for burglary, a crime punishable by two years in prison. The prosecution wishes to enter a certified copy of a prior burglary conviction in which Bob spent two days in prison. What is the best way to characterize this evidence?

- (A) Admissible to prove Bob's character and propensity to commit burglary.
- (B) Admissible to impeach Bob's testimony.

(C) Not admissible, hearsay.

(D) Not admissible, character evidence.

Questions 195 and 196 share common facts:

195. Clumsy Clancy trips on uneven pavement in front of Carl's house. Carl denies that the sidewalk belongs to him, rather Carl asserts it is county property. Clancy sues Carl for injuries and seeks to admit the testimony of Nosy Neighbor who saw Carl repairing the sidewalk a week after Clancy tripped. Is Nosy's testimony admissible?

(A) Inadmissible, repairing a dangerous condition would be discouraged otherwise.

(B) Inadmissible, too much time has passed since the injury.

(C) Admissible, it is evidence of Carl's ownership of the sidewalk.

(D) Admissible, it proves the sidewalk was in a dangerous condition.

196. Nosy is called to the stand by Clancy. Nosy refuses to testify even after being thrown in jail for contempt. Clancy offers Nosy's deposition transcript in lieu of Nosy's testimony. Carl objects. What result?

(A) Admissible, former testimony.

(B) Admissible, prior statement by witness.

(C) Inadmissible, declarant is available.

(D) Inadmissible, hearsay not subject to an exception.

197. Captain Ahab runs his ship aground. The owners of the ship then sue Ahab alleging he negligently failed to order the ship to turn. Ahab testifies that he gave the order to turn, but the helmsman failed to respond in time. All orders given on the ship are recorded in the ship's log. The owners object to Ahab's testimony. What result?

(A) Inadmissible, when the contents of a writing are sought to be proved, the writing itself must be produced.

(B) Inadmissible, hearsay not subject to an exception.

(C) Admissible, Ahab's first hand knowledge.

(D) Admissible, hearsay subject to an exception.

Questions 198 – 200 are based on the following:

Jones is arrested for driving under the influence of a controlled substance, marijuana. The prosecution wishes to introduce a videotape from a pot party showing Jones sucking on a four foot bong and saying "that's great weed, man."

198. Assuming the prosecutor can establish the proper foundation, is this videotape admissible?

(A) Yes, hearsay, admission by party.

(B) Yes, not hearsay.

(C) No, hearsay not subject to any exception.

(D) No, this evidence must be elicited upon cross-examination.

199. At a pre-trial hearing, Jones' attorney alleges that the police did not have probable cause to pull Jones over. At the hearing, the police officer testifies that he was following Jones and saw Jones driving erratically. Jones' attorney then wishes to introduce an affidavit of the officer stating that he pulled Jones over because he "looked like a dirty hippie freak." What result?

(A) Admissible, but only to impeach the testimony of the officer.

(B) Admissible, as substantive evidence of why the officer pulled Jones over.

(C) Inadmissible, hearsay not subject to any exception.

(D) Admissible, unlimited purpose.

200. Jones testifies on his own behalf and states, "I am an honest person. I absolutely did not drive erratically. On cross-examination, the prosecutor asks, "Isn't it true you lied in your divorce trial last year?" Upon objection, what result?

(A) Admissible, goes to Jones' credibility as a witness.

(B) Admissible, so long as the prosecutor produces a certified copy of the conviction.

(C) Not admissible, specific instances of conduct cannot be proved with extrinsic evidence.

(D) Not admissible, irrelevant.

Questions 201 – 203 are based on the following:

Frank is on trial for burglary. Frank was caught when Wally Witness told a Police Officer, "I saw Frank enter that building twenty minutes ago and come out with an armload of stuff." The Officer then went to Frank's house and arrested him. Prior to trial, Wally meets a mysterious and untimely death.

201. The prosecutor wishes to have the Officer testify as to Wally's statement. Is the Officer's testimony admissible?

(A) Yes, present sense impression.

(B) Yes, declarant unavailable.

(C) No, hearsay with no exception.

(D) No, all testimony must be subject to cross-examination.

202. Frank is also tried for the strangulation of a security guard. The County Coroner testifies that the Guard had petechia in the eyelids, which she claims is conclusive for death by asphyxiation. Frank's expert testifies that petechia can be caused by many conditions. The expert then justifies her opinion by citing *Pathology of Asphyxiation* a treatise recognized as authoritative in this subject area. The expert then reads the relevant passage to the jury. If the prosecution objects, what result?

(A) The passage will be read to the jury.

(B) The treatise must be entered into evidence as an exhibit.

(C) The Judge will prohibit the expert from reading the passage.

(D) The Judge will prohibit the expert from referring to the treatise.

203. The prosecutor wishes to introduce a letter signed by Frank addressed to the Prosecutor, which states "Yes, I am guilty of the murder. However, because your best witness is dead, I will plead guilty to littering." Is this letter admissible?

(A) Yes, admission by party.

(B) Yes, statement against interest.

(C) No, plea discussions are inadmissible.

(D) No, hearsay subject to no exception.

204. Caesar is on trial for treason. He takes the stand in his own defense. On cross-examination the prosecutor asks, "Isn't it true that you were convicted of rape three years ago?" Upon objection, what must the prosecutor argue to get his question answered?

(A) That rape has a logical nexus to treason.

(B) Nothing, the Prosecutor may always ask such questions on cross-examination.

(C) That rape somehow involves dishonesty or false statement.

(D) That the prosecutor will offer into evidence a certified copy of the conviction, that rape is punishable by one year or more in prison, and that the probative value outweighs its prejudicial effect.

Questions 205 – 207 are based on the following:

Ethel Expert is called to testify and give her opinion in regards to causation of a certain mechanical failure.

205. Which of the following is not correct in regards to the type of facts an expert may rely upon?

(A) Facts known personally to the expert.

(B) Facts made known to the expert at trial.

(C) Facts of the type reasonably relied upon by experts in the field in forming an opinion.

(D) The facts upon which the expert bases her opinion must be admissible, but not necessarily admitted into evidence.

206. Wally Weasel is called to testify to as to Ethel's reputation for truth and veracity. Wally says, "Ethel does not have a good reputation for truthfulness. In fact, she falsified test data for her Doctoral Dissertation." Which of the following parts of Wally's statement is admissible?

(A) The first sentence only.
(B) The second sentence only.
(C) Both sentences.
(D) Neither sentences.

207. Wally's wife is called to testify about a statement Wally made to Ethel prior to the Wife's marriage to Wally. Can the Wife be compelled to testify?

(A) Yes, the communication occurred before marriage.
(B) Yes, opposing counsel failed to make a hearsay objection.
(C) No, a spouse cannot be compelled to testify against her spouse.
(D) No, despite the lack of objection, the Court may not allow inadmissible hearsay evidence.

208. Dudley is an engineer called by P to testify in regards to automotive engineering standards. Dudley testifies that he has a degree in Mechanical Engineering and has studied automotive engineering standards in his spare time. On cross-examination, opposing counsel asks, "Isn't it true that you have never worked as an automotive engineer?" If Dudley answers "Correct" what result?

(A) He is disqualified as an expert because he has not worked in the field.
(B) His authority as an expert may be undermined in the eyes of the jury.
(C) No adverse results because specific instances of conduct must proved with extrinsic evidence.
(D) Strike the question because it does not go to truth or veracity.

209. What is the best way to authenticate a signature on a document?

(A) Right before trial have a lay witness compare the signature with an already authenticated signature.
(B) Have the jury make a finding of fact that the signature is indeed authentic.
(C) Have an expert compare the disputed signature with an authentic signature.
(D) When the alleged signatory answers "No" when asked if the signature is his follow up with "Are you sure?"

210. P is suing D for fraud. P takes the stand and says, "I was one of D's investment clients for ten years. D defrauded me and several other investors out of our life savings." In rebuttal, D testifies that P was a client for only two years, and ceased to be a client one year prior to the alleged fraud. Is D's rebuttal testimony admissible?

(A) Inadmissible, evidence on a collateral matter is not admissible for impeachment only.
(B) Inadmissible, irrelevant.
(C) Admissible, testimony is substantive evidence of whether D could have been defrauded.
(D) Admissible, impeaches P's credibility.

211. P sues D Accountant for negligent calculation of tax returns. P calls Melson Ferry, an accountant, to present a summary of the taxes reported in the years in which D was P's accountant. If the summaries are to be admitted into evidence, what must occur?

(A) The underlying tax returns must be admitted into evidence.
(B) The witness must testify that the summaries are accurately based upon the tax returns.
(C) Nothing, the summaries are admissible in and of themselves.
(D) The underlying tax returns may not be produced in Court.

Questions 212 and 213 share common facts:

212. Carl Criminal is on trial for "Disturbing the Social Order" for criticizing an elected official. The main witness against Carl is Sally Socialist, the elected official Carl allegedly criticized. Sally identified Carl to a Sheriff's deputy at the time of the seditious criticism. However, at trial, Sally's testimony is that she does not recognize Carl. The prosecution calls the deputy to testify that Sally identified Carl to him at the time of the sedition. Is the deputy's testimony admissible?

(A) No, hearsay without an exception.
(B) No, best evidence requires Sally to testify.
(C) Yes, prior identification of a person.
(D) Yes, hearsay subject to an exception.

213. Carl does not take the stand in his own defense. He does call Percy who will testify that Carl volunteers at the local orphanage to read bedtime stories to the poor urchins. Is the testimony admissible?

(A) Not admissible, not a pertinent character trait.
(B) Admissible, goes to witness bias.
(C) Admissible, an accused may always put on favorable character evidence.
(D) Not admissible, character evidence may not be admitted to prove action in conformity therewith.

214. In Anystate, evidence of a violation of a statute creates a rebuttable presumption of negligence. P offers evidence that D ran a stop sign thus raising the presumption. D offers evidence that there was no stop sign. What instruction should the Court give to the jury?

(A) Negligence is presumed, thus a verdict for P must be returned.
(B) D has the burden of proof in rebutting the presumption.
(C) P has not met his burden, so a verdict in favor of D must be returned.

(D) P has the burden of proof to establish negligence.

Questions 215 and 216 share common facts:

215. P sues D for injuries suffered in an automobile collision. P calls Dr. Evil to testify that during an exam to determine injuries from a collision, P stated, "I had no pain in my back prior to the collision even though I had a prior back injury." Is Dr. Evil's testimony admissible?

(A) No, hearsay not subject to any exception.
(B) No, physician-patient privilege.
(C) Yes, then existing physical condition.
(D) Yes, statement for the purpose of medical diagnosis.

216. On cross-examination, opposing counsel asks, "Isn't it true that P suffers from a congenital defect of the skeleton that is causing the current pain?" P objects. What ruling?

(A) Inadmissible, P has not waived Physician-Patient privilege.
(B) Inadmissible, outside the scope of direct examination.
(C) Admissible, relevant to P's injuries.
(D) Admissible, hearsay subject to an exception.

Evidence
Learning Question Answer Rationales

1. **/A/** The fact is conclusively established when the Court takes judicial notice of a fact in a civil case. **(B)** is incorrect, the fact is conclusively established. **(C)** is not the best answer because it describes the effect of judicial notice in a *criminal* case. **(D)** is incorrect because the fact is conclusively established.

2. **/C/** Unlike a civil case, judicial notice of a fact in a criminal case merely satisfies the prosecution's burden of production on the fact. **(A)** is incorrect because in a criminal case, the defense may still rebut. **(B)** is not the best answer because the prosecution's burden of production has been satisfied, although the defense may still rebut. **(D)** misstates the law: a court may take judicial notice of a universally accepted fact without reference to outside sources.

3. **/D/** This is something that must be proved with evidence. The basic rationale of judicial notice is to save time. However, this is different from the Court ruling as a matter of law that the fact is established, which it can do upon proper motion. However, that is a civil procedure issue, not an evidentiary one, so summary judgment will not be tested. **(A)** would not be error. This fact is known to everybody who does not live in a cave. **(B)** would not be

error. The fact that New York is in New York is not subject to reasonable dispute. **(C)** is not error. This can be readily verified in an atlas or other generally accepted text, making it capable of accurate and ready determination.

4. **/A/** This is a necessary limiting instruction under FRE 105. The evidence is not admissible to prove that the Defendant is more likely than not guilty of the crime, but it is admissible to prove that his testimony is unreliable. **(B)** misstates the rule: the conviction may only be admitted for impeachment purposes. **(C)** is incorrect because a prior conviction's effect on a witness' credibility is for the jury to weigh and decide. **(D)** is incorrect because FRE 105 requires a limiting instruction in this circumstance.

5. **/B/** In a civil case, a presumption can be raised by the evidence and will exist until the other party offers evidence rebutting the presumption. At that point, the presumption disappears and it is simply an issue of fact for the jury to decide. If D did not offer any evidence in rebuttal, then the presumption becomes conclusive and is established as a matter of law. **(A)** is incorrect because D's negligence is presumed only until he offers rebuttal evidence. **(C)** is incorrect because P has proved negligence per se according to the statute, and the jury must find D

negligent unless he adequately rebuts. **(D)** is incorrect because P has proved negligence per se according to state law.

6. **/C/** In a criminal case, a presumption merely satisfies the burden of production. The jury will still determine whether the defendant is criminally liable. **(A)** is incorrect because the jury may merely consider the evidence in its ultimate determination of negligence. **(B)** is incorrect because the jury may merely consider the evidence in its ultimate determination of negligence. **(D)** is incorrect because the prosecution has proved a fact for the jury's consideration in its determination of criminal negligence.

7. **/B/** This goes to lack of due care which makes it relevant. **(A)** is incorrect because it has no tendency to make the existence of D's negligence more or less likely and is thus irrelevant. **(C)** is incorrect because it has no tendency to make the existence of D's negligence more or less likely and is thus irrelevant. **(D)** is incorrect because it has no tendency to make the existence of D's negligence more or less likely and is thus irrelevant.

8. **/B/** Though probative of negligence, it is immaterial to any issue at trial because negligence has already been established. **(A)** is not the best answer because the evidence is probative, it is just not material because negligence has already been established. **(C)** is incorrect because the evidence is not material if negligence has already been established. **(D)** is not the best answer because the evidence is probative but not material because negligence has already been established.

9. **/B/** This fact may show not that D was a pauper, rather that a pauper would not normally be able to buy a sports car. Thus, the jury could then infer that D got the money from the embezzlement. **(A)** is incorrect because poverty alone is not relevant to show motive of embezzlement. **(C)** is not relevant unless it could be established that D had large gambling debts. **(D)** is relevant to the defense's case and does not help the prosecution.

10. **/A/** This question shows a motivation for bias, which is nearly always relevant. A corollary to this is that witness impeachment evidence will never be excluded for irrelevancy, but it must conform to Rules 608-609. **(B)** is irrelevant absent further proof that such a "crime" is probative of a material issue at trial. Also, this type of crime does not meet the Rule 609 criteria for impeachment evidence. **(C)** is irrelevant to any issue at trial. **(D)** is also irrelevant absent proof that W is testifying as a medical expert. W could be a friend testifying upon personal knowledge of the effect of injuries upon P. Don't assume "Doctor" means medical doctor or some type of expert.

11. **/C/** Though probative of D's possible breach, the prejudicial effect of the evidence substantially outweighs the probative value. The witness could testify that D said he had another engagement at that time without problem. The other three answers are prejudicial (as is all evidence) but the prejudice does not substantially outweigh the probative value to the point to where the jury would make a decision based on emotion rather than reason. FRE 403. **(A)** is incorrect because it is relevant and not unfairly prejudicial. **(B)** may

have problems under the hearsay rule, but is not as clear-cut an answer as C. **(D)** would be admitted because it is relevant and although prejudicial, not unfairly so.

12. **/B/** Under FRE 404(a) character evidence may be introduced to rebut character evidence offered by the accused. **(A)** is incorrect because character evidence cannot be used to show a propensity to commit the crime. **(C)** is incorrect because character of the victim's peacefulness can be introduced only to rebut an accused's character evidence of the victim or to rebut a charge that victim was first aggressor when the accused claims self-defense. **(D)** is incorrect because character evidence cannot be used to show a propensity to commit the crime.

13. **/D/** Under FRE 404(b) other crimes, wrongs, or acts may be admissible for other purposes such as to establish the identity of the robber. In this case, since D placed his whereabouts in issue, the fact he was charged with a crime becomes admissible to rebut his claim that the robber was not him. **(A)** is incorrect since this trial is for robbery not assault. **(B)** may be correct if there is other evidence to establish a common scheme or plan between the two assaults. **(C)** is incorrect unless D is charged with murder.

14. **/A/** This would allow the prosecution to introduce the evidence to rebut Heather's claim of mistake. FRE 404(b). Otherwise, the evidence is inadmissible as propensity evidence. **(B)** is incorrect unless the previous crimes conformed to the definition in FRE 609, which we don't know. **(C)** is incorrect because reputation for such acts is

another form of character evidence. **(D)** is obviously incorrect because without Heather's claim of mistake the evidence is inadmissible because it is propensity evidence.

15. **/C/** Character is in issue in this case as it relates directly to fitness as a parent. **(A)** is incorrect because character is in issue in this case as it relates directly to fitness as a parent. **(B)** is incorrect because the evidence may be used to show a propensity of conduct that would render one an unfit parent. **(D)** is incorrect because the evidence may be used as propensity evidence in this case.

16. **/D/** (D) is simply not relevant to any issue at trial. In a defamation case, the truth is a defense. **(A)** would establish the truth of Garrett's statement thus is admissible to establish a defense to defamation. **(B)** would establish the truth of Garrett's statement thus is admissible to establish a defense to defamation. **(C)** would establish the truth of Garrett's statement thus is admissible to establish a defense to defamation.

17. **/A/** This is modus operandi evidence that may be used to link D from the previous burglaries to the current one. **(B)** is incorrect because it may not be used to show that D is a criminal type as that would be general propensity evidence. **(C)** is incorrect because propensity character evidence may not be used to rebut a mere denial otherwise every defendant who denies the crime would be subject to this effectively eliminating the prohibition on propensity character evidence. **(D)** is not the best answer because evidence is not usually relevant solely for the purpose of showing that various witnesses agree with each other.

For example, if all five witnesses were introduced just to prove that the crime happened at night, this would likely be cumulative and irrelevant. Some other reason (like propensity) must be offered.

18. **/C/** Specific instances of conduct may be elicited upon cross-examination only, unless the character trait is an essential element of a charge or claim. In this instance, it is not necessary to use character evidence to convict for perjury. **(A)** is a permissible way to prove character once character evidence is deemed admissible. **(B)** is a permissible way to prove character once character evidence is deemed admissible. **(D)** is a permissible way to prove character once character evidence is deemed admissible.

19. **/A/** FRE 413 allows propensity character evidence in cases of sexual assault. **(B)** is incorrect because although FRE 413 does allow propensity character evidence in sexual assault cases, the evidence must be related to propensity for a sexual crime. **(C)** is incorrect because although FRE 413 does allow propensity character evidence in sexual assault cases, the evidence must be related to propensity for a sexual crime. **(D)** is incorrect because although FRE 413 does allow propensity character evidence in sexual assault cases, the evidence must be related to propensity for a sexual crime.

20. **/C/** This is a routine practice performed in certain circumstances, but not an automatic response. The action of filling out the report is premeditated. **(A)** is habit: an automatic response conditioned by the amount of time elapsed. **(B)** is habit: the length of time establishes this automatic response to sitting

down to eat. **(D)** is habit: an automatic response not involving premeditation.

21. **/A/** Evidence of a subsequent remedial measure is inadmissible to prove negligence. **(B)** is incorrect because evidence of a subsequent remedial measure is admissible for any "other purpose" besides as proof of negligence (notice). **(C)** is incorrect because evidence of a subsequent remedial measure is admissible for any "other purpose" besides as proof of negligence (feasibility of safety measures). **(D)** is incorrect because evidence of a subsequent remedial measure is admissible for any "other purpose" besides as proof of negligence (ownership or control).

22. **/C/** Under FRE 409 an offer to pay a person's medical expenses is inadmissible to prove negligence, but other statements made during the course of such an offer are admissible. This is a narrower restriction on admissibility than is contained in rules 408 and 410. Whether the offer of settlement was verbal or written makes no difference. **(A)** is incorrect because settlement negotiations are inadmissible under FRE 408. **(B)** is incorrect because plea negotiations are inadmissible under FRE 410. **(D)** is incorrect because the letter is a settlement offer. The fact that medical expenses are "discussed" does not make the rest of the settlement letter admissible.

23. **/D/** Evidence of liability insurance is not admissible to prove negligence. **(A)** is incorrect because evidence of insurance may be admissible to prove ownership or control. **(B)** is incorrect because evidence of insurance may be admissible to prove existence of an agency relationship. **(C)** is incorrect

because evidence of insurance may be to prove witness bias.

24. /B/ This is a statement contained in an offer of compromise and is inadmissible. **(A)** is admissible to show control over the sidewalk since D placed control in issue by denying ownership. **(C)** is admissible to show control over the sidewalk since D placed control in issue by denying ownership. **(D)** is admissible because statements other than an offer to pay medical bills may be admissible.

25. /D/ This is a confidential marital communication. Privacy is one of the necessary elements of a privileged communication. **(A)** is missing the element of privacy, one of the necessary elements of a privileged communication. **(B)** is missing the element of privacy, one of the necessary elements of a privileged communication. **(C)** is a communication about a future crime, which is not privileged.

26. /A/ A spouse need not testify against the other either during their marriage or regarding a communication made during marriage. However, in (A) neither is present. The other options have at least one of these two criteria present, so a spouse will not be compelled to testify. Marital privilege is applicable to communications during marriage. Spousal incompetence applies during marriage. These two can overlap. **(B)** is incorrect because one spouse cannot be compelled to testify against the other during their marriage. **(C)** is incorrect because one spouse cannot be compelled to testify against the other during their marriage. **(D)** is incorrect because one spouse cannot be compelled to testify against the other regarding communications made during their

marriage, even if the marriage is now over.

27. /C/ This is a confidential communication where the client is seeking representation for a past crime. **(B)** is incorrect because the client is consulting in the furtherance of a crime. When engaged in a fee dispute or the client sues for malpractice the privilege disappears, so **(A)** is incorrect. **(D)** is incorrect because the "man on the street" is not necessary to the communication as opposed to an interpreter or attorney support staff.

28. /D/ This is correct because it does not constitute an exception to the marital privilege. **(A)** is incorrect because divorce proceedings are an exception to the marital privilege. **(B)** is incorrect because a mental competency proceeding against a spouse is an exception to a marital privilege. **(C)** is incorrect because statements regarding planning or furtherance of a crime are excepted from marital privilege.

29. /A/ Spouses are competent to testify against each other when one is accused of a crime upon the other. **(B)** is incorrect. Although it might be admissible under the exception to marital privilege, it does not affect competence. **(C)** is incorrect. It might be admissible under the exception to marital privilege, it does not affect competence. **(D)** is incorrect. There is no exception to marital privilege for a crime against any person besides the other spouse.

30. /D/ Insanity alone will not disqualify a witness. An insane person may be able to recall events and communicate them with appreciation of truthfulness. Witnesses are not competent if they do not appreciate truthfulness, so **(A)** is incorrect. Witnesses are not competent if they cannot communicate, so **(B)** is incorrect. Witnesses are not competent if they cannot recall events, so **(C)** is incorrect.

31. **/A/** There is no foundation as to the witness' personal knowledge. **(B)** is incorrect because it establishes that witness saw the light and thus has personal knowledge. The fact that witness may use equivocal language goes to weight and not admissibility. **(C)** is incorrect because it establishes that witness saw the light and thus has personal knowledge. The fact that witness may use equivocal language goes to weight and not admissibility. **(D)** is incorrect because it establishes that witness saw the light and thus has personal knowledge. The fact that witness may use equivocal language goes to weight and not admissibility.

32. **/B/** This is a collateral matter that goes only to casting doubt on the witness' memory. Impeachment evidence must be material to the case. The other options are evidence that is material to the case while casting doubt upon the witness' testimony. **(A)** shows that someone other than D threw the brick, so it is substantive evidence that also impeaches witness. **(C)** is material to the case. **(D)** is admissible under FRE 609.

33. **/C/** This shows bias, which is nearly always admissible. **(A)** is inadmissible propensity character evidence. **(B)** is inadmissible propensity character evidence. **(D)** incorrect because it is not material (what the two were doing at the time) that would only cast doubt on the witness, not contradict the fact that Homer and D were together.

34. **/B/** Before bolstering the credibility of a witness with reputation evidence, the credibility must first be attacked. **(A)** would apply to a situation where the prosecution offers character evidence under FRE 404. **(C)** is a correct statement of FRE 607, but is still subject to FRE 608. **(D)** is not applicable because the party is not offering extrinsic evidence.

35. **/C/** This is the only way to question the witness about specific instances of conduct. FRE 608(b). **(A)** is incorrect because extrinsic evidence may not be used to attack a witness' credibility. **(B)** is incorrect because extrinsic evidence may not be used to attack a witness' credibility. **(D)** is incorrect because there is no condition precedent to a party attacking another party's witness.

36. **/A/** Under FRE 609(a)(2), conviction for a crime of dishonesty may be used to impeach any witness. Embezzlement is a crime of dishonesty. **(B)** is incorrect because under FRE 609(a)(1) conviction of a crime other than for dishonesty or false statement cannot be offered against the accused. **(C)** is incorrect because a juvenile adjudication is not admissible against the accused. **(D)** is not evidence of a crime or dishonest behavior. It is irrelevant and inadmissible.

37. **/D/** For instance, a defeasible fee simple estate may require that the grantee remain Catholic. Thus, if the grantee becomes Lutheran, religious belief becomes an issue in a quiet title action. **(A)** is incorrect because evidence of religious belief is inadmissible to bolster or attack a witness' credibility. **(B)** is incorrect because evidence of

religious belief is inadmissible to bolster or attack a witness' credibility. **(C)** is incorrect because evidence of religious belief is inadmissible to bolster or attack a witness' credibility.

38. **/D/** This is a collateral matter, so it is not admissible. If the day the incident happened were in issue then it would not be collateral, but there is not enough information to infer that. **(A)** is a permissible way to impeach a witness with a prior statement under FRE 613 (Just hope that W doesn't lie). **(B)** is permissible extrinsic evidence of a prior inconsistent statement under FRE 613(b). **(C)** is also permissible even though the statement is not directly contradictory of W's testimony. The prior statement need only cast doubt upon W's testimony. Note that the prior statement may be elicited for impeachment evidence only. If offered as substantive evidence, then it is hearsay that must come in under an exception.

39. **/A/** The scope of direct is accounting professional standards. Thus any other professional standards are outside the scope. **(B)** is incorrect because leading questions may be asked on cross-examination. **(C)** is incorrect for the same reason **(A)** is correct. **(D)** is a trick answer. Leading questions may certainly be asked to develop testimony, but as an *exception to the prohibition* on leading questions on direct. This exception is not required on cross-examination, where leading questions are allowed.

40. **/B/** When a writing is used to refresh the witness' memory, the opposing counsel must be allowed to inspect the writing. FRE 612. **(A)** is incorrect because the writing may be offered into evidence, but it is not required merely to refresh the witness' memory. **(C)** is incorrect and is the rule for admitting a Recorded Recollection under FRE 803(5). **(D)** is incorrect because opposing counsel must be allowed to inspect the writing.

41. **/D/** This type of opinion requires an expert as it requires specialized knowledge. Also, it is not clear from the statement that the witness perceived the event. **(A)** is based upon the witness' perception, pertains to subjects not requiring specialized knowledge and will help the jury when stated as a conclusion. **(B)** is based upon the witness' perception, pertains to subjects not requiring specialized knowledge and will help the jury when stated as a conclusion. **(C)** is based upon the witness' perception, pertains to subjects not requiring specialized knowledge and will help the jury when stated as a conclusion.

42. **/B/** An opinion on an ultimate issue of fact is admissible. **(A)** is a legal conclusion, which is not admissible. **(C)** is a legal conclusion, which is not admissible. **(D)** is incorrect because such an opinion is specifically inadmissible under FRE 704(b).

43. **/D/** An expert may be qualified by experience, but medical malpractice requires a medical practitioner. A lay person with experience with a particular injury is not qualified to testify as to medical issues. **(A)** is incorrect because the witness qualifies as an expert based on experience. **(B)** is incorrect because the witness qualifies as an expert based on education. **(C)** is incorrect because the witness qualifies as an expert based on knowledge.

44. /C/ An expert may draw an opinion from facts either perceived by or made known to the witness. **(A)** is wrong because an expert may draw an opinion from facts either perceived by *or* made known to the witness. **(B)** is incorrect because an expert may draw an opinion from facts either perceived by *or* made known to the witness. **(D)** is incorrect because an expert may draw an opinion from facts either perceived by or made known to the witness.

45. /A/ The facts themselves need only be known or perceived by the expert. It is the methods and principles that the expert uses to arrive at an opinion that may be accepted within the scientific community, so **(B)** is incorrect. The facts upon which an expert relies need not be admissible, so **(C)** is incorrect. The facts must be the type relied upon by experts in the field only when the opinion is based on facts not in evidence, so **(D)** is incorrect.

46. /B/ An expert need not testify to facts underlying the opinion unless asked to on cross-examination. FRE 705. An expert need not testify to facts underlying the opinion unless asked to on cross-examination, so **(A)** is incorrect. An expert need not testify to facts underlying the opinion unless asked to on cross-examination, so **(C)** is incorrect. An expert need not testify to facts underlying the opinion unless asked to on cross-examination, so **(D)** is incorrect.

47. /B/ This is a statement that is offered to prove the guilt of defendant, so it is asserting the truth therein. **(A)** is incorrect because in a defamation case, the fact a defamatory statement was uttered is an element of the claim. Thus, the statement is offered to prove that it was uttered, not for the truth of the statement. **(C)** is incorrect because statements offered to show notice to a person does not turn on the truth of the statement. Whether or not the statement is true, it would put the shopkeeper on notice to inspect and remedy a hazardous condition. **(D)** is incorrect because this statement shows that the victim perceived the location of his captivity not that the perception was accurate.

48. /A/ In A, Bob's actions were not meant to communicate to anyone that it was raining out. Assertive conduct is usually in response to an inquiry. **(B)** is incorrect because the conduct is in response to an inquiry, and therefore it is assertive. **(C)** is incorrect because although the secretary was not making a direct inquiry, Bob's conduct of shaking the umbrella was meant to communicate to her the truth of her assertion. **(D)** is incorrect because the conduct is in response to an inquiry, and therefore it is assertive.

49. /A/ Under FRE 801((D))(1) a witness's prior *inconsistent* statement must have been given while under penalty of perjury so a statement to an insurance adjuster is hearsay. **(B)** is not hearsay because the prior inconsistent statement was made under penalty of perjury. **(C)** is not hearsay because the prior inconsistent statement was made under penalty of perjury. **(D)** is not hearsay because statements regarding identification of a person are admissible.

50. /A/ This is hearsay. In the case of intentional torts, the spouse is not a party unless he/she specifically participated in the tort. Therefore the admission is not by a party. FRE 801((D))(2). **(B)** is not hearsay. This is an admission by a party opponent. FRE 801((D))(2). **(C)** is an admission by party-opponent even though the defendant is not necessarily "admitting" liability. An "admission" is almost any statement by a party-opponent. FRE 801((D))(2). **(D)** is not hearsay. A statement by a person authorized by the party to make the statement is an admission by the party opponent. FRE 801((D))(2).

51. **/A/** An adoptive admission requires that the party heard the statement, the statement was not denied, and the party was able to respond. All three are present, so Defendant's silence is an adoptive admission of the statement. **(B)** is incorrect because Defendant could not hear the statement, so it is not an adoptive admission. **(C)** is incorrect because Defendant fainted before he could answer, he was unable to respond to the statement, so is not an adoptive admission. **(D)** is incorrect because D denies the statement, so it is not an adoptive admission.

52. **/C/** C fits under no hearsay exception. It is too attenuated in time to be a present sense impression. **(A)** is a Present Sense Impression, a statement made during or immediately after perceiving the event. **(B)** is an Excited Utterance, a statement made about a startling event while under the stress of the event. **(D)** is a Then Existing Emotional, Mental, or Physical Condition. The statement must describe the declarant's condition at the time the statement is made. Here the declarant is describing her then-current condition.

53. **/B/** The witness must have insufficient recollection to testify *fully* as well as accurately. Thus, total recall

negates this exception. **(A)** correctly states an element of the Recorded Recollection hearsay exception. **(C)** correctly states an element of the Recorded Recollection hearsay exception. **(D)** correctly states an element of the Recorded Recollection hearsay exception.

54. **/C/** Due to the risk manager's statement, these statements were made in anticipation of litigation even if the litigation was not yet underway. This gives the D Corp. a motive to at least slant the statements, if not outright fabricate them. **(A)** is incorrect because failure of *any* of the requirements negates this exception even though this particular requirement was met. **(B)** is incorrect because failure of *any* of the requirements negates this exception even though this particular requirement was met. **(D)** is incorrect because the facts state that the procedure is established, which makes the taking of statements was a regular practice.

55. **/B/** The expert may only read the relevant passage into the record. The treatise itself cannot be admitted into evidence. **(A)** is incorrect because the treatise itself cannot be admitted into evidence. **(C)** is incorrect because the treatise itself cannot be admitted into evidence. **(D)** is incorrect because the treatise itself cannot be admitted into evidence.

56. **/A/** A witness who refuses to testify despite a court order to do so is unavailable under FRE 804(a)(2). **(B)** is incorrect because absence under FRE 804(a)(3) requires that the proponent have been unable to procure the declarant's attendance by reasonable means. The proponent had plenty of time to

subpoena the witness prior to trial, so the proponent's failure to do so does not render the declarant unavailable. **(C)** is incorrect because a declarant is not unavailable if the inability to testify is due to the proponent's wrongdoing. FRE 804(a). **(D)** is incorrect because under FRE 804(a)(3), the declarant must testify to a lack of memory of the subject matter of the statement. Since the declarant remembers most of the subject matter she is available.

57. **/B/** The fact that the declarant did not believe his death was impending, even though he died, does not put the statement under the exception. **(A)** is incorrect because a statement under belief of impending death regarding the cause of the impending death. Since the declarant is making a statement concerning the cause of his (believed) impending death, the exception applies. **(C)** is incorrect because the exception applies in this case because the party against whom the statement is offered had the opportunity to cross-examine the declarant at the first trial. **(D)** is incorrect because it is a statement against interest. This statement was contrary to the declarant's proprietary interest, so the exception applies.

58. **/B/** This is hearsay within hearsay. The record of the doctor and the plaintiff's statement are their own statements each of which must have its own exception. The medical records are Records of a Regularly Conducted Activity and the statement of plaintiff was a Statement for the purpose of Medical Diagnosis. **(A)** is not completely correct because only one of the hearsay statements is addressed. The motor vehicle accident statement is not covered by this exception. **(C)** is incorrect because the recorded recollection exception requires the declarant's lack of knowledge, which is not present here. **(D)** is incorrect as neither exception applies to the doctor's medical records, though they may apply to plaintiff's statement.

59. **/C/** FRE 806 allows impeachment of a declarant who makes a statement under FRE 801((D))(2)(C-E) or a hearsay statement. **(A)** is incorrect because "non-hearsay" statements are not covered by this impeachment rule. **(B)** is incorrect because "non-hearsay" statements are not covered by this impeachment rule. **(C)** is incorrect because "non-hearsay" statements are not covered by this impeachment rule.

60. **/D/** FRE 807. Corroboration of the statement is not required. **(A)** is incorrect because it is a requirement of the residual hearsay exception. **(B)** is incorrect because it is a requirement of the residual hearsay exception. **(C)** is incorrect because it is a requirement of the residual hearsay exception.

61. **/A/** There must be just sufficient evidence from which the trier of fact could conclude that the evidence is what the proponent claims it to be. **(B)** is incorrect because the proponent need only supply sufficient evidence and B overstates the required burden of proof. **(C)** is incorrect because the proponent need only supply sufficient evidence and (C) overstates the required burden of proof. **(D)** is incorrect because the proponent need only supply sufficient evidence, thus answer (D) overstates the required burden of proof.

62. /A/ This type of comparison requires an expert. FRE 901(b)(3). A lay witness who is familiar with the signature may authenticate based on familiarity, but not based on a comparison. FRE 901(b)(2). **(B)** is incorrect because this is an acceptable method of authentication. **(C)** is incorrect because this is an acceptable method of authentication. **(D)** is incorrect because this is an acceptable method of authentication (Note: the statement is not excludable as hearsay because it is an admission by a party opponent and thus falls under that exception).

63. /B/ This is an acceptable method under FRE 901 (b)(1). The word "must" in option **(A)** renders it incorrect even though it is an acceptable method of authentication. It is not *required* to authenticate a photograph, but *may* be used to authenticate a photograph. The word "must" in option **(C)** renders it incorrect even though it is an acceptable method of authentication. It is not *required* to authenticate a photograph, but *may* be used to authenticate a photograph. The word "must" in option **(D)** renders it incorrect even though it is an acceptable method of authentication. It is not *required* to authenticate a photograph, but *may* be used to authenticate a photograph.

64. /B/ This is not sufficient to identify the caller's voice as someone could be posing as Y. **(A)** is not the best answer because it has a higher degree of reliability as a person identifying himself as "Y" was called at a phone number assigned by the phone company to Y. The difference between (A) and (B) is the fact that in (A) 'Y' stated he was returning the previous call. Otherwise, the situation would be the same as (B). **(C)** is incorrect because it has a higher degree of reliability as a person identifying himself as "Y" was called at a phone number assigned by the phone company to Y. **(D)** is incorrect because it has a higher degree of reliability, as a person identifying himself as "Y" was called at a phone number assigned by the phone company to Y.

65. /D/ A document must be in existence 20 years to qualify for authentication under FRE 901(b)(8). **(A)** is an acceptable method of authentication under FRE 901(b)(2). **(B)** is acceptable as a distinctive characteristic under FRE 901(b)(4). **(C)** is acceptable under the lay witness opinion on handwriting.

66. /D/ An ancient document under FRE 901(b)(8) must be in such a condition so as to not raise suspicions concerning its authenticity. Given that the document does not match the others, there are serious questions regarding the reliability of the document's authenticity. **(A)** is incorrect because it satisfies a requirement for an ancient document. **(B)** is incorrect because it satisfies a requirement for an ancient document. **(C)** is incorrect because it would render the need for authentication moot.

67. /A/ This is an exception to hearsay, not a self-authenticating document. **(B)** is self-authenticating under FRE 902(4). **(C)** is self-authenticating under FRE 902(5). **(D)** is self-authenticating under FRE 902(6).

68. /C/ The "Best Evidence" rule simply states that a document must be produced to prove the contents thereof. FRE 1002. **(A)** is incorrect because it is contrary to the Best Evidence rule and describes exactly what the rule forbids. **(B)** is incorrect because it goes to credibility and weight rather than admissibility of the document, which is the focus of the Best Evidence Rule. **(D)** is incorrect because the witness can testify first hand regarding the events, making the Best Evidence Rule irrelevant.

69. /A/ If the document is not central to the case, the contents may be proved by other means. FRE 1004(4). For example, if a witness testifies to remembering a certain fact because "I wrote it down in my diary," it is collateral to issues in the case. Compare with FRE 612 writing used to refresh memory. **(B)** is incorrect because possession by opposing party alone does not remove the requirement of the original, only if the opposing party refused to produce the original. **(C)** is incorrect because the original must be unobtainable through any judicial process or procedure. **(D)** is incorrect because duplicates may be admissible in lieu of the original. See FRE 1003.

70. /B/ This eliminates the need to produce the original under FRE 1007. **(A)** is incorrect because the admission eliminates the need to produce the original under FRE 1007. **(C)** is incorrect because obtainability is not part of the Rule 1007 analysis. **(D)** is incorrect because the arising of a presumption is a matter of substantive law. FRE 301 merely governs the treatment of a presumption once arisen.

71. /D/ FRE 1006. The only requirement of the four is that the underlying documents are made available to opposing parties. **(A)** is incorrect because the underlying documents need not be admitted, though they must be admissible. **(B)** is incorrect because production in court is at the Judge's discretion. **(C)** is incorrect because opposing parties need not stipulate to the admission of the summary.

Evidence
Practice Question Answer Rationales

72. /D/ Eliminate the alternatives. (D) is correct because honesty is not relevant to vandalism. Watch for the accused trying to introduce his own character evidence, which is admissible, so long as it is also relevant. **(A)** is incorrect because Jones is not a witness. **(B)** is incorrect because honesty is not relevant to the issue of a character trait, or lack thereof, to commit property damage. If Jones were on trial for perjury, evidence of his honesty would be relevant. **(C)** is incorrect because character evidence may be introduced by the accused; however, he opens the door to rebuttal by the prosecution. (C) states the opposite of the rule.

73. /A/ This evidence is admissible for other purposes to show identity (Rule 404(b)). Again eliminate the alternatives. **(B)** is not the best answer because the evidence may imply action in conformity therewith, so long as the evidence is admissible for another purpose. **(C)** is incorrect because Rule 609 applies to crimes committed by witnesses only; Jones is not on the stand. **(D)** is incorrect because this answer applies to impeaching witnesses under Rule 608. Watch for answers that seem to impeach the accused when he does not take the stand; such an answer will always be wrong.

74. **/B/** By eliminating the alternatives one arrives at **(B)**. This evidence will prejudice Jones because its shock value outweighs the very slight probative value. **(A)** is attempting to confuse you with reference to the requirements of impeaching a witness with a prior crime. **(C)** is incorrect because this evidence will prejudice Jones (its shock value outweighs the very slight probative value). **(D)** is incorrect because the two incidents are not similar enough to show a scheme or plan.

75. **/C/** This evidence is admissible as establishing Jones' negligence by entrusting Heather with the boat when he knew she would make good on her threat. **(A)** is incorrect because evidence of Heather's character is admissible, not to prove action in conformity therewith, rather to establish Jones' knowledge, thus it is perfectly permissible for the jury to infer Heather's liability therefrom. **(B)** seeks to confuse you with the rules for impeaching witnesses. **(D)** is incorrect because the evidence can be used against Heather, so long as it is admissible for another purpose other than to prove action in conformity therewith.

76. **/C/** Though this evidence in and of itself is not sufficient to sustain the prosecutor's burden, it does have some probative value in proving Gunther's guilt. **(A)** is incorrect; the best evidence rule applies to documentary evidence. **(B)** is incorrect because prejudice must substantially outweigh probative value. This situation is the opposite. Remember that all evidence is prejudicial to some extent. **(D)** is incorrect because evidence need not be sufficient, merely relevant.

77. **/D/** This is the correct answer because drinking a beer does not make the occurrence of the battery any more or less probable. **(A)** is incorrect because Bob's intoxication does not make the fact of the battery any more or less probable. **(B)** is incorrect even if intoxication is a defense to battery because the existence of an affirmative defense does not make the battery any more or less probable. **(C)** is incorrect because the question of relevancy is again the establishment of battery, not an affirmative defense.

78. **/A/** This is the correct answer. Even though it is not direct evidence (such as a witness to the murder) it is circumstantial in that it establishes a motive for the murder. **(B)** is incorrect because the fact Dave is dishonest does not make it more or less likely that her murdered Erin. **(C)** is incorrect because a piece of evidence need not in and of itself sustain a guilty verdict. As stated by McCormick it need only be "one brick in the wall of evidence" that the prosecutor must build to sustain a verdict. **(D)** is incorrect because circumstantial evidence can be very relevant.

79. **/C/** This is the best answer. The fact that Dave is a butcher makes his disposal of the clothes just as consistent with innocence as with guilt. **(A)** is not the best answer because the fact he is a butcher makes this less likely. **(B)** is not the best answer because again an innocent explanation is just as likely. **(D)** is not the best answer because the testimony could be relevant because it may imply he was disposing of the clothes he wore during the murder.

80. **/C/** This is correct because it is a specific instance of conduct (Rule 608(b). **(A)** is incorrect because under Rule 609(a)(1) conviction by crime other than for dishonesty may not be used against an accused. **(B)** is incorrect because Rule 610 prohibits evidence of witness religious beliefs to bolster or attack credibility. **(D)** is incorrect because he must have been *convicted* of perjury, not just arrested.

81. **/A/** This is correct. The letter is extrinsic evidence of a specific instance of conduct under Rule 608(b), which is not admissible. **(B)** is meant to confuse you with Rule 613, prior statement by *witness*. However, the letter was not a statement by Dave. **(C)** is meant to confuse you with Rule 613, prior statement by *witness*. However, the letter was not a statement by Dave. **(D)** is incorrect because the prosecutor is offering the letter itself into evidence, not giving it to Dave to refresh his memory.

82. **/B/** This is correct; a prior written or verbal statement by the witness may be the subject of questioning. Rule 613. **(A)** is incorrect because extrinsic evidence may be used to prove a prior inconsistent statement. **(C)** is incorrect because under Rule 613 the statement need not be shown to the witness prior to questioning. **(D)** is nonsensical because the prosecutor is not producing the letter, merely asking Goler about it.

83. **/C/** This is correct because it shows possible witness bias, which is generally admissible. **(A)** is incorrect because the question is relevant to Goler's bias. **(B)** is incorrect because any prejudice does not substantially outweigh the probative value of Goler's bias. **(D)** is not the best answer. Although bias does go to truthfulness, (C) is a better way of stating it.

84. **/D/** This is correct because statements made during settlement offers are not admissible. **(A)** is incorrect because it is hearsay, but subject to an exception (admission by party opponent). **(B)** is incorrect because the entire statement is inadmissible under Rule 408: the offer itself and statements made during negotiations stay out. **(C)** is incorrect because thought the statement is subject to a hearsay exception, it is still inadmissible under Rule 408.

85. **/C/** Unlike Rule 408, Rule 409 excludes only the offer to pay; it does not exclude an admission made during the offer. Note that if Penelope had said "I'm sorry I was negligent; I'll pay your medical bills *if you agree not to sue me*" it would be a settlement offer. **(A)** is incorrect because Rule 409 excludes only the offer to pay; it does not exclude an admission made during the offer. **(B)** is incorrect because Rule 409 excludes only the offer to pay; it does not exclude an admission made during the offer. **(D)** is incorrect because Rule 409 excludes only the offer to pay; it does not exclude an admission made during the offer.

86. **/A/** The cross-examination is within the scope of direct examination. You can arrive at this answer through elimination. **(B)** is incorrect because the offered evidence is irrelevant; Defendant has stipulated to negligence, thus any evidence of such is not needed. **(C)** is incorrect because the prejudicial effect outweighs the

probative value; there are other ways to prove that victim is dead. **(D)** is incorrect because the cumulative nature of the testimony makes it prejudicial and wastes time.

87. **/A/** This rebuts Doris' allegation that Henry knew or should have known of the dangerous condition. **(B)** is incorrect because it is relevant to an issue in the case; therefore, no limiting instruction is necessary. **(C)** is incorrect because negative evidence is admissible if it is relevant. **(D)** is incorrect because it rebuts Doris' allegation that Henry knew or should have known of the dangerous condition.

88. **/B/** The text must be established as authoritative to fall under the Learned Treatise exception to hearsay. **(A)** is incorrect because the evidence is a reading of the passage not the document itself. **(C)** is incorrect because the text must be established as authoritative to fall under the Learned Treatise exception to hearsay. **(D)** is incorrect because the text must be established as authoritative to fall under the Learned Treatise exception to hearsay. Note that if the treatise were determined as authoritative then (D) would be correct as a treatise passage can impeach and be substantive evidence.

89. **/C/** The issue to be proved is the placement of the stop sign. So long as Polly can testify that the photo is an accurate depiction of the placement of the sign at the time of the collision, the photo is authenticated. **(A)** is incorrect because so long as Polly can testify that the photo is an accurate depiction of the placement of the sign at the time of the collision, the photo is authenticated. **(B)** is incorrect because the creator of the photo need not testify, rather a witness with personal knowledge that it is an accurate depiction of the item to be proved. **(D)** is incorrect because a photo needs to be authenticated.

90. **/A/** A certified public record is self-authenticating (Rule 902(4)) and excepted from hearsay (Rule 803(8)). **(B)** is incorrect because a certified public record is self-authenticating (Rule 902(4)) and excepted from the hearsay rule (803(8)). **(C)** is incorrect because a certified public record is self-authenticating (Rule 902(4)) and excepted from the hearsay rule (803(8)). **(D)** is incorrect because a certified public record is self-authenticating (Rule 902(4)) and excepted from the hearsay rule (803(8)).

91. **/D/** An expert's opinion must be based on facts known to her and her status as an expert must be established to the court's satisfaction. **(A)** is incorrect because, though it is true, it is not applicable to the facts. No hypothetical information has been introduced. **(B)** is incorrect because an expert's credentials must be established in court, not in public. **(C)** is incorrect because an expert need not base her opinion on admissible testimony, but must be based on facts relied upon by the scientific community in reaching such an opinion.

92. **/A/** Sally did not see the collision, so she has no personal knowledge of the car's speed. **(B)** is incorrect because it does not take an expert to establish something as ordinary as the speed of a car. **(C)** is true, but not applicable to these facts because Sally has no personal knowledge. **(D)** is incorrect

because this goes to weight not admissibility.

93. /C/ Due to his longtime use, Jones would most likely be qualified as an expert. **(A)** is incorrect because it goes to credibility, a jury question. **(B)** is incorrect because experience as well as education and training can qualify one as an expert. **(D)** is not the best answer because Jones is an expert. A lay witness could not identify a substance as marijuana, but he could describe the substance.

94. /A/ The technician is an expert based on experience, and his opinion is based on his perception of the facts. **(B)** is incorrect because an expert may opine on an ultimate issue. **(C)** is incorrect because opinions need not be based on facts in evidence, only upon the perception of the expert using methods accepted by the scientific community. **(D)** is incorrect because he does have personal knowledge of the test results.

95. /D/ Communications between spouses are privileged while they are married. However, no privilege exists where there was no expectation of confidentiality, such as in a crowded restaurant. **(A)** is incorrect because the statement is excepted from hearsay as an admission by party-opponent. **(B)** is incorrect for this reason. Marital Communication Privilege should not be confused with spousal incompetence, which is not a choice in this question. **(C)** is meant to confuse you with impeaching of a witness. The issue is marital communication privilege.

96. /C/ The presence of the court reporter in this case does not destroy the privilege because her presence was necessary to the attorney-client communication. **(A)** is incorrect because privilege survives the death of the client. **(B)** is incorrect because the presence of the court reporter in this case does not destroy the privilege because her presence was necessary to the attorney-client communication. **(D)** is incorrect because it is an admission by party opponent, thus not hearsay.

97. /C/ Both statements are then existing state of mind excepted under Rule 803(3). **(A)** is incorrect because it does not matter if Bob is available or not. **(B)** is incorrect because her statement is hearsay; it is not an admission. **(D)** is incorrect because the statements are subject to hearsay exceptions.

98. /D/ Former testimony may be admitted when the declarant is unavailable. One of the factors making a declarant unavailable is beyond process. Rule 804(a)(5). Overseas assignment would most likely qualify. **(A)** would operate to bar Gary's former testimony because procuring a declarant's unavailability negates this hearsay exception. Note that in the first trial, Gary was not the declarant; he was a witness repeating a declaration. His former testimony makes him the declarant at the second trial – the substance of his testimony is hearsay within hearsay. **(B)** is trying to confuse you with Rule 803(3) in which availability is immaterial. **(C)** is incorrect because a Rule 804(b)(2) dying declaration is admissible only for the declarant's perception of the cause of death.

99. /B/ Admission by party opponent. The statement is an admission of owner's knowledge of his culpability. **(A)** is incorrect because the statement is not

hearsay (note the difference from a hearsay statement subject to an exception). **(C)** is incorrect because the statement is not hearsay (note the difference from a hearsay statement subject to an exception). **(D)** is a distracter. The statement being offered is owner's not Richard's.

100. /C/ By elimination. **(A)** may seem correct if this were a criminal case, but it is civil. **(B)** is incorrect because reputation does not show motive, opportunity, intent, or the others listed in Rule 404(b). **(D)** is incorrect because again this is a civil case. If it were a criminal case, Betty could only rebut Ronald's character evidence, not the other way around.

101. /A/ Present sense impression. Rule 803(1). The statement was describing an event as it was happening. **(B)** is incorrect because the statement is hearsay. **(C)** is incorrect because the statement need only be based on the personal observation of the witness. **(D)** is incorrect because the statement was describing an event as it was happening and falls under the present sense impression exception to the hearsay rule.

102. /D/ The logbook is a record of a regularly conducted activity; the church records are records of a religious organization. Both are exceptions to hearsay under Rule 803. **(A)** is incorrect because the logbook is a record of a regularly conducted activity. **(B)** is incorrect because the church records are records of a religious organization. **(C)** is incorrect because the logbook is a record of a regularly conducted activity and the church records are records of a religious organization.

103. /C/ Under Rule 803(16) the blueprints are ancient documents and excepted from hearsay. **(A)** is incorrect because the blueprints are ancient documents and excepted from hearsay. **(B)** is a nonsensical answer. Evidence is either (1) hearsay and is inadmissible, or (2) not hearsay/subject to an exception and is admissible. It is never both. **(D)** is incorrect as the blueprints do meet the definition of hearsay.

104. /A/ You may have thought the statement was one under belief of impending death and therefore subject to a hearsay exception. However, Hauser was confident he would live, so there was no belief of impending death. **(B)** is incorrect because the statement is certainly relevant. **(C)** is incorrect because the statement is not prejudicial (just because it's bad for someone's case doesn't make it prejudicial!). **(D)** is a red herring and incorrect. The examiners will occasionally throw this in to confuse you. The Dead Man's Statute makes a decedent's statements inadmissible when the statement is offered to prove a contractual or other claim against the estate. It would not apply to a statement under belief of impending death.

105. /C/ Rule 612 writing used to refresh memory. **(A)** is incorrect because a witness may refer to notes to refresh her recollection. **(B)** is incorrect. It is possible to have the witness read the notes into evidence under Rule 803(5), but the notes themselves may not be entered as exhibits. **(D)** is incorrect. It is possible to have the witness read the notes into evidence under Rule 803(5), but the notes themselves may not be entered as exhibits. Note that under Rule 803(5) the notes must have been made while the matter was fresh in the witness's memory.

106./A/ In a criminal case, the prosecution's burden of production is satisfied when judicial notice is taken. **(B)** is incorrect because the facts specify that this is a criminal case, not civil. **(C)** is incorrect because the defendant does not need to produce any evidence to the contrary; the prosecutor always has the burden of persuasion. **(D)** is incorrect even in a civil case; the fact would be conclusive.

107./B/ This is the best answer. The identity of defendant as the object thrower is central to plaintiff's case. **(A)** is incorrect because the facts do not state whether or not disclosure is required or occurred. **(C)** is incorrect because there is no prohibition on impeaching one's own witness though it may raise the eyebrows of some jurors. **(D)** is incorrect because there is no condition precedent to having Clancy testify.

108./C/ This is the best answer because though the color of the jacket may cast doubt on Clancy's memory, the color of the jacket is not central to the plaintiff's claim. The memory of a witness can only be attacked with contradictory facts central to the case such as if the videotape showed the policeman throwing an object through the window. **(A)** is incorrect because specific acts are not involved. **(B)** is incorrect because evidence that casts doubt on witness testimony is not automatically admissible. **(D)** is incorrect because evidence that casts doubt on witness testimony is not automatically admissible.

109./C/ Able is offering the testimony for purposes other than proving a likelihood of negligent or wrongful conduct. He is offering it to prove an essential element of breach of contract. **(A)** is incorrect because Able is offering the testimony for purposes other than proving a likelihood of negligent or wrongful conduct. He is offering it to prove an essential element of breach of contract. **(B)** is a hearsay objection, but there is an exception – admission by party opponent. **(D)** is correct, but not the best answer because all relevant evidence is admissible unless otherwise excluded by rule. Though relevant, the fact that the offered evidence regards insurance coverage brings Rule 411 into play requiring an analysis beyond Rules 401 and 402.

110./B/ Rule 801((D))(2)(A) allows for the admission of a party's own statement against him or her. Betty made the statement herself and it is offered against her to prove breach of contract. **(A)** is incorrect for this reason. Though the statement was not made by the declarant (Carol) and is offered to prove the truth of the matter asserted (lack of coverage), it is not hearsay as explained above. **(C)** is not the best answer because the subject of insurance is not offered to prove negligence. It would be admissible. **(D)** is incorrect because even though the *testimony* is made by Betty's employee, the *statement* was made by Betty herself.

111./A/ Rule 413 allows for the admission of evidence of past sexual assaults for its bearing on any relevant matter in a current sexual assault case. This is an exception to the Rule 404(b) prohibition on propensity type character evidence. **(B)** would be correct if the prosecution sought the admission of evidence that Jeff wore a mask during the previous assault under

Rule 404(b) identity. However, the prosecution only sought evidence of the prior conviction, not the wearing of the mask during the prior assault. **(C)** is not the best answer because the ten-year limit on evidence of prior convictions applies to character evidence of witnesses under Rule 609. Nothing in this question indicates the prosecutor is attempting to impeach Jeff. **(D)** is incorrect because evidence of past sexual assaults is admissible in a current sexual assault case.

112./D/ Rule 609(b) prohibits admission of a witness' past crime for impeachment purposes if the witness was convicted or released (whichever is later) more than ten years ago. **(A)** is incorrect because evidence of past sexual assaults is admissible only against an *accused* not a witness. See Rule 413 et seq. **(B)** would be correct if Jeff's conviction or release was less than ten years ago. **(C)** is not the best answer, though technically correct, because evidence of past crimes other than for dishonesty or false statement can be admissible to impeach a witness (though not in this case because of the ten year lapse). See Rule 609(a).

113./C/ Sal's ownership of the rifle is relevant to establish that he possessed the means to kill Tom. **(A)** is not the best answer because it is unlikely that the name and use of the rifle creates prejudice *greater* than the probative value. **(B)** is incorrect because the insufficiency of the evidence does not make it inadmissible. Don't confuse the standards for a directed verdict with the standards for admissibility. **(D)** not the best answer because it is unlikely that the name and use of the rifle

creates prejudice *greater* than the probative value.

114./D/ Evidence of a witness' truthful character is not admissible unless the witness' character has been attacked by the other party. Rule 608(a)(2). **(A)** is incorrect because evidence of a witness' truthful character is not admissible unless the witness' character has been attacked by the other party. **(B)** is incorrect because evidence of a witness' truthful character is not admissible unless the witness' character has been attacked by the other party. **(C)** is incorrect because Sal calling a character witness does not bar Wendy from testifying.

115./A/ When attacking the credibility of a witness, at the Court's discretion, past instances of conduct probative of untruthfulness can be elicited on cross-examination of the witness. Rule 608(b). **(B)** is incorrect because instances of conduct other than *criminal conviction* (provided for under Rule 609) cannot be proved by extrinsic evidence. Rule 609 is not applicable because the employer's suit was civil not criminal. **(C)** is incorrect because instances of conduct other than *criminal conviction* (provided for under Rule 609) cannot be proved by extrinsic evidence. Rule 609 is not applicable because the employer's suit was civil not criminal. **(D)** is incorrect because instances of conduct other than *criminal conviction* (provided for under Rule 609) cannot be proved by extrinsic evidence. Rule 609 is not applicable because the employer's suit was civil not criminal.

116./C/ This is evidence of a habit. Rule 406. The key is the similarity of circumstances between the night in question and every Saturday for the past ten years. If any circumstances had changed, such as Sal not going to the club that night, Bruce's testimony would be barred. **(A)** is incorrect because Bruce's testimony is based on firsthand knowledge, though it implies circumstances beyond his firsthand knowledge. **(B)** is incorrect because the fact Bruce left for church is a collateral matter not used for the purpose of enhancing his credibility. **(D)** is incorrect because Rule 404(b) is not applicable in these circumstances.

117. /D/ Evidence of compromise or offers thereof is admissible to rebut a contention of delay. Rule 408. **(A)** is incorrect because evidence of compromise or offers thereof is admissible to rebut a contention of delay. **(B)** is incorrect because it is an ethics question not an evidentiary question. **(C)** is technically correct, but not the best answer because any evidence other than plea discussions is not barred by Rule 410.

118. /C/ Evidence of offering to pay for Tom's bills is inadmissible to prove liability. Rule 409. **(A)** may be correct, but even if the statement clears the hearsay hurdle it cannot get past Rule 409, so it is not the best answer. **(B)** is incorrect because the statement is not an offer of compromise. **(D)** could be correct, but (C) is the better answer because of the bright line prohibition on payment of medical expense evidence.

119. /A/ Subsequent remedial measures are not admissible to prove negligence, but may be admitted for other purposes such as to prove ownership. Since Landlord, Inc.

has denied ownership Tenant may introduce the installation of the handrail to prove such. **(B)** is incorrect because Tenant has not offered any documentary evidence, only testimonial. **(C)** is incorrect because a subsequent remedial measure is not admissible to prove negligence, but may be admitted for another purpose such as to prove ownership. **(D)** is incorrect because Contractor is merely identifying who hired him; he is not relating an out of court statement.

120. /D/ The call of the question asks for the *best* answer. (D) is not necessarily a good answer for Harold, but it is the best he can accomplish among these four choices. **(A)** is incorrect because Harold and Wanda are no longer married at the time of her testimony. **(B)** is incorrect because the communication was made before their marriage began. **(C)** is incorrect because Harold's statement is an admission by party opponent.

121. /C/ The Attorney-Client privilege is not applicable when the client sues the attorney for malpractice. **(A)** is incorrect because the Attorney-Client privilege is not applicable when the client sues the attorney for malpractice. **(B)** is not the best answer because Cathy's statement is most likely an admission by party opponent; hearsay would not bar her statement. **(D)** is not he best answer because there is a concrete rule available: the exception to Attorney-Client privilege when a client sues for malpractice. Therefore, (D) is not the best way to articulate the rule.

122. /A/ Rule 601 makes every witness competent unless otherwise provided by the Rules. Though he is mentally ill, defense counsel has not proved that Donald does not appreciate truthfulness or cannot recall the events he witnessed. **(B)** is not the best answer because the fact his credibility may be attacked does not support his competency. **(C)** is incorrect because Rule 601 makes every witness competent unless otherwise provided by the Rules. Though he is mentally ill, defense counsel has not proved that Donald does not appreciate truthfulness or cannot recall the events he witnessed. **(D)** is incorrect because the brother's testimony goes to Donald's credibility, not competence. The brother may testify against Donald's character under Rule 608.

123./B/ Do not be distracted by the subject matter of Bob's testimony. The prosecutor is trying to establish Bob's bias. **(A)** is incorrect because evidence inadmissible for one purpose may be admissible for another. In this instance, Bob and Alan's prison time is elicited to show Bob's bias even though it collaterally demonstrates a propensity to commit crime. **(C)** is incorrect because by eliciting character testimony from Bob, Alan has opened the door to prosecution attack of his character. **(D)** is incorrect because being in a gang is not a specific instance of conduct concerning truthfulness. If the facts showed that Bob had lied for Alan in the past, then (D) would be correct.

124./C/ This is classic Rule 608(b) Specific Instance of Conduct. **(A)** is incorrect because the fact that a priest is referenced does not invoke the Rule 610 prohibition of religious beliefs because the prosecutor is trying to attack Bob's credibility by virtue of his lying, not by virtue of his religious affiliation. However, the prosecutor missed a good Rule 610 objection when Charlie testified to Bob's reputation for truthfulness due to his religious beliefs. **(B)** is meant to confuse you by making you think Charlie's answering of the question is extrinsic evidence of Bob's character, but a witness may be impeached by the cross-examination of a second witness when the second witness has testified on direct to the first witness' character. Note that it is arguable whether Alan could solicit Charlie's testimony of Bob's truthfulness because Bob's character has not been attacked (though his bias has been exposed). **(D)** is incorrect and is meant to confuse you with the fact the prosecutor did not object to Charlie's testimony establishing Bob's truthfulness due to his religious beliefs.

125./B/ Under FRE 609 an *accused* who takes the stand can be impeached by crimes only involving dishonesty or false statement. Impeachment by crimes punishable by more than one year in prison applies only to witnesses. **(A)** is not a good answer because it is a Rule 608(b) argument, which applies to conduct *other than conviction of a crime*. Since this involves a crime Rule 609 is applicable. **(C)** is not the best answer because (B) is a much stronger argument (the crime *must* involve dishonesty or false statement to be admitted) than this weaker procedural argument. **(D)** is incorrect because the facts establish that the crime is punishable by imprisonment greater than one year. Obviously, the prosecutor is trying to admit the judgment under Rule 609(a)(1), but did not take the Rigos course!

126./A/ The prosecutor is offering the evidence for a purpose other than propensity evidence. This is evidence of identity due to the unique modus operandi of the robbers in both cases. See Rule 404(b). **(B)** would be correct if the prosecutor were offering the evidence of the past conviction to impeach Alan's own testimony. Rule 609(b). **(C)** is incorrect because a habit is an automatic response to identical stimuli, which these facts are not. **(D)** is incorrect despite the fact that the jury could draw a conclusion that the evidence shows a propensity. The test for admissibility under Rule 404 is not based on what conclusion the jury may reach but rather the reason for which the proponent offers the evidence.

127./D/ Rule 613(a) permits examination of a witness regarding his or her own prior statement. Note that David's prior statement does not meet the definition of hearsay because a hearsay statement is one made by a person other than the witness. See Rule 803(c). **(A)** is incorrect because rule 613(a) permits examination of a witness regarding his or her own prior statement. **(B)** is incorrect (watch out for universal statements with the words "never" or "always") because under Rule 801((D))(1) a prior inconsistent statement that meets the definition of hearsay must have been made under oath subject to the laws of perjury to be admissible. **(C)** is incorrect because this opportunity must be afforded when a prior inconsistent statement is offered using *extrinsic* evidence. Here, the evidence is elicited under cross-examination. Compare Rules 613(a) with 613(b).

128./C/ A prior inconsistent statement of a witness introduced by another witness must have been made under oath. Rule 801((D))(1)(A). **(A)** is incorrect because this question regards a statement, not conduct thus Rule 608(b) is not applicable. **(B)** is incorrect because a prior inconsistent statement of a witness introduced by another witness must have been made under oath. Rule 801((D))(1)(A). **(D)** would be correct if David were a party; an admission must be by a party-opponent to be admissible hearsay.

129./B/ This question is meant to mislead you into a hearsay analysis. However, so long as the prosecutor allows Alan or his attorney to inspect the notes, it is permissible under Rule 612 for David to review the Detective's notes to refresh his memory regarding the statement he gave to the Detective. **(A)** is not applicable because the prosecution has not offered the notes into evidence, so a hearsay analysis does not arise. **(C)** is not applicable because the prosecution has not offered the notes into evidence, so a hearsay analysis does not arise. **(D)** is not applicable because the prosecution has not offered the notes into evidence, so a hearsay analysis does not arise.

130./B/ This is the best answer because the question is very prejudicial and offers little probative value. **(A)** is incorrect because leading questions may be asked of an adverse party on direct examination. **(C)** is incorrect because Plaintiff *is* testifying on direct examination. **(D)** is incorrect because it is a nonsensical objection.

131./A/ Even though this is an opinion, the opinion is admissible because it is based on her perception and is more helpful to the trier of fact than a mere recitation of exactly what she saw. Though **(A)** is also based on an inference, it is the most likely inference. **(B)** is incorrect because the witness makes a conclusion not based on her perception, but upon an inference from what she saw. **(C)** is incorrect because the witness makes a conclusion not based on her perception, but upon an inference from what she saw. **(D)** is incorrect because the witness makes a conclusion not based on her perception, but upon an inference from what she saw.

132./C/ Though it is doubtful any Court would permit this testimony, this is the best answer. Guru Dot is undoubtedly an expert in this area, though not taken seriously by most people. **(A)** is not best because acceptance in the scientific community is merely a factor for the Judge to consider in her discretion, rather than a strict rule of exclusion. **(B)** is not the best because an expert may testify that he or she relied upon statements of others to arrive at the opinion. See Rule 703. **(D)** is not the best because it goes to the weight of the testimony, not the admissibility.

133./B/ Wendy is testifying to a fact she did not witness. **(A)** is incorrect because Wendy is not stating that Doug told her Paul ran the red light. **(C)** is incorrect because the statement's probative value outweighs its prejudice. **(D)** is incorrect because the evidence of Paul running the light is central to the prosecution's case.

134./A/ Now Wendy is testifying not to a fact she did not witness, rather what Doug told her. **(B)** is incorrect because she has personal knowledge of Doug's statement. **(C)** is incorrect because the

statement's probative value outweighs its prejudice. **(D)** is incorrect because the evidence of Paul running the light is central to the prosecution's case.

135./B/ The statement is not offered for the truth of the matter asserted (the presence of ice), rather to prove notice to Albert (the fact the statement was made). This does not meet the core definition of hearsay. **(A)** is incorrect because the statement is not offered for the truth of the matter asserted (the presence of ice). **(C)** is incorrect because the declarant, Bob, is not a party-opponent. **(D)** is incorrect because it is not a prior statement by the witness, David.

136./C/ The husband's holding up of the shoes was intended as a non-verbal assertion that it had rained the previous day, and the testimony is offered to prove the fact that it was raining the day before. **(A)** is incorrect because the husband's holding up of the shoes was intended as a non-verbal assertion that it had rained the previous day, and the testimony is offered to prove the fact that it was raining the day before. **(B)** is incorrect because the holding up of the shoes was not a present sense impression admissible under Rule 803(1) (the assertion was not made contemporaneously with the event). **(D)** is incorrect because the statement is hearsay.

137./A/ Opening the umbrella was not an assertion from the husband to his wife that it was raining, but merely an action. The other options describe assertions, therefore they are incorrect choices. Opening the umbrella was an action but not an assertion, and it does not meet the definition of hearsay, so **(B)** is incorrect. Opening the umbrella was an action but not an assertion, and it does not meet the definition of hearsay, so **(C)** is incorrect. Opening the umbrella was an action but not an assertion, and it does not meet the definition of hearsay, so **(D)** is incorrect.

138./C/ Xavier's testimony does not fall under the Rule 801((D)) definition of non-hearsay because a consistent prior statement may not be admitted unless the witness' credibility is attacked. **(A)** is incorrect because a consistent prior statement may not be admitted unless the witness' credibility is attacked. **(B)** is incorrect because Whitney's statement is not one identifying a person. **(D)** is incorrect because there is no prohibition in the hearsay rules against using extrinsic evidence of a witness' prior inconsistent or prior consistent statement. Compare with the Rule 608(b) prohibition on extrinsic evidence used to prove a witness' prior acts.

139./B/ Dan's statement has independent legal effect regardless of the truth or falsity of his statement. It is not being offered for the truth of the matter asserted, it is also arguable that the statement is an admission by party opponent. **(A)** is incorrect because the statement is not hearsay thus an analysis under Rules 803 is moot and the fact Dan is a party makes him available under Rule 804. **(C)** is incorrect because the statement does not meet the definition of hearsay. **(D)** is incorrect because there is no other rule of exclusion applicable to the testimony.

140./D/ Drake is not offering the statement to prove Piper actually intended to kill his cats, rather he is trying to prove that the statement was made as evidence of the duress. Thus

(A) is incorrect because it is not offered for the truth of the matter asserted. **(B)** is incorrect because testimony can be self-serving (watch for answers that seem out of left field like this one). **(C)** is incorrect because the declarant must be unavailable to take advantage of this exclusion.

141./B/ Peter's statement to David is hearsay, but is excepted from exclusion as an excited utterance. Rule 803(2). **(A)** is incorrect because Peter's prior statement, though inconsistent, was not given under oath thus Rule 801((D)) is not applicable. **(C)** is incorrect because the statement is an excited utterance. **(D)** is incorrect because extrinsic evidence may be used to prove prior inconsistent statements, Rule 613(b), but not specific instances of conduct. Rule 608(b).

142./A/ This is an admission by party opponent, under Rule 801(2)(A) Party's Own Statement. Though his statement is arguably against his interest, **(B)** is incorrect because Jack is a party thus he is available. Note that this statement tends to exculpate Jill, but would not be admissible for that purpose because of a lack of corroborating evidence. The statement is not a Rule 801(2)(E) statement by a co-conspirator because no other evidence of a conspiracy is present thus **(C)** is incorrect. **(D)** is incorrect because this is an admission by a party opponent, under Rule 801(2)(A) Party's Own Statement.

143./D/ This statement is hearsay with no exception. **(A)** is incorrect because there is no evidence that the statement is more probative than any other available evidence. **(B)** is incorrect. A statement by a party-opponent's employee must concern a matter within the scope of the employment to be an admission, or the declarant must be authorized to make the statement. An engineering issue is not within the course and scope of a human resource manager's employment. If this were an employment discrimination case, the result would be different. **(C)** is incorrect because there are no facts supporting a hearsay exception.

144./C/ The statement is a present sense impression. Rule 803(1). Wally is describing an event as it is happening. If he were more excited, the statement would also be an excited utterance. **(A)** is not the best answer because the present sense impression exception applies. **(B)** is incorrect because a statement by a party-opponent's employee must concern a matter within the scope of the employment to be an admission, or the declarant must be authorized to make the statement. **(D)** is incorrect because the statement is a present sense impression and excepted from the hearsay rule.

145./D/ If you thought that the statement was a then existing mental, emotional, or physical condition, you are incorrect. The statement is admissible to prove how Wally was feeling (if it were material to the case), but not to prove that the valve was diverted. **(A)** is not the best answer because there is no evidence that the statement is more probative than any other available evidence. **(B)** is incorrect because a statement by a party-opponent's employee must concern a matter within the scope of the employment to be an admission, or the declarant must be authorized to make the statement. **(C)** is incorrect because the statement falls under no exception.

146./B/ The statement to Sue is excepted from hearsay as either a Present Sense Impression or Then Existing Mental, Emotional, or Physical Condition. Thus **(A)** is incorrect. **(C)** is incorrect because the statement falls under the Present Sense Impression or Then-Existing Emotional or Physical Condition Exceptions. **(D)** is incorrect because Wally himself is offering the statement, it is not being offered by his opponent.

147./D/ With this hearsay exception, the entire statement would be admitted. **(A)** is simply incorrect, as at least part of Bob's statement would be admissible under the three exceptions. **(B)** would allow only complaints of his symptoms, not the statement regarding how he acquired the symptoms. **(C)** would allow only complaints of his symptoms, not the statement regarding how he acquired the symptoms.

148./B/ This is hearsay within hearsay. The report is hearsay, but is excepted either as a Recorded Recollection or a Record of a Regularly Conducted Activity. Because Wally has insufficient recollection the report would be read into evidence. **(A)** is not the best answer because Wally has already stated that he can't recall the event even if he reviews the report. **(C)** is not the best answer because though Joe's statement is hearsay within hearsay, it is excepted as a then existing physical condition, so it can be admitted. **(D)** is not the best answer because Joe's statement is admissible. If (D) did not strike Joe's statement, then it would be an acceptable answer because the report is a Record of a Regularly Conducted Activity. However, the report itself qualifies under either admission, so (D) is not the best answer.

149. /D/ Joe's statement is hearsay within hearsay. The first is the document itself, which falls under the business record exception. However, Joe's statement is also hearsay. Note that the same statement made to his physician would be admissible under Rule 803(4). **(A)** is correct, but not the best answer because it does not recognize the hearsay within hearsay. **(B)** is incorrect because Joe would like to prove the truth of the matter asserted; the fact that he was injured by valve failure. Also, the statement is not being offered against him as is required under FRE 801(D). **(C)** is incorrect because there is a hearsay within hearsay problem.

150. /A/ This is not a record of a regularly conducted activity because this report was prepared in anticipation of litigation. Nor is it a present sense impression of the witnesses because of the passage of time. **(B)** is incorrect because the report is not a record of a regularly conducted activity (the report was prepared in anticipation of litigation). Nor is it a present sense impression of the witnesses because of the passage of time. **(C)** is incorrect because the statements are offered for the truth of the matter asserted: Joe's own fault. **(D)** is incorrect because the statement is hearsay.

151. /C/ Statements for purposes of medical diagnosis or treatment are admissible including statements regarding causation. How the injury occurred is important to the treatment or diagnosis. **(A)** is incorrect, the fact that the statement was made to a physician retained exclusively for expert testimony does not make the entire statement inadmissible. A medical expert still needs to diagnose the problem as any treating physician would. **(B)** is not the best answer because the statement of causation is important to the treatment and diagnosis. **(D)** is incorrect because the statement of defendant's actions is not for the purpose of diagnosis and treatment and would most likely be excluded.

152. /A/ This statement is not a statement under belief of impending death because Bret thought his injuries were not life threatening. **(B)** is incorrect because the statement is hearsay, because the prosecution is offering the statement for the truth of the matter asserted. **(C)** is incorrect because the statement was not made under belief of impending death. **(D)** is incorrect because it is offered for the truth of the matter asserted and is not an admission by party opponent, nor a prior statement by witness.

153. /B/ Typically, a then-existing mental condition cannot be admitted to prove a *prior* existing condition. However, it may be admitted when it relates to the execution of a will. **(A)** is incorrect because the statement does not concern the cause or circumstances of an impending death. **(C)** is incorrect because the statement is used to prove the truth of the matter asserted: the fact Earl was delusional. **(D)** is incorrect because the statement is hearsay.

154. /B/ Whether Donald struck Percy is the central issue at trial. **(A)** is incorrect because "being caught off guard" is not a basis on which to admit or deny evidence. **(C)** is incorrect because a party may certainly impeach its own witness (FRE 607). The fact that Wendy's testimony was detrimental to Percy's case does not prohibit Xavier from testifying. **(D)** is incorrect because "fairness" is a broad policy abstraction, but is very subjective when applied to individual cases.

155./D/ Even though it would cast doubt on Xavier's testimony, Xavier's credibility may not be impeached with this evidence because the fact that he wears glasses is collateral to the issues at trial. **(A)** is incorrect because Xavier's credibility may not be impeached with this evidence because the fact that he wears glasses is collateral to the issues at trial. **(B)** is incorrect because Xavier's credibility may not be impeached with this evidence because the fact that he wears glasses is collateral to the issues at trial. **(C)** is incorrect because there is no prior act being elicited. Xavier should be impeached with evidence that Donald did not strike Percy or that Donald was not present.

156./C/ Ray merely needs personal knowledge of the reputation. FRE 602. He need not know Xavier personally. **(A)** is incorrect because Ray merely needs personal knowledge of the reputation. FRE 602. He need not know Xavier personally. **(B)** is incorrect because character evidence is admissible pursuant to FRE 404(a)(3). **(D)** is incorrect because credibility is not a basis for admitting or excluding evidence.

157./B/ Under FRE 804(b)(1) former testimony is admissible if the declarant is unavailable. Death certainly meets this requirement. **(A)** is incorrect because a then existing physical condition must be the declarant's condition. Here the declarant is talking about someone

else's condition. Note that if the Doctor said, "Paul told me that his arm was broken," it would then fit within this exception. **(C)** is incorrect because an injury is relevant to plaintiff's damages. **(D)** is incorrect because there is a valid exception. Note that the Doctor's statement is hearsay, but it is subject to an exception.

158./C/ This is an admission that he had a prior injury. **(A)** is incorrect because there is no indication that Paul was excited. **(B)** is incorrect because Wanda is not a physician. **(D)** is incorrect because an admission by a party is defined as non-hearsay. FRE 801((D))(2).

159./C/ Because the risk manager wrote the memo to the attorney, it is attorney-client communication. **(A)** is incorrect because the memo was not created as a routine matter following the injury and is not a business record exception to the hearsay rule. **(B)** is incorrect because the risk manager wrote the memo to the attorney so it is attorney-client communication. **(D)** is not the best answer because hearsay would exclude the memo from evidence, but would not prevent its production at trial.

160./C/ This is classic propensity evidence; the prosecution is trying show that Dirk is the kind of person more likely than not to have committed the armed robbery. **(A)** is incorrect because this is classic propensity evidence; the prosecution is trying show that Dirk is the kind of person more likely than not to have committed the armed robbery. **(B)** is incorrect because Dirk has not taken the stand. Even if he did, only character evidence of truth or veracity may be introduced for the limited purpose of impeaching his testimony. **(D)** is incorrect because the prosecution need not notify the defendant of its intent to impeach Dirk. (D) attempts to confuse with the requirement of FRE 807 to disclose the intent for this type of hearsay evidence.

161./B/ A party may make an admission by failing to contradict such a statement when a reasonable person would be expected to contradict such a statement. **(A)** is incorrect because there is no evidence of a criminal conspiracy. **(C)** is incorrect because silence can be an adoptive admission. **(D)** is incorrect because Dave's statement is not offered to prove the truth of the matter asserted, rather that it was said and Tom failed to contradict it.

162./B/ This is the best answer out of the options presented. No valid exception to hearsay is presented. **(A)** is incorrect because the Dead Man's Statute bars claims against a decedent's estate. **(C)** is incorrect because a document must be twenty years old to be ancient. **(D)** is incorrect because it is unknown if the diagnosis is based upon a statement by decedent.

163./C/ FRE 901(b)(2) allows a non-expert familiar with the signature to authenticate it. **(A)** is incorrect because an expert is not required to authenticate a signature. **(B)** is incorrect because the witness need not have seen Jane sign the letter, though if she had, that also would be authentication evidence. **(D)** is incorrect because an expert is not required to authenticate a signature.

164./A/ This goes directly to notice of a dangerous condition. **(B)** is incorrect because lack of prior injuries does not prove Clancy was contributorily negligent and is thus irrelevant. **(C)** is incorrect because

the evidence is offered for control not due care. **(D)** is incorrect because prejudice must substantially outweigh the probative value.

165./D/ This goes directly to the issue of control over the area where Clancy fell. **(A)** is incorrect because it would then be characterized as a subsequent remedial measure if offered for proof of negligence. **(B)** is incorrect because the evidence is not offered to prove negligence. FRE 407. **(C)** is incorrect because it is not relevant to negligence.

166./D/ The color of Lynx's shirt is collateral to the issues at trial. **(A)** is incorrect because even if the color of the shirt is relevant, relevancy is the threshold inquiry still subject to other rules of admissibility. **(B)** is incorrect because relevancy is the threshold inquiry still subject to other rules of admissibility, even though it is good evidence of Lynx's memory. **(C)** is incorrect because the question is relevant to Lynx's memory, but is still excluded under the collateral matters rule.

167./D/ This is an admission by Lynx that he may not have been exercising due care for his own safety. **(A)** is incorrect because a statement against interest is admissible only when the declarant is unavailable. **(B)** is incorrect because there is no prior testimony. **(C)** is incorrect because there is an applicable hearsay exception.

168./B/ This is direct testimony by a witness based on first-hand knowledge. There is no out of court statement. **(A)** is incorrect because this is direct testimony by a witness based on first-hand knowledge. There is no out of court statement. **(C)** is incorrect because this is direct testimony by a witness based on first-hand knowledge. There is no out of court statement. **(D)** is incorrect because the witness was a passenger in the car.

169. **/C/** This statement is hearsay. **(A)** is incorrect because Witness 1 is not a party. **(B)** is incorrect because the declarant is available. **(D)** is incorrect because prejudice must substantially outweigh probative value.

170. **/B/** Excited utterance would also be correct, but (B) is correct because Witness 3 was describing the event as it occurred. **(A)** is incorrect because the statement did not encompass the cause of the declarant's death. **(C)** is incorrect because mere unavailability does not constitute an exception in and of itself. Unavailability is a condition precedent to the exceptions under FRE 804, which do not apply to this question. **(D)** is incorrect because Witness 3 was describing the event as it occurred.

171. **/A/** Despite the presence of both parties, in relation to third parties this conversation was privileged because both parties are required for the communication to occur. **(B)** is incorrect because there is attorney-client privilege. **(C)** is incorrect because of the privilege. Just because a statement may be admissible under a hearsay exclusion, it may still be inadmissible under another rule of evidence. **(D)** is incorrect because it is arguably an admission by party opponent.

172. **/B/** This is permissible because there is no privilege between the two parties present, unless employee's presence was reasonably required

in the meeting. There is no indication of that here. **(A)** is not the best answer because even if relevant, it may still be subject to a privilege. **(C)** is incorrect because it is arguably an admission by a party. **(D)** is incorrect because there is no privilege.

173. **/C/** Subsequent remedial measures are not admissible to prove negligence. **(A)** is incorrect because subsequent remedial measures are not admissible to prove negligence. **(B)** is incorrect because a subsequent remedial measure is inadmissible to prove negligence. **(D)** is incorrect because it argues to the sufficiency of the evidence, not the admissibility. The analysis turns on the purpose for which the remedial measure is offered.

174. **/C/** The diary is an out-of-court statement offered for the truth of the matter asserted. The wife could testify, but this is not an option. **(A)** is incorrect because unavailability is not an exception in and of itself. Also, the marital privilege is inapplicable because the diary was not a marital communication thus she is available as a witness. **(B)** is incorrect because the best evidence rule applies to proving the contents of writings. The wife could testify that the husband stopped taking medication, but not that she wrote that in her diary. **(D)** is incorrect because the best evidence rule applies to proving the contents of writings. The wife could testify that the husband stopped taking medication, but not that she wrote that in her diary.

175. **/A/** This is the best answer, subject to relevancy to the cause of the crash. **(B)** is incorrect because the witness is not testifying to the contents of a writing. **(C)** is incorrect because

the witness is not testifying to the contents of a writing. **(D)** is incorrect because the wife is testifying from personal knowledge of facts not out of court statements.

176./C/ This is an out of court statement offered by Seccna to prove the truth of the matter asserted: the pilot's own negligence. **(A)** is incorrect because the pilot is not a party. **(B)** is incorrect because the fact Seccna is exculpated does not make the statement admissible, though the statement would certainly withstand a relevancy challenge. **(D)** is incorrect because the statement is relevant to a negligence claim.

177./B/ The best evidence rule does not extend to writings collateral to the issues at trial. The issue is what date Bubo left, which he testifies to out of personal knowledge. The fact that he remembers the date because he wrote it down is collateral to the issue of when he left. **(A)** is incorrect because the engagement tablet need not be admitted to prove a collateral matter. If the contents of the engagement tablet were in issue, then the tablet would have to be offered into evidence. **(C)** is incorrect because the engagement tablet need not be admitted to prove a collateral matter. **(D)** is not the best answer because the evidence is testimony regarding the engagement tablet not the tablet itself.

178./C/ Victim is now a party and the confession is an admission. **(A)** is incorrect because there is an exception. **(B)** is incorrect because victim neither died nor was his confession regarding the manner of his impending death. **(D)** is not the best answer, though the availability of victim would preclude the

admission of a dying declaration, witness can testify based on another exception.

179./A/ Admission by party opponent as to the laughing (note the adoptive admission) and the fact the voice identified itself as Justin at his telephone number of record authenticates the voice as his. FRE 901(b)(6). **(B)** is incorrect because there is an admission by party opponent as to the laughing (note the adoptive admission) and the fact the voice identified itself as Justin at his telephone number of record authenticates the voice as his. FRE 901(b)(6). **(C)** is incorrect because the voice was authenticated. **(D)** is incorrect because the statement is an admission by party opponent.

180./C/ So long as Polly states that the photograph accurately depicts the damage to the apartment, the photo is authentic under FRE 901(a); the matter in question is what it is claimed to be. **(A)** is not the best answer as the photographer would also have to testify that the photo accurately depicts the damage, thus the photographer's testimony is superfluous. **(B)** is not the best answer as it does not prove that the photograph depicts what it claims to depict. **(D)** is not the best answer as it is not a detailed as (C), which is best for authentication.

181./D/ The Handyman did not testify that the log was filled out by him. **(A)** is incorrect because the log is not an admission by Justin. **(B)** is not the best answer, though the log is a record of a regularly conducted activity the authentication hurdle to admissibility is not surmounted. **(C)** is incorrect because the log is a record of regular conducted activity.

182./A/ The accused may offer character evidence that shows he is not the type of person that would commit the crime. **(B)** is incorrect because the accused may offer character evidence to show he is not the type of person that would commit the crime. **(C)** is incorrect because religious beliefs are inadmissible to establish credibility of a witness; Justin is not a witness. **(D)** is incorrect because there is no out of court statement.

183./A/ When a witness offers character evidence of another, that witness may be cross-examined on specific instances of that person's conduct under FRE 405(a). **(B)** is incorrect because this evidence cannot have substantive value to show Justin's character for trashing apartments; it may be offered to rebut Justin's character evidence under FRE 404(a)(1). **(C)** is incorrect because FRE 405 does allow the evidence to be offered to rebut Justin's character evidence under FRE 404(a)(1). **(D)** is incorrect because the testimony bears directly on the statement made by George that Justin would not "do that sort of thing," so it is not collateral.

184./D/ FRE 404(a)(2) allows a pertinent character trait of the victim to be admitted. But see FRE 412 et seq. (Sex assault victims). **(A)** is not the best answer because though the evidence is admissible it is not because of a hearsay analysis that it is admissible. **(B)** is incorrect because FRE 404(a)(2) allows a pertinent character trait of the victim to be admitted. **(C)** is incorrect because there is no requirement that the victim must have the opportunity to rebut the evidence.

185./A/ Under FRE 404(a)(2) the prosecution may offer the victim's character under two circumstances: to rebut defense evidence of victim's character or to rebut evidence that a homicide victim was the first aggressor. Here, the only option is under the latter circumstance. Though Polly introduced evidence of Justin's character, this was not an option to this question, but either circumstance would justify the admission of George's testimony. **(B)** is incorrect because it does not state the condition precedent to the prosecutor's offering of such evidence. **(C)** is incorrect because FRE 404 allows such character evidence. **(D)** is incorrect because the Best Evidence Rule applies to documentary evidence only.

186./C/ By claiming self-defense, Polly admits that she shot Justin, thus the statement is irrelevant. If Justin stated that Polly shot him without provocation, then the statement would be relevant. **(A)** is not the best answer though technically correct, the statement does not meet the relevance threshold inquiry. **(B)** is incorrect because unavailability is not in and of itself a hearsay exception. **(D)** is incorrect because prejudice must substantially outweigh probative value.

187./A/ The prosecution may offer a victim's character as evidence once the accused alleges the victim was the first aggressor. FRE 404(a)(2). **(B)** is incorrect because the defendant need not make the victim's character an issue, rather allege the victim was the first aggressor. **(C)** is incorrect because the character of the victim is analyzed differently from the character of the accused under FRE 404. **(D)** is incorrect because the character evidence under FRE 404 has nothing to do with FRE 608 witness character evidence.

188./B/ Justin is unavailable and his statement would subject him to criminal liability (attempted murder) thus it is a statement against interest. **(A)** is incorrect because the statement of Justin's attempt does not go to the cause of his impending death and is not a dying declaration under FRE 804(b)(2). **(C)** is incorrect because Justin needs to be a party for his statement to be excepted under FRE 801. **(D)** is incorrect because there is an exception, statement against interest.

189./C/ Polly is a party and the statement is an admission of negligence. **(A)** is incorrect because Polly is available, thus this exception is not valid. **(B)** is incorrect because there is an applicable exception. **(D)** is incorrect because FRE 704 allows opinions embracing an ultimate issue.

190./A/ All statements made in the course of settlement negotiations are inadmissible. **(B)** is incorrect because all statements made in settlement negotiations are not admissible. **(C)** is incorrect because FRE 704 allows opinions on ultimate issues. **(D)** is incorrect because all statements contemporaneous with settlement negotiations are inadmissible.

191./B/ There are two levels of hearsay in this statement. Polly's statement to Dana and Dana's statement to Wendy. Polly's statement is an admission by a party. However, Dana's statement to Wendy is hearsay without an exception. **(A)** is incorrect because FRE 704 allows opinion on an ultimate issue. **(C)** is incorrect because Dana is not a party. **(D)** is

incorrect because both declarants are available.

192./B/ The writing is used to refresh the witness' memory under FRE 612 and is not required to be entered into evidence though it may be offered into evidence by opposing counsel. **(A)** is incorrect because it is not required to be entered into evidence. **(C)** is incorrect because it is not an FRE 803(5) recorded recollection because the witness must have insufficient recollection of the events recorded. **(D)** is incorrect because the writing need not be a record of a regularly conducted activity to be used to refresh a witness' recollection.

193./D/ An expert may opine on facts not in evidence, so long as the facts are those relied upon by other experts in the field. **(A)** is incorrect because the Doctor testified that the procedures are recognized. **(B)** is incorrect because an expert may base an opinion on facts not in evidence. **(C)** is incorrect because the facts need not be admissible.

194./B/ Impeachment is the only way this evidence could be admitted. **(A)** is incorrect because character evidence is not admissible to prove action in conformity therewith. **(C)** is incorrect because a conviction is a matter of public record excepted from hearsay under FRE 803(8). **(D)** is not the best answer because though it may be character evidence, it is admissible to impeach Bob.

195./C/ FRE 407 allows subsequent remedial measures to be admitted to prove, inter alia, ownership. **(A)** is incorrect, though it is a correct statement of the policy rationale, because the repairs are not offered to prove negligence thus the policy rationale for excluding such evidence is not present. **(B)** is incorrect since the passage of time does not enter an FRE 407 analysis. **(D)** is incorrect because it is directly contrary to the purpose of FRE 407.

196./A/ Nosy's refusal to testify renders her unavailable under FRE 804 thus former testimony is excepted from hearsay under FRE 804(b)(1). **(B)** is incorrect because a prior statement by witness under FRE 801((D))(1) must be inconsistent with present courtroom testimony or consistent with testimony to rebut a claim to the contrary. **(C)** is incorrect because under FRE 804(a)(2) Nosy is not available. **(D)** is incorrect because an exception does exist.

197./C/ Ahab is testifying to his firsthand knowledge of events, not to out of court statements or the log record. **(A)** is not correct; Ahab is not testifying as to the contents of the log but the events as he perceived them first hand; the log would certainly corroborate his testimony. **(B)** is incorrect because he is testifying to events, not to an out-of-court statement. **(D)** is incorrect because Ahab is testifying to events, not to an out-of-court statement, but would be correct if the log itself were being offered since it is a record of a regularly conducted activity.

198./B/ So far as Jones' action is an admission, it is not hearsay under FRE 801(D). **(A)** tries to trick you by defining the action as an admission and calling it hearsay at the same time. **(C)** is incorrect because Jones' action is an admission and is not hearsay under FRE 801(D).. **(D)** is incorrect unless the Prosecution is trying to impeach Jones under FRE 608(b), but he has yet to be a witness and the actions do not go to his character for truthfulness.

199./A/ Impeachment evidence need not comply with hearsay rules because it is not offered to prove the truth of the matter asserted, rather to impeach the witness. This is not a prior statement by witness inconsistent with the declarant's testimony under FRE 801((D))(1)(A) because the affidavit was not a statement made at trial, hearing, or deposition. **(B)** is incorrect because impeachment evidence is not offered to prove the truth of the matter asserted but to impeach the witness. **(C)** is incorrect because impeachment evidence is not offered to prove the truth of the matter asserted but to impeach the witness. **(D)** is incorrect because impeachment evidence is not offered to prove the truth of the matter asserted but to impeach the witness.

200./A/ This is a specific instance of conduct that is admissible to prove the character of the witness under FRE 608(b). Although the illegal conduct did not result in a conviction, it is still admissible, but only upon cross-examination. Note that Jones could lie, and the prosecutor could do nothing about it. **(B)** would be correct if Jones had been convicted of perjury. **(C)** would be correct had the prosecutor called another witness to testify or introduced some document regarding the lie. **(D)** would be correct if Jones were asked about a prior act not concerning the witness' character for truthfulness.

201./C/ Wally is not a party, and though unavailable, his statement does not fall under any hearsay exception. **(A)** is incorrect because he did not make the statement while observing the event. **(B)** is incorrect because mere unavailability is not an exception. **(D)** is incorrect because hearsay exceptions allow for introduction of statements without the opportunity for cross-examination. Note that this statement would be admissible as a prior statement by a witness of identification of a person. FRE 801((D))(1). However, that option was not available for this question.

202. /A/ FRE 803(18) allows for a relevant passage of a learned treatise to be read into evidence once the authority of the treatise is established. **(B)** is incorrect because the treatise itself may not be admitted into evidence. **(C)** is incorrect because the passage may be read into evidence. **(D)** is incorrect because an expert may refer to a treatise.

203. /C/ FRE 410(4) makes any statement made in the course of plea discussions inadmissible. **(A)** would be correct if the statement were not made in the course of a plea discussion. **(B)** is incorrect because under this exception (FRE 804(b)(3)) the declarant must be unavailable. **(D)** is incorrect because but for the plea discussion, the statement is an admission.

204. /D/ FRE 609(a)(1) allows evidence of a conviction punishable by one year or more in prison to be introduced provided the probative value of the evidence outweighs the prejudicial effect. **(A)** is incorrect because a nexus between the current crime and a past crime is not the determinate of admissibility. **(B)** is incorrect because there are limits on what the prosecution may ask regarding conviction of a crime. **(C)** is incorrect because the conviction need not be for dishonesty or false statement.

205. /D/ Under FRE 703 facts upon which the expert bases her opinion need not be admissible into evidence. **(A)** is a proper basis for an expert opinion and therefore an incorrect response. **(B)** is a proper basis for an expert opinion and therefore an incorrect response. **(C)** is a proper basis for an expert opinion and therefore an incorrect response.

206. /A/ The first sentence is reputation testimony admissible under FRE 405 and FRE 608(a). The second sentence is extrinsic evidence of a specific instance of conduct inadmissible under FRE 608(b). Note that specific instances of conduct under FRE 405(b) is admissible only if the character trait is an essential element of a charge or claim. **(B)** is incorrect because the second sentence is extrinsic evidence of a specific instance of conduct inadmissible under FRE 608(b). **(C)** is incorrect because the second sentence is extrinsic evidence of a specific instance of conduct inadmissible under FRE 608(b). **(D)** is not the best answer because the first sentence is reputation testimony admissible under FRE 405 and FRE 608(a).

207. /C/ A spouse may not be compelled to testify against the other regarding any matter. This is marital incompetence, which is different from marital privilege, which covers communications during marriage only. **(A)** is incorrect because marital incompetence still prohibits the testimony. If Wife had divorced Wally prior to trial she could testify. **(B)** would be correct but for marital incompetency, in which spouse may not be compelled to testify against the other regarding any matter. **(D)** is incorrect because an objection not timely made is waived. FRE 103.

208. /B/ This is impeachment evidence that can reduce the witness' credibility in the eyes of the jury. **(A)** is incorrect because a witness can be an expert based on knowledge. FRE 702. **(C)** is incorrect because it misstates the rule prohibiting extrinsic evidence, and even if correctly stated, prior acts may be elicited upon cross-examination. **(D)** is incorrect because the question goes to credibility as an expert, not credibility for truth.

209. /C/ Under FRE 901(b)(3) an expert in handwriting may authenticate a signature with an already authenticated specimen. **(A)** is incorrect because a lay witness must be familiar with the signature for reasons other than purposes of trial. **(B)** is incorrect because the jury must have an authentic specimen with which to compare the contested signature. **(D)** is incorrect because it will prove nothing.

210. /C/ This testimony goes directly to rebut plaintiff's claim of fraud by proving that plaintiff was not a client at the time of the alleged fraud. Thus, the testimony is not regarding a collateral matter, but goes directly to the issues at trial, though it will have the effect of also impeaching plaintiff by casting doubt upon her memory. **(A)** is incorrect because the testimony is not regarding a collateral matter, but goes directly to the issues at trial, though it will have the effect of also impeaching plaintiff by casting doubt upon her memory. **(B)** is incorrect because the testimony is very relevant. **(D)**

is not the best answer because if this were the only reason to admit the testimony it might be viewed as collateral. The fact the testimony impeaches the witness in and of itself does not make it admissible.

211. /B/ This is the best answer: the witness must lay the foundation for the accuracy of the summaries. **(A)** is incorrect because FRE 1006 does not require that the underlying documents be admitted, though there is no prohibition on admission either. **(C)** is incorrect because a witness must at least identify the exhibit as a summary. **(D)** is incorrect because the Court may order the production of the underlying returns.

212. /C/ FRE 801(D)(1)(C) allows an out of court statement of a witness/declarant's identification of a person after perceiving him provided the witness/declarant testifies at trial. **(A)** is incorrect because a prior witness statement is not defined as hearsay. **(B)** is incorrect because the Best Evidence Rule applies to documentary evidence. **(D)** is incorrect because it is not hearsay under FRE 801.

213. /A/ The character of the accused is admissible if offered by the accused and pertinent to the charge. In this case, Carl's compassion for children is not pertinent to the charges against him. **(B)** is incorrect because Carl never took the stand. **(C)** is incorrect because the favorable character evidence must be pertinent. **(D)** is incorrect because an accused may offer evidence of a pertinent character trait that may tend to prove he did not commit the crime.

214./D/ Plaintiff always has the burden of proof in establishing the presumption. **(A)** is incorrect because the presumption is rebuttable and defendant offered rebuttal evidence. **(B)** is incorrect because the establishment of the presumption does not shift the burden of proof to defendant, plaintiff still has the burden of proof and persuasion. **(C)** is incorrect because plaintiff has offered evidence in favor of the presumption.

215./D/ Statements for the purpose of medical diagnosis are admissible. Note that FRE 803(4) allows the description of past symptoms, which would not be admissible under an FRE 803(3) then existing physical condition. **(A)** is incorrect because there is an applicable exception. **(B)** is incorrect because plaintiff waives this privilege by bringing suit where his physical condition is at issue. **(C)** is incorrect because the symptoms must be contemporaneous with the statement.

216./C/ This testimony is relevant to plaintiff's injuries. **(A)** is incorrect because bringing the suit and putting his physical condition in issue waives the privilege. **(B)** is incorrect because direct examination had to do with injuries and pain. **(D)** is incorrect because there is no out of court statement to which the witness is testifying.

Index

CHAPTER 5

CONSTITUTIONAL LAW

RIGOS BAR REVIEW SERIES

MULTISTATE BAR EXAM REVIEW (MBE)

CHAPTER 5

CONSTITUTIONAL LAW

Table of Contents

I.   INTRODUCTION

A. Bar Exam Focus Generally

The MBE will have 33 Constitutional Law questions.

1. 5 Areas: The questions are roughly broken into 5 areas: Federal Courts' Authority (5 questions); Separation of Powers (7 questions); Federalism (6 questions); First Amendment (8 questions); and other Individual Rights (7 questions).

2. Source of Questions: Questions mainly cover old Supreme Court cases and the text of the Constitution that distributes power among the branches. Memorize the powers of Congress and the Executive. Knowing the locations (which Article or Amendment) of certain powers and protections is helpful in remembering who is restricted (federal or state government) and who is protected (e.g., states, people, residents).

B. Checklist Approach

In order to spot and answer the constitutional issues present in most MBE questions, walk through the following checklist:

1. Who is Acting: If individual liberties are at stake, is there state action or an individual acting on the state's behalf? If legislative power is in question, ask "who is enacting the legislation?"

2. Identify Individual Rights or Subject Matter Involved: If legislative power is questioned, what category is the regulation (e.g., economic regulation, safety)? If individual rights are threatened, then ask are these rights "fundamental" (e.g., freedom of speech, religion, liberty), or not? If an agency is acting, are there any crossover issues?

3. Test Applicable: If legislative power has been exercised, then determine the appropriate power. If rights are infringed, then determine which test to apply (strict scrutiny for fundamental rights and suspect classes; intermediate or rational basis scrutiny for other classes). MBE Tips throughout the text help identify which possible answers are frequent red herrings.

4. Eliminate Wrong Legal Standards: If legislative power is challenged, does the government have power over the issue; or may the means (power) used reach the ends achieved? If individual rights are challenged, does the government (strict scrutiny) or the challenger (rational basis scrutiny) have the burden of proof?

5. Be Aware of Subtle Differences: Part of the reason Constitutional Law on the MBE is challenging is because the tests and levels of scrutiny often contain slight variations.

Both of these depend on what Constitutional provision is being challenged. A solid mastery of these variations will prevent confusion.

> **MBE Tip:** The MBE requires specific and detailed knowledge not only of the laws of the Constitution, but also the constructs courts used to evaluating those laws (levels of scrutiny, fundamental v. non-fundamental rights, etc.). Make sure you understand these intricacies.

II. FEDERAL COURTS' AUTHORITY – ORGANIZATION

A. Article III Courts

Article III of the Federal Constitution vests judicial power over all cases and controversies in one Supreme Court. Lower courts (e.g., federal district and appellate courts) may be established by Congress. Federal Courts may hear cases involving diversity of citizenship (e.g., parties from different states) and/or involving a federal question (arising under the Constitution or federal law).

1. Supreme Court: Article III requires one Supreme Court. Congress may establish or eliminate lower courts.

> **MBE Tip:** It is a frequently held misconception that all levels of the federal judicial branch are immune from elimination by an act of Congress. Remember, only the Supreme Court is established and protected by the Constitution.

2. Article III Judges: These judges are appointed by the President, with the advice and consent of the Senate. They have life tenure (dismissal only for cause by act of Congress) and salary protection (Congress may not lower salary).

B. Article I Courts

Congress creates other courts (e.g., Tax Courts, District of Columbia Courts, military courts), which may be vested with administrative as well as judicial functions. They are not necessarily tenured or salary protected.

III. FEDERAL COURTS' AUTHORITY – FEDERAL JUDICIAL REVIEW

A. Original Jurisdiction – Supreme Court

The Supreme Court sits as a trial court in cases involving ambassadors, public ministers, consuls, or any case where a state is a party. Congress may neither enlarge nor restrict the Supreme Court's jurisdiction but may grant concurrent jurisdiction to lower courts. Cases between two or more states must be heard in the Supreme Court; lower federal courts have concurrent jurisdiction to hear other cases where a state is a party.

> **MBE Tip:** On the MBE, there may be a case "between states" where one state is a party via *parens patriae* (which allows a state to sue on behalf of its citizens if there is a separate sovereign injury or interest). This derivative standing does *not* confer original jurisdiction on the Supreme Court.

B. Appellate Jurisdiction – Supreme Court

Congress may broadly regulate which cases may be appealed to the Supreme Court, but may not preclude review of an entire class of cases. Appeals can be made via two different procedures:

> **MBE Tip:** Compare "Congress passes a law denying direct appeal to the Supreme Court of a decision upholding a temporary injunction under the Clean Air Act," which is constitutional; with "Congress passes a law that no decision affecting school prayer may be appealed to the Supreme Court," which is probably unconstitutional.

1. Writ of Certiorari – Discretionary: US Supreme Court may hear cases from a state high court decision when the constitutionality of a treaty or any statute is questioned, including the supremacy clause; and all cases from federal courts of appeal.

2. Appeal – Mandatory: US Supreme Court must hear cases from a three-judge federal district court regarding injunctive relief. However, review need not be by the full court with all the attendant formalities.

C. Judicial Restraint – Justiciability

The Constitution confined federal courts to adjudicating only "cases or controversies." A number of discrete doctrines have evolved from this restriction.

1. Advisory Opinions: Federal Courts may neither offer advisory opinions nor settle abstract or hypothetical disputes. They can only hear actual cases and controversies.

2. Political Question: Courts cannot hear political questions. Factors in deciding if the issue is a political question are:

a. Constitution: Does the Constitution textually commit final decision of the issue to another branch of government (e.g., time to ratify a pending constitutional amendment)?

b. Standards: Is there a lack of judicially manageable standards by which to decide the case (e.g., organizing, disciplining, and arming the military)?

c. Government Unity: Is there a need for a unified pronouncement on the issue by the federal government (e.g. foreign policy matters, respect for states)?

d. Examples of Political Questions: Political questions include most congressional membership issues (e.g., age, residency, and citizenship) or Senate impeachment hearings. Whether the "guarantee clause" (also referred to as "republican form of government") allows a particular structure of government is a political question.

e. Examples of Non-Political Questions: Often tested are non-political questions such as legislative apportionment known as "gerrymandering" cases; or whether a tax is for the purpose of raising revenue. These cases sound like political questions but are not, which is why the examiners like to throw them in.

> **MBE Tip:** Just because an issue involves politics doesn't make it a "political question." Government employees and agencies are bound by laws, and courts adjudicate legal disputes. Remember, political questions are those which the Constitution would prohibit a court from deciding.

3. Ripeness:

a. Balancing Test: A case is ripe if there is a genuine, immediate threat of harm. The balancing test is whether future actions will more narrowly clarify the dispute versus the hardship on the P of waiting.

> **MBE Tip:** To analyze a ripeness question, ask: Has this case been brought too early? What will be the harm if the case if brought later?

b. Examples: Individuals have standing to invalidate a statute suppressing free speech even if it has not yet been enforced against them, because the harm prevented by free speech laws is unlawful prior restraint. However, a state law prohibiting purchase of the game of Scrabble that has not been enforced in 70 years does not threaten imminent harm.

> **MBE Tip:** A threat of future harm can create ripeness, but the harm must be actual, not speculative. For example, if a zoning law directly harms the value of A's property, A has standing. But if the law applies to another neighborhood, and A only suspects that it may be applied to her neighborhood in the future, her suit is probably premature.

c. Finality: To be ripe for review a case must be final. This means that a final order, judgment, dismissal, etc. must have been entered that ended the case at the previous level. The only exception is when a particular issue of law must be settled for the case to proceed, in which case an interlocutory appeal can be filed.

4. Mootness:

a. Test: Is the case brought too late? An actual controversy must exist at all stages, including appeal.

b. Exceptions:

(1) Capable of Repetition, But Evading Review: If the duration of the actual harm is shorter than the typical court cycle, this exception may come into play. It also applies if the D voluntarily stops injuring P, but could resume injuring P at any time.

(2) Class Actions: Even if the class representative's particular case is moot by the time of the court action, the representative may proceed as long as remaining class members' claims are still ripe.

c. Examples:

(1) Mootness: A farmer sues a manufacturer because his cows were poisoned by the manufacturer's illegal disposal of chemicals and will require expensive decontamination. However, halfway through the suit his cows are all killed in a tornado. The farmer's case is moot.

(2) Capable of Repetition: The classic case of "capable of repetition yet evading review" is an abortion law. Inevitably, the party bringing the challenge is no longer pregnant by the time the case goes to trial or appeal.

5. Standing: Is the proper party bringing the suit? P must establish a "personal stake" in the outcome of a "case or controversy." To meet the requirements of standing, P must establish:

a. Injury: An injury in fact, which is usually economic harm or violation of a personal right;

b. Causation: Injury must be fairly traceable to the D's conduct; and

c. Redressability: The relief sought must eliminate the harm alleged. Threat of future harm is required for injunctive relief.

> **MBE Tip:** Frequently tested standing issues on the MBE include: (1) Government Statutes – If the case involves a federal statute and the P is in the "zone of interests" that the statute was enacted to address, then that P will have standing; (2) Standing of Organizations – If there is an injury in fact to members for which those members could sue, and the injury has some connection to the organization, the organization will usually have standing to sue.

6. Third Party Standing: Generally, third-party standing is not allowed. The P must assert his own rights, not the rights of other parties. The major exceptions to this rule are:

a. Close Relationship between P and injured party (e.g., doctor/patient; school/student, labor union/member, association/member), insures adequate representation of real party's interests. An association has standing to assert the rights of its members if the right is related to the association.

b. Special Need to Adjudicate: Injury suffered by P adversely affects his relationship with third parties (e.g., doctor cannot perform abortion if patients' right to abortion is hindered).

c. Limited Taxpayer Standing: Generally, there is no Federal taxpayer standing. One narrow exception is that one may make an Establishment Clause challenge to an expenditure enacted under the congressional tax/spend power. A state taxpayer may have standing to challenge measurable expenditures.

> **MBE Tip:** Generally there is no "citizen standing" (i.e., no right to sue merely as a citizen claiming the government is functioning improperly). Congress may not create standing for an abstract or generalized grievance.

7. Eleventh Amendment:

a. Rule: A State cannot be sued in federal court by its own citizens, citizens of another state, or citizens of a foreign country, unless the state expressly consents. There are many exceptions, so "the state has immunity pursuant to the Eleventh Amendment" is generally a wrong answer.

b. Exceptions: There are numerous exceptions to the rule barring suits against states in federal courts.

(1) Local Governments: Immunity does not bar suits against local agencies (e.g., municipalities, school boards).

(2) Limited Actions Against State Officers:

(a) Injunctions Against Future Constitutional Violations: Even if there are prospective damages, a party can sue a state officer in a federal court to enjoin a future violation of the Federal Constitution.

(b) Personal Actions: A party can sue a state officer in his or her personal capacity in a federal court.

(3) State Consents: If a state gives express consent to be sued in federal court on a particular issue or pursuant to a particular area of law, it is permissible.

(4) Congress Abrogates: Congress can lift a state's immunity from suit in federal court in certain cases arising under the Fourteenth Amendment or under the Commerce Clause, but Congress must clearly and explicitly state that it intended to do so.

> **MBE Tip:** There are so many exceptions to Eleventh Amendment immunity from suit that "Eleventh Amendment immunity precludes a lawsuit" it is usually a wrong answer on the MBE.

8. Abstention:

a. State Law: Federal courts abstain from hearing cases involving underlying questions of state law that are unsettled.

b. Pending Claims: Additionally, federal courts will only hear cases where relief below has been exhausted and is final – pending claims will not be heard unless some sort of showing of bad faith on the part of the D governmental unit is made.

9. Adequate and Independent State Grounds: When the decision coming to the court is based on "adequate and independent state grounds" (i.e., issues of state law), the court will refrain from hearing the case as there is no federal question (required by the jurisdiction granting statute). Failure of criminal Ds to comply with state procedural rules is an adequate state ground if the rule is applied consistently.

> **MBE Tip:** Look for a state statute that violates the state and federal constitutions. A court will not review the case if state grounds are clearly independent from the federal, even if the state court erroneously decided a federal constitutional issue.

> **STOP!** Go to page 221 and work Learning Questions 1 to 9.

IV. SEPARATION OF POWERS – FEDERAL CONGRESSIONAL POWER

Federal Congressional power is limited to the power conferred upon it. Other powers are reserved to the states in the 10th Amendment; the states have a general "police power" to legislate for health, safety, and welfare. Such legislation is subject to rational basis scrutiny if challenged, for example, under the equal protection clause. There is no federal police power.

A. Congressional Enumerated Powers

The enumerated powers are: commerce, admiralty/maritime, military/war, foreign affairs, tax and spend, citizenship/immigration/naturalization, postal, trademark, bankruptcy, and laws for the District of Columbia. These powers are magnified by the necessary and proper clause, which allows Congress to use reasonable means to carry into execution any power granted to another federal branch.

> **MBE Tip:** Though the necessary and proper clause is not an independent source of power, it does confer upon Congress the power to implement those powers specifically delegated to it. Questions regarding the source of congressional power will not ask for this clause by itself.

1. Commerce Power: Congressional power in this area is broad. As there is no national police power, most legislation is enacted via interstate commerce clause power.

a. Means: Congress can regulate channels and instrumentalities of interstate commerce.

b. Ends: Naturally, the commerce power can be used to regulate any commercial activity or any activity affecting commerce.

(1) Vehicles/Traffic: Even if the traffic is not for commercial purposes (i.e., a family vacation), Congress may regulate all interstate traffic/movement/vehicles.

(2) Aggregate: Also, any activity which in the aggregate has a substantial effect on the stream of interstate commerce is subject to regulation. This includes its cumulative impact.

c. Close Scrutiny for Non-Economic Regulation: Congress may achieve purely non-economic purposes (e.g., civil rights) by regulating commerce. Non-economic regulation may be scrutinized, particularly in areas of criminal and tort law. *US v. Lopez* (federal crime to possess a firearm in school zone was not a substantial effect, unless gun traveled across state lines); *US v. Morrison* (federal tort for victims of gender-based violence was not proper use of commerce clause).

d. 10th Amendment Limits: Congress may not regulate states directly, but may regulate via generally applicable laws (e.g., Federal government may require all employers, including states, to pay minimum wage). Congress may not commandeer the legislative processes of the states by directing a particular regulatory program, nor compel the state executive branch to enforce a federal program.

> **MBE Tip:** Generally "the 10th Amendment controls" is a wrong answer if you are asked about the constitutionality of a federal statute. Do not choose an answer that strikes a federal statute because it regulates "an integral state function."

2. Tax and Spend Power:

a. Taxing: Congress may lay and collect taxes, but not "regulate" by imposing penalties. Courts will defer to Congress if the dominant intent is fiscal, meaning the tax produces revenue (or makes money).

b. Spending: Also known as "Federal Appropriations," Congress may attach conditions to its spending. For example, Congress can withhold federal money from states unless the states raise the drinking age and lower the speed limit.

> **MBE Tip:** Congress cannot regulate merely for the general welfare like states can – "general welfare" is not an independent power but a limitation on Congress's power to tax and spend.

3. Postal Power: This is exclusive to the federal government. Mail can be restricted, regulated, priced, and classified, but no individual or group may be excluded from the national postal system.

4. U.S. Citizenship: Congress may establish rules of immigration and naturalization. It may admit or deport aliens as it sees fit.

5. Bankruptcy: Congress may regulate bankruptcies, but its power is not exclusive like the postal power. States may legislate in the field of bankruptcy as long as the laws do not conflict with federal laws.

6. Property: Congress has control over the disposition of all federal property and lands.

7. Takings/Eminent Domain: Congress can appropriate private property for the public good, provided that the private owner is justly compensated for the taking (Fifth Amendment). However, takings power may be exercised only pursuant to some other enumerated Constitutional power. Actual appropriation or physical invasion is a taking.

a. Public Use: Any public use rationally related to a legitimate government purpose will suffice.

b. Regulations: If the reduction in property value is due to a regulation rather than a taking, no compensation is due. However, there is a category of regulation, a "regulatory taking" that will be compensated.

(1) Complete Devaluation: If the regulation deprives the owner of all economic value in the land, this will be a taking unless the law existed at the time the owner acquired the property.

(2) Reduction In Value: If the owner retains some value in the land, there is a balancing test:

(a) Weigh the social goals of the regulation against

(b) The reduction in value and the owner's reasonable expectations vis a vis the property.

8. Investigation: Congress has an implied right to investigate. There must be express or implied authorization by the congressional house conducting the investigation. Witnesses are afforded the protection of the Fifth Amendment (unless they have immunity) and are only required to answer relevant questions.

B. Delegation of Legislative Power

Congress may delegate legislative authority to an agency, committee, the executive, or the judiciary.

1. No Veto: If Congress disagrees with the action of a delegatee, it must pass a law to override. The enabling legislation may not reserve veto power. The Line Item Veto is unconstitutional because the presentment clause requires a bill passed by Congress to be presented to the President for signature or rejection.

2. Powers Not Unique to Congress: The powers to impeach and declare war are not delegable.

C. Fourteenth Amendment, Section 5

Congress may pass laws to enforce the civil rights guaranteed under the Fourteenth Amendment or any other amendment that gives it authority to legislate. This is the main source of any limited "police power" that the federal government may have.

V. SEPARATION OF POWERS – FEDERAL EXECUTIVE POWER

A. Execution of the Laws

The President must faithfully execute the laws. This includes control of the Justice Department that chooses which laws to prosecute, which civil litigation to enforce, etc. Administrative agencies that engage in rulemaking and adjudicative proceedings of their own are also ultimately under the control of the Executive Branch.

B. Appointment

The President, with "advice and consent of the Senate," appoints all ambassadors, Supreme Court Justices, cabinet members, and other officers of the US. Consent is not needed for appointment to certain agencies having administrative powers such as the FTC, FAA, etc. Congress cannot appoint inferior officers (e.g., special prosecutors), but may delegate power to the judiciary or executive branches. The President does not have the power to "fire" appointed officials who are approved by Congress, only those appointees who serve "at the pleasure of the President."

C. Removal of Appointed Officials

The President may remove "at will" any purely executive official unless there is a fixed term of appointment. Congress may place whatever limitations it deems proper, including prohibition on the President's ability to remove quasi-judicial and quasi-legislative officers. This preserves the checks and balances and establishes their independence from the Executive under the Separation of Powers doctrine.

D. Pardons

Art II. Sec I specifies that the President may pardon individuals for federal crimes but not state crimes. This Presidential power cannot be limited by Congress.

> **MBE Tip:** Watch for this issue – a fact pattern where a case involving a state crime goes to the Supreme Court on a Constitutional question, and then a Presidential pardon occurs. Even though the case has been brought by the prosecutor in a federal court, it is the *crime* that dictates whether a pardon is appropriate.

E. Commander-in-Chief

The President may deploy troops during the outbreak of hostilities (even though only Congress may declare war). The President may activate state militias into federal service and is given broad discretion in emergencies.

F. Foreign Policy

President has three power sources for foreign policy: his power as Commander-in-Chief, the treaty power, and congressional authorization (which is a delegation from the commerce power).

1. Treaty Power: This requires at least two-thirds consent of the Senate. If there is a conflict between a treaty and a federal law, the most recent in time controls.

2. Executive Agreement: This is an agreement by the President to conduct day-to-day business with foreign countries. It is less formal than a treaty. Executive Agreements are different from executive orders, which deal with domestic policy.

G. Executive Privilege/Immunity

Executive Privilege provides a reason to refuse disclosure of sensitive information. This right is absolute for military or diplomatic secrets, and is qualified (i.e., limited) for other information. President has immunity against civil suits for money damages resulting from actions taken while in office. S/he is not immune from suit during office for acts occurring before taking office.

> **MBE Tip:** Although Presidential immunity is broad, watch for limiting facts. Criminal actions and actions taken prior to inauguration will not be subject to immunity.

H. Impeachment and Removal of Elected Executives

The President, Vice President and all other civil officers are subject to the impeachment clause. This applies where a majority of the House determines grounds for impeachment exist ("Treason, Bribery, or other high Crimes and Misdemeanors"), and the Senate convicts by a 2/3 vote. If the President is convicted, s/he must leave office.

VI. FEDERALISM – INTERGOVERNMENTAL IMMUNITIES AND TAXATION

A. Taxation and Power

The federal government and its agents are usually immune from state taxation and other regulation.

1. State Commerce Taxation: The state may tax commerce if

a. Non-Discriminatory: The tax must be non-discriminatory between states and between residents of different states. The result may not be protectionist.

b. Nexus: There must be a substantial nexus between a state interest and that activity taxed.

c. Fairly Apportioned: The tax must also be fairly apportioned, so the tax is not disproportionate to the business conducted in the state.

d. Not In Stream of Commerce: States may tax goods at the beginning, end, and any break in transit; but not in the stream of commerce between states.

2. State Tax on Federal Government: States may levy non-discriminatory property tax on federal government buildings, income tax on federal employees, sales tax on items sold from bankruptcy estates, and tax private contractors. The legal incidence of the tax may not fall on the federal government.

3. Federal Property Clause: Article IV, Section III (memorize section number) of the Federal Constitution limits State power – Congress has the power to dispose of and make all needful rules and regulations regarding the territory of and the property of the US.

> **MBE Tip:** To spot a Federal Property clause issue, look for state law or action intruding on federal land, federal buildings or enclaves (group of buildings), military ships and airplanes, wild animals on federal land, or Indian reservations.

4. Federal Taxation of States: The States are *partially immune* from federal taxation. The federal government may only tax the states if:

a. Uniform Tax: The tax is uniform (applied equally to all the states); and

b. On a Proprietary Activity: The activity taxed is "proprietary," meaning one that could also be operated by the private sector. For example, property taxes levied on the state capitol building are not allowed but they would be on a government-operated parking lot.

B. Article IV – Privileges and Immunities Clause

This clause prohibits discrimination by a state against citizens or residents of another state regarding important state rights. An exception applies to nonresidents who are the peculiar source of evil.

1. Fundamental Rights: Only fundamental state rights are protected by the Privileges and Immunities Clause. This includes rights involving commercial activities (right to pursue a livelihood) and civil liberties protections. Note that these rights are different from "fundamental rights" in the context of Substantive Due Process.

2. Exception: If there is a substantial justification for the different treatment because the nonresidents are a particular cause or part of the harm prevented, the state regulation may be upheld. The regulation must be the least restrictive means available.

MBE Tip: Don't confuse Article IV Privileges and Immunities with two other clauses: the Dormant Commerce Clause and 14th Amendment Privileges or Immunities. Keep them straight this way: (1) if the discrimination is against a *citizen or resident* of another state based on a state right, then use Article IV – Privileges and Immunities. (2) If the discrimination is against an *entire business or industry*, then use the dormant commerce clause. (3) If the discrimination is based on a federal right, then look to the 14th Amendment Privileges or Immunities.

C. Supremacy Clause

Even the most trivial federal law, regulation, or order controls. Such federal authority trumps every state law or state constitutional provision.

1. Federal Controls: Federal law supersedes any state law in direct conflict. This is known as "succession." The states may give greater protection (especially health and safety), but may not protect on a lower level than the federal standard. If compliance with both state and federal standards is impossible, then the state law is struck down.

2. Preemption: If Congress intends to occupy the field of regulation in a particular area, the states may not regulate in that area at all.

STOP! Go to page 222 and work Learning Questions 10 to 18.

VII. FEDERALISM – DORMANT COMMERCE CLAUSE

This doctrine is also known as the negative implications of the commerce clause. Congress regulates commerce, and the Supremacy Clause is used to strike inconsistent state laws. States are free to regulate areas where there is no uniform regulation required by the federal government, unless Congress preempts by occupying the field. State regulations must be both non-discriminatory and must not unduly burden interstate commerce.

MBE Tip: Close questions involving the Dormant Commerce Clause are usually resolved in favor of the federal government preemption. When in doubt on the MBE, choose the option in which the state law is struck down.

A. State Commerce Taxation

The state may tax commerce if it is non-discriminatory (not protectionist) and there is a substantial nexus between state interest and the activity taxed (due process). The tax must be fairly apportioned between in-state and out-of-state actors. States may tax goods at the beginning, end, and any break in transit, but not in the stream of commerce.

B. Non-Discriminatory

A state may not favor local interests over foreign interests unless:

1. **Legitimate State Interest:** Any law must further a legitimate state interest. It cannot be purposeful discrimination. If the law produces a discriminatory impact, then it must be the least restrictive means available by which the state can achieve its purpose.

2. **Market Participant:** The state may be a "market participant" (i.e., state is a buyer and seller of goods and services), but may not be a market regulator for the purpose of favoring local interests. A state, acting as a market participant, may favor in-state interest when using taxpayer funds to create the market.

MBE Tip: Be careful of the "market participant" concept on the MBE. If the state actor is trying to control the market through preferential rules and regulations, then the state is not a market participant and favoritism of local interests is improper. However, if the state is actually participating in commerce, buying and selling goods, then it is a market participant and may choose to do business with an in-state interest.

C. Undue Burden

In order to determine whether the state regulation imposes an undue burden, balance the state interest (e.g., safety of citizens, unemployment) against the impact on interstate commerce and determine whether the means is "substantially related" to the state interest.

D. Consent

Congress may enact legislation approving a state's discrimination against out-of-state residents. Such a Congressional act will usually reverse negative court rulings.

E. Types of Taxes

There are a number of different kinds of taxes.

1. **Use Taxes:** These are taxes imposed on the transaction price of goods purchased outside the state but used by the buyer within the state.

2. **Sales Tax (Seller's State):** If the sale takes place physically within the state, a state sales tax is valid even if the buyer removes the item from the state. If the sale takes place outside the state, the tax is invalid.

3. **Sales Tax (Buyer's State):** A sales tax is valid if the seller has substantial contacts with the state, even if the goods are delivered from outside the state.

4. **Ad Valorem Property Tax:** This is a tax based on the value of the property. Commodities in interstate transit are exempt. Instrumentalities of transport (trucks, planes, etc.) may only be taxed if they have sufficient connections (receive benefits or protection of the state), and the tax must be apportioned in a fair relation to the physical presence of the instrumentality.

5. **Net Income, Privilege, License, Franchise, & Occupational Taxes:** These are taxes on doing business. Again, taxes must be apportioned and fairly related to the business activity conducted in that state.

> **MBE Tip:** State taxation should be evaluated first on whether it is contrary to any federal legislation, and if not, then whether it unduly burdens interstate commerce.

VIII. INDIVIDUAL RIGHTS – STATE ACTION

The Constitution prohibits discrimination only by state actors. The action must deprive a right granted by the government. (The only exception is that the 13th Amendment prohibition of slavery does not require state action.) Nevertheless, the actions of private persons may be state actions in the following circumstances:

A. Public Function

This is where a private party carries on an activity that is traditionally a state function. A company town is a state actor, but privately-owned shopping malls are not.

B. Mutual Contacts or Symbiotic Relationship

Significant state involvement, pervasive regulation, or a state subsidy may justify finding a "state action." For example, a private company working under government contract would be a state actor for the purposes of that contract. However, there is no state action by merely granting a liquor license, or for a private utility racially discriminating despite a high amount of state regulatory involvement in the process.

> **MBE Tip:** The MBE often tests the concept of significant state involvement with a private actor. For example, a state-owned building with a business tenant with racially discriminatory policies or a private school with a racist policy that uses state-supplied textbooks.

C. State Command or Encouragement

If the private actor is working at the behest, encouragement, or order of the state, then a private actor becomes a public one for the purpose of constitutional limitation. An example would be the police suggesting to a private actor that the private actor conduct a search.

D. Racially Restrictive Covenants

When a property deed or lease negotiated between private parties contains a covenant excluding a particular race, state action is present if the contract is enforced by a court (this is a narrow rule established in *Shelley v. Kramer*).

> **MBE Tip:** "Federal action" is required in some circumstances to restrict federal government discrimination, but MBE questions usually refer to states' actions on this issue.

IX. INDIVIDUAL RIGHTS – EQUAL PROTECTION

A. Equal Protection Clause

The Fourteenth Amendment Equal Protection analysis is used when similarly situated persons are treated differently by the state. The due process clause of the 5th Amendment similarly restricts the federal government.

1. Facially Discriminatory: The first step in your analysis is to determine if the law is discriminatory on its face. If the law in question is facially discriminatory, go immediately to the next two steps: (1) Identify the class being discriminated against and (2) subject the law to the appropriate level of scrutiny.

2. Facially Neutral: If the law in question is facially neutral, then the P must be able to show both a highly disproportionate impact and a discriminatory intent.

B. Classifications

If the fact pattern includes facial discrimination, or disproportionate impact and discriminatory intent, the next step is to identify the class as either "suspect," "quasi-suspect," or "non-suspect." Your final steps are to allocate the burden of proof and identify and apply the appropriate test.

1. Suspect Class: Memorize the following classifications as suspect.

a. Race: Ethnic ancestry or background.

b. Alienage (or citizenship): State discrimination is subject to strict scrutiny, except where participation in government is involved. Aliens may be excluded from being teachers, police, or jurors; but children of illegal aliens are entitled to free public education. Federal government may legislate alienage under a rational basis standard.

c. National Origin: This is the nation where the individual was born.

2. Quasi-Suspect Class: Sex/gender specific laws and "illegitimacy" laws which benefit children born to married parents and prejudice children not born to married parents are unconstitutional. The state may require a finding of paternity for a child born out of wedlock to receive an intestate share.

3. Non-Suspect Class: All other classifications, including poverty, age, mental retardation, or social and economic welfare measures are subject to rational basis scrutiny.

C. Level of Scrutiny

The applicable level of scrutiny will (usually) depend on the classification. Memorize the following tests:

1. Strict Scrutiny: If the class is a suspect class, then the law must be "necessary to promote a compelling governmental interest." The law must be narrowly tailored (not overly broad and no less intrusive means are available) to achieve the compelling government interest. The government has the burden of proof.

2. Intermediate Scrutiny: If the law affects a quasi-suspect class, it must be "substantially related to an important governmental purpose." The state probably has the burden of proof.

> **MBE Tip:** Notice the "probably" in the burden of proof for intermediate scrutiny. This rule has not been definitively established, which means that fortunately it will not likely be tested. But be aware of the ambiguity if the question involves a quasi-suspect class.

3. Rational Basis Test: If the class is one of age, wealth, handicap, etc., then the law must be "rationally related to a legitimate governmental interest." P has burden of proof.

> **MBE Tip:** Sometimes on the MBE, the options will list the definition of the test, and not the name of it. In other words, you must be able to recognize the "strict scrutiny" test if the option reads "necessary to promote a compelling governmental interest."

D. Affirmative Action

Race-based affirmative action plans (or benign discrimination) are subject to strict scrutiny, but are upheld if used to remedy past discrimination in that particular area. Numerical goals are generally constitutional, but racial quotas are generally unconstitutional.

> **MBE Tip:** Because of the recent Supreme Court decision regarding the University of Michigan, this issue is likely to appear on the MBE. Remember that using race as a factor in university admissions is acceptable, but using it as the exclusive factor or using quotas is unconstitutional.

E. Peremptory Challenges

Peremptory challenge of a potential juror by any party made on the basis of race or sex is unconstitutional in both civil and criminal cases. *Batson*.

F. Interstate Travel

Discrimination or denial of the right to travel (e.g., durational residency requirements) on a limited class of persons is subject to strict scrutiny under Equal Protection.

> **STOP!** Go to page 223 and work Learning Questions 19 to 27.

X. INDIVIDUAL RIGHTS – DUE PROCESS

Individual rights generally arise from those protections guaranteed in the Bill of Rights. Most of the Bill of Rights (first ten amendments to the United States Constitution) apply directly to the federal government and have been selectively incorporated into the Fourteenth Amendment to apply to the states. The rights that do not apply to the states include: right to bear arms, right to a grand jury in criminal cases, right to a jury trial in civil cases, and a right against excessive bail.

A. Procedural Due Process

Procedural due process asks "what process is due?" Notice and opportunity to be heard are required whenever a state deprives a person of a life, liberty, or property interest. The Fifth Amendment restricts the federal government the same way as the Fourteenth Amendment restricts the states. Also, there is a balancing test for determining whether pre-deprivation due process is warranted (*Mathews v. Eldridge*).

MBE Tip: Procedural Due Process does not distinguish between "a right or a privilege." Both are protected.

---

1. Liberty Interests: A liberty interest involves both physical and non-physical liberties. These include: right to contract, right to engage in gainful employment, natural parents care and custody of children, right to refuse unwanted medical procedures, and freedom of movement.

2. Property Interests: A property interest can be tangible or intangible, but usually involves some kind of economic stake. These include: welfare and disability benefits, public education (elementary and secondary), continued public employment absent good cause for termination (e.g., tenured teachers and civil service employees who are not "at will" employees), and a license required to do business.

3. Minimum Due Process: Minimum due process requires notice and a meaningful opportunity to be heard.

    a. Notice: Notice must be "reasonably calculated under the circumstances" to reach the affected person(s). Service of process or some kind of official letter or contact must occur to inform the person threatened with deprivation of the action.

    b. Opportunity to be Heard: The party must have a meaningful right to give input into the process leading to the tribunal's decision.

4. Timing of Due Process: All persons' lives and some liberty and property rights are deemed too important to be taken away without a pre-deprivation due process proceeding. Apply the following test to determine when the hearing should occur, i.e., pre or post deprivation.

    a. *Mathews v. Eldridge* Pre-Deprivation Balancing Test: Balance the importance of the interest and the risk that the interest will be deprived erroneously against the cost and administrative burden on the government to provide additional safeguards.

Importance of individual interest involved + Risk of erroneous deprivation	VS	Cost to government of pre-deprivation procedure + Administrative burden and Availability of additional safeguards

    b. Post-Deprivation Due Process: Sometimes the cost to the government and the administrative burden of additional safeguards outweighs the importance of the deprived interest and low risk of erroneous deprivation. In such a case, the opportunity to be heard may be granted post-deprivation.

> **MBE Tip:** MBE examiners do not usually use the terms "procedural" or "substantive" in due process questions. "Procedural" tells us what and when process is due; "Substantive" due process isn't really "process" at all. It refers to the category of rights and privileges that may not be infringed without proper procedural due process.

B. Substantive Due Process

Substantive Due Process asks "may the government infringe on this individual right?" For the purposes of the bar exam, ask yourself two questions:

1. Category of Right: Is the right one of life, liberty, or property?

2. Fundamental Right: Is the right fundamental? (see list below). If not, then like economic regulation, the challenged law is subject only to rational basis scrutiny. The test to be applied is: "Is the law rationally related to a legitimate state interest?"

> **MBE Tip:** Substantive Due Process protects fundamental rights from laws which affect all persons, compared to Equal Protection, which protects against two persons similarly situated from being treated differently.

3. Liberty Interests: This refers to the basic human freedoms to move about and generally do as one likes. Look for governmental action affecting someone's freedom (e.g., jail, civil commitment).

4. Property Interests: A property interest is a legitimate claim to something of value. The property may be tangible or intangible. Examples on the exam include the right to a public education and to own real and personal property. There is also a right to keep a government job if tenured or the organization's rule book specifies cause is necessary for dismissal.

> **MBE Tip:** Punitive damages may violate substantive due process if they are "grossly excessive" of compensatory damages.

5. Non-Fundamental Right Test: If the right being infringed upon is not fundamental, then the action is presumed valid and must merely be "rationally related to a legitimate governmental interest." The burden is on the challenger to prove the action invalid.

6. Fundamental Right Test: If the right is fundamental, then strict judicial scrutiny will be applied. The government has the burden to show:

a. Compelling Interest: The restriction must advance a compelling governmental interest, and

b. No Less Intrusive Means: There must be no less intrusive means available.

c. Examples: The following rights are fundamental and frequently tested:

(1) First Amendment Rights: This includes the freedoms of religion, speech, press, assembly, and to petition the government for redress of grievances. Due Process analysis will usually be unnecessary in this area because it applies directly to the feds, and to the states via the Fourteenth Amendment.

(2) **Voting:** Reasonable, non-discriminatory voter qualifications and legislative apportionment (population equivalency rules) are permissible. Gerrymandering schemes that deliberately distort voting districts for political purposes are unconstitutional.

(a) **Apportionment:** Geographical boundaries of voting districts may not be defined so as to prevent numerical equality among voting groups (one person, one vote). An exception is a special limited purpose district (e.g., water storage district) which can be limited to landowners and apportioned to the percentage of land owned.

(b) **Ballot Access:** States may make reasonable restrictions (e.g., pay reasonable filing fee, or gather small percentage of voter signatures). The state may require minimum age and residency requirements for candidate eligibility.

(3) **Interstate Travel:** There is a fundamental right to travel freely from state to state in the U.S. This pertains to the right to travel itself, not to the right to do certain activities once the traveler has arrived. For example, if a state prohibits someone from doing business in that state, the right to travel is not implicated, although there might be Commerce Clause or Article IV Privileges and Immunities concerns. If a state requires duration-based residency as a condition of benefits, the right to travel is implicated.

(a) **Residency Requirement:** While the state may require residency for benefits, durational residency requirements are unconstitutional prerequisites to medical aid, welfare benefits, and library services. They are allowed in determining reduced tuition for state universities, marital dissolutions, or voter registration.

(b) **Travel Restraint:** Foreign travel restrictions are reviewed under rational basis scrutiny for national security reasons. A law regulating the right to change residency should be tested under Due Process if it is a general limitation on all persons' ability to travel. See Equal Protection section above.

MBE Tip: If the question deals with the basic right to vote, apply the Fifteenth Amendment. If there is discrimination in voting (e.g., race or sex), apply the Fourteenth Amendment Equal Protection Clause. Duration-based residency requirements are a right to travel issue (Substantive Due Process), not a right to vote issue.

---

(4) **Refuse Medical Treatment:** A mentally competent adult has the right to refuse life prolonging treatment and necessary nutrition.

(5) **Privacy Rights – "CAMPER"** The below rights are fundamental:

(a) <u>**C**</u>**ontraception:** States cannot prohibit the sale of contraceptives to adults.

(b) <u>**A**</u>**bortion:** States may regulate but not prohibit or unduly burden the right to obtain an abortion. Prior to the end of the first trimester of pregnancy (pre-viability period), a state may not interfere with or regulate a physician's decision, reached in consultation with his patient, to terminate a pregnancy. State may require parental consent to abortion for a minor, but it must make a judicial review available. States cannot require spousal consent. Patients have no right to state funding for abortion.

(c) Marriage: Laws may not unduly restrict the right to marry. For example, a state cannot prohibit an ex-spouse from remarrying in order to force him to make child support payments, even if there is a compelling state interest in doing so. Requiring a marriage license is not a restriction on the right to marry per se, but is a condition of receiving certain benefits of the legal status of marriage.

(d) Procreation: Protection against excessive state interference in procreative activities. This is closely related to contraception and abortion rights protections.

(e) Education: There is a right to privately educate children (i.e., home-school). Although there is no right to free public education, a complete deprivation of education is probably unconstitutional.

(f) Relations: Right of related people (nuclear family) to live together, and rights of natural parents to have custody.

MBE Tip: Privacy now protects homosexuals from prosecution under state sodomy statutes. While the Supreme Court has *not* held that there is a fundamental right to engage in such activity, it nonetheless concluded that there is "no legitimate state interest" in criminalizing same-sex sodomy. *Lawrence v. Texas.* This landmark ruling may be tested on the MBE.

STOP! Go to page 224 and work Learning Questions 28 to 37.

XI. OTHER INDIVIDUAL RIGHTS

A. Fourteenth Amendment Privileges or Immunities

This is also known as the rights of national citizenship. This clause protects rights fundamental to national unity from intrusion by the federal government or by a state against its own citizens. Note that these rights are different from "fundamental rights" in the context of Substantive Due Process. The right to travel from state to state is a commonly tested topic right now.

MBE Tip: There are two Privileges [and/or] Immunities clauses. The Article IV Privileges *and* Immunities clause prevents states from discriminating against non-residents regarding important state rights. The Fourteenth Amendment Privileges *or* Immunities clause prevents states or the federal government from infringing on federal rights. In the case of state action against a non-citizen of that state, "Fourteenth Amendment Privileges or Immunities applies" is generally a wrong answer on the MBE. It is more likely that Article IV Privileges and Immunities will apply.

B. Contracts Clause

Article I, Section 10 prevents the states (not the federal government) from substantially impairing public or private contracts unless a significant public need exists. The state's police power (power to regulate for the health, safety, and morals of the state) generally satisfies the public need and the court applies the rational basis test.

> **MBE Tip:** Because of the broad police power, impairment of contracts is generally a wrong answer on MBE. There is a narrow exception if the State action lowers the value of bonds issued by the state, risking the rights of the bondholders.

C. Takings

States, like the federal government, may not take private property for public use without just compensation. Public uses have traditionally included utilities or railroads, Property is taken by eminent domain, inverse condemnation (reduction in value by restricting use), or a regulation which deprives the owner of all reasonable economic use of land. State may restrict use of property using police power without paying just compensation (e.g., land use, zoning).

> **MBE Tip:** However, recently the Supreme Court held that a private developer's building plan intended to stimulate the local economy qualified as a public use. *Kelo v. City of New London.* A similar fact pattern is likely to appear on the MBE.

D. Ex Post Facto Law

After an act has occurred, the government may not then retroactively make that conduct criminal, increase sentencing, or decrease the burden necessary to convict (criminal, not civil). It does not apply to mere procedural changes.

> **MBE Tip:** Striking a law on ex post facto grounds is generally a wrong answer on the MBE.

E. Bills of Attainder

The legislature cannot punish a named group or individual without a judicial trial (criminal or civil punishment). E.g., the state cannot pass a law stripping the license of a named person.

> **MBE Tip:** The suggestion that the action "is an inappropriate bill of attainder" is a wrong answer on the MBE. Remember, for a bill of attainder to exist, the law must single out a named person or group of persons. If the law happens to affect only a small group, but does not name that group, it is not a bill of attainder.

XII. FIRST AMENDMENT RIGHTS – RELIGION CLAUSES

In approaching a freedom of religion issue, first identify the issue as such and then determine whether the law in the fact pattern pertains to the "free exercise" of religion or the "establishment" of religion. If the law interferes with the free exercise of religion, distinguish between the "religious belief" itself and the "conduct" stemming from the belief. If the law endorses or supports religion, look at the purpose of the law, the effect of the law, and whether there is excessive government entanglement between church and state.

A. Free Exercise Clause

When the issue is one of free exercise of religion, identify whether the law pertains to a religious belief or the conduct stemming from the belief. For example, if there is a religion that believes that clothing is evil, distinguish between the belief that clothing is evil and walking around naked in public.

1. Beliefs: Religious beliefs are absolutely protected, no matter how far outside the norm they are. A law that outlaws a particular religious belief is per se unconstitutional. Also, clerics may not be excluded from holding public office, and requiring religious oaths for government jobs is prohibited (an oath to uphold the Constitution is okay).

2. Conduct: Conduct stemming from a particular religious belief may be regulated if there is a secular reason for doing so. Using the above example, the government may not enact a law making it illegal to believe that clothes are evil, but it may make it against the law to walk around naked in public.

3. Scrutiny: The degree of scrutiny for many free exercise claims is uncertain.

a. Lower Scrutiny: If the law is generally applicable and not intentionally discriminatory, then favor the answer that upholds the law, especially criminal laws.

b. Strict Scrutiny: If the law is subject to strict scrutiny, there must be no less restrictive means available to achieve a compelling secular end. For strict scrutiny to apply, one of the following must be proven:

(1) Governmental Intent to Interfere: This applies where there is some evidence or indication that the state was deliberately trying to interfere, prohibit, restrict, or regulate religious conduct.

> **MBE Tip:** The Supreme Court is slow to find government intention to interfere, but if it is very clear or given, then apply strict scrutiny. Look for facts that suggest an obviously devious or improper purpose.

(2) Support by Another Fundamental Right: If the regulation also interferes with another fundamental right then apply strict scrutiny. Compare these examples:

(a) Religion – Control of Child's Education: Amish parents' right to educate kids at home combines religious conduct with the right to educate one's children in a manner the parent chooses. Strict scrutiny will apply.

(b) Religion – Property Right: If a "for cause" state employee quits her job for religious reasons, i.e., a new work rule requiring her to work on her Sabbath day, unemployment benefits cannot be withheld. This is true despite the fact that the loss of work is a "voluntary quit" not normally covered by unemployment compensation laws. Strict scrutiny will apply because a property right (state employment) is combined with freedom of religion.

> **MBE Tip:** Many candidates assume that strict scrutiny will apply whenever any freedom of religion issue is in play. Study the above distinctions and remember that strict scrutiny only applies in limited circumstances. On the MBE, if one of the options in a free exercise question is strict scrutiny, be skeptical.

4. Examples: Examples of permissible regulations that affect religious conduct are:

a. Use of Controlled Substances: Laws prohibiting the use of peyote in religious ceremonies.

b. Polygamy: Prohibitions on the practice of polygamy encouraged by the person's religion have been upheld.

c. Graduation on Sabbath: Frequently tested is a school holding graduation ceremonies on a Saturday, which is the Sabbath for some of the students. The Saturday graduation policy is designed to promote the secular end of administrative and family convenience. This interest must be balanced against the degree of indirect infringement on religious belief. An acceptable alternative used by many institutions is to hold a second event on a Sunday.

B. Establishment Clause

Government may not prefer one religion over another religion or over non-religion. Statutes and regulations must be enacted for a secular purpose, and must not cause the government to become too much involved in religion.

1. The *Lemon* Test: There is a three part test for determining whether an Establishment Clause violation has occurred.

a. Primary Purpose Must be Secular: The purpose of the law must not be religious. It must be for the benefit of the public at large without religious considerations. However, if there is a mixed secular and a religious purpose, this prong is probably satisfied. Sunday business closure laws are permitted.

b. Primary Effect: The law must neither advance nor inhibit religion. While it may have incidental effects, the primary effect must neither advance nor inhibit religion.

c. No Excessive Government Entanglement: The law must not foster excessive government entanglement or require close government monitoring. Allowing a church to veto a liquor license fails this prong.

2. Examples:

a. Religious Activity: Government-sponsored religious activity or teaching religion in public schools is generally unconstitutional (e.g., requiring a moment of prayer, forbidding the teaching of evolution).

b. Financial Aid: Government aid directed solely to private religious schools is unconstitutional at K-12, but probably not at the university level. Government aid to all schools on the same terms, including religious schools, that cannot be used for religious purposes is constitutional.

3. Conflict: Use your common sense instincts to resolve apparent conflict between these two clauses. Government may hire chaplains to work in the military, prisons, or hospitals but not a public school. Religious displays taken as a whole, which celebrate the secular holiday season, are constitutional. Two reindeer, Santa, and a Jewish Symbol was upheld; 18' Menorah and 45' Xmas tree was upheld. Catholic Church putting a nativity scene in a city building was held unconstitutional.

MBE Tip: Recently the Supreme Court decided two cases on the public display of the Ten Commandments and the Establishment Clause. They did not overrule *Lemon*, but in *Van Orden v. Perry*, the Supreme Court noted that it does not consistently use the *Lemon* test and held that a 40+-year-old "passive monument" displaying the Ten Commandments, and set among over 35 other monuments on the Texas State Capitol grounds, did not violate the Establishment Clause. On the other hand, in *McCreary County v. ACLU of Kentucky*, the Supreme Court applied *Lemon* in invalidating the recent posting of the Ten Commandments in courthouses. Suggested approach: in cases matching these fact patterns, determine which case matches the facts more closely (e.g., what is the history of the display?), and apply the reasoning and results. In all other Establishment Clause cases, apply the *Lemon* test.

STOP! Go to page 226 and work Learning Questions 38 to 43.

XIII. FIRST AMENDMENT RIGHTS – FREEDOM OF SPEECH

A. Overall Approach

1. Identify the Law: First, identify the law (regulation, edict, etc.) as one that affects speech. You must know the types of speech, including conduct as speech.

MBE Tip: Even if the law is not aimed at speech or intended to affect speech, there are freedom of speech implications even if speech is only indirectly affected.

2. Content Question: Second, determine whether the law is content-neutral or content-specific. This will be fairly obvious from the facts: if a type of speech is identified, then the law is content-specific.

a. Public or Private Forum: If the law is content neutral (does not specify a type of speech that is prohibited), then identify the forum as public or private.

b. Protected or Unprotected: If the law is content specific, identify the speech as either protected or unprotected speech. If the speech is unprotected, the government may ban it outright. If the speech is protected, the law must be "necessary to promote a compelling governmental interest."

MBE Tip: Freedom of speech analysis is intricate and heavily tested. Examine the nuances of freedom of speech issues and watch your facts carefully for clues about the forum and the type of speech affected.

B. Facial Attacks

A law restricting speech may be attacked as unconstitutional on its face or as applied. A facial attack is one that says the law as written is per se unconstitutional, regardless of the context in which it is enforced. Facial attacks include Vagueness, Overbreadth, and Unfettered Discretion.

1. Vague: A law must give persons reasonable notice of what speech is prohibited. A vague law is so unclear that persons of ordinary intelligence must guess as its meaning. A law which states that one needs a permit to speak about "morally repugnant issues" is unconstitutionally vague, because the concept of moral repugnance is vastly malleable. What is morally repugnant to one person may be morally uplifting to someone else.

2. Overbroad: Overbroad laws are written in such sweeping language that they punish both protected and unprotected speech. The test is whether the regulation restricts substantially more speech than is necessary. For example, a restriction on all speech on government land.

3. Unfettered Discretion: Officials may not have arbitrary discretion to grant licenses (e.g., parade license issued only if police chief says so).

> **MBE Tip:** "Unfettered discretion" is an area where it pays to have familiarity with the interrelated topic of Administrative Law. Any administrative agency or employee must have some kind of minimal legislative guidance in decision-making regarding issues of fundamental rights. Otherwise, constitutional violations are likely.

C. Content Neutral Speech

Content neutral speech may only be regulated by the government as to the time, place, and manner of its expression. Your analysis will differ depending on whether the law affects speech in a public forum or a private forum.

1. Public Forum: A public forum is that in which public business, assembly, and association traditionally has taken place. Traditional public forums include, streets, sidewalks, parks, and town squares. In order to pass constitutional muster, content neutral-restrictions on speech in a public forum must not be facially invalid and must conform to the following:

a. Intermediate Scrutiny: The law must be narrowly tailored (least restrictive means available) to achieve a significant government interest, and

b. Time, Place, and Manner Restrictions: The law must leave open alternative channels of communication. The alternative channels must be somewhat comparable to the channels restricted. For example, restricting all public speeches is not acceptable simply because the speaker could call people on the phone.

> **MBE Tip:** Note that the interest furthered by the government need only be "significant" rather than "compelling." This is an intermediate level of scrutiny. If the fact pattern indicates any reasonable policy reason for the law, it will probably survive this level of scrutiny.

c. Examples: Nazi parades on public streets, virtually all peaceful demonstrations, literature distribution, and charitable solicitations must be allowed in a public forum.

2. Private Forum: Basically this is any space that is not a public forum, including private residences, shopping malls, newspapers, jails, military bases, and courtrooms. Time, place, and manner restrictions on speech in a private forum must not be facially invalid and must conform to the following:

a. Viewpoint Neutral: The law must be viewpoint and subject matter neutral. Both sides must be able to present their opinions and views. Certain subjects may be allowed while others are not.

b. Rationality Test: The law must bear a rational relationship to a legitimate governmental interest. Essentially, it is almost impossible to fail this test unless the law is utterly absurd and meaningless.

> **MBE Tip:** Notice that the scrutiny tests are similar to those described previously, but slightly different. For example, "strict scrutiny" as described in the section XII above is "narrowly tailored to achieve a compelling government interest," but in the context of free speech analysis, the level is closer to "intermediate" scrutiny," which is "narrowly tailored to achieve a significant government interest."

c. Limited Public Forum: This is a government-owned forum opened only to certain subjects or speakers. Possible examples include libraries, schools, and fairgrounds. They may be regulated in the same manner as private forums.

D. Content Specific Speech

Content specific speech may be categorized as protected or unprotected. Unprotected speech is afforded no protection whatsoever. For constitutional analysis purposes, unprotected speech is non-speech. If you have identified the speech prohibitive law as content specific, determine whether it is protected or unprotected speech.

1. Unprotected Speech: The following categories of speech are unprotected:

a. Defamation: The definition of defamation is a "false and defamatory statement, of or concerning the P, intentionally communicated to third persons, which results in injury to P's reputation." Oral defamation is "slander;" written defamation is "libel." The requisite proof for defamation will differ depending on whether the subject of the defamatory statement is a public official or figure, and whether the matter is of public or private concern.

> **MBE Tip:** For a more detailed discussion of defamation, refer to the Torts Chapter in Rigos Bar Review Series MBE Review Volume 1.

(1) Public Official, Candidate, or Figure – Matter of Public Concern: This includes anyone whose job, position, or reputation has a connection to public life or the public welfare. The burden of proof which is on the P, is a preponderance of the evidence. The P must show falsity of the statement and actual malice. "Actual malice" is defined as "knowledge of falsity, or reckless disregard for the truth."

> **MBE Tip:** As discussed in the Criminal Law chapter, "malice" is a pre-Model Penal Code term that is somewhat misleading. There does not need to be any evil or ill will involved for "malice" to occur, only intention or recklessness.

(2) Public Official – Matter of Private Concern: Damages are presumed, the burden is on the D to show the truth of the statement.

> **MBE Tip:** Keep in mind that what is considered a matter of "private concern" when a public figure is involved may be expanded compared to those matters considered private to a private figure. For example, the sexual conduct of a public figure might be considered a matter of public concern if such conduct is considered to compromise that figure's character or suitability for office.

(3) Private Figure – Matter of Public Concern: The burden is on the P, who must show falsity of the statement and negligence by the D.

(4) Private Figure – Not Matter of Public Concern: Damages are presumed, and burden is on the D to show the truth of the statement. Some jurisdictions shift the burden and require to P to show falsity.

b. Fighting Words: These are words that would "naturally arouse violence in the person to whom they are directed." A statute that bans "all fighting words" is unconstitutionally vague. Merely annoying or nuisance speech does not rise to the level of fighting words, the speech must incite violence.

> **MBE Tip:** The Supreme Court has rejected prohibition of "fighting words" that are based on a particular category of speech, for example, a restriction only on racially provocative speech, or speech that inflames based on religion. This is too close to political speech, which is guarded by the First Amendment.

c. Commercial Speech: Commercial speech is generally protected as long as it is truthful and not proposing illegal activity or promoting illegal products.

(1) Commercially Illegal Speech: Advertisements for illegal products or services may be outlawed.

(2) Commercially Misleading Speech: False or deceptive advertising may be prohibited if it significantly misleads the public.

(3) Unique Level of Scrutiny: Censorship of commercial speech that is not about an illegal activity and is not misleading is subjected to a slightly different standard of scrutiny than any described thus far.

(a) Substantial Government Interest: The law must serve a substantial government interest;

(b) Directly Advance: The law must directly advance that government interest;

(c) Narrowly Tailored: The law must be narrowly tailored to protect that interest.

> **MBE Tip:** Commercial speech is essentially all forms of advertising. It is subject to more restrictions than political speech.

d. Obscenity: Obscene material may be banned outright. The test consists of the following elements:

(1) Prurient Interest: The material may not appeal to the prurient interest in sex, using a community standard, and;

(2) Patently Offensive: The material may not depict sexual conduct in a patently offensive way and be an affront to current community standards; and

(3) Lacks Value: The material, taken as a whole, must not lack serious literary, artistic, political, or scientific value or it may be banned.

(4) Standards Used: Elements 1 and 2 apply the contemporary community (local) standards, and 3 is a reasonableness standard. Radio and television broadcasting do not have all of the constitutional protection as other forums, so the government may regulate non-obscene material.

> **MBE Tip:** Private possession of obscene material in the home is protected, but not theaters or other distribution.

(5) Zoning and Liquor Regulations: States may use zoning ordinances to limit location and number of adult theaters or bookstores. States may use the 21st Amendment to regulate non-obscene adult establishments that serve liquor. Seizure of allegedly obscene books to block their distribution must be preceded by a full adversary hearing and a judicial determination of obscenity (see prior restraint).

e. Child Pornography: State can criminalize possession of child pornography anywhere, even in the home. The standard for child pornography is easier for the government to satisfy than other "obscenity." It is simply the visual depiction of any sexual context involving a child, even if the depiction would not be obscene if adults were involved.

f. Incite Unlawfulness: This speech is punishable if it is intended to produce imminent unlawful conduct and is likely to produce it.

> **MBE Tip:** The issue of inciting unlawfulness is a favorite MBE testing topic. Just because speech may rouse the ire of a person or group does not make it unprotected. The speech must specifically encourage, incite, or authorize specific violent action, not simply upset people.

g. Audience Veto: The government must take reasonable steps to allow even unpopular speakers to speak. The audience may not usually threaten violence to make police suppress speech.

2. Protected Speech: Protected speech is the highest form of speech recognized under the Constitution. The following categories of speech are examples of protected speech:

a. Political Speech: This includes all political speech not intended to incite imminent lawless behavior and likely to produce such action.

b. Commercial Speech: This includes commercial speech that is not commercially illegal, false, or misleading.

c. Non-Obscene, Sexually Explicit Speech: Sexually explicit speech that is not "obscene" is protected.

> **MBE Tip:** Remember that even protected speech may be regulated as to the time, place, and manner of its expression (see above section on time, place, and manner restrictions in public and private forums). Because the speech is protected, the time, place, and manner restrictions must be "narrowly tailored to achieve a compelling governmental interest."

E. Freedom of the Press

The press and media generally stand on the same constitutional footing as individuals. Once information is in the public domain, the media can report it. This includes an unconditional privilege to report what occurs in open court or republishing documents in the court file.

1. Some Restrictions: The press is not totally unfettered. For example:

a. Judicial Closure Order: A judge may find that a narrow closure (gag) order is necessary to promote the substantial interest in protecting the identities of children who are victims of sex crimes.

b. Equal Time: Broadcast media may be required to give equal air-time to ideas (not candidates).

c. Government Privilege: Some records may be redacted (portions blocked out) or classified and not available to the press for national security reasons.

d. Grand Jury Testimony: Reporters and other members of the press may be required to testify in grand jury proceedings.

e. Regulations of Broadcast Media: The regulation of broadcast media can be more extensive than print media. The key interest protected is the interest of viewers and listeners to receive information that is of public interest or concern.

> **MBE Tip:** Contrary to popular belief, the press has no greater First Amendment protection than any other citizen. If an MBE question involves freedom of the press, remember to analyze the question from a freedom of speech standpoint as well.

STOP! Go to page 226 and work Learning Questions 44 to 50.

F. Prior Restraints on Speech

A prior restraint is a law that prohibits speech, rather than punishing inappropriate speech after the fact. A common example of a prior restraint on speech is the necessity to get a permit before speaking. Prior restraints on speech are presumptively unconstitutional; the preference is to allow the speech and then punish it if necessary. This presumption may be overcome if the following elements are present:

1. Unprotected Speech: If the speech that is being restrained is unprotected; a number of cases hold that the government has the burden of proof.

2. Important Governmental Interest: If the prior restraint serves an important governmental interest, it will be held enforceable. Examples include military circumstances or prohibiting a speech urging sedition.

3. Not Vague or Overbroad: As elsewhere, the language of the prior restraint must be narrowly drawn and definite.

> **MBE Tip:** Vagueness or overbreadth is a common incorrect answer. Restricting a large category of speech does not make a rule overbroad, nor does restricting a general type of speech make it vague. Generally, vagueness and overbreadth arguments fail.

    4. Reasonable Notice: Reasonable notice of the prior restraint must be given.

    5. Uniformly Applied: The prior restraint must be uniformly applied.

    6. Prompt Judicial Review / Burden on Censor: Upon denial of a permit to speak, prompt judicial review is mandated. The burden of proof is on the government censor to show either an important governmental interest, or that the speech is unprotected.

G. Conduct as Speech

Speech is not always mere words or writings. Other means of expression such as conduct may qualify.

    1. Political Conduct as Speech: Burning an American flag, defacing an effigy, and tearing up a draft card are examples of political conduct as speech. Political conduct as speech is afforded the same degree of protection as political speech. Thus, the government must show that its prohibition is "necessary to promote a compelling governmental interest."

    2. Commercial Conduct as Speech: Wearing a sandwich board or dressing up as a giant stuffed animal and parading around a street corner to lure customers into a used car lot is an example of commercial conduct as speech. Any law prohibiting such commercial conduct must promote a "substantial governmental interest" and the regulation must "directly advance" such interest.

H. Loyalty Oaths

Loyalty oaths as a precondition to public employment are invalid. Exceptions apply to an oath to support and uphold the Constitution and oppose the violent overthrow of the government.

> **MBE Tip:** Loyalty oaths are an example of when the government may not compel a particular kind of speech. While rare on the MBE, look for this type of issue in a free speech context. Another example is the recent case where a farmer could not be compelled to pay for commercial speech (advertising) as a condition of membership in a cooperative farming association.

I. Freedom of Association

Freedom of association is not explicitly protected by the words of the Constitution, but is an unquestionable right that is implied by other language.

    1. Group Membership: Membership in a group cannot be punished, unless the group advocates unlawfulness, the member is a knowing and active member, and the member has specific intent to further unlawful behavior. Membership lists may be compelled only if the government could make membership illegal.

2. Not Absolute: Like any constitutionally protected freedom, the freedom of association is subject to some restrictions, however those restrictions are subject to strict scrutiny. The restrictions will be upheld only if they

    a. Are justified by a **Compelling State Interest**;

    b. Are **Unrelated to the Suppression of Ideas;** and

    c. Are the **Least Restrictive Means** of protecting the interest involved.

> **STOP!** Go to page 228 and work Learning Questions 51 to 54.

XIV. FINAL CHAPTER REVIEW INSTRUCTIONS

1. Completing the Chapter: Now that you have completed your study of the chapter's substantive text and the related Learning Questions, you need to button up this chapter. This includes your preparing your Magic Memory Outlines® and working all of the subject's practice questions.

2. Preparing Your Own Magic Memory Outline®: This is essential to your MBE success. We recommend that you use our software template in this process. Do not underestimate the learning and memory effectiveness derived from condensing the text chapter into your succinct summaries using your own words. This exercise is covered in much more detail in the preface and on the CD-ROM.

    a. Summarize Knowledge: You need to prepare a summary of the chapter in your own words. This is best accomplished using the Rigos Bar Review Series Magic Memory Outlines® software. The words in the outline correspond to the bold headings in the text.

    b. Capture the Essence: Your job is to summarize the substance of the text by capturing the essence of the rule and entering your summarized wording into your own outlines. Go to the text coverage and craft your own tight, concise, but yet comprehensive statements of the law. Take pride in your skills as an author; this is the best outline you have ever created.

    c. Focus: Focus your attention and wording on the required technical elements necessary to prove the relevant legal principles and fine-line distinctions. Integrate any helpful "learning question" information into your outline.

3. Memorize Outline: After you have completed your own Magic Memory Outline® for the whole chapter, read it over carefully once or twice. They are the best book ever written. Refer back to your Outlines frequently.

4. Work Old Questions: The next step is to work all the final questions of each chapter. These vary in degree of difficulty, but the ones towards the end tend to concentrate on fact patterns and issues at the most difficult testing level. Consider using the Question Map on the CD-ROM. Click on the questions under the subject and topic you have just studied. This allows you to cross relate the subjects and related MBE testing.

a. Question Details: Again, it is usually worthwhile to review the explanatory answer rationales as they reinforce the relevant principles of law. If you are still unsure of the controlling rule, refer back to the related portion of the text. This will help you to appreciate the fine-line distinctions on which the MBE questions turn.

b. Do a Few Questions At a Time: Work the final chapter questions in sequence. Make sure you stop after no more than a few to check the answer rationales. Do this frequently so that the facts of the individual question are still in active memory.

c. Work Them All: We have tried to pick questions with an average or higher probability of reappearing on the MBE. You should at least read all the questions and ponder their answers. Every question and answer has some marginal learning and/or reinforcement value. On the MBE you will recognize many of the actual MBE questions as very similar to the ones in your Rigos Bar Review Series review books.

d. Learn From Mistakes: The objective is to learn from your mistakes by reviewing the explanatory rationales while you still remember the factual and legal details of the question. It is good to miss a few; they will help you become familiar with the MBE fine-line distinctions. The examiners' use of distracters, tricks, and red herrings is repetitive.

e. Flag Errors: Put a red star in the margin of the book along side every question you missed. Missed questions should be worked again the day right before the MBE. Do not make the same mistakes on the exam.

f. Essays: Candidates in jurisdictions that administer the Multistate Essay Exam should refer to the *Rigos Multistate Essay Exam Review — MEE* for practice essay questions.

5. Practice Exam: After you complete the last chapter, you should take the 200 item practice exam. There is detailed information covering this simulated MBE test in both the preface and at the beginning of the exam in Volume 2. This is important because you need to build your concentrated attention time span. You also need to get intellectually used to jumping between unrelated topics and subjects.

6. Make Your Own Exam: The Rigos Bar Review Series software allows you to pick 5, 10, 20 or 100 questions at random from all six MBE subjects. This is an important feature because you must become comfortable with switching intellectual gears between different subjects. If you are not an early riser and/or get going slowly when you get up, try working 10 or 20 questions using the "Make Your Own Exam" software the first thing every morning.

7. Update Your Magic Memory Outline®: The fine-line distinctions in the question and answer rationales will improve your understanding of how the MBE tests the law. Consider updating your Magic Memory Outline® while the question testing environment is still fresh in your mind.

8. Next Chapter: It is now time to go to the beginning of the next subject. Begin by previewing the chapter. Scan the typical coverage.

RIGOS BAR REVIEW SERIES

MULTISTATE BAR EXAM REVIEW (MBE)

CHAPTER 5

CONSTITUTIONAL LAW

Magic Memory Outlines®

IV. SEPARATION OF POWERS – FEDERAL CONGRESSIONAL POWER

> Numbers immediately following the topic are the chapter question numbers. The **boldface** numbers preceded by "F" are the final exam question numbers. For example, for the topic "II. A. Article III Courts" below, questions 1, 82, 97, and 130 are in the chapter questions on pages 5-221, 5-235, 5-238, and 5-247, respectively; question **F129** is in the final exam on page 7-481.

IV. SEPARATION OF POWERS – FEDERAL CONGRESSIONAL POWER

MEE Candidates: If your jurisdiction administers the Multistate Essay Exam in addition to the MBE, please refer to the *Rigos Bar Review Series Multistate Essay Exam Review — MEE* for practice essay questions and sample answers covering constitutional law.

Constitutional Law
Learning Questions

1. Which of the following is not within the jurisdiction of the Federal Courts?
(A) Suits between two states.
(B) Admiralty suits.
(C) Suits between one state and the citizen of another state.
(D) Suits against the United States.

2. Which of the following will not be reviewed by the U.S. Supreme Court?
(A) A California Supreme Court decision in a Quiet Title action.
(B) A Michigan Supreme Court decision interpreting the federal Clean Air Act.
(C) A decision of the Ninth Circuit interpreting Texas State Law.
(D) A decision of the Ninth Circuit interpreting state minimum wage regulations.

3. A P's prayer for injunctive relief to stop oil drilling on a federal wildlife reserve is heard in federal court by a three-judge panel. Relief is denied. What will be the result of an appeal to the Supreme Court?
(A) Certiorari will be granted because environmental protection of federal lands is a federal issue.
(B) Certiorari will be denied because the docket is overloaded with more pressing issues.
(C) Appeal will be granted because it is mandatory.
(D) Appeal will be denied because the Supreme Court does not have jurisdiction.

4. A labor union learns that one of its members, a law professor, was wrongfully discharged by the law school. Does the union have standing to file suit?
(A) Yes, because the close relationship between union and member creates third-party standing.
(B) Yes, because when injury occurs to a member of an organization, direct injury to the organization is imputed.
(C) No, because there is no concurrent injury to the union.
(D) No, because third-party standing is not generally allowed.

5. If a citizen files a suit in federal court claiming that his state's governor has not balanced the state budget, what result?
(A) The case will be removed to state court.
(B) The case will be dismissed because there is no "citizen standing" for generalized grievances.
(C) The case will be heard only if the citizen can demonstrate that he has suffered some loss as a result of the governor's malfeasance.
(D) The case will be dismissed because the governor has immunity.

6. The U.S. Forestry Department approves the sale of federally owned forest lands to a logging company. A taxpayer files suit in federal court to stop the sale. What is the likely outcome?
(A) The case will be dismissed because the injury is not redressable.
(B) The case will be dismissed because the P has no standing.
(C) The case will be heard because a challenge to an expenditure enacted under the tax/spend power is an exception the general preclusion of taxpayer standing.

(D) The case will be dismissed unless the P can prove damages.

7. A state enacts a law prohibiting all abortions except to save the life of the mother. A pregnant woman files suit to invalidate the law. By the time the case reaches the Supreme Court, she has traveled to another state to have the abortion. The respondent argues that the case is moot. Will the case be allowed to continue?

(A) Yes, because there may still monetary damages at issue.
(B) No, because the respondent is correct, the case is moot.
(C) No, because the Supreme Court does not engage in a mootness inquiry.
(D) Yes, because the injury in question was one capable of repetition, yet evading review.

8. Which of the following is not an example of a political question?

(A) Whether the U.S. Army should be restructured to eliminate racial disparities.
(B) Whether the President should be impeached.
(C) Whether a legislative district is properly apportioned.
(D) Whether the Guarantee Clause prohibits the use of the electoral college system.

9. "Abstention" refers to

(A) When federal courts delay hearing a case in which an unsettled issue of state law exists.
(B) When federal courts refrain from hearing a case which is not ripe.
(C) When state courts refrain from hearing an issue of federal law.
(D) When federal courts refrain from deciding an issue upon motion for summary judgment.

10. If Congress were to outlaw the growing of wheat over a certain quantity by individual farmers but the wheat is for the farmer's personal consumption only, what is the likely source for that power?

(A) Commerce Clause.
(B) Necessary and Proper Clause.
(C) Exclusive Legislation Clause.
(D) General Welfare Clause.

11. Which of the following is a proper exercise of Congress' power to regulate interstate commerce?

(A) Providing a Federal civil cause of action for victims of gender based violence.
(B) Criminalizing the possession of firearms on state public school property.
(C) Outlawing racial discrimination by hotels not located near any interstate highway.
(D) Prohibiting a person from driving over 55 miles per hour.

12. Which is a proper delegation of Congress' legislative authority?

(A) Granting authority to the Department of Transportation to promulgate regulations, but reserving a legislative "veto" on the regulations.
(B) Granting authority to the President to designate certain acts as criminal and to promulgate an appropriate penalty.
(C) Granting authority to the Supreme Court to promulgate rules of evidence for use by the Federal Judiciary.
(D) Granting authority to the President to reject only certain portions of a bill.

13. Which of the following is not a proper exercise of state taxing authority?

(A) State property tax on federal property.
(B) State income tax on federal employees.
(C) State tax on goods manufactured in a neighboring state.
(D) State tax on all goods warehoused in the state.

14. Congress passes a law establishing that arsenic in water must be less than 50 parts per billion. Which of the following state laws would not be effective?

(A) A law establishing maximum arsenic in water at 100 parts per billion.

(B) A law establishing maximum arsenic in water at 10 parts per billion.

(C) Any law regulating arsenic in the water.

(D) A law establishing maximum lead in water at 100 parts per billion.

15. Congress does not have the power to do which one of the following?

(A) Require employers to limit the workweek to 40 hours.

(B) Prohibit gender discrimination in places of public accommodation.

(C) Change the command structure of the Coast Guard.

(D) Compel the executive branch of a state to enforce a federal jobs program.

16. Which of the following categories is not an enumerated power of Congress subject to rational basis scrutiny?

(A) Admiralty and Maritime.

(B) Trademarks.

(C) Laws of the District if Columbia.

(D) Energy.

17. Congress appropriates $4 billion for domestic abuse prevention programs, to be distributed only to states that enact tougher penalties for perpetrators of domestic violence. Is Congress' action valid?

(A) Yes, because it is an appropriate exercise of its power under the Commerce Clause.

(B) Yes, because Congress may attach conditions to its spending.

(C) No, such action was invalidated by the Supreme Court in *U.S. v. Morrisson* as an improper use of the Commerce Clause.

(D) No, the 10th Amendment prohibits Congress from compelling states to enforce a federal program.

18. For the President to enter into a treaty with a foreign country, he must obtain

(A) The advice and consent of Congress.

(B) 2/3rds consent of the Senate.

(C) 3/4ths consent of the Senate.

(D) An executive agreement.

19. Alabama enacts a law allowing the licensed hunting of sporting game in Greenboughs National Park, which is entirely within its borders. Is the law valid?

(A) No, because the law infringes on Congress' power under the Property Clause.

(B) No, because the law exceeds state power under the Dormant Commerce Clause.

(C) Yes, because minor state intrusion on federal land is permissible if its boundaries are entirely within that state.

(D) Yes, because wildlife is not a fixture and therefore the law does not affect the land directly.

20. Congress has occupied the field of nuclear safety. It passes a law setting the maximum permissible radiation output of a nuclear generator as 100 millirads per day. Pennsylvania enacts a law establishing a maximum output of 50 millirads per day. What result?

(A) The law is valid because it exceeds the federal standard.

(B) The law is valid because states have general police powers.

(C) The law is invalid.

(D) The law is valid because of the vital state interests involved.

21. Which of the following is not "State action" for the purpose of a constitutional violation?

(A) A court ruling upholding a privately negotiated restrictive covenant in a deed that prohibits selling the property to certain racial groups.

(B) A private tenant of a State owned office building that refuses to hire members of a certain racial group.

(C) A private citizen conducts a search of a tenant's room at the behest of police.

(D) A state licensed liquor store that refuses to hire members of a certain racial group.

22. The State of California bans the slaughter of beef within its borders. As a result, the price of kosher beef increases by a factor of three, but the price of non-kosher beef stays the same. Which argument is most likely to prevail within the context of an equal protection violation claim?

(A) The law is facially discriminatory.

(B) The law was intended to discriminate against the Jewish community.

(C) The law will be subject to rational basis scrutiny.

(D) The State has a compelling governmental interest in preventing the consumption of beef.

23. Which of the following is a "non-suspect" class requiring rational basis scrutiny?

(A) Race.

(B) Citizenship.

(C) Disability.

(D) National Origin.

24. Which of the following is a permissible state action?

(A) A law that gives illegitimate children the same inheritance rights as legitimate children.

(B) A law that excludes a foreign national from attendance at state universities.

(C) A law that limits the rights of Pakistanis to own real property.

(D) A law that limits the voting rights of members of a certain racial group.

25. The State of Columbus passes a law giving government job preference to members of a certain racial group. If the state is sued for racial discrimination, what must the state prove?

(A) The law is a quota to bring employment levels of the racial group to reflect their proportion within the population.

(B) The law is narrowly tailored to remedy past discrimination.

(C) The group continues to experience daily discrimination.

(D) The group is a racial minority recognized by the EEOC.

26. Anystate, USA passes a law requiring that anyone who moves into the state be financially self-sufficient. What is the proper analysis that will be used by the court?

(A) Any restrictions on travel are unconstitutional.

(B) The law must be rationally related to a legitimate governmental interest.

(C) The law must be narrowly tailored to achieve a compelling governmental interest.

(D) The law must be substantially related to an important governmental purpose.

27. A peremptory challenge of a potential juror on the basis of gender in a criminal case

(A) Is unconstitutional and prohibited.

(B) Must be proven by the party making the challenge to have a rational basis.

(C) Must be proven by the party making the challenge to serve a compelling interest.

(D) May be made only by the D.

28. In which of the following situations is a fundamental right violated?

(A) The State of Washington prohibits entering the state by swimming across the Columbia River.

(B) A State legislature redraws a Congressional District boundary to reflect the growth in population.

(C) A State legislature requires a certain amount of time residing in the state before a student may get reduced State University tuition.

(D) A State legislature passes a law that states a person may not have a child without attending a state approved child-care class.

29. Which of the following does not involve a fundamental right?

    (A) The purchase of contraceptives by minors.

    (B) Educating one's child at home or at a private school.

    (C) Getting married without a license.

    (D) A father's right to live with his child.

30. If a right is not fundamental, a law infringing upon it is

    (A) Presumed invalid and must be rationally related to a legitimate governmental interest.

    (B) Presumed valid and must forward a compelling governmental interest.

    (C) Presumed valid and must be rationally related to a legitimate governmental interest.

    (D) Presumed valid but there must be no less intrusive means available to achieve the state's goal.

31. Procedural due process is not required when the state deprives a person of

    (A) Welfare benefits.

    (B) Public education.

    (C) Employment.

    (D) The right to engage in gainful employment.

32. Which of these is not a factor in the *Mathews v. Eldredge* balancing test?

    (A) Risk of erroneous deprivation.

    (B) Cost to government.

    (C) Timing of due process.

    (D) Administrative burden.

33. A municipal ordinance provides that no one may vote without showing proof of age. A voter challenges the ordinance. The ordinance will likely be

    (A) Subjected to strict scrutiny and uphheld.

    (B) Subjected to rational basis scrutiny and upheld.

    (C) Subjected to strict scrutiny and overturned.

    (D) Subjected to rational basis scrutiny and overturned.

34. Kansas may not prohibit newly-hired college professors from leaving the state for 180 days because

    (A) It is an unconstitutional restriction on the right to education.

    (B) It is an unconstitutional restriction on the right to interstate travel.

    (C) Such a rule has no rational relationship to a legitimate government interest.

    (D) It is an equal protection violation.

35. Which of the following describes a fundamental right?

    (A) The right of a terminally ill person to receive a painless lethal dose of morphine.

    (B) The right of the wife of a man in an unrecoverable coma to order the withdrawal of artificial life support.

    (C) The right of a mentally competent adult to refuse i.v. nutrition and breathing assistance, when such methods may save his life.

    (D) The right of parents of a mentally competent adult to terminate i.v. nutrition and breathing assistance, when such methods may save his life.

36. All but which of the following are acceptable restrictions on the fundamental right to marry?

    (A) Requiring proof of marriage before allowing a spouse to be covered by the medical plan of a state employee.

    (B) Requiring parties who are divorced to wait 6 months before remarrying.

    (C) Requiring issue of a license if parties intend the marriage to be legally recognized.

    (D) Defining marriage as between one man and one woman.

37. A state agency is accused of racial discrimination regarding the right to vote. A challenge to the action would properly be brought under the
- (A) 14th Amendment.
- (B) 15th Amendment.
- (C) 10th Amendment.
- (D) 16th Amendment.

38. Which of the following is most likely the basis for a successful 14th Amendment Privileges or Immunities Clause challenge?
- (A) A citizen of State A moves to State B but is refused employment at the office of the Secretary of State because of a past felony conviction for fraud.
- (B) A business entity incorporated in State A is refused a license to operate in State B because State B wants an in-state corporation to retain its monopoly.
- (C) A citizen of State A is refused entry to the federal courthouse.
- (D) A citizen of Country Y is refused employment in State A because he is not an in-state resident.

39. "Inverse condemnation" is a principle related to the law of
- (A) Takings.
- (B) Bills of attainder.
- (C) Free exercise.
- (D) 14th Amendment privileges or immunities.

40. The first step in analyzing a freedom of religion issue is identifying
- (A) Whether there is excessive government entanglement.
- (B) Whether the law pertains to a religious belief or conduct stemming from the belief.
- (C) Whether the law pertains to "free exercise" or "establishment."
- (D) The level of scrutiny to be applied.

41. State Q enacts a law restricting the use of 27 kinds of food additives considered dangerous. One such additive is used in preserving kosher meats. Citizen R challenges the law as a burden on his free religious exercise. The law will likely be upheld if
- (A) There are no less restrictive means available to achieve the desired end.
- (B) It is generally applicable and not intentional discrimination.
- (C) It is selectively enforced.
- (D) There is no evidence that one religion is preferred over another.

42. Which of the following is not an example of excessive government entanglement in religion?
- (A) Allowing a church to veto the issuance of a liquor license.
- (B) Allowing a church to install a nativity scene in a city building.
- (C) Government aid given solely to religious private elementary schools.
- (D) A law requiring businesses to be closed on Sundays.

43. Pursuant to its Commerce Clause power, Congress passes a law requiring that all federal public contracts be verified by a separate oversight agency. As a result, executory public contracts are suspended. The law is likely
- (A) Valid, because only private, not public, contracts are subject to the Contracts Clause.
- (B) Valid, because the federal government is not subject to the Contracts Clause.
- (C) Invalid, because there is substantial interference with public contracts without a significant public need.
- (D) Invalid, because the federal government has no broad police power.

44. A law in State M prohibits "speaking about lewd topics within 100 feet of a schoolyard." If challenged, this law will likely be
- (A) Upheld, because it leaves open alternative channels of communication.

(B) Upheld, because it is narrowly tailored to achieve a significant government interest.

(C) Invalidated, because the law is unconstitutionally vague.

(D) Invalidated, because the law is unconstitutionally overbroad.

45. The Chaplin County Council established a local authority to organize, oversee and approve plans for public assemblies and holiday parades. The enabling act authorized a county overseer to "issue appropriate permits to acceptable public and private groups who wish to march and speak." A local group advocating the legalization of marijuana use applies for a permit to march and speak in an upcoming Veteran's Day parade. The permit is denied. Upon challenge, what result?

(A) The decision will be affirmed, because the group's position is inappropriate and the commissioner acted within his discretion.

(B) The decision will be affirmed, because the group advocates unlawful behavior.

(C) The decision will be reversed, because the enabling act is overbroad.

(D) The decision will be reversed and the statute invalidated, because it allows the commissioner unfettered discretion.

46. Content neutral restrictions on speech in a public forum must not be facially invalid and must

I. Be narrowly tailored to achieve a significant government interest.
II. Bear a rational relationship to a legitimate government interest.
III. Be viewpoint and subject matter neutral.
IV. Leave open alternative channels of communication.

(A) I and II.
(B) I, II, and III.
(C) I and IV only.

(D) II and IV only.

47. Defamatory speech is not protected by the First Amendment. What must a public official show to prevail in a defamation case?

(A) Falsity of the statement and negligence by the D.

(B) Falsity of the statement and knowledge of falsity or reckless disregard for the truth by the D.

(C) Damages are presumed and the burden is on the D to show the truth of the statement.

(D) Reckless disregard of the truth by the D.

48. Which of the following is an example of unprotected speech?

(A) A lecture advocating the legalization of prostitution.

(B) A commercial advertisement for a car that suggests its owner will be considered more sexually attractive.

(C) A man shouting "The government wants to jail you, riot, riot!" into a megaphone at a public rally about racial discrimination.

(D) A magazine depicting graphic sexual acts, found in the owner's home.

49. State police set up and execute a successful "sting" operation to seize shipments of allegedly obscene material to block their distribution. Before the material is destroyed, the distributors challenge the police action and demand the return of the material. Was the police action proper?

(A) No, because the seizure was not preceded by a full adversary hearing.

(B) Yes, because obscene material is unprotected speech.

(C) Yes, because police are capable of ascertaining the community standards to judge obscenity.

(D) No, because non-broadcast printed material is protected speech, even if it is considered obscene.

50. A law requiring newspapers to give equal time to all political candidates is likely

(A) Valid, if the information is not in the public domain.

(B) Valid, because "equal time" requirements do not infringe on the freedom of the press to report the news.

(C) Invalid, because only broadcast entities may be subject to equal time requirements.

(D) Invalid, because political speech is protected.

51. A prior restraint on speech is

(A) Presumed unconstitutional, but the presumption can be overcome.

(B) Presumed constitutional unless demonstrated to burden protected speech.

(C) *Per se* unconstitutional.

(D) *Per se* constitutional.

52. Under the 1st Amendment, burning a voter registration card is

(A) Unprotected, because it is not speech.

(B) Protected.

(C) Unprotected, because it is intentional destruction of an important government document.

(D) Unprotected, if the government can demonstrate a rational basis for prohibiting their destruction.

53. A loyalty oath as a precondition to public employment is

(A) Always unconstitutional.

(B) Constitutional if it is an oath to oppose the violent overthrow of the government.

(C) Constitutional only if it does not involve religious language.

(D) Always constitutional.

54. Membership in a group can be punished if

I. The group advocates unlawfulness.

II. The member is a knowing and active member.

III. The member has specific intent to further unlawful behavior.

IV. The member has specific intent to disseminate knowledge of the group's activities to others.

(A) I and II.

(B) I, III and IV.

(C) I, II, and III.

(D) I and III.

Constitutional Law
Practice Questions

55. HardTime Inc., a private corporation, owns and operates a prison in the State of South Carobama. The State needed to outsource some of the overflow of the prison population, due to the increase in penalties for drug crimes. HardTime gets $85 per inmate, per day. Terry McNichols is being kept in solitary confinement costing HardTime $175 per day because the warden is afraid that Terry will be confused with another criminal, and the other inmates will harm Terry. Terry wants to sue to make HardTime move him back into the general population of the prison. The HardTime rules allow the warden complete discretion, but Terry wants to claim that his liberty is infringed. In a suit against South Carobama and HardTime, will HardTime be considered a State Actor?

(A) No, because it is private corporation.

(B) No, because Carobama does not excessively regulate HardTime.

(C) Yes, because running prisons is a public function.

(D) Yes, because the contract encourages cost cutting.

56. The Evergreen State University charges resident students $1,200 per year, and nonresident students $4,800 per year in tuition. The University considers a student a nonresident if the student's primary residence was outside the state at any time during the previous school year. Imma Grant transferred from Sunshine State University to Evergreen as a junior. She paid nonresident tuition that year. She filed a declaratory judgment action against the Evergreen Registrar to have her considered a resident and asked for no money damages. Fourteen groups filed amicus briefs in support of changing Evergreen's protectionist regulation. Now that she is a senior, and spent all of her last year within Evergreen, she is considered a resident student. The federal court should

(A) Dismiss the suit as moot.
(B) Dismiss the suit, because she lacked standing to sue initially.
(C) Hear the case if it appears that Ms. Grant is diligently prosecuting.
(D) Hear the case due to the amicus interests.

57. T.J. Simpson, an African American man, was a D in a civil suit represented by Johnny Tortrun, an African American attorney. Johnny used three peremptory challenges to strike individuals from the jury pool. Johnny struck Barney, an African American man, because of his race. Barney was the only African American on the panel. Johnny struck Albert because he was Catholic. The third strike was against Mark, because Mark was a white racist. Which of these is/are likely unconstitutional peremptory strike(s)?

I. None, because a defense attorney is not a state actor.
II. Barney
III. Albert.
IV. Mark.

(A) II only.
(B) I only.
(C) II, and IV.
(D) II, III, and IV.

58. Evergreen State requires all persons between the ages of 6 and 16 who reside in the state to attend a state accredited elementary or secondary school. The state school system is funded by local property taxes. The accreditation committee is funded by the state's education allotment of the general fund. St. Pious is a private school run by the Catholic Church and accredited by the State. Catherine, a 15 year old, was suspended from St Pious for

refusing to say the Lord's Prayer during the morning announcements and prayer time. Catherine's parents sue St. Pious on her behalf, claiming her First Amendment rights were violated. In the suit, St. Pious will

(A) Win, because the parents have no standing.
(B) Win, because Catherine may not be forced to speak.
(C) Win, because there is no state action.
(D) Win, because the school has a compelling interest in her praying.

59. Salt Lake State has had a criminal statute making it illegal to knowingly interfere with the operation of government with malicious intent. Corry Upt is a computer hacker, who shut down the government's website by infecting it with a virus. The virus entered electronic mail of users and mailed itself to every address listed in each user's address book every two hours. The website was crippled for the last week of January. The State passed a law in February clarifying that knowingly infecting the State's Internet server with a computer virus met the definition of interference. During the criminal trial against Corry, the State introduced an instruction based on the statutory computer virus clarification. The defense objects to the instruction. How should the state court judge rule?

(A) Reject the instruction, based on ex post facto.
(B) Reject the instruction as a violation of due process.
(C) Admit the instruction, because the law was passed before the prosecution was initiated.
(D) Admit the instruction, as a bill of attainder.

60. The National Collegiate Athletic Association (NCAA) is a voluntary association of public and private universities. NCAA adopted rules governing member institutions' recruiting, admissions, academic eligibility, and financial aid standards for student athletes.

Member schools agree contractually to the discipline of NCAA, but may withdraw from the association at will. The NCAA Policing Committee imposed sanctions on Coach N. Tice, the head football coach for Farm State University. NCAA scheduled a hearing for Farm State, at which it would impose further sanctions if the university did not fire Coach Tice. Farm State fired Coach Tice. Tice sued NCAA claiming that the backroom committee violated his rights. Which constitutional right will a court analyze?

(A) None, because NCAA is not a state actor.
(B) Due Process, because Tice had no notice.
(C) Due Process, because Tice had no opportunity to be heard.
(D) None, because Tice contracted away his constitutional rights.

61. Congress passed the Davis Energy Act, which requires commercial energy users to reduce their consumption by a specified percentage, and authorizes the President to set that percentage by executive order. The Act delineates standards for determining the percentage. The provision that allows the President to set the exact amount is probably

(A) Constitutional, because it creates a limited administrative power to implement the statute.
(B) Unconstitutional, because it delegates legislative power.
(C) Constitutional, because the President has inherent power to execute laws.
(D) Unconstitutional, because it violates Due Process.

62. Bob, a Pakistani American, was fired from New Yorsey State University the day after unknown terrorists ran a hotdog cart into the campus Starcups Coffee Shop. Bob claimed the University fired him only because of his heritage. He filed a suit in federal court against his supervisor, Dean Neechurk, pleading for reinstatement and back pay. Bob used a federal statute that created a private civil action for the

violation of civil rights if the D acted "under color of state law" to deny him "equal protection under the law." The dean filed for summary judgment claiming the statute was invalid. The court will take what action on the motion?

(A) Grant it, because the 11th Amendment bars the suit.
(B) Grant it, because there is no substantial effect on commerce.
(C) Deny it, if due process was denied.
(D) Deny it, because Congress validly passed the statute.

63. North Wisconsin State legislature banned the importation of milk from other states to avoid harm to its citizens by adulterated milk. The U.S. Supreme Court struck down the North Wisconsin law as unconstitutional. The President, however, is a connoisseur of cheese and especially likes North Wisconsin's domestic sharp cheddar. While speaking to the North Wisconsin Governor about the problem, he learns that milk is the major ingredient in cheese. The President twists arms on the hill and gets Congress to pass a law forbidding the importation of milk into North Wisconsin. Which of the following best describes the constitutionality of the federal statute?

(A) Constitutional, because federal government may legislate for the general welfare.
(B) Unconstitutional, because the Dormant Commerce Clause forbids it.
(C) Constitutional under the Commerce Clause.
(D) Unconstitutional, because the Supreme Court is the final authority for interpreting the Constitution.

64. Nebraskahoma passed a statute providing for the incarceration of any person with AIDS, regardless of whether that person has engaged in criminal activity, in a special state facility. The incarceration occurs after a full, adversarial trial results in a judicial determination that the person suffers from AIDS. The statute also provides for an attorney for indigent persons, and an appeal as a matter of right. The statute is

(A) Unconstitutional, denial of due process.
(B) Unconstitutional, denial of right to a trial by jury.
(C) Constitutional, as a health and safety measure.
(D) Unconstitutional, denial of equal protection.

65. Stan is a certified public accountant in the State of Kansitaw. Stan used to specialize in debt adjusting until the State passed a law restricting the business to attorneys. Stan sues the Kansitaw Attorney General in state court to enjoin him from enforcing the law claiming it violates his federal constitutional rights of due process and equal protection. Which answer best describes the burden in the case?

(A) Stan must show that the law serves no important government interest.
(B) Kansitaw must show that the law serves an important government interest.
(C) Kansitaw must show a rational relationship to the interest served by the law.
(D) Stan must show that the law serves no legitimate state interest.

66. Alablaintiff State Court entered a judgment for P, Mr. V. Gan, and against D, McDan's, for not disclosing to its customers that its fries contained "animal flavoring." The jury awarded Mr. Gan $4,000 in damages (he ate a lot of fries), and $4 million in punitive damages. Assuming no remitittur is granted, what is McDan's recourse?

(A) Pay $4,004,000, because the judgment is rational economic regulation.
(B) Appeal claiming punitives are so grossly excessive as to violate due process.
(C) No recovery. Jury awards are not reviewed under due process.
(D) Appeal, claiming a taking in violation of the constitution.

67. The State of Tropicanna is composed of dozens of islands. State law criminalizes participating in an abortion performed by anyone other than a licensed physician, but the New East Coast Journal of Medicine and the Association of American Medical People agree that a physician's assistant is qualified to perform the operation. Three fourths of the Tropicana population live on the main island. Candice is four weeks pregnant and wants an abortion. She is on state assistance. She lives on an island were there are no licensed physicians, only physician's assistants and midwives. It would cost a minimum of $125 to take a boat or plane round trip to the main island where there are many licensed physicians. She and her physician's assistant attack the constitutionality of the criminal statute, and in the alternative, they seek state assistance in getting Candice to the main island. The most likely outcome is that the

(A) Criminal statute is a facially unconstitutional violation of due process rights.
(B) Statute violates the contracts clause with respect to the physician's assistant.
(C) Not getting Candice to the main island violates due process and equal protection.
(D) Criminal statute is facially constitutional exercise of police power.

68. Trail State passes a law requiring state civil service employees to retire no later than their 65th birthdays. Congress passes a law in reaction forbidding employers from requiring anyone to retire prior to age 70, unless there is a compelling interest in a younger person performing the job. Cletus has worked for Trail for the past 50 years as a janitor in the state capital building. He is in great shape, and the staff likes his quick wit. Because of the state mandatory step raises, he earns almost as much as the Beaver University Football Coach. Trail will save $40,000 per year by hiring a new employee. Cletus, on his 65th birthday, files in federal court using the federal statute as

protection from mandatory retirement. The Court will likely rule that

(A) Cletus may work, because the Trail law violates equal protection.

(B) Cletus must retire, because the state has a legitimate interest in saving money.

(C) Cletus may work, because the federal law relates to the integral governmental function of operating a public building.

(D) Cletus may work, because the federal law voids the inconsistent state law.

69. The Yellystone National Park is exclusively federal jurisdiction. Federal law prohibits hunting wild animals in the park. Wherehouser hires Rutger and pays for his state-issued hunting license to shoot any spotted owls who try to leave Jellystone and inhabit Wherehouser's adjacent wooded property. Rutger is prosecuted for violating the federal law. What is the strongest argument for upholding the statute?

(A) The law is necessary and proper for protecting federal property.

(B) Hunting is a privilege, not a right, so due process is not affected.

(C) Federal police power supersedes inconsistent state laws.

(D) Animals crossing boundaries are in interstate commerce.

70. The State of Wazacomy passed a law requiring employers to hire only state "residents" to work on the State's new oil pipeline project. A "resident" under this statute is a person who has lived in the state for 20 of the last 24 months. Wazacomy will impose civil penalties against general contractors who hire nonresidents. Cal, who is a nonresident, challenges the statutes constitutionality. Cal's strongest argument is that the statute violates the

(A) Privileges and Immunities Clause of Article IV.

(B) Dormant Commerce Clause.

(C) Equal protection clause.

(D) Ex post facto clause.

71. Charles Dahmer is on trial in Gallows State Court for murder in the first degree. During jury selection, the prosecuting attorney uses peremptory challenges on three Catholics from the jury pool. The Defense objects, but the judge grants the challenges. Dahmer's lawyer appeals claiming the peremptory challenges violate a Gallows State Court Rule and the Federal Constitution. The Gallows Supreme Court overturns the conviction. In the opinion, the State Court says that peremptory challenges violate the court rule and the Federal Constitution. The State appeals to the U.S. Supreme Court claiming State Court error. The U.S. Supreme Court will likely

(A) Accept review, because the Gallows Court misinterpreted the Constitution.

(B) Accept review to clarify that the U.S. Constitution does not protect religion in this manner.

(C) Deny review for lack of standing.

(D) Deny review, because the Gallows Court Rule is an adequate state ground.

72. An earthquake devastated northern Mexico and disrupted water, power, and civil services, including medical and police functions. The President of Mexico pleaded for U.S. involvement. Because Congress was not is session over a holiday break, the President acted on his own. The President sent the 82nd Airborne from North Carolina and other units from Texas in to assist in humanitarian capacity. The Army Corps of Engineers dedicated 1,000 soldiers and $1 million in equipment to clear rubble and debris. Which alternative is true of the President's use of soldiers in Mexico?

(A) Unconstitutional, because the President cannot act without Congress delegating authority.

(B) Valid exercise of the President's power as Commander-in-Chief.

(C) Valid under the plenary powers of the President to use the Army for humanitarian purposes.

(D) Unconstitutional aid to foreign nation, because Congress was not involved.

73. Senator Watt, distinguished gentleman from New Dakota, determined that there should be a uniform law for fluorescent lights used in commercial buildings, and sponsored the Federal Lit Building Act, which was referred to in debate as the Dim Watt Act. Which constitutional provision could most easily be considered as the basis of the Act?

(A) Commerce Clause.
(B) Necessary and Proper Clause.
(C) 3rd Amendment.
(D) Federal Police Power.

74. The Republic of Lone Star, in the United States, passed a law authorizing the use of force and trespass to apprehend terrorists, and posted a $1,000 reward for each terrorist captured. John Ruger, a private citizen, breaks into Lin Bowden's house. John finds evidence of bomb manufacturing, and captures Lin in the home. Will John's actions be considered state action?

(A) No, because John is a private citizen.
(B) Yes, because there is state endorsement.
(C) No, because the 11th Amendment bars the suit.
(D) Yes, if John cashes the check.

75. Young was convicted of his third rape offense in 1989 and sentenced to 20 years in prison by Kansington State Court. The Kansington Legislature passed the Sexual Predator Act of 1990, which allowed for the "civil commitment" of persons found to be sexually violent predators. When he was being released early in 1995 for good behavior, Young was put on trial for being a sexually violent predator. He was given assigned counsel, and after a trial, the jury found him a sexually violent predator. He was civilly committed to the Kansington Rehabilitation Center. He is confined to his cell, or cell unit most of the time. He participates in mandatory group counseling

and individual counseling. In 2001, he filed a habeas corpus suit in federal court after being told that he was no closer to being released. Many experts agree that sexually violent predators have no hope of recovery by the time they reach this level. The federal court will likely have him

(A) Remain, because the state has a compelling interest in treating him and protecting the community.
(B) Released, because it violates the due process clause.
(C) Released, because it violates the ex post facto clause.
(D) Released, because it violates double jeopardy.

76. Kennedy Middle School, a public school, allows groups to rent the gym and cafeteria after school hours and on weekends. Fearing a lawsuit, the school restricts the use of the school to groups with a non-religious purpose. The Great News Club applied for and was denied use of the cafeteria on Sundays. They offered to pay the usual fee, require parental consent from minors, and clean up juice and cookie spills. The school denied the request, because the Great News Club wanted to conduct religious activity on school grounds. Great News filed suit in federal court. The likely outcome based on federal constitutional issues would be that Great News

(A) Prevails, if the school is a limited public forum.
(B) Prevails, because the school violated equal protection.
(C) Loses, because the school has a legitimate fear of lawsuits.
(D) Loses, because the school cannot get entangled with the club.

77. City of Brotherly Love passed a tough gun ordinance. The ordinance prohibits the private ownership of a long list of guns that are "unreasonably dangerous." Under the ordinance, the owner may reside in the city and store the guns outside the city limits. The ordinance becomes effective in 90 days. Fourteen of the seventeen guns owned by Harry Dirt were made illegal under this ordinance. What is the best characterization of the ordinance?

   (A) Unconstitutional, as a violation of the Second Amendment.
   (B) Unconstitutional, as a violation of Privileges of National Citizenship.
   (C) Constitutional, as an exercise of the police power.
   (D) Constitutional, as an exercise under Section 5 of Fourteenth Amendment.

78. In response to growing concern about the use of airplanes in terrorist attacks on the government, the President issued an executive order banning the exportation of flight training or flight simulation materials to a list of 50 countries. Congress had previously passed a law granting the Executive wide authority to restrict foreign trade, and gave standards for selecting methods of new restrictions. Macrosoft, a Redmond State corporation, sells software nationally and internationally. Macrosoft had contracts to sell Plane Simulator software to retailers in 30 of the listed countries. All of these contracts are now expressly prohibited by the executive order. Which of the following statements best describes the order?

   (A) The executive order is constitutional, because the President has inherent power to conduct foreign affairs.
   (B) The executive order is constitutional, because Congress has plenary power to regulate commerce with foreign nations and authorized the President to issue such orders.
   (C) The executive order is an unconstitutional violation of the Contracts clause.
   (D) The executive order is unconstitutional, because Macrosoft has a property interest in the existing contracts.

79. The Dry State legislature is convinced that women mature at an earlier age than men and fight less frequently than men. Dry State passes a law lowering the drinking age for women to 18, but keeping the drinking age for men at 21. What best describes the constitutionality of the statute?

   (A) Unconstitutional, unless the State shows a compelling state interest.
   (B) Unconstitutional, unless the State shows the age minimum is rationally related to a legitimate state interest.
   (C) Unconstitutional if the law is not substantially related to an important government interest.
   (D) Unconstitutional if the law is not narrowly tailored.

80. The State of East Tennessee wanted to protect its citizens from greedy bankers by passing an anti-usury statute. The law made 12% the highest interest rate legally permissible for in-state banks to lend at, with a small exception for credit cards. The interest rate jumped suddenly after the stock markets improved. The Federal Reserve raised rates, and banks followed suit. Soon, inflation began to occur. A Wall Avenue Journal article reported that no bank could make a mortgage loan for less than 15%. It came to the point in East Tennessee that only wealthy people could afford to buy real estate. Is the East Tennessee anti-usury statute constitutional?

   (A) Yes, because the state acted properly to protect its citizens.
   (B) Yes, because the law is not in an area specifically reserved to the federal government.
   (C) No, because the law denies equal protection to less wealthy people.
   (D) No, because it violates the negative implications doctrine.

81. Congress adopted a statute years ago, which provided for student aid at colleges and universities. A recent change requires colleges and universities that receive federal money to offer aid to students solely on the basis of need. Which is the best source of federal power authorizing the statute?

   (A) Police power.
   (B) Power to enforce Equal Protection.

(C) Power to tax and spend for the general welfare.

(D) Power to enforce Privileges and Immunities.

82. After conservatives gained eight seats in the Senate, Congress decided to take action against judges on the left coast. Citing the high percentage of cases from one circuit that have been overturned by the Supreme Court, Congress passes a law making changes to the Supreme Court and the Ninth Circuit. The U.S. Supreme Court will now sit six Justices in Washington D.C., and three Justices in California to hear Ninth Circuit appeals. This provision will bypass the liberal judges in the Ninth Circuit. What is the likely result based on the Constitution?

(A) Unconstitutional, because the Supreme Court must have nine members.

(B) Unconstitutional, because there is only one Supreme Court.

(C) Unconstitutional, because Congress has no power to eliminate a circuit court.

(D) Unconstitutional as a denial of equal protection.

83. Which of the following cases is least likely to be heard under the Supreme Court's original jurisdiction?

(A) *Washington v. Oregon*, over which a state breached its duty to prevent a forest fire.

(B) *New York v. New Jersey*, over which state owns part of an island.

(C) *Texas v. U.S.*, regarding a state challenge to an executive order reducing federal funding to a highway.

(D) *California v. U.S.*, regarding state citizens' interest in continued diplomatic ties with Japan.

84. Congress held hearings regarding the shrinking middle class in America. Economists testified that the wealth gap between rich and poor has not been this big since Louis XIV reigned in France. The wealthiest five percent own 85% of the property when government property is excluded. Reacting to "hate the rich" sentiment in the population, Congress passes a statute reinstating the estate tax. The law eliminates loopholes. The government will get $1 billion from the tax. After the cost of auditing and accounting is accounted for the net revenue generated will be about $10 million. What is the likely result if the Court reviews the constitutionality of the statute?

(A) Constitutional, if the dominant intent of the tax was fiscal.

(B) Constitutional, because Congress has the power to tax the estates of persons.

(C) Unconstitutional, because the revenue does not substantially outweigh the burden on the estate.

(D) Unconstitutional, because the Court will conclude that it is a penalty, not a tax.

85. Brook stored his personal handguns at Flagg's Mini-Storage. Brook became delinquent in payment for his storage space, so Flagg's informed him that his property would be sold pursuant to state law that permitted the private sale of stored goods under such circumstances. Brook filed an injunction against Flagg's in federal court, claiming the sale violated his rights. What constitutional rights are at issue?

(A) 14th Amendment Due Process.

(B) 2nd Amendment Right to Bear Arms.

(C) Dormant Commerce Clause.

(D) None, because no state action.

86. Congress passed an amendment to the tax code. The amendment creates a one-time deduction for a very narrow class of taxpayers. The deduction allows twin brothers who simultaneously inherent a corporation, which owns land that produces farm crops during the taxable year, from the estate of a common paternal parent, if the taxpayer receives one-half share of the corporation and the taxpayer has natural hair color of brown and is thirty-eight years old during the fiscal year. Earnest and Julio Gallon fortunately inherit their father's wine company during the one year that the deduction is effective. John Crest files a declaratory judgment in federal court to have the tax law declared unconstitutional. What is the likely outcome?

    (A) The court will declare the deduction is an unconstitutional bill of attainder.

    (B) The court will declare the deduction is unconstitutional as not rationally related to a legitimate government interest.

    (C) The court will declare the deduction is a constitutional exercise of the tax power.

    (D) The court will not hear John's case on the merits.

87. Attorneys and accountants are bitterly fighting in Evergreen State regarding the ability of attorneys to form partnerships with non-attorneys. Accountants want to be able to hire attorneys to give legal advice to clients of the accounting firm. Accountants accuse attorneys of economic protectionism. Some attorneys view the proposal as a danger to the independent professional judgment of attorneys to work for non-attorney management. The Evergreen Legislature was holding hearings to hear public comment on the issue. Tom Iman called the legislators, who were primarily lawyers, cowards for not allowing the accounting firms to practice law. The Legislature passed a statute declaring that Mr. Iman would never be able to obtain a license to practice law in Evergreen State. What is the best characterization of the statute?

    (A) An unconstitutional ex post facto law.

    (B) An unconstitutional bill of attainder.

    (C) Unconstitutional, because it violates due process.

    (D) Unconstitutional, because it violates his rights of state citizenship.

88. The City of West Angeles needs to protect its beaches from excessive development. Public outrage against the overabundance of beachfront condominiums convinced city planners to increase environmental protections of the waterfront. A commission redrew the local zoning plans. Pursuant to state law, the City stopped issuing new permits for all new building within 200 feet of the high water mark of the ocean. Buildings completed previously must be taken down within 180 days. Fran Kavalon owns an acre of property on the beach. The acre is a long stretch of beach, and only extends 215 feet from the high water mark. She had just signed at contract with a general contractor to build 45 condominiums overlooking the water. The contractor sent her notice of intent to terminate performance under the contract due to the recent changes. The property still has a wonderful view of the ocean. What is Fran's best argument?

    (A) The City owes her money under the inverse condemnation doctrine.

    (B) The City violated due process by taking her land.

    (C) The City violated the Contracts Clause.

    (D) Both C and D.

89. Syscom, a Dover State corporation, had a contract with the federal government to install direct server lines to bring the Internet to "all American Embassies." The President then issued an executive order cutting off foreign relations with Jamaica, because the country lowered trade barriers with Cuba. Marines were scheduled to close the embassy the following day. If Syscom filed suit in federal court to enjoin the closing of the embassy, what would be the most likely outcome?

    (A) Dismissed, because the Court would not consider the action on motion for injunction as it is an issue committed to another branch of government.

    (B) Dismissed, because the Constitution's Takings Clause applies.

    (C) Dismissed, because Constitution's Contracts Clause applies.

    (D) Dismissed, because Syscom lacks an injury in fact.

90. During the World Commerce Organization's convention in Emerald City, several members of the Resist One-World Government (ROWG) protested. Some of the protesters caused damage to the convention center and local businesses. ROWG has many members, some of whom overlap with the ACLU. Members rely on the loose-knit leadership to keep their names secret. Some of the members who work for corporations and local governments fear retaliation for being members. ROWG does not endorse violence or property damage, but many of the members actively profess it. The Emerald City Attorney subpoenaed the organization for the membership list. Emerald asserts that ROWG should have known that some of its members would resort to lawbreaking. ROWG files to resist the subpoena. What is the most likely outcome?

(A) ROWG's motion denied, because ROWG lacks standing to protect individual member rights.
(B) ROWG's motion granted, because the members had the right to peaceably assemble.
(C) ROWG's motion granted, because membership is lawful.
(D) ROWG's motion denied if the State can show a compelling state interest.

91. Alabarkansa Legislature passed a law stating that if state elementary schools teach children about George Washington, then they must also teach children about Moses, a person described in the Bible. What is the likely result if the constitutionality of the statute was tested?

(A) Unconstitutional, because it violates free exercise clause.
(B) Constitutional, unless there is no secular purpose.
(C) Unconstitutional, because the teachers cannot be forced to teach an idea.
(D) Constitutional if applied generally to public and private schools.

92. The City of Rhode, in the State of Pawtucket Island, erects an annual Christmas display during the Christmas season. In the display are Santa Claus and other related characters, colored lights, and a nativity scene with Mary, Joseph, and the infant Jesus. Does the display survive constitutional scrutiny?

(A) No, because it depicts a religious scene.
(B) No, if government employees erected it and taxpayers paid for it.
(C) Yes, if the inclusion of Jesus was to celebrate the season and depict the origins of the holiday.
(D) Yes, if the scene is in a limited public forum.

93. Congress passed a law authorizing and directing the Food and Drug Administration (FDA) to regulate genetically modified crops. Congress was reacting to the fervor of activists and a "20/20 Minutes" television news report suggesting the dangers of genetically altered foods. The law has standards for determining congressional intent and boundaries for the regulation. If the law is interpreted broadly, the FDA will have the authority to pass a regulation allowing it to seize crops and finished products anywhere in the stream of commerce or in the home. Under the law, the FDA will not take action on the crops and produce, until it passes a rule about how the seizure will proceed. Fearing government storm troopers in the homes of its members, the Americans for Liberal Civilities Union files suit in federal court to enjoin the FDA from conducting seizures. What is the court most likely to do?

(A) Dismiss, because the FDA has not passed a rule.
(B) Abstain from ruling, but retain jurisdiction over the case.
(C) Enjoin the FDA from making an unconstitutional rule.
(D) Dismiss, because of 11th Amendment Immunity.

94. Cornhusk City denied the Crew Cut Clan's permit application for the city's

Autumn Parade on November 11th. What is the constitutionality of this denial?

    (A) Unconstitutional, because it is prior restraint on free speech.

    (B) Unconstitutional if the Clan can show that their speech is protected.

    (C) Constitutional if a prompt judicial review finds an important governmental interest for having a veteran's parade that day instead of the Clan's parade.

    (D) Constitutional if the state articulates a viewpoint neutral reason that shifts the burden to the Clan.

95. Congress has passed a statute which provides that no federal court, including the United States Supreme Court, shall have jurisdiction to decide any case involving the validity under the Constitution of any law limiting the rights of children under age 15 to obtain an abortion without parental consent. If properly challenged, the statute would be

    (A) Constitutional because of the plenary power of Congress to determine jurisdiction of the federal courts.

    (B) Constitutional because a series of Supreme Court decisions have upheld the constitutionality of similar statutes.

    (C) Unconstitutional because Congress cannot regulate the jurisdiction of the United States Supreme Court.

    (D) Unconstitutional because Congress may not preclude an entire class of cases from judicial review.

96. Jones, a 21 year-old white male, applied to law school at Missibama State University, a prominent southern university which had been found to have unlawfully refused applicants on account of their race in 1980. His index score, which combines law school aptitude test score and grade point average, was below the lowest score of white applicants admitted. Jones' score was substantially above 15 of the 20 black students admitted. The University agreed to grant bonus points to black students'

index score and had a numerical goal of 20 black students, pursuant to a consent decree entered in 1980. If Jones brings suit to require that he be admitted because the university has unlawfully discriminated against him because of his race, the Court would

    (A) Grant relief because a classification solely based on race, even to achieve a worthy purpose, is not necessary to achieve a compelling state need, and therefore violates the Equal Protection Clause.

    (B) Grant relief because a state may not use race as a criterion in making admissions decisions.

    (C) Deny relief because a state may consider race as a factor in admissions when it is attempting to aid disadvantaged minorities and penalizes no particular group.

    (D) Deny relief because the racial classification is designed to remedy past unlawful discrimination.

97. The State of Vermont is operating a large nuclear power plant on the Connecticut River. The plant uses river water for cooling and discharges water back into the river, ten degrees warmer than it was at the point of entry. While this temperature differential quickly dissipates, it has adversely affected the business of North Pole, a downstream ice-cutting operator, located in New Hampshire. Primarily as a result of North Pole's urging, New Hampshire has sued Vermont in the U.S. Supreme Court, alleging damage to its environment and seeking an injunction against thermal discharge. The U.S. Supreme Court should

    (A) Dismiss the suit because the suit it is barred by the Eleventh Amendment.

    (B) Hear the matter on the merits because New Hampshire is suing in its own right and jurisdiction is proper.

    (C) Dismiss the action because it does not have original jurisdiction.

(D) Hear the matter on the merits because New Hampshire is suing parens patriae.

98. The school-age population in Metro City is 15% black and 85% white. Metro City has fifteen schools within its district. Seventy percent of the pupils in five intercity schools in the city are black. Other schools have no black pupils. Which of the following statements concerning these facts is most accurate?

(A) The facts establish a violation of the Equal Protection Clause of the Fourteenth Amendment.

(B) The facts set forth are not sufficient to establish an Equal Protection violation unless it could be shown that the predominantly black schools were the five oldest schools in the system.

(C) The facts are insufficient to establish a violation of the Equal Protection Clause of the Fourteenth Amendment, but a violation would be established if it could be shown that there was a higher percentage of tenured teachers in the predominantly white schools.

(D) The facts are insufficient to establish a violation of the Equal Protection Clause of the Fourteenth Amendment even if the facts shown in Choices (B) and (C) are established.

99. The town of Arlex has enacted a zoning ordinance that restricts all land in the town to single-family residences that can only be constructed (except for a small business zone in the center) on lots with a frontage of 200 feet and an area of 60,000 square feet. An out-of-state developer who plans to build townhouses in Arlex has brought suit in the federal court to enjoin the operation of the statute.

Which is the weakest argument for the city if it tries to obtain a dismissal of the suit before a trial on the merits?

(A) The case is moot.

(B) There is no case or controversy.

(C) The P lacks standing.

(D) The issues are not ripe.

100. Pursuant to a state enabling statute, the city of Easton enacted a rent control ordinance affecting all residential buildings containing ten or more dwelling units. As of the effective date of the ordinance, the maximum rent charged was the rent charged on that dwelling unit one year prior to the effective date. Lord had entered into a two-year lease with Tent six months prior to the effective date of the ordinance at a rental higher than was charged one year prior to the effective date. If Lord challenges the constitutionality of the ordinance, his most effective argument will be that it

(A) Impairs the obligation of contract.

(B) Violates the Due Process Clause because it operates retroactively.

(C) Violates the Equal Protection Clause because it classifies large landlords differently from small landlords.

(D) Violates the Due Process Clause because the rent charged was controlled without giving him a hearing.

101. Roman is the leader of a religious cult in Thogam City. He holds a weekly "service" in the public park and during his sermon, uses insulting expletives directed at persons in his audience who are not members of the cult. The audience has become boisterous and several times fights have almost broken out between members of the audience and members of the cult. After a particularly boisterous rally, the attorney for the city of Thogam obtained an ex parte injunction prohibiting Roman from conducting any further rallies "which tend to disturb or annoy the average member of the community." If challenged on appeal, a judge would find the injunction

(A) Valid because the threats of imminent violence justify the injunction.

(B) Invalid because the injunction is overly broad and vague.

    (C) Invalid because the injunction was obtained in a manner that violates procedural due process.

    (D) Invalid for the reasons set forth in choices (B) and (C).

102. Dolly Belle was a guest on a television talk show called "Fernwood Today," which is on the air between 4 p.m. and 6 p.m. The host of the show spent five minutes asking Dolly questions about the size and shape of her breasts. Dolly answered all the questions in a full and frank manner. The Federal Communications Commission issued a letter of reprimand to the station because of the program's content, and the station has appealed on the ground that the Commission does not have the constitutional power to issue the reprimand. Which of the following is the strongest argument to uphold the validity of the Commission's action?

    (A) Because the airwaves are public property and limited in number, the government may regulate broadcasts under the police power.

    (B) The pervasive nature of television makes it likely that a show scheduled in the late afternoon will reach an immature audience whom the government has a right to protect.

    (C) The material present on the show was obscene and not entitled to First Amendment protection.

    (D) The show was staged for the purpose of raising advertising revenue, and is therefore commercial speech that is subject to reasonable regulation.

103. William Pierce was addressing an audience in a park in New York on the subject of salvation. He uttered words highly offensive to the religious crowd that gathered to hear him speak. After a while, about three men indicated that if the police officer did not "get that S.O.B. off the stand," that they would do it themselves. At this point, a police officer stepped in to stop a fight from breaking out and demanded that Pierce cease speaking.

When he refused, the police officer arrested Pierce and he was convicted of disorderly conduct. Upon appeal

    (A) The conviction will be reversed by the Supreme Court of the United States because Pierce's arrest constituted an interference with his First Amendment right to freedom of speech.

    (B) The conviction will be reversed by the Supreme Court of the United States because Pierce's arrest constituted undue interference with his audience's right to assemble peaceably under the First Amendment.

    (C) The conviction will be sustained by the Supreme Court of the United States because Pierce had a duty to obey a police officer where there were other times and places to convey his message.

    (D) The conviction will be sustained by the Supreme Court of the United States because his speech caused an immediate and substantial threat to public order.

104. State Q enacts a statute that is narrowly drawn and defines obscenity in accordance with the latest decision of the U.S. Supreme Court. When the police searched D incident to a motor vehicle arrest they found a film in his coat pocket. D is arrested for the illegal transportation of obscene material. Assuming that the material found on his person is an indecent pornographic film, what is his best defense?

    (A) Others have carried similar material with the knowledge of the police and have not been prosecuted.

    (B) He received the film as a gift.

    (C) He only had the film because he just bought it and was taking it home.

    (D) Parts of the film have literary merit.

105. Dandruff is the owner of a beauty shop, which employs only male hairdressers and caters only to female customers. An ordinance of the City of Tinsel makes it unlawful for any person to operate a hairdressing salon catering to female customers if the hairdressers are male. Dandruff brings an action in the federal court challenging the constitutionality of the ordinance. If the D city moves to dismiss the lawsuit on the grounds that Dandruff lacks standing, the city would

- (A) Prevail because the ordinance does not prohibit the operation of beauty salons per se, but only the right of the male employees to service female customers.
- (B) Prevail because only the employees can raise their rights of association.
- (C) Not prevail because the employees and the beauty shop operators have rights that are harmed by the ordinance.
- (D) Not prevail because the ordinance prevents the employees from exercising their First Amendment rights.

106. Smith, a citizen of England, operates an adult theater that shows films that are obscene in the constitutional sense. Pursuant to a narrowly drawn statute, Smith is prosecuted in state court for the exhibition of an obscene motion picture, and asserts as a defense the right of privacy. Which of the following best explains the effectiveness of his defense?

- (A) An alien may not assert an invasion of privacy defense.
- (B) The right to possess obscene material does not extend beyond the home.
- (C) The right of privacy allows the possession of obscene motion pictures.
- (D) Theaters may show obscene films to adults.

107. When he was interviewed on a radio show, an assistant district attorney made three statements:

I. His boss, the district attorney, was on a witch-hunt, trying to convict prominent citizens so that he could further his political career.

II. Many times he did not produce all of the evidence that the police had gathered if he felt that the D should not be convicted.

III. He was going to ask the legislature to appropriate more funds for the public defender's office because he felt that the quality of their representation of criminals was not as good as the state representation by the district attorney's office.

The district attorney could dismiss him for making:

- (A) Statement I.
- (B) Statement II.
- (C) Statement III.
- (D) None of the statements.

108. A zoning ordinance of Carmel prevents the keeping of any animals, except dogs and cats, within city limits. Chusetts is a member of a religious cult which believes in ancestor worship, and which uses monkeys as part of their daily religious worship. Consequently, he keeps a monkey in a separate bedroom in his home. If the town should sue to require Chusetts to remove the animal from the premises because its presence violates the zoning ordinance, and Chusetts challenged the constitutionality of the statute on First Amendment grounds,

- (A) Chusetts will prevail if he proves that the City passed the law with religious motivation, and the zoning ordinance is not narrowly tailored to the state's compelling interest.
- (B) Chusetts will prevail only if he proves that the application of the statute to him is not rational.
- (C) The city will prevail only if it can show that the statute is necessary to satisfy a compelling state need.
- (D) The city will prevail if it can show a rational basis for the statute.

109. Chinook, a resident of State A, was a commercial salmon fisherman who fished for two months per year in the Red River in State B. Effective this year, State B's legislature provided that the fee for a salmon fishing license was $5 per year for a resident and $500 per year for a non-resident. If Chinook challenged the constitutionality of the law under the Privileges and Immunities Clause of Article IV, the Court would find that

    (A) It was constitutional because the state has a proprietary interest in the fish within its borders, and therefore may discriminate against nonresidents.

    (B) It was constitutional because no fundamental interest was infringed.

    (C) It is unconstitutional discrimination against nonresidents because it does not bear a substantial relationship to the fact that there is a limited number of salmon.

    (D) It is unconstitutional because a state may not deny an alien a livelihood unless that action is necessary to satisfy a compelling state need.

110. A new statute in Virginia requires all residents to submit a certificate of fetal health during the fourth month of each pregnancy. The certificate must be signed by a doctor, which declares that the baby is healthy and free of AIDS and genetic defects. The certificate must still be submitted if the prospective mother has an abortion prior to the fourth month. Mary files suit in state court to enjoin the statute. She alleges the law impinges on her federally guaranteed constitutional right to privacy. The state court upholds the statute. The state supreme court upholds the statute on emergency appeal. Mary appeals to the U.S. Supreme Court. In her distress, Mary has a miscarriage prior to oral arguments. Which answer best describes whether the Supreme Court should dismiss the suit?

    (A) Yes, the Court lacks jurisdiction to hear the case because it is moot.

    (B) Yes, the Court lacks jurisdiction to hear the case because it originated in state court.

    (C) No, the Court has jurisdiction because a constitutional issue is raised.

    (D) No, the Court has jurisdiction because she may become pregnant again and be subject to the law yet not reach the high court in time.

111. The city of Madison, Wisconsin, enacts an ordinance that requires a city inspection of all milk products coming into the city from outside the state of Wisconsin. A Wisconsin state law requires an identical inspection of all milk, both intra- and interstate, for health purposes. The Good Milk Company sues, alleging that requiring the city inspection is a Commerce Clause violation. What is the most likely result in the case?

    (A) Madison will prevail because the statute is designed to protect the health and welfare of Madison citizens.

    (B) Madison will prevail because it has been given implicit authority by the Wisconsin statute to conduct the inspection.

    (C) The Good Milk Company will prevail because the city inspection, which is identical to the state inspection, is an undue burden on interstate commerce.

    (D) The Good Milk Company will prevail because the statute is discriminatory on its face.

112. The President of the United States has entered into an executive agreement with the President of Mexico. The agreement provides that all Mexicans in prison in the U.S. will be repatriated to serve the remainder of their sentences in Mexican prison, and all Americans in Mexican prison will be repatriated to serve the remainder of their sentences in American prison. Pursuant to this agreement, federal marshals arrived at a local prison in Texas to take Lopez, a convicted murderer of Mexican citizenship, and deliver him to Mexican authorities. A state statute requires that murderers convicted in Texas must be incarcerated in Texas prison. The local sheriff therefore brings an action in federal court to enjoin the marshal on the ground that he is acting pursuant to an unconstitutional order. The court should:

(A) Grant the injunction because the agreement violates the sovereign powers reserved to the states under the Tenth Amendment.

(B) Grant the injunction because executive agreements cannot supercede state law.

(C) Deny the injunction because of the Supremacy Clause.

(D) Deny the injunction because a sensitive area of foreign policy is nonjusticiable.

113.   Furman has been convicted of a federal offense carrying the death penalty, and has been sentenced to death by a federal court during a time when the death penalty was constitutional. The Supreme Court rejected all appeals, including an appeal claiming ineffective assistance of counsel by Furman's trial attorney. The President of the United States decided that there may have been valid arguments tending to show ineffective assistance of counsel. The President proceeded to commute the sentence from the death penalty to life in prison subject to the condition that Furman would never be eligible for parole. At a later date, the death penalty is declared unconstitutional and Furman seeks parole. The federal district court will decide that

(A) This is a valid exercise of the President's pardoning power under Article II.

(B) The commutation must be set aside because it is not authorized by legislation.

(C) The commutation must be set aside because the President may not decide constitutional issues.

(D) The commutation must be set aside because the death penalty was subsequently declared unconstitutional.

114.   The United States House of Representatives asks the judiciary committee to recommend a law regulating the conditions for marriages and divorces.

The committee would like to respond with a law that would most likely withstand constitutional analysis. That law would

(A) Only apply to marriages and divorces by members of the armed services.

(B) Only apply to marriages performed by federal judges and divorces in federal courts.

(C) Only apply to marriages implemented by an executive agreement seeking to define basic human rights.

(D) Apply only to marriages and divorces in the District of Columbia.

115.   Jersey State sues York State over which state owes Sille Island, which is located in the navigable water between the two states. Jersey files its complaint in the U.S. Supreme Court initially. York brings a motion to dismiss. What is the most likely outcome on the motion?

(A) Dismiss as a political question.

(B) Remand the case to federal district court.

(C) Overrule the motion and hear the case on the merits.

(D) Dismiss the case as a violation of the 11th Amendment.

116.   Pat sues Don in state court for trespass and battery. Pat prevails in a bench trial on the merits, but Don continues to object to evidence admitted regarding a deed. Don claims the deed was erroneously admitted, and violated the rules of evidence. Don appeals his evidence issue to the state supreme court, but the court upholds the trial court in a published opinion. Don files in the U.S. Supreme Court. The Court should:

(A) Refuse to hear the case, unless there is a final judgment on the merits from highest state court.

(B) Deny the writ of certiorari, because the court has no jurisdiction.

(C) Decline to hear oral arguments, if the case can be easily decided.

(D) Decline the appeal, because it is not an interesting issue.

Questions 117 and 118 are based on the following:

City of the Big Apple passed a municipal ordinance making spray painting on public buildings a misdemeanor, if it is done with the intent to criticize a public officer. Spary is arrested and charged for "tagging" the County Jail, which sits inside city limits. Spary painted "Juliani sucks." Spary is assigned a public defender. The public defender believes the ordinance violates both the State and Federal Constitutions.

117. If the public defender files a declaratory action in federal district court on Spary's behalf to have the ordinance declared unconstitutional, the district court would most likely do what to the federal action?

(A) Dismiss, because Big Apple has not consented to suit in federal court.

(B) Abstain, if the prosecution has initiated.

(C) Hear the case, because one party is a city not a state.

(D) Hear the case, because it is a flagrant violation of the Constitution.

118. Assuming the Big Apple continues the prosecution within the state system, the court convicts Spary after a bench trial. Spary's attorney appeals claiming the conviction violates both state and federal constitutional protections of free speech. The highest court in the state concludes that the statute does violate the state constitution, but does not reach the federal issue. The State's Constitution has a free speech provision, but the language and case history are distinct from the Federal Constitution. For that reason, the Americans for Liberal Civilities Union (ALCU) convinces Spary to appeal the decision to the U.S. Supreme Court. What is the weakest argument for declining review by the Supreme Court?

(A) The ALCU has no standing.

(B) Spary's conviction is already overturned.

(C) The decision would be merely advisory.

(D) The case is non-justiciable.

119. Manning Couch received unemployment benefits from Great Lake State for one year more than the state statute allowed. When the federal government sent a memorandum to the Great Lake Attorney General regarding an audit, the state sought to recover the funds from Manning. Kennedy was an assistant attorney general for Great Lake. Kennedy graduated a number of years ago, but only recently passed the bar exam. Kennedy filed an action in federal court against Manning to recover the payments, relying on an obscure regulation that allows jurisdiction to recover government money accepted under misleading circumstances. Manning files a motion to dismiss in federal district court. What is the most likely outcome?

(A) The court will dismiss based on the State's Sovereign Immunity in federal court.

(B) The court will dismiss based on lack of standing.

(C) The court will hear the case.

(D) The court will find for Manning based on the ex post facto clause.

120. Congress enacted a statute prohibiting states from intentionally discriminating in hiring based on the applicant's race. The statute further provided for individuals to file a suit for money damages in federal court based on the violation. What is the best characterization of the statute?

(A) Constitutional exercise of Section Five of the Fourteenth Amendment.

(B) Unconstitutional as an abridgment of the 11th Amendment.

(C) Unconstitutional as a regulation of an integral state function.

(D) Constitutional exercise of the Commerce Clause power.

121. Congress enacted a law limiting the number of passengers allowed in each train car. The bill was drafted the day after a terrorist attack on a passenger train. It also criminalized all of the common law crimes if committed while on a train scheduled for interstate travel. During debate, it became clear that the law would be solely for the purpose of deterring terrorists. What is the constitutionality of the statute?

(A) Constitutional exercise of the commerce clause.

(B) Constitutional exercise of the federal police power.

(C) Unconstitutional regulation in a traditional state area.

(D) Unconstitutional as enacted for a non-economic purpose.

122. The State of Tennesville enacted a law criminalizing certain speech. The legislature intended to punish the use of fighting words. A recent law review article by a third-year law student argued that the law is a fairly well worded, good faith attempt at the constitutional requirements. The student argued that a reasonable person could decide what conduct or speech was prohibited, but that it is borderline constitutional. The law student decided to write the article because there were no state cases interpreting the statute, and the new governor had talked about enforcing it. Americans for Free Speech (AFS) initiate a declaratory judgment action in federal district court. The Governor of Tennesville claims that the law prohibits another, yet unrecognized category of unprotected free speech. The district court will most likely

(A) Not hear the case because the state court has not interpreted the law.

(B) Not hear the case, because the state is immune from suit in federal court.

(C) Hear the case, if the AFS has membership in the state.

(D) Hear the case, because of the law's effects on interstate commerce

123. South Georgia has had a statute on the books prohibiting the use of contraceptives by any person since the year condoms were invented. The State has not prosecuted anyone under the statute in 80 years, and sales have been brisk. Bill and Sally Process are married and living in South Georgia. Bill Process wanted to join a gang of liberals. As an initiation, Bill was ordered to file a lawsuit against the State. Bill sued the State in federal court alleging the old contraceptive law was unconstitutional. What is the court's most likely course of action?

(A) Dismiss the case, as the outcome would have no practical legal effect.

(B) Dismiss the case, because Bill does not have standing.

(C) Dismiss the case as a violation of the 11th Amendment.

(D) Hear the case on its merits and find the law unconstitutional.

124. More than ten years ago, Congress created the United States Sentencing Commission and delegated to it the power to promulgate sentencing guidelines that would bind the federal courts to impose sentences within prescribed ranges. Last year, Congress authorized the Commission to update sentence recommendations in light of prison overcrowding. The Commission adopted new guidelines effective May of this year, but only for drug crimes. The law creating the Commission set general policies and principles to guide the creation of the Guidelines.

In April of this year, Kris Rock was arrested for assault and battery of a postal worker and tried in federal court. He was convicted in June. At the sentencing hearing, the judge imposed a sentence at the high end of the standard range. Had the Commission lowered the sentence range for assault and battery in proportion with how much lower the new drug crime range is, Kris's sentence would be outside the range. Kris's attorney is arguing on appeal that the sentence is improper. What is the likely outcome on appeal?

(A) The sentence violates the Ex Post Facto clause.

(B) The sentence was valid.

(C) The sentence violates the Equal Protection clause.

(D) Congress improperly delegated to the Sentencing Commission.

125. Last Year, the Key Lime Supreme Court struck down the statute that sets the procedure for implementing the death penalty for capital crimes in the state. This year, Key Lime State prosecuted Birddog for murder. On New Year's Day, Birddog shot and killed two nuns and a firefighter in a crosswalk while he was on parole for armed robbery. Key Lime had a statute since 1901 stating that this crime was a capital offense. Key Lime legislature passed a statute that would survive current constitutional standards for the death penalty procedures. In June, Birddog was convicted and sentenced to death in accordance with the new law. What is the likely outcome on appeal of the case?

    (A) The sentence violates the Ex Post Facto clause if the new statute was not in effect when the crime was committed.

    (B) The sentence will be upheld, because it comports with the Constitution.

    (C) The conviction violates the Ex Post Facto clause if the new statute was not in effect when the crime was committed.

    (D) The conviction will be upheld, but the sentence violates the Constitution.

126. The Richmond State Constitution has always had a provision prohibiting aliens from inheriting certain property. The United States signed a treaty over a century ago with Great Britain providing that no restrictions shall be placed on the rights of the citizens of either country to inherit property in the country of the other. Arthur, a citizen and resident of Great Britain, stands to inherit 34 acres of land in Richmond. This type of conveyance falls within the prohibition in the State Constitution. What is the likely outcome?

    (A) Arthur inherits the land if he can show no compelling state interest for the prohibition.

    (B) Arthur inherits the land, because the treaty over-rides the prohibition.

    (C) Arthur does not inherit the land, because the Richmond State constitution prohibits it.

    (D) Arthur inherits the land, because the prohibition violates Equal Protection.

Questions 127 – 130 share common facts:

Illinois requires a license for those "who engage in the trade of barbering." Illinois grants licenses to people who meet three conditions: graduate from an Illinois barber school, reside in the state for two years, and are United States citizens.

127. The requirement that a license applicant have graduated from an Illinois barber school is probably

    (A) Constitutional, because barbering is a privilege not a right.

    (B) Constitutional, because the state does not know the quality of barber schools outside of Illinois.

    (C) Unconstitutional because it is a violation of the 14th Amendment Privileges or Immunities clause.

    (D) Unconstitutional as an undue burden on interstate commerce.

128. The requirement that a license applicant must be a United States citizen is

    (A) Constitutional as an exercise of the state's police power.

    (B) Constitutional as an effort to ensure that barbers speak English adequately.

    (C) Unconstitutional as a denial of equal protection.

    (D) Unconstitutional as a bill of attainder.

129. Which of the following is (are) good argument(s) to challenge the two year residency requirement?

    (A) Art. IV Privileges and Immunities.

    (B) 14th Amendment Privileges or Immunities.

    (C) 14th Amendment Equal Protection.

    (D) Both A and C.

130. Jake Elwood, a resident of Iowa, was not allowed to sit for the hairdresser's licensing exam in Illinois because he graduated from an Iowa barber school. If Jake files a suit in federal court to contest the denial of the license, what is the likely outcome for Jake?

    (A) Dismissed, because of the abstention doctrine.

    (B) Prevail, because Illinois violated due process.

    (C) Prevail, because the law violates the Art. IV Privileges and Immunities Clause.

    (D) Decided on the merits, because federal jurisdiction extends to controversies between two states.

131. Ronald McDowell is convicted for speaking about the oppression of clowns by the state government. Ronald is convicted under a statute prohibiting the "disturbance of the peace by shouting political nonsense." While Ronald was known for his outbursts when he forgot his medication, some of his statements on this occasion could be defensible if interpreted favorably.

On appeal to the state's highest court claiming a violation of his right to free speech, the court refused to hear the case. In a single page decision, the court invoked a widely ignored rule of appellate procedure requiring litigants to attach a copy of the statute in the appendix of the brief. As a result, Ronald's conviction stands. In an appeal to the U.S. Supreme Court, what is the most likely result?

    (A) The Court will hear the case if Ronald claims the state violated due process by applying the appellate rule.

    (B) The Court will hear the case, because the state may not preclude high court review by applying the appellate rule inconsistently.

    (C) The Court will hear the case, because it is a facially invalid statute.

    (D) The Court will not hear the case, because the appellate rule issue is not a federal constitutional matter.

132. Congress passed a statute requiring each state to arrange for the disposal of toxic waste generated within its borders. If the toxic waste is not disposed of or contained pursuant to federal guidelines within five years, the state will be deemed to "take title" to the waste and thereby become liable for tort damages stemming from it. The federal statute contemplates that every state with toxic waste within its boundaries will pass legislation funding containment construction. It will take New Power State five years to build containment facilities to handle all of the nuclear waste it currently has to the new federal standards. New Power files an action in federal court to have the law declared invalid. What is the likely outcome of the case?

    (A) The court will invalidate the law, which improperly requires the state to pass laws to implement a federal program.

    (B) The court will dismiss the case, because it violates 11th Amendment sovereign immunity.

    (C) The court will dismiss, because New Power will not suffer any injury for five years, so the case is not ripe.

    (D) The court will find for the United States, because the law is constitutionally valid.

133. The State of Rhode Island entered into a contract with Roads, Inc., for the construction of a four-lane turnpike. Prior to commencement of construction, the legislature, in order to provide funds for parks, repealed the statute authorizing the turnpike and canceled the agreement with Roads. Roads sued Rhode Island to enforce its original agreement. In ruling on this case, a court will likely hold that the state statute canceling the agreement is

    (A) Valid, because constitutionally the sovereign is not liable except with its own consent.

(B) Valid, because the legislature is vested with constitutional authority to repeal laws it has enacted.

(C) Invalid, because a state is equitably estopped to disclaim a valid bid once accepted by it.

(D) Invalid, because of the constitutional prohibition against impairment of contracts.

Questions 134 and 135 are based on the following:

Green is cited for contempt by the House of Representatives after she refused to answer certain questions posed by a House Committee concerning her acts while serving as a United States Ambassador. A federal statute authorizes the Attorney General to prosecute contempt of Congress. Pursuant to this law, the House directs the Attorney General to begin criminal proceedings against Green. A federal grand jury indicts Green, but the Attorney General refuses to sign the indictment.

134. Which of the following best describes the constitutionality of the Attorney General's action?

(A) Illegal, because the Attorney General must prosecute if the House of Representatives directs.

(B) Illegal, because the Attorney General must prosecute those who violate the federal law.

(C) Legal, because ambassadors are immune from prosecution for acts committed in the course of their duties.

(D) Legal, because the decision to prosecute is an exclusively executive act.

135. If the Attorney General signs the indictment, the strongest defense Green could offer is that

(A) Green may refuse to answer the questions if she can demonstrate that they are unrelated to matters upon which Congress may legislate.

(B) The House may question Green only on matters pertaining to the expenditure of funds appropriated by Congress.

(C) Only the Senate may question Green on matters that relate to the performance of her duties.

(D) Congress may not ask questions relating to the performance of duties executed by an officer of the executive branch.

Questions 136 and 137 are based on the following:

Congress decided that the application of the Uniform Consumer Credit Code should be the same throughout the United States. To that end, it enacted the UCCC as a federal law directly applicable to all consumer credit, small loans, and retail installment sales. The law is intended to protect borrowers and buyers against unfair practices by suppliers of consumer credit.

136. Which of the following constitutional provisions may be most easily used to justify federal enactment of this statute?

(A) The obligation of Contracts Clause.

(B) The Privileges or Immunities Clause of the 14th Amendment.

(C) The Commerce Clause.

(D) Section 5 of the Fourteenth Amendment.

137. A national religious organization makes loans throughout the country for the construction and furnishing of churches. The federal UCCC would substantially interfere with the successful accomplishment of that organization's religious objectives. The organization seeks to obtain a declaratory judgment that the federal law may not be applied to its lending activities. As a matter of constitutional law, which of the following best describes the burden that must be sustained?

(A) The federal government must demonstrate that the application of this statute to the lending activities of this organization is necessary to vindicate a compelling governmental interest.

(B) The federal government must demonstrate that the religious conduct affects commerce.

(C) The organization must prove that the activity is central to their religion and substantially interfered with.

(D) The organization will prevail by showing intentional discrimination by the federal government only if it also shows the law is not narrowly tailored to a compelling government interest.

138. The Federal Endangered Species Act imposes criminal penalties for killing certain specified animals, among which is the rare Plaid Squirrel. Trail State classifies all species of squirrels as varmints, which may be destroyed by anyone with a Trail State hunting license. Rambo, who possesses a Trail State hunting license, regularly shoots Plaid Squirrels who trespass on his land. If Rambo is prosecuted under the federal statute, and challenges the constitutionality of the law, which of the following is the strongest constitutional argument in support of the statute?

(A) The Commerce Power.

(B) The Necessary and Proper Clause.

(C) The Police Power.

(D) The power to regulate federal lands.

139. The Macrosoft Corporation is headquartered in Evergreen State. To keep the corporation within the State, Evergreen passes a massive funding bill, which includes direct subsidies to Macrosoft. Several state attorneys general and private software competitor companies file an injunction against Evergreen subsidizing Macrosoft claiming a violation of the Dormant Commerce Clause. The most likely disposition of this suit will be that the injunction will be:

(A) Granted, because the subsidies violate the Dormant Commerce Clause by unduly burdening out-of-

state companies that must compete with Macrosoft.

(B) Granted, because the subsidies violate the Dormant Commerce Clause by effectively insulating the in-state corporation from out-of-state competition.

(C) Granted, because the Ps have standing to challenge state subsidies as measurable expenditures.

(D) Denied, because the states are allowed to use state tax dollars to subsidize local industry.

140. Washington requires imported apples to be inspected for parasites and diseases to reduce the risk of infecting local crops. The inspections are relatively low in cost and do not delay shipments more than a few hours. Unfortunately, a new breed of apple maggot found only in Oregon cannot be found with any existing test due to its small size. The Oregon Apple Maggot devastates any crop it comes in contact with. Washington apple growers successfully lobbied their state legislature into passing a law banning the importation of apples from Oregon. Those in Oregon challenge the statute as unconstitutional will

(A) Prevail, because the law discriminates against interstate commerce.

(B) Prevail, because the law violates the Article IV Privileges and Immunities of those in Oregon.

(C) Lose, because the law only burdens one state not several states.

(D) Lose, if there is no less restrictive way to prevent the Oregon Apple Maggot infestation from reaching Washington.

141. The U.S. Department of Agriculture distributes surplus farm products acquired in exchange for farm subsidies. To reduce the incidents of fraudulent claims, the agency implemented a test program in its distribution of government cheese. Each household is allowed up to one pound of cheese per month. Any household in which unrelated persons were living together would be ineligible for the cheese. Bill and Hillary, two unmarried people, each applied for surplus cheese and were both denied because they lived together. What is the most appropriate provision for challenging the agency's withholding of the cheese?

(A) First Amendment.
(B) The equal protection implications of the Fifth Amendment.
(C) The Due Process Clause of the Fourteenth Amendment.
(D) The Privileges and Immunities Clause of the Fourteenth Amendment.

142. After two-thirds majorities of the House and Senate passed the Campaign Finance Amendment to the U.S. Constitution, it was submitted to the states for ratification. Several years passed while states were considering the amendment. The state of Mountain's legislature subsequently took up the issue. While the matter was pending before the Mountain legislature, an action was filed in federal district court seeking to enjoin the legislature from voting on the ratification issue. The grounds cited were that the Campaign Finance Amendment was no longer viable because less than three-fourths of the states necessary for ratification had ratified it, and no other states were currently considering whether to ratify it. How should the district court rule on this issue?

(A) Dismiss the matter as untimely, since the Mountain legislature has not yet voted on the issue of ratification.
(B) Dismiss the matter as a nonjusticiable political question.
(C) Abstain so that the state's highest court may authoritatively interpret state law on the subject.
(D) Decide the matter on its merits.

143. The local chapter of the Libertarians wants to succeed from Snohomish County and form Freedom County. In an effort to raise awareness of the oppressive nature of the government, Jeb contacted the advertising department of the local AM talk radio station. Jeb wants to run a campaign of political ads on the radio, and he thinks this station is the best way to reach his target audience. The advertising department manager refuses to run the ads. Jeb files an action seeking a federal court order to force the radio station to air the advertisements. What is the trial court's strongest justification in denying Jeb relief?

(A) The radio station's commercial time is not a public forum.
(B) Jeb has a reasonable alternative to get his message out to his target audience.
(C) The Fourteenth Amendment provides no basis upon which to compel the radio station to air Jeb's ads.
(D) The radio station's decision is based on a content neutral reason.

144. University of Michigan conducted a test, using state tax subsidies, to determine the cause of the recent increase in fatalities from car accidents. Professor Thunderbird concluded that Yokobishi Manufacturing had produced a defective electronic speedometer. Neither Congress nor any other state took any action on the issue. Rather than naming the manufacturer, the Michigan State Legislature banned the use of all electronic speedometers within the state effective 60 days from the passage of the law. What is the best argument to defeat the law?

(A) It is a violation of the Equal Protection Clause because it treats electronic speedometers differently from conventional speedometers.
(B) It is a violation of the Commerce Clause, because it unduly burdens interstate commerce.
(C) It is a violation of the Due Process Clause because it is a taking without just compensation.
(D) It is a violation of the Constitution as a Bill of Attainder.

145. Congress enacted the Health Information Act, which disbursed funds from the federal treasury to the public educational systems of each state ($500 per

pupil enrolled in the state college system). It also provided that the school system included in its curriculum accurate information about the human reproductive system and sexual behavior, including the manner of transmission of the AIDS virus. If these provisions of the federal act are challenged as unconstitutional, they should be held

(A) Invalid, because education about human sexuality is not a proper subject of federal regulation.
(B) Invalid, because Congress may not achieve through conditional grant of funds an object that would be unconstitutional if it were the subject of direct regulation.
(C) Valid, as a proper exercise of congressional power to spend to promote the general welfare.
(D) Valid, but only if the health education has a significant impact upon interstate commerce.

146. Responding to the economic downturn, New Gingrich State passed a law terminating all welfare programs effective in 90 days. Ninety days later, the State cuts off Sally's benefits. Sally, a mother of two who is currently on welfare, files suit. The court will most likely

(A) Find that the hardship on Sally outweighs the administrative convenience of terminating the benefits.
(B) Deny Sally's claim.
(C) Find the action invalid as the State did not provide Sally an opportunity to be heard.
(D) Find that the State must give Sally a post-deprivation hearing to determine her benefits.

147. Soon after a small private plane crashed near the White House, Congress enacted a law prohibiting private planes from flying over Washington, D.C. An organization representing private plane pilots brought suit in the federal court seeking to invalidate this law. The federal statute could best be supported by

(A) The Supremacy Clause.

(B) The General Welfare Clause.
(C) Congress's plenary power to make regulations protecting government property.
(D) Congress's police power over the District of Columbia.

148. Marymore State purchases old, junk cars, or "hulks" and disposes of them. The State purchases from in-state owners for $200, and from out-of-state owners for $10. Were an out-of-state owner to challenge the program, the court would find that it was

(A) Constitutional, because the State created the market using its own funds.
(B) Unconstitutional, because it substantially interferes with interstate commerce.
(C) Unconstitutional, because it violates the negative implications of the commerce clause.
(D) Unconstitutional, because it is in-state economic protectionism.

149. Congress enacts a $100 tax on the sale of any handgun to a private individual not for use in law enforcement or military duties. Will this tax survive a constitutional challenge?

(A) Yes, but only if Congress could have banned possession of handguns outright.
(B) Yes, if the dominant intent of Congress was that the tax would produce revenue.
(C) No, if the tax does not result in any significant collection of revenue.
(D) No, because the tax is clearly intended as a penalty on handgun ownership.

150. Dixie State requires a competency test granting people a license to teach elementary or secondary school within the state. The test covers skills and knowledge taught in high school, as well as other skills. Caucasian test-takers pass the test twice as often as African-American test-takers. Regina, a black woman who failed the test, sues Dixie State. An expert

testifying on behalf of the P opines that Caucasians score 35% higher than minority groups on multiple-choice format tests, but that other formats reduce the margin substantially. The expert further opines that the choice of the multiple-choice format in the face of such evidence is clearly intentional discrimination. The court will most likely find that the competency test is

(A) Constitutional, as rationally related to a legitimate government interest.

(B) Unconstitutional, as a violation of equal protection due to its discriminatory impact.

(C) Unconstitutional, as a violation of equal protection due to its discriminatory intent.

(D) Constitutional, because teachers constitute participation in government.

151. Belt State Legislature sent Belt University, a private religious school, a $1 million cash grant for the school to acquire a new kitchen facility in the student union building. The grant was a part of a larger series of awards of higher education grants to schools. If the grant is challenged by a P who has proper standing, the court will likely find it

(A) Valid, as an incidental benefit to a private school in higher education.

(B) Valid, as property clause disbursement.

(C) Invalid, as an excessive entanglement.

(D) Invalid, as an improper religious benefit

152. Sam Blocky was married to Eve. Eve won custody of their two children and support payments from Sam in the divorce decree. Readjustment was hard on Sam. Sam got behind in his support payments. Then Sam met Rebecca and asked her to marry him. The state refused to issue a marriage license unless he could make a showing that his two children would never have to go on welfare. This denial of the marriage license was pursuant to a state statute. What is the probable outcome if the statute were properly challenged as to its constitutionality?

(A) Valid, as rationally related to the legitimate end of protecting children of a prior marriage.

(B) Valid, as the state has general power to enact legislation.

(C) Invalid, as the statute is not narrowly tailored to fit permissible ends.

(D) Invalid, as the statute does not treat applicants with children the same as similarly situated applicants without children.

153. A state law banning the sale of which substance would be least likely to be subject to strict scrutiny?

(A) Milk.

(B) Condoms.
(C) Rubber Tires.
(D) Both B and C.

154. Mr. Dole is a welfare recipient. The state passed a law ending welfare in the state. The department ceases paying benefits to Mr. Dole in reaction to the law. What best describes the constitutionality of this?

(A) Constitutional, as rationally related to legitimate ends.

(B) Unconstitutional, because the state ended his benefits prior to a hearing.

(C) Unconstitutional, because the state has assumed the duty of his care.

(D) Constitutional, if the state grants him a hearing as soon as practicable after the benefits are ceased.

155. In Farstate, USA the examinations for driver's licensing are contracted out to a private company. The contractor refuses to hire anyone but white males. Assume that there are no state or federal civil rights statutes that would prevent such. Which of the following is the correct analysis and conclusion?

(A) Race is a suspect class, so the policy most likely violates strict scrutiny because there is no compelling governmental interest being advanced.

(B) The private company is not a state actor, so unless there are statutes preventing race discrimination, the action is not prohibited by the equal protection clause.

(C) Because race and gender are both at issue, the proper level of scrutiny is intermediate because the lesser of two classes is evaluated in a "double classification" case. The decision will be for the contractor because driver licensing is an important governmental purpose.

(D) Because there is no constitutional right to drive, the proper level of scrutiny is rational basis.

156. Farstate grants funding to a private nursing home to care for indigent patients. The nursing home has a practice of hiring only women who are members of a minority racial group. Assume that there is no state or federal civil rights statutes to prevent such a hiring practice. Which of the following is the correct analysis and conclusion?

(A) Race is a suspect class, so the hiring practice most likely violates strict scrutiny because there is no compelling governmental interest being advanced.

(B) The nursing home is not a state actor, so unless there are statutes preventing race discrimination the action is not prohibited by the equal protection clause.

(C) Race is a suspect class, but since the hiring practice is remedying past discrimination the practice will satisfy strict scrutiny.

(D) Because government funding is involved, the proper level of scrutiny is rational basis.

157. The Farstate Department of Wealth Equality is an agency dedicated to taking from the rich to give to the poor in the finest Marxist tradition. The head of the department has promulgated the following hiring rule: "Because the rich are the source of all problems of society and cannot understand the plight of the poor, anyone who has a net worth over $10,000.00 is ineligible for employment with this department." Immediately, 25 employees are fired due to their substantial net worth. They sue the state. Which of the following is the correct analysis and conclusion?

(A) The action is arbitrary and capricious, so it is unconstitutional under strict scrutiny.

(B) The action is not by a state actor because wealth redistribution is not an essential government function.

(C) The right to public employment is a protected property interest and the employees would likely prevail because of lack of procedural due process.

(D) Wealth is a quasi-suspect class, so the rule must promulgate an important governmental purpose. Because eliminating poverty is so important, the rule meets this level of scrutiny.

158. The State of Oppression passes a law that authorizes the Department of Environmental Quality to seize "any motor vehicle that pollutes an unconscionable amount." The law then states that the seizure becomes permanent after a "reasonable time." The department decides to be generous in that no seizure will become permanent until after a hearing. The department then posts the hearing dates on its web site. At the hearing, the owner is allowed a fair opportunity to present his or her case. Under this scheme, which option is the correct result?

(A) The owners have been granted sufficient notice and an opportunity to be heard.
(B) The owners do not have sufficient notice.
(C) Notice may be constructive when the regulated subject matter is an important governmental function like pollution.
(D) The owners have sufficient notice, but the hearing itself does not meet due process because the burden of proof beyond a reasonable doubt is not upon the state.

Questions 159-160 share common facts.

159. The State of California has a law that all state employees are "at-will" employees, which means the employees may be fired without cause. Professor Leftofski is an associate professor who attends public rallies critical of U.S. foreign policy. He often cancels his classes and has been late on several deadlines because of his activities. The university president tells the professor "Get your lazy rear end off my campus. You're fired." Which of the following is the correct analysis and conclusion?

(A) Employment is a fundamental right requiring due process. Due process was denied, so the professor's termination was illegal.
(B) A job with the government is a property right requiring due process. Due process was denied, so the professor's termination was illegal.
(C) The professor had no property interest in the job, so his termination did not violate due process.
(D) The professor was exercising his protected free speech rights, and so his termination was unconstitutional.

160. The former Professor is now a private citizen. He gets on a soapbox in downtown and begins a diatribe against the U.S., capitalism, and democracy. The busy capitalists walking by pay no attention to him. In frustration, he throws an American flag to the ground and shoots it with his .357 Magnum to get people's attention. Which is the proper analysis and conclusion?

(A) Freedom of speech is a fundamental right, which includes the right to be heard. Therefore, getting people's attention with the pistol was a protected exercise of expression.
(B) He may be prosecuted for discharging a firearm, but not desecrating the flag. This is because desecrating a flag is protected political speech, but discharging a firearm is not, due to a rational basis in protecting public safety.
(C) He may not be prosecuted for discharging a firearm because the second amendment prohibits such, but may be prosecuted for desecrating a flag if prohibited by State law.
(D) He may be prosecuted for both discharging a firearm and desecrating a flag because there was no prior restraint on his speech.

Questions 161 to 163 are based on the following:

The North American Association to Promote Strictly Traditional Religions (NAAPSTR) has successfully lobbied the State of Texarkana for a statute named "Equal Rights for All Religions." The law requires broadcasters that air segments discussing Christianity to allow equal time for segments on Judaism, Hinduism, and Buddhism.

The American Atheism Association (AAA) is devoted to the study and promotion of the belief that there is no supreme power or creator. AAA has put together a segment about atheism for broadcast on five major television stations in Texarkana. However, four of the five stations have declined to air the segment because they believe it would violate the statute. AAA has sued the four stations and has filed suit against the state challenging the constitutionality of the statute.

161. What is the strongest argument AAA can make in support of striking down the Equal Rights for All Religions statute?
- (A) The First Amendment prohibits government interference with freedom of the press.
- (B) The fact that the statute involves only broadcast media and not print media is an Equal Protection violation.
- (C) The First Amendment prohibits government interference with the free exercise of religion.
- (D) The statute is not narrowly tailored to promote a compelling governmental interest.

162. The state files a motion to dismiss claiming that AAA lacks standing. What result?
- (A) Motion granted, because the stations were under no obligation to air the segment and therefore no injury has occurred.
- (B) Motion granted, because only individual members of AAA (and not the organization itself) have standing.
- (C) Motion denied, because the stations did refuse to air the segment based on the statute.
- (D) Motion granted, because the statute does not actually prohibit the stations from broadcasting the segment.

163. NAAPSTR files suit against the station that agreed to air the AAA segment, claiming that the station violated the statute. What is the likely result?
- (A) The suit will be dismissed because NAAPSTR lacks standing.
- (B) The suit will be dismissed because only the state has the power to enforce the statute.

- (C) NAAPSTR will prevail because the station violated the statute.
- (D) The station will prevail because atheism is not a religious belief and therefore the broadcast did not violate the statute.

Questions 164 and 165 are based on the following:

The states of Allen and Burns share a border straddled by a beautiful mountain range. Atop the range are two state parks, one run by the state of Allen and one run by the state of Burns. Visitors may take gondolas to the top of the mountains and take state-guided tours that overlap both parks. According to the federal Parks & Recreation Employment Act, employees of any park or recreational facility that engages in interstate activities must be paid a minimum wage of $8.00.

Tour guides are employed by both states. Tour guides from Allen are paid $6.75 per hour, which is the minimum wage of that state. Guides from Burns are paid $7.50 per hour, although that state's minimum wage is only $6.00.

164. Employees from the State of Burns sue the state in federal court for back pay, claiming they are entitled to the difference between their wages and the $8.00 per hour wages mandated by the Parks & Recreation Employment Act. What is the likely result?
- (A) The employees will prevail, because of the Supremacy Clause.
- (B) The case will be dismissed or removed pursuant to the Eleventh Amendment.
- (C) The state will prevail, because Congress has no authority to regulate the wages of state employees not engaged in interstate commerce.
- (D) The state will prevail, because the management of state parks is a traditional state function.

165. State of Allen park employees sue the State of Allen in state court for back pay, claiming they are entitled to the difference between their wages and the $7.50 per hour paid to State of Burns park employees. What is the likely result?

(A) The state will prevail, because it is not required to pay its employees the same wage as similarly situated employees in Burns.

(B) The employees will prevail, because of the Article IV Privileges and Immunities Clause.

(C) The employees will prevail, because of the Equal Protection Clause.

(D) The case will be dismissed, because it is barred by the Eleventh Amendment.

166. Rebecca is a married woman living in the State of Serendipity. She has three children and is a homemaker. In which of the following situations is she most likely to successfully challenge the constitutionality of a state statute?

(A) A statute is passed that prohibits unmarried persons from engaging in "unnatural" sexual acts. Rebecca wants to challenge the statute as a violation of the right to privacy and for vagueness.

(B) A statute is passed that gives a state income tax credit to married persons with children. Rebecca wants to challenge the statute under the Equal Protection Clause.

(C) A statute is passed that deprives citizens of the State of Serendipity from receiving unemployment benefits if they were dismissed for refusing to work on their Sabbath day. Rebecca wants to challenge the statute under the Establishment Clause.

(D) A statute is passed that prohibits speeches in Serendipity public squares that "incite strong negative emotions" about the state government. Rebecca has no plans to make any public speeches, but wants to challenge the statute for overbreadth and as a violation of the right to free speech.

167. Due to decades of overfishing by commercial and game fisherman, the South Pacific Red Tuna has become an endangered species. Congress has passed a law that prohibits the importation of the rare tuna into the United States. However, the President, with the consent of two-thirds of the Senate, has a long-standing treaty with the country of Ivaronia that includes trade agreements regarding the importation of South Pacific Red Tuna.

The President has vetoed the law, but both houses of Congress have overridden the veto by a three-fourths majority. What is the best argument for why the importation of tuna from Ivaronia should cease?

(A) Only a two-thirds majority of Congress is required to override a Presidential veto.

(B) When a treaty and a federal law are in conflict, the one that is last in time prevails.

(C) When a treaty and a federal law are in conflict, the federal law prevails whenever the law relates to commerce.

(D) The Executive Branch has ultimate authority regarding foreign affairs.

168. Congress has passed the Career Horizons Act, which provides educational grants to U.S. citizens who meet specific qualifications. Hans Kleimer is a German citizen who has been studying in the United States under a valid visa. Hans applies for a grant under the Career Horizons Act. Despite meeting all of the other specified qualifications, Hans is turned down because he is not a U.S. citizen. If Hans challenges the constitutionality of his denial, what is the most likely decision that a court would reach?

(A) Hans will not prevail, because Congress has the right to attach limiting conditions to its spending.

(B) Hans will prevail, because he is in the country legally and is entitled to constitutional protections.

(C) Hans will not prevail, because Congress has broad powers to restrict the entitlements of aliens.

(D) The case will be dismissed, because aliens have no right to bring suit in courts of the United States.

Questions 169 - 171 are based on the following:

Cheminol is a corporation operating in the State of Nebar. The company produces and ships flammable chemicals for use in the manufacture of certain types of hard plastics. For years, Cheminol has been burying bithium, a toxic waste product, in metal drums in a storage trench on Cheminol property. Some of the drums have suffered metal fatigue and begun to leak, but the company has not instituted clean up procedures.

Kasan, a city in Nebar located near the Cheminol plant, has recently been detecting rising levels of bithium in its groundwater, attributable to the Cheminol dumpsite. One test completed on April 3 revealed that the bithium level had reached 100 parts per billion. The federal government regulations regarding bithium set the maximum permissible level in groundwater at 250 parts per billion. Neither the State of Nebar nor the city of Kasan has any law regarding bithium on the books.

The Kasan City Council is concerned about a new study indicating that even lower levels of bithium – 75 parts per billion – could be dangerous to humans. On July 17, the council passed a municipal ordinance limiting the permissible amount of bithium in groundwater to 50 parts per billion and cites Cheminol for violation. After a full and fair hearing, the city fined Cheminol $100,000 and ordered the immediate cleanup of the dumpsite within 60 days.

169. Cheminol brings suit to challenge the fine. What is the likely result?

(A) The city council will prevail, because it has the right to regulate for the health and safety of its citizens.

(B) The city council will prevail, because Cheminol had notice and an opportunity to be heard.

(C) Cheminol will prevail, because the city ordinance amounts to a bill of attainder.

(D) Cheminol will prevail, because the city ordinance was an ex post facto law.

170. Cheminol also brings suit to challenge the constitutionality of the city ordinance. What is the LEAST effective argument Cheminol could make?

(A) Congress has occupied the field of regulation of toxic waste contaminant levels.

(B) The city ordinance is in conflict with the federal law and is therefore invalid.

(C) The city ordinance was enacted as a result of improper procedural methods.

(D) The city ordinance amounted to a taking of Cheminol's property because there is no way to operate its plant without a minimum contamination rate of 60 parts per billion.

171. Cheminol refuses to obey the order to clean up its site, and after 90 days an additional non-compliance fine of $200,000 is assessed. If the ordinance is valid, can the new fine be enforced?

(A) Yes, because Cheminol had a full and fair hearing and refused to obey the order.

(B) Yes, because Cheminol had no liberty or property interest at stake in performing the cleanup.

(C) No, because the order was an ex post facto law.

(D) No, because the order was in conflict with federal law.

172. In an effort to smooth relations between two troubled countries, the President of the United States signs an executive agreement with the Premier of the Sovereign Nation of Zimtar. The stated purpose of the agreement is for the President to "create the best possible public image" for Zimtar in the U.S. media. The Editor-in-Chief of the New York Times files suit on behalf of the paper, claiming that the agreement violates the First Amendment guarantee of a free press. The President's best argument for the constitutional validity of the executive agreement is

(A) Executive agreements have no actual force of authority or law.
(B) Congress can override an executive agreement if it so chooses.
(C) The executive agreement does not place any restrictions whatsoever on the press.
(D) The President has broad discretion when entering into executive agreements.

173. A state law requires state employees over the age of 60 who drive 3 or more hours a day as part of their job to take a periodic eyesight and reflex test. Males must take the test annually, females must take it biannually. Which of the following, if true, would most likely make this law constitutionally valid?

(A) Studies have shown that males are more likely than females to be involved in automobile collisions.
(B) Studies have shown that males over the age of 60 lose their vision and reflexes twice as fast as females over the age of 60.
(C) Congress has passed a law declaring gender discrimination in state employment to be legal.
(D) In the past, female employees have been subjected to discrimination in hiring for state jobs that require three or more hours of driving per day.

Questions 174 - 176 are based on the following:

After two disasters involving chemical explosions, Palray City enacted an ordinance banning the transportation of flammable chemicals within three miles of the city center. Chemlab, a manufacturer of volatile chemicals, is located in the heart of the industrial sector of Palray, 1 mile from the downtown area.

Employees of Chemlab protested the city's action, carrying signs and banners down to Palray City Hall. Many of them blocked traffic, and a number of city workers inside the building came to the windows when they heard the people below. Six Chemlab employees were arrested pursuant Palray City Ordinance 35.598, which makes it a misdemeanor to "engage in protests, marches, gatherings, or demonstrations that create a disturbance or hinder the work of city employees."

174. Chemlab filed suit in state court, alleging that it was entitled to just compensation pursuant to the Fifth Amendment to the United State Constitution. What is the likely outcome?

(A) Palray will prevail, because the Fifth Amendment does not apply to cities or other non-federal governmental entities.
(B) Palray will prevail, because the regulation does not amount to a taking.
(C) Chemlab will win, unless Palray City can demonstrate that the ordinance serves a compelling interest and is the least restrictive means available.
(D) Chemlab will win, because it has been deprived of economic use of its property.

175. The six employees arrested at the protest filed suit against the city, claiming that Ordinance 35.598 is in violation of the United States Constitution. What is the strongest argument the employees can make in support of their claim?

(A) The ordinance violates the Equal Protection Clause.
(B) The ordinance prohibits exercise of the right to freedom of association.

(C) The ordinance prohibits the exercise of the First Amendment right to free speech.

(D) The ordinance is vague and overbroad.

176. In response to the employees' claim, Palray City argues that the statute is constitutional under Article X Section 5 of the Palray State Constitution, which gives cities greater discretion to regulate for public safety than federal law. This argument will likely

(A) Fail, because of the Supremacy Clause.

(B) Fail, because the federal government has ultimate police power.

(C) Succeed, because the federal government cannot interfere with a state's interpretation of its own constitution.

(D) Fail, because of the 14th Amendment Privileges or Immunities Clause.

Questions 177 - 179 are based on the following:

The State of Waldorf and the State of Statler share a border at their eastern and western edges, respectively. Because Waldorf has a lower sales tax than Statler does, many residents of Statler go to Waldorf to make major purchases, such as automobiles, expensive jewelry, etc. As a result, the otherwise quiet stretch of interstate highway connecting Eastern Waldorf and Western Statler is plagued with constant traffic jams and accidents.

Due to these problems caused by interstate purchasers from Statler, Representative Moneypenny from the State of Waldorf lobbies Congress for the Waldorf Business Defense Act, a bill that would allow Waldorf to tax residents of Statler at a higher rate than residents of Waldorf for single consumer purchases over the cost of $1,000. The bill passes by a narrow majority.

Maggie Mardelene lives in the State of Statler. She takes a vacation to the nearby State of Waldorf to see her sister's new baby. While in Waldorf, Maggie drives her rental car past Sid's Sizzling Streetlegals, a used car lot incorporated and licensed in Waldorf. Sid's is selling a beautiful 1999 Lexus for $9,000. Maggie can't resist the great deal and goes to Sid's to purchase the car. However, when the salesman asks for her identification and discovers she is a resident of Statler, Maggie is charged sales tax amounting to $2400. A resident of Waldorf would have paid only $900 in sales tax.

177. Maggie's best chance for challenging the constitutionality of the sales tax would be to bring a claim pursuant to the

(A) Congressional Tax and Spend Power.

(B) Commerce Clause.

(C) Article IV Privileges and Immunities Clause.

(D) Fourteenth Amendment Privileges or Immunities Clause.

178. Which of the following taxes, if imposed, would be constitutionally permissible in this situation?

I.   A sales tax by Waldorf levied against Sid's.

II. A sales tax by Statler levied against Maggie.

III. A use tax by Statler levied against Maggie.

IV. A net income tax by Waldorf levied against Sid's.

(A) II and III.

(B) I, III, and IV.

(C) II and IV.

(D) III and IV.

179. Sid's experiences a sharp drop in business because of the new tax against residents of Statler. The company files suit challenging the constitutionality of the state tax law. What is the least effective argument that the state can make in defense to Sid's claim?

(A) Sid's claim does not involve a fundamental right.

(B) There is statistical evidence that the problems on Waldorf's eastern highway are caused by residents of Statler.

(C) The Waldorf Business Defense Act is constitutional.

(D) Any other measure would not solve the problem.

Questions 180 to 182 are based on the following:

In a stunning front-page article in the New York Times, it is revealed that the President of the United States, Geoff Brush, has participated in insider trading. On November 7, 2000, Brush was elected to his first term of office. On November 27, he resigned as CEO of his father's tobacco company, Fillup Maurice.

On January 16, 2001, Brush was golfing with the CFO of Fillup Maurice. The CFO said that the company was about to fold. Apparently, there had been some shady bookkeeping going on (of which Brush had no knowledge when he was CEO). On January 18, 2001, Brush dumped his stock. The dump greatly exacerbated the stock's plummet and caused a number of other stockholders to be financially ruined. On January 20, 2001, Brush was inaugurated.

180. On December 10, 2001, Brush is indicted under the Federal Insider Trading Act and is sued by the aggrieved stockholders. He argues that he has Executive Immunity as to the civil suit. Will his argument succeed?

(A) Yes, because the President is immune from suits for money damages while he is in office.

(B) No, because the act that is the basis for the suit took place two days prior to the President's inauguration.

(C) Yes, because only Congress can initiate civil litigation against a sitting President.

(D) No, because the President has also been indicted for a crime, and therefore his immunity to a related civil suit is waived.

181. Brush is tried and convicted of violating the Insider Trading Act. As a result, the House determines that grounds for impeachment exist. The vote is 223 to 212. The Senate convicts by a vote of 56 to 44. What are the consequences for President Brush?

I.   He is impeached.
II. He is removed from office.

(A) I only.

(B) II only.

(C) I and II.

(D) Neither I nor II.

182. Following a similar scandal in 1986, Congress enacted legislation to limit the Executive pardon power so that the Vice President who was the direct successor to an impeached President could not pardon that same President. Brush's successor, Vice President Cheely, is now President and wants to pardon Brush. He files suit in federal court challenging the legislation as unconstitutional. What should the federal court do?

(A) Dismiss the case as a non-justiciable political question.

(B) Strike down the law as contrary to Article II Section I.

(C) Dismiss the case as moot, because the Presidential pardon power extends only to state crimes, not federal crimes.

(D) Uphold the law, because it is permissible under Article IV, Section III.

183. Kelly is a property developer who owns 110 acres in a suburb of Baysurf, California. She has subdivided the property into 1-acre plots and wants to sell them to private parties to build single-family dwellings. She receives all of the necessary licensing and zoning approval, and registers her business with the Secretary of State and other appropriate state agencies.

Concerned about property values and safety, she wants to include in each deed a covenant stating that the purchaser will not resell the property to anyone of Arabic descent.

The O'Neills buy a piece of property and build a house. Three years later, they wish to sell, and get an outstanding offer from a man whose parents are both Syrian nationals. They sell the property and move. However, Kelly files a breach of contract suit in state court for violation of the covenant. Kelly prevails, and the O'Neills appeal, claiming that the covenant amounted to unconstitutional racial discrimination. Kelly argues that there was no state action. What is the best argument that the O'Neills can make in support of their claim?

(A) The housing development is a place of public accommodation.
(B) There are mutual contacts between Kelly and the state.
(C) Housing citizens is a traditional public function.
(D) The lower court enforced the contract.

Questions 184 and 185 are based on the following:

Congress recently passed a new comprehensive Labor and Employment Act, which greatly expanded the rights of American employees. In anticipation of an overwhelming amount of litigation, Congress created the federal Labor and Employment Court. The court's jurisdiction is to hear cases brought pursuant to the Labor and Employment Act. Since litigation will settle much of the controversy surrounding the Act, Congress has provided that the court will be eliminated after 10 years. Since the Labor and Employment Court will have expertise in adjudicating disputes about the act, no appeals will be allowed, and the U.S. Supreme Court will not have the power of judicial review.

The Minimum Wage Act provides that the federal minimum wage will increase by a certain percentage every two years. The next increase will occur in eleven months and will bring the federal minimum wage up to $7.15 per hour. The State of Dakola's minimum wage is currently $7.00 per hour.

184. What is the strongest ground for challenging the constitutionality of the Labor and Employment Act?
(A) It limits the jurisdiction of the Labor and Employment Court.
(B) It eliminates judicial review of an inferior federal court by the U.S. Supreme Court.
(C) It eliminates all possibility of appeal.
(D) It violates the constitutional provision that all federal court judges serve for a life term as long as they do not act improperly.

185. An employer in Dakola challenges the constitutionality of the Minimum Wage Act in the Labor and Employment Court. The employer argues that when the new increases take effect, Dakola's minimum wage will increase and he will not be able to afford to stay in business. The State of Dakola moves to dismiss. What result?
(A) Dismissed, the case is not ripe because the employer has not been injured.
(B) Dismissed, the court does not have jurisdiction.
(C) Motion to dismiss denied, the employer will be injured by the law when it takes effect and the case should be heard by the Labor and Employment Court.
(D) Dismissed, the case is moot because the federal law will have no effect on Dakola's minimum wage.

186. The State of North Caretarna has a law that allows public funds to be used in financial assistance programs to schools. In North Caretarna, a few schools at each academic level are run by religious organizations. In which of the following

situations is the law most likely to be constitutionally valid?

(A) The law allows payment to all elementary schools, provided the school can demonstrate that the funds are not used in furtherance of religion.

(B) The law allows payment to all high schools, provided the funds are used only for athletic programs.

(C) The law allows payment to all high schools, provided the school can demonstrate that students of all religions are admitted without discrimination.

(D) The law allows payment to all colleges, provided the funds are used for athletic programs.

Questions 187 and 188 are based on the following:

An outbreak of waterborne illness has ravaged the State of Pensacola. The illness has been traced to seepage from slaughterhouses engaged in unsafe disposal of animal byproducts. A recently enacted state law requires the "sanitary disposal of all animal carcasses, including organs, at a designated state disposal site." Jerry is a devoutly religious man whose faith requires him to bury a whole goat carcass in his backyard each month as an offering. Two weeks after the law is enacted, he is arrested while performing the act of burial.

187. If Jerry is prosecuted for violating the state law, what is his best defense on constitutional grounds?

(A) Enforcement of the law in Jerry's case is a violation of his freedom of religion.

(B) The act of burying the goat is expressive conduct and is therefore protected speech under the First Amendment.

(C) His belief that his religion requires him to bury a goat is sincere and therefore the prosecution is a Free Exercise Clause violation.

(D) The statute excessively entangles the government with religion, and

is an Establishment Clause violation.

188. Which of the following is the court prohibited from considering in its evaluation of Jerry's constitutional challenge to the statute?

(A) Whether Jerry is the owner of a slaughterhouse.

(B) Whether Jerry's belief in the sanctity of goat-burying is sincere.

(C) Whether the ritual that Jerry performs is mandated by his faith.

(D) Whether a reasonable person would agree that belief in the sanctity of burying a goat is a "religious" belief.

Questions 189 to 191 are based on the following:

The State of Illiho is located on the West Coast the United States. To get from Illiho to almost any other U.S. state requires travelling through Tassen, a neighboring state that shares an eastern border. To the North of Illiho is the State of Starket, the only state accessible to Illiho without going through Tassen.

Ace Trucking Company has its national headquarters in the State of Illiho but ships goods throughout the United States. Due to the heavy use of its roads by trucks from Illiho, Tassen has imposed a privilege tax on trucks from Illiho of $10 for every shipment across Tassen. Trucks from other states are taxed 50 cents per shipment, regardless of the amount of use. Tassen trucks are exempted from the tax, regardless of how much they use Tassen roads. Tassen also imposes a tax of 4% of the value of the goods in each truck that travels through Tassen, regardless of where the truck originated and whether the truck stops in the State of Tassen or not.

189. Ace Trucking files suit challenging the constitutionality of the Tassen privilege tax. Which of the following is the strongest argument in support of Ace's claim?

(A) Tassen is taxing goods in the stream of commerce.

(B) There is no substantial nexus between the state interest and the activity taxed.

(C) The tax is protectionist.

(D) No legitimate state interest is furthered by the tax.

190. In a summary judgment hearing on the privilege tax case, the court determines that the imposition of a privilege tax by Tassen is constitutional, but that Tassen must change its tax code to include a tax on Tassen trucks. Tassen then moves to dismiss. What is the likely result?

(A) Motion denied, there is another issue of apportionment.

(B) Motion denied, there is another issue of preemption.

(C) Motion granted, because there are no other constitutional issues raised.

(D) Motion denied, any privilege tax is an undue burden on interstate commerce.

191. In a separate action, another trucking company from Illiho that ships goods through Tassen challenges the Tassen goods tax under the dormant commerce clause. Is the claim valid?

(A) No. The dormant commerce clause only prohibits states from enacting protectionist legislation that burdens interstate commerce.

(B) Yes. The dormant commerce clause prohibits the taxing of goods in the stream of commerce.

(C) No. States are permitted to tax out-of-state interests at the same rate as in-state interests.

(D) Yes. The dormant commerce clause prohibits states from taxing goods unless a legitimate state interest is served.

192. The House of Representatives conducts a two-year study investigating the negative effects of domestic violence on the larger economic and social fabric of society. It is determined that a decrease in domestic violence would result in an increase in economic productivity nationwide. As a result of the study, Congress enacts a law prohibiting violence against women within the District of Columbia. What is the best argument in favor of the constitutionality of the law?

(A) The law does not violate the Necessary and Proper Clause.

(B) Congress has expansive powers to research and explore issues affecting society.

(C) The law is a proper exercise of Congressional authority pursuant to the Commerce Clause.

(D) Congress has police power over the District of Columbia.

193. In response to a rising problem with homelessness and panhandling, the State of Wollstone enacts legislation that requires those earning less than $20,000 per year to register with the state Department of Health and Human Services. The registration list is intended to track those who may eventually become homeless, and also to register eligibility for certain state services. Earl, a food service worker earning $18,000 per year, challenges the law on Equal Protection grounds. Under what test will Wollstone's law be evaluated?

(A) Earl must demonstrate that the law is not rationally related to an important governmental purpose.

(B) The state must demonstrate that the law is rationally related to a compelling governmental interest.

(C) Earl must demonstrate that the law is not rationally related to a legitimate governmental interest.

(D) The state must demonstrate that the law is substantially related to an important governmental purpose.

Questions 194 and 195 are based on the following:

The State of Calibama enacts a new statute that requires drivers who are stopped and cited for traffic violations which have fines of less than $50 to pay the amount of the fine directly to the officer. The driver may then challenge the citation at a hearing. If the driver wins his or her case, the amount of the fine is returned along with reasonable court costs.

194. If constitutional challenges to Calibama's statute are raised, it will most likely be because the statute threatens rights to
    (A) Procedural due process.
    (B) Substantive due process.
    (C) Equal protection.
    (D) Liberty interests.

195. Joe challenges the validity of the Calibama statute under *Mathews v. Eldredge*. What fact, if true, most strongly supports the state's defense of its procedure?
    (A) The statute is rationally related to a legitimate governmental interest.
    (B) More than 70% of the citations issued under the old law were dismissed at hearing.
    (C) To most people, $50 is a *de minimis* amount of money that is not important.
    (D) Under the old law, citizens rarely paid their tickets and the state incurred substantial costs in pursuing those who evaded the fines.

Questions 196 and 197 are based on the following:

Ty is the owner of a disreputable, run-down theater in the heart of the City of Statley's central business district. He specializes in screening films that "push the envelope of society" and advertises to that end. A number of local residents are upset by the graphic nature of some of his films, and make complaints to the local police. Ty's theater is shut down pursuant to Statley's municipal code prohibiting the public screening of obscene films.

196. Which of the following arguments would assist Ty in his suit to reopen his theater?

I. The films he screens have artistic value.
II. Most of the citizens of Statley agree that the films he screens have serious political value.
III. A reasonable person would agree that the films he screens do not depict any deviant sexual activity.
IV. The films he screens have been shown in theaters all across the United States.
    (A) I only.
    (B) I and III.
    (C) I, III, and IV.
    (D) II and III.

197. Ty wins his lawsuit and his theater reopens. Before he can say "Constitution," he is slapped with another lawsuit regarding his advertisements. Apparently, Statley also has an ordinance prohibiting the publication of advertisements promoting obscene material. For Statley's law to pass constitutional muster, a court must find that
    (A) Statley's definition of "obscene" comports with the federal standard.
    (B) The law serves a compelling governmental interest.
    (C) The law is narrowly tailored.
    (D) The law is rationally related to the Statley's interest.

Questions 198 and 199 are based on the following:

Virgenessee and Alabraska are neighboring states that share the Blue Ridge River as a border. For three years, Virgenesee has been relaxing its environmental laws, including water pollution controls, in the hope of enticing more manufacturing businesses to the state. It worked, and mercury levels in the Blue Ridge River have tripled. Citzens of Alabraska are no longer able to use the river for recreation and fishing. The State of Alabraska files suit in the Federal District Court of Virgenessee, requesting that Virgenessee compensate Alabraska citizens for the harm resulting from the increased mercury levels.

198. Virgenessee files a 12(b)(6) motion to dismiss the case, arguing that the court has no jurisdiction to hear the case. The motion will likely be

(A) Denied, because lower courts have concurrent jurisdiction to hear cases between two or more states.

(B) Denied, because of Alabraska's parens patriae status.

(C) Granted, because the Supreme Court has mandatory original jurisdiction.

(D) Granted, because in cases between states the Supreme Court must first deny certiorari before a suit in a lower court is filed.

199. Alabraska is also suing to have Virgenesee's environmental laws declared invalid. Alabraska will most likely prevail in its suit if which of the following is true:

(A) Virgenessee's water pollution regulations are less stringent than Alabraska's regulations.

(B) The Virgenesee legislature lowered water pollution regulations without conducting a study of the possible impact on Alabraska citizens.

(C) Virgenessee's water pollution regulations do not comport with regulations promulgated by the Federal Water Board.

(D) Virgenessee's water pollution regulations are less stringent than those required under the federal Clean Water Act.

200. With the approval of the majority of Congress, United States President John Taylor appoints Simon LeBon as head of the EPA for a term of 3 years. After a bitter political disagreement, Taylor revokes the appointment on the grounds that LeBon serves "at the pleasure of the President." LeBon protests and files suit. What is the likely result?

(A) LeBon will prevail, because he was appointed for a term.

(B) LeBon will prevail, because Taylor may not remove him without Congress' consent.

(C) Taylor will prevail, because the Executive Branch may dismiss administrative appointees at will.

(D) Taylor will prevail, because the Executive does not need Congressional approval to remove administrative appointees.

Constitutional Law
Learning Question Answer Rationales

1. /C/ Originally this type of suit was within the jurisdiction of the Federal Courts under Article 3 Section 2 clause 1, but was abrogated by the 11th Amendment. **(A)** is incorrect because it is within the jurisdiction of the Federal Courts. **(B)** is incorrect because it is within the jurisdiction of the Federal Courts. **(D)** is incorrect because it is within the jurisdiction of the Federal Courts.

2. /A/ A State Supreme Court is the final word on state law issues; a quiet title action regards property and is a state law matter. **(B)** is incorrect because it contains a Federal issue, so the Supreme Court will review the State Court decision. **(C)** is incorrect because the Supreme Court, absent limitation by Congress, may review Circuit Court decisions. The subject matter of the Circuit Court decision is not dispositive to the analysis. **(D)** is incorrect because the Supreme Court, absent limitation by Congress, may review Circuit Court decisions. The subject matter of the Circuit Court decision is not dispositive to the analysis.

3. /C/ When a case involves injunctive relief and it is heard by a three-judge panel in federal court, appeal to the Supreme Court is mandatory. **(A)** is not the best answer because certiorari involves discretion; the Supreme Court does not have discretion to deny in these circumstances. **(B)** is incorrect because when a case involves injunctive relief and is heard by a three-judge panel in federal court, appeal to the Supreme Court is mandatory. **(D)** is incorrect because when a case involves injunctive relief and is heard by a three-judge panel in federal court, appeal to the Supreme Court is mandatory.

4. /A/ Although third-party standing is not generally allowed, an exception exists for certain close relationships, such as that between union member and union. **(B)** is not the best answer because a direct injury is not imputed, the third party is simply allowed to take the place of the injured party. **(C)** is incorrect because although third-party standing is not generally allowed, an exception exists for certain close relationships, such as that between union member and union. **(D)** is incorrect because although third-party standing is not generally allowed, an exception exists for certain close relationships, such as that between union member and union.

5. /B/ There is no citizen standing for generalized grievances. **(A)** is incorrect because there is no citizen standing for generalized grievances. **(C)** is incorrect because there is no citizen standing for generalized grievances. **(D)** is not the best answer because

standing is a preliminary threshold analysis. An immunity analysis would only be reached after the court was satisfied that the P had standing.

6. **/B/** There is no general "taxpayer standing." **(A)** is not the best answer because theoretically, the injury could be redressed by stopping the sale. **(C)** correctly states the law, but is incorrect because property disposal under the property clause is not included in the exception. **(D)** is incorrect because there is no general "taxpayer standing."

7. **/D/** Because any pregnancy will always be significantly shorter than the appeals process, this falls under the exception. **(A)** is not the best answer because regardless of monetary damages, the mootness exception applies. **(B)** is incorrect because a legal issue surrounding a pregnancy falls under the exception for injuries "capable of repetition yet evading review." **(C)** is incorrect because a legal issue surrounding a pregnancy falls under the exception for injuries "capable of repetition yet evading review."

8. **/C/** Apportionment (a.k.a. "gerrymandering") cases are frequently heard and are not considered political questions. **(A)** represents a political question not addressable by the judicial branch. **(B)** represents a political question not addressable by the judicial branch. **(D)** represents a political question not addressable by the judicial branch.

9. **/A/** Federal courts will abstain from hearing, but keep jurisdiction over, cases in which an unsettled issue of state law exists. **(B)** is incorrect because it describes a legal scenario other than abstention. **(C)** is incorrect because it describes a legal scenario other than abstention. **(D)** is incorrect because it describes a legal scenario other than abstention.

10. **/B/** Even if not an enumerated power, Congress may use means that are not enumerated to achieve enumerated ends. **(A)** is incorrect because the Commerce Clause requires a nexus to interstate commerce. Since the farmer was not engaged in interstate commerce, that clause cannot be the source of this Congressional power. **(C)** is incorrect because Congress exercising exclusive legislation takes place in Washington, D.C., or other property purchased from the states with the consent of the legislature. **(D)** is incorrect because the General Welfare clause refers to taxing and spending.

11. **/C/** This option actually relates to commerce, so it is a subject falling within Congress' power. **(A)** is an actual case and does not have a sufficient nexus to commerce to be regulated. **(B)** is an actual case and does not have a sufficient nexus to commerce to be regulated. **(D)** is incorrect unless some nexus to interstate commerce is demonstrated. States enacted the 55-mile-per-hour law as a condition of receiving federal funding.

12. **/C/** Congress may delegate rule-making ability to other branches of government. **(A)** is incorrect because Congress may not reserve a "veto" on agency rules. Congress cannot give a blank check, so option **(B)** is incorrect because the delegation is too broad. **(D)** is incorrect because a line-item veto is unconstitutional.

13. **/C/** A state may not burden interstate commerce with its tax policy, or favor local interests over out of state interests generally. **(A)** is incorrect because a state may levy property tax on federal property as part of its general property tax scheme. **(B)** is incorrect because a state may also tax the income of federal employees. **(D)** is incorrect because a state may tax all goods that encounter a break in transit.

14. **/A/** A state may set higher health and safety standards than the federal government, but not lower. **(A)** is ineffective because it sets a lower standard. **(B)** is effective because it sets a higher standard. **(C)** is incorrect because the state may regulate as long as it does not fall below the federal standard (unless the federal government has totally preempted the field, which is not indicated in these facts). **(D)** is effective because it pertains to lead, not arsenic.

15. **/D/** The 10th Amendment prohibits Congress from commandeering the legislative or executive processes of the states. **(A)** is not the best answer because as long as the law is generally applicable and is a legitimate exercise of Commerce Clause. **(B)** is incorrect because non-economic ends may be achieved by regulating commerce. **(C)** is incorrect because structure of the military is an enumerated power.

16. **/D/** This is the only choice that is not an enumerated power. **(A)** is incorrect because Admiralty and Maritime law is an enumerated power of Congress. **(B)** is incorrect because Trademark law is an enumerated power of Congress. **(C)** is incorrect because laws of the District of Columbia are an enumerated power of Congress.

17. **/B/** Congress may attach conditions or "strings" to its spending that states may accept or reject. **(A)** is not the best answer because in this fact patter Congress is exercising its Tax & Spend power, not its Commerce Clause power. **(C)** is incorrect because <u>Morrison</u> limited Congress' Commerce Clause power, but did not affect the Tax & Spend power. **(D)** is incorrect because the 10th Amendment only limits Congress power to *directly* control state legislative and executive functions.

18. **/B/** 2/3rds Senate consent is required to enter into a treaty. **(A)** is not the best answer because it refers to "Congress" and does not indicate the level of consent required. **(C)** is incorrect because 2/3rds Senate consent is required to enter into a treaty. **(D)** is incorrect because an executive agreement is separate from a treaty, it is an informal agreement regarding everyday business with foreign countries.

19. **/A/** Article IV, Section III allows Congress to dispose of and make needful rules regarding federal land, and limits state's power in that regard. **(B)** is not the best answer because states have general police powers, and may make laws outside the realm of commerce. **(C)** misstates the law; no such "minor intrusion" is permissible. **(D)** is incorrect because wildlife is property for the purposes of the Property Clause.

20. **/C/** When Congress occupies a field, states may not regulate in that area. **(A)** is incorrect because when Congress occupies a field, states may not regulate in that area. **(B)** is incorrect because when Congress

occupies a field, states may not regulate in that area. **(D)** is incorrect because when Congress occupies a field, states may not regulate in that area.

21. **/D/** This is correct because mere state licensing, without more, is insufficient to constitute significant state involvement or direction. **(A)** is incorrect because it precisely describes the factual situation in *Shelly v. Kramer*, in which the Supreme Court held that state action existed. **(B)** is incorrect because a private lessee of state-owned property is considered to have "significant state involvement" such that state action is inferred. **(C)** is incorrect because a private citizen performing an act at the request or urging of police becomes a state actor for constitutional purposes.

22. **/C/** Because the law is facially neutral and religion is not a suspect class for equal protection purposes, the California law will be subject to rational basis scrutiny. **(A)** is incorrect because the law is facially neutral, and the facts do not reveal any discriminatory intent though the impact is disproportionate. **(B)** is incorrect because religion is not a suspect class for equal protection analysis (Note: The call of the question involves an equal protection claim, not a free exercise challenge. First Amendment protections are still available). **(D)** is not the best answer because it is unlikely a court would find a *compelling* interest, but may find a rational purpose (politics is a strange animal, pun intended).

23. **/C/** Disability is not a suspect class. There is no intuitive way to classify group membership. The level of scrutiny for each class

must simply be memorized. It is easier to memorize the suspect classes (race, national origin, citizenship) and assume the rest to be non-suspect. **(A)** is incorrect because race is a suspect class. **(B)** is incorrect because citizenship is a suspect class. **(D)** is incorrect because national origin is a suspect class.

24. **/A/** Legitimacy is subject to intermediate scrutiny and a law violates equal protection if it prejudices illegitimate children. Here the law benefits that class, so the state action is permissible. **(B)** is incorrect because citizenship may only be a criterion for participation in government or government jobs. **(C)** is incorrect because national origin is subject to strict scrutiny and the purpose of the law probably does not meet a compelling governmental need. **(D)** is incorrect because race is a suspect class.

25. **/B/** This is a requirement of affirmative action programs. **(A)** is incorrect because quotas are not constitutional. **(C)** is incorrect because continuing discrimination need not be proved, only past discrimination. **(D)** is incorrect because the group need not be "recognized" by a government agency.

26. **/B/** Because economic status is not a suspect or quasi-suspect class, the level of scrutiny is rational basis. **(A)** is incorrect because every restriction on travel is not per se unconstitutional. **(C)** is incorrect because the level of scrutiny is incorrect. **(D)** is incorrect because the level of scrutiny is incorrect.

27. **/A/** According to *Batson* a peremptory challenge of a juror on the basis of race or gender in either a civil or

criminal case is *per se* unconstitutional. **(B)** is incorrect because according to *Batson* a peremptory challenge of a juror on the basis of race or gender in either a civil or criminal case is *per se* unconstitutional. **(C)** is incorrect because according to *Batson* a peremptory challenge of a juror on the basis of race or gender in either a civil or criminal case is *per se* unconstitutional. **(D)** is incorrect because according to *Batson* a peremptory challenge of a juror on the basis of race or gender in either a civil or criminal case is *per se* unconstitutional.

28. **/D/** Procreation is a fundamental right that may not be interfered with absent a compelling governmental interest. Since most people are able to raise children without formal education in how to do so (like we have since the dawn of time), there is no compelling interest. **(A)** is incorrect because the legislature is not prohibiting entry into the state, rather only one very dangerous method of doing so. **(B)** is incorrect because apportionment in accordance with population growth is permissible. **(C)** is incorrect because in-state tuition may be subject to residency requirements.

29. **/A/** Sale of contraceptives to adults is a fundamental right, but not to minors. **(B)** is incorrect because it is in the "CAMPER" list of fundamental rights. **(C)** is incorrect because it is in the "CAMPER" list of fundamental rights. **(D)** is incorrect because it is in the "CAMPER" list of fundamental rights.

30. **/C/** This is the proper statement of the non-fundamental right test. **(A)** is incorrect because the law is not presumed invalid. **(B)** is incorrect

because it states an element of the strict scrutiny analysis. **(D)** is incorrect because it states an element of the strict scrutiny analysis.

31. **/C/** Although "for cause" employment is a protected property interest, due process is not required when the employee is "at will." Therefore, a blanket statement that employment is protected is inaccurate. **(A)** is incorrect because welfare benefits are a protected property interest. **(B)** is incorrect because public education is a protected property interest. **(D)** is incorrect because the right to engage in gainful employment is a protected liberty interest.

32. **/C/** The *goal* of the *Mathews* test is to determine the appropriate timing of due process, it is not a *factor* of the test. The test balances the importance of the individual interest + the risk of erroneous deprivation against the cost to the government + the administrative burden and availability of additional safeguards. **(A)** is an element of the *Mathews* test and thus an incorrect answer. **(B)** is an element of the *Mathews* test and thus an incorrect answer. **(D)** is an element of the *Mathews* test and thus an incorrect answer.

33. **/A/** Voting is a fundamental right, and thus infringement is evaluated under strict scrutiny. However, a reasonable non-discriminatory voting rule such as this will likely be upheld because is advances a compelling government interest (ascertaining that all those voting are of the proper age) and there is no less intrusive means available ("proof of age" requirement is narrowly tailored to accomplish the interest). **(B)** is not the best answer because it states the incorrect level

of scrutiny. Voting is a fundamental right and therefore subjected to strict scrutiny. **(C)** is not the best answer because the law is non-discriminatory, advances a compelling government interest, and is narrowly tailored; therefore it will likely be upheld. **(D)** is not the best answer because it states the incorrect level of scrutiny. Voting is a fundamental right and therefore subjected to strict scrutiny.

34. **/B/** Restrictions on the right to enter or leave the state leveled at a specific group is an unconstitutional restriction on the right to interstate travel. **(A)** is not the best answer because the fundamental right to "education" refers to school attendance. **(C)** is incorrect because the right to interstate travel is fundamental and therefore subject to strict scrutiny. **(D)** is not the best answer because an equal protection claim would be harder to prove than the clear restriction on the right to travel implicated by the facts.

35. **/C/** The right to refuse medical treatment is the fundamental right of all mentally competent adults. **(A)** is incorrect because the right to refuse medical treatment does not extend to assisted suicide. **(B)** is incorrect because the right to refuse medical treatment is only available to the person requiring the treatment, not a relative. **(D)** is incorrect because the right to refuse medical treatment is only available to the person requiring the treatment, not a relative.

36. **/B/** A flat restriction on the right to marry when the parties would otherwise be free to marry (i.e., they are not already married, they are adults) is unconstitutional. Requiring proof of legal marriage for the purpose of distributing state benefits is acceptable, so **(A)** is incorrect. Requiring proof of legal marriage for the purpose of distributing state benefits is acceptable, so **(C)** is incorrect. **(D)** is incorrect because it has been established as such by the Supreme Court.

37. **/A/** A challenge of racial discrimination would be a 14th Amendment equal protection challenge. **(B)** is incorrect because the 15th Amendment is applicable when the law deals with restricting the right to vote for everyone. **(C)** is incorrect because a challenge of racial discrimination would be a 14th Amendment equal protection challenge. **(D)** is incorrect because a challenge of racial discrimination would be a 14th Amendment equal protection challenge.

38. **/C/** The right to enter federal lands is a right of national citizenship that is protected by the 14th Amendment. **(A)** is not the best answer because there is just cause for not hiring – he is not refused employment on the basis of his state citizenship. **(B)** is incorrect because 14th Amendment Privileges or Immunities applies to people, not corporations. **(D)** is incorrect because only citizens of the United States are protected by the clause.

39. **/A/** Inverse condemnation refers to a regulation that restricts the use of property, thereby reducing its value and giving rise to a takings inquiry. **(B)** is incorrect because inverse condemnation is a principle related to the law of takings. **(C)** is incorrect because inverse condemnation is a principle related to the law of takings. **(D)** is incorrect because inverse condemnation is a principle related to the law of takings.

40. /C/ The two possible issues in any religious freedom issue are whether the law in question restricts an individual's right to free exercise of his or her religious beliefs, or whether the law creates excessive government entanglement or endorsement of an establishment of religion. The threshold question of whether the law pertains to "free exercise" or "establishment" must be answered before any other analyses can occur, therefore **(A)** is incorrect. The threshold question of whether the law pertains to "free exercise" or "establishment" must be answered before any other analyses can occur, therefore **(B)** is incorrect. The threshold question of whether the law pertains to "free exercise" or "establishment" must be answered before any other analyses can occur, therefore **(D)** is incorrect.

41. /B/ Unless there is evidence of intentional discrimination or the regulation interferes with another fundamental right, a generally applicable law is subject to lower scrutiny. **(A)** is not the best answer because it defines the strict scrutiny standard. **(C)** is incorrect because selective enforcement suggests an invalid law, not a valid one. **(D)** is not the best answer because preference of religion is an establishment clause analysis.

42. /D/ Sunday business closure laws have been permitted, although their purpose is partially religious in nature. **(A)** is an example of unconstitutional entanglement in religion. **(B)** is an example of unconstitutional entanglement in religion. **(C)** is an example of unconstitutional entanglement in religion.

43. /B/ The Contracts Clause (Article I, § 10 of the 14th Amendment) applies only to the states, not the federal government. **(C)** is incorrect because the Contracts Clause applies only to the states, not the federal government. **(D)** is incorrect because the Contracts Clause applies only to the states, not the federal government. **(A)** is not the best answer because the Contracts Clause does include public contracts.

44. /C/ The law does not sufficiently define what "lewd" speech is, making it unclear. **(A)** is incorrect because a law must first survive a facial attack before further analysis becomes necessary. **(B)** is incorrect because a law must first survive a facial attack before further analysis becomes necessary. **(D)** is not the best answer because "lewd" speech, similar to obscene speech, is probably not protected speech, and because free speech rights are more limited in the proximity of a school.

45. /D/ The term "appropriate" places no restrictions on the county overseer. Unfettered discretion in a licensing official makes a law restricting speech facially unconstitutional. **(A)** is incorrect because it assumes the commissioner has appropriate authority to deny the permit. **(B)** is incorrect because it assumes the commissioner has appropriate authority to deny the permit. **(C)** is not the best answer because the enabling act does not punish any particular kind of speech, so it cannot punish protected speech.

46. /C/ The test of a content neutral restriction on speech in public forums is that it must be narrowly tailored and leave open alternative channels of communication. II and III comprise the test for content neutral speech in private forums, so **(A)** is incorrect. II and III comprise the test for content neutral speech in private forums, so **(B)** is incorrect. II and III comprise the test for content neutral speech in private forums, so **(D)** is incorrect.

47. **/B/** This is the appropriate standard of proof in a defamation case involving a public official. **(A)** is incorrect because it describes the standard of proof when the suit involves a private figure regarding a matter of public concern. **(C)** is incorrect because it describes the standard of proof when the suit involves a private figure regarding a matter of private concern. **(D)** is not the best answer because it does not mention the requirement that the statement be proven false.

48. **/C/** Speech that is intended and likely to produce imminent unlawful conduct is unprotected speech. **(A)** is incorrect because it is political speech. **(B)** is not the best answer because only significantly misleading commercial speech is unprotected. **(D)** is not the best answer because obscene material in the home is protected.

49. **/A/** Seizure of printed materials to block their distribution must be preceded by a full adversary hearing and a judicial determination of obscenity. **(B)** is incorrect because seizure of printed materials to block distribution must be preceded by a full adversary hearing and a judicial determination of obscenity. **(C)** is incorrect because seizure of printed materials to block distribution must be preceded by a full adversary hearing and a judicial determination of obscenity. **(D)** is not the best answer because only printed obscene material in private homes is protected, not when it is in the public forum.

50. **/C/** Although radio and television media may be subject to equal time restrictions, the print media are not. **(A)** is incorrect because print media are not subject to "equal time" restrictions. **(B)** is incorrect because print media are not subject to "equal time" restrictions. **(D)** is not the best answer because a freedom of speech analysis does not completely answer the question without examining freedom of the press issues.

51. **/A/** Prior restraints on speech are presumed unconstitutional, but the presumption can be overcome if a number of elements are shown, including that the speech is unprotected, the prior restraint serves an important governmental interest, it is not vague or overbroad, etc. **(B)** is incorrect because political conduct is considered speech. **(C)** is incorrect because the restriction must be shown "necessary to promote a compelling government interest" to pass constitutional muster. **(D)** is incorrect because the restriction must be shown "necessary to promote a compelling government interest" to pass constitutional muster.

52. **/B/** Burning a voter registration card is conduct qualifying as protected political speech. **(A)** is incorrect, because political conduct is afforded the same protection as political speech. **(C)** is incorrect because burning a voter registration card is conduct qualifying as protected political speech. Unless the prohibition is necessary to promote a compelling governmental interest, the conduct may not be prohibited. **(D)** is wrong because it misstates the test: unless the prohibition is necessary to promote a compelling

governmental interest, the conduct
may not be prohibited.

53. /B/ A loyalty oath that only requires
the employee to uphold the
constitution and/or oppose the
violent overthrow of the
government is acceptable, but all
others are not. **(A)** is incorrect
because a loyalty oath that only
requires the employee to uphold the
constitution and/or oppose the
violent overthrow of the
government is acceptable, but all
others are not. **(C)** is incorrect
because a loyalty oath that only
requires the employee to uphold the
constitution and/or oppose the
violent overthrow of the
government is acceptable, but all
others are not. **(D)** is incorrect
because a loyalty oath that only
requires the employee to uphold the
constitution and/or oppose the
violent overthrow of the
government is acceptable, but all
others are not.

54. /C/ The First Amendment freedom of
association protection only allows
punishment for membership in a
particular group if all three of these
elements are shown. **(A)** is
incorrect because First Amendment
freedom of association protection
only allows punishment for
membership in a particular group if
all three of these elements are
shown. **(B)** is incorrect because
First Amendment freedom of
association protection only allows
punishment for membership in a
particular group if all three of these
elements are shown. **(D)** is
incorrect because First Amendment
freedom of association protection
only allows punishment for
membership in a particular group if
all three of these elements are
shown.

Constitutional Law
Practice Question Answer Rationales

55. /C/ This is the best answer, because
HardTime is performing a public
function, as punishment for crimes
is traditionally and exclusively
done by the state. Similar public
functions are running a primary
election, or a company town. **(A)**
is incorrect because although
private actors are generally not
state actors, this situation squarely
fits the public function exception.
(B) is incorrect because although
private actors are generally not
state actors, this situation squarely
fits the public function exception.
(D) is incorrect because although
state encouragement can be an
exception, the fixed contract price
actually encourages not using
expensive solitary confinement.

56. /A/ This is the best answer, because she
is now a resident and did not ask
for money damages. **(B)** is
incorrect because she was the right
P to bring the suit when she was
considered a nonresident. **(C)** is
incorrect because it ignores
mootness. This does not meet the
capable of repetition exception,
because as a senior she will never
again be a nonresident at Evergreen
– unlike *Roe*, who could get
pregnant again. **(D)** is incorrect
because amici are not parties to the
lawsuit, so their interests do not
sustain the case.

57. /A/ Strikes based solely on race or
gender are improper under *Batson*.
(B) is incorrect because peremptory
challenges on the basis of race and
gender are an exception to state
action since *Batson v. Kentucky*.
(C) is incorrect because racists can
be struck (the race of the juror was
not the sole reason for striking
him). **(D)** is incorrect because
racists can be struck, and Albert

can probably be struck for his religion.

58. /C/ This is the best answer. Mere licensing does not make a private actor a state actor. This is a close call and the closest case holding to the contrary was a racially discriminatory private school using state-supplied textbooks. **(A)** is incorrect because there is no standing problem with parents suing on behalf of their minor children. **(B)** is incorrect because the First Amendment does not apply to private actors such as St. Pious. **(D)** is incorrect because even if the First Amendment did apply, it must be a governmental interest, not the school's.

59. /A/ This is the best answer because the ex post facto clause prohibits the government from making something criminal after it has occurred. Prosecution could argue that it is an interpretation of the old law, but that is not a choice given. **(B)** is not the best answer because ex post facto is more clearly on point. **(C)** is incorrect because the law must be effective before the criminal act. **(D)** is nonsensical. Bills of Attainder are also prohibited, and this isn't one of them.

60. /A/ This is correct because there was no state action. Although it is a close call to a "symbiotic relationship," a majority held otherwise in *NCAA v. Tarkanian*. The university made the decision to fire him rather than suffer sanctions, but they could have withdrawn. **(B)** is incorrect because there is no state action. **(C)** is incorrect because there is no state action. **(D)** is incorrect because he was not in contract with NCAA, and couldn't have contracted them away under these facts.

61. /A/ This is a garden-variety delegation of legislative power. Just because it gives limited administrative power to the Executive, that doesn't invalidate the provision. **(B)** is incorrect because giving limited administrative power does not invalidate a delegation. **(C)** is not the best answer because although executing the law requires fixing a percentage, the focus of the question is on the provision of the law, not the Presidential power. **(D)** is incorrect because the facts do not suggest loss of property without due process of law.

62. /D/ This is the best answer because Congress has power to enforce the equal protection clause in section V of the 14th Amendment. The provision "under color of state law" will be interpreted as nearly equivalent to state action, which is met by a state employee, Dean, acting in his job. **(A)** is incorrect because the statute is valid exercise under the 14th Amendment, which will trump the 11th Amendment, and the state is not named. **(B)** is incorrect because Congress is not using the commerce clause, but the 14th Amendment. **(C)** is not the best answer, because the statute says "equal protection" in the language.

63. /C/ Although the Court properly struck the initial state law as a violation of the dormant commerce clause (also known as the negative implications doctrine) (C) is correct, because Congress can consent to state discrimination in commerce and actively legislate it. **(A)** is incorrect because there is no federal general welfare clause (only spending for the general welfare). **(B)** is incorrect because this clause is a limit on the states – not the federal government. **(D)** is incorrect because the State law was only unconstitutional because Congress had not yet authorized it.

64. **/A/** This is correct because a liberty interest is at stake and this is not the least restrictive means to serve the state's interest. **(B)** is incorrect because the right to a jury trial in civil cases has not been selectively incorporated against the states. **(C)** is incorrect because the state's police power may not be used in violation of due process. **(D)** is incorrect because similarly situated persons are treated the same under the law.

65. **/D/** As *Ferguson v. Skrupa* illustrates, to overturn an economic regulation pursuant to the Equal Protection Clause, the challenger (Stan) has the burden of proving that the law is not rationally related to a legitimate government interest. Equal protection analysis would be the same for the class of CPAs under these facts. (D) works best as Stan would win if no legitimate state interest is served. **(A)** states too high an interest and is not the best answer. **(B)** is incorrect because the burden is on the challenger under rational basis scrutiny. **(C)** is incorrect because the burden is on the challenger under rational basis scrutiny.

66. **/B/** As in *BMW* paint case, the court can strike "grossly excessive" punitive damages as a violation of substantive due process. **(A)** is incorrect because the court can strike "grossly excessive" punitive damages as a violation of substantive due process. **(C)** is incorrect because the court can strike "grossly excessive" punitive damages as a violation of substantive due process. **(D)** is

incorrect because the takings clause asks for just compensation for the state taking private property for public use, and judgments have never been seen as takings.

67. **/D/** This is the best answer given. States can regulate for health and safety purposes (police power), unless it unduly burdens the right to an abortion. The state may rationally authorize only physicians to perform abortions, despite credible evidence that it is not necessary. **(A)** is incorrect because while there is a strong argument for the law being unconstitutional *as applied*, it is *facially* valid. Facial attacks prevail if the law cannot be enforced against anyone. This law is valid against the women on the main island who are not unduly burdened by this requirement. **(B)** is incorrect because police power trumps private contracts. **(C)** is incorrect because there is no due process right to assistance in getting an abortion, and poverty is not a suspect class under equal protection (rational basis scrutiny).

68. **/D/** This works, because the supremacy clause voids inconsistent state laws, even against the state as employer if generally applicable. **(A)** is incorrect, because age is not a suspect class. The State could use age 65 as rationally related to the legitimate end of health, safety, or welfare. **(B)** is incorrect, as it states the rational basis scrutiny without accounting for the federal law. **(C)** is incorrect since *Garcia* over-ruled the "integral state function" language.

69. **/A/** This is the best answer because Congress has the power to regulate and dispose of federal property. The right/privilege comparison in **(B)** is incorrect (and is a common incorrect answer) because the

Necessary and Proper Clause does not itself confer any power, it is simply a means by which Congress can carry out its other enumerated powers. **(C)** is incorrect because there is no federal police power. **(D)** is not the best answer because the are no facts giving a jurisdictional hook to a substantial effect on interstate commerce.

70. **/A/** This is the best answer because this is exactly what the clause prohibits and there is no market participant exception to this clause. **(B)** is not the best answer, because the discrimination is against *residents*, not an entire industry, profession, or product. Also at issue is the market participant exception for states. **(C)** is not the best answer, because *residency* is not a suspect class. **(D)** is incorrect because the ex post facto clause restricts criminal punishment.

71. **/D/** This is the best answer because there are adequate state grounds clearly independent from the Constitution that resolve the issue. **(A)** is incorrect because the Court will not hear the case, even though the state court got the constitutional issue incorrect. **(B)** is incorrect because the Court will not hear the case, even though the state court got the constitutional issue incorrect. **(C)** is a good answer, but not the best. There are strong arguments that Gallows has no injury in fact, or that the case is moot, but adequate state grounds is on all fours.

72. **/B/** This is correct, because the Constitution enumerates specific powers of the President, including Commander-in-Chief. **(A)** is incorrect because it assumes the President has no inherent authority. **(C)** is incorrect because the it assumes inherent plenary power, which is too broad a description of the President's enumerated powers. **(D)** is incorrect because it assumes the President has no inherent authority.

73. **/A/** Easily, this is the best answer. The Commerce Clause is the workhorse for the federal government. **(B)** is incorrect because the necessary and proper clause only enhances other enumerated powers, and has no reach of its own. **(C)** is incorrect unless there are quartered soldiers involved. **(D)** is incorrect because there is no federal police power.

74. **/B/** This is the best answer because Lone Star encouraged and endorsed John's conduct. **(A)** is incorrect because John's actions are attributed to Lone Star due to their active encouragement. This is more egregious than *Flagg Bros.* authorizing the sale of delinquent tenant's personal property to pay for rent. **(C)** is incorrect because the question does not ask whether Lin may sue Lone Star in federal court for money damages, but if John is a state actor. **(D)** is not the best answer because the state action probably occurred when John entered the property, not when he cashed the check.

75. **/A/** This is the correct answer by process of elimination. The commitment is civil, not criminal, and due process has been satisfied. **(B)** is incorrect because he was given procedural due process at trial and the statute passes substantive due process by attempting to treat him. **(C)** is incorrect because the commitment is civil treatment, not criminal punishment. **(D)** is incorrect because the commitment is civil treatment, not criminal punishment.

76. **/A/** This is correct, because the Club's free speech rights were impinged by viewpoint discrimination when the school would not allow religious activity. Public schools are state actors, and the restriction was content specific – it did not allow religious activity. **(B)** is incorrect because religion is not a suspect class. **(C)** is incorrect because content specific restrictions must be a compelling interest. **(D)** is incorrect because there was no excessive entanglement (establishment clause) due to it being after school hours and asked for parental consent.

77. **/C/** This is the best answer because the law is a constitutional exercise of police power. Cites and states may regulate guns within reason to protect the public. **(A)** is incorrect because the Second Amendment restricts the federal government, not the states. **(B)** is incorrect because gun ownership is probably not a national citizenship right. **(D)** is incorrect because it authorizes the federal not the state government to enforce the 14th Amendment.

78. **/B/** This is correct, because Congress does have plenary power to regulate foreign commerce, which can be done by delegating authority to the Executive. **(A)** is incorrect because the President's foreign affairs power is largely delegated by Congress – not inherent. **(C)** is incorrect because the Contracts clause restricts states – not the federal government. **(D)** is incorrect because the order is valid. The contract expectancy is probably a valid property interest, but it can be limited.

79. **/C/** On double classification problems, the law must pass both (age, gender). **(C)** properly articulates the mid-tier scrutiny for gender under equal protection. The law would pass the age problem, if that was the only problem. **(A)** is incorrect because compelling is harder to prove than important and is only half the test. **(B)** is incorrect because the challenger has the burden under rational basis, and the law is not saved by passing the age problem alone. **(D)** is incorrect because narrowly tailored is too strict for mid-tier scrutiny.

80. **/A/** This is correct as a disguised way of announcing the police power of the state. **(B)** is not the best answer because the state may be prohibited from passing laws that are not reserved to the federal government. **(C)** is incorrect because poverty is not a suspect class. **(D)** is not the best answer, because the are no given conflicting federal laws and the law burdens in-state banks – not out-of-state banks.

81. **/C/** This is correct, because Congress can always attach strings to the receipt of federal funds and can reach areas outside the commerce clause with spending. **(A)** is incorrect because there is no federal police power. **(B)** is incorrect because equal protection issues are not raised by these facts. **(D)** is incorrect because privileges and immunities issues are not raised by these facts.

82. **/B/** This is the best answer, because judicial power is vested in one Supreme Court. **(A)** is incorrect because nowhere is the number nine specified. **(C)** is not true, Congress can eliminate any lower court. **(D)** is interesting, but no case law suggests a violation based on it.

83. **/D/** This is correct, because it is a state asserting the rights of its citizens –

rather than a right of its own, and probably a political question. The Supreme Court *may* hear any case were a state is a party. **(A)** is incorrect because it is a suit between two states. **(B)** is incorrect because it is a suit between two states. **(C)** is incorrect because it could be heard by concurrent jurisdiction in either Supreme or District Court as a case with a state as party.

84. **/A/** This is correct because the Courts defer to Congress if the intent of the tax is to produce revenue. **(B)** is not the best answer because the tax could be invalid for more than that one reason. **(C)** is incorrect because it incorrectly states the test. **(D)** is incorrect because the Courts defer to Congress if the intent of the tax is to produce revenue.

85. **/D/** This is correct because Flagg's exercise of its statutory right to sell Brook's property does not make Flagg a state actor. **(A)** is incorrect because there is no state action. **(B)** is incorrect because the Second Amendment right to bear arms restricts the federal government, not private actors. **(C)** is incorrect because nothing suggests that the state law conflicts with a federal scheme.

86. **/D/** John has no standing, because he has no injury. Federal taxpayers generally have no standing. **(A)** is incorrect because this is not punishing anyone. **(B)** might be true, but nobody has standing to challenge it. **(C)** is incorrect because the court won't hear the case.

87. **/B/** This is the best answer, because this is legislative punishment of a named person. **(A)** is incorrect because it is not necessarily criminal and does not make any act

a retroactive crime. **(C)** is not the best answer, because the law is clearly an unconstitutional bill of attainder and no due process analysis is required. **(D)** is incorrect because the law is clearly an unconstitutional bill of attainder (although a license to practice is a privilege that can be restricted in some cases).

88. **/A/** This is correct, because the state may take private property for public use, but must pay reasonable compensation. Inverse condemnation is restricting the use of the land to eliminate all reasonable use of the land. **(B)** is incorrect because the state may restrict use of the land under its police power to preserve the environment. **(C)** is incorrect because police power generally trumps contracts clause claims. **(D)** is incorrect because the state may restrict use of the land under its police power to preserve the environment.

89. **/A/** This is correct, because the court will not prevent the executive from closing down a foreign embassy. The political question doctrine applies to issues textually committed to another branch of government. **(B)** is incorrect because the Takings Clause refers to private property being taken for public use, not loss of business opportunities. **(C)** is incorrect because the Contracts Clause does not apply to the federal government, only to states. **(D)** is not the best answer, because (depending on the interpretation of the contract) Syscom only has to allege that it suffered, *or is threatened imminent* economic loss or that the U.S. breached the contract to satisfy the "injury in fact" requirement of standing.

90. /C/ This is correct, because the government cannot compel disclosure of membership – unless it could make that membership illegal. ROWG is a lawful group. **(A)** is incorrect because ROWG can assert association standing on behalf of its members – because its members could assert this privilege. **(B)** is incorrect because the right to be present does not mean they had the right to assert a privilege to resist membership disclosure. **(D)** is incorrect because it misstates the test—the government can only compel disclosure of the membership list if it could make membership illegal due to the illegal nature of the organization.

91. /B/ This is the best answer. The state is trying to prefer one religion over others by teaching a character from the Bible (analogous to requiring the teaching of creation with evolution). The court will likely find either no secular purpose and strike the law, or find both a secular and religious purpose and uphold the law. **(A)** is incorrect because this presents an establishment clause problem – not a free exercise problem. **(C)** is incorrect because this presents an establishment clause problem – not a free speech problem. **(D)** incorrectly states a part of free exercise analysis to an establishment problem.

92. /C/ This is the best answer, because the display must have a secular purpose (prong 1), and may have incidental, but not primary effect of advancing religion (prong 2). **(A)** is too broad of a rule, because the government may depict religious scenes if they pass the *Lemon* test. **(B)** states two factors that may influence the decisions, but the test is three prongs of *Lemon*. **(D)** is

incorrect because limited public forum is a category of free speech – not establishment analysis.

93. /A/ This is the best answer, because the case is not ripe yet. There is no imminent injury, because the FDA could chose to pass a constitutional regulation. **(B)** is incorrect because abstention restricts federal courts from interfering with state court prosecutions. **(C)** is incorrect because the FDA could chose to pass a constitutional regulation. **(D)** is incorrect, because the 11th Amendment is state sovereign immunity – not federal agency immunity.

94. /C/ The government may use prior restraints on protected free speech if a prompt judicial review finds an important governmental interest. **(A)** is incorrect because the government may use prior restraints on protected free speech if a prompt judicial review finds an important governmental interest. **(B)** is incorrect because the government may use prior restraints on protected free speech if a prompt judicial review finds an important governmental interest.. **(D)** misstates the rule for analyzing prior restraints.

95. /D/ This is the best choice because the Supreme Court is the final interpreter of the Constitution and Congress may not include an entire class of cases from all judicial review. **(A)** is incorrect because although Congress has substantial power to regulate the jurisdiction of the federal courts, this power may not be used to effectively overrule a Supreme Court decision. **(B)** is incorrect because although Congress has substantial power to regulate the jurisdiction of the federal courts, this power may not be used to effectively overrule a

Supreme Court decision. **(C)** is incorrect because Congress can regulate the *appellate* jurisdiction of the Supreme Court.

96. **/D/** This is the best answer. The Court will probably analyze the case using strict scrutiny after *Croson*, and the program will survive scrutiny because it is narrowly tailored to achieve a compelling interest – this particular school intentionally discriminated in the past in this particular area of admissions. **(A)** is incorrect because the Court has ruled that the use of racial classifications by school authorities to implement the desegregation of an intentionally segregated school system is not only constitutionally permissible, but mandated by the 14th Amendment. **(B)** is incorrect because the Court has ruled that the use of racial classifications by school authorities to implement the desegregation of an intentionally segregated school system is not only constitutionally permissible, but mandated by the 14th Amendment. **(C)** is not the best answer because of the "penalizes no particular group" language and also because it does not categorize this case as a remedy for past intentional discrimination.

97. **/A/** This is the best choice because the suit is really between North Pole and Vermont, and North Pole is barred by the 11th Amendment sovereign immunity from suing Vermont in federal court. NH has no separate sovereign interest, and has not alleged an injury in fact. **(B)** is incorrect because NH does not have a sovereign interest. NH could sue if the warm water was injuring the state's resources, but that was not given. **(C)** is incorrect because the Supreme Court has original jurisdiction to hear cases

where a state is a party. That jurisdiction is exclusive if between two states, and concurrent if not. **(D)** is incorrect because NH does not have a sovereign interest. NH could sue if the warm water was injuring the state's resources, but that was not given.

98. **/D/** This question tests whether the candidate can select the correct facts, rather than recall the words used in equal protection analysis. The facts are given, so the question does not test burdens of proof. (D) is correct because the facts fail to establish the existence of an intention to discriminate. **(A)** is incorrect because the existence of segregation due to residential patterns or other neutral classification does not, by itself, establish a violation of the Equal Protection Clause. Some intentional act by the state that created the segregation must be proven before a violation of the Equal Protection Clause will be found. **(B)** is incorrect the change in the racial composition of a school does not prove intentional discrimination by the government. **(C)** is incorrect because the fact that there are more tenured teachers in the white schools can be attributed to the individual choices of the teachers and does not show an intention to discriminate by the school board or the city.

99. **/A/** Mootness is the case brought too late. All three of the other answers are similar in that they address the case brought too early, which is ripeness. **(B)** is incorrect This is a strong argument, because the city may argue that since the developer is merely planning the project and has not yet begun to implement his plans, there is not yet a case or controversy. **(C)** is incorrect. While the developer may meet the

constitutional requirement for standing, he may not meet the prudential rules of standing because he has not yet shown how, when or where he plans to build. **(D)** is incorrect. Since the case will be better decided when the developer provides the specifics of his development, the town may argue that the issues are not ripe.

100./A/ The ordinance impairs the obligation of Tent to Lord on a contract in existence on its effective date. **(A)** is the best answer, even though the State would merely need to show reasonable action furthering a legitimate interest. Contracts Clause is a slightly better argument than Equal Protection. **(B)** is incorrect because the statute does not operate retroactively; it sets a future rent to a past benchmark. **(C)** is not the best answer because there is a rational basis for treating them differently. **(D)** is incorrect. The legislature passed the generally applicable law – no hearing necessary.

101./B/ This is correct because the injunction fails to sufficiently define what acts are prohibited. **(A)** is incorrect because there is no threat of imminent violence. **(C)** is not the best answer because freedom of religion alone does not invalidate a law attempting to prevent violence. **(D)** is incorrect because preemptive laws restricting assembly cannot be premised on future possibilities of "disturbance."

102./B/ This is correct because the federal government can regulate the use of airwaves to protect children. **(A)** is incorrect because there is no federal police power. **(C)** is incorrect because it is not bad enough to be obscene if there is

literary merit. **(D)** is incorrect because the speech was not "commercial speech" and states the incorrect rule.

103./D/ This is the best answer because the because the "audience veto" of unpopular speech can only be stopped when there is imminent danger of uncontrolled violence, and the police must use reasonable means to protect speaker's rights. The officer waited and allowed the speaker to continue until the situation was getting out of hand. **(A)** is incorrect because the police officer gave the speaker opportunity to be heard and only intervened when the situation was getting out of control. **(B)** is incorrect because the audience's right to assemble does not grant him his right to speak. **(C)** is incorrect because the police may not require obedience to an unconstitutional law.

104./D/ This is correct because the film may be protected if it has literary, artistic, political, or scientific merit. **(A)** is incorrect because selective prosecution is not a defense. **(B)** is incorrect because possession outside the home can be made illegal (criminal procedure may have a defense for unwitting possession). **(C)** is incorrect because possession outside the home can be made illegal (criminal procedure may have a defense for unwitting possession).

105./C/ This is the best answer because Dandruff and his employees are harmed by the statute and they have standing to contest the ordinance. **(A)** is incorrect because Dandruff alleges a sufficient injury for standing. **(B)** is not the best answer because association is neither the only right, nor the strongest right asserted. **(D)** is incorrect because it presents an issue on the merits – not for standing.

106./B/ This is correct, because the line is drawn at the home for personal use, not the theater. One may possess obscenity in the home. Remember, there is a distinction between "obscenity" and mere pornography. **(A)** is incorrect because the Constitution does protect aliens as persons. **(C)** is incorrect. A person is constitutionally protected to posses (not buy or sell) obscenity in the home. **(D)** is incorrect, because the State may prohibit obscenity, even for adults.

107./B/ This is obviously a free speech question. (B) is the best answer because it is an admission of his failure to discharge his duty as an attorney. **(A)** is weak, because the district attorney is a public figure and the comment is a public concern. **(C)** is incorrect because political activity is protected. **(D)** is incorrect because Statement II is an admission by the ADA that he had failed to discharge his duty, which is grounds for dismissal.

108./A/ The law in this area is not crystal clear, but (A) is the best answer. Like *Hialeah*, the law is subject to strict scrutiny if there is intentional discrimination. **(B)** is incorrect because "irrational as applied" is probably not a defense if the statute is rational as generally applied. **(C)** is incorrect because strict scrutiny would apply only to a generally applicable law if the state is found to be intentionally discriminating, like answer (A). **(D)** is not the best answer because it is not as clear that rational basis applies if the law places a direct burden on his religious practices and does not allow him to practice his religion at all.

109./C/ This is correct because the state must show a substantial relationship. **(A)** is incorrect because a state may not discriminate against a non-resident merely because it has a proprietary interest in the resource. **(B)** is incorrect because earning a living is a fundamental interest. This is distinct from recreational fishing. **(D)** is incorrect because the standard is not strict scrutiny.

110./D/ This is the best answer. An exception to the mootness doctrine is when an injury is repeatable yet will evade review. **(A)** is not the best answer. Mootness is the issue, but this case probably meets an exception. **(B)** in incorrect. Supreme Court has appellate jurisdiction over constitutional issues. **(C)** is not the best answer, because it does not acknowledge the mootness concern.

111./C/ This is the best answer because the application of the inspection rule creates an unnecessary burden on interstate commerce by requiring double inspection and, therefore, the rule is not the least restrictive means of protecting its citizens. **(A)** is incorrect because the state must use the least burdensome means to protect its citizens. **(B)** is incorrect because the federal government must approve restrictions on interstate commerce so state authority does not solve the problem. **(D)** is incorrect because it is the application of the rule that is unconstitutional, not discriminatory on its face.

112./C/ This is correct because executive orders (domestic policy) and executive agreements (foreign policy) invalidate inconsistent state law under the Supremacy Clause. **(A)** is incorrect because it does not pervasively interfere with state sovereignty and does serve an important national interest. **(B)** is incorrect because executive orders (domestic policy) and executive agreements (foreign policy) invalidate inconsistent state law under the Supremacy Clause. **(D)** is not the best answer. This is not a political question. A standard exists by which the court can decide the issue, and that standard is the Supremacy Clause.

113./A/ This is correct because the President has plenary power to pardon offenses against the U.S. (federal law) and set conditions of pardon, including conditions Congress did not establish by statute. **(B)** is incorrect because the President has plenary power to pardon offenses against the U.S.. **(C)** is because the President can pardon for nearly any reason, whether or not based in law. His pardon does not alter the Court's interpretation of the Constitution. **(D)** is probably incorrect because the death penalty was constitutional when the pardon was made, the conditions are enforceable after it was declared unconstitutional.

114./D/ All the answers are arguably plausible, but (D) is the clearest example that could be upheld. The House of Representatives is the body with authority to regulate marriages (traditionally a state function) in D.C. **(A)** is not the best answer because while it might be sustained under the War Power Act, it could be an Equal Protection violation. **(B)** is not the best answer because it could be an Equal Protection violation. **(C)** is not the best answer because it involves a complex use of executive branch power to establish foreign policy, which is not the most likely of these four options to be upheld.

115./C/ This is the best answer because the court actually did hear this case. **(A)** is incorrect because ownership of property within the US is not a political question. **(B)** is incorrect because the high court has original and exclusive jurisdiction over cases between two states. **(D)** is incorrect because the 11th Amendment bars suit by a person against a state in federal court.

116./B/ This is correct because the U.S. Supreme Court may only hear cases that have a federal question (constitutional or other federal law). While interesting issues may be more likely to be heard, the court must have jurisdiction to hear them. One way to the Court is after a final judgment from the state's highest court, but there must be a federal question. **(A)** is incorrect because the U.S. Supreme Court may only hear cases that have a federal question. **(C)** is incorrect because the U.S. Supreme Court may only hear cases that have a federal question. **(D)** is incorrect because the U.S. Supreme Court may only hear cases that have a federal question.

117./B/ This is correct, because the Abstention doctrine restricts federal court review of pending state court criminal prosecutions. **(A)** is incorrect because it hints at 11th Amendment sovereign immunity, and sovereign immunity neither applies to declaratory judgments nor protects municipalities. **(C)** is incorrect because it hints at 11th Amendment sovereign immunity, and sovereign immunity neither applies to declaratory judgments nor protects municipalities. **(D)** is incorrect, because the civil suit was filed after the criminal action began.

118./A/ This is the best answer, because the ALCU does not need standing if it convinces Spary to appeal. The other three answers are three ways to say the same thing. **(B)** is incorrect because the case is an advisory opinion if Spary's conviction is already vacated or overturned. **(C)** is incorrect because federal courts may not issue advisory opinions. **(D)** is incorrect because non-justiciable is another way of describing certain reasons, including advisory opinions and mootness, why the Court will not hear a case.

119./C/ This is the best answer assuming there is a federal question to provide jurisdiction. **(A)** is incorrect because sovereign immunity was waived when the state filed as P. **(B)** is incorrect because the state has standing if it alleges the money was taken fraudulently. **(D)** is incorrect because it applies to criminalizing an act after it occurred.

120./A/ This is the correct answer. Congress can overcome the state's immunity under the 14th Amendment if clearly expressed, so **(B)** is incorrect because Congress may waive 11th Amendment immunity pursuant to the 14th Amendment provided that it does so explicitly. **(C)** is a common incorrect answer on the MBE. **(D)** is incorrect because it is incomplete. Congress can lift states' immunity under the 11th Amendment pursuant to the Commerce Clause *only* if it does so explicitly. Also, the statute described in the facts appears to be enacted pursuant to the Fourteenth Amendment, not the Commerce Clause.

121./A/ This is the best answer because Congress may make criminal statutes and regulate instrumentalities of interstate commerce for non-economic ends. **(B)** is incorrect because there is no federal police power. **(C)** is a common incorrect answer on the MBE because integral state area is not a winning argument. **(D)** is incorrect because Congress may make criminal statutes and regulate instrumentalities of interstate commerce for non-economic ends.

122./A/ This is the best answer because the abstention doctrine restrains federal courts from addressing federal constitutional law until unsettled issues of state law have been resolved. If the state court interprets the law to prohibit fighting words only, then there is no reason to interpret the Constitution further. **(B)** is incorrect because the 11th Amendment does not apply to most declaratory judgments. **(C)** is the not the best answer because although the P needs associational standing to sue in federal court, the court will abstain in this case. **(D)** is incorrect because if the law effects speech, then the Constitution is implicated. Adding the commerce clause to that does nothing to the justiciability of the case.

123./A/ This is the best answer because the answer describes the mootness doctrine, which results in dismissal. **(B)** is not the best answer because it is arguable that Bill has an injury in fact if the law could be enforced, but it is a clear case under mootness. **(C)** is incorrect because the 11th Amendment does not bar declaratory judgments generally where the declaratory P is not seeking money damages. **(D)** is not the best answer because although the the statute is unconstitutional (*Griswold*) Bill's motivation for the suit and the total lack of prosecution of the statute would likely lead a judge to decide the case is moot in the interests of judicial economy.

124./B/ This is the best answer because there seem to be no strong challenges to the sentence. **(A)** is incorrect because this act was criminal long before Kris committed it and the punishment has not changed. **(C)** is incorrect because the class of violent crime convicts is not a suspect class. Rational basis scrutiny will be applied, and there will be a rational basis for distinguishing drug crimes from violent crimes. **(D)** is incorrect. The delegation was proper because it contained guidelines, and it did not violate separation of functions by restricting judges.

125./B/ This is correct because the Ex Post Facto clause prohibits punishing an act that was legal when it was committed and made illegal afterwards, or increases the punishment. The Supreme Court upheld a similar sentence in 1977. **(A)** is incorrect because aggravated murder was a death penalty crime before the act was committed. So, both the conviction and sentence are constitutional under the Ex Post Facto challenge. **(C)** is incorrect because aggravated murder was a death penalty crime before the act was committed. So, both the conviction and sentence are constitutional under the Ex Post Facto challenge. **(D)** is also incorrect because this is an appeal to the entire Constitution. In the given facts, was the fact that the law was drafted to survive current constitutional challenge. So if it doesn't violate Ex Post Facto, then it is valid. An argument, not raised

by the facts, could be legislative intent to influence a particular case.

126./B/ This is the best answer because the Supremacy Clause strikes state laws, including constitutions, that conflict with federal laws, including treaties. **(A)** is not the best answer because the restraint is invalid, whether or not it survives Equal Protection analysis. **(C)** is incorrect because the Richmond State Constitution is preempted by the treaty under the Supremacy Clause. **(D)** is not the best answer because the restraint is invalid, whether or not it survives Equal Protection analysis.

127./D/ This is the best answer because the state is preferring in-state colleges over out-of-state colleges and restricting interstate commerce. **(A)** is frequent incorrect answer on the MBE; the bald statement that something is "not a right" is almost never correct. **(B)** is not the best answer, because the state is not using the least restrictive means to achieve the objective. **(C)** is frequent incorrect answer on the MBE; remember there are two P&I clauses—this question involves Article IV Privileges and Immunities. One state is discriminating against another. 14th Amendment Privileges *or* Immunities involves rights of national citizenship (employment, interstate travel, etc.).

128./C/ This is the best answer. State discrimination on the basis of US citizenship is tested under strict scrutiny (unless it is participation in government). The requirement fails strict scrutiny. **(A)** is incorrect. The state cannot exercise the police power in a manner that violates the Equal Protection clause. **(B)** is incorrect because requiring U.S. citizenship is not a narrowly tailored way of ensuring barbers speak English. **(D)** is incorrect because this is not legislative punishment of a named person.

129./D/ This is the best answer because both (A) and (C) are effective. **(A)** is a specific protection against discrimination of out-of-staters, so it is effective. **(B)** is incorrect because this clause protects rights of national citizenship, like petitioning Congress. **(C)** protects against invidious discrimination, including interstate travel rights, so it is effective.

130./C/ This is correct because Article IV Privileges and Immunities is in play—discrimination by one state against citizens of other states. **(A)** is incorrect because abstention does not apply here, because the state law is unambiguous. **(B)** is not the best answer. The argument for denial of procedural due process is unsupported. **(D)** is incorrect, because it correctly states the original or trial jurisdiction of the US Supreme Court – not the federal district court.

131./B/ The Supreme Court may hear cases appealed from a state's highest court if a constitutional challenge is made, but the state court may not preclude review by applying a procedural rule inconsistently. **(A)** is not the best answer, because the inconsistent application of the rule makes (B) a stronger argument. **(C)** is incorrect because the constitutional issue is First Amendment, which cannot be foreclosed by inconsistent use of procedural rules. The D cannot get around the state high court requirement by asserting that the statute is facially invalid. **(D)** is incorrect because the constitutional issue is First Amendment, which

cannot be foreclosed by inconsistent use of procedural rules. The D cannot get around the state high court requirement by asserting that the statute is facially invalid.

132./A/ This is the best answer, as in *NY v. US*. Congress may not commandeer the legislative process of the states into implementing a federal program. **(B)** is incorrect because the 11th Amendment is state sovereign immunity, not federal. **(C)** is incorrect because the case is ripe, since the state would have to begin building immediately even though fines are five years away. **(D)** is incorrect because Congress may not commandeer the legislative process of the states into implementing a federal program.

133./B/ This is the best answer because state laws impairing a government contract need only have a rational basis. **(A)** is overbroad because the state's sovereignty is limited by the federal Constitution. **(C)** is incorrect because laws override equitable principles. **(D)** is incorrect because a state may generally repeal its own laws if there is a rational basis for doing so.

134./D/ The Executive (branch) must execute the laws of the U.S., and the AG has prosecutorial discretion. **(A)** is incorrect because the executive branch has prosecutorial discretion. **(B)** is incorrect because the executive branch has prosecutorial discretion. **(C)** is incorrect because only the President is immune for acts done in official capacity.

135./A/ Congress has broad ability to investigate for the purpose of finding facts to assist it in passing legislation. **(B)** is incorrect because

Congress' power to investigate extends to more than mere expenditures. **(C)** is incorrect because either house may inquire of the Executive Branch. **(D)** is incorrect because either house may inquire of the Executive Branch.

136./C/ This is correct because the legislation relates to commerce. **(A)** is incorrect because it is a restriction on government power, not a clause conferring power. **(B)** is incorrect because it is a restriction on government power, not a clause conferring power. **(D)** is not the best answer because no rights secured by the 14th Amendment are implicated in the facts given.

137./D/ This is the best answer. See *Church of Lukimi Babalu Aye*. Note that the burden of showing discrimination is on the challenger, but the answer does not state who proved to the court the interest and narrow tailoring. Even though the law affects religion, it is generally applicable. It will probably be reviewed under rational basis scrutiny, unless intentional discrimination is shown. **(A)** is incorrect because it assumes the government has the burden of proof. **(B)** is incorrect because it assumes the government has the burden of proof. **(C)** is incorrect because the organization will have to show more than just substantial interference.

138./A/ This is correct because it has been held that wild animals move in interstate commerce when they cross state lines, and are thus subject to the commerce power. **(B)** is generally an incorrect answer on the MBE; "necessary and proper only extends enumerated powers, it does not create new powers. **(C)** is generally an incorrect answer on

the MBE; the police power at the federal level is very limited—police power is much more expansive at the state level. **(D)** is a close incorrect answer. These animals were killed on private property. Occasionally, the examiners use a similar question involving wild animals on federal land. In that event, the federal property power is the correct answer.

139./D/ This is correct because states can subsidize local industries and "distribute government largess" to state residents. *Reeves v. Stake*. **(A)** is incorrect because it is not the type of protectionism that the clause seeks to prevent. **(B)** is incorrect because it is not the type of protectionism that the clause seeks to prevent. Other companies are free to lobby their own states to grant them subsidies. **(C)** is not the best answer because it purports to make an exception to standing and does not answer the merits.

140./D/ This is the best answer because a state can burden interstate commerce if it is the least restrictive means to a legitimate state interest. **(A)** is incorrect because the dormant commerce clause does not prevent a state from subsidizing in-state businesses. **(B)** is incorrect because states can discriminate against out-of-state citizens or residents if they are the peculiar source of evil, which here they are. **(C)** is the best incorrect answer because undue burden can be one state, it doesn't have to be a multi-state undue burden.

141./B/ This is correct because the Fifth Amendment Due Process Clause does have equal protection implications, which can support a challenge to "household" definitions. **(A)** is incorrect because no First Amendment rights are implicated – not even the right of association. **(C)** is incorrect because the Fourteenth Amendment does not apply to the Federal Government. **(D)** is incorrect because the Fourteenth Amendment does not apply to the Federal Government.

142./B/ In *Coleman v. Miller*, the Court held that the viability of an Amendment is a political question, which prevents a federal court from deciding issues related to viability of Amendments. **(A)** is not the best answer because the suit seeks to enjoin even the consideration of the issue. **(C)** is incorrect because state law does not control federal Constitutional Amendments. **(D)** is incorrect. In *Coleman v. Miller*, the Court held that the viability of an Amendment is a political question, which prevents a federal court from deciding issues related to viability of Amendments.

143./C/ This is the correct answer because the radio station is not a state actor, so the Constitution does not require it to play Jeb's ads. **(A)** hints at First Amendment doctrine, which does not apply to private parties. **(B)** hints at First Amendment doctrine, which does not apply to private parties. **(D)** hints at First Amendment doctrine, which does not apply to private parties.

144./B/ This is the best answer. It is arguably an undue burden on interstate commerce, just as requiring different size mud flaps on trucks. **(A)** is incorrect because the clause protects people not speedometers. **(C)** is not a good choice. The takings clause is separate from Due Process, and this law survives both analyses. **(D)** is flat incorrect. Bills of Attainder are legislative punishment of a named

individual. The question actually states that the legislature did not name anyone.

145./C/ This is correct because Congress is empowered to spend money for the general welfare of the U.S. This power is extremely broad and extends beyond the regulatory power of Congress. **(A)** is incorrect because spending power is not limited by commerce or other powers. **(B)** is incorrect because spending power is not limited by commerce or other powers. **(D)** is incorrect because spending power is not limited by commerce or other powers.

146./B/ **(B)** is the best answer, because there was no state action. The state passed a statute, which is not state action, and terminated her benefits. **(A)** is incorrect because it assumes state action and applies procedural due process analysis. **(C)** is incorrect because it assumes state action and applies procedural due process analysis. **(D)** is incorrect because it assumes state action and applies procedural due process analysis.

147./D/ This is the best answer because Congress has police power over the District of Columbia, and this statute is intended to protect the health and welfare of the citizens of the District. **(A)** is incorrect because the supremacy clause only strikes inconsistent state laws. **(B)** is incorrect because general welfare is a spending provision. **(C)** is not the best answer because it is arguable whether regulation of government property would allow this particular law.

148./A/ This is the best answer because it describes the classic "market participant exception" to the dormant commerce clause. Unlike the New Jersey law prohibiting out of state trash, this State purchases the cars and becomes a market participant creating the market with its own funds. **(B)** is incorrect because ignores the market participant exception to the dormant commerce clause. **(C)** is incorrect because ignores the market participant exception to the dormant commerce clause. **(D)** is incorrect because ignores the market participant exception to the dormant commerce clause.

149./B/ This is the correct answer. The tax power, separate from the power to regulate, is properly used when the dominant intent of a tax is to raise revenue and not merely a penalty. **(A)** is incorrect because the power to tax is independent from the power to regulate. **(C)** is incorrect because the test is whether the tax generates revenue, not significant or substantial revenue. **(D)** is incorrect because taxes are presumed not to be penalties, as long as the tax raises revenue.

150./A/ This is the best answer because the court will apply rational basis scrutiny as the law is not facially discriminatory. **(B)** is incorrect because discriminatory impact requires much higher percentages – nearly 100%. **(C)** is incorrect because discriminatory intent is very difficult to prove and the courts will weigh heavily against this finding. **(D)** is incorrect because the language comes from an exception to discrimination against alienage or citizenship.

151./A/ This is the best answer because cash grants to private colleges are generally upheld. **(B)** is incorrect because the state cannot violate the establishment clause by switching the power used, and the property clause is a federal power. **(C)** is

incorrect because there is no excessive entanglement in cashing a check, and the grant was part of a larger program. **(D)** is incorrect because there is no excessive entanglement in cashing a check, and the grant was part of a larger program.

152./C/ This is the best answer. The statute is a restriction on marriage, which must be narrowly tailored to promote a compelling governmental interest with no less restrictive means. The state can pursue child support in other ways. **(A)** is incorrect because a state may not constitutionally enact a law that violates due process. **(B)** is incorrect because a state may not constitutionally enact a law that violates due process. **(D)** is incorrect, because there is probably a rational basis for the distinction, and indigents and people with children are not a suspect class.

153./A/ This is the best answer because even if the court would strike down a law banning milk, the Court would not employ strict scrutiny. **(B)** is incorrect, because contraceptives are protected by strict scrutiny under substantive due process. **(C)** is not the best answer, because tires would probably be protected under the dormant commerce clause due to their necessity for interstate commerce. **(D)** is incorrect, because contraceptives are protected by strict scrutiny under substantive due process.

154./A/ This is the best answer because the state may terminate its entire welfare program. **(B)** is incorrect because it contemplates procedural due process issues. **(C)** is incorrect because the Court has not recognized this principle in the context of welfare benefits. **(D)** is incorrect because it contemplates procedural due process issues.

155./A/ Because race is at issue, strict scrutiny applies to this state actor. **(B)** is incorrect because the company is contracting to carry out a public function so it is a state actor. **(C)** is incorrect because one cannot boot strap a suspect class onto a quasi-suspect class. **(D)** is incorrect because the subject matter of the state function is not related to the company's employment practice.

156./B/ Funding does not make a nursing home a state actor; only if the home were fulfilling a governmental function would it be a state actor. **(A)** is incorrect because the home is not a state actor. **(C)** is incorrect because even if the home were a state actor, it would still need to prove that the hiring practice is to remedy past discrimination. The facts do not state such, only that the employees are members of a racial minority. **(D)** is incorrect because the home is not a state actor.

157./C/ Procedural due process is lacking for those employees who were fired. **(A)** is incorrect because arbitrary and capricious suggests that the state lacked any reason for the action. In this case, the state's reason is articulated. **(B)** is incorrect because a state agency is a state actor regardless of the function performed. **(D)** is incorrect because wealth is not a quasi-suspect class, and because it ignores the due process problem.

158./B/ Notice must be reasonably calculated under the circumstances to reach the person deprived of property. Actual notice is required. **(A)** is incorrect because posting a hearing date on the web site is not reasonably calculated to reach the person being deprived of the property. **(C)** is incorrect because there is no exception to the notice requirement because of necessity. **(D)** is incorrect because this level of proof applies in criminal trials only.

159./C/ Unless the professorship is tenured, the at-will law negates any property interest in a government job. **(A)** is incorrect because employment by itself is not a fundamental right. **(B)** is incorrect because unless the professorship is tenured, the at-will law negates any property interest in a government job. **(D)** is incorrect because the professor was fired for being "lazy", not for his protected expression.

160./B/ Desecrating the flag is protected speech, but the method of desecration may be prohibited because of the rational basis in protecting public safety. **(A)** is incorrect because there is no "right to be heard." People are free to ignore anyone they like. **(C)** is incorrect because the second amendment guarantees the right to ownership, but does not protect misuse. Also, a state law prohibiting flag desecration would be struck down because the first amendment applies to the states. **(D)** is incorrect because prior restraint is only one method of impermissible government interference with fundamental rights.

161./D/ A statute that prefers certain religions must be narrowly tailored to achieve a compelling secular end. This statute fails that test. **(A)** is not the best answer because a certain amount control over the press, particularly broadcast media, is constitutionally permissible. **(B)**

is not the best answer, because AAA does not have standing to assert such a claim, only one of the media that suffered from the Equal Protection violation. **(C)** is incorrect because the Free Exercise Clause prevents the prohibition of religious beliefs. AAA is not arguing that the statute interfered with its religious beliefs, only with its ability to disseminate information about those beliefs.

162./C/ Whether a party has standing depends on whether there is an injury in fact that is redressable by the court. The stations refused to broadcast the AAA segment based on the Texarkana statute, so AAA has been harmed by the state. **(A)** is not the best answer because even though the states may have been under no obligation to air the segment in the absence of the statute, the reason they cited for refusing to air it was the statute. **(B)** is incorrect because an organization does have standing if it is directly injured. **(D)** is not the best answer because a standing analysis relates to whether an injury has occurred. Whether the statute actually prohibits stations from broadcasting the segment is a substantive legal defense, not a standing argument.

163./A/ NAAPSTR has not been injured by the broadcast. Simply because an organization lobbies for a statute does not automatically confer standing on that organization in every conflict involving the statute. **(B)** is not the best answer because a private party may file suit based on a civil statute, provided that party has been injured. **(C)** is incorrect because NAAPSTR has not been injured and therefore lacks standing to sue. **(D)** is incorrect because NAAPSTR lacks standing and therefore the suit will never be

decided on its merits. Also, atheism is a religious belief and is thus protected by the First Amendment.

164./B/ The Eleventh Amendment grants states immunity from suits by citizens seeking money damages in federal courts. **(A)** is not the best answer because the suit is barred from federal court by the Eleventh Amendment (although if the case were brought in state court, the Supremacy Clause would apply and so the employees would likely prevail). **(C)** is incorrect because according to the facts, the employees are engaged in interstate commerce – guided tours in parks between two states. Also, the Eleventh Amendment bars a suit in federal court. **(D)** is incorrect because it is too generic. Giving guided tours is not a traditional state function, even if state parks management is. Also, the Eleventh Amendment bars a suit in federal court.

165./A/ Although the Allen Employees may have a claim under the federal act, there is no constitutional requirement that a state pay its employees the same wages as employees of other states, even if those employees perform similar functions. **(B)** is incorrect because Article IV Privileges and Immunities protects citizens of one state from discrimination based on citizenship in another state. It does not protect citizens of Allen from "discrimination" by the State of Allen. **(C)** is not the best answer because Equal Protection prevents one sovereign body from treating two similarly situated persons differently. It does not prevent the State of Allen from paying its own citizens a different wage than the State of Burns pays its own citizens. As long as the State of

Allen treats all of its own citizens the same, there is no Equal Protection violation. **(D)** is incorrect because the Eleventh Amendment grants states immunity from suit in federal court, not state court.

166./D/ Any citizen has standing to challenge a prior restraint on protected speech, despite no actual personal harm. An overbreadth challenge is appropriate here because the statute appears to prohibit protected speech as well as unprotected speech. **(A)** is not the best answer because Rebecca is not unmarried, and cannot be personally harmed by the statute. She therefore has no standing to challenge the statute, although the grounds cited would be valid. **(B)** is incorrect because Rebecca has no standing to challenge this statute because she has benefited from the statute, so she has no injury. **(C)** is not the best answer because Rebecca is not currently employed for wages, so she is not eligible for unemployment benefits. She therefore has no standing to challenge the statute because she cannot be injured by it.

167./B/ Since the veto has been overridden, the statute is valid law and trumps the treaty, which was signed earlier. **(A)** is not the best answer. Although (A) is true, it is not an argument for why the statute should prevail over the treaty, it is only an argument for why the veto override is successful. **(C)** is incorrect because there is no such constitutional provision that negates all treaties relating to trade. Had the treaty been signed after the passage of the statute, then the treaty would prevail. **(D)** is incorrect because it is not an argument for why the importation

should cease, but for why it should continue.

168./C/ Article I gives Congress plenary power to regulate the naturalization process. This means that Congress can restrict entitlements for the benefit of U.S. citizens, as this would encourage aliens to become citizens. **(A)** is not the best answer, because the reasoning is not specific enough. Congress does have this right, but there is another option that is more tailored to these facts. **(B)** is incorrect because as an alien, Hans is subject to certain restrictions of Congress. **(D)** is incorrect, because neither Hans nor any other alien has to prove citizenship to file a lawsuit in the United States, so long as personal and subject matter jurisdiction requirements are satisfied.

169./D/ The ordinance was an ex post facto law. Cheminol was not in violation of any bithium regulations until after the city passed the new lower standard. Cheminol was not given the opportunity to comply with the new standard. **(A)** is not the best answer because the right to regulate does not include the right to pass laws and issue punishments ex post facto. **(B)** is incorrect because Cheminol had no notice of the law it was accused of violating, it was an ex post facto law. **(C)** is incorrect because a bill of attainder is a law that punishes an individual without a hearing. Cheminol did have a hearing, and the law did not specifically target Cheminol, but was neutral.

170./B/ The city ordinance sets a higher standard of public safety than the federal law, and therefore does not violate the Supremacy Clause. The federal law simply provides a floor below which the state or city law may not go. A higher standard is acceptable. **(A)** is incorrect because if Congress had occupied the field then a city ordinance would be per se invalid. This would be a valid constitutional argument. **(C)** is not the best answer because improper legislative procedure would be a legitimate constitutional argument. **(D)** is not the best answer because individuals are protected by the takings clause from government actions that deprive them of use of their property (whether this is a successful takings argument is not the issue, the question calls for the least effective constitutional argument).

171./A/ Unlike the fine for the excessive bithium levels, which was ex post facto, Cheminol had a full and fair opportunity to be heard, had notice of the city's cleanup order, and refused to obey. Only then was Cheminol fined the additional $200,000. Therefore, the fine is enforceable. **(B)** is not the best answer because Cheminol did have a property interest – the cost of the cleanup – at stake. **(C)** is incorrect because unlike the fine for the excessive bithium levels, the cleanup order was prospective, and allowed time for Cheminol to comply. **(D)** is incorrect because nothing in the facts indicate that the cleanup order was in conflict with any federal law.

172./C/ The language of the executive agreement only places a burden on the President to create a positive image, not the press. **(A)** is incorrect because executive agreements do have the force of law, although to a lesser extent than treaties or statutes. **(B)** is not the best answer because while true, Congress does not need to override an executive agreement that is not unconstitutional. **(D)** is not the best answer because while the President does have broad discretion, he may not violate the Constitution. Therefore, this is not the best argument for the validity of the agreement.

173./B/ If (B) were true, it would mean that the gender distinction is substantially related to the achievement of an important governmental interest. This would make the distinction constitutionally permissible. **(A)** is not the best answer because it is too general. Collision statistics do not bear any substantial relation to a rule differentiating between men and women over 60 in vision and reflex testing. **(C)** is incorrect because Congress cannot pass a law that the Supreme Court has declared unconstitutional. Gender discrimination in state employment is illegal, and any Congressional edict to the contrary would be overturned. **(D)** is not the best answer because a general history of discrimination against women in those types of jobs does not bear any substantial relationship to a rule regarding eyesight and vision testing.

174./D/ The Takings Clause of the Fifth Amendment, applicable to states and cities via the Due Process Clause of the Fourteenth Amendment, prohibits the taking of private property for public use without just compensation. A regulation can amount to a taking if it deprives the owner of most or all economic use of the property. Chemlab, a chemical manufacturer, has no other use for the property and will have to move. **(A)** is incorrect. The Fifth Amendment applies to state and local bodies via the Due Process Clause of the Fourteenth Amendment. **(B)** is incorrect. Chemlab has been deprived of any economic use of its property and will have to incur great expense to move its factory. **(C)** is not the best answer, because the Takings Clause is applicable even if the law serves a compelling governmental interest (like building a public transportation system through a block of businesses). Just compensation must still be paid.

175./D/ The ordinance is both vague and overbroad. It is vague because ordinary persons must guess at what activities would "create a disturbance" or "hinder the work of city employees." It is overbroad because both protected and non-protected activities appear to be prohibited by the ordinance. **(A)** is incorrect because Equal Protection is not implicated; similarly situated individuals are not being treated differently. **(B)** is not the best answer because while the ordinance does interfere with the right to assembly, it does so only because it is vague and overbroad. Cities and states can regulate assembly and association, as long there is a compelling state interest, there is no attempt to suppress ideas, and there are no less restrictive means available. **(C)** is not the best answer because the government can put reasonable time, place, and manner restrictions on speech. The ordinance does not appear to restrict the content of speech, only the manner in which it is carried out.

176./A/ The U.S. Constitution always trumps state constitutions when they are in direct conflict. The employees have a strong argument under the U.S. Constitution that cannot be countered simply by saying that the Palray State Constitution provides more latitude to the city. **(B)** is incorrect because

the federal government has very little police power compared with the states. Also, although a state's police power is bound by federal laws, the question of which entity has *more* police power is not relevant. The important issue is whether the entity has used its police power in a constitutionally acceptable way. **(C)** is incorrect. A state constitution must always comport with the minimum protections provided by the U.S. Constitution. **(D)** is incorrect. 14th Amendment Privileges or Immunities deals with the rights of national citizenship, like the right to travel and vote.

177./C/ Article IV P&I prevents states from discriminating against residents from other states. **(A)** is not the best answer because the Congressional Tax and Spend power relates to federal taxing and spending, not state. **(B)** is incorrect because the Commerce Clause applies to the federal government, not the states. **(D)** is incorrect because Fourteenth Amendment Privileges or Immunities protects rights of national citizenship, like voting and interstate travel. No national right is implicated here.

178.D/ If a product is purchased outside a state but used in-state, a use tax is permissible. Also, business conducted within a state may be subject to net income, licensing, and occupational taxes. **(A)** is incorrect because a sales tax can be levied only by the state in which the purchase takes place. Maggie made her purchase in Waldorf, not Statler. **(B)** is incorrect because a sales tax is levied against the buyer, not the seller. **(C)** is incorrect because a sales tax can be levied only by the state in which the purchase takes place. Maggie made her purchase in Waldorf, not Statler.

179./A/ Sid's claim involves the right to pursue a livelihood, which is certainly fundamental. **(B)** is not the best answer because this argument supports Waldorf's claim that the nonresidents are the particular source of evil. Waldorf would have to make this claim to counter Sid's argument that the tax is discriminatory in violation of the Article IV Privileges and Immunities Clause. **(C)** is not the best answer because Congress gave express permission to Waldorf to impose this discriminatory tax, so if the Act is constitutional, then almost certainly the tax law is. **(D)** is not the best answer because it shows that Waldorf is using the least restrictive means available to solve the problem. Waldorf would have to make this claim to counter Sid's argument that the tax is discriminatory in violation of the Article IV Privileges and Immunities Clause.

180./B/ The President is only immune from civil suits regarding acts taken while in office, not before. Since the act in question took place two days prior to his inauguration, Executive Immunity does not apply. **(A)** is incorrect because the President is immune from civil suits for acts taken while in office, and in this case the acts in question took place two days prior to his inauguration. **(C)** is incorrect. The issue here is not impeachment, but whether the President has immunity from suit. **(D)** is not the best answer. There is no such rule for waiver of immunity when a crime is involved.

181./A/ Only a majority of House votes are necessary to impeach, but the Senate must convict by a 2/3 margin for the President to be removed. **(B)** is incorrect because the Senate must convict by a 2/3 vote to remove the President from office. Also, he must be impeached before he is removed. **(C)** is not the best answer because although the President has been impeached by a majority of the House, he cannot be removed without a 2/3 vote of the Senate. **(D)** is incorrect because President Brush has been impeached, although he has not been removed.

182./B/ Article II Section I prohibits Congress from limiting the pardon power of the Executive. **(A)** is not the best answer, because it is the job of the courts to interpret the constitution. This task has not been delegated to another branch of government, which is the definition of a political question. **(C)** is incorrect, because the reverse is actually true: the President can only pardon for federal crimes, not state crimes. **(D)** is incorrect. Article IV, Section III is the Federal Property Clause, which has absolutely nothing to do with this question.

183./D/ This scenario falls under the narrow exception carved out in *Shelly v. Kramer*. If a contract contains racially restrictive covenants, state action is present if a court enforces the contract. **(A)** is not the best answer. A place of public accommodation would include a business or school, but not a housing development. **(B)** is not the best answer, because although there are some licensing and zoning contact between Kelly and the state, these kinds of minor regulations do not constitute significant state involvement. **(C)** is incorrect. Housing is not a traditional public function.

184./C/ The Act completely eliminates the right of appeal, which is has been determined to be a Fifth Amendment due process right. **(A)** is not the best answer because federal courts established by Congress can be courts of limited jurisdiction (i.e., Bankruptcy, Admiralty, etc.). **(B)** is not the best answer because Congress does have the power under Article III to limit the jurisdiction of the Supreme Court. **(D)** is incorrect because the Act does not remove federal judges from office, it eliminates the office altogether, which is permissible.

185./B/ The initial fact pattern stated that the Labor and Employment Court had jurisdiction over claims made pursuant to the Labor and Employment Act. This claim is made pursuant to the Minimum Wage Act, over which the court has no jurisdiction. **(A)** is not the best answer because there is immediate harm threatened by the minimum wage increase, and the harm is not speculative. **(C)** is incorrect because the court has no jurisdiction. **(D)** is not the best answer because Dakola's minimum wage will increase as a result of the Supremacy Clause.

186./D/ Courts have been most lenient about public funds to religious schools at the college level. **(A)** is not the best answer because any aid to religious schools at levels lower than college has been almost totally prohibited. **(B)** is not the best answer because any aid to religious schools at levels lower than college has been almost totally prohibited. **(C)** is not the best answer because any aid to religious schools at levels lower than college has been almost totally prohibited.

187./C/ If Jerry is sincere in his belief, then the law as applied may be an violation of his right to religious free exercise. **(A)** is not the best answer because it is not specific enough. **(C)** is a better argument. **(B)** is not the best answer because the facts do not suggest that Jerry was trying to express or communicate any information. A freedom of religion argument is more appropriate. **(D)** is not the best answer because a neutral, generally applicable law that does not create any government approval, oversight, involvement, money, etc. does not offend the Establishment Clause.

188./D/ The First Amendment totally prohibits any restriction on religious beliefs. This would include a court examining a belief to determine if it is reasonably religious. Jerry's opinion regarding the sanctity of his beliefs is the only one that matters. **(A)** is not the best answer, because it speaks to Jerry's sincerity in his religious belief or is a pretext, which the court may examine. **(B)** is not the best answer because a court may examine the sincerity of a religious belief. **(C)** is incorrect because Jerry is only protected if he actually believes that the ritual is required as part of his faith.

189./C/ Since the state does not impose the tax on Tassen trucks, the tax favors in-state interests over foreign interests. **(A)** is incorrect because the *privilege* tax is not a tax on goods (the goods tax is separate). Therefore, a "goods in the stream of commerce" argument is inapplicable. Privilege taxes are permissible, even if the user does not stop in the state. **(B)** is not the best answer because the state has an interest in preserving its roads. This has a substantial nexus with taxing trucking, which is a direct cause of wear and tear to roads. **(D)** is not the best answer because preserving roads is a legitimate state interest.

190./A/ There is still the issue of whether the tax is fairly apportioned between actors from various states and in-state versus out-of-state actors. Illiho trucks are taxed 20 times higher than trucks from other states, regardless of any actual connection to the proportional amount of use of Tassen roads. **(B)** is incorrect. No federal law is indicated to raise a preemption issue. **(C)** is incorrect, there is still the constitutional issue of apportionment of the tax, even if the imposition of the tax is permissible. **(D)** is not the best answer, because the issue of undue burden on interstate commerce at the imposition of the privilege tax was resolved when the court determined the privilege tax to be valid. If the privilege tax imposed an undue burden on interstate commerce, it would have been struck down in its entirety.

191./B/ The Tassen goods tax is taxing some goods that are in the stream of commerce – there is no break in transit as the goods pass through the state. This is not permitted under the dormant (or negative) Commerce Clause. **(A)** is not the best answer because a tax imposed on goods in the stream of commerce *does* burden interstate commerce, even though it is not necessarily protectionist. **(C)** is incorrect because it is really just a restatement of (A). Just because a tax is not protectionist does not end a dormant Commerce Clause inquiry. The tax must also avoid undue burdens on interstate commerce. **(D)** is incorrect. The dormant Commerce Clause regulates the burden placed on interstate commerce, and not taxation of goods in general.

192./D/ Although there is no general federal police power, Congress does have police power over the District of Columbia, as enumerated in Article I. **(A)** is not the best answer because it is not specific enough. Congress has the power to do what is necessary and proper to carry out all of its enumerated powers. But the N&P Clause does not, in and of itself, justify any particular action without reference to an enumerated power. **(B)** is not the best answer because while true, it does nothing to explain why the law is constitutional. **(C)** is not the best answer because it is precisely the argument that was rejected by the Supreme Court when it struck down the federal Prevention of Violence Against Women Act.

193./C/ Poverty is a non-suspect class, which is afforded rational basis scrutiny under Equal Protection jurisprudence. The rational basis test states that the law must be rationally related to a legitimate governmental interest, and the P has the burden of proof. **(A)** is not the best answer, because it combines the rational basis test with intermediate scrutiny. Intermediate scrutiny states that the law must be substantially related to an important governmental purpose, and the state usually has the burden of proof. **(B)** is incorrect, because it confuses the rational basis test with strict scrutiny language, and because the proper test is rational basis. **(D)** is incorrect because it states the intermediate scrutiny test, which applies only to quasi-suspect classes of gender and illegitimacy. Poverty is a non-suspect class.

194./A/ A law that deprives a citizen of property prior to providing a meaningful opportunity to be heard must be carefully scrutinized as a potential procedural due process violation. **(B)** is not the best answer because there is no question that states may impose fines for civil traffic violations pursuant to their police powers. **(C)** is not the best answer because there is no indication that the state is discriminating based on classifications of persons, but instead is establishing different procedures based on the severity of the fine involved, which is acceptable. **(D)** is incorrect. No person's liberty is threatened, because no restraint of movement or activity is involved.

195./D/ One element of the *Mathews v. Eldredge* balancing test weighs the administrative burden and cost to the government of providing a pre-deprivation procedure. The facts in (D) support the state's use of a post-deprivation procedure. **(A)** is incorrect. It states the rational basis test, which is not a factor in the *Mathews v. Eldredge* balancing test. **(B)** is incorrect because this fact, if true, would support Joe's argument. One element of the *Mathews* test that weighs in favor of a pre-deprivation hearing is whether there is a high risk of erroneous deprivation. **(C)** is not the best answer because *Mathews* examines the individual interest at stake in each case. To some people, $50 might be a very important property interest, even if others rate it lower.

196./A/ This is the only argument that will carry any weight with a court trying to determine whether certain speech is obscene. If a film has artistic value according to a reasonable person standard, it will not be classified as obscene. **(B)** is not the best answer because even a film depicting "normal" sexual relations can be obscene if it appeals to prurient interest in sex. **(C)** is not the best answer because how widely a film is distributed has no bearing on an evaluation of its obscenity. The test is whether the film lacks social value, is patently offensive, and appeals to the prurient interest in sex. **(D)** is not the best answer because the question of whether materials have scientific, artistic, or literary merit is determined by a reasonable person standard, not a local standard. Also, even a film depicting "normal" sexual relations can be obscene if it appeals to prurient interest in sex.

197./C/ The unique test for evaluating a law restricting commercial speech is that the law serves a substantial government interest, directly advances that interest, and is narrowly tailored to achieve that interest. Only the wording of (C) matches the language of the test. **(A)** is incorrect because the determination of what is obscene is a complex standard that states and localities may determine themselves (with certain restrictions). **(B)** is not the best answer because the test refers to a "substantial" government interest, not a "compelling" government interest. **(D)** is not the best answer because the test is whether the law "directly advances" that interest, not whether it is "rationally related."

198./B/ In cases between two states where, as here, one state is suing on behalf of its citizens under the parens patriae doctrine, lower federal courts have concurrent jurisdiction with the Supreme Court. **(A)** is not the best answer because it misstates the law. Lower courts have concurrent jurisdiction when one state is a party, or when one state is suing on behalf of its citizens under the parens patriae doctrine. If the suit is between two or more states, and neither state is suing on behalf of its citizens, then the Supreme Court has mandatory original jurisdiction. **(C)** is incorrect because Alabraska is suing on behalf of its citizens under the parens patriae doctrine, therefore the case does not fall within the Supreme Court's mandatory jurisdiction. **(D)** is incorrect because it misstates the law. The Supreme Court *must* hear cases between two states, it does not have certiorari discretion.

199./D/ If Virginessee's regulations are less stringent than federal law, they are invalid. Any state law that provides less protection than a federal law on the same matter is preempted. **(A)** is incorrect because states are not required to have similar regulations to other states, even if they share a border. State laws must comport with federal law, not the laws of other states. **(B)** is not correct because legislation is not necessarily invalid when it is recklessly or thoughtlessly enacted. **(C)** is not the best answer because it is vague – just because the state regulations "do not comport" with the federal regulations does not mean that they are less stringent. If they are more stringent, they are valid.

200./A/ The President may remove administrative appointees, but only if they are not appointed for a fixed term. **(B)** is not the best answer because Congressional approval is not required for appointments to administrative agencies like the EPA. **(C)** is incorrect because the President may not dismiss appointees at will if they are appointed for a fixed term. **(D)** is incorrect. Although it is true that the President does not need Congressional approval, he may not remove officials who are appointed for a fixed term.

Index

CHAPTER 6

CRIMINAL LAW AND PROCEDURE

RIGOS BAR REVIEW SERIES

MULTISTATE BAR EXAM REVIEW (MBE)

CHAPTER 6

CRIMINAL LAW AND PROCEDURE

Table of Contents

I. MBE EXAM COVERAGE

A. Weight

Thirty-three of the 200 MBE objective multiple-choice questions test Criminal Law and Procedure. The testing is approximately 60% criminal law and 40% criminal procedure. Two, three, and four-string questions flowing from a common fact pattern are likely.

B. Emphasis

The MBE focuses on common law criminal law, some modern statutory modifications, and constitutional criminal procedure. If statutory law is tested, the statute will be provided. Since there is no federal criminal common law, the MBE focuses on the majority state common law principles, and will sometimes refer to the rules embodied in the Model Penal Code.

C. The Call of the Question

1. **Criminal Law:** The call will likely be phrased in one of five ways:

a. **Outcome:** Should D be found guilty of the crime(s) alleged, and what rule justifies that outcome?

b. **Best Argument:** What is the best argument for the prosecution/defense?

c. **Most Serious Crime:** Of the alternatives listed, what is the most serious crime of which the D could be convicted?

d. **Best Precedent:** Which precedent best resolves the issue raised by the facts?

e. **Which Crime:** Which of four fact patterns most closely describes a particular crime?

2. **Criminal Procedure:** Look for the following calls:

a. **Best Argument:** What is the best argument that the prosecution/defense could offer at trial regarding the validity of a search?

b. **Admissibility:** Is the evidence offered admissible at trial?

c. **Appeal:** Based on the facts of the investigation, arrest, and trial, are there grounds for an appeal by the defendant?

II. OVERVIEW: GENERAL PRINCIPLES OF CRIMINAL LAW

A. Requirements for Criminal Liability

The elements of a crime are stated in the definition of the crime. The prosecutor must prove each element beyond a reasonable doubt. These elements are:

1. Action (*Actus Reus*): The prosecutor must prove beyond a reasonable doubt that the D performed each act required by the crime.

2. Mental State (*Mens Rea*): The prosecutor must prove the D possessed the mental state required for that specific crime.

> **MBE Tip:** *Mens rea* and *actus reus* should be nearly concurrent. That is to say, the *mens rea* should be the impetus or activating factor of the *actus reus*. For example, if a D has the intent in his mind to commit larceny, and then three days later (with the intent no longer present) he takes the victim's money by mistake, the earlier *mens rea* will not join with the later *actus reus* to create criminal liability.

3. Result: The prosecutor must prove that the specified crime occurred.

4. Causation: The prosecutor must prove the D's actions caused the criminal result.

> **MBE Tip:** Many questions will set up facts where most elements of a crime are given, but one element is not discussed, not proven beyond a reasonable doubt, or not supported by competent evidence. Look for missing elements in the fact pattern. Don't skip this step or you'll be missing obvious correct responses.

B. *Actus Reus*

The D must have committed an unlawful act – *actus reus* or "guilty act." A person is not criminally liable for thoughts alone. The definition of a crime will specify what acts are required for a specific crime. There are two questions involving the criminal liability act requirement: (1) When is an act not an act for criminal law purposes?, and (2) When will a failure to act serve as a culpable act?

1. Nonvolitional Act: Although there may be an "act" in the ordinary sense of the word, it does not qualify as an *actus reus* for the purpose of assigning criminal liability to the actor if it is a nonvolitional act.

a. Rule: An involuntary act that was not controlled by the conscious will of the actor does not qualify as an "act" for criminal liability purposes.

b. Example: If a person is sleepwalking, unconscious, having an epileptic seizure, or is acting under physical force by another, his actions are nonvolitional.

c. Exception: If the person knew he had a defect that might make him a danger but failed to take reasonable precautions, he still may be culpable. For example, an epileptic would still be culpable if he failed to take his medication, but continued to drive knowing a seizure was likely and could put other drivers' lives in danger.

> **MBE Tip:** Watch for subtle issues of causation. If the *actus reus* did not cause the crime, the D is not culpable. Scrutinize the fact pattern for something that breaks the chain of causation. For example, if a parent hits a child, but the coroner lists the cause of death as cancer, the parent will not be convicted of homicide.

2. Omission/Failure to Act: The general rule is that there is no duty to act. If you see someone dying in the street, you have no *legal* duty to act although you may have a moral duty. However, a failure to act can be criminal in certain situations, described below. Keep in mind that the D must be physically able to perform the act if he is to be held liable for the failure.

a. Statute Specifies Failure to Act as *Actus Reus*: When a statute specifically criminalizes the omission (such as not filing one's income tax return or not paying a speeding ticket) then that failure to act will be the *actus reus* of the crime.

b. Legal Duty to Act: Sometimes there is a legal duty to act and D's failure to act substantially contributed to an illegal result. This legal duty can be based on a contract, a statute, a parental duty to a child, the creation of risk by D, or an undertaking.

(1) Contract: A person hired as a lifeguard has a duty by contract to save swimmers in the area. She must make an attempt to rescue if it is reasonable to do so.

(2) Statute: Some hospitals must, by statute, treat indigent patients. If employees of such a hospital knowingly turn away someone who then dies because of lack of treatment, they can be liable for homicide.

(3) Parent for a Child: A parent has a legal duty to care for a child. If a parent neglects to feed her child, seek medical attention, or protect her child from abuse, she can be held criminally liable for that omission.

(4) Creation of Risk: Danger created may impose a duty. At a party, Able pushed Betty into the pool as a joke. When he hears her shout, "Help! I can't swim," he now has the duty to rescue her.

(5) Undertaking: A D may have a duty to assist when she has already begun assisting, particularly if she does so to the victim's detriment or dissuades other potential rescuers.

> **MBE Tip:** Good Samaritan statutes, a recent development, also create a duty to act. Look for this kind of statute on the MBE, and note if there is a failure to act as the *actus reus*. Note that such statutes are entirely different from "Good Samaritan" statutes in the context of tort law.

C. *Mens Rea*

A D who committed the *actus reus* must also possess a specific, unlawful state of mind to be criminally liable. This state of mind is called the "culpable mental state," the "criminal intent," or the "*mens rea*" (guilty mind). The required mental state is included in the elements of the crime. For example, criminal liability for burglary requires that the D specifically intend to enter a dwelling at night to commit a crime therein.

1. Common Law: Under common law, a variety of terms and definitions may be used for the culpable state of mind, however the most common are specific intent, malice, recklessness, and absolute or strict liability. Proof of a more deliberate state of mind automatically proves the lesser states of mind.

a. Specific Intent: A "specific intent" *mens rea* requires the actor to actually intend to commit the act or cause the harm constituting the crime. If a crime requires specific intent, the prosecutor must prove that the D actually had the specific intent to commit the crime. Under common law, larceny, robbery, burglary, assault, attempt, and conspiracy require specific intent.

MBE Tip: Intent is another subtle area often tested. Learn the different levels of intent well and be able to distinguish crimes based on the presence or absence of intent.

---

b. Malice: This is ill will or the desire to harm another. Malice is defined as the intentional doing of a wrongful act without just cause or excuse, with an intent to inflict an injury or under circumstances such that the law will imply an evil intent. Under common law, malice is also evidenced by "extreme recklessness" which is an extreme indifference to the consequence of the act, also called a "depraved or wicked heart." For the common law crimes of arson or murder, the prosecutor must prove the D acted with malice or specific intent.

c. Recklessness: A person is reckless when she consciously disregards a substantial and unjustifiable risk. The disregard must be a substantial deviation from the conduct that a reasonable person would exercise in the same situation. Thus, recklessness is greater than ordinary negligence. The actor must act without regard for the harm that might occur generally, but need not specifically intend to cause the particular harm which occurred. The recklessness crimes are manslaughter, rape, and battery.

d. Criminal Negligence: This is a level of disregard, indifference, or neglect that is below the standard of recklessness. It involves an act that creates an unreasonable risk of harm (use the tort standard to decide what constitutes "unreasonable") and awareness of the risk by the D. It does not constitute criminal liability at common law, but most states and the Modal Penal Code have adopted it.

e. Absolute or Strict Liability: Proof of a particular state of mind is not necessary for a strict liability crime. The conduct alone is proscribed. Statutory rape is an absolute liability crime.

f. Vicarious Liability: When an employee or agent commits the *actus reus* and some culpability can be inferred to the employer or principal, vicarious criminal liability may arise. This is a principle similar to *respondeat superior* in tort law. However, because the intent does not arise directly from the employer's/principal's conduct, liability under this doctrine is always designated by statute and restricted to relatively minor punishments such as fines.

MBE Tip: Remember that a total lack of intent may be at issue in a particular question. Look for an unconscious actor. This would not qualify because intention requires that the act be voluntary.

---

2. Model Penal Code (MPC) States of Mind: In an effort to simplify and define the common law mental states, the MPC defines the mental states as "purposely," "knowingly," "recklessly," "negligently," and "strict liability." The state of mind is included in the definition of each crime and each mental state is clearly defined.

a. Purposely: A person acts purposely when it is his conscious intent to perform the act and cause the result constituting the crime.

b. Knowingly: A person acts knowingly when he is aware that it is practically certain that his act will cause the result constituting the crime.

c. Recklessly: A person acts recklessly when he consciously disregards a substantial and unjustifiable risk that his act will cause a result which constitutes a crime. His disregard of the risk must be a gross deviation from what a reasonable person would do under the circumstances.

d. Negligently: A person acts negligently when he should be aware of a substantial and unjustifiable risk that his act will cause a result which constitutes a crime. Again, his disregard of the risk must be a gross deviation from what a reasonable person would do under the circumstances. Criminal negligence implies gross negligence as a substantial departure from the ordinary standard of due care.

> **MBE Tip:** Some states have adopted statutes making "criminal negligence" sufficient *mens rea* for crimes such as vehicular homicide or child neglect. On the MBE, look for a statute that refers to this *mens rea*. Absent such a statute, assume that criminal negligence is insufficient to create criminal liability.

e. Strict Liability: Essentially the same as under the common law.

> **MBE Tip:** *Mens rea* can be confusing. For example, it is counterintuitive to think of "recklessness" as a "mental state" when it sounds like D was not thinking. Have a thorough understanding of all levels of *mens rea* and remember that the statute or common law definition of the crime will indicate the *mens rea* for you.

3. "Mistakes of Fact" May Negate *Mens Rea*: A person's misunderstanding of the circumstances may prevent the prosecutor from proving that the person possessed the state of mind required for the particular crime. If the crime requires specific intent, an honest mistake will negate that the D possessed specific intent. If the crime requires malice or recklessness, the mistake must be both honest and reasonable.

4. "Mistakes of Law" Do Not Excuse Except in Certain Circumstances: A person's ignorance of the law is generally not a defense. Anyone could say they did not know the law and escape liability. There are three exceptions where ignorance of the law could be a defense.

a. Offense Requires Knowledge of the Law:

(1) Rule: The statute must define the crime so that "knowledge" is a required element that the prosecutor must prove. In this circumstance, mistake is not an affirmative defense raised by the defendant, instead the burden is on the prosecutor to prove knowledge beyond a reasonable doubt.

(2) Example: An anti-pollution statute might specify that the D "willfully fail to report levels of contaminants." "Willfully" indicates that the D must have knowledge of the requirement and fail to report. To avoid ignorance as a defense, the statute will often require only constructive knowledge, not actual knowledge.

b. Mistake of Law Causes a Mistake of Fact:

(1) Rule: If a person mistakenly thinks that the law provides him with rights, it may negate the *mens rea* in some cases. Again, this is not an affirmative defense, but an element that the prosecutor must prove for which the defendant can raise a reasonable doubt.

(2) Example: D's car has been lawfully repossessed, but he thinks it is stolen. He finds it and takes it back. His mistaken belief that the car is lawfully his may negate the *mens rea* for theft.

c. Misinformation From a Public Official:
If a person tries to learn the law by consulting a public official (IRS agent, Department of Land Use inspector, etc.), and that official misinforms the D, this is a defense under the MPC or statutory law but not under the common law. Notice that this exception does constitute an affirmative defense rather than negating any element of the crime.

> **MBE Tip:** Under the common law, mistake is not a "defense" strictly speaking. Rather, it negates the required *mens rea*, causing the prosecution to fail in its task of proving all the elements of a crime.

5. Transferred Intent: Mental states are subject to transferred intent. A defendant cannot avoid criminal liability by claiming that she intended to commit a different crime, or intended to commit the same crime against another subject. Therefore, intent will often transfer between similar crimes/victims, unless there is a radical break in the chain of foreseeability.

a. Between Victims:
Intent will transfer between victims. If D intends to shoot Bill, but hit Sam, D's intent will transfer between victims and D will be liable for the intentional shooting of Sam.

b. Between Crimes:
Intent will also transfer between crimes. If the D breaks into a house intending to commit a robbery, but no one is home so he commits larceny instead, intent will transfer.

> **MBE Tip:** Don't try to stretch transferred intent too far. For example, if A throws a rock into a vacant building intending to break a window (intent to do Malicious Mischief) and unbeknownst to him B is inside the building and is hit (Assault), intent does not transfer. A will not be convicted of intentionally assaulting B although he could be found criminally negligent.

D. Causation

The prosecutor must prove beyond a reasonable doubt that the D's actions caused the result required for the particular crime. For example, if the crime charged is murder, someone must have been killed and the D's actions were both the actual and the proximate cause of the resulting death.

1. Actual Cause: To prove actual cause or cause-in-fact, the prosecutor must prove that "but for" the D's actions the harm would not have occurred or that the D's actions were a substantial factor in causing the harm.

a. "But For" Test: "But for" the D's actions, harm to the P would not have occurred. Under the "but for" test, the D is considered the sole cause of the harm.

b. Substantial Factor Test: Even if another event or actor contributed to the harm, the D is still liable if his actions were a substantial factor in causing the harm. If the D's actions were not enough by themselves to cause the harm, but when combined with other forces would produce the harm, the D's actions are considered the cause-in-fact.

MBE Tip: If the harm would have resulted anyway and the D's actions hasten the harm, the D is liable. For example, killing a terminally ill person is still murder.

---

2. Proximate Cause:

a. Rule: The D's actions were the proximate cause of the harm if the harm was the natural and probable result of the D's actions. Generally, if the D's actions were the actual cause of the harm, the actions will also be the proximate cause of the harm.

b. Exception: Even though the D's actions might have been the actual cause of the harm, there are some results that are so far removed from the D's actions by time, place, or circumstances that it would be unjust to hold the D criminally liable. There may be no proximate cause if:

(1) Intervening Cause: The ultimate harm was set in motion by the D's actions but the harm occurred at the end of an unforeseeable chain of events (*"intervening" cause*); or

(2) Superseding Cause: The ultimate harm was the result of an unforeseeable, independent event beyond the D's control (*"superseding" cause*).

MBE Tip: On the MBE, be wary of questions that imply intervening or superseding causes. Rarely will these help the D escape liability, unless the intervening event is wholly independent of the criminal act (example: D poisons V without V's knowledge and V is immediately killed in an unrelated auto accident), or there is some unforeseeable criminal behavior by a third party (example: D scratches V with a fingernail and treating physician recklessly infects V with a deadly disease).

E. Accomplice Liability

One D can be convicted of the crime committed by another D under the theory of accomplice liability if the D aids, abets, facilitates, or encourages the perpetrator in the commission of the crime. If the facts indicate that a D is liable as an accomplice, he is liable for the *underlying crime* committed.

MBE Tip: This is a common point of confusion. Being an accomplice is *not* a separate crime, but merely a means of prosecuting helpers. For example, if a D is an accomplice to a burglary, he himself is charged with burglary. If an option suggests that a D can be "charged with the crime of being an accomplice" or something to that effect, discard it.

---

1. Complicity: This is general agreement and cooperation in the crime.

> **MBE Tip:** Complicity frequently involves the companion crimes of attempt, solicitation, and conspiracy. MBE string questions will often involve multiple issues among these three crimes. If complicity is suggested in the fact pattern, remember to look for an accomplice trying to withdraw from complicity before the crime occurs. An act of warning or prevention of the crime is also necessary for the accomplice to avoid liability.

2. Intent: The majority rule under the common law requires that the D specifically intend for the crime to be committed.

3. Assistance: The D must actually assist in the crime by actual participation (getaway driver, lookout, etc.) or by encouraging the perpetrator to commit the crime.

4. Victim: A person cannot be convicted of a crime if the person is in the class of persons the statute means to protect. For instance, an underage person cannot be convicted of statutory rape even if that person aided, abetted, facilitated, or encouraged the perpetrator to commit statutory rape. She is in the class of persons the law means to protect, thus she is a victim, not an accomplice.

5. Conviction Not Dependent on Fate of Others: Again, the D will be charged, tried and convicted of the crime committed by the perpetrator, not with the crime of "complicity" or "accomplice." The complicit D can be convicted even if the primary perpetrator is not convicted.

> **MBE Tip:** The MBE will often test the "act" requirement for accomplice liability. Remember: a silent onlooker, even one with criminal intent, is not enough for accomplice liability. Verbal encouragement, however, is usually enough to fulfill the act requirement.

F. Merger – Lesser Included Crimes

All crimes whose elements are included in a greater crime are implicitly charged by charging the crime with the greater degree. For example, robbery is larceny plus additional elements. A D cannot be charged with both larceny and robbery. An exception is for burglary. The underlying felony must be charged separately.

> **STOP!** Go to page 371 and work Learning Questions 1 to 10.

III. DEFENSES

A. Insanity

The insanity defenses measure whether the D was mentally ill at the time of the crime. The D raises the issue of insanity and must either produce a "scintilla" of evidence or raise a "reasonable doubt" as to his sanity (depending on the jurisdiction). The D need not plead "guilty" to raise this defense. Again, depending on the jurisdiction, the D will either have to prove insanity by a preponderance, or the prosecutor will have to prove sanity beyond a reasonable doubt.

1. *M'Naghten* Test: To establish the defense of insanity, the *M'Naghten* test requires that the D prove he was unable to comprehend the act, or unable to tell right from wrong as a result of mental disease or defect at the time of the offense. The defense of insanity must be established by a preponderance of the evidence. This defense puts the mental health of the D at issue, which waives the doctor-patient privilege.

2. Irresistible Impulse: Some states, including half of those that use *M'Naghten*, use the "irresistible impulse" insanity defense if the D was unable to control his actions. The test provides that even if the D did know what he was doing was wrong, he was unable to control his actions to conform to what he knew was right.

3. MPC Substantial Capacity: This is a lesser standard than *M'Naghten*; it requires the D to be totally incapable of realizing what he was doing, knowing if it was right or wrong, or being able to control his actions. The substantial capacity test will find the D not guilty by reason of insanity if he was substantially incapable of knowing right from wrong, or incapable of controlling his actions (essentially combining the *M'Naghten* and irresistible impulse tests).

4. Durham Test: This is also called the "Product Rule." When the unlawful act was the product of a mental defect/disease, then the D will not be held criminally liable. This is the most expansive of the insanity tests, and therefore the most criticized and least used.

MBE Tip: It is likely that in law school you learned the test for your particular state's jurisdiction, so make sure you are aware of the MPC substantial capacity test. If the MBE question does not specifically name the *M'Naghten* or Irresistible Impulse test as the governing law, assume the MPC Substantial Capacity test applies.

---

5. Competence to Stand Trial: Competence to stand trial, in contrast, measures the mental illness at the time of trial. If a person is unable to understand the proceedings or assist in his defense, it jeopardizes his constitutional right to a fair trial.

B. Intoxication

No act committed by a person while in a state of voluntary intoxication shall be deemed less criminal by reason of his condition. However, if the crime requires specific intent, it is a defense if the D can prove he was so intoxicated that he was unable to form the required specific intent. Voluntary intoxication will never be a valid defense to a malice or recklessness crime because the act of becoming intoxicated itself shows disregard for consequences and thus malice or recklessness.

MBE Tip: Involuntary intoxication may be a valid defense to all crimes as it may be considered equivalent to temporary mental illness. However, intoxication is unlikely to be a successful defense on the MBE. If involuntary intoxication is an option, be wary. Was the D truly not responsible for his/her intoxicated state?

C. Infancy

The level of intent imputed to children, and the venue (juvenile v. adult) court depends primarily upon the age of the child.

1. Under Seven: Children under the age of seven years are conclusively presumed to be incapable of forming the intent to commit a crime.

2. Seven to Thirteen: Children over seven and under fourteen years old are presumed to be incapable of intending a crime, because of insufficient capacity to understand the act was wrong. The prosecutor must submit clear and convincing proof that the child had sufficient capacity to understand the act (or neglect), and to know that it was wrong.

3. Fourteen to Eighteen: There is no presumption of incapacity for children fourteen to eighteen years old. However, all children under 18 are tried in juvenile court. An exception to this is if the crime is a serious violent offense and the D is 16 or 17.

D. Duress

If a D was threatened with harm to himself or another, and that threat compelled him to commit a crime, the D may raise the defense of duress in certain circumstances.

1. When Available: Duress is available as a defense if the person was threatened with imminent death or great physical harm to himself, a member of his family, or others and he reasonably believed that he had to commit the crime to avoid the threatened harm outlined below.

2. When Not Available:

a. Only Property Threatened: Threats against property are not sufficient to raise the defense of duress.

b. Murder or Manslaughter: Duress also is not an available if the crime charged is murder or manslaughter.

c. D Created Situation: The D cannot intentionally or recklessly place himself in a situation where it was probable he would be subject to duress, and then claim the defense.

MBE Tip: Duress is frequently tested on the MBE. The fact pattern will likely describe a very sympathetic D, who was placed in an intolerable situation of duress. This will tempt you toward acquittal as your response. However, remember that if murder or manslaughter is charged no amount of duress, however dire, will exonerate the D.

E. Entrapment

Entrapment is a defense when the idea of the crime originated with the police and the D would not have committed the crime in the absence of the enticement of the police. The defense of entrapment is not established by a showing that the law enforcement officials merely afforded the actor an opportunity to commit a crime; there must be inducement present.

MBE Tip: On the MBE, an answer which suggests that D is acquitted because of the defense of entrapment is almost always wrong. The fact pattern must state that the D was not predisposed to commit the criminal act and the idea to engage in such an unlawful act originated from the law enforcement officer. Only in those rare instances will the answer concerning a defense of entrapment be the right one.

F. Defense of Self

1. Reasonable Force: A person who reasonably believes he is being attacked can use reasonable force to protect himself. The person must reasonably believe his actions were necessary to protect himself from an imminent, unlawful attack.

  a. Must Be Imminent: The threat of future harm is not sufficient to justify the present use of force.

  b. Reasonable Force: The person may use only the amount of force he believes is reasonably necessary to prevent harm to himself, i.e., force proportional to the attack. Deadly force may be used if deadly force is threatened or if deadly force is necessary to defend oneself.

MBE Tip: Use of deadly force resulting in homicide is heavily tested. The defense will be unsuccessful if the deadly force is used in defense of property.

---

2. Honest Mistake: An honest, reasonable mistake as to the facts of a situation may be sufficient for self defense to be available. If the D makes an honest but *un*reasonable mistake in the amount of force necessary to defend himself, self defense is not available. However, it may reduce the charge from murder to manslaughter as the mistake prevented the formation of the required mental state.

3. Aggressors: Self defense is sometimes available to a first aggressor, but this depends primarily on the subsequent actions of the first aggressor and the victim.

  a. Non-Deadly v. Deadly Force: If an aggressor uses non-deadly force, he can claim self defense if the victim responds with deadly force. However, if the aggressor uses deadly force in the first place, he cannot claim self defense.

  b. Withdrawal By First Aggressor: If the aggressor withdraws from his aggression and communicates that to the victim, he regains his right to self defense. In this circumstance, the victim can no longer claim self defense.

4. Retreat Rule: Under the MPC, the victim must first try to retreat if it is safely possible to do so, before she is entitled to use deadly force. The common law has no requirement to retreat.

MBE Tip: Retreat is another tricky area in that the MPC differs from the common law. If the fact pattern does not mention the MPC, assume no duty to retreat.

G. Defense of Others

1. Others: Under common law, there needed to be a relationship between the victim and the defender for the defender to use force to protect the victim. In the modern view, the victim can be a total stranger unless limited by statute.

2. Reasonable Force: This standard is essentially the same as for self defense.

a. Majority View: The majority view determines whether the amount of force was appropriate according to the defender's belief as to the amount of force necessary to protect the victim.

b. Minority View: The minority view, in contrast, would allow the defender to use only as much force as the victim himself could use. Thus, if the seeming victim was the original aggressor who had used deadly force, the defender cannot use force because the aggressor had forfeited her right to self defense. If the victim is being lawfully arrested, neither victim nor defender are entitled to use force against the police officer.

H. Defense of Property

Deadly force cannot be used to protect property. Reasonable non-deadly force can be used to defend property. If a threat to property also threatens to harm people rules for defense of self and others apply.

I. Fleeing Felon

If D is fleeing from the scene of a felony, a private citizen can use deadly force if the suspected felon poses an immediate threat. Note that the citizen/D must know and be correct in the knowledge that the D is a fleeing felon.

MBE Tip: Insanity, self defense, defense of property and fleeing felon are frequently tested defenses. You must understand the intricacies of when these defenses are available, and under what circumstances they will likely succeed/fail.

STOP! Go to page 372 and work Learning Questions 11 to 20.

IV. INCHOATE OFFENSES

A. Solicitation

Common law solicitation consists of encouraging another person to commit a felony or serious misdemeanor with the intent that the other person commit the crime.

1. Encouragement: The encouragement may consist of only words either written or spoken. Many different terms have been used besides "encourage:" If you "advise," "command," "convince," "counsel," "entice," "entreat," "incite," "induce," or "urge" another to commit a crime, you are guilty of solicitation.

2. Felony or Serious Misdemeanor: Solicitation can only be charged if the crime solicited is any felony or a serious misdemeanor that breaches the peace or obstructs justice. A parking violation will not suffice.

3. Intent: The state of mind required for solicitation is specific intent even if the state of mind for the underlying crime is only malice or recklessness.

4. Completion: The crime of solicitation is complete as soon as the other person hears the solicitation, even if that person immediately rejects the offer.

5. Protected Class: As with accomplice liability, a person who is in the class of persons to be protected cannot be convicted of solicitation. The prime example is statutory rape.

6. Merger: If the other person agrees to commit the crime, a conspiracy is formed and the solicitation merges into conspiracy and/or into the crime, if the crime is in fact committed. Thus, the solicitor becomes an accomplice to the crime.

7. Renunication: Under the MPC, if the solicitor immediately renounces or disavows the solicitation (for reasons other than fear of criminal prosecution), the solicitor may have a defense. However, this is rare.

> **MBE Tip:** Keep solicitation in mind when reading the next two subsections: there is some overlap between solicitation, conspiracy, and attempt. Bare solicitation is not automatically attempt, but solicitation plus acts in furtherance implicate attempt as well as conspiracy. Remember that a solicitor can be charged with solicitation even if the solicitee immediately refuses.

B. Conspiracy

Common law conspiracy is an agreement, spoken or unspoken, between two or more persons to commit an unlawful act. Most jurisdictions now also require at least one of the conspirators take an actual, overt step in furtherance of the conspiracy. Example include buying supplies to use in the crime, staking out or observing the victim or location, making phone calls and arrangements, etc.

1. Agreement: As long as the parties have the intent to agree and to commit an unlawful act, the agreement does not have to be spoken. Feigned agreement, such as when the person agrees to a crime in order to escape the situation and report the conspiracy to law enforcement does not qualify as "conspiracy."

2. Two or More Persons: A conspiracy must consist of at least two people. If the underlying crime such as bribery requires two people, they cannot also be charged with conspiracy.

a. Common Law: Under the common law, if one of the "conspirators" is someone with no intent to commit the crime, there is no conspiracy. For example, if an undercover police officer is the "conspirator," the D cannot be charged with conspiracy. However, a person can be convicted of conspiracy even if none of the co-conspirators can be convicted due to incapacity (insanity, infancy, etc.).

b. Modern Rule: The modern rule is that one person, with intent to conspire and intent to commit a crime, can be charged with conspiracy even if the other person had no intent to commit a crime.

> **MBE Tip:** Whenever there is a substantial step towards a crime that involves planning by more than one person, consider conspiracy as a correct answer.

3. Unlawful Act: Under the common law, the unlawful act did not have to be a crime, but could also be a tort or breach of contract. Under the modern rule, the unlawful act must be a crime.

4. Foreseeable:

a. *Pinkerton* **Rule:** A conspirator can be held liable for all foreseeable crimes committed in furtherance of the conspiracy whether or not he specifically agreed to that particular crime. This is the *Pinkerton* rule.

b. Example: If a bookie sends someone to "collect," he is liable for whatever crimes (burglary, assault, robbery) his messenger commits. Under the MPC/*Pinkerton*, the bookie need only specifically agree to the original crime (extortion, larceny, etc.).

c. Minority Rule: The *Pinkerton* rule regarding foreseeable crimes has not been adopted in all states. Some states still only allow a conspirator to be culpable only for those crimes to which he specifically agreed.

MBE Tip: If the MPC is mentioned, *Pinkerton* is in play. All co-conspirators may be charged with all crimes committed. Although it is unlikely that the MBE will test the minority view, review the fact pattern for an indication of the jurisdiction. If the jurisdiction has not adopted the MPC or *Pinkerton*, then each co-conspirator can only be charged with the crimes to which he agreed, regardless of how foreseeable the other crimes were.

---

5. Withdrawal: If a conspirator successfully withdraws, he is not liable for future crimes committed by the other conspirators.

a. Cease Acts: To successfully withdraw, he must cease to commit acts in furtherance of the conspiracy.

b. Communicate Withdrawal: The D must also communicate his withdrawal to all co-conspirators in time for them to cease to commit acts in furtherance of the conspiracy.

c. Take Action: Under the MPC, the withdrawing conspirator must take some action to stop the conspiracy and prevent the commission of future crimes.

MBE Tip: Conspiracy is frequently tested. Watch for decoys like a person who assists without the agreement or knowledge of other conspirators. Such a person cannot be charged with conspiracy, although he may be otherwise chargeable (attempt, aiding & abetting, etc.)

C. Attempt

Common law attempt required that the actor specifically intend to commit the crime and take steps to bring himself into "close proximity" to completing the crime. Under contemporary law, only a substantial step is required, not "close proximity". Under the MPC, it is an affirmative defense if the person abandons the attempt after a substantial step was taken but before the crime is actually committed.

MBE Tip: Once the actor has expressed intent to commit a specific crime and a substantial step has been taken, the crime of criminal attempt has occurred even if the actor subsequently changes her mind and the underlying crime is abandoned. Also, examine the fact pattern and decide whether the actor has abandoned the attempt because of her conscience or because the crime has become too difficult. There is no defense for factual impossibility.

---

1. *Mens Rea*: As with solicitation, specific intent is required, even if the *mens rea* for the underlying crime is lower (e.g. recklessness, negligence).

2. Substantial Step: Any act taken in furtherance of the underlying crime.

3. Mistake: Factual impossibility does not negate attempt (e.g., it's still attempt when D shoots V thinking V is merely asleep but, in fact, V is already dead).

4. Merger: Attempt merges with the crime if it is completed. However, attempt does not merge with conspiracy.

INCHOATE CRIMES ANALYSIS CHART

	Initial Act	Substantial Step Required?	Merger?	Defenses?
Solicitation	Encouragement to commit a crime	NO	Merges with conspiracy if solicitee agrees; Merges with completed crime	Renunciation
Attempt	Intent to commit a crime and an act in furtherance	YES	Merges with completed crime	Abandonment
Conspiracy	Agreement to commit a crime (between two or more persons)	YES, in most jurisdictions	Does not merge with completed crime	Withdrawal

V. HOMICIDE

> **MBE Tip:** We have compiled this section by focusing on the elements that compose the crimes. The types and degrees (1°, 2°, 3°) are particularly important. Note however, that the statutes will often be provided. Where they are not, you will likely be examining the more general common law requirements and you can worry less about degrees.

A. Murder

Common law murder is the unlawful killing of another human being with malice aforethought. If a D intends to kill or cause serious bodily harm to someone, but his actions end up killing another person, the D's intent is transferred to the person actually killed.

1. Malice Aforethought: The mental state requirement for common law murder can be demonstrated by proving the D had (1) intent to kill, (2) intent to cause serious bodily harm, (3) extreme recklessness, or (4) intent to commit a felony. Any of these four mental states is sufficient. "Malice aforethought" is therefore a somewhat misleading term; it does not require malice, ill will, pre-planning, or intent to kill in all cases.

a. Intent to Kill: This requires proof of the D's conscious desire to kill the victim or his substantial certainty that his actions will result in the victim's death. Thus actual specific intent to kill is not required. This state of mind can be demonstrated through the D's actions or statements.

b. Intent to Cause Serious Bodily Harm: A D intends to cause serious bodily harm if he intends to inflict an injury which creates a substantial risk of death or causes a protracted impairment to the victim's health.

c. Extreme Recklessness: This is greater than the mental state of recklessness and is shown as total indifference to the possibility of someone being killed or seriously injured. This does not require proving the intent to kill or cause serious bodily harm.

d. Intent to Commit a Felony:

(1) Rule: If a human being is killed, intentionally or not, during the commission of a dangerous felony, the intent to commit the felony satisfies malice aforethought. The D will be liable as an accomplice for murders committed by co-participants in the felony. In many states, the D can also be liable for the death of a co-participant killed by police, victims, or other co-participants during the felony.

(2) Example: If the D intends to commit arson and someone is killed during the arson (from the time of "attempt" to "escape"), the D can also be convicted of felony murder.

MBE Tip: Homicides are frequently tested on the MBE. Watch carefully for requisite intent to do the act (not to be confused with motive or ill will, which are not required), including intent to cause serious bodily harm, which is sufficient for a murder charge even if death was not intended. For felony murder to apply, the felony must be dangerous and the killing must occur while the felony is in progress.

---

2. Causation: The prosecution must show that the D's actions were the actual and proximate cause of the victim's death. Actual cause is shown if the victim would not have died but for the D's actions or the D's actions were at least a substantial factor in the victim's death. Proximate cause is shown if the victim's death was the natural and probable result of the D's actions.

3. Human Being: The D must have killed a human being. Under common law, a human being exists between birth of a live child and legal death.

a. Legal Death – Historically: Legal death used to be defined as the time when a person stopped breathing and his heart stopped beating.

b. Legal Death – Current View: With medical technology a person can be kept breathing and his heart beating on life support equipment, so now the test is "irreversible cessation of brain function."

> **MBE Tip:** Causing or hastening the death of a person with a terminal illness is still murder. The ultimate fate of the victim is irrelevant as long as the victim was legally alive at the time of the killing.

4. Statutes: Most states have enacted statutes which divide murder into degrees with varying punishments.

a. First Degree: First degree murder generally requires premeditation and deliberation or felony murder.

(1) Premeditation: Some kind of advance thought or planning is considered premeditation, even if it is not prolonged. Some states consider that premeditation can occur in an instant.

(2) Felony Murder: If a death occurs during the course of a dangerous felony, the perpetrator may be charged with felony murder regardless of whether the death was intentional. Foreseeability is the test. Some states specifically list which particularly dangerous felonies qualify for first degree felony murder. Others hold that a killing during any felony committed in a dangerous manner qualifies as first degree felony murder.

> **MBE Tip:** Because of the differing laws in the various states, first degree murder questions will most likely include the applicable statute or rule. If it does not, err on the side of the common sense rule: If the felonies committed seem particularly heinous or there is any suggestion of advance thought prior to the homicide, first degree murder is probably in play.

b. Second Degree: Second degree murder is any common law homicide that does not qualify as first degree murder, but that rises above manslaughter. Focus on the *mens rea* to determine where the homicide falls in the spectrum.

> **MBE Tip:** Consider second degree murder as the correct option in any question about homicide if the facts indicate that there was no consideration or advance thought whatsoever, or where a felony was not in progress.

B. Manslaughter

Common law manslaughter is the unlawful killing of a human being without malice aforethought.

1. Involuntary Manslaughter: A person kills another human being through a voluntary but reckless act, but not with malice, extreme recklessness, or specific intent. Mere recklessness is a significant departure from ordinary care or disregard of a significant risk of harm. It is more than mere negligence or a departure from ordinary care.

2. Voluntary Manslaughter: This is intentional killing committed in the heat of passion caused by excusable provocation.

a. Excusable Provocation: The common law majority rule limited excusable provocation to a predetermined list of provocations such as being assaulted or finding one's spouse in bed with another. The minority view is that excusable provocation is a question of fact for the jury whether the provoking event was one that would cause an ordinary reasonable person to lose all self-control.

b. Heat of Passion: Regardless of whether the provocation was excusable, the jury must also find that the D was actually acting in the heat of passion. The D must have committed the killing shortly after the provoking event while still in a rage.

3. Misdemeanor Manslaughter: This is similar to felony murder but the crime was a misdemeanor instead of a felony. Misdemeanor manslaughter has been abolished by statute in most states, and is not recognized by the MPC. In those states which still recognize it, the misdemeanor must be conduct that is inherently wrong, not merely statutorily wrong (such as driving with an expired license).

MBE Tip: All crimes whose elements are included in a greater crime are implicitly charged by charging the crime with the greater degree (i.e., First Degree Murder includes Second Degree, Third Degree, etc.). The one exception is for burglary. The underlying crime must be charged separately. For example, even though larceny is technically a "lesser included" offense to burglary, the prosecutor must charge both separately.

C. Negligent Homicide

The MPC requires a gross deviation from a reasonable person standard of care for negligent homicide. Most states have statutes proscribing negligent homicide in recognition of the dangerousness of automobiles. The negligence must be a significant deviation from ordinary care, thus more than ordinary negligence.

MBE Tip: There is no negligent homicide under the common law because the common law does not impose criminal penalties for mere negligence. Again watch the facts for the applicable law.

STOP! Go to page 373 and work Learning Questions 21 to 30.

VI. OTHER CRIMES

A. Theft

The English common law recognized larceny, larceny by servant, and larceny by trick. The English Parliament created the crimes of embezzlement and obtaining property by false pretenses. The modern view is to combine all these overlapping offenses into "theft." Statutory theft generally has degrees based upon the value of the stolen property.

1. Larceny: Common law larceny is the trespassory taking and carrying away of tangible personal property in the possession of another, with the intent to permanently deprive that person of his property.

a. Intent to Permanently Deprive: Larceny is a specific intent crime and the D must have intended to permanently deprive the possessor at the time of the taking or at a later time while the D had unauthorized custody of the property. D must intend to keep the property, hold it long enough to deprive the possessor of most of its economic value, or dispose of the property in a manner that would make it unlikely that the possessor would get it back.

(1) At Time of Taking or a Later Time: D must intend to permanently deprive the possessor at the time of the taking. If he decides to return the property at a later time, it does not negate the intent at the time of the taking.

> **MBE Tip:** Mere intent to borrow negates the element of intent to permanently deprive, and thus is not larceny. However, if the D took the property without the intent to permanently deprive the possessor and later decides to keep the property, he has formed the required intent and it relates back to the time of the taking.

(2) Mistake of Fact: If in good faith the D mistakenly believes he is entitled to the property or takes the property in satisfaction of a claim or debt, the D lacks the intent to permanently take "the property of another." An example is someone taking the wrong coat leaving a restaurant. The person mistakenly believes the coat is hers and there is no intent to deprive. An honest mistake, even if it is not a mistake that a reasonable person would have made, negates intent.

> **MBE Tip:** Larceny is one of those crimes where mistake is a defense because it negates an element of the crime. This is not the case with most other types of crimes. Therefore, it is frequently tested on the MBE.

b. Trespassory: This describes the lack of permission of the possessor. If express or implied permission is lacking, then entering is automatically trespassory.

c. Taking: The D obtains complete dominion and control over the property. Control of the property may be control by another person at the D's direction.

d. Carrying Away: The slightest degree of movement of the property satisfies the carrying away requirement. Taking the property out of the store is not required. Even taking the property into one's own hands is enough.

e. Tangible Personal Property: The common law excludes real estate, things attached to the real estate such as minerals, trees, etc., and intangibles such as financial rights. There are other torts and property concepts that cover the improper appropriation or invasion of these kinds of property. See Torts and Property Chapters.

f. In Possession of Another: The property must be owned by another exclusively and must be taken from one who has possession. If the D has joint ownership of the property, he cannot be convicted of larceny in common law.

> **MBE Tip:** Larceny is a crime of possession; even the true owner can commit larceny against someone who has possession, for example, taking items pawned without paying the redemption amount. This makes it possible to commit larceny against a thief. It is not a defense that the possessor did not have legal ownership. Be on the lookout for a tricky fact scenario like this on the MBE.

2. Embezzlement: Embezzlement is when the D takes property from a person with whom the D has a fiduciary relationship with the intent to permanently deprive the owner thereof. The fiduciary has control of the property before the embezzlement takes place. There must be a fiduciary relationship such as employee, agent, attorney, banker, guardian, or trustee. Unauthorized use (such as long distance phone calls) is also embezzlement.

MBE Tip: Note this key distinction between larceny and embezzlement. Embezzlement only applies where the taker is a *fiduciary* who is *legally in control* of the property when it is taken. If the taker is a fiduciary but was not in control of the property (e.g., a banker who goes into the store of one of his customers and steals from the cash register, rather than from the bank account) the crime is larceny. See the chart below for the distinctions between larceny and embezzlement.

3. Embezzlement/Larceny Distinctions Chart:

Embezzlement	Larceny
Property legally in possession of D	Property legally in possession of another
Property "converted" – high standard	Property "carried away" – lower standard, even slight movement or interference will do
Fiduciary relationship – D must be in a position of responsibility and trust	No fiduciary relationship

4. False Pretenses: The D obtains property by false pretenses when, with the intent to permanently deprive the owner thereof at the time, he fraudulently induces the victim to voluntarily deliver possession and title of tangible, personal property to the D. The intent to permanently deprive the owner must be present at the time the D induces the victim to give him the property, not later.

5. Larceny by Trick: Larceny by trick is similar to false pretenses but only requires transfer of possession, not transfer of title. Transfer of title depends on the intent of the owner, whether or not he expects to regain possession of the property. If he does not expect to get the property back, he has transferred title as well as possession, and the crime is false pretenses.

MBE Tip: Larceny is the most heavily tested of the pure theft crimes (larceny, larceny by trick, embezzlement, false pretenses). Memorize all the elements of larceny, and when dealing with a larceny question on the MBE make sure all elements are satisfied.

6. "Bad Check" Statutes: Check fraud has been specifically prohibited by statute in every jurisdiction. Although it is a subset of larceny, it has one element that differs: the D need not have actually deprived the victim of any property. If the account has insufficient funds, the D can still be held liable as long as she had intent to permanently deprive the victim.

B. Receiving Stolen Goods

The crime of receiving stolen property is: (1) the acquisition or control of stolen tangible personal property, (2) knowing the property is stolen, (3) with the intent to permanently deprive the possessor of the property.

1. Acquisition or Control: This can be accomplished by any one of three methods:

a. Actual Possession: The D actually takes physical possession of the stolen property.

b. Deposit on D's Behalf: The thief deposits the stolen property in a place designated by the D.

c. D as Middleman: The D brings together the thief and a receiver of the stolen property.

2. Knowledge: The D must actually believe the property is stolen when he receives the property.

MBE Tip: If the D believes the property was not stolen, the prosecutor can still demonstrate that a reasonable person should have known the property was stolen because the D paid an unreasonably low price, or the transaction occurred under suspicious circumstances. Look for this on the MBE, as it is a less obvious form of "knowledge."

---

3. Intent to Permanently Deprive: Receiving stolen goods is a specific intent crime. The D must have the intent to permanently deprive the true owner of their property either at the time he received the property or later.

C. Robbery

Common law robbery is larceny plus (1) the property must be taken from the owner's person or presence, and (2) this must be accomplished by force or intimidation.

1. Person or Presence: Property is on the victim's person when victim is touching it, such as a wallet, jewelry, or clothing. Property is in the victim's presence when it is in an automobile or room with the victim.

2. By Force or Intimidation: There must be a causal relationship between the use of force and the taking of the property. Force can be any action such as bumping into the victim to pick his pocket. Intimidation is any minimal threat of immediate force to harm the victim, his family, anyone in his company, or to destroy his house. The D doesn't have to have the actual ability to carry out the threat as long as he has the apparent ability. For example, a realistic toy gun would suffice.

MBE Tip: Larceny is the foundation of robbery; make sure all larceny elements are met. Also note that pickpocketing without the victim's knowledge or any use of force is larceny, not robbery.

D. Burglary

Common law burglary is the intentional breaking and entering of the dwelling house of another in the nighttime with the intent to commit larceny or a felony inside.

1. Breaking: The physical or constructive opening of anything closed for the purpose of gaining entry. No force or violence is required. Nothing need be actually broken or destroyed. The D must only open a door or window or enlarge an opening to enter. If the D uses fraud or threat of force to induce someone to let him in, it also constitutes breaking.

2. Entering: Any unlawful physical intrusion beyond that necessary for breaking into the house is entering. If the D has actual or implied consent of the occupants, it is not entry as required by the definition of burglary. The D does not need to fully enter the building; a hand or foot preventing closure of the door is sufficient.

3. Dwelling House of Another: Under the common law, only entry into a building, tent, or houseboat, etc., presently used as a dwelling for habitation or sleeping constitutes burglary. The presence of the inhabitants is not necessary, but the building cannot be abandoned. If the building is both a business and a dwelling, entry into either is burglary.

> **MBE Tip:** Most jurisdictions have eliminated the dwelling requirement for burglary. Breaking and entering any structure will do. Don't be fooled if one of the MBE options suggests that burglary has not occurred because the structure was not a dwelling, unless the facts specifically state that the common law applies.

4. At Nighttime: Under the common law, nighttime is when there is not enough sunlight to recognize the burglar. Most jurisdictions have also eliminated the nighttime requirement. Burglary can occur at any time of day or night.

5. With Intent to Commit a Felony or Larceny: Burglary is a specific intent crime and intent is required at the time of the entry. If the intent to commit a felony is formed later, the D cannot be charged with burglary. He can, of course, be charged with the felony. If the D enters with the intent to commit a felony but changes his mind and does not commit the felony, he can still be charged with burglary. Because larceny of low-value property can be a misdemeanor, larceny is specifically included due to the danger when someone breaks and enters.

> **MBE Tip:** Burglary is frequently tested, as well as criminal trespass without intent to commit another crime. Note that burglary does not merge with the crime that the burglar intended to commit once inside.

6. Underlying Crime: The underlying crime does not need to be actually committed. If the D had the intent to commit the crime when he entered and subsequently changed his mind, he can still be charged with burglary. Burglary does not merge with any other crimes. The D can be convicted of burglary and the crime the burglar intended to commit when he entered if he actually committed the underlying crime.

7. Statutory Burglary: Most states recognize degrees of burglary depending on such factors as whether a dwelling was entered, the D was armed, or a person was injured during the course of the burglary.

> **MBE Tip:** Intent to commit a felony or larceny at the time of entry is the most frequently tested element of burglary. Intent to commit the crime must exist at the time of entry for burglary to be charged. Conversely, failure to commit the crime does not negate a burglary charge if the intent existed at the time of entry.

E. Battery

Common law battery is the intentional or reckless unlawful application of force to the person of another, directly or indirectly, that results in physical harm or an offensive touching.

1. Intentional or Reckless: Actual specific intent is not required although it may be present; only recklessness is required for common law battery. Recklessness is the conscious disregard of a substantial and unjustifiable risk of injury to the victim.

2. Unlawful: The touching or force is unlawful unless the victim consents or the contact is privileged as in self defense, defense of others, or law enforcement.

3. To Person of Another: Coming into contact with the property of another is not sufficient. The contact must be with the body of another.

4. Directly or Indirectly: The D can either touch the body of the victim with his own body, or strike the victim with a object in his hand or thrown at the victim.

5. Physical Harm or Offensive Touching: Physical harm can be any injury or even temporary pain. Offensive touching can be any contact even if no physical injury or pain results. Some states do not recognize offensive touching in their battery statutes.

F. Assault

Common law assault is either attempted battery or intentionally placing another in reasonable apprehension of immediate bodily harm.

1. Attempted Battery: Under the common law, some states recognize only the attempted battery form of assault. The D must specifically intend to batter the victim, must take all steps necessary to batter the victim, but not succeed in actually battering the victim, to be charged with attempted battery.

2. Apprehension: The D must intentionally cause the victim to feel a reasonable apprehension of an immediate battery. The D must specifically intend to cause the victim either bodily harm or apprehension of harm. The victim must feel apprehension but the apprehension does not need to be actual fear. The victim must be aware of the threat (an unconscious victim does not qualify) and the threat must be one that would cause a reasonable person to feel apprehension of immediate contact.

3. Merger: Attempted battery assault merges into battery if the battery is actually completed (on the second swing, so to speak).

> **MBE Tip:** Most states recognize both of the above forms of assault. Some states combine battery and assault in their criminal codes with degrees depending on the seriousness of the injury or whether a weapon was used. This is another area where the MBE question will sometimes include the statute. Always read your facts carefully to make sure you applying the appropriate rule.

G. Rape

Common law rape is forced sexual intercourse with a female, not the spouse of the D, without her consent. Modern statutes have expanded the definition of rape to include spouses, males, and other forced sexual acts not amounting to sexual intercourse.

1. Consent: The prosecutor must prove lack of valid consent. There is no valid consent if the victim is unconscious or mentally impaired, if her consent was obtained by immediate threat of harm to the victim or members of her family, or fraud. Under the common law, the victim had to show she resisted to demonstrate lack of consent. Now physical resistance is not always necessary because the D may coerce the victim by threats, not necessarily with the actual use of force.

2. Statutory Rape: Common law statutory rape is sexual intercourse with a female under the age of consent (varies between ages 14 to 16) regardless of whether she actually consented. Statutory rape is a strict liability crime. The crime itself is prohibited no matter what state of mind the D possessed. Modern statutes have expanded statutory rape to include males and sexual acts not amounting to sexual intercourse. Many statutes have degrees which depend on the relative ages of the D and victim.

MBE Tip: Rape is not frequently tested. If it is at issue, look for an intoxicated D (voluntary intoxication is not a defense unless D was unaware of having intercourse) or a statutory rape scenario (consent/intent are irrelevant; statutory rape is a strict liability crime).

H. Kidnapping/False Imprisonment

Common law false imprisonment is the intentional and unlawful confinement of a person. Kidnapping is false imprisonment with movement of the person to another location. A charge of false imprisonment merges into kidnapping once the D moves the victim.

1. Intent: False imprisonment and kidnapping require specific intent on the part of the D to confine the victim or substantial certainty that his actions will result in confinement of the victim.

2. Confinement: The D must block the victim's movement in all directions. Physical force or restraint is not required; threat of immediate physical force or falsely pretending to have lawful authority also qualify. Physical resistance by the victim is not required. Any measurable period of confinement is sufficient. The victim does not have to attempt escape as long as no avenue of escape is known to the victim.

3. Movement: Moving the victim is kidnapping.

MBE Tip: The difference between kidnapping and false imprisonment is abduction versus mere restraint. Remember abduction requires either deadly force or a secret place.

---

4. Statutes: Many jurisdictions recognize degrees of kidnapping. Some states do not require movement, or require substantial movement or a substantial time period.

I. Arson

Common law arson is the malicious burning of the dwelling house of another.

1. Malice: The D must either intend to burn the house or manifest extreme indifference to the consequences of his behavior.

2. Burning: Any slight burning or charring is sufficient. The building does not need to be destroyed. Mere blackening by smoke or heat does not suffice under common law, but may under modern statutes.

3. Dwelling House: Common law arson must be the burning of a dwelling house. Most states have eliminated this requirement and arson can be the burning of any structure.

4. Of Another: Common law did not recognize burning one's own house or building, but modern statutes do, especially if the D was trying to defraud the insurance company.

MBE Tip: Arson is similar to burglary in that the common law recognizes the crime only as it pertains to a dwelling, but modern statutes apply it in the context of any building. It is not likely that the common law of arson will be tested, so note the modern improvements.

STOP! Go to page 375 and work Learning Questions 31 to 41.

VII. OVERVIEW: GENERAL PRINCIPLES OF CRIMINAL PROCEDURE

A. Federal Constitution

The Due Process Clause of the Fourteenth Amendment applies the Fourth, Fifth and Sixth Amendments of the United States Constitution to the individual states.

1. Fourth Amendment:

a. Security from Unwarrantable Search and Seizure: The Fourth Amendment provides, "The right of the people to be secure in their persons, houses, papers, and effects, against unreasonable searches and seizures, shall not be violated, and no warrants shall issue, but upon probable cause, supported by oath or affirmation, and particularly describing the place to be searched and the persons or things to be seized."

b. State Intrusion on a Legitimate Expectation of Privacy: There must be (1) a state action, (2) intrusion on private citizens who (3) have an expectation of privacy.

(1) State Action: The party making the intrusion must be a state actor or there is no issue. The state actor need not be a police officer, but can also be such state officials as probation officers, school teachers, welfare case workers, or fish and game wardens. Private citizens under the direction and/or control of a police officer are treated as state actors. Private citizens are not state actors when they act on their own even if they hope to give what they have seized to the police.

(2) Legitimate Expectation of Privacy: This is an objective test standard. Would a reasonable person have a legitimate expectation of privacy in this situation? Areas where there is a reasonable expectation of privacy include a person's own home, place of business, automobile (in a limited sense), and own personal effects.

(3) No Expectation of Privacy:

(a) Public Property: Commercial stores are public places that afford no no legitimate expectation of privacy to anyone. Situations such as a drug-smelling dog on public property, a police officer on public property looking over into private property, or a private residence used as a "drug house", also do not create a legitimate expectation of privacy.

(b) Control of Another: If someone else also has control of the location, there is no legitimate expectation of privacy.

(c) Public Place: If the area is exposed to the public, there is no legitimate expectation of privacy. An example would be a private home with the blinds open. Similarly, a person in a car driving around in public, a prisoner in a jail cell, a high school student in a class, etc., may have no expectation of privacy, or a limited expectation.

> **MBE Tip:** Being in a public place does not always vitiate the right to privacy. Note, however, that a person can assert a reasonable expectation of privacy and thus a Fourth Amendment claim in a public place such as a phone booth. Similarly most guests have a reasonable expectation of privacy in a hotel or motel room.

(d) Held Out to the Public: A person does not have a reasonable expectation of privacy for things held out to the public at large. Examples of this are voice or handwriting samples or public utility records.

(e) Open Fields Doctrine: As long as the fields are outside the curtilage of a home (outside the area of the buildings immediately adjacent to the house), there is no expectation of privacy.

(f) Garbage Left For Collection: A search of curb side garbage does not require a warrant because the creator of the garbage has no reasonable expectation of privacy once the garbage is put out for collection by another party.

> **MBE Tip:** The topic of searches is well-tested and the nuances should be understood thoroughly. First, examine where the search took place and under what circumstances: Was there an expectation of privacy? Do the circumstances suggest that there is a justification for violating that privacy (probable cause, articulable suspicion, etc.)?

2. Fifth Amendment: The text of the Fifth Amendment reads as follows: "No person shall be held to answer for a capital, or otherwise infamous crime, unless on a presentment or indictment of a grand jury, except in cases arising in the land or naval forces, or in the militia, when in actual service in time of war or public danger; nor shall any person be subject for the same offense to be twice put in jeopardy of life or limb, nor shall be compelled in any criminal case to be a witness against himself, nor be deprived of life, liberty, or property, without due process of law; nor shall private property be taken for public use, without just compensation."

3. Sixth Amendment: The text of the Sixth Amendment reads as follows: "In all criminal prosecutions, the accused shall enjoy the right to a speedy and public trial, by an impartial jury of the state and district wherein the crime shall have been committed, which district shall have been previously ascertained by law, and to be informed of the nature and cause of the accusation; to be confronted with the witnesses against him; to have compulsory process for obtaining witnesses in his favor, and to have the assistance of counsel for his defense."

VIII. SEARCH AND SEIZURE

The Fourth Amendment requires that prior to all searches and seizures, the state actor must have probable cause and a warrant or a special exception to a warrant. Any trustworthy information may be considered in determining whether probable cause exists, even if the information would not ultimately be admissible at trial. The standard of proof for probable cause is less than the preponderance of the evidence in a civil matter, but more than an articulable suspicion.

A. Arrest

Arrest is taking legal custody of a person, depriving him of liberty and requiring him to answer a criminal charge. Arrest must always be reasonable. Arrest is considered reasonable if there is probable cause. Excessive force during arrest is not allowed. Deadly force used against a fleeing suspect not posing a risk of death or serious physical injury is unreasonable. Arrest is a heightened form of detention for which the police can move the suspect to jail.

B. Probable Cause to Arrest

In order to have sufficient probable cause to arrest a suspect, it must be likely that

1. Violation: A violation of the law has occurred, and

2. Suspect Committed: The suspect arrested committed the violation. This is also true when there is a seizure of the person to the extent that it is similar to an arrest (detainment of the suspect where the suspect does not feel free to leave).

C. Warrant

Even if probable cause exists, a warrant is required before a search or seizure can be made unless exceptional circumstances apply.

1. Warrant Required: Prior to the issuance of a warrant, a neutral and detached judge or magistrate must be satisfied that probable cause exists based on the surrounding facts and circumstances. A warrant is required to arrest the suspect if the crime is a misdemeanor unless the crime is committed in the presence of a police officer. In the case of a non-emergency where the suspect is in a home, the law officers must obtain a warrant.

2. Warrant Not Required: An officer must have probable cause for a warrantless search or arrest. The burden is on the government to justify a warrantless search or seizure (arrest).

a. Felony Suspect in Public Place: A warrant is usually not required if a felony has been committed and the suspect is in a public place.

b. **Misdemeanor in Officer's Presence:** A misdemeanor which is committed in a police officer's presence does not require a warrant. For example, if an officer witnesses a minor shoplifting a case of beer from the local mini-mart, the officer does not have to wait for the issuance of a warrant.

c. **Exigent Circumstances:** This would include circumstances where there is reason to believe the suspect of a serious crime will flee, evidence may disappear, or public safety is jeopardized.

D. Effect of Unlawful Arrest

1. Prosecution Still Valid: The prosecution may move ahead with its case if there is supporting evidence. An unlawful arrest does not necessarily destroy the prosecution's case.

MBE Tip: On the MBE, a frequent wrong answer is "The D cannot be prosecuted due to an illegal arrest." Evidence may be suppressed, but the prosecution can proceed if there is enough other evidence.

---

2. Fruits of the Poisonous Tree Excluded: An unlawful arrest may lead to suppression of evidence acquired during the course of the arrest. Evidence most likely suppressed in this instance would be a post-arrest confession or physical evidence of the crime seized during the search incident to arrest.

MBE Tip: If the search that led to the arrest was illegal (insufficient prior justification to go on to the premises), the arrest is a "fruit" and is also tainted.

E. Detentions

Detention is a temporary (brief and reasonable) restraint of a person's liberty (person does not feel free to leave).

1. Investigative *Terry* Stop: In order for there to be an investigative stop by a police officer without the presence of probable cause, there must be a reasonable suspicion based on specific and articulable facts known to the officer at the time of the stop, when looking at the totality of the circumstances, including the officer's training.

MBE Tip: Recently, the Supreme Court upheld the conviction of a man who violated a Nevada statute by refusing to provide his name during a *Terry* stop. Many other states have similar "stop and identify" statutes.

---

2. Automobile Stops and Roadblocks: Sobriety roadblocks (where the police stop every car, every other car, or every tenth car, etc.) are allowed under the Fourth Amendment and in the majority of jurisdictions. The police cannot stop a car at random unless they have articulable suspicion. In November 2000, the U.S. Supreme Court held that drug roadblocks using drug-sniffing dogs were unconstitutional.

3. Police Station Detention: In order to bring a suspect to the police station for a line-up, fingerprinting, or questioning, an officer must have full probable cause for arrest.

4. Detention During House Search: When police are searching a house for contraband pursuant to a search warrant, they may detain the occupants while the search continues.

F. Probable Cause to Search

If a search is not valid, the evidence seized is not admissible in court. In order to have sufficient probable cause to search a premises, it must be likely that two circumstances apply:

1. Connected: The items searched for must be likely connected to criminal activity. A general search for non-criminal items is not allowed, even if there is a possibility of finding criminally connected items.

2. In the Location: The items must be likely to be found in the place to be searched. The Fourth Amendment does not prohibit searches of property under the control of persons not suspected of a crime at the time of the search.

G. Warrant Search

Most searches must be conducted pursuant to a valid warrant. Probable cause is only the first step toward establishing a valid warrant search.

1. Prerequisites:

a. Probable Cause: Probable cause is always required. Warrants must be supported and based upon a showing of probable cause. This may be shown by an officer's affidavits, and hearsay may be used (i.e., confidential informants).

b. Neutral Magistrate: The magistrate determining probable cause at the hearing and issuing the warrant must be neutral, detached, and otherwise unbiased. If the neutrality of the magistrate is challenged, there must be case-specific reasons offered for the alleged bias.

c. Factors Considered With Informant Tips: Among the factors to be considered by the judge in issuing a warrant are the following:

(1) Reliable Information: The information must be inherently reliable (not obviously false or contrary to logic). This is a vague standard and easy to meet.

(2) Reliable Informant: The informant must have been in a position to have a factual basis for the information (i.e., personal knowledge). There must be a factual basis for the credibility of the informant to the extent that he is a reliable witness. However, reliability can also be established if the police have corroborating information independent of the informant's tip. The affidavit can be attacked if it contained a false statement that was material to the finding of probable cause.

d. Knock and Announce Requirement: The police must "knock and announce their purpose" when executing the warrant. Force may be used if there is a failure to respond after a reasonable time. An exception to the knock and announce requirement is when emergencies require the immediate entry upon the premises. Emergencies are generally limited to life, safety, and preservation of property (evidence). A judge may issue a "no-knock warrant" in advance for the same reasons.

e. Must be Executed Without Delay: The warrant must not be stale. If delayed, there may be an absence of probable cause which is required above. It must be reasonably likely the evidence is still there.

2. Scope of Warrant: The scope of the authorized search must not be exceeded.

> **MBE Tip:** Look for a warrant to search a home and the police search other adjacent buildings such as a garage or tool shed. These may be all right if outbuildings are specified in the warrant; the house next door is not.

3. Fruits of Search May be Seized: Police may generally seize any contraband that they discover while they are properly executing a warrant. This is true even if the items are not specified in the warrant.

> **STOP!** Go to page 376 and work Learning Questions 42 to 50.

H. Exceptions to a Warrant

1. Search Incident to Arrest: The general rule is that a search may be made prior to the arrest only if the police had probable cause to arrest the person prior to the search. Police are allowed to conduct a warrantless "search incident to" (after) a lawful arrest for a reasonable time. If an arrest is unlawful, then any search incident thereto is also unlawful. The scope of the search is generally the "wingspan" of the suspect; an example is a closed glove box or briefcase within reach ("wingspan") of the driver suspect, but not the entire vehicle.

a. Protective Sweep: A "protective sweep" may be made of the house for dangerous persons. However, the scope of a protective sweep extends only to those places in which a person could reasonably be hiding. The police may effect a pat-down for weapons of anyone present to ensure officer safety. The police may detain other persons present in the house ("investigative detention") for the purpose of ensuring officer safety.

b. Search of Persons While on Premises: If individuals are named in the search warrant, police may search such individuals. The police may also search individuals present if there is probable cause to arrest them, or if the police have a reasonable fear for their own safety sufficient to justify a pat-down search for weapons. Otherwise, the police may not search persons found on the premises who are not named in the warrant.

2. Automobiles:

a. Stop: To stop a vehicle, only an articulable suspicion is required; speeding or even a taillight out probably qualifies.

b. Search: The police must have probable cause to believe that the vehicle contains contraband or evidence of a crime prior to the search. In the event an automobile will be unavailable by the time a warrant is obtained, the "exigent circumstances" exception may be applicable. This exception allows an automobile to be searched if the automobile is reasonably believed to have been used in a crime.

c. Locked Places: There are only a couple of circumstances under which officers can search a locked container or locked trunk of an automobile. They are:

(1) Probable Cause: When the officers have probable cause (an articulable suspicion is insufficient) to search the trunk or other locked space.

(2) Impound Upon Arrest: When the vehicle has been impounded subsequent to an arrest.

> **MBE Tip:** Automobile searches are a very tricky area. All the various exceptions should be noted: articulable suspicion; exigent circumstances; "wingspan" (within suspect's control); plain view; search incident to arrest; search upon impound; and probable cause. In other words, if you see an automobile search, have a prepared "laundry list" of exceptions to check before determining that the search is illegal.

3. Stop and Frisk: Police may stop a person without probable cause for arrest if they had an "articulable and reasonable suspicion" of criminal activity. This is also known as a "*Terry* frisk." A protective search is valid only if the police reasonably believe that the person may be armed and dangerous. This search is limited to a pat-down of the outer clothing for concealed weapons. Admissibility of any evidence seized depends upon whether or not the officer "reasonably believed" the item seized was a possible weapon.

> **MBE Tip:** A hammer, ax, or similar object may qualify as a weapon if it could inflict substantial harm.

4. Plain View: Police may make a warrantless seizure only when they are justified in being present on the premises, inadvertently discover contraband or items used in a crime, have knowledge (prior to the search) that the object in plain view is seizable or contraband, and when the police can show some "exigent circumstance" that requires an immediate seizure. Smelling by drug-sniffing dogs is considered in "plain view."

> **MBE Tip:** Note that this exception only applies if the police had probable cause to enter the premises. The exam frequently poses facts where unusual and suspicious circumstances are present such as neighbor saw a trespasser, or police came on evidence of forcible entry. The contraband must not be hidden, such as in a box.

5. Inventory:

a. Property at Jail: This search must be incident to a lawful arrest and subject to a search policy that is consistently enforced.

b. Impound of Automobile: An automobile may be inventoried when it is impounded. A locked trunk or locked containers can be searched. The police must allow a third party an opportunity to move the car, unless the car contains evidence, is suspected to contain evidence, or will itself be held as evidence. An automobile may be impounded when one of the following is true:

(1) Incapacitation: The driver is incapacitated, either unconscious, intoxicated, or otherwise unable to move the vehicle.

(2) Arrest: The driver is arrested and taken into custody by police.

(3) Public Danger: The automobile presents a public danger, for example being halfway on the road or by leaking dangerous chemicals.

6. Consent: Police can search without a warrant if a search of the person or premises has been consented to by the person or the owner, or other person with control of or other rights to the premises. The consent must be express, voluntarily, and intelligently made. Consent may be revoked at any time.

MBE Tip: It is important to note that consent may be given by one who actually controls the premises or by one who has apparent control (but not necessarily actual control) of the premises. This may include housemates (as to common areas) or live-in partners, but not usually guests.

---

7. Exigent Circumstances: Immediate action must be required.

a. In Hot Pursuit, Emergencies: Police in hot pursuit of a fleeing felon may conduct a search without a warrant and seize items, and may also pursue the suspect into private dwellings.

b. Evanescent (Disappearing) Evidence: Police may seize evidence without a warrant if it is likely to disappear before a warrant can be obtained. An example of "disappearing evidence" is a blood sample which may contain drugs or alcohol.

c. Automobiles: Because automobiles are easily moved, they may sometimes fall under this exception.

8. Wiretapping/Eavesdropping: Wiretapping, eavesdropping (including an electronic device on a phone that records the numbers dialed) and other forms of electronic surveillance violate the expectation of privacy and constitute a search under the Fourth Amendment. A warrant or consent by one party is thus required. The following are exceptions:

a. Non-Private Public Speech: When the speaker makes no attempt to keep the conversation or his voice private, a warrant is not required.

b. Consent by One Party: Consent by one party to the conversation is adequate to avoid the warrant requirement if there is a fire, medical emergency, crime, disaster, extortion, or hostage holder.

c. Announcement by One Party: If one party to the conversation announces to the others that the conversation is about to be recorded, the recording becomes admissible.

STOP! Go to page 377 and work Learning Questions 51 to 57.

IX. CONFESSION AND INTERROGATION

Coercion by improper police conduct violates the Fifth Amendment. Coerced confessions are inherently unreliable and are therefore inadmissible. In order for a confession to be valid, and therefore admissible, there are two requirements. A confession may be introduced against the person who made it only if the confession was (1) voluntary (not coerced by the police) and (2) otherwise in compliance with the *Miranda* rules (i.e., if the suspect was given the *Miranda* warnings prior to interrogation and subsequently confessed).

A. Voluntary

A confession will only be admissible against a D if it was given voluntarily. Even if *Miranda* warnings were administered, an involuntary confession will not be allowed into evidence.

1. Test: The test for determining the "voluntariness" of a confession is the absence of police coercion. If the police coerce a confession, it is involuntary and must be excluded from the prosecution's case in chief; in addition, it cannot be used to impeach the D's testimony.

2. Exception: Note, the key factor here is the possibility of police coercion. Thus, confessions made by a cellmate (suspect brags about the crime), or made by a suspect due to serious mental illness (he heard "voices" telling him to confess) or coercion by the average citizen (a neighborhood acquaintance threatened harm to the suspect if he did not confess), are not considered "police coercion" and may, therefore, be admissible.

> **MBE Tip:** Voluntariness analysis is separate from *Miranda* analysis. Don't be fooled by facts that suggest *Miranda* is satisfied but imply police coercion. If the police fail either the *Miranda* analysis or the voluntariness analysis, the confession/statements will be suppressed.

B. *Miranda*

Miranda holds that when a suspect is questioned in custody by the police, his confession will not be admissible against him unless he has received the *Miranda* warnings. The rationale is that questioning of the suspect while in custody is likely to induce confessions made in violation of the Fifth Amendment. The police must give *Miranda* warnings even if the suspect is already aware of his rights.

1. Fifth Amendment Protection: *Miranda* is based in the Fifth Amendment's privilege against self-incrimination (not the Sixth Amendment right to counsel).

2. Applies to State and Federal Courts: The *Miranda* rules govern the admissibility of confessions in both state and federal courts.

3. Custody: *Miranda* warnings are necessary only when the suspect is taken into custody for "custodial interrogation." If the police question someone they have not yet formally detained, *Miranda* is not triggered. An objective test is used to determine whether or not the suspect is in custody. A person is "in custody" if a reasonable person in that situation would not have felt free to leave or who felt compelled to stay until dismissed.

4. Interrogation: Interrogation by the police covers both direct and indirect questions aimed at the suspect. Interrogation occurs if the police submit questions to a suspect that are likely to elicit an incriminating response from the suspect.

a. Questioning: It is only where the confession is the result of questioning that *Miranda* is triggered. If the suspect blurts out a statement voluntarily without police questioning, it is admissible.

b. Police: *Miranda* is triggered only when both the custody and the questioning are by the authorities. *Miranda* does not apply if Joe Citizen elicits a confession from the suspect after detainment and questioning. Incriminating statements voluntarily made by a suspect to a cellmate are admissible. If the "cellmate" elicits the incriminating statements, however, the environment takes on the character of a custodial interrogation and the admission must be excluded at trial.

5. Four Protected Warnings – RARI: A suspect may exercise his rights at any time. If, during questioning, the suspect at any time exercises his rights to silence or to an attorney, the questioning must cease – even if the suspect originally did not invoke those rights. The four required RARI components (i.e., *Miranda* warnings) are:

    a. You have the **Right to remain silent**.

    b. **Anything you say can be used against you** in the court of law.

    c. You have the **Right to the presence of an attorney**.

    d. **If you cannot afford an attorney, one will be appointed** for you prior to questioning if you so choose.

6. Waiver of *Miranda*: A suspect's waiver of his right to silence and to an attorney during questioning is valid only if it is knowingly, intelligently, and affirmatively waived. The suspect's silence is not a waiver of his rights.

7. Grand Jury Testimony Not Protected: A witness testifying before a grand jury is not entitled to have an attorney present or receive *Miranda* warnings.

MBE Tip: The wording used by the suspect to waive invocation of the right to counsel is often fuzzy on the exam. Such a "waiver" is to be carefully scrutinized and if ambiguous is usually ineffective.

C. Effect of Assertion of *Miranda* Rights

Once the suspect invokes his right to silence or right to counsel, the interrogation must cease, even if the suspect previously waived those rights.

1. Right to Silence Invoked: If the suspect invokes his right to silence, the police may resume questioning after waiting several hours and giving new *Miranda* warnings.

2. Right to Counsel Invoked: If the suspect clearly and unequivocally invokes his right to counsel, the police may not resume questioning until counsel has been made available to the suspect, or the suspect himself initiates communication with the police.

3. Subsequent Waiver or Assertion of Rights: A D who originally asserted his rights can subsequently waive them. Also a D who originally waived his rights may later assert his rights. The assertion must be unambiguous and unequivocal.

MBE Tip: *Miranda* is heavily tested. Do not confuse the standard for waiver of the right to counsel during *questioning* (the invocation must be clear and unambiguous, otherwise waiver of the right is presumed) and the standard for waiver of the right to counsel during *formal proceedings* (the waiver must be knowing and intelligent and is never presumed).

D. Confession Admissibility Flow Chart

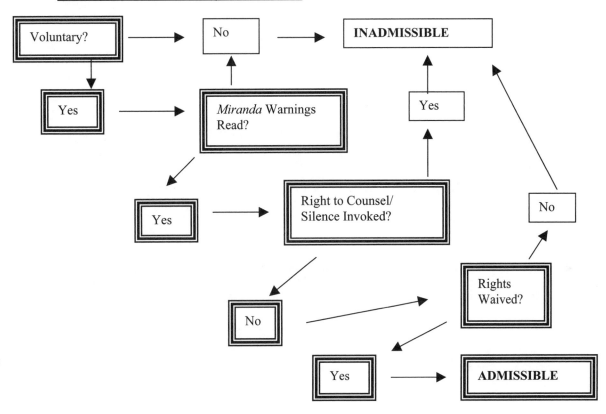

X. PRE-TRIAL PROCEEDINGS

A. Sixth Amendment Right to Counsel

Once formal criminal proceedings have commenced, a suspect has a right to have counsel present at all pre-trial confrontation procedures. Such confrontations include line-ups (witness picks the suspect out of a group of "suspects") and show-ups (witness is shown the suspect and asked whether the suspect is the perpetrator). The right does not apply where a witness views still or moving pictures of the suspect for identification.

B. Waiver of Right to Counsel

Waiver of one's Sixth Amendment right to counsel must be made affirmatively, knowingly, and intelligently. In effect, the suspect must be told of this right, understand it, and affirmatively waive it.

C. Due Process and Identification Procedures

The danger of some identification procedures is the possibility that a witness will identify the suspect at trial based on the police station session and not from remembering the details of the actual crime scene.

1. Totality of the Circumstances: The validity of an identification procedure is reviewed by a judge based on the totality of the circumstances.

2. Unnecessarily Suggestive: If the identification procedure was so "unnecessarily suggestive" and so "conducive to mistaken identification" as to be deeply unfair to the D, the D may challenge the resulting identification on due process grounds. For example, if the suspect was known to be over 6 feet tall, and the D was placed in a lineup with men all under 5 feet 8 inches tall.

3. Reliable and Not Conducive to Error: An identification procedure does not violate due process if it is reliable or "not conducive to likely error" even if it is somewhat suggestive. For example, if the witness had a long time to view the suspect under adequate light and close up, then suggestive identification procedures are more likely to be held as fair to the D. Also, an independent source may make an identification at trial even if the identification of the lineup witness is suppressed.

4. Photo Identifications: Where a witness identifies the suspect through the use of photographs, the "totality of the circumstances" test is used to determine whether the D's due process rights have been violated. A due process violation will be found only if the photo identification session is very likely to have produced a misidentification.

> **MBE Tip:** Whether the identification was unnecessarily suggestive is a question of fact. For example, police statements to the witness such as, "We have the man," may qualify if the witness sees the police with only one suspect.

D. Indictment or Information

The initial pleading by the state is an "indictment" from a grand jury or an "information" filed by the prosecuting attorney. The indictment or information is a concise and definite statement identifying the D and giving the essential facts constituting the offense charged and signed by the prosecuting attorney. For each offense charged, the prosecution must cite the statute, rule, regulation, or other provision of law that the D is alleged to have violated.

E. Preliminary Hearings

The D has a right to counsel at a preliminary hearing.

1. Probable Cause: If a person is indicted or arrested without a warrant, a magistrate must evaluate the officer's probable cause at a *Gerstein* hearing. This must occur within 48 hours of detainment or the suspect must be released.

2. Bail Hearing: Bail is generally available in connection with all crimes except in the case of a capital offense (i.e., where the death penalty applicable). Otherwise, bail can be denied to secure a D's presence at trial (i.e., where flight is feared), to prevent the commission of a serious crime (e.g., the D is threatening harm to another) or to otherwise prevent an interference with case proceedings. Bail must not be excessive.

3. Determination of Competence: A hearing may be held by the trial court to determine the D's competence. The D's ability to understand the charge and assist counsel during the trial process are the leading factors.

F. Guilty Pleas

1. Plea Bargain: A plea bargain is viewed as a contract between the prosecutor and the D. The D has the right to counsel in plea negotiations. Once the prosecutor and the D have agreed to a plea bargain, it is presented to the judge who may or may not accept it.

2. Waiver of Sixth Amendment Right to Trial: A guilty plea waives a D's right to a jury trial as provided under the Sixth Amendment.

3. Voluntary and Intelligent: The judge must determine that the plea is voluntary and intelligent by questioning the D. The judge must personally inform the D of the elements of the crime he is charged with, of the D's rights not to plea, and of the potential sentence in consequence of pleading guilty or not guilty.

4. Withdrawal of Guilty Plea: The D's guilty plea is subject to collateral attack if the court lacked jurisdiction to take the plea, if there was ineffective assistance of counsel to the extent that the D did not make an intelligent decision, if the plea was not made knowingly or voluntarily, or if the prosecution failed to keep the bargain.

STOP! Go to page 378 and work Learning Questions 58 to 66.

XI. TRIAL

A. Right to a Speedy Trial

The right to a speedy trial is guaranteed by the Sixth Amendment. There is no fixed length of time in the federal courts to determine whether or not there has been a speedy trial. It is based on a number of factors discussed below.

1. Factors: There are four factors to be balanced:

a. Length of Delay: The length of delay between charging or arrest and trial.

b. Reason: The reason or reasons for the delay are key. If the delay is due to the fault or request of the D, it is unlikely that speedy trial rule has been violated without other intervening circumstances.

c. When Right Asserted: Whether and when the D asserted the right to a speedy trial is considered. The longer the D waits, the more likely it is that the D was not truly concerned about the speediness of the trial.

d. Prejudice: Whether the D was prejudiced by the delay is also important.

2. Result of Violation: If the court finds that the D's right to a speedy trial was violated, the charges must be dismissed or the conviction reversed.

B. Right to a Public Trial

The Sixth Amendment provides that the criminally accused has a right to a public trial. Thus, any suspect in a criminal prosecution may elect to have a closed trial, but may not be forced to have a closed trial. However, a judge does not violate the constitutional rights of an accused if he/she refuses a closed trial.

C. Right to a Trial by Jury

All serious criminal cases (i.e., those that involve more than 6 months in jail) are to be heard by a fair and impartial jury. There is no constitutional right to a jury of more than six persons or that the verdict be unanimous. However, there are rules to be followed that have been promulgated by the courts.

1. Jury Size: If the jury is only six persons, the verdict must be unanimous. If a jury is 12 persons, a 9 to 3 vote in favor of conviction is sufficient.

2. Jury Composition/Selection: Jury pools must represent an accurate cross-section of the community, although the actual seated jury doesn't have to. Jurors may be stricken for cause (unlimited) or peremptorily (limited number). There can be no peremptory challenges based on race or gender. *Batson.*

D. Right to a Separate Trial

A D may be represented by counsel who is also representing another D in the same case. If the D's interests may be jeopardized by a joint trial (particularly in the use of confessions), she may move to sever the proceeding into a separate trial and obtain separate counsel.

E. Right to be Present at Trial

The Sixth Amendment provides the basis for the D's right to be present during his trial. The D may forfeit this right by disruptive behavior.

F. Rights Provided by the Confrontation Clause

The Sixth Amendment provides every criminal D with the right to be "confronted with the witnesses against him." The Confrontation Clause applies to the state as well as to the federal government, but is not absolute. For example, a D may voluntarily leave the courtroom. Or, if the D is an alleged child molester, the D may be in another room or behind a screen so that the child would not see him.

G. Right to Counsel

1. Appointment of Counsel: Every D has a right to counsel and the court will appoint counsel if the D is indigent. Under the *Faretta* case, a D may waive the right to counsel and defend himself (*pro se*). There is no right to be co-counsel with an appointed attorney. Nor does the right to counsel entitle a D to exceptional counsel.

2. Effective Counsel: The deprivation of the right to effective counsel applies only if the assistance was not reasonably effective and there is a "reasonable probability" that the trial court's outcome would have been different without counsel's misfeasance or nonfeasance. The right to "effective representation" applies at every "critical stage."

H. Right to Remain Silent

The Fifth Amendment provides that no person shall be compelled to be a witness against himself in a criminal case; nor may the D's silence be argued as an inference against him. The

Fifth Amendment privilege against self-incrimination involves taking the stand at trial. This privilege may be invoked in both criminal and civil settings.

    1. D: The D may assert this privilege and in doing so does not have to take the stand. The prosecutor may not comment on the D's refusal to testify. If the D testifies once, he has waived his Fifth Amendment right and is subject to cross-examination.

    2. Witness: A witness must take the stand (and be sworn in) if called, and after listening to each question individually, specifically invoke the privilege as it would apply to each question. If the witness is granted immunity by the prosecutor, the witness may be compelled to answer questions.

> **MBE Tip:** Remember, only a witness may selectively invoke the Fifth Amendment after each question. The D must either refrain entirely from testifying or he has waived the right and must then subject himself to cross-examination and answer all questions.

    3. Testimonial Evidence: Only testimonial evidence (the witness' own words) is affected by this privilege. This privilege cannot be invoked against physical evidence (fingerprints, blood, or DNA samples).

I. Burden of Proof

In order for the D to be convicted of a criminal offense, the prosecution must prove every element of its case beyond a reasonable doubt. In some states, self-defense is not an affirmative defense. The prosecution must disprove self-defense beyond a reasonable doubt. Insanity and duress are affirmative defenses and the defense has the burden of proof.

> **STOP!** Go to page 380 and work Learning Questions 67 to 73.

Go to page 380 and work Learning Questions 67 to 73.

XII. DOUBLE JEOPARDY

The Fifth Amendment provides that no person shall "be subject for the same offense to be twice put in jeopardy of life or limb." This is the guarantee against "double jeopardy." Via the Fourteenth Amendment, the guarantee applies to state trials as well as federal. The classic application and intent of the Double Jeopardy Clause is to prevent re-prosecution after the D has been acquitted.

A. Jeopardy Attached

It is only after jeopardy has "attached" that the protection against double jeopardy applies.

    1. Bench Trial: If the case is tried by a judge without a jury, jeopardy attaches when the first witness has been sworn.

    2. Jury Trial: If the case is tried by a jury, jeopardy attaches when the jury has been impaneled and sworn (when the entire jury has been selected and taken the oath).

B. Separate Charges Brought Separately

Prosecuting separate offenses in succession, even if they arise from the same set of factual events, is not a double jeopardy violation.

1. Same Facts, Different Crimes: For example, during the course of a bank robbery, the D shoots and kills the teller. The prosecutor is not obligated to try the robbery charge and the murder charge at the same time, because they are separate offenses. Normally, prosecutors will charge and try separate crimes arising from the same conduct together, but this is not constitutionally required.

2. Same Facts, Different Victims: It also does not violate double jeopardy to try a D for the commission of a crime against two different victims, even if the two victims were harmed under the same factual circumstances, unless they are absolutely indistinguishable. For example, a D could be tried successively for killing a bank teller and also a bystander. However, if a D burglarizes a home shared by three roommates, successive prosecutions cannot be brought by each roommate for burglary.

C. Exceptions

1. Mistrial: If after the trial has begun it is terminated by a mistrial, the prosecution is usually not barred from retrying the D. This could occur because of "manifest necessity," hung jury, too few jurors left on the panel, or mistrial at the D's request.

2. After Conviction: Where the D is convicted at trial, and then gets the verdict set aside on appeal, the double jeopardy rule usually does not apply and the state may then re-prosecute. However, if the appellate court reverses the decision because the evidence at trial was insufficient to support a conviction (i.e., the evidence presented at trial was insufficient to convict the D), a retrial is barred.

D. Separate Sovereigns

A conviction or acquittal by one jurisdiction does not bar a re-prosecution by another jurisdiction such as federal and a state.

E. Lesser Included Offenses

This exception arises only where one charge is a lesser included offense of the other. Lesser included and greater offenses are treated as the same offense and are therefore subject to the double jeopardy rule. For example, if a D is tried for first degree murder and is acquitted, he cannot subsequently be tried for manslaughter of the same V. If each offense has an element different from the other then they are not the same offense but are separate offenses, and are not subject to the double jeopardy rule (see Section B, above).

XIII. REMEDY FOR VIOLATIONS OF CONSTITUTIONAL PROTECTIONS: THE EXCLUSIONARY RULE

The exclusionary rule applies following the grant of a motion to suppress. This is a remedy against violations of the Fourth, Fifth, and Sixth Amendments. This rule provides that evidence obtained by violating the D's constitutional rights may not be introduced by the prosecution at the D's criminal trial for the purpose of providing direct proof of the D's guilt. While there are limited exceptions, it is a powerful tool for the defense.

A. Enforceable Right

The D has a right to a hearing outside the presence of the jury to determine the admissibility of evidence. During that hearing, the D has a right to testify without fear that anything he says will be admitted against him at trial. The prosecution must prove admissibility by a preponderance.

B. Fruits of the Poisonous Tree

In general, all illegally obtained evidence must be excluded; all evidence flowing from the illegally obtained evidence must also be suppressed. This includes any evidence obtained from an illegal search, arrest, or confession.

C. Limitations on the Exclusionary Rule

A number of exceptions to the exclusionary rule have been carved out. They are generally based on a principle of "harmless error," where the lack or invalidity of a search warrant has not harmed the evidentiary process. There is also an exception for warrants that appear in all respects to be valid and were relied upon in good faith, but were later shown to be invalid.

1. Good Faith Reliance on Search Warrant: Evidence is admissible if it is obtained from a good faith reliance on a facially valid search warrant that was later proved invalid.

2. Independent Source: Where evidence is obtained from a source independent from the original illegal source, it is admissible.

3. Inevitable Discovery: If the prosecutor can show that the police would have discovered the evidence even if they had not violated the constitutional protections, it will be admissible.

4. Live Witness: A witness identified through illegally obtained evidence may testify if he does so voluntarily.

5. Impeachment Purposes: Excluded evidence may be used to impeach the testifying D.

D. Harmless Error

The prosecution must prove, on appeal, that the evidence that should have been excluded was harmless error. This usually means a showing that there was enough other evidence to convict the D even without the tainted evidence.

STOP! Go to page 380 and work Learning Questions 74 to 79.

XIV. FINAL CHAPTER REVIEW INSTRUCTIONS

1. Completing the Chapter: Now that you have completed your study of the chapter's substantive text and the related Learning Questions, you need to button up this chapter. This includes your preparing your Magic Memory Outlines® and working all of the subject's practice questions.

2. Preparing Your Own Magic Memory Outline®: This is essential to your MBE success. We recommend that you use our software template in this process. Do not underestimate the learning and memory effectiveness derived from condensing the text chapter into your succinct summaries using your own words. This exercise is covered in much more detail in the preface and on the CD-ROM.

a. Summarize Knowledge: You need to prepare a summary of the chapter in your own words. This is best accomplished using the Rigos Bar Review Series Magic Memory Outlines® software. The words in the outline correspond to the bold headings in the text.

b. Capture the Essence: Your job is to summarize the substance of the text by capturing the essence of the rule and entering your summarized wording into your own outlines. Go to the text coverage and craft your own tight, concise, but yet comprehensive statements of the law. Take pride in your skills as an author; this is the best outline you have ever created.

c. Focus: Focus your attention and wording on the required technical elements necessary to prove the relevant legal principles and fine-line distinctions. Integrate any helpful "learning question" information into your outline.

3. Memorize Outline: After you have completed your own Magic Memory Outline® for the whole chapter, read it over carefully once or twice. They are the best book ever written. Refer back to your Outlines frequently.

4. Work Old Questions: The next step is to work all the final questions of each chapter. These vary in degree of difficulty, but the ones towards the end tend to concentrate on fact patterns and issues at the most difficult testing level. Consider using the Question Map on the CD-ROM. Click on the questions under the subject and topic you have just studied. This allows you to cross relate the subjects and related MBE testing.

a. Question Details: Again, it is usually worthwhile to review the explanatory answer rationales as they reinforce the relevant principles of law. If you are still unsure of the controlling rule, refer back to the related portion of the text. This will help you to appreciate the fine-line distinctions on which the MBE questions turn.

b. Do a Few Questions At a Time: Work the final chapter questions in sequence. Make sure you stop after no more than a few to check the answer rationales. Do this frequently so that the facts of the individual question are still in active memory.

c. Work Them All: We have tried to pick questions with an average or higher probability of reappearing on the MBE. You should at least read all the questions and ponder their answers. Every question and answer has some marginal learning and/or reinforcement value. On the MBE you will recognize many of the actual MBE questions as very similar to the ones in your Rigos Bar Review Series review books.

d. Learn From Mistakes: The objective is to learn from your mistakes by reviewing the explanatory rationales while you still remember the factual and legal details of the question. It is good to miss a few; they will help you become familiar with the MBE fine-line distinctions. The examiners' use of distracters, tricks, and red herrings is repetitive.

e. Flag Errors: Put a red star in the margin of the book along side every question you missed. Missed questions should be worked again the day right before the MBE. Do not make the same mistakes on the exam.

f. Essays: Candidates in jurisdictions that administer the Multistate Essay Exam should refer to the *Rigos Multistate Essay Exam Review — MEE* for practice essay questions.

5. Practice Exam: After you complete the last chapter, you should take the 200 item practice exam. There is detailed information covering this simulated MBE test in both the preface and at the beginning of the exam in Volume 2. This is important because you need to build your concentrated attention time span. You also need to get intellectually used to jumping between unrelated topics and subjects.

6. Make Your Own Exam: The Rigos Bar Review Series software allows you to pick 5, 10, 20 or 100 questions at random from all six MBE subjects. This is an important feature because you must become comfortable with switching intellectual gears between different subjects. If you are not an early riser and/or get going slowly when you get up, try working 10 or 20 questions using the "Make Your Own Exam" software the first thing every morning.

7. Update Your Magic Memory Outline®: The fine-line distinctions in the question and answer rationales will improve your understanding of how the MBE tests the law. Consider updating your Magic Memory Outline® while the question testing environment is still fresh in your mind.

XI. TRIAL

A. Right to a Speedy Trial ....
    1. Factors ....
        a. Length of Delay..
        b. Reason ....
        c. When Right Asserted ....
        d. Prejudice ....
    2. Result of Violation ....
B. Right to a Public Trial ....
C. Right to a Trial by Jury ....
    1. Jury Size..
    2. Jury Composition/Selection ....
D. Right to a Separate Trial ....
E. Right to be Present at Trial...
F. Rights Provided by the Confrontation Clause...
G. Right to Counsel..
    1. Appointment of Counsel ....
    2. Effective Counsel ....
H. Right to Remain Silent ....
    1. D...
    2. Witness..
    3. Testimonial Evidence ....
I. Burden of Proof..

XII. DOUBLE JEOPARDY

A. Jeopardy Attached...
    1. Bench Trial..
    2. Jury Trial ....
B. Separate Charges Brought Separately..
    1. Same Facts, Different Crimes ....
    2. Same Facts, Different Victims ....
C. Exceptions...
    1. Mistrial ....
    2. After Conviction..
D. Separate Sovereigns ....
E. Lesser Included Offenses ....

XIII. REMEDY FOR VIOLATIONS OF CONSTITUTIONAL PROTECTIONS: THE EXCLUSIONARY RULE

A. Enforceable Right..
B. Fruits of the Poisonous Tree ....
C. Limitations on the Exclusionary Rule..
    1. Good Faith Reliance on Search Warrant...
    2. Independent Source...
    3. Inevitable Discovery ....
    4. Live Witness..
    5. Impeachment Purposes...
D. Harmless Error ....

> Numbers immediately following the topic are the chapter question numbers. The **boldface** numbers preceded by "F" are the final exam question numbers. For example, for the topic "II. B. 1. Nonvolitional Act" below, question 148 is in the chapter questions on page 6-395; question **F102** is in the final exam on page 7-475.

VII. OVERVIEW: GENERAL PRINCIPLES OF CRIMINAL PROCEDURE

XIII. REMEDY FOR VIOLATIONS OF CONSTITUTIONAL PROTECTIONS: THE EXCLUSIONARY RULE

MEE Candidates: If your jurisdiction administers the Multistate Essay Exam in addition to the MBE, please refer to the *Rigos Bar Review Series Multistate Essay Exam Review — MEE* for practice essay questions and sample answers covering criminal law and procedure.

Criminal Law and Procedure Learning Questions

1. If a defendant stabs a victim with the intent to kill him, but the victim had already died of a heart attack six hours before, the defendant cannot be found guilty of murder because the prosecution cannot prove

(A) Actus reus.
(B) Mens rea.
(C) Causation.
(D) Result.

2. An omission or a failure to act can create criminal culpability if

I. A statute or other law creates a duty to act.
II. The defendant had a duty under contract.
III. The defendant could have assisted

without harm to himself.

IV. The defendant created the risk to the victim.
(A) I only.
(B) II and III.
(C) II, III and IV.
(D) I, II and IV.

3. Under the common law, specific intent is always required to prove the crime of

(A) Felony murder.
(B) Manslaughter.
(C) Robbery.
(D) Statutory rape.

4. If a crime is one of strict liability, proof of intent to commit the crime

(A) Must be beyond a reasonable doubt.
(B) Is not required.

(C) Must be proved by a preponderance of evidence.
(D) Is impossible to procure.

5. The criminal law doctrine of "transferred intent" means

(A) Intent to commit one type of crime transfers to any other type of crime.
(B) Intent to harm one victim transfers to another victim.
(C) Intent by one conspirator to commit a crime transfers to all other conspirators.
(D) Intent to seize certain evidence transfers to other unrelated evidence seized.

6. Under the MPC, mistake of law can exonerate a defendant if

(A) The statute does not specify that knowledge of the law is presumed.
(B) The defendant can prove his mistake by a preponderance.
(C) The defendant was acting upon misinformation from a public official.
(D) The defendant is a non-US citizen and unfamiliar with the legal system.

7. Suppose A shoots B, intending to kill him, and then 20 minutes later, C shoots B also intending to kill him. Neither wound alone would be fatal, but the two combined cause B to bleed to death. According to the substantial factor test

(A) A is guilty of murder and B of attempted murder.
(B) B is guilty of murder and A of attempted murder.
(C) A and B are both guilty of murder.
(D) Both A and B are guilty of attempted murder.

8. If Y helps Z commit a burglary by driving Z to the scene and acting as a lookout, and Z completes the crime, Y can be charged with

    (A) Burglary.
    (B) Accomplice to burglary.
    (C) Attempted burglary.
    (D) None of the above.

9. If the victim's harm is a natural and probable result of the actions of a defendant, then that defendant's actions are said to be the _____

_____

_____ of the harm.

    (A) Presumed cause.
    (B) Proven cause.
    (C) Actual cause.
    (D) Proximate cause.

10. A defendant who breaks into a home intending to steal a stereo and instead steals $500 in cash can be found guilty of both larceny and burglary because

    (A) The two crimes are identical.
    (B) The elements of burglary have been met.
    (C) Larceny is a lesser included offense of burglary.
    (D) Burglary does not merge.

11. In a jurisdiction that has adopted the Model Penal Code, a defendant can be found not guilty by reason of insanity if he

I.   Lacked the capacity to distinguish right from wrong.
II. Was unable to control his actions as a result of some mental defect.
III. Was totally incapable of realizing what he was doing.
IV. Acted out of terror as a result of a threat of substantial physical harm.

    (A) I only.
    (B) II only.
    (C) I, II, and III.
    (D) II and IV.

12. A criminal defendant must be capable of understanding the criminal proceedings and effectively assisting her lawyer because

    (A) If she can't, it violates her constitutional right to a fair trial.
    (B) If she can't, she was likely unable to comprehend the nature of her crime at the time she committed it.
    (C) She must appear as a witness in her own defense.
    (D) She must tell her lawyer when to make objections.

13. Q goes to a bar and orders a number of virgin daiquiris. Unbeknownst to him, the bartender makes them with alcohol. Q, who never drinks, becomes quite drunk and batters V. On the battery charge, Q will likely be found

    (A) Guilty, because intoxication is not a defense.
    (B) Guilty, because a reasonable person would have known that the drinks contained alcohol.
    (C) Not guilty, because involuntary intoxication is a defense.
    (D) Guilty, because battery is a strict liability crime.

14. If a child is 12 years old at the time he is charged with murder

    (A) He is conclusively presumed incapable of forming the requisite intent.
    (B) He is presumed incapable of forming the requisite intent and the prosecutor must provide clear and convincing proof of capacity.
    (C) He is presumed incompetent to stand trial.
    (D) He may be tried as an adult.

15. A commits burglary because B threatens to sink A's yacht if A does not comply. Charged with burglary, A will likely be found

    (A) Guilty, because duress is not an available defense to burglary.
    (B) Not guilty, because under duress A could not have formed the requisite specific intent.
    (C) Not guilty, because A was acting under duress.

(D) Guilty, because a threat to property is insufficient for a duress defense.

16. Entrapment is available as a defense when
(A) Police create the opportunity for the defendant to commit the crime.
(B) The defendant has a predisposition to committing the crime.
(C) The police induce the defendant to commit a crime that he otherwise would not have committed.
(D) The defendant was predisposed to commit the crime, but did not intend to commit that particular crime prior to encountering the police setup.

17. In a busy restaurant, A tells B, "If you don't pay this debt by 5:00 tomorrow, I'm coming to your house to cut your arms off." B, in terror, shoots A. B is charged with murder and argues self-defense. His defense will fail because
(A) He had a duty to retreat.
(B) He used deadly force when deadly force was not threatened.
(C) He was threatened with future, not imminent, harm.
(D) He recklessly put himself in a dangerous situation.

18. A defendant who makes an honest but unreasonable mistake in using deadly force as self-defense against an aggressor will likely
(A) Be charged with murder, because mistake is not acceptable when the use of deadly force is involved.
(B) Be charged with manslaughter, because the mistake negated the required mental state for murder.
(C) Be acquitted, because he acted in self-defense.
(D) Be acquitted, because he had no criminal intent.

19. The majority view on defense of others is that a defender may use as much force as he reasonably believes is required to protect the victim. The minority view holds that

(A) A defender may use as much force as he reasonably believes is required, but only if he has a personal relationship to the victim.
(B) A defender may not use any force but must summon help from a law enforcement officer.
(C) A defender must use only non-deadly force unless he has a personal relationship to the victim.
(D) A defender can only use that amount of force that the victim himself would be legally allowed to use.

20. Quincy witnesses Abram robbing Jones, although he sees no weapon. As Abram flees from the scene he runs by Quincy, who hits Abram in the head with a golf club, killing him instantly. If charged with murder, Quincy will likely be
(A) Convicted, because Abram did not pose an immediate threat.
(B) Acquitted, because Abram was a fleeing felon.
(C) Convicted, because private citizens may never use force to apprehend suspects.
(D) Convicted, because Quincy was not correct in his belief that Abram was a felon.

21. Over a couple of beers, Don tells Mathew that he should go over to his ex-girlfriend's house and beat up her new boyfriend. Mathew says "You're nuts, man, I'm not that stupid" and leaves. Charged with solicitation, Don would likely be
(A) Convicted, because he intentionally encouraged another to commit a felony.
(B) Acquitted, because Mathew immediately refused.
(C) Acquitted, because Don did not offer anything of value to Mathew for committing the crime.
(D) Acquitted, because the proposed crime was never committed.

22. Sarah, age 14, approaches Ben, age 19, at a party and suggests that they have sex.

They do so. Ben is arrested for statutory rape, and Sarah for solicitation. Ben is acquitted. Sarah will likely be
- (A) Acquitted, because the solicitor cannot be convicted if the solicitee is acquitted.
- (B) Acquitted, because she is within the class of persons that the statute was enacted to protect.
- (C) Acquitted, because she consented and therefore she was not soliciting a crime.
- (D) Convicted, because the crime of solicitation is completed when the offer is made.

23. "In a criminal conspiracy, every co-conspirator may be charged with each crime committed, whether or not he agreed to each crime." This statement is a description of the
- (A) *Pinkerton* rule
- (B) *M'Naghten* rule
- (C) *Miranda* rule
- (D) *Gerstein* rule

24. If two people commit a crime that by definition requires two persons to commit
- (A) They can also be charged with conspiracy if they had a previous verbal agreement.
- (B) They cannot be charged with conspiracy under any circumstances.
- (C) One person will be charged with solicitation.
- (D) Only one can be charged because the other must be granted immunity and testify.

25. The mens rea which must be proven for attempt is
- (A) The same as the mens rea for the underlying crime attempted.
- (B) Specific intent.
- (C) Recklessness.
- (D) None, attempt is a strict liability crime.

26. A murder defendant, who did not specifically intend to kill his victim or cause him serious bodily harm, may still be convicted of murder if
- (A) It can be proven that the defendant had a motive for the killing.
- (B) He had recently threatened the victim.
- (C) He was totally indifferent to the possibility of seriously injuring or killing someone.
- (D) He violated a statute.

27. In a murder case, if it is proven that a defendant did not intend to kill his victim, but instead intended only to "shoot him in the leg to scare him" the defendant will likely be convicted of
- (A) Murder.
- (B) Voluntary manslaughter.
- (C) Involuntary manslaughter.
- (D) None of the above.

28. Disconnecting the life support of a victim who is still breathing and whose heart is still beating, but who has irreversible cessation of brain function is not murder because
- (A) The victim is not legally a human being.
- (B) It is voluntary manslaughter.
- (C) There is no causation.
- (D) It is merciful.

29. X is driving 100 mph on a deserted country road late at night. As he comes around a corner, he collides with a vehicle that was pulling out of a driveway, killing a passenger. If the jury finds that X was reckless, he should properly be convicted of
- (A) Second degree murder.
- (B) Involuntary manslaughter.
- (C) Voluntary manslaughter.
- (D) Reckless endangerment.

30. In a jurisdiction governed by the MPC, the mens rea for negligent homicide is
- (A) Extreme recklessness.
- (B) Mere negligence.
- (C) A gross deviation from the standard of care.
- (D) Nothing; the MPC does not recognize negligent homicide.

31. Which of the following scenarios would most likely result in a conviction for larceny?

(A) Tim goes to his neighbor's house, hoping to borrow his weed whacker. His neighbor is not home, but the tool is sitting out. Tim takes it, but it is quite old and breaks before he can return it.

(B) Tim goes to his neighbor's house, intending to take back his own weed whacker that the neighbor borrowed months ago. Unbeknownst to Tim, his neighbor had already returned the tool to Tim's wife. Tim mistakes his neighbor's tool for his own and takes it.

(C) Tim goes to his neighbor's house intending to borrow his weed whacker. His neighbor isn't home, but the tool is sitting out. After a few days, he decides that he likes his neighbor's tool better. He returns his own tool to his neighbor, hoping his neighbor won't notice.

(D) Tim goes to his neighbor's house, intending to steal his weed whacker. He sees the tool in the open garage, and is about to pick it up when he abruptly changes his mind and leaves.

32. An employee who uses his computer at work to run his own secret for-profit enterprise would be most appropriately charged with

(A) Embezzlement.
(B) Larceny.
(C) False pretenses.
(D) Robbery.

33. The difference between larceny by trick and false pretenses is

(A) One involves fraud; the other does not.
(B) One involves transfer of title and possession; the other only involves transfer of possession.
(C) One involves tangible property; the other does not.

(D) Nothing; they are the same crime.

34. Maurice gets a call from Ron, who in the past has sold him top-quality car stereos at a great price. Ron tells Maurice, "Hey, I got 300 stereos I'll sell you for $10 each." Ron says "Great! Leave them in my warehouse on Bleecker." Ron does so. But when Maurice sees them, he says, "Half of these are broken – I won't pay." As it turns out, the stereos are stolen. Charged with receiving stolen goods, Maurice will likely be

(A) Acquitted, because he did not actually take possession.
(B) Acquitted, because he had no actual knowledge that the property was stolen.
(C) Acquitted, because he did not complete the transaction.
(D) Convicted.

35. Stan cases a liquor store with an unloaded gun in his hand, hoping for a chance to get some cash. He sees the clerk go in the back room, dashes in, breaks open the cash register, and makes off with $400 before the clerk returns. Charged with robbery, Stan will likely be

(A) Acquitted, because the clerk was not present.
(B) Acquitted, because the gun was not loaded.
(C) Convicted, because he forced the cash register drawer open.
(D) Convicted, because he was carrying a gun.

36. Biff goes to Jackson's house at 3:30 p.m. intending to break in and take Jackson's TV. When he arrives, he finds the door wide open and no one at home. He walks in and takes the TV. The most serious crime that Biff could be convicted of is

(A) Larceny.
(B) Robbery.
(C) Burglary.
(D) Embezzlement.

37. A defendant can be convicted of common law battery if he possessed a mens rea of

I. Recklessness.
II. Gross negligence.
III. Specific intent.
IV. Negligence.
   (A) III only
   (B) I and III.
   (C) I, II, and III.
   (D) II and IV.

38. To be convicted of assault, a defendant must
   (A) Cause a victim to fear serious bodily harm.
   (B) Cause a victim to fear immediate battery.
   (C) Ultimately succeed in battering a victim.
   (D) Be holding a weapon or object capable of inflicting serious bodily harm.

39. Doug has sexual intercourse with Linda without her consent. She tells him "No" repeatedly, but he is too drunk to realize that she has not consented. Charged with rape, Doug will likely be
   (A) Convicted, because he should not have had intercourse while intoxicated.
   (B) Convicted, because intoxication negates the mens rea only when the defendant was too drunk to realize he was having intercourse.
   (C) Acquitted, because Linda did not demonstrate any physical resistance.
   (D) Acquitted, because his intoxication prevented him from realizing there was a lack of consent, which is an element of rape.

40. Kidnapping is defined as the intentional and unlawful confinement of a person with movement of that person to another location. However, a defendant is not guilty of kidnapping if
   (A) The victim is not physically restrained.

   (B) The victim does not attempt escape.
   (C) The victim is only confined for a short time.
   (D) The defendant does not intend to confine the victim.

41. Mel is painting his car in his garage, surrounded by flammable chemicals. He steps outside to take a smoke break, and falls asleep with the cigarette in his hand. The cigarette ignites some fumes and burns the garage down. Charged with arson under most modern statutes, Mel will likely be
   (A) Convicted, because his actions were reckless, sufficient mens rea for arson.
   (B) Acquitted, because he did not burn down a dwelling.
   (C) Acquitted, because the garage was his own property.
   (D) Acquitted, because he did not intend to start the fire or manifest extreme disregard for the danger.

42. A business owner reviewing an employee's personal emails on a work computer does not violate the Fourth Amendment because
   (A) There is no legitimate expectation of privacy.
   (B) The computer is the property of the owner, and it is therefore the equivalent to a man searching his own wallet.
   (C) The business owner is not a government employee.
   (D) It is not a search.

43. The Open Fields doctrine holds that
   (A) If there is no fence or other barrier to private property, an officer may enter the premises and search.
   (B) There is no expectation of privacy in fields not immediately adjacent to a dwelling.
   (C) A computer may be searched if there is no password protection.
   (D) A car parked in a open field may be searched.

44. In order to have probable cause to arrest, there must be

I. A likelihood that a violation of the law occurred.
II. A likelihood that the person arrested committed the violation.
III. A warrant.
IV. A likelihood that the suspect will be convicted.
  (A) I only.
  (B) I and II.
  (C) I, II, and III.
  (D) II and IV.

45. A warrantless arrest is legally permissible if
  (A) The suspect committed a felony and is in a public place.
  (B) The officer has an articulable suspicion that the suspect was involved in a crime.
  (C) The suspect is in a location not under his control.
  (D) The suspect committed a misdemeanor in front of an eyewitness.

46. If a defendant is successful in challenging the validity of the warrant, it will have the following effect
  (A) His case will be dismissed.
  (B) He will be found not guilty, because there will be no evidence against him.
  (C) Any evidence obtained as a result of the arrest will be excluded as evidence.
  (D) No effect.

47. In order to bring a suspect to the police station for a lineup, an officer must have
  (A) An articulable suspicion.
  (B) Some physical evidence linking the defendant to criminal activity.
  (C) A warrant.
  (D) Full probable cause to arrest.

48. A probable cause affidavit for a search warrant
  (A) Cannot be based on hearsay.

  (B) Must exist before stopping an automobile.
  (C) Must specify the items to be seized and their location.
  (D) Cannot be based on the testimony of an informant alone.

49. A proper search warrant must specify
  (A) The particular rooms in a structure in which evidence is suspected to be located.
  (B) The particular structure in which evidence is suspected to be located.
  (C) The particular person who owns the structure to be searched.
  (D) The particular crimes which are expected to be charged after the search is completed.

50. Incident to a lawful arrest, a warrantless search may be made
  (A) Of all the suspect's property.
  (B) Of anything within the suspect's reach.
  (C) Of the suspect's home.
  (D) Of the suspect's car, including the trunk.

51. While executing a search warrant for illegal weapons in Stuart's home, Officer Jones frisked Greg. When he felt a large metal object, he reached in Greg's jacket and found an iron pipe. Later, it was discovered that the pipe had been used as a murder weapon. Greg's motion to exclude the pipe as evidence should be
  (A) Denied, because Officer Jones had the right to pat down Greg to ensure his own safety.
  (B) Granted, because the search of Greg's person was outside the scope of the warrant.
  (C) Denied, because a *Terry* frisk is always legal.
  (D) Granted, because Officer Jones did not have an articulable suspicion to validate the search.

52. To validate an automobile search under the "exigent circumstances" warrant exception, the officer must be able to demonstrate that

(A) The officer reasonably believed the automobile was used in a crime.
(B) The automobile was in working order and therefore capable of being moved.
(C) The driver was acting suspiciously.
(D) The evidence sought was in plain view.

53. Paul's neighbor notices suspicious persons on Paul's property and calls the police. When they arrive, they find a broken window. They knock, and hearing no answer, enter. Sitting on the living room table, they see a wooden box. Inside, they find a handgun. As a convicted felon, Paul is not allowed to own a handgun. Paul's motion to suppress the handgun as evidence should be
   (A) Granted, because there was no proof that the handgun was Paul's.
   (B) Denied, because the handgun was in plain view.
   (C) Denied, because the police entered illegally.
   (D) Granted, because the handgun was not in plain view.

54. An automobile may be searched and inventoried when impounded. It may be impounded when

I.   The driver is unconscious.
II. The driver is arrested.
III. The automobile is suspected to have been used in a crime.
IV. The automobile is abandoned in the middle of the freeway.
   (A) II and III only.
   (B) II, III, and IV.
   (C) I, II, and IV.
   (D) I, II, and III.

55. Police may search without a warrant if express, voluntary, and knowing consent is given. Once consent is given, it may be revoked
   (A) If the officer exceeds the scope of the consent.
   (B) For any reason at any time.

(C) If it is demonstrated that the person giving the consent did not have authority.
(D) After a reasonable period of time.

56. An example of evanescent evidence is
   (A) An automobile.
   (B) A handwriting sample.
   (C) A suspect's blood that may contain drugs.
   (D) A confession.

57. Kyle tells the police that Ted is going to call him in two days to arrange a murder for hire. The police conduct a warrantless wiretap of the phone call, and arrest Ted for solicitation of murder. Ted's motion to suppress the recording as evidence should be
   (A) Denied, because Kyle consented and the conversation related to a crime.
   (B) Denied, because a wiretap is not a "search" under the Fourth Amendment.
   (C) Granted, because Ted had a legitimate expectation of privacy.
   (D) Granted, because the police had sufficient time to obtain a warrant.

58. A confession will generally be admissible against a defendant if

I.   It is in the form of a signed affidavit.
II. *Miranda* warnings were given.
III. The defendant was not being interrogated when he confessed.
IV. The confession was made voluntarily.
   (A) II, III, and IV.
   (B) II and IV only.
   (C) I, II, and III.
   (D) II only.

59. If it is established that a confession was coerced by the police, then
   (A) It can be used, but a limiting instruction must be read to the jury.
   (B) It is excluded from the prosecution's case in chief, but can be used for impeachment purposes.
   (C) The prosecution may still proceed.

(D) The charges against the defendant are dismissed.

60. Joe is arrested and is read the *Miranda* warnings. He chooses not to speak to police until he speaks to a lawyer. While is in jail waiting for his lawyer, his "cellmate," an undercover officer, begins asking Joe about his arrest. Eventually Joe confesses that he is guilty. Joe's motion to exclude the confession should be

    (A) Denied, because he received and understood his *Miranda* rights.
    (B) Granted, because the questions were a custodial interrogation.
    (C) Denied, because Joe did not know that his cellmate was an officer and therefore his confession was voluntary.
    (D) Granted, because his confession was coerced.

61. When testifying to a grand jury, a witness has the right to

I. Receive *Miranda* warnings.
II. Have an attorney present.
III. Have cigarette breaks.
IV. Be confronted with the witnesses against him.
    (A) I and II only
    (B) I, II and IV only.
    (C) I, II, III, and IV.
    (D) None of the above.

62. The right to be represented by counsel during formal court proceedings

    (A) Must be affirmatively, knowingly, and intelligently waived.
    (B) Must be clearly and unambiguously invoked.
    (C) Cannot be refused.
    (D) Is protected by the Fifth Amendment.

63. Bob, an Asian American, is arrested for armed robbery. An eyewitness who claims the robber was of Asian descent is brought in for a lineup. In the lineup are two African Americans, two Caucasian Americans, one Native American, and Bob. Under these circumstances

    (A) The identification procedure will probably be found unnecessarily suggestive, and the charges will be dismissed.
    (B) The identification procedure will probably be found unnecessarily suggestive, and the witness identification will be excluded as evidence.
    (C) Another lineup should be prepared for the witness, this time with Bob surrounded by other Asian Americans.
    (D) A judge would likely find the lineup identification to be admissible.

64. If a person is indicted or arrested without a warrant

    (A) The warrant can be issued ex post facto.
    (B) An arraignment must be held within 72 hours.
    (C) He cannot be held for more than 24 hours.
    (D) A *Gerstein* hearing must be held within 48 hours of detainment.

65. A competency hearing may be held by the trial court to determine

    (A) If counsel is competent to provide adequate representation.
    (B) If the defendant was of sound mind at the time he committed the crime.
    (C) If the defendant is capable of understanding the proceedings and assisting counsel.
    (D) If the defendant will be able to receive a fair trial within the jurisdiction.

66. If the prosecution and defendant reach a plea agreement

    (A) No further proceedings are necessary.
    (B) A judge has discretion to accept or reject the plea.
    (C) The defendant still has the right to a jury trial.
    (D) It may not be withdrawn.

67. If the judge in a criminal case determines that a defendant's right to a speedy trial has been violated,

(A) The conviction is set aside and a new trial is granted.
(B) A trial must be held within 72 hours.
(C) The charges are dismissed or the conviction reversed.
(D) The defendant is entitled to compensation.

68. Brenda, a respected and reputable accountant, is about to be tried for embezzlement. At a pretrial hearing, she requests a closed trial to prevent damage to her reputation in the community. Without comment or explanation, the judge refuses. The judge's decision is

(A) Proper, because there is no constitutional right to a closed trial.
(B) Proper, because sufficient grounds for requesting a closed trial did not exist, therefore the judge had discretion.
(C) Improper, because the judge did not enter written justification in the record.
(D) Improper, because a closed trial must always be granted upon request.

69. In a trial with a twelve-person jury, a conviction is only proper if

(A) The verdict is unanimous.
(B) At least 9 jurors vote in favor of conviction.
(C) The jurors are all the same race as the defendant.
(D) The majority of jurors vote in favor of conviction.

70. The Sixth Amendment right to be present at trial

(A) Is absolute.
(B) Only applies through the Confrontation Clause, so if there are no witnesses, the trial may be conducted without the defendant.
(C) May be forfeited if the defendant is continually disruptive.
(D) Only applies to felonies.

71. The right to effective counsel is violated if

(A) The defendant is convicted despite the existence of questionable evidence.
(B) Counsel neglected to make an appropriate objection.
(C) The defendant can demonstrate that he disagreed with counsel's strategy.
(D) There is a reasonable probability that the outcome would have been different without counsel's misfeasance or nonfeasance.

72. Marla is on trial for arson. Peter, an eyewitness, takes the stand. To everyone's surprise, on cross-examination it begins to seem as though Peter may have had a hand in the crime. Peter begins to invoke his Fifth Amendment right after each question. Defense counsel requests that the witness be compelled to answer. The judge should

(A) Compel Peter to answer, as failure to do so would violate Marla's rights under the Confrontation Clause.
(B) Compel Peter to answer, as he waived his Fifth Amendment right to remain silent when he took the stand.
(C) Refuse to compel.
(D) Compel Peter to answer, as he is not the defendant on trial and thus the privilege against self-incrimination is applicable.

73. To secure a conviction in a criminal case, the prosecution must

(A) Prove every element of the charge beyond a reasonable doubt.
(B) Prove key elements of the charge beyond a reasonable doubt.
(C) Prove every element of the charge by clear and convincing evidence.
(D) Prove every element of the charge by a preponderance of the evidence.

74. When a defendant is convicted and the verdict is set aside on appeal

(A) Double jeopardy bars a retrial.

(B) A retrial is barred only if the appellate court determines that the evidence was insufficient to support a conviction.

(C) The appellate court may conduct a de novo trial.

(D) A retrial may be held only if it is conducted by a different sovereign.

75. Kylie is tried for burglary and acquitted. Upon an exit poll of the jury, the prosecutor discovers that the jury would have convicted her for larceny, if they had understood that they could. The prosecutor files a larceny charge against Kylie. Kylie moves for dismissal. The motion should be

(A) Denied, because burglary and larceny are different charges.

(B) Denied, because the jury made a reversible legal error.

(C) Granted, because double jeopardy bars prosecution of the larceny charge.

(D) Granted, because a lesser charge can only be tried before a greater one, not after.

76. The prosecution must prove that evidence is admissible

(A) By a showing of probable cause.

(B) By a preponderance.

(C) By clear and convincing proof.

(D) Beyond a reasonable doubt.

77. Evidence obtained in violation of the Fourth Amendment

(A) Is always inadmissible.

(B) Is usually admissible to impeach the defendant.

(C) Is admissible in the prosecution's case if the trial judge determines that is would be harmless to do so.

(D) Is admissible if the police believed their actions were proper.

78. "Fruits of the poisonous tree" are

(A) Criminal charges that are based on excluded evidence.

(B) Jurors that have personal biases that exclude them from hearing a case.

(C) Items of evidence that would not have been obtained without the help of prior illegally obtained evidence.

(D) Arguments that are based on excluded evidence.

79. A live witness who was identified through illegally obtained evidence

(A) Is considered "fruit of the poisonous tree" and may not testify.

(B) May testify only to impeach the defendant.

(C) May testify only in favor of the defendant.

(D) May testify if she does so voluntarily.

Criminal Law and Procedure
Practice Questions

80. In a Motion to Suppress hearing

I. The defendant's statements may not be used against him at trial.

II. The jury may not be present.

III. The burden is on the defense to prove evidence inadmissible.

IV. The defendant does not have a right to counsel.

(A) I only.

(B) I and II only.

(C) I, II, and III.

(D) II and III.

Questions 81 and 82 are based on the following:

Tom buys $100 worth of heroin from Mike. When Mike's product turns out to be bogus, Tom goes to Mike's house to break in and get his $100 back. When he arrives he finds the house empty. An envelope containing $500 is wedged halfway under the door. He takes $100, replaces the envelope, and goes.

Mike's neighbor sees Tom poking around and calls the police. As Mike is leaving, the police arrive and arrest him.

81. On a charge of 1st degree burglary, Tom's best defense is
  - (A) He lacked intent, since he only went there to recover his own property.
  - (B) He did not enter the house, but only stood out front.
  - (C) The amount of money taken is so small that it is only a misdemeanor, not a felony.
  - (D) No one was present in the house at the time.

82. Upon Tom's arrest, the police discover the previous transaction between Mike and Tom. According to Tom, he and Mike agreed to meet in a hotel room Mike had reserved and make the exchange. Tom and Mike are both charged with conspiracy to traffic in illegal narcotics. Mike's defense at trial is that although he did originally agree to meet Tom and sell him the drugs, prior to the actual exchange, Mike had a change of heart. He purposely gave Tom fake heroin to prevent him from getting real heroin somewhere else.

Mike's defense will likely
  - (A) Succeed, because he lacked the necessary mens rea.
  - (B) Fail, because he initially agreed to commit the crime, and failure to complete it is not a defense to conspiracy.
  - (C) Succeed, because no substantial step was taken in furtherance of the crime.
  - (D) Fail, because he committed fraud.

83. Shawn and Tanya break into Umberto's house at night and are arrested and charged with burglary and conspiracy to commit burglary. At trial, the prosecutor presents evidence that they had planned the break-in, but does not successfully demonstrate what they intended to do once inside. Shawn and Tanya will likely be
  - (A) Convicted, because agreement and substantial step is enough for conspiracy, even if the crime is not committed.
  - (B) Convicted, because they broke into a dwelling at night and therefore an inherently dangerous situation was created.
  - (C) Acquitted, because the conspiracy merged with the burglary once it was actually committed.
  - (D) Acquitted, because the prosecution failed to prove agreement or intent to commit the substantive crime of burglary.

84. Max enters a liquor store, pulls out a gun, and demands that the cashier empty the register. As he nervously looks around for police, the cashier reaches out and attempts to grab the gun. Max nervously drops it, it accidentally discharges, killing a nearby customer. Max is charged with first degree murder. On these facts, he will likely be
  - (A) Acquitted, because he lacked the necessary intent required for first degree murder.
  - (B) Acquitted, because the cashier's actions were the proximate cause of the death.
  - (C) Convicted, because any death that is a natural and probable consequence of a felony is first degree murder.
  - (D) Convicted, because intent to commit serious bodily harm is assumed when a deadly weapon is used.

Questions 85 – 87 are based on the following:

The next three questions each describe an offense. Select from the choices the most serious offense of which the defendant could be properly convicted.

85. Lawrence removes Victor's wallet from his jacket pocket while Victor is wearing the jacket. Victor notices Lawrence as he is running away and tackles him after only a few feet.
  - (A) Larceny.
  - (B) Burglary.

(C) Robbery.
(D) None of the above

86. William goes to John's home at 10 p.m. to demand repayment of a loan. He knocks repeatedly, but gets no answer. Hearing the cries of a hurt dog coming from inside, he breaks a window and crawls in. He finds John's dog underneath a fallen bookshelf, and rescues him. On his way out the front door, he notices $50 on a table and takes it.

(A) Larceny.
(B) Burglary.
(C) Robbery.
(D) Embezzlement.

87. Gary walks up to Tim with a hot pink plastic toy gun, points it at Tim, and with a grin on his face states, "Give me your wallet or I'll shoot you." Tim, being rather dim witted, believes the gun to be real and, hands over his wallet. Gary, dumbfounded at his luck, takes the wallet and walks away.

(A) Larceny.
(B) Burglary.
(C) Robbery.
(D) None of the above.

88. In a jurisdiction which has adopted only the *M'Naghten* test, which of the following scenarios could provide defendant with a colorable insanity defense?

(A) D is charged with first degree murder. He is a clinically diagnosed schizophrenic and claims that demonic voices commanded him to stab the victim.
(B) D is charged with second degree murder. He claims he was enraged over the discovery of his wife's affair and lost control, hitting the victim with his fists and breaking his neck.
(C) D is charged with vehicular manslaughter. He is a clinically diagnosed psychotic and claims he thought he was riding a horse in an open pasture, not driving a car.

(D) D is charged with arson. He has been diagnosed as a pyromaniac, unable to control his urges to burn buildings.

Questions 89 and 90 are based on the following:

Gerald tells Nancy that he is planning to confront Dan, a known gang member, and "beat him senseless." Nancy, whose sister was attacked by a member of the same gang, thinks this a great idea and tells Gerald the name of a park which she knows Dan frequents. When Gerald gets there, he assaults Dan in front of Barry. Barry watches the entire attack, smiling, but does nothing to stop it.

89. On these facts, Nancy can be charged with

(A) Solicitation.
(B) Rendering Criminal Assistance.
(C) Assault.
(D) None of the above.

90. Barry is also charged with assault on a theory of accomplice liability. His best defense to that charge is

(A) He was too frightened to act in Dan's defense.
(B) He did not take any action to assist Gerald.
(C) He owed no legal duty to rescue Dan.
(D) He did not have criminal intent.

Questions 91 – 93 are based on the following:

A bank robbery takes place and 2 eyewitnesses state the getaway car was a gray Honda Accord. Minutes later, Dave is stopped in his blue Honda Accord 3 blocks from the scene. The officer sees a locked briefcase on the back seat and asks Dave to open it. When Dave refuses, the officer pries the briefcase open and finds cocaine.

91. Dave's motion to suppress introduction of the cocaine as evidence will most probably be

(A) Granted, because insufficient probable cause existed for the search.
(B) Denied, because the briefcase was in plain view and therefore subject to search.
(C) Granted, because the briefcase was locked and Dave refused consent.
(D) Denied, because the briefcase was within Dave's "wingspan."

92. Dave is arrested and charged with possession of cocaine with intent to distribute. The prosecutor wants to bolster her case regarding intent, and executes a search warrant for Dave's apartment. No drugs or other evidence are found. They do discover, however, that Dave often spends the night at the apartment of his girlfriend, Debbie.

The prosecutor applies for a warrant to search Debbie's apartment for cocaine. The magistrate, a former prosecutor, issues the warrant. In the pantry of Debbie's apartment, a Tupperware container is found containing a small amount of cocaine. The container has Dave's fingerprints on it.

Dave's motion to suppress introduction of the cocaine as evidence will most probably be
(A) Granted, because Debbie was not a suspect and her residence could not be subject to a valid warrant.
(B) Granted, because the warrant was invalid due to lack of probable cause.
(C) Denied, because the warrant was issued subsequent to a valid arrest.
(D) Granted, because the magistrate was biased.

93. At trial, Dave decides to take the stand. On cross-examination, the prosecutor begins to ask questions about Dave's drug activities, and Dave responds "I refuse to answer on the grounds that I may incriminate myself." The judge orders Dave to answer, and he is convicted, based largely on his own testimony. On appeal,

Dave's request that his conviction be reversed will likely be
(A) Granted, because Dave's attorney should have prevented him from taking the stand, and thus was not reasonably effective.
(B) Granted, because a witness may invoke the Fifth Amendment selectively as each question is asked.
(C) Denied, because the judge's decision constitutes harmless error.
(D) Denied, because Dave waived his right to avoid self-incrimination once he took the stand.

Questions 94 and 95 are based on the following:

On a tip from a reliable informant that Mark is planning a bank robbery, Officer Lewis, in uniform, pays a visit to Mark's house. Mark is not home, but his wife Sheila answers the door. Officer informs Sheila of his purpose and requests her consent to search the house. Sheila says "Certainly, we have nothing to hide" and steps aside. Looking in the closet in the master bedroom, Officer finds floor plans of First National Bank and documents containing strategies for breaking in. When Mark returns home, Officer arrests him.

94. On a motion to suppress the evidence found at his home, Mark will most likely
(A) Succeed, because Sheila was not told that she had the right to refuse consent.
(B) Succeed, because Officer Lewis should have first obtained a warrant.
(C) Fail, because consent to search by third persons is effective if they have joint authority over the premises.
(D) Succeed, since the officer had no warrant and the evidence was not in plain view.

95. After Mark's arrest without warrant, he is booked, a complaint is filed charging him with attempted robbery, and he is immediately indicted and arraigned. His trial begins five weeks later. On appeal, Mark could raise the issue that

    (A) The delay was a violation of his right to a speedy trial.

    (B) A preliminary hearing with live witnesses in front of a magistrate should have been held prior to indictment.

    (C) The failure to hold an immediate arraignment was a due process violation.

    (D) There was insufficient evidence to file a complaint.

Questions 96 and 97 are based on the following:

Officer Stanley pulls over John's station wagon when he sees it has a broken tail light. Upon approaching the car, Officer notices Harry sitting on the passenger's side and sees a handgun and several purses sitting in the rear compartment of the station wagon, beyond the back seat. He asks John about the items, and John replies, "Harry did it, all I did was give him a lift." Both are arrested and charged, and four days later make their first court appearance and are indicted.

96. On appeal, John and Harry can both argue

    (A) The failure to hold a *Gerstein* hearing was improper.

    (B) The stop was illegal because no articulable suspicion existed.

    (C) The illegal items were not within the "wingspan" of any occupant.

    (D) The arrest was unlawful because the Officer did not have a warrant.

97. John is charged with rendering criminal assistance. In a pretrial hearing, John moves to have his statement "Harry did it, all I did was give him a lift" suppressed. John's motion will likely

    (A) Fail, because he was not under custodial interrogation at the time he made his statement.

    (B) Fail, because it is an exculpatory statement and not a confession.

    (C) Succeed, because he had not been read his *Miranda* rights before he made the statement.

    (D) Succeed, because it is hearsay.

98. Hank is arrested on suspicion of arson. He is read his *Miranda* warnings and then interrogated. At one point during interrogation, he says to Officer, "Don't I get a lawyer if you're going to ask me questions?" Officer responds, "Sure, if you think you need one." John replies, "Well, I guess I don't." He then confesses and pleads guilty to a lesser charge. While awaiting sentence, a cellmate informs him that he may have been hasty in his decision. He then requests representation and appeals his conviction. An appellate court looking at the case will likely

    (A) Uphold, because he knowingly and voluntarily entered into a beneficial plea bargain.

    (B) Reverse, because interrogation continued after he had invoked his right to counsel.

    (C) Reverse, because his waiver of the right to counsel was not knowing and intelligent.

    (D) Uphold, because if the right to counsel is not clearly invoked, it is deemed waived.

99. Tom is arrested and charged with vehicular homicide. Despite repeated explanations and warnings by the police and the prosecutor, he chooses to represent himself. Before initial proceedings, the court questions Tom and discovers he has only an 8th grade education and no legal knowledge or experience. The court appoints counsel based on its reasonable belief that defendant is incapable of adequately representing himself. Defendant is convicted. An appellate court will likely

    (A) Reverse, because Tom should have been allowed to represent himself.

    (B) Reverse, because defendant received ineffective assistance of counsel.

    (C) Uphold, because the decision to appoint counsel was harmless error.

(D) Uphold, because the trial judge's decision adequately protected defendant's right to counsel.

100. Tim, while demonstrating the capabilities of his new assault rifle, pulls the trigger believing the rifle to be unloaded. A single bullet discharges, passes through Mary's body and hits Jack. He is charged with the murder of both victims. Trial for the murder of Mary ends in a hung jury. Prior to the commencement of the trial for Jack's murder, defense counsel moves for dismissal. The motion will likely be

(A) Granted, because double jeopardy attached after the jury was sworn in Mary's case.

(B) Granted, because Tim lacked the necessary intent for murder.

(C) Denied, because double jeopardy does not apply when the first trial ends in a hung jury.

(D) Denied, because the murder of each victim is a separate crime and double jeopardy does not apply.

101. Officer hears breaking glass and sees Stan run out of a darkened liquor store at 3 a.m. as the alarm blares. Stan runs around the corner, out of Officer's view and hops into a car. Officer sees Stan drive away and pursues, lights flashing. Stan pulls over and Officer arrests him. Seeing nothing in the passenger compartment, officer pops the trunk of the car and finds cash and a baseball bat. Stan's motion to suppress the cash and baseball bat as evidence will likely be

(A) Denied, because the officer had probable cause to search the trunk.

(B) Denied, because a search incident to a valid arrest in an automobile always includes the trunk.

(C) Granted, because the trunk area was out of the range of Stan's control.

(D) Granted, because the arrest was illegal and therefore the evidence is fruit of the poisonous tree.

102. Bill commits a burglary and seems to get away with it. Two weeks later, the victim's brother, suspicious of Bill, comes to his house and threatens to kill Bill's daughter if Bill does not confess. Bill goes down to the police station, and confesses. Bill's motion to suppress his confession will likely be

(A) Granted, because the confession was coerced.

(B) Granted, because no other evidence linking Bill to the crime existed aside from his confession.

(C) Denied, because the police were not involved in any coercion.

(D) Denied, because Bill's belief that the threat would be carried out was not reasonable.

103. Mike is arrested on suspicion of larceny. After receiving and acknowledging his *Miranda* rights, he is questioned. When he refuses to confess, the officer tells him that he has connections in the prison that could make Mike's life there "unpleasant" if he does not confess. Mike confesses. At trial, the confession is not used in the prosecution's case-in-chief, but is admitted to impeach his testimony. On appeal, Mike's conviction will likely be

(A) Upheld, because he confessed with full understanding of his right to remain silent, and that his statements could be used against him.

(B) Upheld, because his conviction would probably have been secured regardless of the admittance of his confession, and the decision was harmless error.

(C) Upheld, because the confession may be admitted to impeach.

(D) Reversed, because a coerced confession is never admissible.

104. On the tip of an informant, the police go to Dan' house looking for illegal narcotics. Finding only Dan's 12-year-old daughter at home, the police ask her permission to come in and look around. She agrees, and upon entry, the officers find several types of narcotics and drug paraphernalia. In a pretrial motion, Dan argues to suppress the evidence as fruits of an illegal search. After hearing the evidence and arguments, the trial court admits the evidence and Dan is convicted. Dan's habeas appeal on the grounds that the search was illegal should be

(A) Granted, because his daughter did not have authority to consent to the search and was too young to knowingly consent.
(B) Granted, because a warrant should have been obtained.
(C) Denied, because Dan had the opportunity for full and fair litigation of his 4th Amendment claim at the trial level.
(D) Granted, because the trial court committed reversible error.

Questions 105 – 107 are based on the following:

Michael's wife, Terry, is suffering from end stage cancer and is in terrible pain. Michael, Terry's sister Brenda, and the doctor discuss Terry's situation in the waiting room. Michael asks the doctor to turn up the intravenous drip of morphine to a lethal level. The doctor initially agrees; Brenda says nothing but nods. However, a few moments later the doctor changes his mind and tells Michael. Michael returns to Terry's room followed by Brenda and the doctor. Michael turns up the drip himself, as Brenda looks on. The doctor tries to restrain Michael and calls security. Terry dies as a result of the morphine overdose.

105. What is the most serious crime of which Michael can be convicted?
(A) Involuntary manslaughter.
(B) Voluntary manslaughter.
(C) Murder.
(D) None of the above.

106. In a Model Penal Code jurisdiction, what is the most serious crime of which the doctor can be convicted?
(A) Attempted murder.
(B) Conspiracy to commit murder.

(C) Murder.
(D) None of the above.

107. What is the most serious crime of which Brenda can be convicted?
(A) Murder.
(B) Attempted murder.
(C) Conspiracy to commit murder.
(D) None of the above.

Questions 108 – 110 are based on the following:

Eddie (who has been twice previously convicted of bank robbery) convinces Zelda (who has no criminal record) to help him break in to Dave's Discount Diamonds and take some jewelry to sell for cash. They enter at night through an open window in an adjacent apartment building and steal $14,000 worth of necklaces, earrings, etc., from the store. Three days later, a police department informant with a 5% history of accuracy tells Officer Briggs that Zelda has stolen jewelry in her apartment. Briggs asks a judge for a warrant, which is issued. Briggs goes to Zelda's apartment. Zelda answers and Briggs declares that he has a warrant and is there to search. He searches the entire apartment, finally finding the jewelry in the freezer. Zelda immediately confesses, but claims that Eddie planned the crime and threatened to kill Zelda's daughter, who was in the next room, if Zelda didn't participate.

108. On these facts, if Eddie is charged with burglary he will most likely be
(A) Convicted.
(B) Acquitted, because the window was open, so he did not break into the store.
(C) Acquitted, because he did not have intent to commit a felony inside.
(D) Acquitted, because he did not enter a dwelling.

109. At trial, Zelda moves for the jewelry to be excluded as evidence because it was obtained due to an improper search. Her best argument in support of her motion is

(A) She did not receive her *Miranda* warnings before the search was conducted.
(B) She did not consent to the search.
(C) There was insufficient probable cause for the warrant.
(D) The search was outside the scope of the warrant.

110. Zelda's defense at trial is that she committed the crime under duress. This defense will likely
(A) Fail, because the threat of harm was not immediate.
(B) Fail, because duress is not available when the crime charged is burglary.
(C) Fail, because the threat of harm was not against Zelda herself.
(D) Succeed.

111. Slick and Stan are in an automobile collision. Slick gets out of his car and runs over to Stan's car, knocking on the window. Stan rolls down his window and Slick screams profanities, shaking his fist. Stan gets out of his car and Slick, seeing Stan's immense stature, backs away toward his own car and tries to get back into it. Stan grabs Slick by the collar and slaps him across the ear. Slick yelps and gets back in his car. If charged with battery, Stan will likely be
(A) Convicted, because he intentionally engaged in a harmful touching.
(B) Acquitted, because Slick was the first aggressor and Stan was acting in self-defense.
(C) Acquitted, because the physical harm to Slick was minor and temporary.
(D) Acquitted, because Slick's aggressive behavior created an assumption of risk of offensive bodily contact.

112. During Tom's trial for robbery, two witnesses testified. Nancy, the victim, stated that Tom pulled a gun on her from behind and said "hand over your purse or I'll kill you" and then grabbed her purse off her shoulder and ran. A passerby testified that Tom ran up from behind, grabbed the purse and ran, but that no weapon or threats were used. Tom can be convicted of
(A) Either robbery or larceny.
(B) Larceny only.
(C) Neither robbery nor larceny.
(D) Both robbery and larceny.

113. Bryce owns a liquor store in the State of Atley, which has a statute making it a strict liability offense to sell alcohol to anyone under the age of 21. Bryce hires Ben to work as cashier. Mel, who is 17, comes in and asks to purchase alcohol. Ben asks to see Mel's identification. Mel shows Ben a phony driver's license. Ben glances at it, and sells Mel a six pack of beer. If charged with sale of alcohol to a minor, Ben will likely be
(A) Convicted, because he failed to take the proper steps to ensure that Mel was 21.
(B) Acquitted, because Bryce as the owner of the store is solely responsible.
(C) Acquitted, because Ben believed the identification to be genuine.
(D) Convicted, because Ben made the sale and Joe was underage.

Questions 114 – 116 are based on the following:

Detective Johns received information from Taylor, a police informant who had given reliable information in the past, that Wanda had a large amount of PCP in her apartment. Taylor specified that he knew Wanda socially, and that six weeks prior, he had been at Wanda's apartment and seen the drugs there, inside a large wooden chest in the living room. Detective Johns, upon inquiry, discovered that Taylor did in fact know Wanda. Johns drew up an affidavit, went before a neutral magistrate, and got a search warrant for half a kilo of PCP. The next day, in Taylor's apartment, inside of a shoebox in the hall closet, Johns found a small amount of PCP and a baggie of marijuana.

114. The warrant procured by Johns is

(A) Valid, because it was based on reliable information from a reliable informant.

(B) Valid, because magistrate was impartial.

(C) Invalid, because there was no corroboration to the informant's claims.

(D) Invalid, because the information was too remote in time to justify a finding of probable cause.

115. Assuming the warrant is valid, what is the best argument Wanda could make that the search was improper?

(A) The warrant was not executed without delay.

(B) The shoebox was outside the scope of the warrant.

(C) A warrant alone is not sufficient to search a residence, the officer must also have consent.

(D) The PCP did not belong to Wanda, but to her brother.

116. In the State of Woollahra, a statute defines bribery as "the offer and acceptance of money in exchange for the consideration of a public official in the course of his or her duties." Belinda, a lobbyist for the Save the Spotted Owl Society, offers Sophie, a Senator, $500 to vote yes on an important referendum. Sophie takes the money, but then votes no. Both are charged with bribery and conspiracy to commit bribery. Sophie will likely be

(A) Acquitted, because she did not vote yes and so there is no proof of conspiracy.

(B) Convicted, because an agreement was made and money was exchanged, which is a substantial step in furtherance.

(C) Acquitted, because bribery as defined by the statute requires two persons.

(D) Convicted, because she considered Belinda's request and took the money.

Questions 117 and 118 are based on the following:

117. Q and R are hanging out at Q's house looking at rifles. Q, intending to demonstrate the action on his newest acquisition, fires a shot toward his neighbor's yard, even though he knows his neighbor is at home and likely to be out in his yard. The bullet hits S, a meter reader in the neighbor's yard. What is the most serious crime of which Q can be convicted?

(A) Murder.

(B) Voluntary manslaughter.

(C) Involuntary manslaughter.

(D) Q cannot be convicted.

118. If Q had intended to shoot his neighbor, and shot the meter reader by mistake, the appropriate charge would be

(A) Murder.

(B) Voluntary manslaughter.

(C) Involuntary manslaughter.

(D) Negligent homicide.

Questions 119 and 120 are based on the following:

Tim shoplifts a candy bar from a convenience store, in full view of video cameras. Officer Bevis is also watching and tails Tim out of the store. Just as Tim gets home and closes his front door, Bevis knocks on it. Tim opens the door and Bevis arrests him. Upon searching Tim's home, Bevis finds an empty candy bar wrapper and no receipt.

119. Tim's argument that the warrantless arrest was unlawful will likely

(A) Fail because he committed a misdemeanor in an officer's presence.

(B) Succeed, because Bevis did not knock and announce his intentions.

(C) Succeed, because once a suspect is home a warrant is always required.

(D) Fail, because Bevis had an articulable suspicion.

120. If Tim loses his argument that the arrest was unlawful, his motion to exclude the candy bar wrapper as evidence will likely be

(A) Granted, because an officer may only pat-down for weapons incident to an arrest

(B) Granted, because Bevis could not have specified the location of the candy bar wrapper prior to the search.

(C) Denied, because a full search is permissible incident to a lawful arrest.

(D) Granted, because Bevis did not have a reasonable apprehension of danger.

Questions 121 and 122 are based on the following:

Officer Stevens properly obtains a warrant to search the home of Trey Parkins looking for cocaine. After a thorough search turns up nothing, Stevens notices a mobile home, owned by Parkins and parked 500 feet from Parkins' house. He searches the mobile home and finds heroin.

121. A motion to suppress the heroin as evidence should be

(A) Denied, because the mobile home was an adjacent outbuilding.

(B) Granted, because the mobile home was outside the scope of the warrant.

(C) Granted, because heroin was not specified in the warrant as an item to be seized.

(D) Denied, because Parkins owned the mobile home.

122. During the motion to suppress hearing, it is revealed that the search occurred 35 days after the warrant was obtained. This presents a problem for the prosecution primarily because

(A) The case will be dismissed because the Sixth Amendment right to a speedy trial has been violated.

(B) It conclusively establishes a presumption of police misconduct that the jury must consider.

(C) It means that the defense may argue police misconduct to the jury in closing arguments.

(D) All of the evidence obtained as a result of the warrant is now probably fruit of the poisonous tree.

Questions 123 – 125 are based on the following:

In a jurisdiction governed by the Model Penal Code, Ted and Sandra go on vacation, leaving their 10 year old daughter Lea in charge of the house and their 9 month old infant. While they are away, the infant becomes ill. The illness is treatable, but Lea ignores the baby's cries and watches TV. The infant dies of fever.

123. Ted and Sandra are charged with negligent homicide. It is likely that

(A) The case will be dismissed because the MPC does not impose criminal liability for negligence, only tort liability.

(B) They will be acquitted, because the prosecution will not be able to prove that Ted and Sandra were practically certain that their act would result in the death of their infant.

(C) They will be convicted, because their actions were a substantial departure from the ordinary standard of due care.

(D) They will be convicted, because child neglect is a strict liability crime.

124. If Lea is charged with criminally negligent homicide, she will likely be

(A) Convicted, unless the defense can prove by clear and convincing evidence that she did not know her actions were wrong.

(B) Acquitted, unless the prosecution can prove by clear and convincing evidence that she know her actions were wrong.

(C) Acquitted, because she is conclusively presumed incapable of forming the intent to commit a crime.

(D) Acquitted, unless the prosecution can prove beyond a reasonable doubt that she did not know her actions were wrong.

125. Ted confesses to the police. Sandra requests her own lawyer and moves for a separate trial. The motion should be

(A) Denied, because she cannot establish any facts that distinguish her case from Ted's.

(B) Denied, in the interests of judicial economy.

(C) Granted, because two defendants can never be tried together if their interests conflict in any way.

(D) Granted, because Ted's confession jeopardizes Sandra's interests.

Questions 126 – 129 are based on the following.

A criminal statute in the State of Nalya makes it a gross misdemeanor to sell firearms to anyone under 18. Violators are strictly liable for the crime. Pete's Gun Emporiorama has a strict policy to check for identification before making any sale. Bubba works at Pete's, but routinely fails to check for i.d. Pete has knowledge of Bubba's transgressions, but does not take any action to remedy the situation. One afternoon, Bubba comes in to work after a lunch consisting of a six-pack of beer. At work, he sneaks another two beers and promptly passes out behind the counter. Dale, who is 14, comes in to the store and sees Bubba's condition. He takes a $500 handgun out of the unlocked case and, misreading the sign, leaves $50 cash on the counter, thinking it is payment in full.

126. Bubba is arrested for violating the statute. He will likely be

(A) Acquitted, because he lacked the requisite intent.

(B) Convicted, because voluntary intoxication is never a defense.

(C) Acquitted, because he did not perform the actus reus.

(D) Convicted, because the statute makes this a strict liability crime

.

127. Dale is charged with larceny. His best defense is

(A) He was mistaken as to the price, which negated the "trespassory" element of larceny.

(B) As a minor, he was legally incapable of forming the necessary intent.

(C) He was under duress because his friend Xavier told him if he didn't get a gun, Xavier would wreck his car.

(D) The gun did not work and therefore was not worth $5, let alone $500.

128. Pete is arrested and charged with violating the gun sale statute. He will likely be

(A) Acquitted, because he was unaware of the existence of the statute.

(B) Convicted, because he knew of Bubba's transgression and failed to supervise Bubba, which led to the violation.

(C) Convicted, because as the owner of the shop he is responsible for the "sale."

(D) Acquitted, because the statute only imposes liability for the act of a sale.

129. If Dale is acquitted on the larceny charge, then re-arrested and charged with violation of the gun sale statute, he will likely be

(A) Acquitted, because the statute only criminalizes the sale and says nothing about the purchase.

(B) Convicted, because he is strictly liable for violating the statute.

(C) Acquitted, because double jeopardy prevents prosecution of the misdemeanor.

(D) Acquitted, because he was acquitted on the larceny charge.

Questions 130 – 132 are based on the following:

Cisco and Hopalong are sitting in a coffee shop. Cisco says, "Hey, wanna know how we can make some fast money?" Hopalong says, "Sure, lay it on me." Cisco says, "I know where this rich dude's kid goes to school, out at Westside. We can grab him outside and hang on to him until the old man pays up big." Hopalong frowns and says, "No way. I'm on parole. Find another toady." Hopalong then leaves, but Cisco decides to do the job anyway.

That afternoon, as Cisco is waiting outside the school, Hopalong shows up. They nod at each other quickly. Cisco shifts his eyes toward a young boy, and Hopalong pulls him into the van. They drive into a far corner of the school parking lot and wait. Cisco makes a call on his cellular phone to the boy's father and demands a ransom. Much to their dismay, however, when they put the boy on the phone to prove they have him, they realize they have grabbed the wrong child. They quickly hang up the phone and release the boy. However, the father has caller i.d. and Cisco and Hopalong are quickly apprehended.

130. Hopalong and Cisco are both charged with kidnapping the boy. They will likely be
- (A) Acquitted, because they did not move the boy to a different location.
- (B) Convicted.
- (C) Acquitted, because their mistake as to the boy's identity negated their intent to kidnap him.
- (D) Acquitted, because they only held the boy for a brief period.

131. Hopalong and Cisco are also both charged with conspiracy to commit kidnapping. They will likely be
- (A) Convicted, since they had a tacit agreement to commit the crime.
- (B) Acquitted, since they made no agreement prior to the act.

- (C) Acquitted, because conspiracy merges with the completed crime.
- (D) Convicted, since two of them were involved.

132. Hopalong is also charged with battery. By state statute, offensive touching is not recognized as a form of battery. Hopalong's best defense would be
- (A) The boy did not feel any apprehension.
- (B) He did not have the specific intent to harm the boy.
- (C) He did not inflict any physical harm.
- (D) Battery is a lesser included offense to kidnapping.

133. Aaron fires a shotgun into a dwelling at night, killing someone sleeping inside. He is charged with murder. He may succeed in having the charge reduced from second degree murder to involuntary manslaughter by arguing
- (A) The victim was a trespasser who assumed the risk.
- (B) He believed the house to be abandoned.
- (C) He was intoxicated and failed to form the requisite intent.
- (D) He did not have specific intent to kill.

Questions 134 and 135 are based on the following:

Beaker is a veteran police officer of 20 years. One night while off duty, he is pulled over. He consents to the standard battery of intoxication tests including a blood alcohol test, which comes back above the legal limit. Beaker is arrested for drunk driving. As the officer puts the handcuffs on, he says, "You know the routine. Do I have to go through it?" Beaker says, "No, I'm quite familiar, thanks." The officer then questions him and says, "You know Honeydew (the prosecutor). If you admit it, he'll probably cut you a break." Beaker then confesses.

134. Beaker's motion to suppress the confession should be
- **(A)** Denied, because he acknowledged and voluntarily waived his *Miranda* rights, and his statement was voluntary.
- **(B)** Denied, because it could be demonstrated by a preponderance that he was familiar with the *Miranda* warnings.
- **(C)** Granted, because his confession was coerced.
- **(D)** Granted, because the *Miranda* warnings were not read.

135. Beaker also moves to suppress the blood alcohol content (BAC) test administered at the scene as fruits of the poisonous tree. That motion should be
- **(A)** Denied, because Beaker consented to the test and it was administered prior to the arrest.
- **(B)** Denied, because only the confession itself is inadmissible; physical evidence obtained as a result of an illegal confession is admissible.
- **(C)** Granted, because blood alcohol tests are inherently unreliable.
- **(D)** Granted, because Beaker had strong evidence indicating that he had not been drinking.

136. Ted and Daniel are at a restaurant. Mitch approaches from behind and, thinking Ted is someone else, he playfully reaches out to smack Ted lightly on the shoulder. Ted has Mitch arrested for battery. On these facts, Mitch will likely be
- **(A)** Convicted, because he intentionally slapped Ted, an offensive touching.
- **(B)** Convicted, because there is an eyewitness and battery is a strict liability offense.
- **(C)** Acquitted, because Mitch's mistake as to Ted's identity negates the mens rea.
- **(D)** Acquitted, because the slap was not serious enough to cause pain.

Questions 137 – 140 are based on the following.

Tanya has a plan to get rid of her troublesome husband and her demanding boyfriend and make some easy money in the process. First, she takes out a hefty life insurance policy on her husband, with herself as the beneficiary. The policy states that the proceeds will not be paid in the event that the beneficiary causes the death. She then calls her boyfriend who comes over while her husband is out. Tanya tells her boyfriend, "Hey, if you really want us to be together, I know a way. Take these shears and cut the brake line in his car. By the time he gets to the bottom of the hill, our troubles will be over." The boyfriend hesitates, and Tanya says if he doesn't agree, she will kill herself. He then agrees.

The boyfriend waits in the bushes until the husband returns, cuts the brake line, and leaves. The next day, the husband is killed when his brakes fail as he drives down the steep hill from his house. The police rule the death an accident, and Tanya applies for and receives the insurance proceeds. She then tells the police that she suspects someone murdered her husband. She gives them the shears and name of her boyfriend. Betrayed, the boyfriend confesses and tells the entire story. Tanya is arrested.

137. As relates to the death of her husband, Tanya could potentially be convicted of
- **(A)** Murder.
- **(B)** Conspiracy and murder.
- **(C)** Solicitation, conspiracy, and murder.
- **(D)** Solicitation and conspiracy only.

138. The boyfriend's best defense to a murder charge would be
- **(A)** He did not think that the husband would actually be killed in the collision.
- **(B)** He was under duress as a result of Tanya's threat to harm herself.
- **(C)** He is only 17.
- **(D)** He actually cut the line to the air conditioning, not the brakes.

139. The insurance company could press charges against Tanya for
- (A) False pretenses.
- (B) Embezzlement.
- (C) Larceny.
- (D) Larceny by trick.

140. Unbeknownst to Tanya, her husband had been secretly tape-recording the goings-on in the house because he suspected her. The police find the tape recorder and seize it. Tanya's motion to suppress the recording of her conversation with her boyfriend about the killing should be
- (A) Granted, because neither party to the conversation consented to having it recorded.
- (B) Granted, because tape recordings are never admissible evidence.
- (C) Denied, because Tanya had no legitimate expectation of privacy.
- (D) Denied, because her husband made the recording.

Questions 141 and 142 are based on the following:

Jamie and Franz are enjoying a quiet evening at home in their spacious 10-bedroom mansion. Suddenly, Jamie hears a noise downstairs. Franz goes to check it out, and comes back saying he saw a man creeping around downstairs in the dark. Jamie says, "Let's take the back stairs and go to the neighbors' house." Franz grabs his gun and says, "No way, I'll see what's going on." Franz heads downstairs and finds the man in the kitchen. He calls out, "Hey, what are you doing?" The man turns around with something in his hand that looks like a gun. Franz shoots the man in the chest and he dies almost instantly. When Franz turns on the light, he realizes to his horror that the man was holding a zucchini – he was unarmed and had been looking for food.

141. Franz could be charged with
- (A) First degree murder.
- (B) Second degree murder.
- (C) Involuntary manslaughter.

- (D) None of the above.

142. Franz argues self-defense. In a jurisdiction governed by the MPC, his defense will likely
- (A) Succeed, because his mistake about the weapon was honest and reasonable.
- (B) Succeed, because self-defense is conclusively presumed when one is in one's own home.
- (C) Fail, because he did not retreat when Jamie suggested it.
- (D) Succeed, because the amount of force used was reasonable.

Questions 143 – 145 are based on the following:

Heidi is schizophrenic. She often sees people and hears voices that are not there telling her to do things that she knows are wrong. One day she hears a voice tell her, "If you don't burn down that bank over there, you're going to die." Heidi cannot resist the voice, but waits until the bank closes so that at least no one will be killed. She throws a firebomb in the window and the building goes up in flames. A night watchman is trapped inside and dies.

143. Heidi will have an insanity defense in a jurisdiction governed by

I. *M'Naghten*
II. Irresistible impulse
III. MPC Substantial Capacity
- (A) I only.
- (B) III only.
- (C) II and III.
- (D) I, II, and III

144. If her insanity defense is unsuccessful, Heidi will likely be convicted of
- (A) Arson.
- (B) Arson and murder.
- (C) Arson and manslaughter.
- (D) Manslaughter.

145. Heidi requests a 12 person jury, but her request is refused by the judge. The judge's decision is

(A) Proper, because there is no constitutional right to a 12-person jury.

(B) Improper, because a defendant in a capital case has the right to a 12-person jury.

(C) Improper, because a jury request may not be refused for any reason.

(D) Proper, because there is no absolute constitutional right to a jury trial.

146. Kylie is 15 but looks older, and has a fake driver's license that states she is 21. She approaches Ben in a bar and strikes up a conversation. They hit it off and begin dating. After six dates, Ben suggests they have sexual intercourse, which they do. Kylie's mother discovers the relationship and confronts her. Kylie denies that she consented, and her mother calls Ben. He is shocked and dismayed to learn her true age, and truthfully insists that he had no idea she was underage. Ben is charged with statutory rape. He will likely be

(A) Convicted, because he was reckless in having intercourse without verifying her age.

(B) Convicted, because Kylie did not consent.

(C) Acquitted, because he had made an honest, reasonable mistake of fact about Kylie's age.

(D) Convicted, because he is strictly liable.

Questions 147 and 148 are based on the following.

Tamara is an epileptic. She must take her medicine regularly to avoid seizures. One afternoon, she is in a hurry to beat the traffic out of town, and leaves the house without taking her medication on time, figuring she can take it at the first rest stop. She gets on the freeway and suddenly blacks out. When Tamara awakens, she is in the hospital. Her father tells her she had a seizure while driving and collided with another vehicle, killing the driver.

147. Tamara is charged with vehicular manslaughter. She will likely be

(A) Convicted, because she was reckless in driving without taking her medication.

(B) Convicted, because she failed to act when she had a legal duty.

(C) Acquitted, because she lacked the proper mens rea for manslaughter.

(D) Acquitted, because she acted involuntarily and thus is not culpable.

148. While in the hospital and being administered medication, Tamara has another attack. The nurse comes in to restrain her, and Tamara's arm jerks and hits him across the face, breaking his nose. Tamara is charged with battery. She will likely be

(A) Convicted, because battery is a strict liability crime.

(B) Acquitted, because there is no causation.

(C) Acquitted, because she acted involuntarily.

(D) Acquitted, because Tamara acted in self-defense.

Questions 149 – 153 are based on the following:

Sanford, Byron, and Reese all own stores down near the waterfront. Sanford hears about a shipment of brand new clock radios and decides to help himself to a few cases to boost his sagging appliance business. He tells Reese his plan; Reese says nothing. Sanford drives over to the docks late one night, and much to his surprise, boxes and boxes are just sitting on the docks. He loads his pickup truck with boxes. When he gets back to his store, however, he realizes that he has locked himself out. He parks the truck inside Byron's warehouse.

When Byron and Reese show up the next morning to open their stores, Sanford asks Byron if he would be willing to hang on to the radios until Sanford can find a locksmith. Byron asks him where the radios came from. Sanford says, "I appropriated them from a shipment that came in last night." Byron thinks that

Sanford means he ordered them and they were finally delivered. Reese, who knew beforehand what Sanford had planned, says nothing and goes into his own store. The police eventually track the missing radios to Byron's store.

149. Charged with receiving stolen goods, Byron will likely be
(A) Convicted, because he had control of the goods.
(B) Acquitted, because he did not know or have reason to know that the goods were stolen.
(C) Acquitted, because he only planned to hold the goods temporarily.
(D) Convicted, because he is strictly liable.

150. Under an accomplice theory, Reese can be charged with
(A) Larceny only.
(B) Receiving stolen goods only.
(C) Larceny and receiving stolen goods.
(D) Nothing; Reese cannot be charged.

151. In addition to larceny, Sanford is also charged with solicitation (asking Byron to hold the goods). On the solicitation charge, Sanford will likely be
(A) Convicted.
(B) Acquitted, because the solicitation merged with the completed crime.
(C) Acquitted, because what he asked Byron to do was not a crime.
(D) Acquitted, because the solicitation was unsuccessful.

152. As it turns out, the "shipment" of radios was actually part of a massive sting operation by the police, and were just useless casings that had been discarded by the manufacturer. Sanford's best defense to the larceny charge would be
(A) Entrapment.
(B) Because the radios were discarded before the police got them, they were not in the possession of another.
(C) He honestly and reasonably believed the radios were being

given away, because they were just sitting on the docks.
(D) He was under duress because his business was failing.

153. Charged with larceny and receiving stolen goods under an accomplice theory, Reese will likely be
(A) Convicted, because knew and approved of both crimes.
(B) Acquitted, because he took no action.
(C) Convicted, because he assisted.
(D) Acquitted, because an accomplice cannot be charged unless he specifically agrees to a crime.

Questions 154 and 155 are based on the following:

Sarah and Kelly live and work in Waratah State, the penal code of which makes it a crime to "Knowingly buy, sell, transport, or distribute marijuana." The state courts have interpreted "distribute" as "disperse, share, or give." Sarah and Kelly have lockers next to each other at work. One day, Sarah notices that Kelly has a baggie in her locker of some dried green leafy substance. She asks Kelly about it; Kelly tells her the substance is marijuana. Kelly then asks Sarah if she would like to smoke some. While she is reaching for the baggie, Sarah refuses and starts to leave. Kelly says, "You better not say anything, or I'll flush it all and you'll look like an idiot." She tells her boss, who calls the police. They come and search Kelly's locker and arrest her after finding the baggie.

154. Charged with violation of the penal code section mentioned above, Kelly will likely be
(A) Convicted, because she transported marijuana.
(B) Acquitted.
(C) Convicted, because she solicited Sarah.
(D) Convicted, because she possessed marijuana.

155. If the prosecutor wants to secure the severest possible sentence for Kelly, she may also charge
- (A) Attempt to distribute and conspiracy to distribute.
- (B) Attempt to distribute and solicitation.
- (C) Solicitation only.
- (D) Attempt to distribute, conspiracy to distribute, and solicitation.

156. Kelly moves to suppress the marijuana as evidence because it was obtained in violation of the Fourth Amendment. Her motion should be
- (A) Denied, because there was probable cause and exigent circumstances.
- (B) Denied, because her employer was the owner of the locker and could give valid consent to the search.
- (C) Granted, because she had a legitimate expectation of privacy.
- (D) Granted, because the police should have obtained a warrant.

Questions 157 and 158 are based on the following:

Stedman plans to kidnap Susie. He follows her for weeks, learning her routine. He buys chain and padlocks. He prepares a room in his home to use as a holding pen; he soundproofs it and boards up all the windows. He waits in an alley with his van one late evening as Susie is leaving work. He waits for her to walk by, and when she does, he runs up behind her and grabs her. But hearing his footsteps, Susie had time to grab her pepper spray. She blasts him in the face and runs for it. He does not run after her. He decides it is too much trouble and goes home.

157. Charged with kidnapping, Stedman will likely be
- (A) Convicted, because he had intent, and confined the victim.
- (B) Convicted, because a victim's escape does not negate the act of kidnapping.
- (C) Acquitted, because he abandoned his crime and turned himself in.

- (D) Acquitted, because the prosecution cannot prove result.

158. However, if charged, Stedman will likely be convicted of
- (A) Attempted battery assault, attempted kidnapping, and battery.
- (B) Attempted kidnapping only.
- (C) Attempted kidnapping and battery.
- (D) Battery only.

Questions 159 – 161 are based on the following:

Roger and Pete are long time friends and belong to the same bowling league. One evening, Pete tells Roger he is feeling ill and is not going bowling. Not having much fun, Roger leaves the alley early and goes by Pete's house to see if he feeling better. As he approaches the front door, Roger hears his own wife, Sarah, laughing. He peeks in the window and sees Pete and Sarah, half undressed with a glass of wine in her hand. In a rage, he kicks in the door, picks up a chair, and hurls it at Pete. Pete is knocked unconscious. He then pushes Sarah to the hardwood floor and hits her repeatedly in the face. Pete suffers minor injuries; Sarah dies several days later of massive head trauma.

159. Choose the precedent that best resolves this case.
- (A) A finds out from an anonymous letter that B has been molesting A's daughter. A grabs a gun, drives to B's house, and kills him. A is guilty of voluntary manslaughter.
- (B) After following her for several weeks, A finally confirms his long-held suspicion that his wife has been having an affair. He goes home and sits with his gun, which he bought when he first began to suspect the affair. When his wife comes home, he asks her about the affair, and she denies it. They argue for over an hour, and then he shoots her. A is guilty of first-degree murder.

(C) A has a prized record collection that took years to accumulate. B, the babysitter, listens to them one night and accidentally scratches a particularly valuable one. A comes home, discovers what B has done, and hits her across the face. She is thrown against a concrete wall and dies of massive head trauma. A is guilty of second-degree murder.

(D) Distraught over his wife's death, A has several drinks at a bar and gets in his car to go home. On his way home, a child runs into the street unexpectedly. Because of his diminished capacity, A is not able to stop in time and hits the child, who dies several days later of head trauma. A is guilty of involuntary manslaughter.

160. Which fact, if proved by the prosecution, should most persuade a jury to convict Roger of murder?

(A) He is a former professional boxer.

(B) He had actually known about the affair for months.

(C) He had displayed a severe temper in the past.

(D) His wife had a life insurance policy with him as beneficiary.

161. Which fact, if proved by the defense, should most persuade a jury to acquit Roger?

(A) He had gotten drunk at the bowling alley before he stopped by Pete's house.

(B) He neither believed that his wife would die from the injuries nor intended to kill her.

(C) He had never been violent in the past.

(D) His wife had come at him with a knife.

162. Xander was sick and tired of his store getting burglarized every other week. He set up a shotgun, pointed at knee level and rigged to fire if the door was forced open. Glen, a career burglar, comes by for his usual "hit" on Xander's store. He kicks open the door and is shot in the thigh. Unwilling to summon help because of fear of getting caught, he hobbles home and eventually bleeds to death. Xander will likely be convicted of

(A) Murder.

(B) Involuntary manslaughter.

(C) Negligent homicide.

(D) None, because he acted in defense of his property.

Questions 163 – 165 are based on the following.

Carey is a junkie and also an alcoholic. He constantly has a red nose and haggard, half-open eyes. His clothing frequently smells of liquor and he has permanent slurred speech. He often stumbles and lurches when he walks because of decreased coordination and motor function. One morning, Carey is on his way to the liquor store, sober but not planning to remain that way. Meanwhile, Officer Tompkins is sitting in an unmarked police car across from the liquor store, taking her breakfast break. She watches Carey stumble and weave down the street, trip over the curb, and head into the liquor store. Officer Tompkins cannot see the sales counter, she can see only a few feet past the front door.

Carey approaches the clerk, who looks skeptical. The clerk asks Carey if he has been drinking. Carey tells him no. The clerk puts Carey through a couple of tests that the police use to determine intoxication, and Carey passes them. The clerk smells no trace of alcohol on Carey's breath, although his clothes have a faint stench. The clerk sells Carey a bottle of vodka but forgets to give Carey his receipt. Carey leaves. Officer Tompkins sees Carey emerge with the paper bag containing the vodka in his hand, from which he removed the cap and takes a sip. She immediately makes her move and arrests Carey, then takes him in handcuffs into the store and arrests the surprised clerk.

163. Charged pursuant to a state statute that prohibits the "knowing sale of alcohol products to any intoxicated person or any person having the appearance of being intoxicated" the clerk will likely be

(A) Convicted.
(B) Acquitted, because Carey was in fact not intoxicated.
(C) Acquitted, because he took reasonable steps to verify that Carey was not intoxicated.
(D) Acquitted, because no one actually witnessed the sale, and so there is no evidence of the crime.

164. Charged pursuant to a state statute that prohibits public intoxication, Carey will likely be

(A) Convicted, because he appeared intoxicated.
(B) Acquitted, because he was not intoxicated.
(C) Convicted, because he had planned to drink the rest of the vodka in a nearby park.
(D) Convicted, because he drank alcohol in public.

165. At trial, the clerk testifies that he was told that he was only prohibited from sales to persons actually intoxicated. When asked who told him that, he states that he was confused by the statute's wording and called a member of the liquor control board to inquire. If true, in a jurisdiction that has adopted the MPC this would

(A) Exonerate the clerk, because he made a mistake of fact.
(B) Exonerate the clerk, because he was acting on misinformation from a public official.
(C) Not exonerate the clerk, because ignorance or mistake of law is not an excuse.
(D) Not exonerate the clerk, because the statute was clear.

Questions 166 – 168 are based on the following:

Talia is walking home from her bus stop late at night on a brightly lit street when she stops and sets her purse down to dig out her keys from her pocket. Corey, a thrice-convicted pickpocket comes up from behind her and snatches her purse off the ground. When she pursues him, he tosses a stick at her to slow her down, but she ducks and it just misses. She continues to pursue him, but after a few blocks gets too tired and stops.

She goes immediately to the police station and reports the theft. She describes Corey's hair, face and clothes in detail. Two officers are radioed the description and told to pursue. Talia waits at the police station to give a full report and look at some mug shots. As Talia is going through the mug shots, the officers bring in Corey in handcuffs saying, "We've got the purse snatcher." A few pages later, Talia identifies Corey's mug shot from the book.

166. On these facts, Corey could be convicted of

(A) Larceny and robbery.
(B) Robbery and battery.
(C) Robbery only.
(D) Larceny and battery.

167. On a charge of assault, Corey would likely be

(A) Convicted, because he threw the stick at her intending to slow her down.
(B) Acquitted, because he never touched her.
(C) Acquitted, because he did not verbally threaten her, so she was never in apprehension of a battery.
(D) Convicted, because he took her property.

168. Corey's motion to suppress Talia's mug shot identification as evidence should be

(A) Denied, because she got such a good look at him that she would have identified the photo anyway.
(B) Denied, because there was no intentional police misconduct.
(C) Granted, because the totality of the circumstances suggest that the photo session was likely to produce a misidentification.

(D) Denied, because there was other independent evidence to suggest Corey's guilt.

Questions 169 and 170 are based on the following:

State X has adopted the MPC. Tad is driving in X with a .03 blood alcohol level. By statute anyone driving with a .02 alcohol level or above has "conclusively committed a misdemeanor," although Tad is unaware of this because the statute was enacted only 4 months ago. He swerves to avoid a cat and hits a child that has suddenly run into the road. The child is killed.

169. Charged with misdemeanor manslaughter, Tad will likely be

(A) Acquitted, because he did not intend to kill the child.

(B) Convicted, because the killing occurred while Tad was committing a misdemeanor that was inherently wrong.

(C) Convicted, because this is the type of crime the misdemeanor manslaughter rule is intended to prevent.

(D) The MPC does not recognize the misdemeanor manslaughter rule.

170. Charged with violating the .03 blood alcohol rule, Tad will likely be

(A) Acquitted, because his friend had told him the statutory limit was .06.

(B) Convicted, he is strictly liable.

(C) Acquitted, because he was unaware of the recent statute's enactment.

(D) Acquitted, because he did not know his level was above .03.

171. Shana gets mugged in broad daylight and Oliver witnesses it. As the mugger struggles with Shana's purse, he reaches in his coat pocket and pulls out a lead pipe. Oliver intervenes, knocking the pipe out of the mugger's hand and striking him several times in the face and stomach. The mugger falls to the ground, bleeding. He dies later that day from internal injuries. Charged with second degree murder, Oliver will likely be

(A) Acquitted, because he used reasonable force to defend Shana.

(B) Convicted, because Shana was a stranger.

(C) Convicted, because only the police may use force in the prevention of a crime.

(D) Convicted, because the amount of force was disproportional.

Questions 172 – 175 are based on the following:

Avery, Hewlett, and Packard are bankers who have developed a plan for early retirement. Avery has designed a computer program that moves small amounts of money, undetectable as individual transactions, into a secret account that will aggregate over time into a hefty nest egg. Hewlett installed the program in a low-profile corner of the mainframe. Packard set up the secret account. They meet to check the account periodically, although they have not yet built up enough of a balance to bother making a withdrawal. Mac, a co-worker, gets wind of the plan and threatens to expose the group. Hewlett pulls Mac into a secluded storeroom and says, "You'd better be careful, or you're gonna get it."

When Packard gets wind of the threat, he decides he is getting in over his head. He closes the account and goes to the police. At the station, he sits down with an inspector who questions him as he tells the whole story. Meanwhile, Avery secretly removes an office computer from a storage room and takes it home so that he can better monitor the progress of his program, intending to return it when the job is done. When he uses it and realizes how fast it is, he decides to keep it. As Hewlett is leaving work, he punches Mac in the face without warning and says "Just a reminder." Avery, Hewlett, and Packard are arrested later that evening.

172. Charged with assault of Mac, Hewlett will likely be
- (A) Convicted, because Mac had apprehension of harm.
- (B) Convicted, because Hewlett threatened deadly force.
- (C) Acquitted, because the threat of harm was not immediate.
- (D) Acquitted, because Mac did not believe the threat to be serious.

173. With respect to taking the computer, Avery can be charged with
- (A) False pretenses.
- (B) Larceny.
- (C) Embezzlement.
- (D) Burglary.

174. In a jurisdiction that has adopted the *Pinkerton* rule, Packard can be charged with
- (A) Conspiracy, embezzlement, larceny, battery.
- (B) Conspiracy only.
- (C) Conspiracy and embezzlement.
- (D) Conspiracy and attempted embezzlement.

175. Packard pleads guilty, Avery and Hewlett plead innocent. Avery and Hewlett move to suppress Packard's confession to the police. The motion should be
- (A) Denied, because it did not occur during a custodial interrogation.
- (B) Denied, because Packard is the only defendant with the right to move to suppress his own confession.
- (C) Granted, because Packard was never read his *Miranda* rights.
- (D) Granted, because Packard was coerced.

176. Ray and Belinda are walking along the pier late at night. Thinking it will be a funny joke Belinda blindfolds Ray, telling him she has a surprise for him, and neglects to warn him that he is about to step off of the pier. Ray falls a couple of feet and lands in relatively deep water. Ray begins to shout that he can't swim. Belinda thinks he is playing a joke on her for revenge, so she does nothing. When she doesn't hear him after a couple of minutes, she becomes concerned, but it is too late. Ray has drowned. Charged with murder, Belinda moves for dismissal, arguing that the prosecution cannot prove actus reus. The motion will likely be
- (A) Granted.
- (B) Denied, because the prosecution need not always prove actus reus.
- (C) Denied, because she intended to cause serious bodily injury.
- (D) Denied, because her failure to act was the actus reus.

Questions 177 – 179 are based on the following:

Lonnie and Burt are getting divorced, and Lonnie has moved out. Burt has told her that she may not reenter the house without his permission, and Lonnie tells him she will not. Lonnie mistakenly believes that half of everything in the house is hers. One day she comes by when Burt is not home and, using her old key, she takes some of Burt's prized and expensive artworks, such as his rare "Dogs Playing Poker" and velvet Elvis paintings, that he acquired before the marriage.

177. What is the most serious crime with which Lonnie can be charged?
- (A) Larceny.
- (B) Larceny by trick.
- (C) Burglary.
- (D) Lonnie cannot be charged.

178. What is Lonnie's best defense at trial?
- (A) She was mistaken as to her legal status regarding the property, and regarding her legal right to enter the house.
- (B) She was under duress as a result of the divorce proceedings.
- (C) She believed that Burt had possession of some of her property, and she thought this would make them even.
- (D) She was drunk, and her judgment was impaired.

179. Lonnie's defense counsel fails to call any witnesses, make any objections, or perform more than a cursory cross-examination. She is convicted. On appeal, Lonnie argues ineffective assistance of counsel. The argument will likely

    (A) Prevail, because his misconduct is per se evidence of ineffective assistance of counsel.

    (B) Prevail, only if she can show that there is a reasonable probability that the outcome would have changed if her attorney had performed differently.

    (C) Fail, unless she can conclusively prove that she would have been acquitted if her attorney had performed differently.

    (D) Fail, because she admitted that she took the items in question.

180. In which of the following circumstances is the defendant most likely to be convicted of the charged crime?

    (A) Alma intends to shoot Bertha, but misses and hits the tire of a passing car. The car veers out of control and crashes, killing the driver. Alma is charged with murder.

    (B) Celine intends to drive to Dave's house and kill Dave with a knife. She pulls a knife out of her kitchen drawer and heads for her car, but changes her mind and goes back in the house. Celine is charged with attempted murder.

    (C) Ernie intends to surprise Fabian, putting a bucket full of confetti over the door that will spill when Fabian comes through. The bucket accidentally comes loose and falls on Fabian's head, cutting him. Ernie is charged with battery.

    (D) Gunther intends to shoot Helga, but the gun misfires. Helga knocks the gun out of Gunther's hand and stabs him in the leg with a knife, intending to wound him so that he can be subdued. Gunther dies from the stab wound. Helga is charged with murder.

181. Intending to play a joke on Kim, Zed took Kim's dog's collar and set it on the back porch, intending to make her think her dog had gotten out into the huge fenced back field and would have to be chased down and retrieved. Kim saw the collar and thought her dog had been stolen. She had a heart attack and died. Zed, charged with involuntary manslaughter, should argue

    (A) He did not intend for Kim to die.

    (B) There is no causation.

    (C) He did not know she had a weak heart.

    (D) His actions were not reckless.

182. David mistakenly believed that Sean had stolen his lawnmower. He crept into Sean's garage late at night to look around. His flashlight batteries burned out and he lit a match. When he didn't find the mower, he blew out the match, dropped it and left. The match, still smoldering, fell into a small pool of flammable solvent, igniting some old newspapers and burning down Sean's house. David is charged with arson. He will likely be

    (A) Convicted, because he was trespassing when fire was started.

    (B) Convicted, because his actions were the actual cause of the fire.

    (C) Acquitted, because he did not act with intent or with extreme indifference to the consequences of his behavior.

    (D) Convicted, because he was negligent.

183. Intending to teach the mischievous neighborhood kids a lesson, Mr. Hooper sets a bear trap in his yard, hoping to injure one of the kids to keep them all from trespassing. A child with a rare physiological disorder where his blood fails to clot gets a leg caught in the trap and bleeds to death at the hospital. Hooper is charged with murder. He will likely be

    (A) Acquitted, because he never intended to kill the child.

    (B) Acquitted, because the fact that the child had a rare disorder was the superseding cause of the death.

(C) Acquitted, because the death was unforeseeable.

(D) Convicted.

Questions 184 and 185 are based on the following:

Intending to set fire to Glen's cabin, so that he and Glen can split the insurance money, William pours gasoline all over the cabin and tries to light a match. However, it suddenly and violently begins to rain. William cannot get the match lit and the gasoline is washed from the cabin. He comes to his senses and walks away, leaving the empty gas can a mile away behind a tree. Three days later, a bolt of lightning strikes a tree near the gas can, which heats up and, explodes the trace gasoline left in it, starting a massive forest fire and incinerating the cabin.

184. William is likely not guilty of arson because

(A) Glen had agreed to the crime.

(B) The lightning strike was a superseding cause.

(C) The actual destruction of the cabin was too remote in time from William's attempt.

(D) He was not acting out of malice.

185. Charged with attempted arson, Glen will likely be

(A) Convicted.

(B) Acquitted, because he took no substantial step toward accomplishing the crime.

(C) Acquitted, because William and Glen agreed to the crime and the attempt merges with the conspiracy.

(D) Acquitted, because William abandoned the attempt before it was completed.

Questions 186 – 190 are based on the following:

In Telstra State, it is a felony to impersonate a police officer. Not aware of this, Tony, Tina, and Tommy all plan to impersonate police officers, crash their friend's party (where illegal drugs will be in use) and scare everyone for a good laugh. They rent realistic looking uniforms and wear sunglasses so they won't be recognized.

On September 8, they go to the party in the uniforms. They knock on the door, and when it is opened, several partygoers scream, "Raid!" Total chaos ensues, and several attendees try to descend the fire escape in the back. They all fall to their deaths. Thinking no one recognized them, the three impersonators flee in horror, and hide the uniforms at Tony's house.

On October 4, officers show up at Tony's door on a completely unrelated case – they have suspicion that Tony's house contains illegal weapons, but no probable cause or warrant. Tony initially consents to the search, confident that he has no such weapons. However, as the police begin searching, Tony remembers the uniforms and tells them, "Okay, you've had your chance, I want you to leave now." But the officers refuse and continue searching. When they find the uniforms, they remember the police report regarding the deaths at the house party the month before. They take Tony in for questioning. They read him his *Miranda* rights and tell him if he doesn't confess, he could be in for some "cruel and unusual punishment." He confesses in a signed affidavit.

The same day, the police station receives a letter, postmarked October 1. It is the confession of Tina, who was overcome by guilt but too terrified to turn herself over to the police in person. She recounts the events, including the flight and stashing the uniforms at Tony's house. She includes Tony's address. Tina and Tommy are arrested later that day.

186. Charged with felony murder, Tony, Tina, and Tommy will likely be

(A) Convicted.

(B) Acquitted, because the deaths were unintentional.

(C) Acquitted, because the felony committed was not inherently dangerous.

(D) Acquitted, because the deaths occurred after, not during, the felony.

187. Charged with conspiracy, Tony, Tina, and Tommy will likely be

(A) Acquitted, because by definition, three persons were not required to commit the crime.

(B) Acquitted, because each acted separately from the other.

(C) Acquitted, because they did not know the act they conspired to commit was unlawful.

(D) Convicted.

188. Tony's motion to suppress the uniforms as evidence should be

(A) Granted, because he withdrew his consent for the search.

(B) Granted, because the uniforms were outside the scope of the search.

(C) Denied, because their discovery was inevitable and Tina's letter was an independent source.

(D) Denied, because Tony could not withdraw his consent once it was given.

189. Tina's motion to suppress her confession as evidence should be

(A) Granted, because she was not aware of her *Miranda* rights.

(B) Granted, because her boyfriend coerced her into confessing.

(C) Denied, because she was not in custody and confessed voluntarily.

(D) Denied, because without it, Tommy could not be prosecuted.

190. Tony's motion to suppress his own confession should be

(A) Denied, because he was administered his *Miranda* rights and waived them by confessing.

(B) Granted, because he did not have a lawyer present when he confessed.

(C) Denied, because the amount of police coercion involved was not enough to cause a reasonable person to confess.

(D) Granted, because the police coerced him into confessing.

191. Theodore and Franklin get into a heated argument about who can eat the most boiled eggs in a sitting. Theodore, in a rage, picks up a baseball bat and hits Franklin, splitting his skull open. Franklin dies on the way to the hospital. In order to successfully reduce the Theodore's crime from murder to voluntary manslaughter, his attorney must demonstrate

(A) That a reasonable person would have reacted similarly.

(B) That Theodore was acting in the heat of passion.

(C) That Theodore was acting in the heat of passion and that a reasonable person would have reacted similarly.

(D) That Theodore's actions were reckless, not intentional.

Questions 192 – 194 are based on the following:

Danny, a 25-year-old-male shoe salesman, is obsessed with women's feet to the point of compulsion. He is particularly enamored of the feet of Trisha, a frequent customer whom he believes is 17 (she is actually 15). One night, he follows Trisha home, in the hope of gaining access to her bedroom and fondling her feet. He is concerned that his actions are wrong, but cannot stop himself. Once all the lights go out, he slides open a window and enters the house.

He accomplishes his deed, but a neighbor spotted him sneaking in and he is quickly arrested. Although he was unaware of this, there is a state statute that makes it a strict liability gross misdemeanor to touch a child under 16 unknown to the perpetrator on any part of the body except genitals. It is a felony to touch a child under 16 on the breasts, genitals, or buttocks.

192. Danny should be charged with
- (A) Burglary and misdemeanor touching of a child.
- (B) Burglary only.
- (C) Misdemeanor touching of a child only.
- (D) Neither burglary nor misdemeanor touching of a child.

193. In a jurisdiction that has adopted only the *M'Naghten* test, Danny's insanity defense will
- (A) Succeed, if he can demonstrate that it was impossible for him to resist the urge to touch Trisha's feet.
- (B) Succeed, if he can prove he has a mental disease or defect.
- (C) Fail, because he knew right from wrong.
- (D) Fail, because he is strictly liable.

194. If the prosecution can prove that Danny intended to fondle Trisha's genitals when he entered the house, but then he got scared and decided not to, he can be charged with
- (A) Burglary and felony touching of a child.
- (B) Burglary and attempted felony touching of a child.
- (C) Burglary only.
- (D) Attempted felony touching of a child only.

Questions 195 – 198 are based on the following:

Keenan goes to Damon's house, hoping to convince Damon to loan Keenan his portable stereo. Unbeknownst to Damon, Keenan has no intention of returning the stereo, as he is about to leave town for good. Unbeknowst to Keenan, Damon knows Keenan is about to leave town. Also, the stereo is broken and useless. The two of them chat for a while and Keenan asks if he can borrow the stereo. Damon says, "Heck, you're such a good friend, you can have it for $10 bucks." Keenan figures this is a good deal. He gives Damon the money and takes off. In this jurisdiction, larceny is punishable by 2 years in prison,

false pretenses by 1 year in prison, larceny by trick by 6 months in prison and $2,500 fine.

195. Charged with burglary, Keenan will likely be
- (A) Convicted.
- (B) Acquitted, because he did not intend to commit a felony at the time of entry.
- (C) Acquitted, because he did not break and enter.
- (D) Acquitted, because he obtained the stereo by legal means.

196. As a prosecutor, you would most likely charge Damon with
- (A) Larceny.
- (B) Larceny by trick.
- (C) False pretenses.
- (D) Nothing – he has not committed a crime.

197. Damon is indigent and requests an attorney, but he is told he does not qualify to receive one because it is believed he has hidden fortunes. In a plea agreement, he pleads guilty to larceny by trick. What punishment can he most likely expect?
- (A) 6 months in prison.
- (B) $2,500 fine.
- (C) 6 months in prison and $2,500 fine.
- (D) No punishment, his conviction will be overturned.

198. Keenan is acquitted on the burglary charge. The prosecutor charges him with attempted larceny. He will most likely be
- (A) Convicted, because he attempted to gain possession of the stereo by fraud without intent to return it.
- (B) Acquitted, because the prosecution violates double jeopardy.
- (C) Acquitted, because he is actually guilty of attempted false pretenses, a more serious crime.
- (D) Convicted, because he took substantial steps toward committing the crime.

Questions 199 and 200 are based on the following:

Barry and Sandra are on a date. They have several drinks and go back to her apartment. Barry pushes Sandra on to the bed and tries to undress her over her sincere protestations. Finally, she kicks him in the stomach and he leaves in agony.

199. Barry is charged with attempted rape of Sandra. His best defense would be
- (A) He honestly and reasonably believed she had consented.
- (B) He is impotent and therefore rape of Sandra was impossible.
- (C) He was intoxicated.
- (D) His actions did not constitute attempted rape.

200. During Barry's trial, he repeatedly protests his innocence during the prosecution's case, and addresses the jury directly, yelling, "You can't do this to me!" Finally, the judge has him removed. His conviction will likely be
- (A) Upheld, because the judge had discretion to have him removed.
- (B) Overturned, because a defendant has a constitutional right to be present at trial.
- (C) Overturned, because his behavior was grounds for a mistrial.
- (D) Overturned, because of ineffective assistance of counsel.

Questions 201 – 204 are based on the following.

Meg's husband Bull is a career criminal, mostly petty theft. He wants to give Meg a special Christmas gift. Having no money, he heads down to the mall to see what might be an easy grab. He strolls into a jewelry shop and sees some inexpensive items near the cash register. He picks out a blue heart-shaped pendant and, giving the cashier a sideways glance, slips it into his pocket. The cashier turns and says, "Hey what did you put in there?" The cashier grabs Bull's arm, and Bull wrenches it

away violently, causing the cashier to reel around. He makes a run for it and escapes.

On Christmas Eve, Bull gives Meg the gift neatly wrapped. She opens it and puts it on, delighted. Christmas morning, Bull and Meg get into a huge argument about Bull's mother. In a fury, Meg takes off the necklace and flings it at Bull, saying, "You can have this ugly thing back!" Bull says, "That's okay, I ripped it off anyway!" He then storms out. Meg is shocked and furious, but she actually loves the necklace, so she picks it back up, puts it on, and begins to pack some things to go to her parents' house.

Meanwhile, back at the mall, the cashier identifies Bull as the thief. One officer, who has had previous run-ins with Bull, heads over to Bull and Meg's house and pounds on the door. Meg opens it, and the officer immediately arrests her. He unzips her jacket, sees the necklace, and seizes it as evidence.

201. Bull can be charged with
- (A) Larceny.
- (B) Burglary.
- (C) Robbery.
- (D) Embezzlement.

202. Meg can be charged with
- (A) Larceny.
- (B) Receiving stolen property.
- (C) Robbery.
- (D) No crime.

203. If Bull presses charges against the cashier for battery, the cashier will likely be
- (A) Convicted.
- (B) Acquitted, because his actions do not meet the elements for battery.
- (C) Acquitted, because he acted in self-defense.
- (D) Acquitted, because Bull has previously been convicted of theft.

204. A motion to suppress the necklace as evidence should be
- (A) Granted, because it was seized incident to an invalid arrest.

(B) Denied, because it was discovered upon search incident to a valid arrest.

(C) Granted, because the officer had no search warrant.

(D) Denied, because it would have inevitably been discovered.

Questions 205 – 207 are based on the following:

Ridiculously Rich Rascals, Inc. (RRR), a major developer, has designs on a particular area of Stubenville to build a mega-mall. Only one obstacle exists: the stubborn long-time residents of this choice acreage. Two residents in particular, Jim and Jack, notice RRR's pattern of buying up property in the neighborhood and begin talking. They call a meeting of residents and organize a protest at RRR's headquarters, saying that residents should be prepared to defend their land "by any means necessary." In fact, Jim and Jack suggest that everyone brings some kind of protection to defend himself in case RRR "gets violent."

The next day, 200 locals show up at RRR headquarters with signs and bullhorns. About 20 bring baseball bats, tire irons, and the like. In response to the shouting and marching, the RRR public relations executive comes out to calm the situation. He begins talking to the crowd, but only incites them further. One resident, Bill, comes after the PR man with a baseball bat. The first swing misses by inches. Jim and Jack roar with approval and scream, "Too bad you missed him!" The rest of the crowd becomes silent, realizing that this is going too far. The second swing connects with the man's leg and he collapses in agony.

The police arrive and break up the protest, arresting Bill. In the squad car on the way to the station, Bill begins babbling, protesting his innocence and blaming Jim and Jack. The officer says, "But they aren't the ones who swung the bat, are they?" Bill says, "No, but they gave me the idea and cheered me on the whole time." Once at the station,

Bill is read his *Miranda* rights and booked, after which he agrees to sign a confession.

205. The prosecutor wants to file the most serious charge(s) possible against Bill. On these facts, she can file

(A) Assault and battery.

(B) Battery and attempted murder.

(C) Battery only.

(D) Attempted murder only.

206. If Bill is convicted, and Jim and Jack are charged with battery, they will likely be

(A) Acquitted, because it has been proven that Bill was the perpetrator.

(B) Convicted, because they encouraged Bill to bring a weapon.

(C) Convicted, because they cheered him on.

(D) Acquitted, because they can only be charged as accomplices to battery, not battery.

207. Jim and Jack's motion to suppress Bill's statements in the police car that implicated them should be

(A) Granted, because Bill was trying to exonerate himself and the statements are inherently untrustworthy.

(B) Denied, because they were spontaneous, voluntary utterances.

(C) Denied, because Bill did not retract them after *Miranda* rights were read.

(D) Granted, because they were made during a custodial interrogation without prior administration of the *Miranda* warnings.

Criminal Law and Procedure
Learning Question Answer Rationales

1. /C/ Since the defendant did not cause the death, he cannot be found guilty of murder. However, he may be found guilty of attempted murder. **(A)** is incorrect because defendant performed the act of stabbing the victim. **(B)** is incorrect because defendant had the intention to kill. **(D)** is not the best answer because although the defendant did not cause it, the result of death has been achieved.

2. /D/ All of these situations create a duty to act except III. Just because a defendant could act without risk to himself does not mean he is under a legal duty. **(A)** is incorrect because all of these situations create a duty to act except III. **(B)** is incorrect because all of these situations create a duty to act except III. **(C)** is incorrect because all of these situations create a duty to act except III.

3. /C/ Robbery requires specific intent under the common law. **(A)** is incorrect because felony murder does not require any intent. **(B)** is incorrect because manslaughter could be the result of recklessness. **(D)** is incorrect because statutory rape is a strict liability crime.

4. /B/ Strict liability means the defendant is guilty regardless of his state of mind. **(A)** is incorrect because proof of intent to commit the crime is not required under strict liability.

(C) is incorrect because proof of intent to commit the crime is not required under strict liability. **(D)** is incorrect because proof of intent to commit the crime is not required under strict liability.

5. /B/ This is correct statement of the doctrine of transferred intent. **(A)** is a misstatement of the law; intent transfers only to similar crimes. **(C)** describes a different principle of law. **(D)** is nonsensical— "intent" by police to seize evidence is not usually analyzed, only procedure.

6. /C/ Misinformation from a public official may exonerate a defendant by negating the mens rea of the crime. **(A)** is incorrect because the mens rea specified in a law has no bearing on whether a mistake of law is permitted. **(B)** is incorrect because a mistake of law is generally not a defense. **(D)** is incorrect because ignorance of the legal system is not usually a defense.

7. /C/ The substantial factor test for causation states that if the defendant's actions were not enough by themselves to cause the harm, but combined with other forces do produce the harm, the defendant's actions are considered the cause in fact. **(A)** is not the best answer because under the substantial factor test, both are guilty of murder. **(B)** is not the best answer because under the substantial factor test, both are

guilty of murder. **(D)** is not the best answer because under the substantial factor test, both are guilty of murder.

8. /A/ An accomplice is charged with the underlying crime committed. There is no such thing as a charge of "accomplice" so **(B)** is incorrect. Attempt is an inchoate crime, and cannot be charged if the crime is completed, as here, so **(C)** is incorrect. Y can be charged with one of the named offenses, so **(D)** is incorrect.

9. /D/ The statement is the definition of proximate cause. **(A)** is incorrect because "presumed cause" is not genuine criminal law terminology. **(B)** is incorrect because "proven cause" is not genuine criminal law terminology. **(C)** is incorrect because "actual cause" is the direct cause of the harm, not simply the "natural and probable result."

10. /D/ Burglary, unlike other crimes, does not merge with the larceny even though larceny is an element of burglary. **(A)** is incorrect because burglary has additional elements to larceny. **(B)** is not the best answer because the facts indicate burglary has occurred. **(C)** is incorrect because a defendant cannot be convicted of both a lesser included and greater offense, and because larceny is not a "lesser included" offense to burglary.

11. /C/ The Model Penal Code recognizes all three of these conditions as acceptable for an insanity defense. **(A)** is not the best answer because it is incomplete. **(B)** is not the best because it is incomplete. **(D)** is incorrect because Option IV describes the defense of duress, not insanity.

12. /A/ This is the standard for competency to stand trial, which is

constitutionally required. **(B)** is incorrect because "competency to stand trial" and "insanity at the time the crime was committed" are examined separately. **(C)** misstates the law – a defendant need not appear as a witness. **(D)** is incorrect – usually the lawyer will use her judgment to determine when to object.

13. /C/ *Voluntary* intoxication is not a valid defense, but *involuntary* intoxication can be a defense to any crime, equivalent to temporary insanity. **(A)** is incorrect because *involuntary* intoxication is a defense. **(B)** is not the best answer because no such reasonableness standard is required for involuntary intoxication. **(D)** is incorrect because battery is not a specific intent crime.

14. /B/ Children ages 7-14 are presumed incapable of intending a crime, but the presumption is rebuttable. **(A)** describes the rule for children under 7. **(C)** is incorrect; children may be tried if they are capable of understanding the proceeding. **(D)** is incorrect because children under 18 are tried in juvenile court unless they are accused of serious violent crimes and are 16 or 17.

15. /D/ Duress requires imminent threat of serious bodily harm or death to oneself or a third party which the defendant reasonably believed would be carried out. **(A)** is incorrect because duress is available for all crimes except murder and manslaughter. **(B)** is incorrect because duress does not negate intent, it is a defense to the crime. **(C)** is incorrect because duress requires imminent threat of serious bodily harm or death to oneself or a third party that the defendant reasonably believed would be carried out.

16. **/C/** This is the only correct scenario for an entrapment defense. **(A)** is incorrect because mere creation of the opportunity to commit a crime is not enough for entrapment. **(B)** is incorrect because it helps to establish that there was *no* entrapment. **(D)** is incorrect because predisposition to commit the crime negates an entrapment defense

17. **/C/** This is the best answer because a threat of harm must be imminent for self-defense to be applicable. Response **(A)** is not the best answer because even if B had retreated, and then shot A, he would not be entitled to argue self-defense. Response **(B)** is incorrect because an imminent threat of serious bodily harm is sufficient for deadly force to be justified. **(D)** is incorrect because one may always act reasonably in self-defense, even if one has not chosen the wisest course of action beforehand.

18. **/B/** This is the best answer because mistake about the amount of necessary force does not exonerate a defendant, but can be sufficient for reducing the charge from murder to manslaughter. **(A)** is not the best answer because mistake about the amount of necessary force will likely be sufficient to reduce the charge from murder to manslaughter. **(C)** is incorrect because deadly force may only be used in self-defense if deadly force is threatened. **(D)** is incorrect, because the intent was to inflict serious bodily harm or death.

19. **/D/** This is the best answer because it accurately states the minority view. The defender need not have a personal relationship to the victim in any jurisdiction, so **(A)** is incorrect. The defender may always act if reasonable, rather than waiting for police, so **(B)** is not the best answer. The amount of force allowed does not turn on the defender's relationship to the victim, so **(C)** incorrect.

20. **/A/** This is the best answer because although Abram is a fleeing felon (he committed a robbery) Quincy has no basis for the belief that Abram is an immediate threat. **(B)** is not the best answer, because Quincy has no basis for the belief that Abram is an immediate threat. **(C)** misstates the law; a citizen may use force apprehend a fleeing felon if that felon poses an immediate threat. **(D)** is incorrect because Quincy witnessed Abram committing robbery, which is a felony.

21. **/A/** Don has committed textbook solicitation. He has intentionally encouraged another to commit a felony or serious misdemeanor. **(B)** is incorrect because solicitation is complete once the offer is complete, regardless of acceptance or refusal. **(C)** is incorrect because no value need be offered, mere words of encouragement are enough. **(D)** is incorrect because while solicitation does merge with conspiracy if the crime is committed, solicitation is itself a crime regardless of the ultimate result.

22. **/B/** One who is in the class of persons that a statute was enacted to protect cannot be charged with solicitation. Statutory rape laws were enacted to protect minors. **(A)** misstates the law: the solicitor can be convicted regardless of the outcome of charges against other parties. **(C)** is incorrect because statutory rape is a strict liability crime. **(D)** correctly states the law, but is not the best answer because of the protected persons exception.

23. /A/ This is the correct response; the statement describes the *Pinkerton* conspiracy rule. **(B)** is incorrect because *M'Naghten* is a rule regarding the defense of insanity. **(C)** is incorrect because *Miranda* concerns reading of Constitutional rights to a suspect. **(D)** is incorrect because *Gerstein* has to do with holding probable cause hearing within 48 hours of a warrantless arrest.

24. /B/ If a crime by its definition requires two persons to commit, those two persons cannot be convicted of both the underlying crime and conspiracy. **(A)** is incorrect because if a crime by its definition requires two persons to commit, those two persons cannot be convicted of both the underlying crime and conspiracy. **(C)** is not the best answer because it is not always true that solicitation is just because there is a two-person crime. **(D)** is incorrect because other evidence may be sufficient to convict both.

25. /B/ This is correct. The mens rea for attempt is always specific intent, regardless of the mens rea for the underlying crime. **(A)** is incorrect because the mens rea for attempt is always specific intent, regardless of the mens rea for the underlying crime. **(C)** is incorrect because the mens rea for attempt is always specific intent. **(D)** is incorrect because the mens rea for attempt is always specific intent.

26. /C/ This describes the mens rea of extreme recklessness, which is sufficient malice aforethought to support a charge of murder. **(A)** is incorrect because motive suggests specific intent to kill, which the

facts of the problem already preclude. **(B)** is incorrect because threats without specific intent to kill (which the facts already preclude) are not enough. **(D)** is incorrect only if the defendant was committing a dangerous felony at the time (felony murder), which the facts do not specify.

27. /A/ Intent to cause serious bodily harm (substantial risk of death or prolonged injury to victim) is sufficient mens rea for murder. **(B)** is incorrect because intent to cause serious bodily harm is sufficient mens rea for murder. **(C)** is incorrect because intent to cause serious bodily harm is sufficient mens rea for murder. **(D)** is incorrect because intent to cause serious bodily harm is sufficient mens rea for murder.

28. /A/ "A human being" legally exists between live birth and legal death, described as irreversible cessation of brain function. **(B)** is incorrect because legal culpability for any death depends first upon the status of the victim as a human being. **(C)** is not the best answer because there is causation to the extent that the heart and lungs ceased to function as a result of the action of the defendant. **(D)** is not the best answer because it is a moral, not a legal, consideration.

29. /B/ The mens rea for involuntary manslaughter is mere recklessness. Second degree murder requires at least extreme recklessness, so **(A)** is incorrect. Voluntary manslaughter is intentional but in the heat of passion, so **(C)** is incorrect. Reckless endangerment does not involve a death, so **(D)** is incorrect.

30. /C/ This is correct; a gross deviation from the "reasonable person"

standard of care must be shown. **(A)** is incorrect because it overstates the mens rea. **(B)** is incorrect because it understates the mens rea. **(D)** is incorrect because the MPC recognizes negligent homicide, typically as it relates to the operation of vehicles.

31. /C/ Larceny is the taking and carrying away of property in the possession of another with the intent to permanently deprive the owner. Although Tim initially intended to borrow the tool, his subsequent intention to permanently deprive relates back to the time of the taking. **(A)** is incorrect because there was never intention to permanently deprive. **(B)** is incorrect because Tim's reasonable mistaken belief of ownership negates the element of property "in possession of another." **(D)** is not the best answer because Tim does not "carry away" the tool.

32. /A/ Unauthorized use is a form of embezzlement. The employee is in a fiduciary relationship with the employer. **(B)** is incorrect because no tangible property has been carried away. **(C)** is not the best answer because the employee has not induced the employer to surrender title to any tangible property. **(D)** is incorrect because no property was taken by force from a person's body or presence.

33. /B/ False pretenses is when a defendant fraudulently induces an owner to transfer title and possession to personal property. Larceny by trick is similar, but involves only transfer of possession, not title. Both crimes involve fraud, so **(A)** is incorrect. Either crime can involve personal property, so **(C)** is incorrect. Larceny by trick is similar, but involves only

possession, not title, so **(D)** is incorrect.

34. /D/ Maurice has committed the crime of receiving stolen goods. Constructive knowledge such as unreasonably low price is sufficient for "knowing" that the goods were stolen. **(A)** is incorrect because the delivery of goods by the thief to a location designated by the defendant is enough for receipt. **(B)** is not the best answer because even if the defendant did not have actual knowledge, he had constructive knowledge due to the unreasonably low price, which is sufficient. **(C)** is incorrect because the crime is complete when property is received, regardless of whether the defendant paid for it or sold it himself.

35. /A/ Robbery is larceny by force from a person or in the presence of a person. There must be a causal relationship between the use of force and the taking of property. **(B)** is irrelevant because the clerk was not present, so the quality or amount of force used is not at issue. **(C)** is incorrect because the force must be used against the person for robbery to be in play. **(D)** is irrelevant because the clerk was not present, so the quality or amount of force used is not at issue.

36. /C/ Entering the dwelling house of another with the intent to commit a felony or larceny inside is burglary. No forced entry is required, and in most jurisdictions, a nighttime entry is no longer necessary. **(A)** is not the best answer because although larceny has occurred, it is not the most serious crime he has committed. **(B)** is incorrect because no person was present. **(D)** is incorrect because no fiduciary relationship is indicated.

37. **/B/** Recklessness or specific intent must be present to warrant a battery charge. **(A)** is not the best response because there is more than one correct mens rea listed in the available responses. **(C)** is incorrect because negligence and gross negligence are insufficient. **(D)** is incorrect because negligence and gross negligence are insufficient.

38. **/B/** Assault is defined as the intentional creation of apprehension of an immediate battery. Threat of serious bodily harm is not required, just as it is not required for a battery conviction, so **(A)** is incorrect. If the defendant succeeds in battering the victim after an attempted battery assault, the assault merges with the battery, so **(C)** is incorrect. Threat of serious bodily harm is not required, just as it is not required for a battery conviction, so **(D)** is incorrect.

39. **/B/** Intoxication is not a defense to rape unless the defendant is so intoxicated that he does not realize that he is having intercourse. **(A)** is incorrect because having consensual intercourse while intoxicated is fine. **(C)** is incorrect because physical resistance is no longer generally required to be proven by the victim. **(D)** is incorrect because intoxication is not a defense to rape unless the defendant is so intoxicated that he does not realize that he is having intercourse.

40. **/D/** For a charge of kidnapping, specific intent or substantial certainty that confinement of the victim will result is required. Physical restraint is not required; a threat is enough, so **(A)** is incorrect. The victim need not attempt to escape, so **(B)** is incorrect. Any measurable confinement time can

qualify, so **(C)** is not the best answer.

41. **/D/** This is the required mens rea for arson. **(A)** is incorrect because recklessness is not a sufficient mens rea for arson. **(B)** is incorrect because most modern statutes have eliminated the "dwelling" requirement. **(C)** is incorrect because most modern statutes have eliminated the exception for burning down one's own property.

42. **/C/** This is the best answer, because no matter how egregious a violation of privacy, if there is no state action (a government officer, police, etc.) the Fourth Amendment does not apply. **(A)** is not the best answer because there is a limited expectation of privacy at a place of business. **(B)** is incorrect because the search is not of the computer, but of the messages, which amount to the "personal effects" of the employee. **(D)** is incorrect because reviewing personal communications is a search, e.g. wiretapping.

43. **/B/** This is a correct statement of the Open Fields doctrine. **(A)** is not the best answer because it misstates the doctrine—entry of premises is not permitted. **(C)** is incorrect because the open fields doctrine does not relate to computer searches. **(D)** is incorrect because it is not a correct statement of the open fields doctrine. Also, a car is still somewhat private even if parked in an open field—an articulable suspicion would still be required.

44. **/B/** For probable cause to arrest, there must be a likelihood of violation of the law and a likelihood that the person arrested committed the violation. A warrant is not always required, such as if the arrest is of a felony suspect in a public place, or a misdemeanor suspect when the misdemeanor was committed in the officer's presence. **(A)** is incorrect because another element is required for probable cause to arrest. **(C)** is not the best answer because a warrant is redundant; procurement of a warrant must based on probable cause. **(D)** is incorrect because probable cause does not require a likelihood of conviction.

45. /A/ A felony suspect in a public place may be arrested without warrant, although a *Gerstein* hearing must be held within 48 hours to establish probable cause. **(B)** is incorrect articulable suspicion, required for a *Terry* frisk, is not probable cause, which is required for an arrest. **(C)** is incorrect because the suspect could be in a dwelling other than his own in which case a warrant would be required. **(D)** is incorrect because the misdemeanor exception is only when the misdemeanor is committed in front of a police officer, not a private citizen.

46. /C/ This is correct. Illegally obtained evidence will be excluded, but the case will go forward. **(A)** is incorrect because an unlawful arrest does not result in dismissal of the case. **(B)** is incorrect because there may be other evidence independent of the unlawful arrest. **(D)** is incorrect because any evidence seized during a search subsequent to arrest would be excluded as fruits of the poisonous tree.

47. /D/ Full probable cause to arrest must exist before any detention where the suspect does not feel free to leave. **(A)** is incorrect because it understates the standard—full probable cause to arrest must exist. **(B)** is incorrect because it understates the standard—full probable cause to arrest must exist.

(C) overstates the requirement—if an officer has full probable cause to arrest he may detain the suspect, even without a warrant.

48. /C/ This is the best answer. **(A)** is incorrect because hearsay is acceptable evidence for establishing probable cause. **(B)** is incorrect because an articulable suspicion is sufficient to stop an automobile. **(D)** is incorrect because if an informant is historically reliable and the information he provides appears reliable, his affidavit is sufficient for probable cause.

49. /B/ A proper warrant must specify the location to be searched. **(A)** is incorrect the warrant need not identify the particular rooms. **(C)** is incorrect because who owns the property may not be relevant and need not be specified. **(D)** is incorrect because charges must be included in an indictment or information, but not a warrant.

50. /B/ Incident to lawful arrest, an officer may search within the suspect's reach, or "wingspan." **(A)** is incorrect a search of all property would require probable cause or a warrant. **(C)** is incorrect because a search of the suspect's home would require probable cause or a warrant. **(D)** is incorrect because a search of the suspect's trunk or anything out of his "wingspan" would require probable cause or a warrant.

51. /A/ While executing a valid search warrant, an officer may conduct a protective sweep for dangerous persons and a pat-down of other persons present. Since the warrant was for illegal weapons, Officer Jones was reasonable in conducting the pat-down. **(B)** is incorrect because the warrant was for illegal weapons and Officer Jones was

reasonable in conducting the pat-down. **(C)** misstates the law; a *Terry* frisk requires an articulable suspicion to be legal. **(D)** is incorrect because the warrant was for illegal weapons and Officer Jones was reasonable in conducting the pat-down.

52. **/A/** Exigent circumstances apply when an automobile is believed to have been used in a crime. Generally this means that the automobile itself constitutes evidence, and might be unavailable by the time a warrant is obtained. **(B)** is incorrect because it is not enough simply that the car is working. If it were enough, the exigent circumstances exception would automatically apply to all vehicles, and it doesn't. **(C)** describes a probable cause situation and is not the best answer. **(D)** describes the plain view exception, so it is not the best answer.

53. **/D/** Contraband hidden in a container is not in plain view, even if the container is. **(A)** is incorrect because it goes to proving the criminal charge, not to the validity of the search. **(B)** is incorrect because contraband hidden in a container is not in plain view, even if the container is. **(C)** is not the best answer because given the circumstances; the police had probable cause to enter.

54. **/C/** In circumstances I, II, and IV, a vehicle may be impounded. **(A)** is incorrect because suspicion that the automobile may be evidence is not enough for an impound, the driver must be arrested or a warrant to search the vehicle obtained. **(B)** is incorrect because suspicion that the automobile may be evidence is not enough for an impound, the driver must be arrested or a warrant to search the vehicle obtained. **(D)** is incorrect because suspicion that the automobile may be evidence is not enough for an impound, the driver must be arrested or a warrant to search the vehicle obtained.

55. **/B/** This is the best answer. When a consent search is conducted, there are no limitations on when and why consent may be revoked. **(A)** is not the best answer because there are no limitations on when and why consent may be revoked. **(C)** is not the best answer because there are no limitations on when and why consent may be revoked. **(D)** is not the best answer because there are no limitations on when and why consent may be revoked.

56. **/C/** Evanescent evidence is physical evidence that might "disappear" before a warrant can be obtained, thus justifying a warrantless seizure. **(A)** is incorrect because an automobile is evidence that will not "disappear," (although it could be moved or destroyed) which is the definition of evanescent evidence. **(B)** is incorrect because a handwriting sample can always be reproduced. **(D)** is incorrect because a confession is not physical evidence.

57. **/A/** Consent by one party when the conversation relates to a fire, medical emergency, crime, disaster, extortion, or hostage situation is enough to avoid the warrant requirement. **(B)** is incorrect because a wiretap is a search. **(C)** is not the best answer because consent by one party when the conversation relates to a fire, medical emergency, crime, disaster, extortion, or hostage situation is enough to avoid the warrant requirement. **(D)** is not the best answer because consent by one party when the conversation relates to a fire, medical emergency,

crime, disaster, extortion, or hostage situation is enough to avoid the warrant requirement.

58. **/A/** All of the circumstances in II, III, and IV weigh in favor of a confession's admissibility. That the defendant was not being interrogated weighs in favor of admissibility, so **(B)** is not the best answer. That the defendant was not being interrogated and *Miranda* warnings were given weighs in favor of admissibility, so **(C)** is not the best answer. Signed affidavits do not make confessions any more or less admissible. This is not a factor to be considered, so **(D)** is not the best answer.

59. **/C/** A coerced confession may not be used by the prosecution for any purpose, but the case may proceed on other evidence. **(A)** is incorrect because the prosecution may not use a coerced confession for any purpose. **(B)** is incorrect because the prosecution may not use a coerced confession for any purpose. **(D)** is incorrect because the case may proceed on other evidence.

60. **/B/** Despite the trickery, this is a custodial interrogation. **(A)** is not the best answer because he had exercised his *Miranda* rights and could not be interrogated without his lawyer. **(C)** is incorrect because of the special exception of a cellmate interrogation. **(D)** is not the best answer because a confession must be both voluntary and obtained in compliance with *Miranda*.

61. **/D/** A grand jury witness has none of these rights. **(A)** is incorrect because a grand jury witness has none of the rights listed. **(B)** is incorrect because a grand jury witness has none of the rights

listed. **(C)** is incorrect because a grand jury witness has none of the rights listed.

62. **/A/** The waiver of the right to counsel during formal proceedings must be affirmative, knowing, and intelligent. Clear and unambiguous invocation only applies to the right to counsel during questioning, so **(B)** is incorrect. On rare occasions, a judge will permit a pro se criminal defendant, so **(C)** is incorrect. The right to counsel during formal proceedings is protected by the Sixth Amendment, so **(D)** is incorrect.

63. **/B/** This kind of lineup would be conducive to mistaken identification, and the witness might identify Bob based on the police station session rather than memory of the crime. **(A)** is incorrect because the charges would not necessarily be dismissed; another, independent i.d. would still be admissible. **(C)** is not the best answer because the witness has already identified Bob based on the tainted session, and this would influence her. **(D)** is not the best answer because under the circumstances, it is unlikely a judge would find this lineup acceptable.

64. **/D/** A *Gerstein* probable cause hearing must be held within 48 hours of detainment upon any warrantless arrest or indictment. **(A)** is incorrect because warrants must be issued prior to arrest. **(B)** is incorrect because it misstates the deadline for an arraignment, which is 14 days. **(C)** is not the best answer because suspect arrested on probable cause without a warrant may be detained for 48 hours until a *Gerstein* hearing is held.

65. **/C/** A competency hearing is held to determine whether the defendant is competent to stand trial. **(A)** is incorrect because a competency hearing relates to the competency of the defendant, not counsel. **(B)** is not the best answer because competency relates to the defendant's ability to stand trial, not the defendant's state of mind when he allegedly committed the crime. **(D)** is incorrect because a competency hearing relates to the defendant's competency, not the competency of the jurisdiction.

66. **/B/** A judge always has the final say in whether to accept or reject a plea bargain, even if both sides agree. **(A)** is incorrect because the plea agreement must be presented to a judge. **(C)** is incorrect because a voluntary and intelligent plea agreement waives the Sixth Amendment jury trial right. **(D)** misstates the law: a plea may be withdrawn if the court lacked jurisdiction, the defendant received ineffective assistance, etc.

67. **/C/** This is the only proper remedy for violation of the right to a speedy trial. **(A)** is incorrect because a new trial is not held. **(B)** is incorrect because once the violation has occurred, any trial held subsequently will still be in violation. **(D)** is not the best answer because compensation is not granted for constitutional rights violations in the context of a criminal proceeding.

68. **/A/** There is no constitutional right to a closed trial, only to an open trial. **(B)** is incorrect because the judge has total discretion. **(C)** is incorrect because the judge has total discretion. **(D)** is incorrect because there is no constitutional right to a closed trial, only an open trial.

69. **/B/** On a 12-member jury, a 9 to 3 vote is sufficient for conviction. Only a 6-member jury need be unanimous, so **(A)** is incorrect. To select jurors based on race violates *Batson*, so **(C)** is incorrect. A majority is not enough in a criminal case, so **(D)** is incorrect.

70. **/C/** The right may be forfeited if the defendant is disruptive. **(A)** is incorrect because the right may be forfeited if the defendant is disruptive. **(B)** is incorrect because it misstates the law; the right to be present is independent of the Confrontation Clause. **(D)** is incorrect because provided the defendant does not forfeit his right to be present, it is otherwise available for every criminal proceeding regardless of the charge.

71. **/D/** This is a correct statement of the test for effective assistance of counsel. **(A)** is not the best answer because questionable evidence might have been ignored by the fact finder. **(B)** is incorrect because failing to make an appropriate objection may have had no effect on the outcome. **(C)** is incorrect because counsel's strategy may have been correct; it might have been misfeasance to obey the client.

72. **/C/** A witness may invoke the Fifth selectively, it is only the defendant who waives the Fifth by taking the stand. **(A)** is incorrect because the Confrontation Clause does not entitle a defendant to the answer to every question posed to a witness (for example, the information may be privileged). **(B)** is incorrect because a witness may invoke the Fifth selectively; it is only the defendant who waives the Fifth by taking the stand. **(D)** misstates the law because the Fifth Amendment

applies to any person testifying in a criminal or civil proceeding.

73. /A/ Every element must be proven beyond a reasonable doubt. **(B)** is incorrect because every element must be proven beyond a reasonable doubt. **(C)** misstates the standard of proof, which is "beyond a reasonable doubt." **(D)** misstates the standard of proof, which is "beyond a reasonable doubt."

74. /B/ A retrial is barred only if the appellate court reverses because the evidence was insufficient to support a conviction. **(A)** is incorrect because double jeopardy is not offended if the verdict is set aside. **(C)** is incorrect because an appellate court reviews the record, it does not restart the trial process. **(D)** is not the best answer because "separate sovereigns" is not the only exception that would allow a retrial.

75. /C/ Double jeopardy prevents prosecution of two separate charges based on the same events unless each charge has an element separate from the other. **(A)** is incorrect because whether or not the charges are different, double jeopardy is offended if the charges arise from the exact same event. **(B)** is incorrect because an acquittal may never be reversed. **(D)** is incorrect because regardless of whether the lesser or greater offense is tried first, double jeopardy prevents subsequent prosecution of the other.

76. /B/ Prosecution must demonstrate admissibility by a preponderance of evidence. **(A)** misstates the standard of proof. **(C)** misstates the standard of proof. **(D)** misstates the standard of proof.

77. /B/ Generally, such evidence will be admissible for impeachment purposes, if it directly contradicts the defendant's testimony. **(A)** is incorrect because evidence obtained in violation of the Fourth Amendment is admissible in some circumstances. **(C)** is incorrect because the harmless error analysis is at the appellate, not the trial, level. **(D)** is incorrect because there is only a limited exception based on the good faith reliance of the police on a facially valid search warrant – such good faith does not generally exonerate illegal behavior.

78. /C/ Evidence that is obtained through previous illegal sources are "fruits of the poisonous tree" and are generally excluded. **(A)** is not the best answer because the doctrine relates to evidence, not charges. **(B)** is incorrect because the doctrine relates to evidence, not jurors. **(D)** is incorrect because the doctrine relates to evidence, not arguments.

79. /D/ A live witness may always testify voluntarily, regardless of how she was discovered. **(A)** is incorrect because a live witness may always testify voluntarily, regardless of how she was discovered. **(B)** is incorrect because a live witness may testify voluntarily on any subject, regardless of how she was discovered. **(C)** is incorrect because a live witness may testify voluntarily on any subject, regardless of how she was discovered.

Criminal Law and Procedure
Practice Question Answer Rationales

80. /B/ A motion to suppress hearing to determine if evidence is admissible must be conducted outside the presence of the jury, and the defendant's statements therein may not be used as evidence at the trial. **(A)** is incorrect because a motion to suppress hearing to determine if evidence is admissible must be conducted outside the presence of the jury, and the defendant's statements therein may not be used as evidence at the trial. **(C)** is incorrect because the burden is on the prosecution. **(D)** is incorrect because the prosecution has the burden.

81. /B/ This is the best answer, because although some states recognize degrees of burglary based on whether the defendant enters, this would not be considered 1st degree burglary. **(A)** is incorrect because even if he could prove that Mike unlawfully deprived him of his property, it is possible to commit burglary against someone who is not the true owner of the property taken. **(C)** is incorrect because misdemeanor larceny is a sufficient underlying offense to burglary, because of the danger created by breaking and entering a dwelling. Persons need not actually be present in a dwelling for a burglary to be committed, so **(D)** is incorrect.

82. /B/ This is the best response because conspiracy involves an agreement between two or more persons to commit an unlawful act, and a substantial step in furtherance of the conspiracy. Actual commitment of the crime is a separate offense, unless it merges. **(A)** is insufficient because Mike did have the necessary mens rea at the time the conspiracy was formed. **(C)** is not the best answer because reserving the hotel room is a substantial step. **(D)** is incorrect because whether or not he committed fraud is not relevant to the issue of conspiracy to commit the drug offense.

83. /D/ This is the best answer, because the prosecution must prove all elements, and an element of burglary is intent to commit a felony or larceny. **(A)** is incorrect because the agreement must include the mens rea of a crime as well as the actus reus. **(B)** is incorrect because it describes a factor in determining the degree of burglary, not an element of the crime. **(C)** is incorrect because conspiracy does not merge, but rather attempt.

84. /C/ This is the best answer because it is an accurate restatement of the felony-murder rule. **(A)** is not the best answer because while intent is normally required for murder, the felony-murder rule is an exception. **(B)** is incorrect, because the cashier's actions were reasonable and predictable under the circumstances. **(D)** is incorrect, because the felony-murder rule does not "assume" intent, it eliminates the element of intent. Intent is rarely assumed; it is either an element of the offense or it is not.

85. /A/ This is the best answer, because Lawrence committed the taking and carrying away of the property of another with intent to steal. That he only made it a few feet does not negate the charge. **(B)** is incorrect because burglary involves entering a structure. **(C)** is not the best answer because although the property was taken from Victor's person, there was no force or threat of force used, a required element of robbery. **(D)** is incorrect because one of the listed crimes has been committed.

86. **/A/** This is the best answer, because William has committed the trespassory taking and carrying away of the property of another with intent to steal. His belief that the property is rightfully his does not invoke the recapture of chattels rule because he was not in pursuit of the chattel directly after the taking. **(B)** is not the best answer because at the time he entered the dwelling, he did not have intent to commit a crime therein. **(C)** is not the best answer because the owner of the property was not present and no force was used or threatened against him. **(D)** is incorrect because William is guilty of one of the listed crimes.

87. **/C/** This is the best answer because he has committed robbery, defined as larceny with the two additional elements of 1) taking the property from person or presence of the owner, and 2) accomplishing the taking by force/putting the owner in fear. The reasonable person standard is *not* applied in this situation – it does not matter that a reasonable person would not have had any apprehension of harm. It is enough that the apprehension was created in the victim. **(A)** is not the best answer because of the additional elements transforming this action from larceny to robbery. **(B)** is not the best answer because burglary requires entry in to a dwelling or structure with intent to commit a crime. **(D)** is incorrect because William is guilty of one of the listed crimes.

88. **/C/** This is the best answer because it describes the requisite state of mind to pass the *M'Naghten* test: the presence of a mental disease or defect coupled with an inability to comprehend the nature and quality of the act. **(A)** is not the best answer because it suggests an acknowledgement of awareness that an act is incorrect, which is overridden by an uncontrollable urge created by mental illness. In a jurisdiction governed by the "irresistible impulse" test, it might fly. **(B)** is not the best answer because there is no mental disease or defect at work, at best the defendant's sudden violent outburst might save him from first degree premeditated murder charge. **(D)** is not the best answer because it suggests an acknowledgement of awareness that an act is incorrect, which is overridden by an uncontrollable urge created by mental illness. In a jurisdiction governed by the "irresistible impulse" test, it might fly.

89. **/C/** This is the best answer because Nancy's conduct meets the elements for accomplice liability; she has the required mens rea for the substantive crime and she acts to aid or encourage Gerald. Accomplice liability creates liability for the target crime, in this case assault. **(A)** is not the best answer because solicitation requires an offer to exchange value for a crime. **(B)** is not the best answer because rendering criminal assistance occurs after a crime has been committed, in concealing or assisting flight from a crime. **(D)** is incorrect because Nancy is guilty of one of the listed crimes.

90. **/B/** This is the best answer because an action, even if it is just words of encouragement, is required to create accomplice liability. **(A)** is not the best answer because Barry's smile during the attack suggests that he was not frightened. **(C)** is

not the best answer because a "no legal duty to rescue" defense is applicable to a tort action, not a criminal one. **(D)** is not the best answer because onlookers who hope for the criminal result are considered to have the same criminal intent as the actor.

91. /C/ This is the best answer because the right of officers to search automobiles under exigent circumstances (with probable cause) but without a warrant does not apply to locked cases. **(A)** is not the best answer because the eyewitnesses' description of the car and the proximity of the car to the scene, establish sufficient probable cause. **(B)** is not the best answer because the plain view rule applies to contraband that is in plain view (e.g., a clear baggie containing suspected drugs) not to opaque containers that happen to be visible. **(D)** fails because Dave was not yet under arrest, so the "wingspan" exception allowing a warrantless search incident to an arrest is not applicable.

92. /B/ This is the best answer, because there was no evidence that there was cocaine at Debbie's apartment, the prosecutor was merely speculating that drugs might be there. **(A)** is not the best answer because a suspect's residence is not the only location that can be subject to a valid warrant. **(C)** is not the best answer because a valid arrest alone is not sufficient for a valid warrant. **(D)** is not the best answer, because the standard for evaluating bias is whether the magistrate had a "stake in the case" (e.g., a current prosecutor) not simply that the magistrate may sympathetic to prosecutors in general.

93. /D/ This is the best answer, because defendants have a right not to take the stand and remain silent, but once they do, Fifth Amendment protection against self-incrimination is waived. **(A)** is not the best answer because there are no facts suggesting that Dave's attorney did not advise him properly, and a client always has the right to decide. **(B)** is incorrect because only witnesses, not defendants, must take the stand and invoke the Fifth Amendment as each question is asked. **(C)** is not the best answer because there are no facts to suggest that Dave's testimony was not critical to his conviction. The outcome might have been different if he had not testified.

94. /C/ This is the best answer because voluntary consent is effective if the person consenting has authority over the premises/property to be searched. **(A)** is incorrect because knowledge of the right to refuse consent is only one element in evaluating voluntary nature of consent, it is not a requirement for a valid consent search. All other facts suggest that the consent was voluntary. **(B)** is not the best answer because although a warrant could be obtained on reliable information from a dependable informant, it is not required if voluntary consent is obtained. **(D)** is not the best answer, because a consent search applies to all places which could reasonably contain the items seized, and all property over which the consenting party has authority, so the bedroom closet counts.

95. /B/ This is the best answer because in a felony case, a preliminary hearing must be held (usually with witnesses) for a magistrate to determine whether there is probable cause to believe that the defendant committed the crime charged. **(A)**

is incorrect because less than 60 days have passed, which is the standard time allotted before speedy trial issues attach. **(C)** is incorrect because arraignment always follows the indictment/filing of information. **(D)** is not the best answer because the extensive documentary evidence combined with the statement of a reliable informant is probably enough for the filing of a complaint.

96. /A/ This is the best answer because whenever a warrantless arrest is made, a *Gerstein* hearing is required to be held within 48 hours in front of a magistrate to establish probable cause. **(B)** is incorrect because the broken taillight is an infraction that makes the stop legal. **(C)** is incorrect because the "wingspan" rule applies to search incident to arrest, and in any event is trumped by the "plain view" rule. **(D)** is incorrect because arrest warrants are not required in exigent circumstances with probable cause. In this case, the exigent circumstance of the suspects being in a car justifies immediate arrest.

97. /A/ This is the best answer because confessions in the absence of *Miranda* warnings are only excluded if they are given during interrogation when the suspect is not free to leave. Voluntary utterances prior to arrest are neither custodial nor the result of interrogation and are admissible. **(B)** is incorrect because the statement is incriminating as to the charge – rendering criminal assistance. **(C)** is not the best answer because an officer is only required to administer *Miranda* warnings upon arrest. **(D)** is not the best answer because an admission by a party opponent is not hearsay.

98. /C/ This is the best answer because waiver of the right to counsel (*during legal proceedings*) must always be knowing and intelligent, and is particularly scrutinized when a guilty plea is entered. **(A)** is incorrect because an advantageous plea bargain does not negate any Constitutional improprieties that may have occurred in reaching the plea. **(B)** is not the best answer because (*in the context of invocation of the right to counsel in a custodial interrogation*) John's question was not a clear invocation of the right to counsel, Officer's response was appropriate, and John sufficiently waived his right to have counsel present. **(D)** is not the best answer, because the facts deal with the right to counsel during formal court proceedings, not interrogation. Also, the rule for the right to counsel during formal proceedings is quite the contrary – waiver must be voluntary, knowing and intelligent.

99. /A/ This is the best answer because even if a judge reasonably believes a defendant will do an incompetent job, the right to self-representation is absolute. **(B)** is incorrect because no facts indicate that the appointed attorney was ineffective. **(C)** is not the best answer because no facts indicate whether the error affected the outcome. **(D)** is incorrect because while the right to counsel may have been protected, the right to self-representation was violated.

100./C/ This is the best answer because re-prosecution after a hung jury is not considered double jeopardy. **(A)** is not the best answer because while it is true that double jeopardy attaches after the jury is sworn, a hung jury negates it. **(B)** is not the best answer because the hung jury in Mary's trial suggests that Tim's intent is at least a debatable issue, and is an unlikely candidate for judgment as a matter of law. **(D)** is not the best answer because two crimes are different for double jeopardy purposes only if each requires proof of one additional fact that the other does not.

101./A/ This is the best answer, because although normally an automobile search incident to arrest is restricted to area's within the suspect's control, the existence of probable cause overrides this restriction. **(B)** is not the best answer, because in an automobile search incident to arrest, the trunk may not be searched unless probable cause exists. **(C)** is not the best answer because the "wingspan" or "control" rule only applies when the officer does not have probable cause to believe the trunk may contain evidence of a crime. **(D)** is incorrect because the officer's observance of Stan's actions and behavior gave him ample cause to arrest.

102./C/ This is the best answer because police coercion is required for a confession to be considered involuntary. **(A)** is not the best answer because the police did not participate in the coercion. **(B)** is not the best answer because the facts are insufficient to make this determination, and a confession need not be corroborated by other evidence to be admissible. **(D)** is incorrect because the facts do not support it, and belief in the likelihood of a threat is probably not relevant to the issue of voluntariness of a confession.

103./D/ This is correct because the facts suggest that the confession was coerced by improper police conduct. **(A)** is incorrect because

the *Miranda* requirements are separate from voluntariness requirements. Even a confession procured in compliance with *Miranda* is not admissible if coerced. **(B)** is not correct because the facts do not suggest this, and a Constitutional violation is not "harmless error." **(C)** is incorrect – a coerced confession may not be admitted to impeach, although a confession in violation of *Miranda* may be admitted to impeach.

104./C/ This is the best answer because a defendant may not argue a search and seizure claim in a habeas appeal if he has had opportunity for full and fair litigation of the issue at the trial level. This is true even if the federal court believes that the state court reached the incorrect result. **(A)** is not the best answer because while these may be good arguments at the state court level, they may not be entertained in a habeas proceeding if they were fully litigated below. **(B)** is not the best answer because a consent search is at least theoretically permissible, and therefore a warrant is not an absolute prerequisite for searching a house. **(D)** is incorrect because the issue was fully litigated below.

105./C/ This is the best answer because Michael had intent to kill, which is defined as "malice aforethought" despite his good intentions. The fact that Terry would have died shortly anyway does not negate causation, because her death was hastened. **(A)** is incorrect because the mens rea for involuntary manslaughter is recklessness. **(B)** is incorrect because voluntary manslaughter is committed in the heat of passion, and the facts indicate premeditation. **(D)** is incorrect because Michael is guilty of one of the listed crimes.

106./D/ "None of the above" is the best answer because the doctor fulfilled the MPC requirements for withdrawal from a conspiracy; he ceased participation and attempted to prevent illegal acts of other conspirators. He did this before a substantial step was taken in furtherance of the crime. **(A)** is incorrect because the doctor withdrew from the crime before a substantial step was taken, and thus has an affirmative defense. **(B)** is incorrect because conspiracy also requires an overt step in furtherance of the conspiracy, and the doctor withdrew immediately. **(C)** is incorrect because the doctor did not perform the actus reus for murder.

107./A/ This is the best answer because Brenda "agreed" through her nodding during the discussion and her subsequent actions. Verbal or written agreement is not required for conspiracy. Conspirators are directly liable for all foreseeable crimes to which they agree, even if they do not commit the act. **(B)** is not correct because the attempt merges with the completed crime. **(C)** is not the best answer because once the conspiracy is completed, co-conspirators may be charged with the underlying crime. Murder is more serious than conspiracy, and the call of the question is for the *most serious* crime. **(D)** is incorrect because Brenda is guilty of one of the listed crimes.

108./A/ This is the best answer, because Eddie has fulfilled all the requisite elements for a burglary. He broke in (physical force is not required) and entered a building at night (connected to a dwelling, although most jurisdictions no longer require this) and had the intent to commit larceny at the time of entry. **(B)** is incorrect because "breaking" only requires lack of permission; no actual force is needed. **(C)** is not the best answer, because intent to commit any larceny is sufficient for a burglary charge. **(D)** is incorrect because the store was connected to an apartment building (and furthermore, most jurisdictions have eliminated the "dwelling" requirement, any structure will do).

109./C/ This is the best answer because a proper warrant based on the word of an informant requires that (1) the informant be reliable, and (2) the information received appear reliable under the circumstances. Neither one appears to be the case here. **(A)** is incorrect because *Miranda* warnings are required before a custodial interrogation, and have nothing to do with a search. **(B)** is not the best answer because a warrant search does not require consent although the warrant was not proper and therefore a lack of consent *could* be a good argument, it is not the *best* argument, as the call of the question demands. **(D)** is incorrect because "outside the scope" means any location not named in the warrant, or any hiding place that could not reasonably contain the items to be seized. The freezer qualifies.

110./D/ The defense will likely succeed based on the available facts. The threat of serious bodily harm or death against one's family member is sufficient to qualify as duress if belief that the threat will be carried out is reasonable. No facts indicate otherwise. **(A)** is incorrect because the threat of harm is probably imminent if the threatened person is nearby. **(B)** is incorrect because only murder and manslaughter exclude duress as a defense. **(C)** is not the best answer because threatened harm against a family member is sufficient for duress.

111./A/ Stan will likely be convicted on these facts. He intentionally and harmfully touched Slick's body directly, which constitutes all the elements of battery. **(B)** is incorrect because Slick had retreated back to his car and was no longer a threat to Stan, so he cannot claim self-defense. **(C)** is incorrect because even minor and temporary pain is sufficient for battery. **(D)** is incorrect because there is no "assumption of risk" principle in criminal battery; assumption of risk is a tort principle that does not apply here.

112./A/ This is the best answer because Tom can be convicted of robbery or larceny depending on whom the jury believes. Robbery is larceny by force in a person's presence, so if Nancy's testimony is believed, Tom will be convicted of robbery. If the purse was simply taken with no force involved, Tom will be convicted of larceny. **(B)** is incorrect because if Nancy is believed, robbery is proved. **(C)** is incorrect because on these facts, either robbery or larceny has been committed. **(D)** is incorrect because larceny is a lesser included offense to robbery, so Tom could not be convicted of both crimes.

113./D/ A strict liability crime requires no mens rea for culpability. The mere actus reus is enough. It does not matter whether Ben knew or should have known that Mel was underage, the fact that he made the sale is all that is required for liability. **(A)** is not the best answer because although Ben could have avoided culpability by ensuring that Mel was 21, his failure to do so is not the reason for his culpability – the statute is strict liability. **(B)** is

incorrect because the actus reus of the statute is the sale of alcohol, regardless of who is the owner of the store. **(C)** is incorrect, because this is a strict liability statute, culpability is not at issue.

114./D/ Probable cause sufficient for a warrant exists when information is presented that would lead a reasonable person to conclude that seizable evidence will be found. The six-week delay raises serious doubts as to whether the evidence would still be in Wanda's apartment. **(A)** is incorrect because a warrant must be based on probable cause to be valid regardless of whether other formalities are observed. **(B)** is incorrect because a warrant must be based on probable cause to be valid regardless of whether other formalities are observed. **(C)** is not the best answer because reliable information from a reliable informant is sufficient and needs no corroboration.

115./B/ This is the best answer because the warrant specified ½ kilo of PCP, which could not possibly fit in a shoe box. Even a search pursuant to a proper warrant is limited to those places where the evidence to be seized could reasonably be. **(A)** is incorrect because one day later is not sufficient delay to invalidate a warrant. **(C)** is a misstatement of the law. Consent is not required if a warrant is valid. **(D)** is irrelevant to the inquiry. To whom the drugs belong has no bearing on the validity of the search, only to Wanda's ultimate culpability.

116./C/ If a crime by its definition requires two persons to commit, those persons cannot be convicted of both the underlying crime and conspiracy. **(A)** is incorrect because a conspiracy can be formed by agreement and a substantial step, even if the crime is not completed. **(B)** is not the best answer because if a crime by its definition requires two persons to commit, those persons cannot be convicted of both the underlying crime and conspiracy. **(D)** is not the best answer because if a crime by its definition requires two persons to commit, those persons cannot be convicted of both the underlying crime and conspiracy.

117./A/ Q is probably guilty of murder. Extreme recklessness is sufficient mens rea for murder, and Q's actions seem to fill the bill. **(B)** is not the best answer because extreme recklessness is sufficient mens rea for murder. **(C)** is not the best answer because extreme recklessness is sufficient mens rea for murder. **(D)** is incorrect because Q can be convicted of murder by causing the death through his extreme recklessness.

118./A/ Intent to kill transfers from one victim to another. If Q intended to kill or inflict serious bodily harm on this neighbor, that intent would transfer to the meter-reader, and Q could be charged with her murder. **(B)** is incorrect because the doctrine of transferred intent applies. **(C)** is incorrect because the doctrine of transferred intent applies. **(D)** is incorrect because the doctrine of transferred intent applies.

119./A/ When a suspect commits a misdemeanor in an officer's presence, the officer need not wait for a warrant to arrest. **(B)** is incorrect because the "knock and announce" requirement relates to search warrants, not arrests when the crime was in a officer's presence. **(C)** is not the best answer, because while generally a suspect at home can only be arrested pursuant to a warrant, in this case Tim's arrival at home was a technicality, the officer was in continuous pursuit. **(D)** is incorrect because articulable suspicion is a lesser form of probable cause, and is not enough to arrest.

120./C/ Incident to a lawful arrest, an officer may conduct a full search of the suspect. **(A)** is incorrect because incident to a lawful arrest, an officer may conduct a full search of the suspect. **(B)** is incorrect because being able to specify the location of evidence to be seized is a rule relating to the formalities of obtaining a search warrant. **(D)** is incorrect because incident to a lawful arrest, an officer may conduct a full search of the suspect.

121./B/ This is the best answer because the mobile home was sufficiently independent and remote from the house and was not specified in the warrant. **(A)** is incorrect because the mobile home was sufficiently independent and remote from the house and was not specified in the warrant. **(C)** is not the best answer because fruits of a search may be seized. **(D)** is incorrect because a warrant to search a particular dwelling does not cover every dwelling or building owned by that person (e.g., property on another block, in another state.)

122./D/ A warrant must be executed without delay to avoid becoming stale. If not, the warrant could be declared invalid and the evidence obtained would be inadmissible. **(A)** is incorrect because the right to a speedy trial only attaches after arrest/detention. **(B)** misstates the law, no such conclusive presumption exists. **(C)** is not the best answer because excluded vital evidence is a more serious problem than counsel's potential arguments.

123./C/ Their actions appear to meet the test for criminal negligence under the MPC. **(A)** is incorrect because the MPC does recognize criminal negligence, although the common law does not. **(B)** is incorrect because it describes the mens rea "knowingly" under the MPC. **(D)** is incorrect because it misstates the law.

124./B/ A child between 7 and 14 is presumed incapable of intending a crime, but the presumption may be rebutted by clear and convincing evidence. **(A)** is incorrect because the burden of proof is on the prosecution. **(C)** is incorrect becaus it describes the rule for a child under 7. **(D)** is incorrect because the standard is "clear and convincing evidence," not "beyond a reasonable doubt."

125./D/ If a defendant's interests are threatened by a joint trial, a motion for separate trial and counsel should be granted. **(A)** is not the best answer because Sandra's interests are threatened, and she should receive a separate trial. **(B)** is not the best answer because Sandra's interests are threatened, and she should receive a separate trial. **(C)** misstates the law; joint trials are permissible, if the conflicting interests are negligible or collateral.

126./C/ The statute proscribes the sale of firearms to minors. Bubba did not perform the actus reus of the sale, so he cannot be criminally liable. **(A)** is incorrect because strict liability requires no proof of intent. **(B)** is incorrect because Bubba did not perform the actus reus of the sale, so he cannot be criminally liable. **(D)** is incorrect because

Bubba did not perform the actus reus of the sale, so he cannot be criminally liable.

127./A/ If Dale presumed that anyone who paid $50 had permission to take the gun, then he would have assumed that he had permission, and thus the taking was not trespassory. **(B)** is incorrect because only infants under 7 are conclusively presumed incapable of intending a crime. **(C)** is incorrect because duress is only a defense if there is an imminent threat of harm to persons, not property. **(D)** is not the best answer because the intent at the time of the crime was not trespassory, so the actual value is not relevant.

128./D/ Like Bubba, Pete did not commit the act of a sale, and the statute does not impose liability for failing to supervise, or any kind of liability to an owner as "respondeat superior." **(A)** is incorrect because ignorance of the fact that certain behavior is proscribed is almost never a defense. **(B)** is incorrect because Pete did not commit the actus reus of a sale, and the statute does not impose liability for failing to supervise, or any kind of liability to an owner as "respondeat superior." **(C)** is incorrect because Pete did not commit the actus reus of a sale, and the statute does not impose liability for failing to supervise, or any kind of liability to an owner as "respondeat superior."

129./A/ The purchase of firearms by minors is not proscribed, only the sale. **(B)** is incorrect because the purchase of firearms by minors is not proscribed. **(C)** is incorrect because each offense contains an element that the other does not, and therefore double jeopardy is not offended by prosecution of both. **(D)** is incorrect because acquittal on one charge does not exonerate a defendant charged with a wholly separate crime, even if it arises from the same circumstances.

130./B/ The thugs appear to have committed all the elements of kidnapping. They moved him to another part of the parking lot (any movement is kidnapping) so **(A)** is incorrect. They had specific intent, which transfers to this boy, so **(C)** is incorrect. They confined him (a lengthy period is not required) so **(D)** is incorrect.

131./A/ Although Hopalong initially refused, his actions in meeting up with Cisco by the school and their shared nod are enough to prove an agreement existed and a substantial step was taken. **(B)** is incorrect because Hopalong's actions in meeting up with Cisco by the school and their shared nod are enough to prove an agreement existed and a substantial step was taken. **(C)** misstates the law, conspiracy does not merge. **(D)** is not the best answer, since two participants do not automatically create a conspiracy. The defining characteristics of a conspiracy are an agreement and a substantial step taken in furtherance.

132./C/ If offensive touching is excluded by statute, then inflicting physical harm is the only way to achieve a battery. **(A)** is incorrect because apprehension is an element of assault, not battery. **(B)** is not the best answer because recklessness is also sufficient mens rea for battery, so specific intent is not required. **(D)** is incorrect because battery is not a lesser included of kidnapping.

133./B/ If he believed the house was empty, it would reduce his mens rea from extreme recklessness to mere recklessness, which could reduce the charge. **(A)** is incorrect

because there is no assumption of risk principle in criminal liability. **(C)** is incorrect because voluntary intoxication is not a defense unless it prevents the defendant from realizing what he is doing. In this case, voluntary intoxication, followed by firearm use, would constitute extremely reckless behavior. **(D)** is incorrect because specific intent is not required for murder; extreme recklessness will suffice.

134./D/ *Miranda* warnings must be read to the suspect even if the police know or have reason to know that a suspect is familiar with his rights, otherwise a confession is not valid. **(A)** is incorrect because *Miranda* warnings must be read to the suspect even if the police know or have reason to know that a suspect is familiar with his rights. **(B)** is incorrect because *Miranda* warnings must be read to the suspect even if the police know or have reason to know that a suspect is familiar with his rights. **(C)** is not the best answer because a suggestion of a possible beneficial plea agreement does not amount to coercion.

135./A/ Fruits of the poisonous tree are items of evidence obtained as the result of an illegal search or confession – the BAC was obtained independently and is admissible. **(B)** misstates the law – physical evidence obtained as a result of an illegally procured confession is fruit of the poisonous tree. **(C)** is irrelevant and a factual misstatement. **(D)** is not the best answer, it goes to weight, not admissibility.

136./C/ This is the best answer, because Mitch did not intentionally or recklessly injure Ted. He made a mistake of fact that negated the mens rea for battery. If Ted and Mitch were friends, the touching would not have been offensive. **(A)** is not the best answer because although Mitch intentionally slapped Ted, he would not have done it if he realized Ted was a stranger. **(B)** is incorrect because it misstates the law, battery requires intent or recklessness. **(D)** is incorrect because slapping a stranger, even a light slap, could be categorized as an offensive touching.

137./B/ Tanya and her boyfriend had an agreement to commit an unlawful act, murder, and completed that act. **(A)** is not the best answer because conspiracy also applies. **(C)** is incorrect because conspiracy does not merge with the completed crime, but solicitation does. **(D)** is incorrect because co-conspirators are liable for the crimes to which they agreed (and in some jurisdictions, *all* foreseeable crimes).

138./D/ This is the best defense because, if true, it negates causation and the boyfriend can be convicted of attempted murder at best. **(A)** is not the best answer because his actions constituted extreme recklessness at best. **(B)** is incorrect because duress is not a defense to murder or manslaughter. **(C)** is not the best answer because if the prosecution could prove by clear and convincing evidence that he knew his actions were incorrect, he would be culpable.

139./A/ Tanya intended to permanently deprive the insurance company of title to and possession of its property by way of fraud. **(B)** is incorrect because the company gave up the money voluntarily. **(C)** is incorrect because the company gave up the money voluntarily. **(D)**

is incorrect because larceny by trick results when the true owner only gives up possession of his property – he expects to get it back. The company did not expect the money would be returned by Tanya at the time they gave it to her.

140./D/ A private party made the recording so there is no state action, and thus no Fourth Amendment violation. **(A)** is incorrect because a private party made the recording so there is no state action, and thus there is no Fourth Amendment violation. **(B)** misstates the law – tape recordings are certainly admissible if authenticated and relevant. **(C)** is incorrect because a private party made the recording so there is no state action, and thus there is no Fourth Amendment violation.

141./B/ On these facts, Franz is probably culpable for second-degree murder. **(A)** is incorrect because Franz did not premeditate or plan the killing. **(C)** is incorrect because Franz's act was deliberate and not reckless. **(D)** is incorrect because Franz is chargeable with one of the listed offenses.

142./C/ The MPC requires a victim to retreat if it is safely possible to do so before the use of deadly force is permitted. **(A)** is not the best answer, although it would be had Franz been unable to retreat. **(B)** misstates the law. **(D)** is not the best answer because—setting aside Franz's mistake—a gun versus a zucchini is not reasonable force.

143./C/ Irresistible impulse and substantial capacity both recognize a defense where the defendant was unable to control her actions as the result of a mental disease or defect. **(A)** is incorrect because the *M'Naughten* test only allows the defense where the defendant cannot determine right from wrong. **(B)** is incorrect because the "irresistible impulse" and "substantial capacity" tests both recognize a defense where the defendant was unable to control her actions as the result of a mental disease or defect. **(D)** is incorrect because the *M'Naughten* test only allows the defense where the defendant cannot determine right from wrong.

144./B/ Heidi intentionally burned a structure, which is arson. Because arson is an inherently dangerous felony, she is also guilty of felony murder. **(A)** is not the best answer because Heidi is also guilty of felony murder. **(C)** is not the best answer because Heidi is guilty of felony murder, not manslaughter. **(D)** is not the best answer because Heidi is guilty of arson and felony murder, not manslaughter.

145./A/ There is only a constitutional right to 6-person jury, the verdict of which must be unanimous. **(B)** is incorrect because there is only a constitutional right to 6-person jury. **(C)** is incorrect; although a request to *have* a jury trial should not be refused, but a request as to jury *size* may be. **(D)** is incorrect because there is only a constitutional right to 6-person jury, the verdict of which must be unanimous.

146./D/ Statutory rape is a strict liability crime. **(A)** is incorrect because mens rea is of no consequence in a strict liability crime. **(B)** is not the best answer because on a charge of statutory rape, consent is irrelevant. **(C)** is incorrect because mens rea is of no consequence in a strict liability crime.

147./A/ Putting herself in a position where she was likely to be a danger makes Tamara reckless, which is

sufficient mens rea for manslaughter. **(B)** is not the best answer because it is the definition of a criminal act of omission. Although Tamara's failure to take her medication did lead to the criminal act, the failure to take it was not itself the criminal act. **(C)** is incorrect because Tamara's recklessness put her in a position where she was likely to be in danger. **(D)** is not the best answer – although she did act involuntarily at the time of the accident, her act of driving without her medication was voluntary.

148./C/ This time, Tamara is off the hook. She is not culpable for failing to take her medicine, and so she is not culpable for any involuntary acts she may commit which having an attack. **(A)** is incorrect because it misstates the law – battery requires intent or recklessness. **(B)** is incorrect because there is causation – her arm hit his nose and broke it. **(D)** is incorrect because first aggressor is a self-defense principle. Tamara did not act in self-defense, she acted involuntarily.

149./B/ To be convicted of receiving stolen goods, the defendant must have known, or the prosecution must be able to show that a reasonable person should have known, that the goods were stolen. It does not appear from the circumstances that Byron had any reason to suspect. **(A)** is incorrect because it does not appear from the circumstances that Byron had any reason to suspect. **(C)** is incorrect because receiving stolen goods is completed once the goods are received, regardless of how long the defendant plans to keep them. **(D)** misstates the law.

150./D/ Reese committed no act of assistance or encouragement, so he cannot be charged as an accomplice, even if he had criminal intent. **(A)** is incorrect because Reese committed no act of assistance or encouragement, so he cannot be charged as an accomplice, even if he had criminal intent. **(B)** is incorrect because Reese committed no act of assistance or encouragement, so he cannot be charged as an accomplice, even if he had criminal intent. **(C)** is incorrect because Reese committed no act of assistance or encouragement, so he cannot be charged as an accomplice, even if he had criminal intent.

151./B/ Solicitation merges with the crime solicited, if the crime is completed. **(A)** is incorrect because solicitation merges with the crime solicited, if the crime is completed. **(C)** is not the best answer because it misstates the facts. **(D)** is not the best answer because it misstates the facts.

152./C/ If Sanford honestly and reasonably believed that the radios were being given away, it would negate the intent to deprive the true owner at the time of the taking, a required element of larceny. **(A)** is incorrect because Sanford was predisposed to commit the crime. **(B)** is not the best answer because at the time of the taking, Sanford believed the radios were in possession of another. Also, the police were in possession of them. **(D)** is incorrect because only threat of serious bodily harm to oneself or another qualifies for a duress defense.

153./B/ An accomplice must take some kind of action to be culpable, even if it is just verbal encouragement. **(A)** is incorrect because mere criminal intent and knowledge is not enough without action. **(C)**

misstates the facts – Reese did not assist. **(D)** is incorrect because agreement is an element of conspiracy – an accomplice can assist without agreement.

154./B/ Interpreting the statute strictly, Kelly should be acquitted, because on the facts given, there is no evidence that she did any of the acts specified. **(A)** is incorrect because she did not transport it (at least there is no evidence of that). **(C)** is incorrect because solicitation does not create liability for the underlying crime if incomplete. **(D)** is incorrect because the statute does not proscribe possession.

155./B/ Kelly had intent and made a substantial step in furtherance, which was reaching for the drugs. **(A)** is incorrect because there was no agreement. Even if there were, the crime of distribution by definition requires two people to accomplish so conspiracy could not be charged. **(C)** is incorrect because Kelly's act of reaching for the drugs is a substantial step, which is enough for attempt. She also intentionally verbally enticed Sarah to take part, which completes solicitation, although Sarah refused immediately. **(D)** is incorrect because there was no agreement. Even if there were, the crime of distribution by definition requires two people to accomplish so conspiracy could not be charged.

156./A/ Under the circumstances, there was probable cause to search the locker and Kelly's statement gave the police reason to believe that the evidence would be destroyed if there were any delay. **(B)** is incorrect because even at work, there is a limited expectation of privacy in a locked locker. **(C)** is incorrect because under the circumstances, there was probable cause to search the locker and Kelly's statement gave the police reason to believe that the evidence would be destroyed if there were any delay. **(D)** is incorrect because under the circumstances, there was probable cause to search the locker and Kelly's statement gave the police reason to believe that the evidence would be destroyed if there were any delay.

157./D/ To be convicted, the defendant must actually achieve the result that the crime prohibits. **(A)** is incorrect because kidnapping includes confinement *and* movement of the victim. **(B)** is not the best answer because the defendant must first complete the act of kidnapping before this rule comes into play. **(C)** is incorrect because it misstates the facts – he did not turn himself in.

158./C/ He has fulfilled the elements for attempted kidnapping: intent and a substantial step toward completion; and battery: an intentional unlawful offensive direct touching to the person of another. **(A)** is incorrect because attempted battery assault followed immediately by a battery merges with the completed battery. **(B)** is incorrect because Stedman has fulfilled the elements for attempted kidnapping: intent and a substantial step toward completion; and battery: an intentional unlawful offensive direct touching to the person of another. **(D)** is incorrect because Stedman has fulfilled the elements for attempted kidnapping: intent and a substantial step toward completion; and battery: an intentional unlawful offensive direct touching to the person of another.

159./A/ Voluntary manslaughter is an intentional killing in the heat of passion due to excusable provocation. Generally the provocation must be at least extreme enough to cause a reasonable person to lose self-control. **(B)** is not the best answer because there is no surprise – A has known for some time and even bought the gun, a sign of some premeditation. **(C)** is incorrect because the provocation is not severe enough. **(D)** is not the best answer because the killing was not intentional.

160./B/ Had Roger known about the affair instead of being surprised, this would tend to negate the "heat of passion" element of voluntary manslaughter – he would have had time to cool down from his anger. **(A)** is not the best answer because Roger's ability to inflict more severe injury than another man could is irrelevant – in the heat of passion all self-control and judgment is lost. **(C)** is not the best answer because Roger's propensity for violence is irrelevant – in the heat of passion all self-control and judgment is lost. **(D)** is not the best answer because this kind of insurance arrangement is common between spouses. The insurance alone does not prove that the killing was premeditated rather than in the heat of passion.

161./D/ If Roger hit his wife after she came at him with a knife, she would be the aggressor, and Roger's use of force would be reasonable and proportional to hers. Therefore, Roger would have been acting in self-defense, and should be acquitted. **(A)** is incorrect because voluntary intoxication is not a defense. **(B)** is incorrect because even if he did not believe she would die, he did intentionally inflict serious bodily harm, which is sufficient mens rea for murder or manslaughter. **(C)** is incorrect because past tendency for peacefulness does not excuse current acts of violence.

162./A/ Xander set his trap with intent to cause serious bodily harm, and knew almost to a certainty that such harm would be inflicted. Glen's failure to seek medical attention is irrelevant because he would not have died but for the injuries inflicted by Xander. **(B)** is incorrect because it presumes that Xander acted without intent. **(C)** is incorrect because it presumes that Xander acted without intent. **(D)** is incorrect because deadly force may never be used in defense of property.

163./A/ The statute as written prohibits the knowing sale of alcohol to a person who *appears* intoxicated as well as those actually intoxicated, so the clerk has committed the offense. **(B)** is incorrect because the statute as written prohibits the knowing sale of alcohol to a person who *appears* intoxicated as well as those actually intoxicated. **(C)** is incorrect because the statute as written prohibits the knowing sale of alcohol to a person who *appears* intoxicated as well as those actually intoxicated. **(D)** is not the best answer because Carey went into the store empty handed and calmly emerged with a paper bag containing a brand new bottle of vodka. This is probably enough circumstantial evidence to convict.

164./B/ The statute as written prohibits the actus reus of public intoxication, which suggests intoxication in fact. **(A)** is incorrect because the appearance of intoxication is not prohibited. **(C)** is not the best answer because Carey cannot be convicted for what he planned to do, only what he actually did (the actus reus). **(D)** is not the best

answer because the statute prohibits public intoxication, not public drinking, and Carey could not have been intoxicated immediately after taking one sip of alcohol.

165./B/ Under the MPC, a person who consults a public official and receives misinformation has a defense. **(A)** is incorrect because the clerk acted on a mistake of law, not fact. **(C)** is incorrect because under the MPC, a person who consults a public official and receives misinformation has a defense. **(D)** is not the best answer, because regardless of the clarity of the statute, the clerk honestly did not understand, sought clarification, and the official misinformed the clerk.

166./C/ Although he initially committed larceny by snatching the purse with no concurrent use of force, he later used force in throwing the stick, and therefore could be charged with robbery. **(A)** is incorrect because larceny is a lesser included offense to robbery and so he could not be convicted of both. **(B)** is incorrect because he did not actually touch Talia, so he cannot be charged with battery. **(D)** is incorrect because he did not actually touch Talia, so he cannot be charged with battery.

167./A/ When Corey threw the stick, he intentionally caused Talia reasonable apprehension of immediate bodily harm. **(B)** is incorrect because in assault there is no touching – only apprehension of a touching. **(C)** is incorrect because verbal threats are not required – a simple swing of the fist will do. **(D)** is incorrect because taking property relates to larceny or robbery, not assault.

168./C/ No matter how certain a victim might be that an identification is accurate, when circumstances make it highly likely that an i.d. will produce a misidentification it will be suppressed. Here, the appearance of the officers with the suspect prior to the mug shot i.d. are highly suggestive to the victim. **(A)** is incorrect because whether the victim would have properly identified the defendant in spite of an improper identification session is impossible to know. **(B)** is incorrect because the intent of the police is irrelevant if the session is truly tainted. **(D)** is not the best answer because the availability of other evidence weighs in favor of, not against, suppressing a possibly illegal piece of evidence (because the value of that evidence is decreased).

169./D/ The MPC does not recognize the misdemeanor-manslaughter rule. [Note: A combination of (B) and (C) would probably be enough for a misdemeanor manslaughter conviction in a state that recognized the rule.] **(A)** is incorrect because even if the MPC recognized the misdemeanor-manslaughter rule (it doesn't), the rule would likely be enforced like the felony murder rule and intent would not be an element of the crime. **(B)** is incorrect because the MPC does not recognize the misdemeanor-manslaughter rule. **(C)** is incorrect because the MPC does not recognize the misdemeanor-manslaughter rule.

170./B/ The word "conclusively" in the statute makes the offense a strict liability misdemeanor. **(A)** is incorrect because mistakes of law based on misinformation are only excused if the misinformation came from a public official. **(C)** is incorrect because ignorance of a law is generally not a defense. **(D)** is incorrect because intent is irrelevant to a strict liability crime.

171./A/ Reasonable force used in defense of others is an available defense to murder. **(B)** is incorrect because modern statutes no longer require the person defended to be a friend or family member. **(C)** is incorrect because it misstates the law – force may be used by private persons in self-defense or defense of others. **(D)** is incorrect under the circumstances, the use of fists was reasonable and proportional to the mugger, armed with a deadly weapon.

172./C/ To be convicted of assault, the defendant must have created an apprehension of immediate harm or an offensive touching. Vague future threats do not constitute assault, no matter how serious. **(A)** is incorrect because to be convicted of assault, the defendant must have created an apprehension of immediate harm or an offensive touching. **(B)** is incorrect because to be convicted of assault, the defendant must have created an apprehension of immediate harm or an offensive touching. **(D)** is not the best answer because regardless of Mac's belief, a vague future threat cannot constitute assault.

173./B/ Avery committed a trespassory taking and carrying away of the tangible personal property in the possession of another with the intent to permanently deprive the owner. Although he intended to return it at the time of the taking, he later intended to keep it, which relates back to the time of taking and creates a larceny. **(A)** is incorrect because the employer did not voluntarily transfer possession and title to Avery. **(C)** is not the best answer because embezzlement does not involve property in the control of the owner, but rather in control of the fiduciary. **(D)** is incorrect because Avery did not break and enter the building without the owner's permission.

174./C/ Although the *Pinkerton* rule allows a co-conspirator to be prosecuted for all foreseeable crimes committed by any other co-conspirator, Packard successfully withdrew (stopped his unlawful activity and took steps to prevent other crimes) prior to the larceny and battery, so **(A)** is incorrect. However, he did conspire to embezzle and did embezzle. **(B)** is incorrect because regardless of the fact that the money was never in his hands, he did deprive his employer of it, so he has also committed embezzlement. **(D)** is incorrect because regardless of the fact that the money was never in his hands, he did deprive his employer of it, so attempted embezzlement merges into the completed crime of embezzlement.

175./A/ Packard voluntarily appeared and the police station and gave the confession of his own free will. Although police questioned him, he was not arrested until later nor was he told he was not free to leave. **(B)** is incorrect because it misstates the law: any evidence offered against a defendant may be subject to suppression, regardless of the source. **(C)** is incorrect because Packard was not in custody, which is a prerequisite for *Miranda* to be at issue. **(D)** is incorrect because it misstates the facts: there is no evidence of coercion.

176./D/ Belinda created the danger and had a duty to rescue, thus her failure to act becomes the actus reus of the crime. **(A)** is incorrect because Belinda created the danger and had a duty to rescue, thus her failure to act becomes the actus reus of the crime. **(B)** misstates the law – the prosecution must always prove mens rea, actus reus, causation, and result. **(C)** is not the best answer because intent is not enough without action, and also because it misstates the facts.

177./C/ Lonnie committed burglary when she entered Burt's residence without permission with the intent to commit larceny therein. The fact that she has a key or that she used to live there is irrelevant; she currently does not have permission so any entry, forced or not, is considered breaking and entering. **(A)** is not the best answer because Lonnie has also committed burglary, of which larceny is a lesser included offense. **(B)** is incorrect because larceny by trick involves obtaining property by fraud perpetrated on the owner. **(D)** is incorrect because Lonnie can be charged with one of the listed crimes.

178./A/ Although ignorance of the law is not a defense to violation of that law, mistake of the law or one's legal status may create a mistake of fact which negates the mens rea of the crime. If Lonnie believed she had a legal right to enter the house and take the property, this would negate the mens rea for burglary and larceny. **(B)** is incorrect because duress is only available if there is a threat of serious bodily harm to oneself or another. **(C)** is incorrect because a belief that one is "owed" is not a defense to theft, unless one believes that the specific property taken is one's own. **(D)** is incorrect because voluntary intoxication is not a defense unless one is unaware of one's actions entirely.

179./B/ To win an ineffective assistance of counsel argument, the defendant must be able to show that counsel was not reasonably effective and that there is a reasonable probability that the outcome would have changed. **(A)** is incorrect because the defendant must be able to show that counsel was not reasonably effective and that there is a reasonable probability that the outcome would have changed. **(C)** is incorrect because the defendant must be able to show that counsel was not reasonably effective and that there is a reasonable probability that the outcome would have changed. **(D)** is not the best answer because admitting the actus reus, causation, result is only part of proving culpability – mens rea and defenses can still be argued.

180./A/ Alma's intent transfers from Bertha to the driver of the car, and so Alma is guilty of the driver's murder just as she would be guilty of Bertha's murder. **(B)** is not the best response because Celine withdrew long before he actually committed the crime, and that is an affirmative defense. **(C)** is not the best response because Ernie had no intent to injure Fabian and was not reckless in his actions. **(D)** is not the best answer because Helga used reasonable proportional force in self-defense to Gunther's attack.

181./D/ To prove involuntary manslaughter, the prosecution must prove that the defendant acted recklessly, disregarding a significant risk of harm or departing from the ordinary standard of care. Zed's best defense is that the joke was harmless, and that an ordinary reasonable person would agree. **(A)** is incorrect because intent is not an element of involuntary manslaughter. **(B)** is incorrect because Zed's actions were the proximate and actual cause of the death. **(C)** is incorrect because there is a stronger response that relates directly to an element of the crime—intent.

182./C/ This answer correctly describes the mens rea for arson, and David's actions do not meet the test. **(A)** is incorrect because it is irrelevant whether or not David was trespassing. **(B)** is not the best answer because causation is not enough to convict without the correct mens rea. **(D)** is not the best answer because mere negligence is not enough to prove arson.

183./D/ Hooper intended to cause serious bodily harm, which is mens rea enough for murder. **(A)** is incorrect because intent is not required. **(B)** is incorrect because to exonerate a defendant, a superseding cause must be so far removed from the defendant's actions as to make it unjust to hold the defendant criminally liable. **(C)** is incorrect because serious bodily injury at least was foreseeable, and therefore so was a death.

184./B/ Even though William's actions were the actual cause of the fire, the lightning striking near the empty gas can and lighting the forest fire was too remote from William's actions to be attributed to him. **(A)** is not the best answer because a defendant need not be acting contrary to the victim's interests to be convicted of arson. **(C)** is not the best answer because remoteness in time need not means lack of causation; William could have started a slow burning fire that took days to smolder. **(D)** is incorrect because "malice" means only intent, not actual ill will or hatred.

185./A/ As a co-conspirator, Glen is culpable for all crimes agreed to (or all foreseeable crimes, if the *Pinkerton* rule governs.) William is guilty of attempted arson (intent and substantial step) so Glen is guilty also. **(B)** is incorrect because a co-conspirator need not take any steps to be culpable as long as another co-conspirator does so. **(C)** misstates the law: conspiracy and attempt do not merge. **(D)** is incorrect because William abandoned, but did not withdraw – he did not take steps to make sure the crime would not take place (i.e., contacting the police).

186./C/ Felony murder requires that the deaths occur during the course of an inherently dangerous felony. **(A)** is incorrect because impersonating a police officer is not inherently dangerous. **(B)** is incorrect because felony murder requires no showing of intent. **(D)** is not the best answer because the felony was still going on at the time the deaths occurred.

187./D/ The three defendants clearly agreed to commit this illegal action together. **(A)** misstates the law: if three persons were required to commit the crime, then they could not be guilty of conspiracy. If three are not required, then conspiracy is available. **(B)** is incorrect because three co-conspirators can act separately in furtherance of the same crime and still be guilty of conspiracy. **(C)** is incorrect because ignorance of the law is generally not a defense.

188./C/ If the prosecution can prove that illegally obtained evidence would have inevitably been discovered, the evidence is admissible. **(A)** is incorrect because Tina's letter would have led the police to Tony's house looking for the uniforms anyway. **(B)** is incorrect because

fruits of a search are usually admissible, as long as the evidence is discovered in a location that could reasonably contain the evidence that is the original object of the search. **(D)** is incorrect because the evidence was obtained illegally after Tony validly withdrew his consent.

189./C/ A voluntary, spontaneous confession when the defendant is not in custody is admissible in the absence of *Miranda* warnings, which are required only prior to a custodial interrogation. **(A)** is incorrect because a voluntary, spontaneous confession when the defendant is not in custody is admissible in the absence of *Miranda* warnings. **(B)** is incorrect because coercion must be by the police or other state actor to render a confession inadmissible. **(D)** is incorrect because the fact of a confession's necessity to the prosecution's case does not affect the issue of whether it was illegally obtained.

190./D/ The definition of a voluntary confession is the absence of police coercion. **(A)** is incorrect because if police coercion is present, the confession is inadmissible, regardless of *Miranda* analysis. **(B)** is not the best answer because the absence of a lawyer does not by itself prove inadmissibility. **(C)** is incorrect because there is no "threshold" by which coercion goes from legal to illegal – any coercion is improper.

191./C/ Theodore must have been acting in the heat of a passion that would have caused a reasonable person to react in a similar manner to have the crime reduced. **(A)** is incorrect because it only addresses one element of the test. **(B)** is incorrect because it only addresses one element of the test. **(D)** is incorrect because the mens rea for voluntary manslaughter is intent, not recklessness.

192./C/ Danny has violated the statute and committed a misdemeanor, and is strictly liable. **(A)** is not the best answer because he did not intend to commit a felony at the time of entry and should not be charged with burglary. **(B)** is incorrect because Danny is strictly liable for the misdemeanor. **(D)** is incorrect because Danny is strictly liable for the misdemeanor.

193./C/ The *M'Naghten* test only allows an insanity defense where a mental disease or defect prevented the defendant from being able to tell the difference between right and wrong. **(A)** is incorrect because "Irresistible impulse" is not recognized under *M'Naghten*. **(B)** is not enough – the mental disease/defect is only part of the defense. **(D)** is not the best answer because strict liability means only that the prosecution need not prove mens rea: defenses are still available to the defendant.

194./B/ The intent to commit a felony turns this entry into a burglary. Also, he has likely taken enough steps toward commission of the felony touching to be charged with that. **(A)** is incorrect because Danny did not commit the actus reus of the touching, and cannot be charged with that. **(C)** is not the best answer because Danny can also be charged with the attempted felony touching. **(D)** is incorrect because Danny entered the house without permission with the intent to commit a felony, so he can be charged with burglary.

195./C/ Keenan was present with the permission of Damon, so he did not

break and enter. **(A)** is incorrect because Keenan had Damon's permission to be on the premises. **(B)** is incorrect because Keenan intended to commit larceny (larceny by trick). **(D)** is incorrect because intent at the time of entry is the proper inquiry for burglary.

196./C/ Damon has deprived Keenan of possession and title to his money (he does not intend to give the money back) by way of fraud. **(A)** is incorrect because Damon had Keenan's permission to take the money. **(B)** is not the best answer because Keenan did not expect to get his money back at some future date. **(D)** is incorrect because Damon has committed one of the listed crimes.

197./D/ The right to counsel is protected by the Sixth Amendment and may only be waived affirmatively, knowingly, and intelligently. **(A)** is incorrect because his conviction will be overturned due to a flagrant Sixth Amendment violation. **(B)** is incorrect because his conviction will be overturned due to a flagrant Sixth Amendment violation. **(C)** is incorrect because his conviction will be overturned due to a flagrant Sixth Amendment violation.

198./B/ Larceny is a lesser included offense to burglary, and would have been available during the burglary prosecution as a lesser charge. Since Keenan was acquitted on the burglary charge, he cannot be charged with larceny based on the same set of facts without offending double jeopardy. **(A)** is incorrect because Keenan was acquitted on the burglary charge and cannot be charged with larceny based on the same set of facts without offending double jeopardy. **(C)** is incorrect because possible guilt of a more serious crime does not preclude prosecution of a lesser crime—it is at the discretion of the prosecutor. **(D)** is not the best answer because Keenan was acquitted on the burglary charge and cannot be charged with larceny based on the same set of facts without offending double jeopardy.

199./A/ Honest belief of consent is a valid defense to a rape charge. **(B)** is incorrect because impossibility does not preclude a conviction for attempt. **(C)** is incorrect because voluntary intoxication is not a defense unless the defendant was totally unaware of his actions. **(D)** is incorrect because it does not fit the facts.

200./A/ When a defendant is being severely disruptive, he waives his right to be present at trial and the judge has discretion to have him removed. **(B)** is incorrect because severe disruption by a defendant can constitute waiver of his right to be present at trial. **(C)** is not the best answer because the defendant's own behavior caused the disruption and the judge had discretion to remove him. **(D)** is incorrect because no facts indicate that counsel was ineffective.

201./C/ The force used against the cashier when he tried to stop Bull is enough to elevate the crime from a larceny to a robbery. **(A)** is incorrect because the force used against the cashier when he tried to stop Bull is enough to elevate the crime from a larceny to a robbery. **(B)** is incorrect because this is a public place. **(D)** is incorrect because Bull has no proprietary relationship to the owner of the property.

202./D/ Meg has not committed acts that fulfill the elements of any of these crimes. She did not take and carry away the necklace from the true owner, so **(A)** is incorrect. Meg did not know the necklace was stolen at the time she received it, so **(B)** is incorrect. Meg did not use force against a person in taking the necklace, so **(C)** is incorrect.

203./B/ Battery involves the intentional *unlawful* application of force to the person of another. The cashier acted lawfully in trying to prevent the theft, and used reasonable force. **(A)** is incorrect because the cashier acted lawfully in trying to prevent the theft, and used reasonable force. **(C)** is incorrect because he was not defending himself from harm when he touched Bull. **(D)** is incorrect because the legal status of the alleged victim is not relevant to establishing battery.

204./A/ The arrest of Meg was without warrant and without probable cause. The cashier identified Bull, not Meg, as the thief. **(B)** is incorrect because even if the officer had come to arrest Bull, he would have needed a warrant because the theft happened several days before and there were no exigent circumstances. **(C)** is incorrect because assuming a valid arrest, no warrant is required to search the person arrested. **(D)** is incorrect because there are no facts to indicate that discovery of the necklace was inevitable.

205./B/ Bill clearly committed a battery. He also intended to cause serious bodily harm using a potentially deadly weapon, or at the very least was extremely reckless in disregarding a substantial risk of serious bodily harm. This would be enough to support an attempted murder charge. **(A)** is not the best answer because Bill also intended to cause serious bodily harm using a potentially deadly weapon, or at the very least was extremely reckless in disregarding a substantial risk of serious bodily harm. **(C)** is not the best answer because Bill also intended to cause serious bodily harm using a potentially deadly weapon, or at the very least was extremely reckless in disregarding a substantial risk of serious bodily harm. **(D)** is incorrect because Bill clearly committed a battery.

206./C/ Criminal intent and verbal encouragement are sufficient to convict Jim and Jack of battery under an accomplice theory of liability. **(A)** is not the best answer because accomplices can also be convicted of the same crime as the perpetrator. **(B)** is incorrect because encouraging someone to bring a weapon for self-defense purposes alone is probably not sufficient to sustain a charge of battery. **(D)** is incorrect because accomplices are charged with the underlying crime.

207./D/ Bill had been arrested and was not free to leave, and the police questioned him without reading the *Miranda* warnings. Therefore, his statement is inadmissible. **(A)** is incorrect because Bill's motivation in making the statements goes to their weight, not their admissibility. **(B)** misstates the facts: the police did ask him a question. **(C)** implies a non-existent legal rule: there is no opportunity to retract earlier statements made, simply because *Miranda* rights are subsequently given.

RIGOS BAR REVIEW SERIES

MULTISTATE BAR EXAM REVIEW (MBE)

CRIMINAL LAW AND PROCEDURE

Index

CHAPTER 7

FINAL EXAM

RIGOS BAR REVIEW SERIES

MULTISTATE BAR EXAM REVIEW (MBE)

CHAPTER 7

FINAL EXAM

Practice MBE Exam Instructions

The final exam consists of two parts. Each part contains 100 exam questions. The questions are in random order by topic (Constitutional Law, Contracts, Criminal Law & Procedure, Evidence, Property, and Torts).

For each part, you have 3 hours to complete all 100 questions. Read each question carefully, noting the call of the question. Also, remember that in some instances, one fact pattern governs a sequence of 2, 3, or 4 questions.

When you are done, check your answers against the answer key provided. Read each answer completely. Not only will this help you to understand the reasoning, it is a good review of the information you need to learn. Track missed questions so that you may review those topics in which you have difficulty.

Here are some tips to help you to success on the practice final exam:

1. Solid Block of Time: One group of the questions should be worked in the morning and the second group in the afternoon. Do each set in a straight-through 3-hour session. Take a one-hour lunch break in between the sets. Time yourself and work as quickly as you can without sacrificing accuracy. Put a question mark alongside every question you are unsure of.

2. Answer Corrections: When you refer to the explanatory solution to correct your answers, be sure to understand why you picked the wrong choice. Again, it is usually worthwhile to review the answer explanatory solutions to all the alternatives because they reinforce the details of the relevant principles of law.

3. Stay Within Time Allocation: Pace yourself. Carefully manage your time as you proceed through the questions. There are 100 questions in each of the two 180-minute (3 hour) sessions. This is an average of 1.8 minutes per question. It is important to work as quickly as possible without sacrificing thoroughness and accuracy. If a particular question is giving you difficulty, either skip it or make your best educated guess and mark it in the margin.

4. Series Questions: Many of the MBE questions include a common fact pattern followed by a series of 2 to 4 related questions. On a time per question basis, analyzing the facts in these questions is usually more efficient than single questions. Still, if you find them too taxing, perhaps skip the series question for subjects in which you feel weak the first time through. If you omit questions, make sure you omit the corresponding box on the bubble answer sheet.

5. Analyze Facts and Law: You need to analyze both the facts and the law. Try to understand the facts of the question separately from the four alternative choices presented below. The facts are always developed chronologically. As you read the facts, circle all the people's names; every new person adds another potential legal relationship and set of claims.

6. Go Through Questions Twice: Initially, go through all the questions in order. Time is so precious it is usually a mistake to not do every question in order the first time through. Still, some candidates use a two-step approach.

    a. First Time Through: The first time through, every question should be put into one of three categories.

        (1) Sure of Subject: If you are reasonably competent in the subject, answer all the subject's questions and move on. This applies even if you are not sure of the exact topic being tested within the subject. Circle your alternative choice on the question sheets.

        (2) No Clue: If you have great difficulty with a question's subject or if the particular question would take too long, skip it. Do not get frustrated by the skipped questions or spend more than 10 seconds before deciding to skip.

        (3) Unsure? Take Your Best Shot: If you have some idea, but are unsure which alternative is the best answer, make your best educated guess. If you eliminate the wrong alternatives, you will usually be down to two choices. Perhaps it is time to use the appropriate default rule discussed in the preface. Answer the question, but mark it in the margin so you can come back later and check the answer if you have time. Don't get bogged down.

    b. Second Time Through: After you have gone through all 100 questions once, look at the time left and count the skipped questions. Calculate the time per question you have left. Keep on your new time schedule.

        (1) Do Skipped Questions First: The second time through, work the skipped ones first. Do not exceed the average remaining time per question. Do not get hung up; some of the series questions intentionally have very long and complicated fact patterns. If you are still unsure after a reasonable intellectual effort, use your default rules.

        (2) Do Marked Questions Last: After the skipped questions are completed, turn to the questions you marked in the question book to determine if you see anything new. The questions you have worked may have jogged your memory. If the uncertainty is still present, don't change your first judgment as it is probably your best intuitive shot at the correct answer.

    7. Answer Sheets are Critical: Attention to detail here is extremely important. A mistake in marking the right number on the official bubble answer sheet can be fatal. Circle your choice on the examination book just before you mark the answer sheet. Every 20 questions (36 minutes on average) you should conscientiously crosscheck the numbering on both documents to be sure you did not make a transposition error. This is especially necessary if you have skipped answering some of the questions the first time through.

Questions 1 and 2 are based on the following:

The Federal Automobile Safety Act establishes certain safety and performance standards for all automobiles manufactured in the United States. The Act creates a five-member "Automobile Commission" to investigate automobile safety, to make recommendations to Congress for new laws, to make further rules establishing safety and performance standards, and to prosecute violations of the act. The chairman is appointed by the President, two members are selected by the President pro tempore of the Senate, and two by the Speaker of the House of Representatives. Compcar, Inc., a minor car manufacturer, seeks to enjoin enforcement of the Commission's rules.

1. The best argument that Compcar can make is that
    (A) Legislative power may not be delegated by Congress to an agency in the absence of clear guidelines.
    (B) The commerce power does not extend to the manufacture of automobiles not used in interstate commerce.
    (C) Compcar is denied due process of law, because it is not represented on the Commission.
    (D) The Commission lacks authority to enforce its standards because not all of its members were appointed by the President.

2. Assuming Compcar is allowed to bring the suit, the court is likely to
    (A) Allow the Commission to continue investigating automobile safety and making recommendations to Congress.
    (B) Allow the Commission to prosecute violations of the act, but not allow it to issue rules.
    (C) Forbid the Commission to take any action under the act.
    (D) Order that all members of the Commission be appointed by the President by and with the advice and consent of the Senate.

3. Plaintiff Warehouse sues Defendant Shipping Company for loading $5,000.00 worth of merchandise from the loading dock. Defendant states that their driver only loaded $2,000.00 worth of merchandise from the dock and a bill of lading proving such is admitted into evidence. Plaintiff calls their shipping manager who will testify that he saw Defendant's driver load $5,000.00 worth of merchandise into the truck. Is the manager's testimony admissible?
    (A) Yes, the testimony goes to an issue at trial.
    (B) Yes, the driver can authenticate the bill of lading.
    (C) No, the Best Evidence Rule prohibits testimony contradicting a written document in evidence.
    (D) No, Plaintiff must offer its own writing.

4. Rachel owned a plot of land that she subdivided into 10 parcels. The configuration of the parcels appears as two rows of five equally sized lots. Rachel sold off lots 1, 2, 4, and 5 of the north row to the City of Sleepy Hollow. She kept lot number 3 from both the north row and number 3 of the south row for herself. She

sold the four remaining lots in the south row to other private citizens. One year later, the city council of Sleepy Hollow announced they planned to use their lots for an elementary school. They condemned Rachel's lot three in the northern row to provide five lots in a row for the construction of the new school grounds. Rachel objects, because she had planned to build her house on both of her remaining lots (3 north and 3 south). The value of all of the other parcels ranged from $25,000 to $28,000 each when sold. The city offered her $12,000 when it condemned lot 3 north. If Rachel brings an action, what is the likely outcome from the following choices?

    (A) Rachel will receive $12,000 from the city because school lots are generally worth about half of what residential lots are worth.

    (B) Rachel will receive $25,000 from the city, because that approximates the market value of the lot.

    (C) Rachel will be able to stop the unconstitutional taking of her property with an injunction.

    (D) None of the above.

5. Laura Lawn had a large yard at her home and a very efficient lawn mower worth $400 which was in her open garage. Her next door neighbor, Nancy Neighbor, came over and "borrowed" the lawn mower. Nancy mowed all of her own lawn with Laura's mower. As she was returning the mower to Laura's garage, she decided to mow the front portion of Laura's lawn. While mowing Laura's lawn, Nancy hit a protruding rock thus breaking the lawn mower rotating blade and causing $200 damages. If Laura Lawn sues Nancy for conversion, the likely result is that Laura will

    (A) Prevail for the damages to the lawn mower of $200.

    (B) Not prevail because Nancy only borrowed the lawn mower.

    (C) Not prevail because at the time of the loss, the lawn mower was working to benefit the plaintiff.

    (D) Prevail for $400, which was the lawn mower's value before the tort.

6. On May 1, Perry Boat Sales sent an email to James offering to sell James a boat for $4,000. James received the offer the morning of May 3. That afternoon, James delivered a letter of acceptance to the post office. Due to an error by the U.S. Postal Service Perry never received the acceptance. Which of the following is correct?

    (A) Perry is bound to a contract even though the letter of acceptance was never received.

    (B) Perry is not bound to a contract because the mail service error excused him of any responsibility.

    (C) Perry would be bound to a contract only if James had sent his acceptance by e-mail.

    (D) If Perry had sold the boat to Evans, without James' knowledge, before James delivered his acceptance to the post office, Perry would still be bound in contract to James.

7. Betty Buyer entered into an agreement with Sam Seller to purchase 1,000 ordinary widgets. Betty was to provide detailed specifications to Sam for assembly. She assumes that Sam will assemble the widgets himself, but the contract does not so specify and they are readily available on the market. In which of the following situations will Betty be most likely to prevail against Sam if he does not deliver the assembled widgets on the specified tender date?

    (A) Sam and his crew develop a highly contagious form of the flu, cannot work at all and complete production.

    (B) The building Sam is using to complete the assembly burns down.

    (C) Betty fails to provide Sam with the detailed specifications.

    (D) The city government passes a new law making Sam's production process illegal.

8. Fantasy Flight is a regional airline that charges passengers less than their competitors do. It does this by ruthlessly cutting costs and subcontracting out all possible functions to the lowest bidders. One of the functions subcontracted out was routine pre-flight maintenance of the airplanes to Lowest Cost Maintenance Inc. Lowest Cost failed to lubricate the tail stabilizer in one of the airplanes during the pre-flight maintenance. In the following flight, the plane's stabilizer froze and the pilots were unable to steer the aircraft. The plane crashed and the representatives of the deceased passengers brought suit against Fantasy Flight. The likely outcome is that the passengers' lawsuit will

(A) Prevail because Fantasy is strictly liable for all injuries suffered in its airplane.

(B) Not prevail because Lowest Cost Maintenance Inc. is an independent contractor.

(C) Not prevail if Lowest Cost Maintenance Inc. and Fantasy Flight have a contract in which Lowest Cost agrees to hold harmless and indemnify Fantasy.

(D) Prevail if the pre-flight maintenance is determined to be a non-delegable duty.

9. Joshua leased a storefront in a strip mall for a period of 12 years for a martial arts studio. A clause in the lease agreement specifically prohibited Joshua from subletting his interest. After using the property for three years, Joshua's business began to fail, so he assigned his lease to Glenn, his uncle, for the original monthly rent amount. Glenn established a dance studio there in the storefront. Oscar, the property owner, was incensed at this, because he had written the anti-sublet clause into the contract to be able to control the types of businesses in his strip mall, and he had a personal grudge against dancers and all those "theater types." Will the assignment stand up in court?

(A) No, because the term subletting includes all types of assignments.

(B) No, because even without a express prohibition of assignments in a lease, the common law requires a tenant to obtain the landlord's permission before assigning.

(C) Yes, because restraints on alienation of property rights are not enforceable.

(D) Yes, because the restraint on subletting does not include assignment.

10. The Defendant in an admiralty case hires Walter Witness to testify as an expert regarding the standard of care in commanding a commercial vessel at sea. Walter is a former Coast Guard certified ship's master who has commanded vessels at sea for 25 years and has written numerous articles regarding the proper way to command a ship at sea. Walter will testify that based upon his review of the ship's log (the log was ruled inadmissible) the ship's master was not negligent. Walter further testifies that it is routine for investigators like him to review a ship's log to render an opinion on the events. Will Walter's testimony be admissible as expert opinion?

(A) No, the facts upon which an expert relies must at least be admissible.

(B) No, Walter does not have formal education in commanding vessels.

(C) Yes, Walter has formed an opinion based on facts made known to him of which he has special knowledge.

(D) Yes, Walter has is certified as an expert by the Coast Guard.

Questions 11 and 12 are based on the following:

Dan and Molly have been dating for six months when Dan gets a job transfer to another city. Molly is driving Dan to the airport when suddenly she has a plan to make him see reason and stay with her. She drives him to their favorite secluded spot and says, "Let's talk about this. I really don't want you to go." Annoyed, Dan says, "Molly, there's nothing to talk about, I have to leave." She refuses to drive, and he tries to get out of the car. She uses the automatic locks, which has a child safety mechanism that means they can only be opened from the driver's side. Dan, becoming alarmed, says, "Come on Molly, this isn't funny, I have to go." She keeps him there for two hours until he relents. She drives him home, and as soon as he gets out of the car, he takes off and goes to the police. Molly is arrested and charged with kidnapping. The information filed by the prosecuting attorney states, "Molly Simpson is accused of first degree kidnapping pursuant to § 2.204.8 of the state penal code. /s/Pros. Atty."

11. Charged with kidnapping Molly will likely be
   (A) Acquitted, because there was confinement but no movement.
   (B) Acquitted, because Dan could have overpowered Molly, thus providing a possible means of escape.
   (C) Convicted.
   (D) Acquitted, because Dan and Molly had a prior relationship.

12. The information filed by the prosecuting attorney is improper because
   (A) It does not identify the charge with sufficient specificity.
   (B) It does not allege any facts in support of the charge.
   (C) It was not handed down by a grand jury.
   (D) It is not signed by a judge or magistrate.

13. In the 1960s, Gibson was appointed to a tribunal established pursuant to a congressional act. The tribunal's duties were to review claims made by veterans and to make recommendations to the Veterans Administration on their merits. Congress later abolished the tribunal and established a different format for review of such claims. Gibson was offered a federal

administrative position in the same bureau at a lesser salary. He then sued on the ground that Congress may not remove a federal judge from office during good behavior nor diminish his compensation during continuance in office. Government attorneys filed a motion to dismiss the action. The court will likely
   (A) Deny the motion because the independence of the federal judiciary is constitutionally guaranteed.
   (B) Grant the motion, because Gibson was not given Article III protection.
   (C) Deny the motion, because Gibson had a property right to his government employment.
   (D) Grant the motion as Gibson lacked standing to bring suit.

14. Sam and Bob enter a purchase and sale agreement to convey Sam's house and lot to Bob for consideration of $150,000. Bob writes a check for $5,000 as earnest money on the deal. The agreements specifies that Sam is selling Bob the property at 123 Main Street, and gives a proper metes and bounds description. The agreement also specifies that the closing will be conducted on December 1st by Eagle Escrow, LLP, and that the closing is contingent on Bob obtaining conventional financing. Three weeks later, Bob finds a house he would rather buy, and fails to submit pay stubs and bank statements to his mortgage bank, causing the bank to cancel his application. He notifies Sam of the failure to obtain the loan and requests his earnest money back. Sam refuses. What is a likely result of litigation?
   (A) Bob would receive his earnest money back from Sam because the contract was contingent upon a condition subsequent that failed.
   (B) Bob would receive his check back because the contract is unenforceable until the contingency is satisfied.
   (C) Sam would prevail, and may keep the earnest money as liquated damages.

(D) Sam would prevail, and may force Bob to close on the deal through specific performance.

Questions 15 – 18 are based on the following:

Tailortown has a gambling ordinance that prohibits "Placement of wagers on any sporting event." "Placement" is defined as "offering of money." Police in Tailortown are organizing a major sting operation to crack down on the city's illegal gambling operations. They send in undercover officers to get friendly with suspected ringleaders and gather information.

Kim and Mike are assigned as undercover officers to one particular secret betting parlor. Van, a regular patron, enters and tells Kim to place a wager on Saturday's game for him. Not wanting to blow Mike's cover, Kim allows Van to leave, then requests and is issued a warrant for Van's arrest, and goes to his house to arrest him.

Meanwhile, Mike observes Tully, one of the higher-ups in the organization, doing the monthly books without filing a 20(k)(2) form. Section 20(k)(2) of the penal code makes it a misdemeanor criminal offense to "knowingly fail to file the proper tax form as required by this statute, reporting all income earned from non-retail and non-investment business sources." Mike arrests Tully immediately. Tully says, "What's the charge?" Mike says, "Failing to file your 20(k)(2) form." Tully says, "What the hell is that? I've never heard of it. Is it a serious crime?" Mike says, "I'll explain it down at the station."

At the station, Tully and Van are placed in the same holding cell awaiting interrogation. Tully recognizes Van and says, "You'd better keep your trap shut or you can kiss your kneecaps goodbye." Van is brought into the interrogation room, where he is told, "You have the right to remain silent. Anything you say can be used against you. You have the right to an attorney, if you can afford one. Are you willing to talk to me about the charges against you?" Van replies, "Yes, I guess so." He is then interrogated and confesses.

15. Charged with violating 20(k)(2), Tully argues that he was unaware of the statute's requirements. He will likely be found
(A) Guilty, because ignorance of the law is not a defense.
(B) Guilty, because he is strictly liable.
(C) Not guilty, because his offense required knowledge of the statute.
(D) Guilty, because Mike witnessed the violation.

16. Charged with "conspiracy to place an illegal wager," under the modern rule Van will likely be
(A) Acquitted, because Kim never had intent to place the wager.
(B) Convicted, because one person can be guilty of conspiracy even if the other is an undercover officer.
(C) Convicted, because he entered the betting parlor.
(D) Acquitted, because by definition the offense requires two participants.

17. A motion to suppress Van's confession should be
(A) Granted, because he was not administered proper *Miranda* warnings.
(B) Denied, because he waived his *Miranda* rights.
(C) Granted, because he was coerced by his cellmate.
(D) Denied, because he confessed voluntarily.

18. At Tully's pre-trial hearing, the prosecution asks to admit as evidence a number of sworn statements by eyewitnesses who are available to testify. The motion should be

(A) Granted, if the prosecution can demonstrate their reliability by clear and convincing evidence.

(B) Granted, if the defense cannot prove by a preponderance why they should not be allowed.

(C) Denied, unless the prosecution can set forth a compelling reason why the witnesses cannot testify in court.

(D) Denied, unless the defense cannot set forth a compelling reason why the live witnesses should be produced.

Questions 19 and 20 are based on the following:

Slugger and Nasty were members of the Patriotic Rifle Association (PRA). The PRA believes that owning machine guns is a citizen's right that should never be restricted. One evening, the PRA had a pep rally featuring a speech by an inspirational speaker named Hestor Charles. As Slugger and Nasty left the meeting, they came upon a lone peacenik named Michael Mild. Michael was carrying a protest sign which stated "Guns Kill Innocent People." Slugger encouraged Nasty to attack the peacenik and they both jumped on Michael. Both of the attackers punched Michael repeatedly in the face. Michael suffered a broken jaw and brought suit against Slugger and Nasty. The jury found for Michael and decided that he suffered $20,000 in damages and that Slugger was 60% at fault while Nasty was 40% at fault.

19. What form should Michael's judgment take?

(A) $20,000 against both defendants because both are legally responsible for the entire damages.

(B) $10,000 against each defendant because both are responsible for the $20,000 total damages.

(C) $10,000 against each defendant because both defendants will be entitled to contribution from each other.

(D) $12,000 against Slugger and $8,000 against Nasty.

20. Michael registered his judgment and levied on the defendants' bank accounts. He was able to realize most of the $20,000 judgment from Slugger's bank accounts. If Slugger brings an action for contribution and/or indemnity against Nasty, the likely outcome is

(A) Slugger will recover some amount from Nasty for indemnity and contribution.

(B) Slugger will recover some amount from Nasty for indemnity but nothing for contribution.

(C) Slugger will recover some amount from Nasty for contribution but nothing for indemnity.

(D) Slugger will recover nothing from Nasty for indemnity and contribution.

21. Minnesota has a quota for awarding its public contracts in order to ensure that a certain percentage of public works projects go to Mexican-American contractors. Williams, a white male, was the lowest bidding contractor, but he was not awarded the contract. What answer best supports Minnesota's awarding the contract to Jose Martinez, a contractor who fits the statutory definition of Mexican-American?

(A) In the past Mexican-Americans construction contractors have suffered discrimination in Minnesota.

(B) The statutory quota was imposed by an initiative passed by ninety-nine percent of the voters.

(C) The quota for each minority group is roughly the same percentage as the group has as a percentage of Minnesota's population.

(D) The quota is only 5% of government contracts and supports an important government interest.

22. Doral, Inc., wished to obtain an adequate supply of lumber for its factory extension which was to be constructed in the spring. It contacted Ace Lumber Company and obtained a 75-day written option to buy its estimated needs for the building. Doral supplied a form contract that included the option. The price of lumber has risen drastically and Ace wishes to avoid its obligation. Which of the following is Ace's best defense against Doral's assertion that Ace is legally bound by the option?

    (A) Such an option is invalid if its duration is for more than two months.

    (B) The option is not supported by any consideration and does not specify a quantity.

    (C) Doral is not a merchant.

    (D) The promise of irrevocability was contained in a form supplied by Doral and was not separately signed by Ace.

Questions 23 and 24 are based on the following:

Microhard was a software corporation which was rapidly expanding. The corporation is developing a large office building and the plans their architects have created are quite complex. Microhard wants to get the building constructed at a very low cost and pushes the bidders for the lowest price. George General was a general contractor in the local area and was asked to submit a total price bid on all aspects of the project. General, in turn, had a group of specialty subcontractors that made bids on various projects on which George was the general contractor.

Sally Strong was a framing subcontractor and had worked for George General in the past. At General's request Sally submitted a bid on May 1 of $250,000 to frame one portion of the building. Unfortunately, Sally made a substantial arithmetic error in calculating the bid which was submitted to General. The next lowest framing bid was $450,000. General bid $600,000 for the whole project. On May 5 Sally realized she

had made a mistake and informed General that she was revoking the bid. On May 10 Microhard awarded the general contract to General. General then informed Sally that they intended to hold her to her bid and that they would bring a suit for damages or specific performance if she refuses to perform.

23. Regarding the general and subcontractor agreements which of the below statements are legally correct.

  I. Sally's bid was revoked on May 5.

  II. The Sally to General offer came into effect on May 1.

  III. Microhard may enforce the contract against General.

  IV. General may enforce the May 1 bid against Sally.

    (A) I, II, and III.

    (B) II, III and IV.

    (C) I and II.

    (D) II and III.

24. In the above question, assume that General feels obliged to fulfill its bid to Microhard at $600,000. If General files a motion seeking an order of specific performance against Sally, Sally's best defense would be that

    (A) The contract is for common law personal services and thus specific performance is not allowed.

    (B) The court would have considerable difficulty determining what should constitute satisfactory performance.

    (C) They have no liability because General knew or should have known of their mistake in the bid.

    (D) Microhard should pay them if they have to do the work because they benefited from the lower cost and it would be inequitable to allow such an unjust enrichment.

25. Paul is rear-ended by driver of Defendant Corporation who was acting within the course and scope of his employment. The driver gets out and says,

"I am so sorry. I was very negligent in rear-ending you." If Paul sues the Corporation, but not the driver, may Paul tell the jury the driver's statement?

(A) Yes, admission by party-opponent.
(B) Yes, statement against interest.
(C) No, hearsay because driver is not a party.
(D) No, the driver is available.

26. Tranquil Farm was situated in a race-notice jurisdiction. Albert owned Tranquil Farm in fee simple absolute. He conveyed it to his daughter Belinda, who did not record the deed. Albert continued to live on the farm after the transfer. Three years later, Belinda sold the farm to Carter, who promptly recorded the deed. After three more years, Albert, who by now had forgotten he had given the land to his daughter, sold it to Dale. Before closing, Dale had checked the record title of Tranquil Farm, but because the deed from Albert to Belinda was not recorded, he did not find that transaction nor the subsequent sale to Carter. The recording statute for that state said, "unless recorded, a deed shall have no effect as to a subsequent purchaser for value who takes in good faith and who first records his or her deed." In a lawsuit over the title to the farm, who should win?

(A) Carter, who was first to record.
(B) Dale, because if Carter only had a quitclaim deed, there was no guarantee to title.
(C) Carter, if he paid value for the land.
(D) Dale, because he had no notice of the prior conveyance and because he is a bona fide purchaser for value.

27. Frederick is on trial for treason. He takes the stand in his own defense and testifies that he is loyal to the United States. The prosecution offers a certified copy of Frederick's fifteen year old conviction for assault. What is the best basis for an objection?

(A) Authenticity cannot be established.
(B) The conviction is fifteen years old.

(C) The crime is not regarding dishonesty.
(D) The conviction is extrinsic evidence.

28. Congress passes the Small Business Support Act, which requires all retailers selling from any public place other than a permanent building to purchase a special street vendor license for a fee. Rebecca was helping her daughter sell Camp Girl Fire Logs as a fundraiser. Rebecca was arrested, strip searched, and eventually fined for violating the Act. If proved, which of the following statements would compel the court to declare the Act unconstitutional?

(A) Regulation of street vendors is not rationally related to improving the general welfare of the citizens of the United States.
(B) The fee does not raise a substantial amount of net revenue.
(C) Sales by street vendors, isolated or aggregated, do not substantially affect interstate commerce.
(D) Camp Girls would have 100,000 left over Fire Logs if they could not sell on the street, so the large number of logs would become an economic liability.

29. Albert Attorney sent a final bill to Deadbeat Client for $5,000.00. Client refuses to pay, so Albert brings an action to collect on the bill. Albert claims $20,000.00 in damages. Client offers the bill into evidence. Attorney objects. What result and why?

(A) Inadmissible, privilege.
(B) Inadmissible, hearsay.
(C) Admissible, contradictory to Albert's claim.
(D) Admissible, admission by party.

30. Rex ran Perfect Pizza, a small restaurant specializing in homemade thick crust pizza and all natural ingredients. When his lease commenced, Rex installed a special pizza oven with custom ventilation hoods. This required installing bolts into the concrete

slab floor, as well as cutting into the ceiling to install the ventilation ductwork. What answer best describes what happens to the ovens and hoods when the lease expires?

(A) Because of the means by which they are attached to the building, these items are fixtures. Therefore they are Oscar's property and must remain in the building.

(B) The items are not fixtures, and Rex can simply detach the items and take them with him.

(C) The items are not fixtures, but Rex must pay for the holes in the floor and ceiling if he removes the items.

(D) The items are trade fixtures, and they remain Rex's property, but he must pay for any damage that removal causes.

31. Citizens of Lumberjack State were concerned about the increasing population overburdening the state's infrastructure. Lumberjack offers its citizens a public education, public transportation, and regulated utilities. The Lumberjack legislature passed a law prohibiting residents from having more than two children. The legislation also provided that for each racial, ethnic, or national group, members of that group could apply for a special waiver. If the total population of that group was not producing enough children to keep that group at its current level, the waivers could be granted allowing additional children to account for those residents who chose to have one or zero children.

Otto and Sabine are the proud parents of Gertrude, a five-year old, and Wilhelm, a toddler. Otto and Sabine wanted another baby. When they applied for a waiver, they were informed that the population was balanced and that no waivers were available. They brought an action in federal district court to have the legislation declared unconstitutional and to enjoin enforcement of that legislation as to them. What is the most accurate statement

evaluating the constitutionality of the statute?

(A) Constitutional, if the state can demonstrate that a compelling state interest justifies the limitation on family size.

(B) Constitutional, if the state shows that its legislation is rationally related to a legitimate government interest.

(C) Unconstitutional, if the plaintiff establishes that no compelling state interest requires that family size be limited in the state.

(D) Unconstitutional, if the plaintiff proves that the legislation on family size is not rationally related to any legitimate state interest.

32. Sally broke into her former employer's office to copy her electronic personnel file onto a floppy disk. All the files had been scanned into a restricted computer and Sally did not have the code to access them. Sally mistakenly believed that retrieving her personnel file was a felony. Charged with burglary, Sally should be

(A) Convicted, because she broke into the office and she had the necessary mens rea.

(B) Convicted, because factual impossibility is not a defense to burglary.

(C) Acquitted, because making a copy of one's personnel file is not a crime.

(D) Acquitted, because she failed to retrieve the file.

33. Harold is on trial for driving while intoxicated. Several prosecution witnesses testify that immediately prior to his driving away, he had been drinking, was staggering, had slurred speech, and vomited in his own lap. The prosecution intends to call Dr. Tallen Encer, a toxicologist who is a world renowned expert on alcoholic intoxication. Dr. Encer will testify that, based upon the witness' descriptions, Harold was more probably than not intoxicated. Will the Judge allow this testimony?

(A) Yes, Dr. Encer is an expert in this field.

(B) Yes, the witness descriptions are facts used by experts in the field.

(C) No, opinion on an ultimate issue.

(D) No, not helpful to the trier of fact.

34. Otis, owner of Greenwood Forest, entered into a written agreement with Jack Lumberman. The agreement, which was notarized and recorded at the local county courthouse, gave Jack the right for 5 years to cut up to 50 trees per month and remove them from the property, so long as he replanted the areas he forested. Jack was to make monthly payments to Otis based on the quantity of lumber he harvested. Under the agreement, Jack's right was exclusive to all others except Otis, who reserved the right use the property for any purpose including cutting trees if he so desired.

One year after they signed the agreement, the state brought a condemnation action to turn Greenwood Forest into a huge superhighway cloverleaf interchange. Otis and Jack both claim entitlements to compensation. Who prevails?

(A) The state need not compensate either, because the right of eminent domain allows them to acquire the property through condemnation.

(B) Otis is entitled to compensation as an owner, but Jack is not because his right is only in contract to Otis.

(C) Jack is entitled to compensation because his contract provides him a property right in the timber.

(D) Otis and Jack are both entitled to compensation for this taking.

35. Falcon, by telegram to Southern Wool, Inc., ordered 30 bolts of cloth, first quality, 60% wool and 40% dacron. The shipping terms were F.O.B. Falcon's factory in Norwalk, Connecticut. Southern accepted the order and packed the bolts of cloth for shipment. In the process it discovered that one half of the bolts packed had been commingled with cloth which was 50% wool and 50% dacron. Since Southern did not have any additional 60% wool cloth, it decided to send the shipment to Falcon as an accommodation.

The goods were shipped and later the same day Southern wired Falcon its apology informing Falcon of the facts and indicating that the 15 bolts of 50% wool would be priced at $15 a bolt less. The carrier delivering the goods was hijacked on the way to Norwalk. Under the circumstances, who bears the risk of loss?

(A) Southern, since they shipped goods which failed to conform to the contract.

(B) Falcon, since the shipping terms were F.O.B. Falcon's place of business.

(C) Southern, because the order was not a signed writing.

(D) Falcon, since Falcon has title to the goods.

Questions 36 – 38 are based on the following:

Charlie Cattlerancher grazed large herds of cattle as a business in Dallas, Texas. When the animals achieved a pre-determined weight, they were slaughtered. The slaughtering process involved butchering the meat into small portions and flash freezing the pieces into airtight plastic containers. This method ensured the meat was not contaminated when it left Charlie's slaughterhouse.

Rebecca Retailer owned and operated an exclusive specialty meat store in Boston. To get her wholesale meat, she used a large refrigerated delivery truck company that picked up select pieces of meat from only the highest quality slaughterhouses. The truck's refrigerated unit broke during the trip from Boston to Dallas to pick up the beef. Nonetheless the driver loaded the frozen meat at Cattlerancher's for the two-day trip to Boston. It was a very hot two-day trip and the meat thawed. During unloading many of the packages broke open and meat became infected. There had never been an instance of infected meat when all the proper refrigeration procedures were followed.

Harriet Host went into Rebecca's Meat Market and purchased some of the tainted meat at a half-price sale without asking why the meat was discounted. That evening, she cooked dinner for herself and her friend Nancy Neighbor. Nancy ate a large amount of the tainted, rare beef and became quite ill from food poisoning.

36. If Nancy sues Harriet for her damages, the likely outcome is that the suit will
- **(A)** Prevail for strict liability for serving spoiled meat.
- **(B)** Not prevail unless Harriet's conduct was in reckless disregard of Nancy's safety.
- **(C)** Not prevail because Nancy was a mere social guest and did not pay for her dinner.
- **(D)** Prevail if Harriet was negligent.

37. If Nancy sues Rebecca Retailer's Meat Market for her damages, the likely outcome is that the suit will
- **(A)** Prevail under the theory of strict liability in tort.
- **(B)** Not prevail because the Meat Market discounted the tainted meat by 50%.
- **(C)** Not prevail because Nancy was not the purchaser of the tainted meat.
- **(D)** Prevail under the theory of res ipsa loquitur.

38. If Nancy sues Charlie Cattlerancher for negligence under the doctrine of res ipsa loquitur, the likely outcome is that the suit will
- **(A)** Prevail because Charlie as the source of the meat and packer for transit is strictly liable.
- **(B)** Not prevail because of the 50% price reduction in the retail purchase.

- **(C)** Not prevail because the meat was transported in a vehicle with a malfunctioning refrigeration system.
- **(D)** Prevail because the meat was packed in secure plastic containers.

39. Derrick is on trial for assaulting a police officer. The prosecution did not offer any kind of character evidence against Derrick. Derrick calls George to testify that Derrick is an attorney with a reputation in the general community as being scrupulously honest. Is this testimony admissible?
- **(A)** Yes, evidence of a pertinent trait of character offered by the accused.
- **(B)** Yes, the accused may always offer evidence of his own character.
- **(C)** No, irrelevant.
- **(D)** No, the prosecution did not "open the door" to Derrick's character.

40. In Anystate U.S.A., any illegal substances found in a person's abode are statutorily presumed to be in that person's possession if the state offers evidence that the defendant had control and dominion over the premises (constructive possession). The defendant can rebut the presumption by offering contrary evidence. Police officers found methamphetamine in a house owned by Greg. At Greg's trial, the prosecution offers a certified copy of a deed granting the property to Greg. There is further testimony from a County Clerk who testifies that she searched the title records and could not find a deed from Greg granting the property to anyone else. Greg introduces and authenticates a lease document demonstrating that Doug was renting the house at the time the methamphetamine was found. Which of the following is correct?
- **(A)** The Jury must find that Greg had constructive possession of the methamphetamine.
- **(B)** The Jury may rely upon the presumption of possession if it

finds that Greg had dominion and control over the premises.

(C) The Jury must find that Greg did not have constructive possession of the methamphetamine.

(D) The Jury must find that Doug had constructive possession of the methamphetamine.

41. The Sunshine State has a policy of hiring employees from its own state whenever possible. The State funds an art endowment, which sometimes shoots movies. Duncan is let go of his job filming the riveting documentary "Seven Angry Men: Inside the Supreme Court" when his boss found out that Duncan lived in New Apple State and was merely staying with his cousin in the Sunshine State. Assuming a proper challenge on the merits, what will the court likely find about the discharge?

(A) Unconstitutional as a violation of the Privileges and Immunities clause.

(B) Constitutional, because the State is funding the position.

(C) Constitutional, because the state has a legitimate state interest in maintaining its reputation as the movie capital of the world.

(D) Duncan does not have standing to sue if his employer was not a state actor.

42. Terrance opened a small deli on the second floor hallway of a very old building. The neighbor on one side was a coffee shop, while the other was a beauty parlor. His lease was for two years, with rent due on the first of each month. After two months in the building, a fire of unknown cause broke out, destroying the entire second floor. Lawrence the landlord claimed the source of fire must have been a chicken Terrance was roasting in his rotisserie oven. Terrance disagreed, and ceased paying rent. He moved to another building a few blocks away and opened a new deli, signing a lease with Alice for two years. Lawrence brought an action against Terrance to recover past rent. This is a common law state that has not modified its landlord-tenant relationships with statutes. Assume that Terrance was NOT the cause of the fire, but it originated in one of his neighbors' premises. What is the likely result?

(A) Judgment for the Lawrence; Terrance breached the lease agreement when he vacated the premises.

(B) Judgment for Lawrence; the common law requires payment for the term of the lease when the premises are destroyed.

(C) Judgment for Terrance; he was constructively evicted because of inhabitability.

(D) Judgment for Terrance; he was not responsible for payment of rent after the premises are destroyed.

Questions 43 – 46 are based on the following:

Wendy and Lisa have an operation in which they approach elderly people at nursing homes and tell them of a "great investment opportunity." The two crooks then convince their victims that with a simple contribution of $1,000 the "investors" will see a 150% return guaranteed. Of course, Wendy and Lisa pocket the cash and send a letter stating that the market forces are unpredictable, etc., and the money is gone. Before someone wises up and notifies the authorities, the two leave the state and start all over again in a new one.

Unknown to Wendy or Lisa, Lisa's brother Prince has been running the scam on a smaller scale in his hometown, hoping to earn enough money to prove himself to the two women and convince them to cut him in on their operation. After running the scam in seven states, Wendy and Lisa are finally caught by the state police, who, without a warrant, sent an undercover officer to a nursing home and recorded a "presentation" made to several residents on the front lawn. Eventually, Prince is brought in for questioning and reveals his own activities. He is subsequently arrested.

43. Aside from any racketeering or other organized crime implication, Wendy, Lisa, and Prince's illegal activity is best categorized as
- (A) Larceny.
- (B) False pretenses.
- (C) Larceny by trick.
- (D) Robbery.

44. On a charge of conspiracy, Prince will most likely be
- (A) Convicted, because he intended to participate in the illegal activity and took steps in furtherance.
- (B) Convicted, because the crime by definition requires less than three people.
- (C) Acquitted, because he withdrew.
- (D) Acquitted, because there was no agreement between him and the other participants.

45. A motion to suppress the recording made by the undercover officer will likely be
- (A) Denied, because the defendants had no expectation of privacy.
- (B) Denied, because its admission would be harmless error.
- (C) Granted, because a warrant should have been obtained.
- (D) Granted, because no one consented to the taping.

46. Wendy and Lisa are acquitted. A federal prosecutor files racketeering charges against them, hoping that this time she can secure a conviction. The defendants move for dismissal. The motion will likely be
- (A) Granted, because the new prosecution violates the double jeopardy clause.
- (B) Denied, because the crime currently charged is not identical to the crime for which they were acquitted.

- (C) Granted, because there is no new evidence on which to base the new prosecution.
- (D) Denied, because the state and federal governments are separate sovereigns.

Questions 47 and 48 are based on the following:

On May 2, Handy Hardware sent Ram Industries a signed purchase order that stated, in part, as follows:

> "Ship for May 8 delivery 300 Model A-X socket sets at current dealer price. Terms are a 2% discount if paid in 10 days, but otherwise all is due in 30 days."

Ram received Handy's purchase order on May 4. On May 5, Ram discovered that it had only 200 Model A-X socket sets and 100 Model W-Z socket sets in stock. Ram shipped the Model A-X and Model W-Z sets to Handy without any explanation concerning the shipment. The socket sets were received by Handy on May 8.

47. Which of the following statements concerning the shipment is correct?
- (A) Ram's shipment is an acceptance of Handy's offer.
- (B) Ram's shipment is a counteroffer.
- (C) Handy's order must be accepted by Ram in writing before Ram ships the socket sets.
- (D) Handy's order can only be accepted by Ram shipping conforming goods.

48. Assuming a contract exists between Handy and Ram, which of the following implied warranties would result?

I.   Implied warranty of merchantability.
II. Implied warranty of fitness for a particular purpose.
III. Implied warranty of title.
- (A) I only.

(B) III only.
(C) I and III only.
(D) I, II and III.

49. Peggy Petlover was a pet lover who had owned many cats. Baby kittens were her favorites. To see if she could breed some larger kittens, Peggy purchased a small cougar. The cat-cougar herd grew in population and the average physical size of the cats increased. Tony Timid lived across the alley from Peggy and occasionally played with some of the cats in the alley. Tony had a weak heart condition which was unknown to Peggy. One morning Peggy let the animals out into the alley to play. Tony stepped out into the alley on his way to work and was attacked by Peggy's cougar when he tried to pet a smaller cat. Besides some significant scratches and skin loss, Tony suffered a massive stroke which left him paralyzed. Will Tony prevail in the lawsuit against Peggy?

(A) Yes, unless Tony was contributorily negligent in petting the cats.
(B) No, because the facts do not indicate that Peggy failed to exercise reasonable care.
(C) Yes, because Peggy was strictly liable.
(D) No, because Tony's weak heart condition was not reasonably foreseeable by Peggy.

50. Fort Lotsa Woods is located in Missouri, a state that taxes liquor. Which transfer may not be taxed?

(A) Liquor producer to the Army.
(B) Liquor producer to the store on the base.
(C) Liquor sold by the store on the base to soldiers.
(D) Liquor sold by the Army to soldiers at a social function.

51. Happy Valley is a subdivision founded by Acme Homebuilders, Inc. When Acme subdivided the 200-acre parcel and recorded the individual deeds, it recorded covenants in each deed that stated: "To preserve the character of the neighborhood, property owners are prohibited from parking recreational vehicles or trailers in their front yards, from having external television antennas of any type, and from having ham radio antenna towers. Twenty years later, John and Abigail decided to buy a property in Happy Valley, but John wanted to erect a ham radio tower, because he was an avid short-wave radio enthusiast. Under what conditions would John most likely be permitted?

(A) On a pre-purchase drive-through of the neighborhood, John and Abigail counted about 25% of the homes with external television antennas.
(B) On a pre-purchase drive-through of the neighborhood, John and Abigail counted 45% of the homes with either a trailer or RV parked on the front lawn.
(C) On a pre-purchase drive-through of the neighborhood, 15 residences had ham radio antenna towers in excess of 50 feet in height.
(D) All of the above.

52. Wally Waterer owned a fine house in the best neighborhood of town. He was very into gardening and cultivated his lawn and well kept gardens with a strong passion. One day he was tilling the soil in his rose garden at the front of his home next to the city sidewalk. Donna Dryer was walking past on the city sidewalk near the rose garden when Wally spotted her. He turned the full force of the hose on her face. Donna ran off the sidewalk and the next day brought a lawsuit against Wally alleging battery. Wally's best defense is that

(A) He mistakenly believed that Donna was about to assault him.
(B) Donna suffered no actual damages.
(C) He had a mental illness, which caused him to mistakenly believe that Donna was on fire and he was therefore saving her life.
(D) He had a mental illness, which caused him to mistakenly believe

that Donna was a rabid dog about to attack him.

53. Brutus always drives over his neighbor Popeye's mailbox when going to and from the garage. Popeye files in federal court under an obscure statute allowing mailbox owners an action for damages, injunctive and declaratory relief. Popeye seeks damages and an order enjoining Brutus from running over the mailbox. Brutus certifies his answer saying he has stopped running over the mailbox and tendered payment for the fourteen mailboxes he has run over. How is the federal court likely to rule on an early motion to dismiss?

(A) Popeye may continue to seek declaratory relief.

(B) Brutus's promise to stop bars Popeye's suit, until the promise is broken.

(C) Popeye cannot show a likelihood of imminent harm.

(D) Popeye's suit is dismissed as the tender of payment satisfies any judgment sought.

54. Ralph and Chuck owned adjacent lots on Lake Ki. Chuck has owned his lot for 25 years, and in order for him to access the lot, he has had to cut across the northeast corner of Ralph's property. Ralph acquired his property one year ago in a quitclaim deed from his grandmother. The first time Ralph visited the property, he noticed the worn tracks across his property leading to Chuck's land, and he visited Chuck and asked him to stop trespassing. Chuck responded that he could have cut a road through the forested back portion of his lot, but that since he had used the shortcut for years, he didn't see why it was such a big deal. Ralph became angry and the following week erected a locked chain gate across the entryway to his land, blocking Chuck out. In the ensuing litigation, what is the likely result?

(A) The court will rule that Chuck is a trespasser.

(B) The court will rule that Chuck has an easement under the doctrine of necessity.

(C) The court will rule that Chuck has an easement under the doctrine of prescription.

(D) The court will rule Chuck has a property right under adverse possession.

55. An off-duty police officer injures himself on a hazardous condition while on the property. The property was owned by Gary but leased by Louise. The officer sues Greg under a theory of premises liability, alleging Greg had control over the property. The officer offers the deed to establish Greg's control. Greg offers the lease, which contains a clause that the lessee assumes complete control over the property. What result will the jury reach?

(A) The Jury must find that Greg had control over the property.

(B) The Jury may find that Greg had control over the property and is liable as a matter of law.

(C) The Jury must find that Greg did not have control over the property.

(D) The Jury may find that Greg had control over the property.

Questions 56 – 58 are based on the following:

Orange Co. computer engineers were designing a new Anti-Microhard Internet hardware and software system. Orange had secured a launch contract to sell the new system to Moon Microsystems. The new system required a very fast processing chip. Hintel offered Orange a chip that would run at 3,000 bits per second and was very excited about being a supplier on the Moon contract. Orange placed an order for 100,000 chips at $1.00 per chip specifying 3,000 bits per second processing speed. Within a month, Hintel delivered the 100,000 chips and Orange paid the full amount of the $100,000 invoice in 30 days.

Two months later, the Orange engineers began testing the Hintel chips for installation into the new software system. They immediately discovered that the Hintel chips only ran at 2,000 bits per second processing speed. Orange immediately informed Hintel that the chips were nonconforming and demanded the right to reject. Hintel refused to accept any returns on the basis that payment after one month constitutes full, unqualified acceptance. Orange was able to use one quarter of the defective chips in the system previously contracted by Moon Microsystems but was required to take a $10,000 discount on the system's price before the customer would accept the slower processing speed. Orange sent the remainder (75,000) of the defective chips back to Hintel.

56. Orange legally accepted:
(A) None of the chips.
(B) All the chips.
(C) All the chips only if they can resell the remaining three-quarters of the chips.
(D) One-quarter of the chips.

57. Regarding the Hintel chips received by Orange:
(A) Orange waived the right to test the chips because of payment after one month.
(B) Orange waived the right to test the chips because they failed to inspect and promptly test the chips.
(C) Orange retained the right to test the chips even though they paid for them.
(D) Orange did not have the right to test the chips because testing was not specified in the contract.

58. Regarding any claim that Orange has against Hintel for the $100,000 paid the likely outcome is that
(A) Orange will be entitled to nothing back.
(B) Orange will entitled to $75,000 back.

(C) Orange will be entitled to $85,000 back.
(D) Orange will be entitled to $100,000 back.

59. Ryan Robber was a heroin addict. One evening, he was on the hunt for a person from whom he could take some cash to purchase more drugs to feed his addiction. He spotted Doug Defender at a cash machine and watched him withdraw several hundred dollars out of the machine. When Doug left the lighted area, he walked back to his car in the parking lot. He got into his car and saw Ryan staggering towards him, demanding all the cash he had just withdrawn. Doug refused and Ryan attacked him, viciously hitting him through the open car window with his fist and a small log he picked up in the parking lot. Doug was terrified and believed he was about to be killed. He pulled a gun and shot Ryan, causing his death. If Ryan's personal representative brings suit against Doug, the most likely reason the personal representative will prevail is
(A) Deadly force cannot be used to defend property.
(B) Doug could have driven off in his car.
(C) The force used was excessive.
(D) Deadly force cannot be used to defend oneself.

Questions 60 – 62 are based on the following:

Congress passed legislation under the spending clause creating the Uniform Standards in Education Agency (USEA). USEA was created to ensure all students received a basic education and met national minimum standards verified through standardized testing. Schools that had more than 25% of their students receive sub-standard test scores were supplemented with USEA funded teachers and books. All of the schools that needed USEA supplementation in Massachusetts were private schools. All of those schools were religiously affiliated. USEA did not test religious knowledge, so all of its teachers taught secular classes. USEA sent two social studies teachers to Holy Blessed Covenant Middle School.

60. What must a challenger show to establish standing to proceed with a federal court lawsuit against USEA?

(A) That he is a federal taxpayer.

(B) That he is a citizen of the state where Holy Blessed is located.

(C) That he is a citizen, who has religious beliefs different from that of Holy Blessed Covenant.

(D) That he has children who attend a public school in the same state.

61. Assuming a proper plaintiff challenged the government action, identify the best argument the government can present to justify its action.

(A) Poor education limits the flow of interstate commerce, just as possessing guns or drugs near schools impacts commerce.

(B) Minimum standards in education further a compelling government interest.

(C) USEA textbooks remain the property of USEA, and USEA instructors are not allowed to teach religion.

(D) Generally, public schools need more assistance nationwide than private schools.

62. The challenger additionally alleges that most of the students benefited by USEA are white. Now, what is the minimum showing this challenger can make to find a constitutional violation based on the whole complaint?

(A) The legislature intended to benefit white students.

(B) The primary effect of the legislation benefits white students.

(C) The non-white students score lower than white students to a statistical significance of two standard deviations.

(D) The primary effect of the legislation benefits religion.

63. Wilma Witness saw a collision involving Plaintiff and Defendant. When she returned home that evening, she told her husband, "I saw defendant run the stop sign." At trial, Wilma testifies that she saw defendant run the stop sign. Upon cross-examination, the defense attorney asks, "Isn't it true that you are Plaintiff's employee?" Wilma admits so. Plaintiff then calls Wilma's husband to testify to the statement that Wilma made to him on the day of the collision. Is the husband's testimony admissible?

(A) Yes, rebuttal of an implied charge of Wilma's improper motive.

(B) Yes, present sense impression.

(C) Yes, so long as opposing counsel is allowed to examine Husband about the statement.

(D) Yes, Wilma is Plaintiff's agent. Therefore the statement is an admission by party opponent.

64. Bill is charged with robbing the Speedy-Mart. The clerk Tim will testify that a masked man came into the Speedy-Mart demanded a large soft drink at gunpoint and did the jitterbug upon leaving the store. The prosecution offers the testimony of three other convenience store clerks who will state that an unmasked Bill robbed each of them at gunpoint demanding a soft drink and doing the jitterbug upon leaving the store. Is the testimony of the three clerks admissible?

(A) Yes, to rebut any favorable character evidence Bill may offer.

(B) Yes, to identify Bill as the perpetrator.

(C) No, character evidence offered to prove action in conformity therewith.

(D) No, Bill must first testify before his character may be impeached.

65. Roger purchased a house on a suburban lot from Sally. The contract contained terms that Roger would pay Sally $1500 a month rent until closing so that he could take immediate possession. Roger then contracted with Anytown Mutual for a policy of fire insurance on the home. Roger was grilling hot dogs on his back porch and negligently sprayed too much starter fluid onto the already burning charcoal, causing flames to torch the overhang to his home. The fire ultimately destroyed the entire building.

Roger made a claim to Anytown Mutual for the damage, but they refused to pay on the grounds that he lacked any insurable interest because closing had not yet occurred. Roger sued for breach of contract. Assume the jurisdiction recognizes the doctrine of equitable conversion. What is the likely result?

    (A) Roger will prevail, because the risk of loss passed to him as soon as he contracted to buy the house.

    (B) Roger will prevail, because the risk of loss passed to him as soon as he took possession of the house.

    (C) Anytown Mutual will prevail, because Sally is the legal owner of the property.

    (D) Anytown Mutual will prevail, because at the time of the fire, Roger had no insurable interest.

66. Virginia is a lawyer who has just received a large retainer from a new client. She uses part of the retainer to pay her mortgage, intending to replace the money, but her client soon drops the case and requests the retainer back. She does not have the money, but promises to pay it back when her next settlement agreement goes through. Charged with embezzlement, Virginia will likely be

    (A) Convicted, because she was a fiduciary in control of the owner's property and deprived the owner thereof.

    (B) Acquitted, because she offered to pay back the money and had the means to do so.

    (C) Acquitted, because she committed an ethical violation, and therefore could not have committed a legal one.

    (D) Acquitted, because she did not have the intent to permanently deprive the client of the money.

Questions 67 – 69 are based on the following:

Pleasant Flights Inc. sold Pattie Pilot a new Skyflyer 4-seater single-engine airplane which had been manufactured by Acme Airplane Company. The next Sunday afternoon, Pattie and her friend Julie Joyride took the plane up for an afternoon flight. Thirty minutes into the flight the plane began to misfire because of an internal electrical ignition problem. Pattie hoped she could glide the plane to a safe landing. She turned away from the urban area towards a farming area alongside a lake. Julie told her to glide into the lake and that they could swim to shore. Pattie did not want to sink her new plane, so she attempted to land in an open field. Unfortunately as she glided in the plane, the plane hit Farmer Fred on his tractor injuring herself, Julie, and Fred.

67. If Farmer Fred brings suit against Pattie Pilot for his personal injury, the likely outcome is that the suit will

    (A) Prevail because Fred's personal injuries were a result of the defect in the internal electrical ignition in her airplane.

    (B) Not prevail because the decision she made to land on the field rather than in the lake is properly the judgment of the pilot.

    (C) Not prevail unless she was negligent in failing to discover the defect in the ignition.

    (D) Prevail if the choice of the field rather than the lake was not a reasonable choice under the emergency circumstances.

68. If Pattie Pilot brings a strict product liability claim against Acme Airplane Company for her personal injuries, the likely outcome is that the suit will

- **(A)** Prevail because an airplane manufacturer is strictly liable for personal injuries resulting from use of its product.
- **(B)** Not prevail unless there was a defect in the electrical ignition when it left the manufacturer and that defect was responsible for the forced landing.
- **(C)** Not prevail because Pattie had the last clear chance to avoid her injuries.
- **(D)** Prevail if she had no contributory negligence in choosing the landing site and gliding the plane down to the field.

69. If Julie Joyride brings suit against Acme Airplane Company for strict products liability, the defendant's least viable defense is that

- **(A)** Pleasant Flights was expected to and did in fact install a new high-speed internal electrical ignition.
- **(B)** The standard internal electrical ignition installed by Acme was not defective.
- **(C)** Julie lacked both vertical and horizontal privity so her remedy was to sue Pattie Pilot.
- **(D)** Julie's damages did not result from the defective ignition but rather the negligence of Pattie Pilot in choosing the wrong place to land.

70. Ike Infant is living in Everystate USA, a jurisdiction that recognizes the age of capacity at 18. When Ike was 17 1/2 years old he went into the Main Motorcycle shop and purchased a twin Harley super-duper motorcycle for $2,500. He paid $1,000 down and promised to pay the balance in one year. Ike rode the motorcycle for six months and became mildly bored with the vehicle. On his 18th birthday, he wrote Main Motorcycle and stated "I will only pay $1,000 more; even that is more than this bike is worth." At the time of the writing the fair value of the motorcycle was $1,750. If Main Motorcycle brings a breach of contract action against Ike Infant, the maximum amount they will recover is

- **(A)** $1,500, the amount due on the balance of the original contract.
- **(B)** $1,000, the amount Ike promised to pay on his 18th birthday.
- **(C)** $750, the reasonable value ($1,750) less the amount paid ($1,000).
- **(D)** -0- because the contract to purchase the motorcycle was not enforceable.

71. Blake is on trial for the murder of Bonnie. The prosecution offers the testimony of Officer Duke who testifies that Bonnie's mother called him in a state of panic saying, "I just found my daughter shot to death! Before she died, she told me that Blake finally made good on his promise to kill her by shooting her!" The mother has since passed away. What part, if any, of the statement will be admitted?

- **(A)** All of it.
- **(B)** The fact the mother stated Bonnie's identification of her killer.
- **(C)** The fact the mother stated Bonnie's identification of the killer and Blake's threats.
- **(D)** None if it.

72. Barney borrows his neighbor's lawnmower with the intent to use it, then return it. He uses it to mow his 15-acre weed and rock-covered property, but before he is done, the lawnmower breaks down. Barney sheepishly returns the mower, but it is unfixable. Charged with larceny, Barney will likely be

- **(A)** Convicted, because he took the mower without permission and is strictly liable.
- **(B)** Convicted, because he intended a use that would likely destroy the property at the time of the taking.
- **(C)** Acquitted, because he intended to return the property.

(D) Acquitted, because he in fact did return the property.

Questions 73 – 75 are based on the following:

Mort purchased property from Edgar for $200,000. Mort put down $30,000 of his own money, closing costs were $10,000, and he took out a mortgage from 1st Mutual Bank for $180,000. First Mutual recorded the mortgage in the courthouse of the county seat where the property was located. Three years later, Mort needed capital for his new "dot com" startup company, so he had his property appraised, and it was now worth $280,000. He promptly took out a second mortgage for $50,000 with Second Bank, which was also duly recorded. His only means of income was from his new dot com company.

About a year later, the stock market began to fall and many dot com startups began to falter in performance. Mort's company was no different. He kept making payments on the first loan, but had to stop paying on the second. Second Bank foreclosed. At the sheriff's sale, the property sold for $215,000, and Mort still owed $170,000 on the first mortgage and $49,000 on the second.

73. What happens to the money?
- **(A)** First Mutual receives 180,000, the amount of the original first mortgage.
- **(B)** Second Bank receives $50,000, the amount of the second mortgage.
- **(C)** Second Bank receives $49,000, the amount still owed to them.
- **(D)** First Mutual receives $170,000 and Second Bank $45,000.

74. Assume in the previous question that First Mutual had somehow forgotten to record the mortgage. All other facts are the same. How would that affect the outcome? (Assume no other creditors).
- **(A)** Second Bank receives $49,000; First Mutual receives nothing.
- **(B)** Second Bank receives $50,000; First Mutual receives $165,000.
- **(C)** Second Bank receives $49,000; First Mutual receives $166,000.
- **(D)** None of the above.

75. Assume that prior to the sheriff's sale on the foreclosure, Mort wins the lottery and wants to recover his land under the theory of redemption. How much will he have to pay to get it back?
- **(A)** $219,000 plus costs.
- **(B)** $170,000 plus costs
- **(C)** $49,000 plus costs.
- **(D)** He cannot get it back at that point under redemption; he must use some other means.

Questions 76 and 77 share common facts.

76. Robert is called as a witness in an adverse possession case. He testifies that squatters have been on the property for over ten years, the minimum statutory period for adverse possession claims. On cross-examination, Robert admits that he was present at the deposition of Daryl who is now deceased and that Daryl testified that the squatters were present only five years. Characterize the testimony.
- **(A)** Admissible as impeachment evidence only.
- **(B)** Admissible as impeachment and as substantive evidence.
- **(C)** Inadmissible as hearsay without an exception.
- **(D)** Inadmissible as extrinsic evidence.

77. The squatters call Frank who testifies that the opposing party told him, "Yes, I know those squatters have been on the property for over ten years." Is this statement admissible?
- **(A)** Yes, admission by party.
- **(B)** Yes, statement against proprietary interest.
- **(C)** No, hearsay with no exception.
- **(D)** No, Best Evidence.

78. Jake and King are friends. They are walking through the central business district late at night when Jake tells King, "Go over to that building and burn it down, or I'll shoot you." He pulls out a gun and points it at King, who is dumbstruck. King goes over to the building, takes a match and some newspaper, and throws it in. The building is soon engulfed in flames. A firefighter runs inside to sweep for people trapped, and becomes trapped himself and dies. Charged with felony murder, King will likely be

(A) Convicted, because arson is an inherently dangerous felony.
(B) Convicted, because duress is not a defense to murder.
(C) Acquitted, because duress is a defense to arson.
(D) Acquitted, because the firefighter's death was unforeseeable.

79. Tiger Drill Press Company makes drill presses for use in manufacturing lines. Tiger sold a large drill press to Mega Manufacturing for $50,000 to use in their tractor production line. Mega has 20 employees who worked on the line full time 40 hours a week at an average hourly wage of $18. Late Friday afternoon, the drill press exploded due to a defect in its assembly caused by Tiger Drill Press. The explosion injured a workman who suffered $15,000 physical damages. It also destroyed the drill press and adjoining pieces of equipment on the assembly line worth $75,000. The line was closed for a week and all 20 employees were laid-off without pay. Tiger is sued under a products liability theory for all possible damages. The plaintiffs will likely recover

(A) $50,000.
(B) $65,000.
(C) $140,000.
(D) $154,400.

80. A theater owner invites his lawyer friend over for dinner and a few drinks. He then asked the lawyer if a new movie would be considered illegal to show in the theater. The new movie has a controversial subject matter and is quite explicit. The owner suggests several statements about the movie. The lawyer says that assuming those statements are true, the movie is constitutionally permissible to show. Which did the lawyer probably rely on the most in determining that the film was not obscene?

(A) The film has a certain scientific value.
(B) The film depicts normal sexual relations.
(C) The film has some artistic value overall.
(D) The film appeals to the prurient interests in sex.

Questions 81 – 83 are based on the following:

Peter Plaintiff and Dan Defendant were neighbors owning adjacent ski cabins in the high country outside of Aspen, Colorado. They jointly hired a road contractor to bulldoze a new winter access road from the main highway to their two cabins in the winter. Both Peter and Dan paid the contractor, but at the end of the construction, Peter believed that he had paid more than Dan. A disagreement occurred between them as to who paid how much and the relative benefits each received. After a feisty confrontation, Dan said "I want to avoid litigation, so if you agree not to sue me for reimbursement, I will hire a workman to keep the winter access road free from snow during the winter." Peter agreed.

In October, Dan decided he was going to spend the skiing season at Cortina, Italy because he heard that the skiing in the Dolomites was better than the Rockies. His brother Dumbbell Defendant had just failed out of law school and decided to ski in Aspen for the season. Dan told Dumbbell he could live in the cabin as long as he kept the winter access road open. Dumbbell agreed and moved into Dan's cabin, but in late November decided to try the skiing at Whistler Mountain in Canada. Dumbbell did not tell either Peter or Dan he was moving from the area. Peter went to his cabin for the holiday break but had to hire another person to keep the winter access road open.

81. If Peter wants to sue Dan, he may
    (A) Sue for his original reimbursement deficiency in paying the road contractor.
    (B) Sue for the costs he spent for the new person who kept the winter access road open.
    (C) Either A or B.
    (D) Both A and B.

82. Assume for this question only that Peter and Dan had actually paid the road contractor the same amount. Was Dan Defendant's promise to hire a workman to keep the access road open supported by adequate consideration?
    (A) No, because Peter's claim for reimbursement was not legally valid.
    (B) No, because Dan did not believe that Peter had a legally valid claim for reimbursement.
    (C) No, because Dan's promise to hire a workman to keep the access road open in the winter was aleatory.
    (D) Yes.

83. Assume that there was a valid contract between Dan and Dumbbell. Does Peter have a cause of action against Dumbbell?
    (A) No, because there is no privity of contract between Peter and Dumbbell.
    (B) Yes, because Peter is a third party creditor beneficiary of the contract.
    (C) Yes, because Peter is a third party donee beneficiary of the contract.
    (D) No, because Peter is only an incidental beneficiary of the contract.

84. Grandma Lizzy promised to give her granddaughter Linda her home after Linda turned 21. Grandma's plan was to give the property to Linda, but to retain possession of it until she died. Grandma had her real estate agent draw up the papers, and she properly executed the deed and placed it in her safe deposit box. Two years later, she died. Her will named her son Stephen as the executor and only beneficiary under her will. The will did not specify that she owned any real estate. Linda discovered that Stephen had found the executed deed in Grandma's safe deposit box, and because she was unsuccessful with her appeal to Stephen for the house, she sued the estate. What is the likely result?
    (A) Because the deed was executed, the Statute of Frauds is satisfied and Linda is the true owner.
    (B) Linda may file the deed at this time and thereby become the true owner.
    (C) The conveyance is ineffective.
    (D) Linda has a basis for a claim due to her reliance on Grandma's promise.

85. Which of the following may the federal government tax?
    (A) Municipally operated parks and bathing beaches charging admission.
    (B) State operated railroad providing use of tracks and transporting goods.
    (C) State owned liquor stores selling liquor.
    (D) All of the above.

Questions 86 and 87 are based on the following:

New York Nuclear Power Inc. had a major nuclear power plant located in a remote area of upstate New York. One of the reactors unexpectedly malfunctioned, causing the vapor escape chimneys to fail and emit a substantial amount of radioactive vapor. There were four families living directly downwind from the plant who were thus exposed to dangerous amounts of radiation. This exposure was serious enough that qualified medical experts believe the families' chances of developing cancer will quadruple. It is not clear, however, when any cancer caused by this exposure will become detectable. Further, if cancer does develop in the family members, it may not be possible to state with certainty if the cause was this exposure or if the cancer would have developed in any event.

86. If the families bring suit against New York Nuclear Power Inc. immediately, which of the following statements would not present a substantial issue?

(A) Will the families be able to prove that any harm they may suffer was caused by the defendant?

(B) Will the court recognize that the families have suffered a present legal injury?

(C) Will the families be able to liquidate their damages into dollars?

(D) Will the families be able to prevail without showing evidence of the defendant's specific negligence?

87. The families hired an attorney to pursue their claims against New York Nuclear Power Inc. The attorneys defending the claim are considering asserting the statute of limitations as a defense. The state does not have an applicable statute of repose. The best rule of the application of the statute of limitations in this case is

(A) The limitation period begins to run on the date the radioactive vapor escaped.

(B) The limitation period begins to run only when the family members are individually diagnosed with cancer.

(C) The limitation is tolled until the family members are individually diagnosed with cancer.

(D) There is no limitation time period because radioactive injury is subject to strict liability for which no statute of limitations applies.

88. Lorne owned a large parcel of land called The Ponderosa. He deeded the land "to nephew Joe for life, remainder to niece Jan, but if the land should ever be used for anything other than ranching, to the Friendly Foundation, a non-profit charitable organization." What kind of interest does Friendly Foundation have? Assume the deed met all the required formalities.

(A) Vested remainder subject to divestment upon a condition subsequent.

(B) Contingent remainder.

(C) Shifting executory interest.

(D) Springing executory interest.

89. Seaman Smith is being prosecuted for failure to report for his watch on board the United States Coast Guard Cutter "Ambition." In his defense, the Officer of the Deck testifies, "I saw Seaman Smith report for his watch and I remember that particular day because I asked him if he had placed his name on the watch list. He answered, 'Yes, Sir.' and showed me the watch list with his signature on it." Is this testimony admissible?

(A) Yes, to prove the fact that Smith put his name on the watch list.

(B) Yes, to prove the fact that Smith was present for his watch.

(C) No, the Best Evidence Rule requires that the watch list be offered into evidence.

(D) No, hearsay with no exception.

90. Federal agents have been losing the war on drugs. In its effort to stem the flow of drugs into the country, Congress passes a law forbidding any person in California or Florida from divulging information obtained by the interception of communications, written or electronic, intended as confidential, except as authorized by a federal law enforcement officer.

Bernstein, an investigative reporter in Florida, published a series of reports on the failure of the Drug Enforcement Agency to keep up with the criminals. Much of the information was based on messages he overheard while monitoring his CB radio and another frequency scanner. Bernstein was charged with violating the federal law. Bernstein's strongest argument that the law is unconstitutional will be

(A) The law burdens interstate commerce.
(B) The law violates the First Amendment.
(C) The law denies him equal protection.
(D) The law denies him liberty without due process.

Questions 91 – 93 are based on the following:

Theresa is two months pregnant, but she is not aware of it. She and her husband are having a fight and he punches her in the stomach, causing internal bleeding. She feels pain but does not seek medical attention until it is too late. She dies from her injuries. Her husband is arrested. During an autopsy, it is discovered that there is evidence of past beatings. The fetus is also discovered, but it is revealed that Theresa had a tumor which ruptured, causing the internal bleeding, and which would have made it physically impossible for her to carry a live fetus past the third month of pregnancy.

91. Theresa's husband will likely not be charged with murder relating to the death of the fetus because

(A) It was medically impossible for the baby to have been born alive, therefore causation cannot be proven.
(B) The fetus was not legally a human being.
(C) He was unaware of the existence of the fetus, and could not have intended its death, therefore he could not have formed the mens rea for murder.
(D) Theresa's initial wounds were not fatal, it was her failure to get

medical help that caused her death, therefore causation cannot be proven.

92. Relating to Theresa's death, the husband's best argument for reducing the charge from murder to manslaughter is

(A) He was not aware that the amount of force he used was sufficient to cause a fatal injury.
(B) If she had sought medical attention sooner, her injury would not have been fatal.
(C) Her words had made him angry enough to kill, and would have had a similar effect on a reasonable person.
(D) The tumor was the intervening cause of death.

93. After his arrest, the husband is read his *Miranda* rights and says, "I'm not saying anything until I have a lawyer." Three hours later, another officer comes in, readministers *Miranda* and asks if he will now be willing to answer questions. He reluctantly agrees and confesses. He motion to suppress the confession will likely be

(A) Granted, because he did not initiate communication with the police after invoking his right to counsel.
(B) Denied, because sufficient time had passed and *Miranda* was properly readministered.
(C) Denied, because his right to counsel was not clearly invoked.
(D) Denied, because he knowingly, voluntarily, and intelligently waived his right to remain silent.

94. Bart is charged with attempt to criticize a government official. The prosecution intends to call Bart's ex-wife who will state that Bart told her prior to their divorce, "I ought to spray paint 'Hillary Clinton is a crook' on the billboard outside her house." Bart objects to the ex-wife's testimony. What result?

(A) Admitted, Bart is no longer married to wife, thus no privilege.

(B) Admitted, criminal intent trumps privilege.

(C) Excluded, marital privilege.

(D) Excluded, hearsay with no exception.

95. The Midwest State election code provides that in a special-purpose election for directors of a state watershed improvement district, the franchise is limited to landowners within the district. This is because those landowners are directly affected by the outcome. Each vote is weighted according to the proportion of the holding of that individual in relation to the total affected property. Which is the best argument in support of the statute against the application of the "one man, one vote" principle?

(A) That principle does not apply to statutes directly affecting real property.

(B) That principle only applies to the election of candidates to statewide public offices.

(C) That principle is limited in special purpose districts specifically affecting rights of landowners.

(D) That principle does not trump state's rights protected by the Tenth Amendment.

Questions 96 – 99 are based on the following:

Oliver Option owned a piece of property named Greenacre in a desirable neighborhood that had just been rezoned for apartment house development. Fred Flipper wanted to get the property under option because he knew potential buyers who were interested in an apartment house development in that area. Oliver declined his request for an option because he wanted the freedom to sell to another, but did offer to sell Greenacre to Fred for $100,000 cash. Fred did not have that much cash but said "make me a written, 10-day offer to sell Greenacre for $100,000 revocable at will and I will pay you $500."

Oliver agreed since he thought this would allow him to sell to another buyer. He signed an agreement stating "I offer to sell to Fred for 10 days my property, Greenacres, but this offer is revocable at will prior to acceptance /s/ Oliver Option."

Two days later, Oliver was approached by Ron Realtor who said "I know a developer who would likely buy Greenacre for $125,000." Oliver asked for the identity of the buyer and Ron said he was Dan Developer. The next morning, Ron phoned Oliver and said "If you do sell to Dan, I will expect the usual 7% commission;" Oliver did not respond. The next day, Oliver called Fred and said "My written offer is revoked and please send me the $500 fee as you promised." Fred refused to pay the $500. Oliver sold the property to Dan, but refused to pay the commission Ron demanded.

96. Which of the following best describes the legal theory or principle that is the basis of any duty or responsibility created by Fred's oral and Oliver's written agreements?

(A) Unilateral Contract.

(B) Firm option agreement.

(C) Pre-contractual liability by promissory estoppel.

(D) Quasi-contractual liability.

97. Oliver Option sues Fred Flipper to recover the $500. Which of the following arguments could plausibly support Oliver's recovery?

I. Although Oliver's was an offer that Oliver could revoke or withdraw at will, such an arrangement was exactly what Fred had bargained for.

II. Despite its wording, Oliver's writing was in effect a legal irrevocable offer for 30 days given in consideration for Fred's promise to pay $500.

III. Although Oliver's writing does not list any consideration for his agreement of making the offer revocable, the promise to pay the $500 constitutes consideration and that can be proved by parol evidence.

(A) I and II only.
(B) I and III only.
(C) II and III only.
(D) All of I, II, and III.

98. Oliver Option sues Fred Flipper to recover the $500. Which of the following arguments would plausibly support Fred's position?

I. Since Oliver's offer, if any, was in writing and involved real estate, it could not be revoked by telephone.
II. Any promise by Oliver was illusory since the terms of the offer were that it could be revoked at will.
III. Since the offer was only open for two days, requiring payment of $500 would defeat Fred's reasonable expectation of a right to sell Oliver's property.

(A) I and II only.
(B) I and III only.
(C) II and III only.
(D) I, II, and III.

99. Ron Realtor sued Oliver for a commission on the sale of the property to Dan Developer. Which of following arguments would support Oliver's position?

I. The statute of frauds requires a writing.
II. Ron and Oliver did not enter into an effective offer and acceptance.
III. Oliver did not promise to pay a commission to Ron.
IV. Even if Oliver did promise to pay a commission, there was no bargained-for consideration to support the promise.

(A) One of the above arguments.
(B) Two of the above arguments.
(C) Three of the above arguments.
(D) All four of the above arguments.

100. George left a will with the following clause: I direct that out of the proceeds of my estate, $10,000 be given to each of my grandchildren and great-grandchildren who reach the age of 25. At the time of his death, he had one child, age 16, but no other descendants. Three years later, his only child has a baby girl, Beth, who survives to age 24. At age 23, Beth has twins, Albert and Brandon. Albert lives to age 25, and Brandon lives to age 78. Which of the descendants will receive part of his estate under this clause in George's will?

(A) Albert and Brandon.
(B) Brandon only.
(C) Albert only.
(D) None of the above.

101. Cadet Kelly was discharged from the police academy in Evergreen State for failing to adhere to the dress code. Mr. Kelly refused to wear the required headgear for the Evergreen State Patrol. Mr. Kelly stated that his religion forbade him from wearing headgear other than his religious headdress. The Evergreen State Patrol wears a distinctive hat with a stiff, round brim. Mr. Kelly refused to wear it. Were Mr. Kelly to challenge the discharge, a court would likely find in favor of:

(A) State, because Kelly's interest in refusing to wear the hat is outweighed by the interests of the police in uniformity and morale of the force.

(B) State, because Kelly has no constitutional right to be a state trooper.

(C) Kelly, because the hat is an undue burden on his religious practices.

(D) Kelly, because there is no rational basis for compelling a grown man wear that hat.

Questions 102 and 103 are based on the following:

Milo, 18, has sexual intercourse with Tanya, a 15-year-old girl.

102. Milo's best defense to a charge of statutory rape would be

(A) She had intercourse with him while he was passed out, and was totally unaware he was having intercourse.

(B) He honestly and reasonably believed she was also 18 years of age.

(C) She consented.

(D) He was not aware that his conduct was illegal.

103. Tanya will likely not be charged with solicitation of statutory rape because

(A) She did not ask for money in exchange for sex.

(B) She is in the class of persons protected by the statutory rape law.

(C) She is a minor and is conclusively presumed incapable of forming any criminal intent.

(D) No evidence suggests that she was the one to propose sex.

104. Justin is charged with seditious criticism of a government bureaucrat. Justin takes the stand in his own defense and states that he has always had nothing but respect for our masters in government. The prosecution then confronts Justin with a certified copy of his prior conviction for criticizing an elected official. Justin objects to the evidence of his prior conviction. What result?

(A) Excluded, prejudicial effect outweighs the probative value.

(B) Excluded, prior acts cannot be proved through extrinsic evidence.

(C) Excluded, hearsay with no exception.

(D) Excluded, lack of authentication.

Questions 105 and 106 are based on the following:

Billy Boozer was out for a night on the town. He stopped at three bars between 8:00 p.m. and midnight and became quite intoxicated. Billy stumbled out of the last bar and began to walk home. While going over a footbridge his foot slipped and he fell into the field alongside the road, breaking his leg. Robert Rescue was driving by, saw Billy in the field, and stopped his car to help. But when he examined Billy, he saw that he was drunk and his broken leg was bleeding very badly. Robert did not like drunks and did not want the blood to stain the upholstery in his car. He then decided to leave the scene and not provide any assistance to Billy. Shortly thereafter Nancy Negligence was driving on the same street. Nancy was inattentive and her car veered off the road into the field hitting Billy who suffered serious injury.

105. If Billy asserts a claim against Robert for his damages, the case will likely

 (A) Prevail if a reasonable person under the circumstances would have aided Billy.
 (B) Not prevail unless in some way Robert made Billy's injury worse.
 (C) Not prevail because Billy created the risk of harm by becoming voluntarily intoxicated.
 (D) Prevail because by stopping and examining Billy, Robert assumed a duty to aid him.

106. If Billy asserts a claim against Nancy, the likely outcome is that the claim will

 (A) Prevail if Nancy was negligent in going off the road.
 (B) Not prevail if Nancy did not see Billy before her automobile hit him since she must have lacked intention.
 (C) Not prevail because but for Billy's intoxication and slipping from the bridge, Billy would not have been in the field at all.
 (D) Prevail because Billy was unconscious and was thus in a helpless condition.

Questions 107 and 108 are based on the following:

Furious D and Cool Mo are hanging out on the street corner. They are joined by Mr. Big, who is an undercover police officer.

107. Mo says to D, "That is some expensive jewelry you are wearing. You must have been the one who knocked over that jewelry store last week." D says nothing. D is later arrested for the heist and Mr. Big testifies that upon the accusation

by Mo, D was silent. Upon objection, which result?

 (A) Admitted, admission by party-opponent.
 (B) Admitted, witness' personal knowledge.
 (C) Excluded, hearsay with no exception.
 (D) Excluded, only spoken utterances can be hearsay.

108. The police interview the owner of a jewelry store. They show him a photo lineup that comports with constitutional requirements. The owner tells them, "Yes, that's him," pointing to a picture of Furious D. The owner then says, "During the robbery I was very upset because I used to change Furious D's diapers." The owner is available as a witness, but is not called. The prosecution offers the testimony of the interviewing officers to relate to the jury the owner's statements. Upon an obvious objection, what result?

 (A) Admitted, prior identification by witness.
 (B) Admitted, then existing emotional condition.
 (C) Excluded, hearsay with no exception.
 (D) Excluded, witness is available.

Questions 109 – 111 are based on the following:

Colleen is a drug addict and a mentally disturbed woman who often thinks she hears voices telling her that various people are inhabited by demons and need to be exorcised. She frequents local nightclubs, waving a crucifix at patrons and chanting. One night, a nightclub owner decided he was fed up with Colleen disturbing his customers. He grabbed her by the neck, and dragged her from the bar toward the street. Realizing the owner had been seized by a powerful demon who wanted to kill her, Colleen pulled a knife and slashed the owner's throat. When the police arrive, Colleen is still standing there, thrashing and waving the knife. She screams repeatedly, "I'm sorry, I had to do it, he was going to kill me!" One officer tackles her from behind and she hits her head on the ground hard. She suffers a concussion and a huge gash on her forehead.

109. If Colleen is acquitted on a charge of second degree murder and released, it will be because

(A) She pleaded insanity.
(B) She was on drugs.
(C) The prosecution failed to prove malice aforethought in its case-in-chief.
(D) She acted in self-defense.

110. In a jurisdiction that has adopted the MPC, Colleen pleads insanity. She will most likely succeed if

(A) She claims she did not know right from wrong.
(B) She claims she was incapable of controlling her actions as a result of the voices.
(C) She was diagnosed with a mental disease or defect prior to committing the homicide.
(D) She has no memory of the incident.

111. The police officer who tackled Colleen will likely not be charged with battery because

(A) Colleen is insane and cannot be called as a witness.
(B) Police officers have absolute immunity from criminal prosecution.
(C) The application of force was not unlawful.
(D) Her injuries are only temporary.

112. Terrance is called as a witness in One-Eyed Pete's Jones Act lawsuit against United Fishmongers (UF). Terrance testifies very favorably for Pete. UF calls as a witness, Mr. Smee, who states that Terrance has a reputation amongst the general sea-going community as a liar and a thief. In rebuttal, Pete calls Terrance's priest who testifies that Terrance would never lie. On cross-examination, the priest is asked, "Isn't it true that Terrance was once caught taking money from the

collection plate?" What result upon objection?

(A) Excluded, religious beliefs are inadmissible to bolster the credibility of a witness.
(B) Excluded, specific instances of conduct cannot be proved through extrinsic evidence.
(C) Admitted, substantive evidence to an issue at trial.
(D) Admitted, impeachment evidence.

Questions 113 and 114 are based on the following:

Congress passes a comprehensive bill changing laws in many areas to allow the country to defend itself better against terrorism. Congress also creates the Office of Homeland Defense. Congress creates the positions of Secretary of Homeland Defense, which is a cabinet position, and the Deputy Secretary, who will assist the Secretary in executing the new anti-terrorism laws. Congress wants to maintain maximum control over this office to protect civil liberties.

113. What is the most far-reaching restriction Congress may constitutionally impose on the process of appointment to the position of Deputy Secretary?

(A) Advice and consent of the Senate in appointment.
(B) Congressional appointment.
(C) Two-year non-renewable term limit.
(D) Judicial appointment.

114. What is the most far-reaching restriction Congress may constitutionally impose on the process of removal from the Deputy Secretary's position?

(A) Congressional removal.
(B) Removal only for cause.
(C) Removal at will by the Secretary.
(D) Removal at will by President.

115. William owned a large farm that he wanted to keep in the family after his death. He gave his brother Daryl a life estate, remainder to Daryl's son Junior. Both interests were contingent upon not selling the land outside the William's bloodline, or if they did, the land would revert to William. Daryl died twenty years later, and Junior didn't want to farm property, so he entered into a purchase and sale contract with Nino, a non-relative. William, who was now quite elderly, became furious and demanded his land back. Junior refused and proceeded with the sale. William sued. What is the likely result?

(A) William will prevail because he has a remainder interest.
(B) William will prevail because he has an interest in reverter.
(C) Junior will prevail because his interest is fee simple absolute.
(D) Junior will prevail because the restriction only applied to the life estate portion, which was his father's.

116. Marine Manufacturing company sold propeller shafts for medium-size sailboats with small motors. Speedy Boat company manufactured a 25 foot inboard speed boat and considered changing from their present source of propeller shafts to Marine. Marine's propeller shafts sold at 25% less than Speedy Boat's previous supplier but the sales brochure did not indicate any warranty. Speedy sent a purchase order to Marine that stated "Send the goods with the warranty that the propeller shafts will perform adequately for two years." Marine's invoice sent with the goods stated "no express or implied warranties." The result of these communications are that

(A) No contract exists since the parties did not agree.
(B) A contract exists subject to the implied warranty of merchantability.
(C) A contract exists with the 2-year warranty covering the propeller shaft.
(D) A contract exists with no express or implied warranties.

Questions 117 and 118 are based on the following:

Smalltown, USA was a city that had experienced a large number of automobiles striking pedestrians. It seemed that many of the citizens jaywalked when they were in a hurry rather than crossing in the designated crosswalks. To reduce the accidents, the City Council passed an ordinance. The ordinance made it illegal to cross a street at any location not designated as an official crosswalk and for any vehicle to block a crosswalk. Connie Careful was walking down the sidewalk and wanted to cross the street. A bus was blocking the designated crosswalk so Connie stepped into the street and walked around the rear of the bus. As she cleared the street side of the bus, she was run down by an automobile being driven negligently by Nathan Negligence. The accident occurred outside the designated crosswalk. Contributory negligence is recognized in the jurisdiction of Smalltown, USA.

117. If Connie sues Nathan, the fact of her failure to be in a designated crosswalk will

(A) Bar Connie's recovery as a matter of law.
(B) Bar Connie's recovery unless Nathan saw her in time to swerve into the left hand lane and thus avoid the accident.
(C) Be considered by the trier of fact as a factor of Nathan's liability.
(D) Not be a relevant factor in determining the rights of Connie.

118. If Connie sues the bus company, the most likely result is that Connie will

(A) Prevail because the bus company's violation of the statute prohibiting blocking a crosswalk creates strict liability.
(B) Prevail because the likely legislative purpose of the statute was to prevent such harm to pedestrians in crosswalks.
(C) Not prevail because Connie assumed the risk of injury by

jaywalking outside the designated crosswalk.

(D) Not prevail because Nathan's driving was the actual cause-in-fact of Connie's injuries.

Questions 119 – 121 are based on the following:

Ox is known throughout his college campus as a violent bully. He especially likes harassing Pete, a high profile member of the gay community on campus. Pete has taken to carrying a small, heavy club around as protection from Ox. One day, the two men cross paths on campus. Ox gives Pete a sour look but says nothing. Pete thinks, "I'm gonna finish this guy off now, I'll say it was self defense." He pulls out his club and takes a swing at Ox's head. Ox reacts quickly by pulling out a knife and stabbing Pete in the chest. Pete is severely wounded and is taken to the hospital. Ox is taken to the police station for questioning. The police do an inventory search of his pockets and find a baggie of heroin. He is arrested and charged with possession of heroin, battery, and attempted murder.

119. On the charges of battery and attempted murder, Ox will likely be found
  (A) Not guilty of either offense.
  (B) Guilty of attempted murder only.
  (C) Guilty of battery only.
  (D) Guilty of battery and attempted murder.

120. When Pete is released from the hospital, he will probably
  (A) Not face criminal charges.
  (B) Be charged with assault and attempted battery.
  (C) Be charged with battery.
  (D) Be charged with attempted murder.

121. On the charge with possession of heroin, Ox moves to suppress the drugs found on him at the jailhouse. His motion will likely be
  (A) Granted, because the search was not incident to a lawful arrest.

(B) Granted, because there was no probable cause to bring him to the station.
(C) Denied, because he consented to the search by voluntarily going to the station.
(D) Denied, because he had no legitimate expectation of privacy.

122. Bert is on trial for driving while intoxicated. In his defense, he calls his mother who testifies that for three hours immediately prior to his being pulled over, he was with her and drank two beers. Bert's attorney then asks, "Did those two beers make Bert intoxicated?" Red-faced, the prosecutor leaps to her feet screaming objection and moving for sanctions. What result to the objection?
  (A) Overruled, helpful to a determination of a fact in issue.
  (B) Overruled, facts upon which an opinion is based may be made known to the witness at trial.
  (C) Sustained, Mom has yet to be qualified as an expert witness.
  (D) Sustained, opinion on ultimate issue is allowed by expert witnesses only.

123. A flash flood washed out a large portion of Harry Homeowner's driveway. He saw an ad in the yellow pages placed by Leroy who owned Lowest Cost Driveway repairs. Harry called Leroy and explained the problem. Leroy faxed Harry a written bid of $4,000. When the bid was received, Harry wrote on the paper "I will only pay $3,500 for the driveway repair" and faxed it back to Leroy. Leroy in turn sent a note back to Harry saying "I will do the job for $3,750." 10 days later, having not heard from Harry, Leroy wrote him saying "I have changed my mind and will now agree to do the job for $3,500. I will start next Monday unless I hear from you to the contrary." Harry received the note but did not reply since he was about to leave on a vacation. The next Monday Leroy and his crew went out to Harry's home and filled and black topped Harry's driveway. The pavement repair job added $3,000 to the

value of Harry's home. Which of the following best characterizes the above relationship?

(A) There was a contract and Leroy will collect $4,000.
(B) There was a contract and Leroy will collect $3,750.
(C) There was a contract and Leroy will collect $3,500.
(D) There was not a contract and Leroy will collect $3,000 in quasi contract.

124. Craig Creditor was owed $100,000 by Donnie Debtor evidenced by a written promissory demand note dated January 1, 1997. Donnie made no payments on the note and on November 15, 2002 Craig hired the law firm of Delay & Postpone to file suit on the note. Unfortunately, the law firm did not file the suit until January 15, 2003, which exceeded the six-year state statute of limitations for a written contract. Donnie's attorney secured a dismissal based on the pleadings and the Court of Appeals affirmed on the basis the statute of limitations had run. Apparently there were two lawyers assigned to the case at Delay & Postpone and each thought that the other had filed the case. Craig was quite upset and hired a new attorney to file a malpractice claim against Delay & Postpone. The case is being tried to the jury. Craig, the plaintiff,

(A) Must establish that he did not negligently contribute to the failure to finally file the promissory note case.
(B) Can rely upon the legal expertise of the judge in advising the jury whether there was a breach of the applicable duty level.
(C) Can not rely on the application of the jurors' common knowledge as to whether there was a breach of the applicable duty level.
(D) Must prove that but for Delay & Postpone's negligence he would have recovered on the promissory demand note.

125. Joseph gives his 13-year-old daughter half an ounce of wine every Sunday as a part of a religious ceremony. Joseph is prosecuted under a state statute prohibiting serving or selling of alcohol to minors. Joseph defends himself against the criminal proceedings asserting his constitutional rights. In which analysis is the trial court prohibited from engaging?

(A) Finding whether Joseph sincerely believes wine is necessary.
(B) Finding whether Joseph's professed religion actually requires him to serve his daughter wine.
(C) Determine whether the statute is constitutional as applied to Joseph.
(D) Determine the reasonableness of the belief that wine service is necessary.

126. Professor Benedict taught courses in political science. Professor Benedict was terminated from Hampshire State College for failing to comply with a new state statute. The statute required him, as a public employee, to swear or affirm that he will do two things: uphold and defend the state and federal constitutions, and oppose the violent overthrow of the government. Which is the best argument for the state in support of the statute?

(A) The state has a compelling need to keep disloyal persons out of government positions of discretion.
(B) The oath is only a commitment to abide by constitutional processes.
(C) Government employment is a privilege, not a right.
(D) The First and Fourteenth Amendments permit a state to fix the conditions of state employment.

127. Tim Crown, brother of Thomas, attempts a very sophisticated burglary of "Dogs playing poker" from the Metropolitan Art Museum. There was no eyewitness to the actual burglary, but a witness did see a man roughly matching Mr. Crown's description wearing a bowler hat hurrying from the museum clutching a flat, wrapped item. After hearing about the daring burglary, witness contacted police giving a description of the perpetrator and identifying a picture of Mr. Crown as the man she saw. Upon searching Mr. Crown's residence a bowler hat was found. Can the witness testify regarding the prior identification of the picture?

(A) Yes, the discovery of the bowler hat gives independent credibility to the witness' testimony.

(B) Yes, prior identification by a witness is admissible.

(C) No, the witness' testimony is insufficient to sustain a guilty verdict.

(D) No, the witness did not identify Mr. Crown at the time of the burglary.

128. Professor Rob Jones has a tenure contract with his employer, Southern State University (S.S.U.). The contract states that Professor Jones may only be terminated for cause. The contract allows the Dean to find good cause to terminate a professor, and the professor is entitled to next day post-termination review by a committee of five faculty members. The Dean found good cause to fire Professor Jones, when Jones posted drawings and diagrams of the Dean's genitals on the internet. Professor Jones claims his free speech was violated by the termination. Which statement best describes the legal effect of the contract?

(A) The University may fire Jones at will and force Jones to prove breach of contract.

(B) Jones is entitled to due process

(C) The Dean may terminate him because the contract allows it.

(D) The University can limit Jones's interest by contract, so the termination and review are constitutional.

129. Congress enacts a tax on bearer bonds. South Carolina sells bearer bonds to fund its state highway system and build new professional sporting facilities. The state had benefited by offering an interest rate lower than the market rate, because the interest was not previously included in federal income tax. South Carolina sues in the United States Supreme Court and seeks to have the tax declared unconstitutional as applied to South Carolina's bonds. What is the likely result?

(A) Constitutional, as a proper, non-discriminatory tax by the federal government.

(B) The Court will not rule on the merits, because it has no jurisdiction.

(C) Unconstitutional, as it violates the Tenth Amendment.

(D) Unconstitutional, as it exceeds the tax and spend clause.

130. Manny Moneymadness was a very aggressive finance student in undergraduate school who was engaged to marry Ingrid Impatient. He had a favorite Uncle Harry who was a M.B.A. graduate of Harvard. He strongly encouraged Manny to attend the Harvard M.B.A. program including paying for a review class to increase Manny's Graduate Management Admission Test (GMAT) score. The review course worked and Manny was admitted. Manny remained apprehensive about being married while pursuing his M.B.A.. Uncle Harry was proud of Manny and offered "to pay $50,000 cash and your M.B.A. tuition if you will attend Harvard and you postpone your wedding plans with Ingrid." Manny considered the offer seriously and finally concluded this was the only way he could financially get through business school.

Manny told Ingrid of the delay and she promptly broke off the engagement. Manny did attend the first year of the M.B.A. program but in the Spring his Uncle Harry died. Between his grief and loss of Ingrid, Manny dropped out of Harvard. Manny filed a claim against Uncle Harry's estate for the $50,000. The likely outcome is that Manny's claim will

(A) Prevail because the contract is enforceable.

(B) Not prevail because uncle Harry's death terminated the offer.

(C) Not prevail because the agreement stopping the wedding violated public policy.

(D) Prevail in equity because he lost both his fiancée and his Harvard M.B.A. education because of Uncle Harry.

Questions 131 and 132 are based on the following:

Grant died, leaving his farm to his four grandchildren as joint tenants. Their names were Alissa, Bentley, Connie, and Delbert. Alissa sold her share to Evan. Delbert died, and his will left all his worldly possessions to his niece Francine.

131. What is Evan's property interest?
   (A) Evan is a tenant in common with Bentley and Connie.
   (B) Evan is a tenant in common with Bentley, Connie, and Francine.
   (C) Evan is a joint tenant with Bentley and Connie.
   (D) Evan is a joint tenant with Bentley, Connie, and Francine.

132. What is Francine's property interest?
   (A) Francine is a joint tenant with Bentley and Connie, but a tenant in common with Evan.
   (B) Francine is a joint tenant only with Bentley and Connie.
   (C) Francine is a joint tenant with Bentley, Connie, and Evan.
   (D) None of the above.

133. Eli Expert is retained to testify regarding the possible negligence of the Captain of the "Baldez" when it ran aground in Prince Henry Sound. Eli reviewed the transcribed statements of the Captain and crew. If the Captain is sued, can Eli give an opinion on the Captain's negligence?
   (A) No, the crew's statements are hearsay.
   (B) No, unless the crew testifies at trial.
   (C) Yes, if the statements are those typically relied upon by experts in the particular field.
   (D) Yes, an expert may rely upon hearsay statements in forming an opinion.

Questions 134 – 137 are based on the following:

Darlene Driver went outside her flat one morning to drive to work. Her car would not start that morning and it was her turn to drive in the car pool. She went back into her flat and woke up her roommate Florence Friendly. Florence offered to loan Darlene her second car that was parked in the basement of the flat. Darlene left driving Florence's car. After Darlene left, Florence realized she had forgotten to warn her about the car's brakes, which a mechanic had told her might fail in an emergency if the brake pedal was stomped down hard. She did know one of the car pool riders named Patty Passenger and called her explaining about the potential brake problems. Darlene picked up Patty and the other car pool rider and proceeded to drive to work. Unfortunately Patty forgot to relay the message about the potential brake problem to Darlene.

Darlene exited the freeway into the downtown area. She was driving on a surface street when Harry Hotrod came out of an intersection against the red light. Darlene slammed on the brakes to avoid hitting Hotrod, the brakes failed and the two cars collided. If the brakes had not failed, Darlene could have stopped Florence's vehicle in time to avoid the accident. Darlene and both the carpool riders were injured.

134. If Darlene asserts a claim against Florence, the likely outcome is that the suit will
   (A) Prevail under a theory of strict liability because the car was a defective product and Florence provided it without a warning.
   (B) Not prevail because the sole cause of the damages was the failure of Patty to warn Darlene about the potentially defective brakes.
   (C) Not prevail because Florence was not a commercial rental agency, but rather was an uncompensated friend.

(D) Prevail under negligence because Florence knew the brakes were potentially defective and failed to warn Darlene.

135. If Darlene asserts a claim against Hotrod, the likely outcome is that the suit will

(A) Recover only a proportion of her damages because Patty was also at fault

(B) Not recover because the brake failure was the immediate cause of the collision.

(C) Not recover because Patty's fault is vicariously imputed to the driver of the vehicle.

(D) Recover the full amount of her damages because Darlene herself had no fault.

136. If Darlene asserts a claim against Florence, the best defense Florence can assert is

(A) Darlene was guilty of contributory negligence.

(B) Hotrod's actions were a superceding cause.

(C) Patty should have passed on the warning to Darlene.

(D) Florence was not compensated for the rental of the vehicle and thus should have no duty.

137. The jurisdiction has adopted "pure" comparative negligence statute. If Patty sues Hotrod, the likely outcome is that she will

(A) Not recover because she should have told the driver Darlene about the possible brake failure problem.

(B) Recover in full for her injuries because the driver Darlene was without fault.

(C) Recover a proportion of her damages based on the respective proportionality of her negligence and that of Hotrod.

(D) Not recover because but for the failure of the brakes the accident would not have occurred.

138. George Garage decided to rebuild the garage on his property. He orally negotiated with Bruce Builder to build the garage for $5,000. The flat price of $5,000 included both Bruce's labor and the lumber necessary to build the garage. Later, Bruce decided he did not want to do the job and so informed George. If George brings suit for breach of contract the likely outcome is that George will

(A) Prevail only if the lumber value is less than $500.

(B) Not prevail if the lumber value is more than $500.

(C) Not prevail unless there is a writing containing a signature of the party to be charged.

(D) Prevail.

Questions 139 – 141 are based on the following:

John cases a donut shop for several weeks hoping to score from the cash register. He buys a hot pink plastic water pistol and stuffs it in his pocket, and enters the store near closing time. He holds up the water pistol, still in his pocket, and says to the cashier, "Okay, no funny business, take all the cash out and give it to me." The cashier does not think the gun is real and says, "Oh yeah, let's see your gun." John is taken aback and freezes. The cashier reaches under the counter for his own real pistol. John reaches across the counter, grabs some change out of the "Take a penny, leave a penny" dish and runs.

139. Charged with burglary, what would be John's best defense?

(A) Robbery was a factual impossibility because the cashier didn't believe he had a real gun.

(B) He did not complete his intended crime.

(C) The shop was open to the public.

(D) He did not commit larceny, because the pennies were free to be taken by anyone.

140. Charged with attempted robbery, John will likely be

(A) Acquitted, because the gun was fake therefore no actual force was used against the cashier.

(B) Acquitted, because he withdrew.

(C) Convicted.

(D) Acquitted, because he is guilty of the lesser-included offense of larceny.

141. John asks for a jury trial, but the request is denied. John is convicted. On appeal, the conviction will likely be

(A) Reversed.

(B) Upheld, unless the defense can demonstrate that the trial judge committed plain error.

(C) Upheld, if the appellate court concludes that the trial judge committed harmless error.

(D) Upheld, unless the defense can demonstrate that the trial judge was biased.

142. Fred Failing operated Fred's Furniture Store that retailed to the public. Fred's location was in a close-in suburb that had increasingly turned from a residential to a business community. As a result, Fred's business had decreased for years and he finally decided it was time to close. As a result, he held a "going-out-of-business" sale and began to mark down his inventory. He advertised in the local newspapers "both of our remaining recliners that normally sell for $500 each will be sold for $300 each." Fred's cost was $250 per chair. Harriet Homeowner e-mailed Fred stating "I will buy both recliners at $300 each and will send my truck for them tomorrow." Fred returned the e-mail stating "I accept your offer for $600 total and look forward to you picking up the recliners tomorrow." The next morning Harriet sent another e-mail to Fred stating, "Sorry, I changed my mind." Fred subsequently sold the two recliners to Jean for $600. If Fred sues Harriet for breach of contract, the likely result is that the court will award damages of

(A) $-0- because Fred suffered no damages.

(B) $600 (2 recliners at $300 each).

(C) $500 (2 recliners at FMV [$500 each] less cost [$250 each]).

(D) $100 (2 recliners at $50 each profit).

143. Alaska has its own timber company. Alaskan Timber sells its wood to Alaskan residents at 10% below market price. Brice builds homes for poor people in Mexico. Brice does not qualify for the discount, because he is from California. Brice files in federal district court to have Alaskan Timber's policy declared unconstitutional. What is the likely outcome?

(A) Constitutional, because Alaskan Timber may discriminate in this manner.

(B) Constitutional, because there is no state action.

(C) Unconstitutional, because it violates the dormant commerce clause.

(D) Unconstitutional, because it violates the privileges and immunities clause.

144. Percy Plaintiff sues Dirk Defendant for breach of contract. Percy contends that Dirk sent him a written offer, which Percy signed and deposited into the mail with Dirk's correct address and sufficient postage. Dirk claims that he never received the signed document. Which is the most likely jury instruction the Judge will give the Jury?

(A) It is established as a matter of law that the Defendant received the signed document, so your verdict must be for Plaintiff.

(B) If you find that Defendant received the signed document, your verdict must be for the Plaintiff.

(C) Plaintiff has not offered evidence from which you can find that Defendant received the signed document, so your verdict must be for Defendant.

(D) You may not speculate as to whether either party has liability insurance.

145. Naomi owned a 20-acre parcel of land on Lake Watonga. Naomi had an easement across Micah's property for access to and from her land. The easement was duly recorded in Micah's deed. The access consisted of a packed dirt road that required no maintenance. Naomi decided to raise some cash, so she divided her land into one-acre parcels, and sold 19 and kept one for herself. All 20 of the new residents used the same easement road to access their property. Micah was angry because the additional use kept a perpetual dust cloud over his property, and because the noise and vibration from all the traffic disturbed him. What is the most likely remedy a court will grant?

(A) Block the access with a fence, thereby ending the easement.

(B) Injunction for overuse.

(C) Permit Naomi to use the easement; charge others with trespassing.

(D) Sue in tort for nuisance.

146. Fred Fog was driving west on Sunset Boulevard a little under the posted speed limit in a residential neighborhood. As he drove towards the ocean, the fog blanket got thicker and thicker and visibility decreased accordingly. A young child was crossing the street in the middle of the block. Because of the thick blanket of fog, Fred did not see the child until he was right on her. He then slammed on his brakes, but was unable to stop in time. If the child's guardian sues Fred Fog, the likely outcome is a verdict for

(A) The child unless the heavy fog was sudden and unexpected.

(B) Fred because he exercised reasonable care in driving within the speed limit.

(C) Fred unless the plaintiff can prove that Fred should have been exercising more than reasonable care under the circumstances.

(D) The child if it is proven that Fred failed to exercise reasonable care under the circumstances.

147. Benevolent State law prohibits publicly funded hospitals from refusing emergency room services based upon a person's inability or appearance of inability to pay for the service. Furthermore, emergency services must be given to indigent persons without charge. Benevolent State recently amended the statute so that non-U.S. citizens who were indigent may be billed for any emergency services. Bob, a Canadian, illegally slipped into the country. Bob was injured in a tragic can-opening incident and needed emergency care. Bob was treated at Public Hospital for his injury and was billed $2,000 for the treatment. Bob alleges the statute is unconstitutional. A court will likely find the statute:

(A) Unconstitutional because the state may not discriminate against non-citizens.

(B) Unconstitutional, if the court concludes that the state's interest is not compelling.

(C) Constitutional, if Benevolent meets its burden of that the law is substantially related to an important government interest.

(D) Constitutional, if Benevolent had a legitimate interest in charging alien indigents.

148. Rowan divided his real estate parcel into two parts. He built on the southern lot, which provided a wonderful view of nearby Mt. Shasta. He sold the other lot to Martin, and provided in the deed for an express easement to ingress and egress to Martin's property. As soon as the deal closed, Martin erected a 3-story home that blocked Rowan's view of the mountain, thereby severely impacting the value of his property. What would be the likely outcome of Rowan's claim against Martin?

(A) Rowan would prevail because he has a right to leave the airspace above his house undisturbed.

(B) Rowan would prevail because his house was built before Martin's construction began.

(C) Martin, because there is no right to an undisturbed mountain view.

(D) Martin, unless he was aware he was obstructing the view.

149. A Marine surveyor entered into agreements with Sally Sailor to inspect a sailboat she was thinking about purchasing. The contract they signed stated that any claim arising from the contract had to be formally asserted within 9 months. The marine survey was completed and, based upon the unqualified opinion, Sally purchased the sailboat. Fourteen months later Sally discovered concealed rot in the boat which was not disclosed in the survey. The state statute of limitation for actions on a written contract was three years. If Sally brings a lawsuit against the marine surveyor based upon breach of contract the likely outcome is that the court will

(A) Dismiss the claim because the contract statute of limitations has run.

(B) Allow the claim to go to the jury because the UCC rule on statute of limitations does not allow the parties to reduce the recovery period to less than one year.

(C) Allow the claim to go to the jury because the period of limitation is only triggered on discovery of the defect.

(D) Allow the claim to go to the jury because the plaintiff is entitled to the longer of the period specified by the agreement or that specified under state law.

150. Richard is at a political rally featuring a famous senator from Nuevo York. When Senator Hally is speaking, Richard heckles, "Socialism is dead and so should you." In addition to being chastised for bad grammar, Richard is charged with assault, which is placing a person in imminent fear of bodily harm. He is found guilty. Hally then sues Richard for the tort of assault claiming that she was in imminent fear of bodily harm. Since she is not a very good attorney, she offers a certified copy of the conviction to prove liability, so she only has to produce evidence of damages. Is the prior conviction admissible?

(A) Yes, but only to impeach Richard if he denies making the statement.

(B) Yes, for the purpose of substantively establishing that Richard assaulted Hally.

(C) No, hearsay subject to no exception.

(D) No, Hally must offer direct witness testimony to establish the assault.

151. Southern State University has 30,000 full-time students on its campus, including 1,000 students from over-seas. Ten thousand stay in dormitories on campus. The dormitories have a policy that Southern State citizens will not share a room with a person, unless that person is a U.S. citizen. Assuming a proper plaintiff brings a challenge, what is the likely result?

(A) State must show a legitimate state interest to discriminate against the alien.

(B) State must show that the alien students are a particular source of an important problem.

(C) State must show excluding aliens from rooming with its citizens is substantially related to an important government interest.

(D) State must show a compelling state interest in excluding aliens from rooming with its citizens.

Questions 152 and 153 are based on the following:

Roy and Dale live in a non-community property state. Roy's dad, Gene, died and left his ranch and Palomino stallion "Trigger" to "Roy and Dale to share jointly."

152. Assume Roy and Dale are married. What is the most likely property interest they hold?

(A) Tenancy by the entirety.

(B) Joint tenancy

(C) Tenancy in common

(D) None of the above.

153. Now assume Roy and Dale have never married, but instead they just ride the "happy trails" together. Also, assume the will instead stated "to Roy and Dale" but did not elaborate further. What is the most likely property interest?

(A) Tenancy by the entirety.
(B) Joint tenancy.
(C) Tenancy-in-common.
(D) None of the above.

154. A newly enacted statute criminalizes the following: "No person shall utter to another person in a public place any annoying, disturbing, or unwelcome language." Johnson is an African American resident visiting from a neighboring state. Johnson followed a city councilwoman down the street yelling an impressive array of highly offensive four-letter words. The woman showed heroic patience. She repeatedly asked him to stop when the reasonable person would have lashed out at Johnson. In the subsequent criminal prosecution of Johnson, can the state convict him?

(A) Cannot convict, because the speech of this sort is protected by the First and Fourteenth Amendments.
(B) Can convict because Johnson uttered obscenities or fighting words.
(C) Cannot convict, unless he is also prosecuted under another statute that meets constitutional standards.
(D) Can convict.

155. Indiana Idiot was a 19-year-old boy who was mentally and physically handicapped, but he was not insane. His disability involved a phobia under which he believed that all people with red hair were from the planet Mars and conspiring to enslave the human race. As he was walking along the street he came upon Ryan Rid, a middle-age red-haired accountant. As he walked by Indiana dropped a bag of marbles on the sidewalk in front of Ryan. Ryan lost his footing as he stepped onto the marbles and fell suffering a concussion. If Ryan sues Indiana for negligence, the court will

(A) Instruct the jury that it must consider Indiana's mental and physical handicaps in determining

whether he acted as a responsible person in the circumstances.
(B) Instruct the jury that it should disregard Indiana's mental and physical handicaps in determining whether he acted as a reasonable person in the circumstances.
(C) Instruct the jury that it may consider Indiana's mental and physical handicaps in determining whether he acted as a reasonable person in the circumstance.
(D) Instruct the jury that it should not consider Indiana's mental and physical handicaps in determining whether he acted reasonable in the circumstance.

156. Bill is charged with perjury. The main prosecution witness is his wife, Hally, who has knowledge of the truth or falsity of Bill's statements. Upon questioning by the prosecutor, Hally responds, "Uh, I don't recall." The prosecution then offers a transcript of her testimony from her own perjury trial where she comments on the truth or falsity of Bill's statement. Upon Bill's objection, what result?

(A) Inadmissible, executive immunity.
(B) Inadmissible, the witness is available to testify.
(C) Admissible, direct evidence of guilt.
(D) Admissible, former testimony.

Questions 157 and 158 are based on the following:

Cathy Client hired Alice Attorney to prepare an estate plan and will. Alice had taken all of the tax and estate planning courses her law school offered. The parties agreed to a $5,000 fee for the engagement.

157. Alice desires to gift $5,000 to her favorite niece Sunbeam and Cathy agrees to pay Sunbeam in the written fee agreement. Later, Alice learned Sunbeam had dropped out of college and got Cathy to agree not to pay Sunbeam. Sunbeam may file a collection action against Cathy

(A) Immediately upon Cathy's promise to pay her.

(B) Immediately when she learns of Cathy's promise favoring her.

(C) Only when she materially changes her position in reliance on Cathy's promise.

(D) At any time because the promise by Cathy was irrevocable.

158. Cathy and Alice began a will and estate plan engagement in which Cathy promises to pay Alice's law firm. The law firm is short on cash to meet their current expenses and seeks to borrow from Bountiful Bank. Bountiful takes an assignment of Cathy's accounts receivable and promptly notifies Cathy she must pay the $5,000 to them and not Alice's law firm. Cathy refused to pay and Bountiful brought suit against Cathy. Her best defense is

(A) There was no consideration to support the assignment.

(B) She did not agree to an assignment of her promise to pay the $5,000.

(C) Alice's performance was negligent.

(D) The contract did not contain a provision authorizing the assignment of the contract.

Questions 159 and 160 are based on the following:

Tammy and Heather are on a camping trip. They set up their tent in a remote area of the woods and build a fire. Avid gun collectors, they have each brought a favorite handgun for some shooting practice. They begin shooting their guns into the sky, aiming at birds. Unbeknowst to them, Craig is camping not far from them, and has brought his brand new shiny SUV. A couple of the bullets ricochet off of tree branches and strike Craig's windshield. He hears the glass breaking, and thinks that hooligans are shooting at his car for kicks. He gets out his shotgun and fires, thinking he will scare away the vandals. He kills Tammy instantly and barely misses Heather. Heather screams and begins running. Craig, seeing what he has done, wants to destroy the evidence. He

takes a burning stick from Heather and Tammy's campfire and throws into the brush, starting a forest fire that consumes Tammy's body. Heather tries to escape on foot but is eventually overcome by smoke and dies in the fire.

159. Charged with second-degree murder of Tammy, Craig will likely be found

(A) Guilty, because he acted with extreme recklessness.

(B) Not guilty, because he was acting in defense of his property.

(C) Guilty, because he tried to cover up his crime.

(D) Not guilty, because Tammy was the first aggressor and used deadly force.

160. Craig is also charged with felony murder related to the death of Heather. His best defense would be

(A) He did not intend to kill Heather by setting the fire.

(B) He is not guilty of arson, only reckless burning, which is a gross misdemeanor.

(C) He believed that the fire could be contained to a small area.

(D) Heather and Tammy had abandoned their fire, and therefore a forest fire was inevitable.

161. Edward, an English citizen, traveled to the State of New England. Edward is traveling on a work visa as a physical therapist. He received his training at Oxford University in England. A wealthy family in New England sponsored his arrival to give their daughter therapy for her tennis elbow. New England has a state statute requiring physical therapists to be licensed. To acquire a state license, the applicant must submit proof of the following: United States citizenship, residence within New England for the previous year, and physical therapy training by a New England accredited institution. Edward is denied a license. How would a trial court likely rule?

(A) For Edward, because the in-state training requirement is an undue burden upon interstate commerce.

(B) For Edward, because the in-state training requirement violates the Privileges and Immunities Clause.

(C) For the state, because there is no constitutional right to practice any particular profession.

(D) For the state, because the in-state training requirement is a rational means to ensure the safety of patients.

162. The estates of several seamen lost at sea during a storm when a wave swept them off the deck of the commercial fishing vessel "Jody V" bring suit under the theory of respondeat superior against the vessel owner. The evidence establishes that the Captain brought the bow of the ship 45 degrees in to the approaching waves. The expert for the estates testifies that holding the bow at 45 degrees to approaching waves was negligent. On cross-examination, the defense attorney asks the expert if the "Manual for the Command of Ships at Sea" published by the United States Department of Transportation under the auspices of the U.S. Coast Guard is authoritative. The expert says, "Yes." The attorney then asks the expert to read from chapter 12, which states in part, "It is necessary to hold the bow 45 degrees to oncoming waves in order to prevent capsizing even though such may expose any crew members on deck to danger." Upon objection, what result?

(A) The treatise passage may be read into evidence.

(B) The excerpted passage must be admitted as an exhibit.

(C) The passage will neither be admitted nor read because the authority of the treatise was not established on direct examination.

(D) The passage will neither be admitted nor read because the defendant's own witness must testify as to the treatise's authority.

163. Betty Blind began to lose her sight in her 30s and was declared legally blind at the age of 40. She still enjoyed a daily walk in her neighborhood. Because she had lived in the same house in the same neighborhood since she was born she knew every step of the sidewalk on her block. One day Betty was walking on her block without her cane. She fell into a sewer hole breaking her leg. The Sewer Company had put very large "caution" signs up around the hole, but did not put up a barricade. Betty sued the Sewer Company for her damages and the defendant asserted contributory negligence as a bar. The jurisdiction does recognize contributory negligence. The likely result of the suit is that Betty will

(A) Prevail because the defendant had an absolute duty to use barricades to stop pedestrians from being injured.

(B) Not prevail if the jury finds a reasonable blind person would have been carrying and using a cane.

(C) Not prevail because the court will hold as a matter of law that Betty failed to act as a prudent person in protecting herself.

(D) Prevail only if it was found that the defendant failed to exercise reasonable care in only having signs warning pedestrians of the danger.

164. Trent leases a three-bedroom apartment from Lloyd for $450 a month. The terms of the lease specify "month to month" and that the rent is due on the first of each month. There is no clause in the lease that specifies how much notice the tenant must provide before vacating. Trent paid the September rent but moved out without notice on the 15th of the September. Through what date does he owe rent?

(A) He owes through the end of September.

(B) He owes through the 15th of October.

(C) He owes through the end of October.

(D) He owes nothing above what he paid at the beginning of September for that month's rent, because

Lloyd received rent for half a month without a tenant.

165. Plaintiff's father is mortally injured by an automobile when walking across the street. As the father is lying in the street he tells Witness, "The car ran the red light." He dies moments later. Plaintiff calls Witness to testify to the father's statement. That statement is the only proof of defendant's negligence. Is the statement admissible?
- (A) Yes, dying declaration.
- (B) Yes, present sense impression.
- (C) Yes, excited utterance.
- (D) Yes, because the declarant is unavailable.

Questions 166 – 168 are based on the following:

Tom and Nancy are fighting in a crowded bar. Nancy takes a swing at Tom, and Tom ducks the swing. Nancy puts her hands up in front of her, palms forward, and says "I'm sorry, I won't do that again." Tom is angry and hits back. He misses Nancy and hits Donald, who is standing behind her.

166. Charged with battery of Donald, Tom will likely be
- (A) Acquitted, because he acted in self-defense.
- (B) Acquitted, because he intended to hit Nancy, not Donald.
- (C) Convicted, because of the doctrine of transferred intent.
- (D) Convicted, because he was negligent to take a swing in a crowded bar.

167. Charged with assault, Nancy's best defense would be
- (A) She only intended to scare Tom, not to actually hit him.
- (B) She withdrew.
- (C) She actually succeeded in hitting him.
- (D) He was drunk and capable of violence.

168. At Tom's trial, the first witness is sworn in and testifies, after which the judge finds there is insufficient evidence to continue and dismisses the case. The prosecution finds another witness and re-files the charges. The prosecution
- (A) Is precluded from re-filing because double jeopardy has attached.
- (B) May proceed if the judge determines that the new evidence is sufficient.
- (C) May proceed, but may not call the witness who testified in the prior proceeding.
- (D) Is precluded from trying the case to a judge, but may try it to a jury.

169. In Anystate, U.S.A., it is illegal for a convicted child molester to seek or obtain employment in a school, preschool, or other position of trust with children. John sought and obtained employment at a pre-school where he was accused of molesting children. John is charged with seeking and obtaining employment while a convicted child molester. The prosecution calls the manager of the pre-school who testifies that he hired John and John never disclosed the prior conviction. The prosecution then offers a certified copy of John's conviction of molestation from five years ago. If John objects what result?
- (A) The prior conviction is not admitted because it is character evidence to prove that John has a propensity to molest children.
- (B) The prior conviction is not admitted because the prejudicial effect substantially outweighs any probative value.
- (C) The prior conviction is admitted to prove an element of the crime charged.
- (D) The prior conviction is admitted because it is a felony conviction less than ten years old.

Questions 170 – 172 are based on the following:

Orange Hat Computing, Inc. intended to create a new operating system for Palm computers. To write the whole program is estimated to take three years. Orange orally hired Peter Programmer's company to lead the software design. Peter began working for Orange under an employment agreement specifying delegation was not allowed. Peter received an offer for more money from a much better software house. Peter had a friend named David who had just graduated from a software engineering college. Peter entered into an agreement with David to sell him the software business. Peter agreed to "assign the Orange Hat contract" as part of his business sale. Peter informed Orange Hat that David was going to do the remaining work.

170. If Orange Hat brings a claim against Peter, the court will probably hold for

    (A) Orange Hat since David did not personally promise to perform the Orange Hat job as part of his agreement.

    (B) Peter Programmer because the original oral agreement was not enforceable under the statute of frauds.

    (C) Peter Programmer since his sale to David implied a delegation and termination of all his obligations under the contract with Orange Hat.

    (D) Orange Hat since Peter's statement announcing the assignment was anticipatory repudiation.

171. In the notification that David had purchased Peter's business, Peter requested that Orange Hat send all the programming information to David. Orange Hat did not forward the programming information but did request in writing that David show sufficient experience to assure them that he was capable of completing the software design. David did not respond at all until he sued Orange Hat for damages. The likely outcome for the case is that the court will find for

    (A) David because Orange Hat failed to send the programming information to him on request.

    (B) Orange Hat because there was no privity between them and the plaintiff.

    (C) Orange Hat because David failed to assure them that he was capable of completing the software design.

    (D) David because Orange Hat continued to have rights against Peter.

172. Assume that David completed the software design for Orange Hat. While the system worked initially it seemed to crash every other day. After repeated warnings by Orange Hat and attempts to fix the system by David, Orange Hat told him to stop working. If Orange Hat brings suit against Peter and David, they will likely

    (A) Prevail against David but not against Peter because David was the sole cause of the malfunctioning system.

    (B) Prevail against Peter but not against David because Orange Hat's contract was only with Peter.

    (C) Prevail against neither Peter nor David since a programmer is never a guarantor that the program will not have problems.

    (D) Prevail against Peter and David.

173. Traffic Stop Incorporated is a privately owned company that contracts with local governments. Traffic Stop installs and maintains cameras at traffic signals and cameras connected with radar guns on roadsides. Traffic Stop prints pictures of vehicles speeding and disregarding traffic signals. These pictures contain the vehicle's license plates. Traffic Stop coordinates with the state Department of Licensing to correlate the car with the registered owner and the owner's address. This information is mailed out to the vehicle's owner in the form of a notice of a civil traffic infraction.

Traffic Stop entered into a contract with Quiet Town. Spee Dracer resides in Quiet Town. Spee Dracer received a notice from Traffic Stop for driving 40 mph in an area restricted to 25 mph. Mr. Dracer challenges the constitutionality of the process. How will the court likely rule?

- (A) Dracer's challenge is not ripe until he has to pay for the ticket.
- (B) Dracer's challenge is rejected as the Constitution does not apply to Traffic Stop.
- (C) The court will consider the constitutionality of Traffic Stop's actions.
- (D) There is no standing to challenge Traffic Stop.

174. Ophelia owned a 2-acre lot in fee simple absolute. The lot was accessed through a road that traversed the western part of the lot and ended in the eastern part. The access road was the only possible connection to the city streets nearby due to the terrain. Ophelia subdivided the lot into two parcels, east and west. She built a house on the west part, nearest the road, and sold the eastern portion to Bjorn. Naturally, Bjorn's only access to the main city street was across the pre-existing road that required him do drive across Ophelia's lot to ingress and egress his property. Which of the choices below best describes Bjorn's property right to traverse Ophelia's land?

- (A) Easement by prescription.
- (B) Easement by implication.
- (C) Easement in gross.
- (D) Easement by express grant.

175. Linda Landowner had an estate with a super-deluxe swimming pool. The whole yard is enclosed by a picket fence. The residence is in a neighborhood that has a number of families with young children. These children wandered and explored the neighborhood more or less oblivious to property lines. Danny Diver, an 8-year-old boy, trespassed onto Linda's residence when there was no one home by jumping over the picket fence. Danny decided to dive off the 20-foot high roof of Linda's house rather than the low diving board. Unfortunately Danny did not hold his hands firmly over his head as he hit the water and he went right to the bottom, hitting his head. He was knocked unconscious and subsequently died. To the best of the knowledge of all the neighbors, no children had ever trespassed and swam in Linda's swimming pool before. If his parents subsequently bring suit against Linda for wrongful death, the best defense Linda can assert is

- (A) The boy made an unforeseen hazardous use of the artificial condition swimming pool, which in and of itself presented no unusual danger.
- (B) A trespasser takes any condition on the property as he finds it.
- (C) A trespasser using a swimming pool on the property of another without permission waives any right to object to any injuries they might sustain.
- (D) The expense of fully protecting against injury, such as installing an electric fence which would stop people from climbing to the house's roof, would be a large compared to a small risk of serious injury.

Questions 176 – 178 are based on the following:

Larry owns Blackacre in fee simple absolute. He wants to provide for his good friends, Mo and Curly after his death. His will states "To Mo, Blackacre, for his possession and full use during his life, then to Curly, if he should survive Mo, otherwise to Mo's daughter Morticia.

176. Shemp visits Mo immediately after Larry's death and falls in love with Blackacre. He offers to buy Mo's interest in Blackacre. Mo does not wish to disclose the nature of the arrangement, but is persuaded by Shemp's pleas. He deeds the property to Shemp with the following: "To Shemp I quitclaim all of my interest in Blackacre." Shemp immediately records the deed and takes possession of the property. Shemp, in his will, states, "To my daughter Cassandra, Blackacre." Shemp then keels over dead. Assume the formalities of Shemp's will are all in order.

Also assume Mo predeceased Shemp. Who holds the current estate in Blackacre?

  (A) Mo's estate.
  (B) Shemp's daughter, Cassandra.
  (C) Curly.
  (D) Morticia.

177. At the time Larry dies, what are the property interests of the following (in this order): Mo, Curly, Morticia, Cassandra?

  (A) Life estate, vested remainder, contingent remainder, none.
  (B) Life estate, life estate, remainder, none.
  (C) Life estate, contingent remainder, contingent remainder, none.
  (D) Life estate, defeasible fee simple, contingent remainder, contingent remainder

178. What if Shemp was a purchaser for value and gave full consideration for the land? Does either Shemp or his estate have any claim against Mo for not fully disclosing that the title was not in fee simple absolute?

  (A) Yes, under the rules for statutory warranty deeds, Mo breached his duty to disclose.
  (B) Yes, because he knowingly withheld information, he committed fraud.
  (C) No, because life estates may be conveyed inter vivos.
  (D) No, because the quitclaim deed is without warranty.

179. The President negotiates an agreement with Mexico regarding the international trucking industry. The agreement is in tension with current statutory law. What must happen to form a treaty with Mexico?

  (A) The presidents of the two countries must sign the agreement.
  (B) The President must submit the treaty to Congress for approval.
  (C) The President must have the treaty ratified by two thirds of the Senate.
  (D) Congress must enact it as law and the presentment clause requires the President's signature.

Questions 180 and 181 are based on the following:

Stanley Sports was a very well known sports figure/baseball player. While Stanley liked the attention and regularly gave interviews to build attendance at the baseball games, he religiously protected his private life. He did this because his first wife had taken her own life which created much grief, anxiety, and embarrassment for both Stanley and his children. Stanley remarried 6 months after his wife's death.

Years later, a reporter from the National Observer interviewed Stanley. Stanley bragged about the history of his family life and the reporter investigated. The reporter then wrote an article about Stanley's life that was published nationally. The article alleged that Stanley's first wife committed suicide because Stanley was unfaithful and having an extramarital relationship with the woman Stanley subsequently married. The reporter believed the story to be accurate since it came from two sources that had been accurate in the past.

180. Stanley's second wife was outraged by the story. She suffered emotional distress and became very depressed. If she brings suit for defamation, the likely outcome is that she will

  (A) Prevail if the story was false.
  (B) Not prevail for defamation if the National Observer exercised ordinary care in investigating whether the story was true or false.
  (C) Not prevail unless the National Observer printed the story with reckless disregard for the truth or knowledge that the statement was false.
  (D) Prevail for emotional distress if the story was published negligently.

181. Stanley was not physically or emotionally distressed by the newspaper story. However, two of his largest sponsors decided that Stanley no longer projected the proper image. If Stanley sues National

Observer for defamation, the worst defense that National can assert is

(A) The statement was true.
(B) Stanley consented by granting the reporter an interview and put the question of his family life at issue.
(C) There is a qualified privilege to print newsworthy items about a public figure and the reporter lacked malice.
(D) There is an applicable absolute privilege which is protected by the First and Fourteenth Amendments to the Constitution.

Questions 182 and 183 are based on the following:

182. Wendy is walking along a sidewalk when she trips on an uneven part of the sidewalk. She brings suit against the City. The City claims that the particular portion of the sidewalk is leased to Business Corp. who has exclusive control over the sidewalk. Wendy offers the testimony of three witnesses who will state that the very next day they saw a City maintenance crew repairing that portion of the sidewalk. What result upon objection by the City?

(A) Inadmissible, it must be established that the City knew of the injury.
(B) Inadmissible, the repairs cannot be used to prove the City's negligence.
(C) Admissible, admission by party opponent.
(D) Admissible, goes to an issue at trial.

183. The City calls its Risk and Claims Manager to testify that in 30 years there have been no formal claims upon the City for injuries resulting from hazardous conditions. Will this testimony be admissible?

(A) Yes, goes to the City's lack of knowledge.
(B) Yes, proves that the City exercised reasonable care in maintaining its sidewalks.

(C) No, unless it is proved that the Risk and Claims Manager has been in that position for those thirty years.
(D) No, the evidence is irrelevant to the issues at trial.

184. Scott's Friendly Realty Development Company founded a subdivision called Shangri-La. Scott recorded the following into each of the deeds of each parcel in the development: "Shangri-La Valley is surrounded by picturesque mountains in every direction. To preserve the views from each house in the subdivision, owners shall not build homes or any other structure on their properties higher than one story, and the peaks of all roofs will extend no more than 28 feet in height." Which answer below cannot qualify as a valid description of the above restriction?

(A) Negative easement.
(B) Restrictive covenant.
(C) Negative servitude.
(D) Easement in gross.

185. Oscar Owner hired Billy Builder to build him a luxury custom home in accordance with plans and specifications drafted by Albert Architect. The contract price for complete performance was specified to be $200,000 with all payment due on completion. Billy sues Oscar for restitution and at trial proves that the 90% completed luxury home added $250,000 in value to the building lot. Oscar, in turn, proves at trial that had Billy completed the house his total building costs would have been $225,000 resulting in a $25,000 loss. Assuming Oscar is held to have wrongfully terminated Billy the court could enter a restitution award of

(A) $180,000.
(B) $200,000.
(C) $255,000.
(D) $250,000.

Questions 186 and 187 are based on the following:

The federal government established the Education Agency to counter the critics of standardized testing. Also that year, the government expanded the responsibility of the existing Occupational Safety and Health Agency (OSHA) to include students. Congress gave OSHA guidelines for implementing its new jurisdiction. OSHA passed several regulations calling for ergonomic desks, better lighting, and restrictions on book size. OSHA regulations require schools to have at least 50% of their assigned textbooks available in paperback, so the weight each child would have to carry home would be lightened. The Education Agency has no regulation requiring the use of either paperback or hard cover books, but the agency's director has indicated his preference for the durability of hard cover books in his quarterly newsletter. State law requires at least one half of the high school textbooks to be hard cover.

Lincoln High is a public school in the state of Washboard. Lincoln received 300 new desks from the Education Agency last year, and the desks do not meet OSHA standards. The Education Agency Director gave a news conference and stated, "If Lincoln throws away all those desks and books, that'll be the last of their funding."

186. Lincoln High files a declaratory judgment action in federal court asking that the OSHA regulations be found unconstitutional. What best describes why the court will or will not hear the case on its merits?
- **(A)** There is an imminent threat of loss of funding if the school complies with the law.
- **(B)** Lincoln High has lost all economic use of the desks.
- **(C)** The threat to cut off funding is speculative.
- **(D)** Funding is a political question.

187. Which answer best describes whether Lincoln will or will not need to assign paperback books.
- **(A)** Both the OSHA regulation and the state law are constitutional.
- **(B)** The OSHA regulation is unconstitutional, as selection of

textbooks is an integral state function.
- **(C)** The OSHA regulation is unconstitutional, as it runs against the clearly established Education Agency policy.
- **(D)** The OSHA regulation is constitutional, and the state law is superseded unconstitutional.

188. June and Ward purchased a new home from Edward Haskell, Sr., a local homebuilder. The home had an unconditional warranty on all new appliances, the furnace, and air conditioner for one full year, and a limited warranty on the roof and structure for three years, however, the foundation, sidewalks, driveway, and curbs were specifically exempted from the warranty. June and Ward purchased the home in the middle of the summer, when the weather was hot and dry.

Seven months later, while walking across the carpet in the basement, they noticed it was sopping wet. They pulled up the wall-to-wall carpeting and found a large crack in the foundation, through which water was seeping. The next morning, they hired a geophysical engineer who told them the house was sitting on an underground spring, and recent rainfall had caused flow of that spring to be more pronounced. They sue Edward Haskell Sr. for damages. Given this fact pattern, what is the likely result?
- **(A)** Haskell prevails; the foundation is exempt from his warranty.
- **(B)** June and Ward prevail: the foundation is covered by implied warranty.
- **(C)** Haskell prevails; he is not responsible for the underground spring.
- **(D)** June and Ward prevail because Haskell hid the defective foundation.

189. Fred and Florence Family had lived in the neighborhood for sixteen years when they began to have children. In the next five years, they had four children. In the fifth year, Robin Rocking, the drummer in a heavy metal band, purchased the house next door. The band practiced every morning and afternoon and this disturbed the young children's naps. If the Family brings suit for nuisance, the claim should

(A) Prevail because the Family's interest in the quiet environment for their children has priority over the neighbors' use of their property.

(B) Not prevail because Rocking's interest in the use of his own property has priority over the Family's children.

(C) Not prevail unless the heavy metal music constitutes a substantial and unreasonable disturbance to persons of normal sensibilities.

(D) Prevail if the heavy metal music constitutes a substantial interference with the Family's use and enjoyment of their family residence.

190. The owners of the Sailing Vessel "Peerless" bring suit against the builders for breach of contract. The owners allege that the plumbing was to be made of "Reading Pipe" and was agreed to in an addendum to the written contract. The builders deny that any employee of the builder signed the addendum. The owners offer an addendum with a signature purported to be that of the builder's sales manager. In order to get the addendum admitted into evidence, what must the proponent do?

(A) Have someone who is familiar with the sales manager's signature identify the signature on the addendum as his.

(B) Have someone testify as to the contents of the addendum if the signature cannot be authenticated.

(C) Question the sales manager on cross-examination because the addendum is extrinsic evidence.

(D) Convince the Judge that the addendum is a statement against interest.

191. Gerald agreed to sell his 25 acres of wheat field farm property on the edge of town to Mark for $50,000 an acre. They both signed the contract. In addition to listing the price, it properly described the property by metes and bounds, and it specified the method of financing (cash) and closing place and date. Mark paid $25,000 in earnest money. Two weeks later, before closing had occurred, Paul approached Gerald with a better offer: he had a famous chain of large discount stores, and offered $80,000 an acre for the property so he could turn it into a P-Mart. Gerald jumped at the chance, and entered a second contract with Paul for the greater amount. The contract with Paul also complied with the Statute of Frauds. When Mark found out, he wrote to Gerald, threatening to sue. Gerald's response was that he could sue all he wanted, because he suffered no damages: Gerald was willing to sell him an identical parcel of land just 5 miles out of town for the same price as the original contract. Mark comes to you as his attorney for advice, because he still wants the original parcel of land. What remedy do you recommend to him?

(A) Sue for monetary damages in the amount of the P-Mart price minus his contracted price.

(B) Sue for specific performance.

(C) Sue for partial performance, since earnest money was collected.

(D) None of the above.

192. Excellent Electric Co. entered into an agreement with Central City to provide the municipality with electricity at a predetermined price per kilowatt for a two year term. The requirement contract was in writing but did not specify the quantity. Happy Hospital was a large user of electricity. Excellent wrote Central City informing them that due to the then energy shortage they may not be able to perform. The legal effect of this situation is

(A) To allow Central City to escape their obligation by treating the contract as repudiated.

(B) To allow Central City to request an assurance that their electricity will be available.

(C) That Central City has no rights because there is no quantity stated in the contract.

(D) That Excellent Electric has no ongoing duty to Central City.

193. Randall leased a small bungalow from Lars for a period of two years for $950 a month, which included all utilities. Because they were good friends, Lars didn't insist on a written contract. After two months, he decided to leave because he thought the bungalow was too small for his needs. He surrendered the keys to Lars, but Lars refused them and also refused to let Randall out of the lease. Randall ceased paying rent and left. Lars sued for breach. What is the likely result?

(A) The entire lease is enforceable due to partial performance.

(B) The entire lease is enforceable because Randall failed to give adequate notice.

(C) The lease is unenforceable because of the Statute of Frauds.

(D) The lease is unenforceable because Randall surrendered the keys.

194. Mr. Slugger had an 11-year-old son named Simon Slugger. Simon had exhibited physical aggressiveness with younger boys and had been accused of being a bully. Mr. Slugger had a business associate who operated a private summer camp for boys ages 6 to 10. Mr. Slugger overstated Simon's experience to his business associate in order to convince him to hire Simon as a camp counselor. Based upon the recommendation, the camp hired Simon. The first two days at the camp, Simon physically attacked and seriously injured two younger boys. If a lawsuit is filed on behalf of the victims against Mr. Slugger to recover for the damages inflicted by Simon, the best reason to impose liability is

(A) The father was negligent.

(B) The father had an absolute duty to supervise his son.

(C) The father was vicariously liable for all of his son's intentional torts.

(D) The father was liable under the doctrine of respondent superior.

195. On February 1, Nugent Manufacturing, Inc. contracted with Costello Wholesalers to supply Costello with 1,000 integrated circuits. Delivery was called for on May 1. On March 15, Nugent notified Costello that it would not perform and that Costello should look elsewhere to satisfy its requirement. Nugent had received a larger and more lucrative contract on February 27 and its production capacity was such that it could not fulfill both orders. On April 1, Nugent purchased a new production facility and contacted Costello stating they would now deliver on May 1. The facts

(A) Are not sufficient to clearly establish an anticipatory repudiation.

(B) The March 15 notification prevents Nugent from retracting its repudiation of the Costello contract.

(C) Will permit Costello to sue on March 15.

(D) Will permit Costello to sue on May 2.

196. Plaintiff is injured due to the possible negligence of Defendant. Defendant visits Plaintiff in the hospital and in the presence of several witnesses tells Plaintiff, "I feel very badly for not paying attention to the red light. Because of this, I will pay for all of your medical expenses and give you $500,000.00 if you don't sue me." Is the Defendant's statement admissible?

(A) Yes, admission by party-opponent.

(B) Yes, but only the statement admitting negligence, not the part offering to pay medical expenses.

(C) No, offer of compromise.

(D) No, hearsay without an exception.

197. Gary has a home that is growing too big for him. He decides to convey it to his daughter Jan, but he is worried about her wild life style, particularly her use of illegal

drugs. Gary conveys his property "to Jan, as long as she does not use illegal drugs on the premises." Jan takes possession, and six months later, she is busted for selling crack cocaine in her back yard. Ignoring all the potential impacts due to her crime, what now happens to her property interest in the home?

(A) Nothing, because it is a fee simple subject to condition subsequent, she does not lose possession unless Gary reenters.

(B) Her property interest reverts back to Gary.

(C) Nothing, because restraints on alienation are void. Therefore, her interest is in fee simple absolute.

(D) None of the above.

198. Microhard Software Co. hired Bill Bates as their chief software engineer for a three year term. Bill began by doing the work himself, but other opportunities began to develop for him. After 14 months, he delegated the performance duty to Don Delegattee. Don Delegattee agreed, but Microhard Software decided they did not want him working on their project. The worst argument that Microhard can assert in support their rejection of Don is

(A) The risk of unacceptable performance has materially increased.

(B) The employment contract Microhard had with Bill Bates prohibited assignment and delegation.

(C) There was no consideration to support the Bill Bates to Don Delegattee contract.

(D) The software development required the personal skill of Bill Bates.

199. Concerned with overworking the high court, a benevolent yet conservative Congress passes a law stating that the U.S. Supreme Court will no longer hear appeals from state court decisions based on alleged Fourth Amendment violations or ineffective assistance of counsel. The law states that prisoners may still file habeas corpus petitions with federal district courts. What is the constitutionality of this statute?

(A) Unconstitutional, as it deprives due process.

(B) Constitutional, as Congress has power over the Supreme Court's appellate jurisdiction.

(C) Unconstitutional, as it violates Article III.

(D) Unconstitutional, as it violates a cornerstone of American jurisprudence to deprive the right to petition the Supreme Court.

200. Sandy Sensation was an up-and-coming actress trying to make it big in Hollywood. She helped advance her career by appearing on as many television celebrity shows as possible. One night she was in New York on the Donna Letterwomen show. Donna told Sandy on the air that the show had hired a private detective, who discovered that Sandy's mother was a prostitute and drug addict. This so disturbed Sandy that she ran off the stage. Subsequently, she suffered emotional depression and filed suit against the Donna Letterwomen show. The likely outcome of the suit is that the claim will

(A) Prevail because Donna's statements hold Sandy up to ridicule and contempt.

(B) Not prevail because the right to privacy is personal.

(C) Not prevail if the Donna Letterwomen show could prove the statements about Sandy's mother were true.

(D) Not prevail because the Donna Letterwomen show lacked malice in that their only intent was to entertain viewers.

SIDE 1

BE SURE EACH MARK IS DARK AND COMPLETELY FILLS THE INTENDED OVAL, AS SHOWN IN THE ILLUSTRATION AT THE RIGHT. COMPLETELY ERASE ANY MISTAKES OR STRAY MARKS.

Ⓐ ● Ⓒ Ⓓ

A JURISDICTION CODE

B APPLICANT NUMBER

C DATE OF BIRTH
Month | Day

Jan.	
Feb.	
March	
April	
May	
June	
July	
Aug.	
Sept.	
Oct.	
Nov.	
Dec.	

JURISDIC-TION CODE

Ala.	01		
Alaska	02		
Ariz.	03		
Ark.	04		
Calif.	05		
Colo.	06		
Conn.	07		
Del.	08		
D.C.	09		
Fla.	10		
Ga.	11		
Hawaii	12		
Idaho	13		
Ill.	14		
Ind.	15		
Iowa	16		
Kans.	17		
Ky.	18		
La.	19		
Maine	20		
Md.	21		
Mass.	22		
Mich.	23		
Minn.	24		
Miss.	25		
Mo.	26		
Mont.	27		
Nebr.	28		
Nev.	29		
N.H.	30		
N.J.	31		
N.Mex.	32		
N.Y.	33		
N.C.	34		
N.Dak.	35		
Ohio	36		
Okla.	37		
Oreg.	38		
Pa.	39		
R.I.	40		
S.C.	41		
S.Dak.	42		
Tenn.	43		
Tex.	44		
Utah	45		
Vt.	46		
Va.	47		
Wash.	48		
W.Va.	49		
Wis.	50		
Wyo.	51		
Guam	52		
NM Is./Saipon	53		
Virgin Is.	55		
All Other	56		

SIDE 1

A — JURISDICTION CODE

JURISDIC-
TION
CODE

Ala.	01
Alaska	02
Ariz.	03
Ark.	04
Calif.	05
Colo.	06
Conn.	07
Del.	08
D.C.	09
Fla.	10
Ga.	11
Hawaii	12
Idaho	13
Ill.	14
Ind.	15
Iowa	16
Kans.	17
Ky.	18
La.	19
Maine	20
Md.	21
Mass.	22
Mich.	23
Minn.	24
Miss.	25
Mo.	26
Mont.	27
Nebr.	28
Nev.	29
N.H.	30
N.J.	31
N.Mex.	32
N.Y.	33
N.C.	34
N.Dak.	35
Ohio	36
Okla.	37
Oreg.	38
Pa.	39
R.I.	40
S.C.	41
S.Dak.	42
Tenn.	43
Tex.	44
Utah	45
Vt.	46
Va.	47
Wash.	48
W.Va.	49
Wis.	50
Wyo.	51
Guam	52
NM Is./Saipon	53
Virgin Is.	55
All Other	56

B — APPLICANT NUMBER

C — DATE OF BIRTH

Month: Jan., Feb., March, April, May, June, July, Aug., Sept., Oct., Nov., Dec.

Day

BE SURE EACH MARK IS DARK AND COMPLETELY FILLS THE INTENDED OVAL, AS SHOWN IN THE ILLUSTRATION AT THE RIGHT. COMPLETELY ERASE ANY MISTAKES OR STRAY MARKS.

Ⓐ ● Ⓒ Ⓓ

1. **/D/** The correct answer because an agency with the power to enforce laws is generally an executive branch agency and requires appointment by the President with advice and consent. Appointment of Committee members is an executive appointment. **(A)** is incorrect because Congress has broad authority to delegate, and this act has intelligible standards. **(B)** is incorrect because the commerce power is far-reaching and can regulate automobiles. **(C)** is incorrect. There has been no government action against Compcar yet. Notice and opportunity to be heard does not include having a representative on the Commission.

2. **/A/** The correct answer because the court will allow the constitutional functions of a congressional committee to continue. This question gives the test-taker a clue as to the answer in the previous question. **(B)** is incorrect because prosecution is an Executive function. **(C)** is incorrect because the court will allow the constitutional functions of a congressional committee to go on. You should not have picked (C) based upon standing, because the question asked you to assume it. **(D)** is incorrect because the court will not re-write the statute to allow for Executive appointments.

3. **/A/** The testimony goes to an issue at trial and this alternative is preferred to all the others. Also, there is no rule that keeps the testimony out; it meets the basic tests of relevance and being more probative than prejudicial. **(B)** is incorrect because the bill of lading is not being offered, rather the manager's testimony is being offered. **(C)** is incorrect because the Best Evidence Rule prohibits only proving the contents of a writing with testimony. In this case, it is not the contents of the bill of lading that is disputed, rather the amount of merchandise taken. The bill of lading is merely one party's evidence of the amount taken. **(D)** is incorrect because testimonial evidence may be offered to contradict written evidence.

4. **/B/** Rachel is entitled to fair market value, which will likely be in the range of $25,000 to $28,000, unless she has some other way to demonstrate the value is now different. **(A)** is incorrect because the property is not valued at its proposed use, but at its "highest and best use" value in the owner's hands. **(C)** is incorrect because condemnation and taking for public use is constitutional under the doctrine of eminent domain; the city must simply compensate the owner at fair market value. **(D)** is incorrect because one of the other alternatives is correct.

5. **/D/** Conversion goes beyond trespass to chattels and Plaintiff is entitled to the full fair market value of the converted asset. **(A)** is incorrect because these damages would be the

proper amount for trespass to chattels; here we have conversion. **(B)** is incorrect since the Defendant did wrongfully exercise control over the Plaintiff's property, which is the definition of conversion. **(C)** is incorrect because there was a conversion even if the Defendant was benefiting the Plaintiff without authority.

6. **/A/** Under the mailbox rule, acceptance by authorized means is effective upon dispatch even if the acceptance is never received by the offeror. **(B)** is incorrect because Perry is bound. **(C)** is incorrect because it is only necessary to use reasonable means to get mailbox treatment under the UCC; not the fast or faster required under the common law. **(D)** is incorrect because an offeror's revocation is effective prior to the offeree's posting even under the mailbox rule.

7. **/B/** The question asks which alternative will not excuse performance. The assembly plant burning down will not discharge the obligation because Sam could purchase the widgets from another source to satisfy the contract requirement. **(A)** is not the best answer because inability to work at all implies Sam would not be able to delegate performance or purchase the goods from another source. **(C)** is incorrect because if cooperation which is necessary is not provided it may discharge the other parties performance duty. **(D)** is incorrect because supervening illegality discharges the contract.

8. **/D/** If pre-flight maintenance is determined to be a non-delegable duty, Fantasy will retain the legal responsibility for the damages. **(A)** is not the best answer because an airline is not always strictly liable; some showing of fault is usually

necessary. **(B)** is incorrect because the responsibility for some potentially dangerous functions cannot be delegated. **(C)** is incorrect because a hold harmless and indemnity agreement between a delegator and a delegatee is not binding on a third party Plaintiff.

9. **/D/** If a landlord wishes to prevent subletting and assignment of a lease, both must be mentioned in the contract. **(A)** is incorrect, because assignment is a separate category, not a subset of subletting. **(B)** is incorrect because the law does not require landlord permission for assignment unless the lease so states. **(C)** is incorrect because restraints on leaseholds are common, they are just strictly construed: in other words, if the lease only mentions subletting, the prohibition does not extend to other restraints such as assignment. Note that this is different from restraints on alienation for sales of property, which generally result in property title being conveyed in fee simple absolute as a default.

10. **/C/** Assuming Defendant properly laid the foundation for Walter's testimony, Walter's experience and the fact that he is basing his opinion on facts used by others in the field makes him an expert and his opinion admissible. **(A)** is incorrect because the facts need not be admissible so long as the facts are such as are relied upon by other experts in the field. FRE 703. **(B)** is incorrect because education is only one factor in qualifying an expert. FRE 702. **(D)** is incorrect because certification does not necessarily prove that Walter is an expert by knowledge, skill, experience, training, or education. If there was evidence of the

qualifications for certification then the certification may be sufficient.

11. **/C/** Molly intentionally confined Dan and moved him in the car to another location. **(A)** is not the best answer because although the confinement happened after movement had ceased, both did occur. **(B)** is not the best answer because a possible means of escape is not necessarily reasonable. Molly might have had a weapon, or Dan might have injured Molly or himself in an attempt to overpower her. **(D)** is incorrect because the relationship between defendant and victim is not relevant to the kidnapping inquiry.

12. **/B/** An indictment or information must allege basic facts in support of the charge. **(A)** is not the best answer because the charge is specifically named, including degree. **(C)** is incorrect because an indictment is handed down by a grand jury, but an information can be filed by the prosecutor without a grand jury hearing. **(D)** is incorrect because a prosecutor signs the information, not a judge.

13. **/B/** Gibson was not an Article III federal judge, so the protections do not apply. **(A)** is incorrect because Gibson was not an Article III federal judge, so the protections do not apply. He was in an Article I tribunal, not Article III. **(C)** is not the best answer because Gibson may be terminated at will, unless he is promised otherwise or is protected as a life tenured federal judge under Article III. **(D)** is incorrect. Gibson sustained an injury in fact directly caused from government action.

14. **/C/** Sam prevails because the contingency requires a good faith effort by Bob to find financing. Bob acted in bad faith by causing the financing process to fail, and he thereby breached the contract. Sam has the option of keeping the earnest money as liquidated damages or selling to another to determine actual damages. **(A)** is incorrect because the contingency required a good faith effort by Bob, which was lacking here. **(B)** is incorrect because the contract is enforceable unless the contingency is not satisfied after a good faith effort by Bob. **(D)** is incorrect because in property transactions, specific performance is a remedy available only to the buyer, not the seller.

15. **/C/** The statute as written requires knowledge of its existence to violate. Therefore, ignorance of it can be a defense unless there is proof that Tully did know or had reason to know of its existence. **(A)** is incorrect because the statute as written requires knowledge of its existence to violate. **(B)** is incorrect because the statute as written requires knowledge of its existence to violate. **(D)** is incorrect because the statute as written requires knowledge of its existence to violate.

16. **/B/** Under the modern rule, both parties need not have actual intent to commit the offense for one party to be convicted of conspiracy. **(A)** is incorrect. Under the modern rule, both parties need not have actual intent to commit the offense for one party to be convicted of conspiracy. **(C)** is incorrect because merely entering the building is insufficient to prove conspiracy. **(D)** is not the best answer because the offense is

placing an illegal wager, which as defined by the statute requires only one person.

17. **/A/** The proper *Miranda* warnings must say, "You have the right to an attorney" and also include, "If you cannot afford an attorney, one will be appointed for you." **(B)** is incorrect because improper *Miranda* warnings render a subsequent voluntary confession inadmissible, regardless of waiver. **(C)** is not the best answer because the *Miranda* violation makes any inquiry into voluntariness moot. **(D)** is not the best answer because the *Miranda* violation makes any inquiry into voluntariness moot.

18. **/C/** The Confrontation Clause requires that a defendant has a right to be confronted with the witnesses against him, although the right is not absolute. The burden is on the prosecution to demonstrate why the witnesses cannot appear. **(A)** is not the best answer because the Confrontation Clause requires that a defendant has a right to be confronted with the witnesses against him, although the right is not absolute. The burden is on the prosecution to demonstrate why the witnesses cannot appear—whether the statements are reliable is irrelevant to the inquiry. **(B)** is not the best answer because the burden is on the prosecution to demonstrate why the witnesses cannot appear. **(D)** is not the best answer because the burden is on the prosecution to demonstrate why the witnesses cannot appear.

19. **/A/** The tort liability is joint and several and both defendants, Slugger and Nasty, are liable for the full $20,000 judgment. The relative fault of each of the joint tort-feasors does not limit the Plaintiff's recovery of the full amount from each of the tort-feasors. **(B)** is incorrect because it involves contributions; the defendants are jointly and severally liable. **(C)** is incorrect because it involves contributions; the defendants are jointly and severally liable. **(D)** is incorrect because it involves contributions; the defendants are jointly and severally liable.

20. **/D/** Indemnity and contribution are not usually available between intentional tort-feasors even though they are jointly and severally liable for the whole judgment. Intentional torts are different from negligence where comparative fault may support indemnity and contribution. Here, the facts make it clear that Slugger and Nasty were engaged in the intentional torts of assault and battery without any viable privilege or defense. **(A)** is incorrect because indemnity and contribution are not usually available between intentional tort-feasors even though they are jointly and severally liable for the whole judgment. **(B)** is incorrect because indemnity and contribution are not usually available between intentional tort-feasors even though they are jointly and severally liable for the whole judgment. **(C)** is incorrect because indemnity and contribution are not usually available between intentional tort-feasors even though they are jointly and severally liable for the whole judgment.

21. **/A/** States may implement "reverse discrimination" programs only if there is a record of past discrimination in the sector at issue. There may be a problem by calling it a quota as opposed to a numerical goal, but this question asks for the best argument. **(B)** is incorrect. Were the quota to violate equal

protection, it would make no difference that it is a statute or by what means or by what majority the statute was implemented. **(C)** is incorrect. Showing that the program is narrowly tailored is only half of the strict scrutiny test. **(D)** is incorrect. Showing a "compelling" state interest is the other half of strict scrutiny, which by itself is insufficient.

22. **/D/** The signature of the party to be charged is required by the statute of frauds. **(A)** is incorrect because the firm offer rule extends the revocability period to three months. **(B)** is incorrect because consideration is not an absolute necessity under the UCC firm offer principle made by a merchant. In addition, requirement contracts do not have to specify a quantity under the UCC. **(C)** is incorrect because only the seller must be a merchant under the firm offer rule.

23. **/D/** There is no question that the Sally to General offer came into effect on May 1. Further, there is nothing that indicates that the owner Microhard does not have the right to enforce the contract against the general contractor. **(A)** is not the best answer because I is incorrect. A subcontractor's bid becomes irrevocable until the general contractor is awarded the prime contract. **(B)** is not the best answer because I is incorrect. A subcontractor's bid becomes irrevocable until the general contractor is awarded the prime contract. **(C)** is not the best answer because IV is incorrect. General knew or should have known that Sally's bid price was unreasonably low and this would excuse Sally's unilateral mistake.

24. **/C/** If Sally can demonstrate she is not liable under contract law, no remedy for breach of contract, including specific performance would exist. **(A)** is not a good defense because construction contracts are not always personal service contracts. **(B)** is not a good defense because an architect could determine satisfactory performance. **(D)** is incorrect because there is no showing that Microhard had any knowledge of Sally's unilateral mistake; this is usually a prerequisite for an in quasi contract recovery.

25. **/A/** Even though driver himself is not a party, he is the agent of a party thus his admissions are deemed made by the employer. **(B)** is incorrect because a witness must first be unavailable to take advantage of this exception. **(C)** is incorrect because the driver is an agent of the party. **(D)** is incorrect because witness unavailability is not a prerequisite to all hearsay exclusions, rather only certain ones.

26. **/A/** Because this is a race-notice jurisdiction, Carter wins because he was first to file and notice was not a factor for him (no prior conveyance that conflicted). **(B)** is incorrect because having a quitclaim deed (as opposed to a statutory warranty deed) does not affect the validity for filing purposes. **(C)** is incorrect because whether Carter paid value is irrelevant: the for value criterion only applies to subsequent purchasers. Since he filed first in time with no prior title conflicts, he wins. **(D)** is incorrect because in a race-notice jurisdiction, his filing later than Carter still defeats his claim.

27. /B/ This is the best answer because the others are wrong. It would be helpful to know if assault is punishable by one year in prison and when Frederick was released from prison. **(A)** is incorrect because the conviction is a certified copy of a public record under FRE 902(4). **(C)** is incorrect because a prior crime need not be exclusively about dishonesty. **(D)** is incorrect because the prohibition on extrinsic evidence applies to non-criminal acts.

28. /C/ The best answer because if the court found that those sales did not substantially affect interstate commerce, then it would be an impermissible use of the commerce clause. **(A)** is incorrect as the general welfare is not a source of congressional power. **(B)** is incorrect, as it is a limitation on the tax power. The fee will be upheld. **(D)** is incorrect, as the remedy for a "taking" is just compensation, not striking the statute.

29. /D/ The bill can be introduced as an admission by Attorney that his damages are really $5,000.00. **(A)** is incorrect because the client holds the privilege (note that privilege is also waived in disputes between lawyer and client). **(B)** is incorrect because the bill is an admission. **(C)** is incorrect because the fact evidence is contradictory does not make it admissible.

30. /D/ These are classic examples of trade fixtures. Unlike regular fixtures, they do not become the property of the landlord, but may be removed when the tenant leaves. The tenant is generally responsible for costs of restoring the property to its prior state. **(A)** is incorrect because they are not generic fixtures, but trade fixtures, and do not become the landlord's property. **(B)** is incorrect because Rex is responsible for any damage. **(C)** is incorrect because the items are "trade fixtures" as opposed to simple "fixtures." If (D) was not available, this would be the next best answer. However, (D) is more complete, therefore it is a better answer.

31. /C/ The last two answers (C) and (D) are troublesome, because they could be read as implying that the challenger has the burden of proof. (C) is an accurate statement and the best answer. If the state cannot meet its burden of showing a compelling state interest in limiting family size, the legislation falls. This is a very difficult and lengthy question involving strict scrutiny of substantive due process and equal protection. **(A)** is incorrect, because it asserts only half of the test and ignores the narrow tailoring and the entire equal protection problem. **(B)** is incorrect, because both the right to have children and be free from governmental racial discrimination are both qualify for strict scrutiny. The answer assumes rational basis scrutiny. **(D)** is not the best answer as it suggests a more difficult case than would prevail under strict scrutiny. While true, (C) is a better answer as it is a more accurate showing of the level of proof.

32. /C/ Burglary involves the breaking and entering of a structure at night with the intent to commit a felony or larceny therein. **(A)** is incorrect because the crime intended must actually be a felony; it is not sufficient that the defendant mistakenly believe it is a felony. **(B)** is incorrect because it misstates the issue – given that Sally did not intend to commit a felony, burglary is a legal impossibility, not a factual one. Legal impossibility is a defense. **(D)** is incorrect because completion of the crime is not required for a burglary charge, if the crime is a felony, it is sufficient that the defendant intended that crime at the time of entry.

33. **/D/** Intoxication is a matter that does not require specialized knowledge. The jury can infer such from the witness descriptions. **(A)** is incorrect because even though an expert, expert testimony must be helpful, not redundant. **(B)** is incorrect because there is no testimony that experts use witness statements to make opinions. Even if there were, it is only relevant to the analysis when the facts are not admissible. FRE 703. **(C)** is incorrect because an expert may opine on an ultimate issue to be decided by the trier of fact.

34. **/D/** Otis is entitled to compensation for the taking of his property. Jack is entitled to compensation because his property right is a profit a prendre protected by the due process clause. **(A)** is incorrect because eminent domain gives the state the right to take, but it must compensate for the takings. **(B)** is incorrect because it is incomplete: it only gives one party's compensation. **(C)** is incorrect because it is incomplete: it only gives one party's compensation.

35. **/A/** The breaching party retains risk of loss until the non-breaching party has insurance coverage. **(B)** is incorrect because the goods didn't arrive at Falcon's place of business. **(C)** is incorrect because a possible violation of the UCC's statute of frauds would not affect the risk of loss. **(D)** is incorrect because Falcon did not have title.

36. **/D/** The best answer based on elimination of the other alternatives and the fact that Harriet Host could be found negligent. The half price of the meat might have been notice that there was some irregularity in the product. This could have created a duty to investigate the reason for the low price. If this investigation had been made, Harriet might have cooked the meat more thoroughly, thus avoiding the effect of the spoiling. **(A)** is incorrect because strict liability applies to a merchant in the business of selling the product producing the damages; here, Harriet was a casual party not in the business of selling steak dinners. **(B)** is incorrect because it misstates the duty in negligence; it is not necessary to prove a reckless disregard – only a failure to exercise reasonable care. **(C)** is incorrect because anyone injured by a defective product can usually bring a negligence or strict liability claim if it was foreseeable that they might be injured.

37. **/A/** The meat was defective when it left the Defendant's store and they were in the business of selling those goods. Further, (A) is a better answer than alternative (D) since res ipsa loquitur only applies to negligence. **(B)** is incorrect because it implies the 50% discount is a proper warning and thus the purchaser assumed the risk. The discount was not a proper warning since it did not refer to the danger or defects and the goods were not sold "as is." Further, such a defense would only be applicable to a negligence claim and here, the more likely claim is for strict liability. **(C)** is incorrect because under both

strict liability and negligence theories, privity has been abolished as long as it should have been foreseeable such Ps would suffer injury from the defective product. **(D)** is not the best answer because res ipsa loquitur is only applicable to a negligence action in which circumstantial evidence is sufficient to infer that such damages would not have occurred in the absence of the Meat Market's negligence.

38. **/C/** This is the best alternative because it correctly identifies the cause of the injury and clarifies that this cause was not under the control of Charlie. **(A)** is incorrect because res ipsa loquitur does not apply to strict liability and the meat did not leave Charlie's control in a dangerously defective condition. **(B)** is not the best answer because the question of contributory negligence or applied assumption of risk due to the 50% price reduction does not impact the doctrine of res ipsa loquitur. If there is direct evidence of negligence, res ipsa loquitur does not apply; this direct evidence is that the retailer's trucking company was negligent. **(D)** is incorrect because it assumes the harm created was in the packaging rather than in the lack of refrigeration caused by the retailer's trucking company.

39. **/C/** FRE 404(a)(1) requires that the accused's character trait be pertinent, thus requiring some relevance to the issues at trial. His honesty is not on trial. Since Derrick never took the stand his reputation for honesty cannot be admitted. **(A)** is incorrect for this reason. **(B)** is another way of stating (A), and is incorrect since Derrick never took the stand and put his honesty at issue. Watch for universal statements. **(D)** is incorrect because the prosecution

may not "open the door," but may walk through it if opened by the accused.

40. **/B/** The Jury may rely upon the presumption to find Greg in possession. The other answers would require the jury to conclude one way or the other. Therefore, **(A)** is incorrect because of the word "must." In a criminal case, the presumption never conclusively establishes a fact. In a civil case, the fact may be established by the presumption unless rebutted. **(C)** is incorrect because of the word "must." In a criminal case, the presumption never conclusively establishes a fact. In a civil case, the fact may be established by the presumption unless rebutted. **(D)** is incorrect because of the word "must." In a criminal case, the presumption never conclusively establishes a fact. In a civil case, the fact may be established by the presumption unless rebutted.

41. **/A/** The best answer because this clause prevents a state from discriminating against another state's citizens, and there is no market participant exception. **(B)** is incorrect. This clause prevents a state from discriminating against another state's citizens, and there is no market participant exception. **(C)** is incorrect, because rational basis is not the standard. **(D)** is totally incorrect. A proper challenge on the merits is given, and standing is not on the merits. Also, state action and standing are two different doctrines.

42. **/D/** Under the common law, a tenant is responsible to continue paying for premises that are destroyed. An exception applies if the tenant is only renting space in a building and not the building and land. **(A)** is

incorrect because it is not a breach to vacate destroyed premises if they were only part of a building. **(B)** is incorrect because it is not a breach to vacate destroyed premises if they were only part of a building. **(C)** is incorrect because this is not constructive eviction or a breach of the warranty of habitability; it is a separate category under the common law for destroyed premises. Constructive eviction would have required a landlord interference with the enjoyment of property; this was a third party, not the landlord. Also, breach of the warranty of habitability requires a breach of the landlord's duty. Here, there was no such breach – again a third party destroyed the property.

43. **/C/** The victims gave their money temporarily, in the expectation that it would be returned with interest. This is larceny by trick— possession, but not title, is given voluntarily by the victim as a result of the defendants' fraud. **(A)** is not the best answer because the victims gave their money voluntarily. **(B)** is incorrect because the victims gave their money temporarily, in the expectation that it would be returned with interest. **(D)** is incorrect because there was no threat of force against the victims.

44. **/D/** Even with criminal intent and acts in furtherance, a defendant has not participated in a conspiracy unless there is agreement with the other participants. **(A)** is incorrect because Wendy and Lisa did not know or agree to Prince's participation, so he cannot be convicted of conspiracy. **(B)** is irrelevant because of the lack of agreement. **(C)** misstates the facts.

45. **/A/** Non-private public speech carries no expectation of privacy, therefore taping by police is not a Fourth Amendment violation. **(B)** is incorrect because harmless error is an appellate review standard, not a trial court standard to determine admissibility. **(C)** is incorrect because non-private public speech carries no expectation of privacy, therefore taping by police is not a Fourth Amendment violation. **(D)** is incorrect because no consent is required when the speech is public.

46. **/D/** The separate sovereigns exception to the double jeopardy rule applies when the there is a state prosecution followed by a federal prosecution. **(A)** is incorrect because the separate sovereigns exception to the double jeopardy rule applies when the there is a state prosecution followed by a federal prosecution. **(B)** is not the best answer because the crimes must each contain an element separate from the other to avoid offending double jeopardy – merely being "not identical" is insufficient. **(C)** is incorrect because the separate sovereigns exception to the double jeopardy rule applies when the there is a state prosecution followed by a federal prosecution.

47. **/A/** The unilateral offer was accepted by shipment. Acceptance is different than full performance. The performance was breach because the goods did not conform and there was no time left for a cure. **(B)** is incorrect because this was an acceptance and a breach. **(C)** is incorrect because acceptance of an unilateral contract is by performance. **(D)** is incorrect because acceptance was effective by

shipping, regardless of whether the goods conformed.

48. **/C/** The implied warranties of merchantability and title result. The implied warranty of fitness for a particular purpose requires a buyer asking the seller to use their expertise in selecting the most appropriate item for a buyer's particular purpose. Unless disclaimed all goods carry an implied warranty of merchantability and title. **(A)** is not the best answer because another selection is also correct. **(B)** is not the best answer because another selection is also correct. **(D)** is not the best answer because the facts do not indicate a situation that would qualify for the implied warranty of fitness.

49. **/C/** Strict liability is imposed for damages created by wild animals. The cougar is not a domestic animal so strict liability applies. **(A)** is incorrect because contributory negligence or fault is not a complete defense to strict liability. **(B)** is incorrect because even assuming the Defendant letting the cats out into the alley did not violate due care, the standard to be applied is one of strict liability. **(D)** is incorrect because the Defendant takes the victim as she finds him.

50. **/A/** The state can tax private contractors provided the legal incidence of the tax does not fall on the federal government. The Army probably cannot be taxed. **(B)** is incorrect. The store can be taxed if it is privately owned. **(C)** is incorrect. Soldiers can be taxed by a non-discriminatory liquor sales tax. **(D)** is not the best answer. The incidence of the tax falls on the individual soldiers and not the government directly.

51. **/C/** A covenant is considered abandoned if it has ceased to be enforced in the affected community or subdivision. Ham radio towers are fairly rare, so if 15 had been erected, one could conclude that particular covenant had been abandoned. **(A)** is incorrect because abandonment of one covenant is not automatic abandonment of all others. **(B)** is incorrect because abandonment of one covenant is not automatic abandonment of all others. **(D)** because one of the other alternatives is correct.

52. **/D/** Battery is an intentional harmful or offensive contact with a person; a dog is not a person, so the requisite intent to harm a human person is missing. A negligence action would still be possible. **(A)** is incorrect because there is nothing in the facts to suggest force was necessary nor did the Plaintiff do anything to provoke or justify Defendant's mistaken belief. **(B)** is incorrect because nominal damages are recoverable for battery. **(C)** is not the best answer because a mistake caused by the Defendant's mental illness is not a defense if the wrongful act was done with intention. Such a mistake is not reasonable.

53. **/A/** Popeye may seek injunctive relief because Brutus' offer does not create mootness, which occurs when the defendant voluntarily stops injuring but may restart at any time. **(B)** is not the best answer. Although Brutus may have a good argument for turning over a new leaf, knocking over 14 mailboxes is good evidence that he may do it again. **(C)** is not the best answer. Although Brutus may have a good argument for turning over a new

leaf, knocking over 14 mailboxes is good evidence that he may do it again. **(D)** is incorrect because Popeye sought both money damages and injunctive relief.

54. /C/ Chuck most likely has an easement under prescription. Prescription requires the "CHO" elements of adverse possession, but not the "E": exclusive possession is not required during the adverse use period. **(A)** is incorrect because Chuck appears to have met the elements of prescription. Until he had met all the requirements for prescription, the remedy to eject him was an action for trespass, but now it is too late. **(B)** is incorrect because the doctrine of necessity requires no other reasonable route into the property. Chuck has at least one alternative – clearing a road through his own property. **(D)** is incorrect because he has not actually exercised sufficient control over the land to constitute possession, and his use has not been exclusive. Therefore, it more closely fits prescription.

55. /D/ Because Greg rebutted the presumption, the jury is not required to find that Greg had control of the leased property, but it may find such. If Greg did not rebut the evidence, then the presumption is established, but liability may not be presumed because the police officer still has the burden of persuasion. **(A)** is incorrect because Greg rebutted the presumption. The jury is not required to find that Greg had control, but it may find such. **(B)** is not the best answer because the police officer still has the burden of persuasion on the issue of liability. **(C)** is incorrect because Greg rebutted the presumption. The jury

is not required to find that Greg had control, but it may find such.

56. /D/ A buyer may accept some units of a non-conforming tender and by using one-quarter of the chips this amount was deemed accepted. [UCC 2.601] **(A)** is not the best answer since there was a partial acceptance and the law allows a subsequent revocation if the goods are non-conforming. **(B)** is incorrect because only one-quarter of the chips were accepted and the rest rejected upon notice being received by Hintel. **(C)** is incorrect since it seems to assume that the buyer's sole remedy on a seller's breach is to resell the non-conforming goods. [UCC 2.608]

57. /C/ The best answer since a buyer always has a reasonable right to inspect the goods before final acceptance. If the hidden defect can only be discovered through a performance test, as here, that test is allowed even after payment. **(A)** is incorrect because payment, without more, does not operate as a waiver. **(B)** is not the best answer, even though the UCC does require a rejection because of non-conformity to be made within a reasonable time of receipt. Two months does not appear to be an unreasonable time period for Orange to begin testing in and the notification was made as soon as the defect was discovered. **(D)** is incorrect because testing was not prohibited in the contract and a buyer always has an inspection right; where the defect is hidden or of a performance nature, testing is allowed. [UCC 2.607]

58. /C/ The court would likely interpret the contract as divisible and hold that the buyer elected to use only one-quarter of the total or 25,000 chips.

A buyer may accept any commercial unit and reject the rest of non-conforming goods. [UCC 2.601] The list price would have been $25,000 and the $10,000 incidental damages that the buyer was forced to take as a discount would be deducted leaving a net amount of $15,000 cost, so $85,000 of the $100,000 should be refunded. [UCC 2.710] **(A)** is incorrect because a buyer of non-conforming goods who has paid the seller is entitled to a refund. **(B)** is incorrect because the law will require some payment for the 25,000 chips since the buyer sold the system; the incidental damages would be deducted for this lot. **(D)** is incorrect because the law will require some payment for the 25,000 chips since the buyer sold the system, realizing a benefit.

59. **/B/** The best answer because had the Defendant made this feasible escape, the encounter would not have occurred. **(A)** is incorrect because while deadly force may not be used to defend property, it may be used to defend one's self. **(C)** is not the best answer since this goes to the reasonableness of the Defendant's reaction to the Plaintiff's aggression which would be a contested question of fact. **(D)** is incorrect because deadly force may be used to defend one's self as long as such use is not unreasonable under the circumstances.

60. **/A/** The exception to denying federal taxpayer standing is an establishment clause challenge to a law passed under the tax and spend power of Congress. **(B)** is incorrect. While state citizens may have standing to challenge measurable expenditures of the state, the federal government passed this law and funds the program. **(C)** is incorrect, because it is a generalized grievance against the policy of the government. **(D)** is incorrect, because there is no causal link to his injury, assuming he can show none other than taxpayer standing.

61. **/D/** The best answer, because the *Lemon* test requires a secular purpose for government actions to stay within bounds of the Establishment Clause. One state is a focus arguably too narrow for federal legislation. **(A)** is incorrect, because the Commerce Clause may not be exercised in violation of a limit on government power, and it is given that the law is passed under the spending clause—not the commerce clause. **(B)** is incorrect, because it states an element of the incorrect test. **(C)** is incorrect. Ownership of the books remaining with USEA would not save the program if the primary purpose or effect is to advance religion.

62. **/D/** The best answer because it states one element of the *Lemon* test for the establishment clause. This question calls for equal protection and establishment clause analysis. **(A)** is incorrect. Primary effect is probably easier to show than intentional discrimination. **(B)** is incorrect. Equal protection protects from intentional discrimination, not merely disproportionate benefits. **(C)** is incorrect as it tends to show discriminatory impact, not intent. Impact is merely the means to show discriminatory intent (or motivation).

63. **/A/** Defendant is trying to imply that Wilma is biased and may have an improper motive to fabricate her story. The hearsay is admissible to rebut this under FRE 801(d)(1)(B): it is consistent with Wilma's testimony and is offered to rebut a charge against the declarant of recent fabrication. **(B)** is incorrect because Wilma's statement was not contemporaneous with the event. **(C)** is incorrect because Husband is testifying to Wilma's statement not his own prior statement. See FRE 613. **(D)** is incorrect because Wilma was not acting in the course and scope of her employment because she was already home.

64. **/B/** Evidence of other crimes may be introduced to establish the identity of Bill as the perpetrator. FRE 404(b). **(A)** is incorrect because Bill must offer the character evidence first. The prosecution may then rebut the evidence with character evidence of its own. **(C)** is incorrect because even if the evidence tends to infer action in conformity therewith it is offered for another purpose: establishing identity. **(D)** is incorrect because this evidence is not impeachment evidence, rather identity evidence.

65. **/A/** Under the doctrine of equitable conversion, risk of loss (including from fire) passes to the buyer as soon as the contract is executed. The seller maintains legal title until closing. Because the risk of loss passed to the buyer, he has an insurable interest. **(B)** is incorrect because the risk passes upon contract execution, not upon possession by the buyer. **(C)** is incorrect because even though Sally is the legal owner, Roger is the equitable owner and therefore bears the risk of loss. **(D)** is incorrect because Roger had an interest as discussed above.

66. **/D/** An element of embezzlement is the intent to permanently deprive the owner of his property. Without that intent, embezzlement cannot be proved. **(A)** is incorrect because an element of embezzlement is the intent to permanently deprive the owner of his property. **(B)** is not the best answer because willingness to make reparations does not excuse criminal liability. **(C)** is incorrect because a transgression may be both an ethical and a legal violation.

67. **/D/** The Plaintiff will win if the Defendant was negligent. The only particular choice available to the Defendant was which landing to attempt to minimize the expected damages. If her choice was unreasonable, she will be liable. **(A)** is not the best answer because a Defendant is not necessarily liable for damages resulting from products she used unless there was also some fault on her part. **(B)** is not the best answer because the judgment of a pilot in an emergency must still be reasonable under the emergency circumstances. **(C)** is incorrect in that the Defendant is not the manufacturer of the product so any duty to inspect would only arise if there were some notice or warning and here the facts state that the defect was internal.

68. **/B/** The best answer because the manufacturer will be liable if the plane's electrical ignition was in a defective condition when it left the Defendant's control. **(A)** is not the best answer because the manufacturer's liability must be based on a defect which created the injury; no defect was mentioned in this alternative. **(C)** is incorrect because "last clear chance" of Defendant is intended to help the Plaintiff overcome contributory negligence and comparative fault and there is nothing in the facts to

indicate that applies here. **(D)** is incorrect because contributory negligence is not a defense in strict products liability actions.

69. /C/ The least viable defense is that the Plaintiff lacked privity since the Defendant's duty extends to anyone foreseeably endangered by the product. **(A)** is incorrect (and thus a viable defense) because if the product was expected to undergo significant changes before it reaches the user, strict products liability may not apply. **(B)** is incorrect (and thus a viable defense) because strict products liability requires the product to be in a defective condition when it left the Defendant. **(D)** is not the best answer (and thus a viable defense) because the Defendant manufacturer could still be liable under strict products liability if it was foreseeable that the plane's pilot would have to make an emergency landing after the plane's ignition failed. Notice this question specified the recovery theory was in strict products liability, not negligence.

70. /B/ The original contract was voidable at Ike's options since he lacked capacity, so Main Motorcycle can only collect the amount the infant ratified. **(A)** is incorrect because there was a contract ratification after the promisor had capacity; had ratification not occurred, Main could have sought return of the motorcycle through restitution. **(C)** is incorrect in that the motorcycle is not a necessary; had it been, the fair value might have been the recovery amount. **(D)** is incorrect because it disregards the fact that Ike ratified the luxury purchase so at least the ratified amount would be recoverable.

71. /A/ This is triple hearsay, but each level of hearsay falls under an exception. Blake's threat is an admission by party-opponent, Bonnie's statement to the mother is a dying declaration, and the mother's statement to the officer is an excited utterance. Each level must have its own exception. Thus the other answers are incorrect. **(B)** is not the best answer because each level of hearsay falls under a hearsay exception, so the entire statement is admissible. **(C)** is not the best answer because each level of hearsay falls under a hearsay exception, so the entire statement is admissible. **(D)** is not the best answer because each level of hearsay falls under a hearsay exception, so the entire statement is admissible.

72. /B/ Although permanent deprivation was not specifically be intended, Barney intended to use the property in a manner that made it unlikely the owner would get it back. **(A)** is not the best answer because it misstates the law – taking without permission does not create strict liability for larceny. **(C)** is incorrect because it ignores his intended use, which was likely to deprive the owner of the property. **(D)** is incorrect because he returned the property devoid of any value.

73. /D/ First Mutual receives $170,000 and Second Bank only receives $45,000, because the amount available is only $215,000. Because First Mutual is first in line as a creditor, their debt is satisfied first. Second Bank receives only the remainder up to the amount of the foreclosure sale. If there had been excess money left after satisfying both the first and second mortgages, Mort would have received that. **(A)** is incorrect because First Mutual is first in line as a creditor, so their debt is satisfied first. Second Bank receives only the remainder up to the amount of the foreclosure sale. **(B)** is incorrect because First Mutual is first in line as a creditor, so their debt is satisfied first. Second Bank receives only the remainder up to the amount of the foreclosure sale. **(C)** is incorrect because First Mutual is first in line as a creditor, so their debt is satisfied first. Second Bank receives only the remainder up to the amount of the foreclosure sale.

74. /**C**/ Because Second Bank is the only perfected creditor, it is first in line for repayment on the foreclosure sale. First Mutual then receives the remainder of the sale proceeds as a general creditor. **(A)** is incorrect because First Mutual is still a general creditor; its debt will be repaid with any remaining funds after all secured parties have been paid. **(B)** is incorrect because Second Bank is only owed $49,000 at the time of foreclosure. **(D)** is incorrect because another alternative is the correct solution.

75. /**C**/ Because Mort never defaulted on the mortgage with First Mutual, he can recover by paying the entire debt on the second mortgage. Second Bank is the only entity that has a cause of action against him (assuming that First Mutual had no acceleration clause that required payment in full if he defaulted on ANY loan related to that property). **(A)** is incorrect because the correct amount due to Second Bank is $49,000, the amount due at time of default. **(B)** is incorrect because the correct amount due to Second Bank is $49,000, the amount due at time of default. **(D)** is incorrect

because under the theory of equitable redemption, he can get the property back by paying off the debt that is in default up to the time of the foreclosure sale.

76. /**B**/ Hearsay evidence may both impeach Robert and substantively establish the time period in which the squatters possessed the land. **(A)** is incorrect because hearsay evidence may both impeach Robert and substantively establish the time period in which the squatters possessed the land. **(C)** is incorrect because former testimony of an unavailable witness is admissible. **(D)** is incorrect because the testimony is not of a prior act.

77. /**A**/ This is the best answer. **(B)** is incorrect because this exception requires that the declarant be unavailable. **(C)** is incorrect because of the admission exception. **(D)** is incorrect because there are no contents of documents being proved.

78. /**C**/ Duress is an available defense to arson. **(A)** is incorrect because if King cannot be convicted of the underlying felony, he also cannot be convicted of the resulting murder, even if the felony was inherently dangerous. **(B)** is not the best answer because the duress applies to the arson. **(D)** is incorrect because the death of rescuers in a deadly situation is always foreseeable.

79. /**C**/ The question turns on the measure of damages allowed under strict products liability. The drill press cost of $50,000 would be recovered as would the injury to the workman of $15,000. The adjoining pieces of equipment on the assembly line worth $75,000 would also be

recoverable. This totals $140,000 (50,000 + 15,000 + 75,000) The laid-off employees' wages of $14,400 would not be a part of damages under strict products liability. These are consequential damages which would only be recovered under negligence. **(A)** is incorrect because that combination of damages would not be recoverable under strict products liability. **(B)** is incorrect because that combination of damages would not be recoverable under strict products liability. **(D)** is incorrect because that combination of damages would not be recoverable under strict products liability.

80. **/C/** This statement is probably enough to allow the film to be shown. The test for obscenity requires a lack of literary, artistic, political, and scientific value. **(A)** is too limited in scope to succeed. **(B)** is incorrect as it tends to show obscenity. Even normal sex can be depicted in a manner that appeals to the prurient interest and is patently offensive. **(D)** is incorrect as it tends to show obscenity.

81. **/C/** Dan's promise to hire a workman to keep the winter access road open was an accord that he failed to satisfy. Peter (the obligee) may sue on either the original obligation or the accord. **(A)** is not the best answer because Dan's promise to hire a workman to keep the winter access road open was an accord that he failed to satisfy. Peter (the obligee) may sue on either the original obligation or the accord. **(B)** is not the best answer because Dan's promise to hire a workman to keep the winter access road open was an accord that he failed to satisfy. Peter (the obligee) may sue on either the original obligation or the accord. **(D)** is incorrect

because Dan's promise to hire a workman to keep the winter access road open was an accord that he failed to satisfy. Peter (the obligee) may sue on either the original obligation or the accord.

82. **/D/** A detriment to the promisee – forbearing from filing a valid legal claim – constitutes adequate consideration if it is bargained for, which appears to be the situation here. **(A)** is incorrect because even if the legal claim was invalid, the consideration is adequate if Peter had a good faith belief it was valid. **(B)** is incorrect in that the test is whether the party forbearing to sue perceived the agreement to be legally valid. **(C)** is incorrect because this is not an aleatory contract, but if it was, it could be enforceable if a future pre-defined event occurred.

83. **/B/** If other than the promisor and promisee are contemplated to receive rights from performance of a contract they are characterized as third party beneficiaries. If the third party is owed a pre-existing duty they are a creditor beneficiary; here, Peter was owed a duty by the delegator, Don. **(A)** is incorrect because lack of privity does not prohibit an obligee's legal recovery against the delegatee; the obligee becomes a third party beneficiary of the delegation contract between Don and Dumbbell Defendant. **(C)** is incorrect since Peter is a creditor beneficiary because he was owed a pre-existing duty. **(D)** is incorrect; Peter was intended to receive rights under the delegation contract and he is an intended creditor beneficiary.

84. **/C/** The conveyance is ineffective because Grandma never delivered the deed. **(A)** is incorrect because

it ignores the non-delivery. **(B)** is incorrect because filing now would not satisfy delivery. **(D)** is incorrect because there is no indication of detrimental reliance in this fact pattern.

85. /**D**/ All of the above is correct. Federal government may tax all proprietary state businesses, which are easily operated by a private entity. Each of these has been found taxable in case law. **(A)** is not the best answer because each of these selections has been found taxable in case law. **(B)** is not the best answer because each of these selections has been found taxable in case law. **(C)** is not the best answer because each of these selections has been found taxable in case law.

86. /**D**/ A substantial issue is not present about strict liability since the activity is dangerous in and of itself. Thus it is not necessary that the Plaintiff show evidence of specific acts of negligence by D. **(A)** is incorrect; there is a substantial issue whether Plaintiff can prove causation. **(B)** is incorrect; there is a substantial question whether the court will recognize that the Ps have suffered a present damage. **(C)** is incorrect; there would seem to be a substantial question whether the Plaintiff will be able to liquidate whatever damages they suffered into a dollar amount.

87. /**B**/ The best answer because this is a special situation under the discovery rule where the injury accrues over time. The trigger date is when the injury has become apparent; the mere possibility of injury is not sufficient. This would seem to be the date when the Plaintiff is diagnosed with cancer. **(A)** is

incorrect because the tort discovery rule would apply. **(C)** is not the best answer (even though the result would be the same) because tolling only occurs after the statute of limitations has been triggered. **(D)** is incorrect because even strict liability claims are subject to a maximum period within which Plaintiff must formally initiate their claim.

88. /**C**/ An executory interest is one that will become possessory upon the termination of a prior estate. A shifting executory interest "divests" or cuts short a prior legal interest from one grantee to another upon the occurrence of a condition subsequent. **(A)** is incorrect because a remainder is a future interest that will become possessory upon termination of a prior estate, which is inevitable. The termination of nephew's and niece's estates are not inevitable. **(B)** is incorrect because a remainder is a future interest that will become possessory upon termination of a prior estate, which is inevitable. The termination of nephew's and niece's estates are not inevitable. **(D)** is incorrect because a springing interest cuts off the possessory right of the grantor, not grantee.

89. /**B**/ The Officer may testify that Smith was present based on his personal knowledge and perception of the events. His testimony regarding Smith's response and his name on the list is collateral to whether Smith was present for the watch. If the only evidence were Smith's name on the watch list, then the list would have to be admitted. **(A)** is incorrect because the issue is Smith's presence, not the presence of his name on the list. **(C)** is

incorrect because it is not the presence of Smith's name on the list that is being proved. **(D)** is incorrect because the Smith's statement is collateral to the issues and not substantive evidence.

90. /B/ His best argument is that he is being punished for conveying information he is allowed to publish under the First Amendment. **(A)** is incorrect. Federal government is allowed to impede interstate commerce. **(C)** is not right. There are no suspect classes, so this law will pass rational basis scrutiny. **(D)** is not right. It might be a violation of substantive due process, but the analysis will come back to the First Amendment as a defense.

91. /B/ A human being is legally defined as existing between live birth and the irreversible cessation of brain function. For murder or manslaughter to obtain, the victim must fulfill this definition. **(A)** is incorrect because even hastening a death that would have occurred anyway does not affect a murder charge (for example, stabbing someone with terminal cancer). **(C)** is incorrect, because specific intent does not always have to be present for a murder charge, for example felony murder. **(D)** is incorrect because the intentional infliction of serious bodily harm that later results in death is sufficient causation for a murder charge.

92. /C/ Voluntary manslaughter is a killing in the heat of passion after excusable provocation. If both of these conditions existed, the charge might be reduced. **(A)** is not the best answer because the defendant need not be cognitively aware of the danger of his actions if they are extremely reckless. **(B)** is incorrect

because a victim is not required to mitigate her injuries by seeking medical attention such that the defendant may escape criminal liability. **(D)** is incorrect because the tumor may have only been a substantial cause, she might have died anyway.

93. /A/ When a suspect has invoked his right to counsel during questioning clearly and unambiguously, questioning must cease until counsel is present or the suspect himself reinitiates conversation. Otherwise, *Miranda* is violated. **(B)** describes the rule relating to the waiver of the right to remain silent, not the right to counsel, and is therefore incorrect. **(C)** misstates the facts. **(D)** is not the best answer because, again, the issue is the right to counsel during questioning, not the right to remain silent.

94. /C/ The marital privilege applies to current or former spouses regarding communications made during a marriage. Marital incompetence prevents a current spouse from testifying against the other spouse. **(A)** is incorrect because marital incompetence prevents a current spouse from testifying against the other spouse. **(B)** is incorrect because privileges protect against any such evidence. **(D)** is incorrect because this is an admission by party-opponent.

95. /C/ Special purpose districts for things such as water rights are the exception to the rule of one person, one vote. **(A)** is incorrect. It states too broad of a rule. **(B)** is incorrect, it misstates the principle – it applies at all levels. **(D)** is a common incorrect answer – many state laws are preempted by federal principles.

96. /A/ A unilateral contract is an offer promise which requests performance as a means of acceptance. Here the promise to pay $500 was seeking a 10-day option and a reasonable at-will agreement as performance. **(B)** is incorrect; a firm option is allowed without consideration by a merchant for the sale of goods. Here, the subject of the contract is land which falls under the common law. In addition, the right to revoke makes this an illusory option. **(C)** is incorrect because promissory estoppel applies where consideration is lacking; even a bargained-for revocable option is some benefit to the promisor. **(D)** is incorrect because a quasi-contractual liability is an equitable remedy that applies only where a contract is lacking; here there is a contract.

97. /B/ I and III only. Alternative I would be a good argument to support the $500 recovery since this is what happened and it was bargained for. Alternative III would support a recovery. The parol evidence rule would exclude extrinsic evidence containing a term, which is also contained in the integrated agreement. Here the agreement does not contain any mention of payment, so this extrinsic evidence would not be excluded by the parol evidence rule. **(A)** is incorrect because alternative II is not plausibly supported by the facts; the written agreement stated that the offer was revocable and the $500 was never paid. **(C)** is incorrect because alternative II is not plausibly supported by the facts; the written agreement stated that the offer was revocable and the $500 was never paid. **(D)** is incorrect because alternative II is

not plausibly supported by the facts; the written agreement stated that the offer was revocable and the $500 was never paid.

98. /C/ II and III only. A revocation applies when the offeree learns of a word or act by the offeror inconsistent with keeping the offer open. Alternative II would support Fred's position because it recognizes that the lack of consideration is fatal to the creation of a common law option agreement. Alternative III is a plausible argument for Fred because under the theory of mutual assent the party's reasonable intentions are to be examined. If they are not met the promise is illusory and thus unenforceable. **(A)** is incorrect because alternative I is not a plausible argument to support Fred's position; while the statute of frauds requires a writing for the sale of land, there is no such writing requirement for a revocation. **(B)** is incorrect because alternative I is not a plausible argument to support Fred's position; while the statute of frauds requires a writing for the sale of land, there is no such writing requirement for a revocation. **(D)** is incorrect because alternative I is not a plausible argument to support Fred's position; while the statute of frauds requires a writing for the sale of land, there is no such writing requirement for a revocation.

99. /D/ Items I, II, III and IV of these arguments would support Oliver's position not to pay the commission. I is a good defense because agreements to employ an agent or broker to sell real property for a commission must be written in most jurisdictions. II is a good defense because without an effective offer and acceptance an enforceable contract can not result. III is a good defense because there was no express promise to pay a commission by the owner. Note, however, that there might have been a duty to respond to the statement expecting a commission and absent an affirmative statement a promise might be implied. IV is a good defense because a lack of consideration would defeat a contractual recovery even if Oliver had made a promise. Notice that the potential buyer's name was given before Ron requested the commission; past consideration is no consideration. **(A)** is not the best answer because more than one argument supports Oliver's position. **(B)** is not the best answer because more than two arguments support Oliver's position. **(C)** is not the best answer because more than three arguments support Oliver's position.

100./D/ None of the descendants are eligible because of the Rule Against Perpetuities (RAP). In order to qualify, all recipients must vest within 21 years of a life in being at his death. Since none of the people in this fact pattern meet that criterion, all are ineligible. **(A)** is incorrect because the devise violates the RAP. **(B)** is incorrect because the devise violates the RAP. **(C)** is incorrect because the devise violates the RAP.

101./A/ The interests of the police force in maintaining uniformity to promote the esprit de corps of the force outweighs the individual interest in his appearance. **(B)** is not the best answer – freedom of religion is not contingent upon other constitutional rights. **(C)** is incorrect. There is a burden on his religious practice, but the balance favors the state in this circumstance. **(D)** while arguably the better policy, is incorrect.

102./A/ This defense, if believed by the jury, would make the intercourse a nonvolitional act on Milo's part, and he would not be culpable. **(B)** is incorrect because statutory rape is a strict liability crime. **(C)** is incorrect because statutory rape is a strict liability crime. **(D)** is incorrect because statutory rape is a strict liability crime..

103./B/ This is the best answer because the class of persons protected by the statute may not be charged with soliciting another person to violate that statute. **(A)** is incorrect because no value need be offered for solicitation to occur – simple encouragement is sufficient. **(C)** misstates the law, only children under 7 are conclusively presumed incapable of forming criminal intent. **(D)** is not the best answer because even if evidence did suggest that sex was Tanya's idea, she would not be charged, as explained in **(B)**, above.

104./A/ This is the best answer because the others are incorrect. **(B)** is incorrect because the prohibition on extrinsic evidence is not applicable to prior convictions. **(C)** is incorrect because public records are excepted from hearsay. FRE 803(8). **(D)** is incorrect because certified public records are self-authenticating. FRE 902(4).

105./B/ The correct alternative since there is no duty to aid another unless there is a special status between the rescuer and the victim, the rescuer's negligence caused the harm or the rescuer began a rescue which made the Plaintiff's situation worse. **(A)** is incorrect because what a reasonable person might have done is only important in determining a duty level if there was a duty at all. **(C)** is incorrect because while Billy's self-inflicted intoxication might establish comparative fault by the Plaintiff, it does not replace the duty requirement that is missing. **(D)** is incorrect because merely stopping and examining the Plaintiff does not usually create a duty for an uncompensated non-involved rescuer.

106./A/ This is the best answer because to prevail would require that the Defendant be negligent. Nancy was inattentive and thus there was a failure to exercise reasonable care. **(B)** is incorrect because the reason that the Defendant did not see the Plaintiff was because she was inattentive and thus negligent. Notice this distinction and the distracter of intentional torts does not apply. **(C)** is incorrect because Nancy's inattentive driving caused Billy's injury and the resultant damages. Notice that Billy's drinking did not create a foreseeable danger of an inattentive driver going off the road; even if it did, it would not create comparative fault by the Plaintiff. **(D)** is not the best answer because it implies that the last clear chance defense would apply. If it applied, the last clear chance principle eliminates comparative fault by Plaintiff if the Defendant could have avoided the injury. The Defendant's lack of attention would have been tortious regardless of the Plaintiff's condition.

107./C/ Furious' silence is being offered as an out of court assertion that he is guilty of the crime. **(A)** is incorrect because it must be shown that a reasonable declarant would have had reason to deny the accusation. If Furious knew that Mr. Big was a police officer then his silence could be an admission. Note that the 5th Amendment was not an option in this question. **(B)** is incorrect because personal knowledge is not an exception to the hearsay rule. **(D)** is incorrect because assertive conduct can be an admission.

108./C/ Both statements are hearsay with no exception. **(A)** is incorrect because to be a prior witness identification, the witness must be testifying at trial, which the owner is not doing. FRE 801(d)(1). **(B)** is incorrect because a then-existing emotional, physical, or mental condition must be made at the time the condition is being experienced. FRE 803(3). The exception does not apply to a statement describing a past condition. **(D)** is incorrect because witness availability applies to exceptions under FRE 804 only.

109./D/ Self-defense is a complete defense to murder if the deadly force used was reasonable under the circumstances. If Colleen acted in self-defense, even based on an honest and reasonable mistake of fact, she will be acquitted. **(A)** is not the best answer because an insanity plea would not result in acquittal, but in involuntary commitment to a psychiatric hospital. **(B)** is incorrect because voluntary intoxication is not a defense. **(C)** is incorrect because malice aforethought is the mens rea for first degree murder. Intent need not be proven for a second degree murder charge, extreme recklessness will do.

110./B/ The MPC substantial capacity test allows for an insanity defense either if the defendant did not know right from wrong *or* was incapable of controlling her actions. **(A)** is not the best answer because Colleen's statements "I'm sorry..." indicate that she did know right from wrong. **(C)** is not the best answer because she need not necessarily have been diagnosed prior to the incident – if she is diagnosed now, that will be sufficient. **(D)** is incorrect because the defendant's current lack of memory of a crime does not go far in proving what the defendant's state of mind was at the time the crime was committed.

111./C/ The police officer had a limited privilege in the use of force to subdue Colleen. Considering her agitated and armed state, the amount of force used was reasonable. **(A)** is incorrect because other witnesses could testify. **(B)** misstates the law – officers have a privilege, not total immunity. **(D)** is incorrect because temporary injury can be sufficient for a battery charge.

112./D/ Under FRE 608(b)(2) one witness may testify to specific instances of conduct of another witness if the witness is testifying as to the other witness' character for truth or veracity. **(A)** is incorrect because the priest is not testifying as to Terrance's religious beliefs, though the jury can certainly infer such from the presence of the priest. **(B)** is incorrect because the rule allows such testimony; however, if the priest were not testifying regarding Terrance's character, the question could not be asked upon cross-examination. **(C)** is incorrect because Terrance's actions are not an issue at trial.

113./D/ This position is an inferior officer in the Executive Branch because it executes the anti-terrorism laws. Like the special prosecutor appointed by the three-judge panel, the judiciary can appoint inferior officers. **(A)** describes principal officers (e.g. cabinet members), not inferior officers. **(B)** is forbidden, unless the office is legislative, not executive. (D) is better than **(C)** because the goal is to protect civil liberties. The judiciary is probably more suited to this task than merely limiting the term of the office, because then the President will likely be allowed to chose the next officer.

114./B/ The best answer, assuming the purpose of restrictions is to insulate the Deputy Secretary from political pressure when he protects civil rights. Congress may limit the removal of an inferior officer, unless it interferes with the President's ability to carry out his constitutional duty to execute the laws. **(A)** is incorrect. Congress may not remove an executive officer. **(C)** is allowable, but does not restrict the President as much as (B). **(D)** is allowable, but does not restrict the President as much as (B).

115./C/ Junior will prevail because such restraints on alienation on the sale of property are generally void, and the property therefore passes in fee simple absolute. **(A)** is incorrect because William has no interest in the land. **(B)** is incorrect because William has no interest in the land. **(D)** is incorrect because the restriction did not apply to either Daryl or Junior – it was void.

116./B/ The best answer. Marine's clause materially altered Speedy's offer by attempting to negate standard warranties. Thus both the parties conflicting terms are to be "knocked out" and the UCC "gap filling" provisions – standard implied warranty of merchantability – will be imposed. [UCC 2.314] **(A)** is incorrect because there will be a contract containing the UCC "gap filling" term. **(C)** is incorrect because when each party's term materially alters the bargain they are to be "knocked out" and the UCC default rule – implied warranty of merchantability – imposed. **(D)** is incorrect because when each party's term materially alters the bargain they are to be "knocked out" and the UCC default rule – implied warranty of merchantability – imposed.

117./C/ The best answer. If Connie failed to exercise reasonable care to protect herself by not using the crosswalk, contributory negligence could bar her recovery. The statute prohibiting crossing outside a designated crosswalk will be relevant but so will the bus blocking the sidewalk since it may indicate violating the statute should be excused. **(A)** is incorrect because negligence per se would only apply if the bus being in the designated crosswalk did not excuse the Plaintiff from compliance with the statute. **(B)** is not the best answer because it implies that the Defendant had the last clear chance to avoid the accident (If so, it would excuse any contributory negligence on the Plaintiff's part). But here there is no showing that the Plaintiff was negligent at all; thus (B) is not the best answer. **(D)** is incorrect because the Plaintiff's failure to cross in the designated crosswalk would be a factor to be considered in determining the Defendant's liability.

118./B/ The best answer because it focuses on the question of whether the statute was intended by the legislature to prevent the type of harm the Plaintiff suffered and the Plaintiff was a member of the protected class. **(A)** is not the best answer because the facts do not indicate that the statute imposed strict liability. Absent this authority a statutory violation could at best be considered negligence per se. (Note that contributory negligence is not a bar to a recovery for strict liability but is to negligence per se). **(C)** is incorrect because an assumption of the risk would have to been made knowingly and with an appreciation of the risks assumed. If that standard were met, it would relieve the Defendant of any duty. That standard is not met in this case. **(D)** is incorrect because Nathan's driving would probably not be considered a superseding force since it should have been foreseeable that parking illegally in the designated crosswalk would create a danger to a pedestrian who would walk around the bus to cross the street. Thus the bus driver's negligence was at least a substantial factor in Plaintiff's injury.

119./A/ Ox acted in self-defense. His use of force was reasonable and proportional to the amount of force used by Pete. Therefore, he should be acquitted on both charges. **(B)** is not the best answer because Ox acted in self-defense. **(C)** is not the best answer because Ox acted in self-defense. **(D)** is not the best answer because Ox acted in self-defense.

120./D/ Pete had intent and took a substantial step toward killing Ox. This is sufficient for an attempted murder charge. **(A)** is incorrect because Pete had intent and took a substantial step toward killing Ox. **(B)** is not the best answer because these two charges are identical to each other. **(C)** is incorrect because Pete did not actually make contact with Ox, which is required for a battery charge.

121./A/ An inventory search at a jailhouse or police station must be incident to a lawful arrest and follow a standard procedure. **(B)** is not the best answer because there was PC to bring him to the station – his involvement in the stabbing of Pete. **(C)** is incorrect because Ox had not been arrested at the time the search was performed, therefore the evidence should be suppressed. **(D)** is incorrect because Ox had not been arrested at the time the search was performed, therefore the evidence should be suppressed.

122./A/ Because intoxication is within the common understanding of most people, a lay witness may offer an opinion thereon if the opinion is helpful to understanding the testimony or determining a fact in issue. FRE 701. **(B)** is incorrect because this statement applies to experts lay witness opinions must be based on the perception of the witness. FRE 701. **(C)** is incorrect because a lay witness need not be an expert to testify to matters within common understanding. **(D)** is incorrect because FRE 704 is not limited to expert witnesses only. This fact pattern is distinguishable from the prior question where the expert was going to render an opinion on intoxication. An expert's testimony on issues within the common understanding of a jury is not helpful to the trier of fact under FRE 702.

123./C/ The first two communications from Leroy ($4,000 and $3,750) were both offers, which were never accepted by Harry. Harry's offer of $3,500 was not rejected by the $3,750 communication, which was probably a "mere inquiry;" thus the offer stayed open. Acceptance was thus not express but rather implied by performance under the "last shot" rule. This was at $3,500. **(A)** is not the best answer because the first two communications from Leroy ($4,000 and $3,750) were both offers that were never accepted by Harry. **(B)** is not the best answer because Harry's offer of $3,500 was not rejected by the $3,750 communication, which was probably a "mere inquiry;" thus the offer stayed open. **(D)** is not the best answer because there was a contract when Leroy accepted Harry's last offer by performance. Thus a quasi-contract equitable remedy is not applicable.

124./D/ The best answer since it focuses on one of the required elements Plaintiff must prove to make with a prima facie case. A legal duty, breach, and damages seen pretty clear; causation is also required. Plaintiff must prove that he would have recovered on the note had the underlying lawsuit been timely filed; this has been called "a case within a case." **(A)** is not the best answer because this is not a required element of Plaintiff's case but rather a defense that Delay & Postpone

would have to raise. **(B)** is incorrect because whether the Defendant breached their duty to their client is a question of fact, not law. Judges are not competent witnesses and they cannot offer expert testimony (FRE 605). **(C)** is incorrect since the Plaintiff may rely upon the jurors' common knowledge in determining the simple fact of whether Delay & Postpone met the statutory filing time limit. This question does not require specialized knowledge and therefore can be determined by the jury (FRE 702).

125./D/ This question is asking in which analysis the court may NOT engage and belief (v. conduct) is protected under this analysis. This alternative involves "belief." **(A)** is incorrect because a court may always determine whether a person is lying or telling the truth. **(B)** is incorrect, because a court may determine whether the religion actually requires a practice. **(C)** is incorrect because an "as applied" analysis is always appropriate.

126./B/ First Amendment protects people from government compelled speech, but narrowly drawn loyalty oaths are permissible conditions of certain government employment. **(A)** is incorrect, because it might overstate the test. Content specific regulations might require strict scrutiny, but loyalty oaths are analyzed separately. **(C)** is a common incorrect answer because it is not the best argument. **(D)** is not the best answer. It correctly states the rights involved, but is not as accurate as (B).

127./B/ Under FRE 801(d) a prior identification by a witness is not hearsay and admissible. **(A)** may be a correct statement, but has no bearing on the admissibility of the witness' identification. **(C)** is incorrect because sufficiency does not go to admissibility. **(D)** is incorrect because it goes to the weight of witness' testimony not the admissibility.

128./B/ S.S.U. is a state actor because it is a state school. Jones has a property interest in the job, because the state gave him one by requiring good cause for termination. Now the state must give him procedural due process to take that job away. **(A)** is incorrect because it ignores this requirement. **(C)** is incorrect because it ignores this requirement. **(D)** is the due process theory that lost. Due process means the state takes the good with the bad. Whether or not the contract gives him due process is a different issue.

129./A/ A generally applicable tax does not violate the constitution. **(B)** is incorrect. Controversies in which a state is a party fits in the Court's "original jurisdiction". **(C)** is incorrect. The tax applies to all bonds, and does not regulate the state as a state. **(D)** is incorrect, because the tax is generally applicable.

130./A/ Manny's postponing his wedding to Ingrid was acceptance of Uncle Harry's promise to pay the $50,000; thus, this unilateral contract was enforceable. **(B)** is incorrect because Manny validly accepted creating a contract so the subsequent death of the promisor is not effective to revoke the offer; the offer became merged into the contract. **(C)** is incorrect; while a general prohibition on marriage has been held to be against public policy, this was only an agreement to postpone a wedding. **(D)** is not the best answer since any equitable remedy would only be available if there was not a contract at law.

131./A/ If an interest in a joint tenancy is sold, the buyer becomes a tenant in common with the remaining tenants who remain joint tenants with respect to each other. After Delbert's death, the joint tenants receive his share, so it does not pass to Francine regardless of his will. **(B)** is incorrect because Delbert's share passes to the other tenants, not Francine. **(C)** is incorrect because the property right after the sale is a tenancy in common, not a joint tenancy. **(D)** is incorrect because Francine does not receive an interest in the joint tenancy.

132./D/ None of the above is the best answer. Francine has no property interest because Delbert's share passed to the other joint tenants who survived him. **(A)** is incorrect because it assumes the will effectively gave Francine some property interest. **(B)** is incorrect because it assumes the will effectively gave Francine some property interest. **(C)** is incorrect because it assumes the will effectively gave Francine some property interest.

133./C/ Under FRE 703 an expert may rely upon facts or data not in evidence, so long as those facts are of the kind relied upon by experts in the field. **(A)** is not the best answer because an expert may rely upon hearsay in forming an opinion. **(B)** is not the best answer because the crew need not testify at trial (though it would eliminate the need to establish that those facts are those relied upon by experts in the field). **(D)** is not the best answer because to rely on hearsay, it must be established that the hearsay contains the kind of facts relied upon by experts in the field.

134./D/ The best answer since it is the proper theory of recovery; a reasonable person would have made the warning directly to the driver especially since Florence knew the vehicle was to be used in a carpool. **(A)** is incorrect because strict liability involves an absolute duty of care without a showing of negligence. Here, the car was not a defective product and the component brakes were only dangerous if stomped on. There may be a duty to warn under these facts, but that would require Plaintiff to show negligence. **(B)** is incorrect because while Patty's failure to transmit the warning to Darlene was also a substantial factor in causing the injuries, it was not the sole cause (or cause-in-fact). This does not relieve Florence of the duty to warn the driver. **(C)** is incorrect because no matter how slight the duty to warn, Florence breached it; there will still be some responsibility.

135./D/ The central reason Darlene will recover her full damages from the tort-feasor is that she had no fault. Hotrod's negligence in running the red light was a substantial factor in the injury and the Plaintiff's injury was foreseeable as being within the scope of risks Hotrod created. While Florence and Patty were also at fault, this will not exonerate Hotrod in the *Darlene v. Hotrod* lawsuit in which Darlene should collect her full damages. **(A)** is not the best answer because Patty's fault is not relevant to Hotrod's negligence in failing to stop at the red light. Darlene had no fault; as between Darlene and Hotrod, he would be liable for all her damages. While there may be others who are also negligent, Hotrod's lack of care was a substantial factor in causing the damages. For multiple independent causes, the "but for"

causation test is replaced by a "substantial factor" test. **(B)** is incorrect because the brake failure will not exonerate Hotrod of liability. **(C)** is incorrect because vicarious liability usually requires a principal and agent relationship where the principal controls the course and scope of the agent's duties. Here, we have only a driver and passenger relationship. Notice that this question does not involve a *Patty v. Hotrod* claim.

136./B/ This is the best defense because Hotrod's action was a superseding cause. A superseding cause will break the chain of causation, thus relieving the original tort-feasor of liability. It could be argued that Hotrod running a red light was not connected to the risk which Florence's negligent conduct set in motion. **(A)** is not the best answer because contributory negligence would go to a defense; this would not be as helpful as being able to show Plaintiff could not meet an element necessary to establish a prima facie case. **(C)** is not the best answer because Patty is not a party in the *Darlene v Florence* lawsuit. **(D)** is incorrect because while the lack of compensation may lower the duty level, it does not eliminate the duty.

137./C/ The best answer because it describes the operation of the "pure" comparative negligence statute. The trier of fact apportions the damages between the parties so that the Plaintiff recovers the percentage of the injuries caused by the Defendant. **(A)** is incorrect because under a "pure" comparative fault statute, the Plaintiff's fault only diminishes the recovery; under contributory negligence, any fault by Plaintiff operates to bar all recovery. **(B)** is incorrect because lack of any fault by Darlene has no bearing on the *Patty v. Hotrod* lawsuit: Darlene's innocence is not imputed to the Plaintiff allowing her to avoid a reduction for her own negligence. **(D)** is incorrect because where there are multiple causes, the "but for" causation test is replaced by the "substantial factor" test.

138./D/ This agreement was a mixed contract involving both common law (labor) and UCC (lumber) topics. As such, the predominate reason for the contract controls; here, that is the common law so the UCC statute of frauds for goods over $500 does not apply. **(A)** is not the best answer because the value of the lumber is not important as long as it does not become the predominate reason for the contract. **(B)** is incorrect because the plaintiff will prevail as long as the lumber was not the predominate reason for the contract. **(C)** is incorrect because it is not necessary that there be any writing; an oral agreement is enforceable.

139./C/ Burglary is the breaking and entering of a structure with the intent to commit a felony therein. The shop was open to the public at the time John entered, so burglary was a legal impossibility. **(A)** is incorrect because the factual possibility of completing the crime is irrelevant to a burglary charge – what matters is intent at time of entering. **(B)** is incorrect because completion of the crime is not necessary. The factual possibility of completing the crime is irrelevant to a burglary charge – what matters is intent at time of entering. **(D)** is irrelevant because larceny or robbery, the shop was open to the public, so burglary was impossible.

140./C/ John had the intent and took a substantial step toward the completion of the crime of robbery, which is enough for attempt. **(A)** is incorrect because factual impossibility is not a defense to attempt. **(B)** is incorrect because he did not withdraw before the attempt was committed, only before the actual robbery was committed. **(D)** is incorrect because larceny is a lesser included offense of robbery, but not attempted robbery.

141./A/ There is an absolute constitutional right to a jury trial. Failure to grant one upon request of the defendant invalidates a conviction. **(B)** is incorrect. There is an absolute constitutional right to a jury trial. Failure to grant one upon request of the defendant invalidates a conviction. **(C)** is incorrect. There is an absolute constitutional right to a jury trial. Failure to grant one upon request of the defendant invalidates a conviction. **(D)** is incorrect. There is an absolute constitutional right to a jury trial. Failure to grant one upon request of the defendant invalidates a conviction.

142./A/ The remedy of rewarding an aggrieved seller the lost profit is based upon the theory that the seller could have made a second profit on the sale of a similar item to another buyer. Here there were no more recliners to sell so such a remedy would allow the seller to pile up damages. **(B)** is incorrect because only where it is impossible to resell the goods at market for mitigation is the total contract price imposed. **(C)** is incorrect because the measure of any damage award would be the contract price of $300, not the higher retail value. **(D)** is incorrect because the lost profit damage figure assumes that the seller could have made two sales; that is not possible since they were going out of business and had no more of these goods in inventory.

143./A/ Alaska may sell to its residents and citizens at a discount because it is a market participant. **(B)** is incorrect, because Alaskan Timber is probably a state actor. **(C)** is incorrect, because the market participant is an exception to the dormant commerce clause. **(D)** is incorrect. Privileges and Immunities clause protects his legal rights, but not his right to state owned cheap timber.

144./B/ Plaintiff's testimony established a presumption of receipt, but Defendant's testimony rebutted that presumption, so it is for the jury to decide whether or not the document was received. **(A)** is incorrect for this reason. If Defendant had not offered any evidence of non-receipt, the presumption would be established as a matter of law. **(C)** is incorrect because the presumption is sufficient to meet plaintiff's burden of production. **(D)** is technically correct, but not applicable to this question.

145./B/ The most common remedy for overuse of an easement is injunctive relief. **(A)** is incorrect because physical blockage is permitted for some easements, but not express easements. **(C)** is incorrect because this type of splitting has no basis in law. **(D)** is not the best answer (but is in second place) because it is not clear there are any damages aside from discomfort.

146./D/ Reasonable care under the circumstances is all that is required. Reasonable care would usually require a driver to slow down in heavy fog because the normal vision would be limited. **(A)** is not the best answer because the alternative contradicts the facts in the question stating that the fog grew heavier and heavier so the sudden and unexpected situation of limited visibility would not excuse the failure to slow down. **(B)** is incorrect because the question is what driving speed was reasonable under the fog conditions in this residential neighborhood? **(C)** is incorrect because only reasonable care is required; the standard is not elevated but what qualifies as reasonable conduct may depend upon the circumstances.

147./B/ This alternative correctly articulates part of the strict scrutiny analysis. Bob is an alien, and the court generally reviews state discrimination against aliens under strict scrutiny. **(A)** is too broadly stated. **(C)** is incorrect because it mentions intermediate scrutiny. **(D)** is incorrect, because it mentions part of rational basis scrutiny.

148./C/ There is no right to an unobstructed view unless there is a valid covenant in place. That is not the case here. **(A)** is incorrect because he only has the right to airspace immediately above his house, not the space over his neighbor's property. **(B)** is incorrect because preceding the neighbor's construction has no legal weight. **(D)** is incorrect because intent or knowledge do not create a duty for Martin not to obstruct the view.

149./A/ While the boat is a "good" under the UCC, the marine survey is a personal service contract and thus under the common law. Under the common law the statute of limitations is triggered (or begins to run) upon accrual which is when the breach occurred. Further, the parties may agree to deviate from the statutory default time period. **(B)** is incorrect because the UCC rule does not apply to a common law topic. **(C)** is incorrect because the discovery rule applies to tort actions, not contract claims. **(D)** is incorrect in that there is no election as to the time period under most state law statute of limitations.

150./B/ A prior conviction can be admitted as substantive evidence. **(A)** is incorrect because impeachment is not the only reason a prior conviction may be offered into evidence. **(C)** is incorrect because the public records exception to hearsay applies in this situation. **(D)** is incorrect because hearsay may be substantive evidence.

151./D/ This is the best answer, because it properly states a part of the strict scrutiny test. State discrimination against alienage (or citizenship) is generally analyzed under strict scrutiny. **(A)** is incorrect, because it uses rational basis scrutiny language. **(B)** is incorrect. It uses a phrase from the privileges and immunities clause. That clause may be an issue, but it should be applied to out-of-staters, not aliens. **(C)** is incorrect, because is uses intermediate scrutiny language.

152./A/ A joint tenancy between husband and wife is usually considered a tenancy by the entirety in most jurisdictions. **(B)** is probably the second best answer, because it would be correct if they were not married and a joint ownership was intended. **(C)** is incorrect because a joint tenancy between husband and wife is usually considered a tenancy by the entirety in most jurisdictions. **(D)** is incorrect because there is another alternative which is correct.

153./C/ A tenancy in common is presumed as a default interest if there is no indication of intent for a joint tenancy. **(A)** is incorrect because a tenancy by the entirety involves married parties. **(B)** is incorrect because of the tenancy in common presumption. [Note how this differs very slightly from the answer in the preceding question. It appeared in that question that there was an intent to convey the property to them as joint tenants, and thus the presumption of tenancy in common is overcome.] **(D)** is incorrect because there is another alternative which is correct.

154./C/ The best answer because the statute is overbroad. Overbreadth spoils the statute as against any defendant, whether or not that defendant's speech was actually protected. **(A)** is incorrect. Johnson's speech can be prohibited if it is fighting words, or restricted by time, place, and manner otherwise. He probably uttered fighting words, because "the reasonable person would have lashed out at him." **(B)** is incorrect because the statute is overbroad. Overbreadth spoils the statute as against any defendant, whether or not that defendant's speech was actually protected. **(D)** is incorrect because the statute is overbroad. Overbreadth spoils the statute as against any defendant, whether or not that defendant's speech was actually protected.

155./C/ The general rule is that only extreme mental deficiency (insanity) may relieve Indiana from liability. This is to be contrasted to the situation of physical impairments which the jury may consider in determining whether reasonable care was exercised. Here it appears to be in the gray area in between. Probably the best answer is (C) where the jury is not required ("must" or "should") to consider the Defendant's handicap but that it "may" consider. **(A)** is incorrect because the jury instruction should state the determination is whether he acted as a reasonable person in the circumstances. **(B)** is incorrect because the jury instruction should state the determination is whether he acted as a reasonable person in the circumstances. **(D)** is incorrect because the jury instruction should state the required determination is whether he acted as a reasonable person in the circumstances.

156./D/ FRE 804(b)(1) allows former testimony to be admitted if the witness is unavailable to testify. Because Hillary does not recall, she is unavailable under 804(a)(3). **(A)** is incorrect because executive immunity is not a rule of evidence. **(B)** is incorrect because a witness can be unavailable under the definition of the rule even when physically present. **(C)** is incorrect because direct evidence of guilt goes to weight not admissibility. Direct evidence can still be inadmissible for any number of reasons.

157./C/ The best answer because a donee beneficiary must usually make some affirmative movement in reliance on the promise before the rights vest. **(A)** is incorrect because the original party could revoke the promise prior to the vesting. **(B)** is not the best answer; merely learning of the promise by a donee beneficiary is not usually sufficient without some movement that demonstrates affirmative reliance. **(D)** is incorrect because the original parties to the contract can modify or revoke the contract prior to beneficiary's rights vesting.

158./C/ The assignee's suit against the promisor is subject to any defense which the promisor has against the promisee. (Note that an account receivable is not a negotiable instrument that a holder-in-due course might take free of the defense of failure of consideration.) **(A)** is incorrect because the consideration for the assignment was the detriment the assignee incurred by making the loan. **(B)** is incorrect because it is not usually necessary that the promisor agree to an assignment of a contractual right unless there is a non-assignment clause in the contract. **(D)** is incorrect because the general rule is that all contractual rights are assignable unless the agreement specifies to the contrary.

159./A/ The second degree murder charge can be sustained with proof of extreme recklessness. Craig knew there were people close by and deliberately shot in that direction, with extreme disregard for the high risk of death he was creating. **(B)** is incorrect because deadly force may not be used in defense of property. **(C)** is not the best answer because proof of a guilty conscience is not the same as proof of a crime. **(D)** is incorrect because this is the standard for evaluating a claim of self-defense, and there are no facts to indicate that Craig was acting in self-defense.

160./B/ Arson is the intentional burning of a dwelling or other structure – Craig has burned the forest. If Craig has not committed a felony, then he cannot be guilty of felony murder. **(A)** is incorrect because Craig is not guilty of arson (intentional burning of a dwelling or other structure). **(C)** is incorrect because Craig is not guilty of arson (intentional burning of a dwelling or other structure). **(D)** is incorrect because Craig is not guilty of arson (intentional burning of a dwelling or other structure).

161./A/ The in-state training requirement places an undue burden on interstate commerce by discriminating against out-of-state providers of physical therapy. Distinguish in-state training from **(B)**, which would be a better answer if the discrimination was more focused on the individual's residency or citizenship. **(C)** is incorrect, because the state may not restrict Edward using unconstitutional means. **(D)** is incorrect. State laws that unduly burden commerce are void whether or not they are rationally related to a legitimate interest.

162./A/ Under FRE 803(18) a learned treatise passage may be read into evidence once the treatise is established as authoritative. **(B)** is incorrect because the treatise may not be received as an exhibit. **(C)** is incorrect because the authority need only be established by the witness, another expert, or judicial notice. **(D)** is incorrect for the same reason.

163./B/ The test for measuring the contributory negligence of a physically disabled Plaintiff would be that degree of care a reasonable person would exhibit if they were blind; this would probably be a jury question. **(A)** is incorrect because this implies strict liability and sewer repairing is not an abnormally dangerous activity. The damages were from the failure to put up a barricade, not the underlying activity. **(C)** is incorrect; this would likely be a jury question and the degree of required care is one of fact, not of law. **(D)** is not the best answer because it does not address the central concern of a physically impaired Plaintiff's contributory negligence.

164./C/ Unless changed by statute, most jurisdictions require a periodic tenancy to have one period's notice before vacating. On a month to month periodic tenancy, this is normally rounded up to the next month. **(A)** is incorrect because one month notice is required to terminate a periodic tenancy. **(B)** is incorrect because one month notice is required to terminate a periodic tenancy. **(D)** is incorrect because one month notice is required to terminate a periodic tenancy.

165./B/ A declarant's statement describing an event as it happens or immediately thereafter is excepted from hearsay. FRE 803(1). **(A)** is incorrect because a dying declaration must concern the cause of declarant's death made while the declarant thought that death was imminent. There is no evidence that declarant thought he was going to die. **(C)** is incorrect because the declarant must be under the stress or excitement of the event. **(D)** is incorrect because a hearsay exception applies where the availability of declarant is immaterial.

166./C/ The intent to hit Nancy transfers to Donald, and Tom is guilty of battery, the unlawful application of direct or indirect force resulting in injury or offensive touching. **(A)** is not the best answer because Nancy had indicated that she had ceased her aggression, thereby making Tom the first aggressor and precluding self-defense. **(B)** is incorrect because intent to commit a battery transfers between victims. **(D)** is incorrect because the mens rea for battery is intent or recklessness, not negligence.

167./C/ Attempted battery assault (creation of apprehension of a battery in the victim) merges with the completed battery, therefore Nancy could only be charged with battery, not assault, if she hit Tom. **(A)** is incorrect because "scaring" the victim is the definition of assault. **(B)** is incorrect because the assault was completed before she ceased her aggression. **(D)** is not the best answer because Tom's general propensity for violence does not excuse Nancy's act of first aggression in this particular instance.

168./A/ In a bench trial, double jeopardy attaches when the first witness is sworn. The judge has acquitted Tom, and double jeopardy precludes his prosecution on the same charge for any reason whatsoever. **(B)** is incorrect because in a bench trial, double jeopardy attaches when the first witness is sworn. **(C)** is incorrect because in a bench trial, double jeopardy attaches when the first witness is sworn. **(D)** is incorrect because in a bench trial, double jeopardy attaches when the first witness is sworn.

169./C/ John is charged with seeking employment as a convicted molester. Thus an essential element is that he is a convicted molester. He is not charged with another molestation. If that were the case, then his prior conviction could only be used to impeach his own testimony. Thus **(A)** is incorrect because the prior conviction is evidence of an element of the crime charged. **(B)** is incorrect because the prior conviction is overwhelmingly probative of the crime charged the prejudicial effect does not substantially outweigh the probity. **(D)** is incorrect because John has not taken the stand thus there is nothing to impeach.

170./D/ Since the contract involved the personal skill of the obligor and stated that delegation was not allowed, the delegation is to be treated as anticipatory repudiation. **(A)** is incorrect because an "assignment of the contract" includes both an assignment of rights and a delegation of duties and presumably binds both parties. **(B)** is incorrect because the employment agreement between Orange Hat and Peter was "at will;" the three year term reference was to the project's development period. **(C)** is incorrect because a delegation (between the delegator and delegatee) does not relieve the obligor-delegator unless a modification or release is executed by the obligee Orange Hat.

171./C/ A delegation of performance of personal service contract creates grounds for sufficient insecurity that a written demand for assurances must be complied with. Failure to comply excuses the other party's performance duty. **(A)** is incorrect because there was no duty to provide trade secret information until the obligee accepts the delegatee. **(B)** is not the best answer because Peter's assignment to David included all rights including sufficient privity to bring a lawsuit. **(D)** is incorrect; while it is true that Orange Hat continued to have rights against Peter (absent a novation or release) this does not necessarily mean the obligee is liable to the delegatee.

172./D/ Both Peter and David are potentially liable. Peter was an original party to the Orange Hat contract. Orange Hat was a third party creditor-beneficiary of the delegation contract between Peter and David. This third party creditor-beneficiary status provides the privity necessary for the obligee to sue the delegatee. **(A)** is not the best answer because both Peter and David are potentially liable. Peter was an original party to the Orange Hat contract. Orange Hat was a third party creditor-beneficiary of the delegation contract between Peter and David. This third party creditor-beneficiary status provides the privity necessary for the obligee to sue the delegatee. **(B)** Peter and David are potentially liable. Peter was an original party to the Orange Hat contract. Orange Hat was a third party creditor-beneficiary of the delegation contract between Peter and David. This third party creditor-beneficiary status provides the privity necessary for the obligee to sue the delegatee. **(C)** Peter and David are potentially liable. Peter was an original party to the Orange Hat contract. Orange Hat was a third party creditor-beneficiary of the delegation contract between Peter and David. This third party creditor-beneficiary status provides the privity necessary for the obligee to sue the delegatee.

173./C/ The public function doctrine probably best explains why Traffic Stop is a state actor. It is performing a traditionally exclusive state function of law enforcement. **(A)** is incorrect. Dracer's challenge is ripe, because he can raise his constitutional challenge in the same proceedings as a defense to the infraction. **(B)** is incorrect. The public function doctrine probably best explains why Traffic Stop is a state actor. It is performing a traditionally exclusive state function of law enforcement. **(D)** is incorrect and is just a distraction. Dracer can raise constitutional rights as a defense to a civil infraction.

174./B/ This is a case of easement by implication, because it was an existing use of a parcel that has been subdivided. Technically, it is also an easement by necessity, because Bjorn's only access is across Ophelia's parcel. However, necessity was not one of the options given. **(A)** is incorrect because the CHO elements of prescription are not present. **(C)** is incorrect, because this easement by implication is a form of an easement appurtenant, and therefore not an easement in gross. An easement in gross is easy to spot because it involves only one parcel of land – the servient estate. Since the fact pattern discussed two parcels, you therefore should have immediately ruled out easement in gross. **(D)** is incorrect because the fact pattern did not discuss an intent by Ophelia to create and record an express easement.

175./A/ This appears to be the best defense. The argument would be that had the swimming pool been used properly there would have been no unusual danger. Had the boy not dived from the roof or had someone else been with him there would have been no unusual danger. **(B)** is incorrect because the attractive nuisance doctrine may impose near strict liability upon a property owner for damages incurred by a child trespasser and the word "any" is too broad. **(C)** is incorrect because it is doubtful if a child of 8 would understand the severity of the risk sufficiently to effect a waiver and the word "any" is too broad. **(D)** is not the best answer (but is in second place). The risk to the children seemed very slight since there had never been a child trespassing and swimming in the pool before and the cost of an electric fence would have been high.

176./C/ Curly, who has a remainder after Mo's life estate. When Mo quitclaimed his interest to Shemp, Shemp only received as much as Mo possessed, which was a possessory estate with Mo as the measuring life. After Mo's death, remainder still goes to Curly, because Mo had no power to convey the remainder. **(A)** is incorrect because the remainder interest has been determined by Larry, and it is Curly/Morticia, not Mo's estate. **(B)** is incorrect because even though the formalities of the will are valid, Shemp has no interest he can pass to Cassandra. **(D)** is incorrect because Curly was still alive at Mo's death.

177./C/ Mo has a life estate. Curly has a remainder that at first appears to be vested, because he is alive and identifiable at Larry's death, but the problem is that the status of his interest is contingent until Mo dies. Likewise, Morticia's remainder remains contingent until Mo dies to see if Curly predeceases. Cassandra, as discussed in the question above, never has an interest because Shemp cannot convey the remainder interest. (Note that if Shemp had died before Mo, the life estate could have passed under his will to Cassandra, but that was not in the fact pattern). **(A)** is incorrect. Morticia's remainder remains contingent until Mo dies to see if Curly predeceases. **(B)** is incorrect. Morticia's remainder remains contingent until Mo dies to see if Curly predeceases. **(D)** is incorrect. Cassandra, as discussed in the question above, never has an interest because Shemp cannot convey the remainder interest.

178./D/ Quitclaim deeds exist so that a person may pass whatever interest they may have without any warranty. **(A)** is incorrect because a quitclaim deed has no warranty. **(B)** is incorrect because with a quitclaim deed, withholding relevant information is not a failure to disclose. There are no facts indicating fraud. **(C)** is incorrect because even though life estates may be conveyed inter vivos, that has no bearing in this fact pattern or whether Shemp or his estate have a claim against Mo for not fully disclosing that the title was not in fee simple absolute.

179./C/ Treaties are entered into by the President and two thirds of the Senate. The last in time governs between a treaty and other statutory law. **(A)** is an incorrect answer appealing to contract law. **(B)** is incorrect, because the House of Representatives does not sign treaties. **(D)** is incorrect, because a treaty may supersede statutory law.

180./B/ To prevail for defamation, a party suing a media defendant for publication of a story that is newsworthy must show that at least Defendant was negligent (failed to exercise ordinary care). A sports figure is a public figure. In addition, the matter is arguably newsworthy even though it may involve a private matter. The modifier "if" is followed by a rationale that is plausible under the facts since the reporter did rely upon two sources he believed to be accurate. **(A)** is not the best answer because to prevail against a media defendant for a newsworthy story requires at least some degree of fault. **(C)** is not the best answer; it states a level of required proof which is too high. A showing of malice (much less a disregard or knowledge of falsity) is not required – only that the Defendant was negligent. **(D)** is incorrect because to recover, the Plaintiff must show at least reckless (willful and wanton) behavior so that there is a high probability that emotional distress will follow from the publication; this clearly goes beyond the facts in the question.

181./D/ This is probably the worst defense. The absolute privilege against defamation is limited to statements made in the course of judicial proceedings, legislative proceedings and debates, and statements by government officials. **(A)** is a better defense because truth is an absolute defense. **(B)** is a better defense because the Plaintiff's implied consent is present since Stanley granted the interviews. **(C)** is a better defense because the qualified privilege would apply to statements made in discharge of the reporter's duty and the facts do not indicate the reporter had malice towards Plaintiff.

182./D/ An issue at trial is the City's control over the sidewalk. FRE 407 prohibits subsequent remedial measures for the purpose of proving negligence; however, subsequent remedial measures are admissible for other purposes. **(A)** is incorrect because knowledge of the injury is not an element of negligence that Wendy must prove, only knowledge of a hazardous condition. **(B)** is not the best answer because the repairs are admissible for another purpose. **(C)** is not the best answer because even if the repairs are assertive conduct one must still surmount an FRE 407 challenge.

183./D/ No prior injuries does not prove presence of due care. All that is proved is that any possible negligence has yet to cause an injury. **(A)** is incorrect because lack of knowledge of injuries does not disprove lack of knowledge of a dangerous condition. **(B)** is incorrect because the City could have failed to exercise due care even if no injuries occur. **(C)** is incorrect because so long as the Manager has personal knowledge, he need not have been in that position the entire time.

184./D/ This is not an easement in gross because it deals with more than one parcel. **(A)** is an incorrect answer because this is a classical negative easement: a restriction recorded in the deed which restrains the servient tenements from building structures that restrict access to views, light, air, support, etc. **(B)** is an incorrect answer because as a negative easement, it is therefore a form of restrictive covenant. **(C)** is not a correct answer, because this could also qualify as a negative servitude because is it meets the two major elements: it was part of a common scheme set out by the developer to be mutually enforceable, and owners have notice. Notice in this case is constructive notice due to the filing of the restriction in each deed.

185./D/ Restitution applies where Defendant wrongfully repudiates the contract before completion. Plaintiff's recovery is valued at Defendant's enrichment, even if such benefit exceeds the contract price; the facts state that there was $250,000 added value. **(A)** is incorrect because 90% of the contract price of $200,000 is not the restitution amount since the contract was not divisible. **(B)** is incorrect because under restitution the enrichment to the Defendant may exceed the contract price. **(C)** is incorrect because the measure of recovery under restitution is the Defendant's enrichment even if the

Plaintiff would have lost money had the contract been completed.

186./B/ This is the best answer, because the desks are economically useless if no student can use them as a desk. This is probably an injury-in-fact as a loss of property. **(A)** is unnecessary to decide, because there is a sufficient injury. **(C)** is unnecessary to decide, because there is a sufficient injury. While **(D)** might be a true statement, Lincoln probably has standing due to the loss of the desks.

187./A/ This is the preferred answer because Congress has delegated power to an agency. The supremacy clause strikes down inconsistent state laws. These laws can be construed as consistent; the school must buy 50% hardcover, 50% paperback. **(B)** is a common incorrect answer. **(C)** is incorrect as the "policy" of one agency does not supersede the regulations of another. **(D)** is incorrect, because the supremacy clause strikes down inconsistent state laws.

188./B/ The house is covered by the implied warranty of habitability. **(A)** is incorrect, because the seller cannot disclaim habitability on a new house. **(C)** is incorrect because regardless of the spring, Haskell is responsible for the foundation that has a crack in it. **(D)** is incorrect because there is no indication in the fact pattern that Haskell failed to disclose. Had there been a failure to disclose, this would have also been a valid answer.

189./C/ The best answer because the interference must be substantial and unreasonable to a Plaintiff of normal sensibilities; note that this standard does not mean that the Family will necessarily lose their lawsuit. **(A)** is incorrect because the test is one of the degree of interference; notice though that the Family did not move to the nuisance. **(B)** is incorrect because the test is one of the degree of interference. **(D)** is incorrect because the test is the sensibility of the average person with normal sensibilities.

190./A/ This meets the requirement of FRE 901(b)(2) for authenticating the signature. Note that the proponent will also need to argue that the addendum falls under the business record exception or is an admission by party-opponent. However, that is not one of the options in this question. **(B)** is incorrect because the contents of a document can only be proved by the document itself. FRE 1002. **(C)** is not the best answer because FRE 613 does not apply to admissions by party-opponent, and FRE 608 applies to the character of a witness introduced for impeachment, not substantive evidence. **(D)** is incorrect because a statement against interest relates to hearsay, not authentication.

191./B/ If the buyer wants the land and not damages, he must sue for specific performance. That remedy in equity is available to buyers when sellers breach because land is unique. **(A)** is not the best answer because it doesn't answer the client's question. However, if the client wanted money rather than the land, it is a valid legal alternative. **(C)** is incorrect because merely putting earnest money down does not constitute partial performance. Normally there must be other factors present: taking possession, making substantial improvements, etc. **(D)** is incorrect because one of the other alternatives is correct.

192./B/ If Electric's statement rises to the level of a potential repudiation it triggers the right of the other contracting party to request written assurances of performance. If an adequate response is not received within 30 days the requesting party may treat the contract as repudiated. **(A)** is incorrect because the non-repudiating party does not escape all their obligation unless the repudiating party fails to respond to a request for assurances. **(C)** is incorrect because the lack of quantity is not fatal in a requirement contract. [UCC 2.306] **(D)** is incorrect because if there is a failure of a presupposed condition the seller is required to notify the buyer of the expected allocation amount. [UCC 2.615]

193./C/ Most jurisdictions require leases for over one year to comply with the Statute of Frauds. If the intent is to enter a lease for more than a year, but there is no writing, the lease will normally revert to a tenancy at will or a periodic tenancy, depending on jurisdiction. **(A)** is incorrect because the doctrine of partial performance does not apply to these facts. **(B)** is incorrect because notice is irrelevant here. If the tenancy had reverted to a periodic tenancy, at most Randall would owe for one month's notice. **(D)** is incorrect because if a lease is valid, surrendering of the property must be accepted by the landlord to release the tenant from his obligation.

194./A/ The father's knowledge that his son had a dangerous propensity to bully and physically intimidate younger boys created a duty to warn the boys' camp owner. The omission is actionable. The harm to the boys at the camp was foreseeable to Mr. Slugger. **(B)** is incorrect because there is not an absolute duty to supervise one's children. Here, it would probably not be reasonable to expect a father to accompany the son to the camp. **(C)** is not the best answer because it ignores the father's negligence in failing to warn the camp owner. In addition, vicarious liability for <u>all</u> torts is too broad. **(D)** is not the best answer because Respondent Superior would only apply if Simon Slugger was operating as an agent for his father.

195./C/ On March 15, the aggrieved party can bring suit. **(A)** is not the best answer since Nugent's statement seems an unequivocal repudiation. **(B)** is incorrect since the party can retract its repudiation prior to the contract date as long as the other party has not detrimentally changed their position. **(D)** is incorrect because the aggrieved party may pursue all legal remedies immediately upon receiving notice of default; it is not necessary to wait until the contract performance date.

196./C/ Because the Defendant is offering money to avoid a lawsuit, this is an offer of compromise and statements made during the course of settlement negotiations are not admissible. FRE 408. **(A)** is not the best answer because though it is an admission by party-opponent for hearsay purposes, the statement is still inadmissible. **(B)** would be correct if there were no offer to compromise, but only an offer to pay medical expenses. Under FRE 409 only the offer to pay is inadmissible, not a contemporaneous statement. **(D)** is incorrect because the statement is an admission by party-opponent.

197./B/ The estate Gary created was a fee simple determinable. Therefore, no action is required by Gary; the property automatically reverts back to him. **(A)** is incorrect because the key language is "so long as." To be subject to a condition subsequent, it must have language such as "on condition that," "provided that," or "but if." **(C)** is incorrect because while certain restraints on alienation are void, a fee simple determinable is usually still permitted. **(D)** is incorrect because one of the other alternatives is correct.

198./C/ A lack of consideration may impair the rights of the delegatee against the delegator but should not affect the right of the obligee to prohibit the delegation. **(A)** is incorrect because delegation is not allowed if it results in imposing a material risk or burden. **(B)** is incorrect because where delegation is prohibited by the contract, the duty is not delegable under the common law. **(D)** is incorrect because if the performance only involves the personal skill of the obligator it is non-delegable.

199./B/ The best answer because Congress does not have such power and the Supreme Court can still hear such a controversy on appeal from a Federal District Court and Circuit Court of Appeals. **(A)** is incorrect because Congress has the express power over the Supreme Court's appellate jurisdiction. **(C)** is incorrect, because Congress has the express power over the Supreme Court's appellate jurisdiction. **(D)** is incorrect because Congress has the express power over the Supreme Court's appellate jurisdiction.

200./B/ The best answer because the right to privacy is personal and does not extend to family members. **(A)** is incorrect because perhaps the statements hold Sandy's mother up to ridicule and contempt but not

Sandy. **(C)** is not the best answer because truth is not a defense to the tort of the invasion of privacy. **(D)** is not the best answer because lack of malice is not a defense to the tort of the invasion of privacy.

RIGOS BAR REVIEW SERIES

MULTISTATE BAR EXAM REVIEW (MBE)

Volume 2 Index

Constitutional Law

Criminal Law and Procedure

RIGOS BAR REVIEW SERIES MBE REVIEW

COURSE EVALUATION FORM

Once again, thank you for choosing **Rigos Bar Review Series**! We hope you feel that these materials have given you the tools and confidence to tackle the Multistate Bar Exam!

We are constantly striving to provide the best possible study materials available. We want to hear from you! If you would kindly take a few minutes to fill out the form below and mail it back to us at 230 Skinner Building, 1326 Fifth Avenue, Seattle WA 98101, or fax it to us at (206) 624-0731. Let your voice be heard in the effort to improve the **Rigos Bar Review Series MBE Review**. THANK YOU!

****

For each of the categories listed below, please rate **Rigos Bar Review Series MBE Review** on a scale of 1 to 5.

| 5 = Excellent | 4 = Very Good | 3 = Good | 2 = Fair | 1 = Poor |

How do you rate the overall presentation of Rigos Bar Review Series?

Arrangement of Materials	5	4	3	2	1
Colors/Typography	5	4	3	2	1
Convenient Binder Format	5	4	3	2	1
Ease of Use	5	4	3	2	1
Professionalism	5	4	3	2	1

How do you rate the Rigos Bar Review Series materials in terms of accuracy (typographical, legal, etc.)?

Chapter Texts	5	4	3	2	1
MBE Tips	5	4	3	2	1
Questions/Answers	5	4	3	2	1
Magic Memory Outlines®	5	4	3	2	1
Question Distribution Maps	5	4	3	2	1

How do you rate the helpfulness of each component of Rigos Bar Review Series?

Chapter Texts	5	4	3	2	1
Questions/Answers	5	4	3	2	1
Magic Memory Outlines®	5	4	3	2	1
Question Distribution Maps	5	4	3	2	1
Final Exam	5	4	3	2	1

How well has Rigos Bar Review Series prepared you for each of the following aspects of the MBE?

Substantive Knowledge	5	4	3	2	1
Multiple Choice Format	5	4	3	2	1
Time Management	5	4	3	2	1
Helpful Tips/Common Mistakes	5	4	3	2	1
Confidence Level	5	4	3	2	1

Continued on back of page

If you felt that some chapters of the Rigos Bar Review Series MBE Review were better than others, rate them individually below:

VOLUME 1

Contracts & UCC Sales Article 2	5	4	3	2	1
Torts	5	4	3	2	1
Real Property & Future Interests	5	4	3	2	1

VOLUME 2

Evidence	5	4	3	2	1
Constitutional Law	5	4	3	2	1
Criminal Law and Procedure	5	4	3	2	1

Did you prepare a Magic Memory Outline® for all 6 subjects?
Yes _____ No _____

Did you use the Make Your Own Exam software feature?
Yes _____ No _____

Did you pass the MBE?
Yes _____ No _____ Don't know yet _____ MBE Score _____

If you have any additional comments, critiques or suggestions about **Rigos Bar Review Series MBE Review**, please tell us about them below. Please feel free to attach pages.

_____

_____

If you wish to, please give us the information below. It will allow us to attribute your comments and to follow up on your concerns.

NAME: _____ PHONE: _____ EMAIL: _____

LAW SCHOOL: _____ GRAD DATE: _____ ADDRESS: _____

MBE SCORE: _____

What is the likelihood that you would do each of the following?

Recommend **Rigos Bar Review Series** to others

5   4   3   2   1

Keep **Rigos Bar Review Series** for future reference

5   4   3   2   1

Buy other products from this company in the future

5   4   3   2   1

Did you study all of the text?
Yes _____ No _____

Did you work all of the learning and practice questions?
Yes _____ No _____

Did you take the Final Exam?
Yes _____ No _____